MASS SOCIETY, PLURALISM, AND BUREAUCRACY

Explication, Assessment, and Commentary

Richard F. Hamilton

Westport, Connecticut
London

Library of Congress Cataloging-in-Publication Data

Hamilton, Richard F.
    Mass society, pluralism, and bureaucracy : explication, assessment, and commentary /
Richard F. Hamilton.
        p.   cm.
    Includes bibliographical references and index.
    ISBN 0–275–96986–X (alk. paper)
    1. Mass society.   2. Pluralism (Social sciences).   3. Bureaucracy.   I. Title.
    HM866.H36   2001
    301—dc21   00–032374

British Library Cataloguing in Publication Data is available.

Library of Congress Catalog Card Number: 00–032374
ISBN: 0–275–96986–X

First published in 2001

Praeger Publishers, 88 Post Road West, Westport, CT 06881
An imprint of Greenwood Publishing Group, Inc.
www.praeger.com

Printed in the United States of America

The paper used in this book complies with the
Permanent Paper Standard issued by the National
Information Standards Organization (Z39.48–1984).

10   9   8   7   6   5   4   3   2   1

Contents

Tables

Acknowledgments

These comments borrow from and paraphrase the statement appearing in my previous work, *Marxism, Revisionism, and Leninism*, the companion volume to the present one.

Commenting on the intellectual enterprise, Aristotle wrote—I quote from distant memory—that "we cannot collectively fail." The notion was, and still is, appealing to me, even though I know it is mistaken. The best we can hope for is minimization of error. The more widely we consult, the better the final product. The best results depend on the help of capable and willing coworkers.

The following persons fit that description: Mark Chaves, Philip Converse, Frederick Crews, Claude S. Fischer, William H. Form, Norval Glenn, Andrew M. Greeley, Pamela Paxton, Stanley Rothman, Michael Smith, and James D. Wright. I wish to thank all of these collaborators. Their generous assistance is very much appreciated.

My friend, colleague, and coworker, Bill Form, deserves special commendation. For his services, a summa cum laude. He has read the entire manuscript, several times over, and provided many pages of comments.

Special thanks are due also to the Mershon Center, Ohio State University, for financial support and for many other kinds of assistance. I am much indebted to Richard Ned Lebow, the center's director, and to Mershon's superb staff, most especially to Wynn Kimble. A special note of thanks and appreciation goes to Young Ho Kim, my research assistant during much of this work and author of the Appendix. For exceptional diligence and dedication, he too deserves a summa cum laude.

The many contributions of Irene Hamilton are gratefully acknowledged.

Introduction

This volume will explicate, assess, and critique three major social theories. As used here, the word theory refers to a set of general statements purporting to describe and explain a complex reality. In social affairs one is dealing with an infinitude of events. Finite minds cannot handle such quantity. All thought, therefore, whether one recognizes it or not, involves some arrangement for simplification; that is, some theory or theories.

The social, political, and economic arrangements of the world's richest countries are based on liberal principles (to be sure, with many modifications). First formulated in the eighteenth century, the intellectuals of the Enlightenment provided a critique of the old regimes that in later elaboration came to be called liberalism. Armed with that powerful critique, the liberals gradually dismantled the old regimes, ultimately replacing them with the new rational, free arrangements.

All of the other major social theories—those appearing in the nineteenth and twentieth centuries—derive in one way or another from liberalism. Some are critiques of the liberal achievement, the most obvious being those of Marxism and its derivatives. Some others are best seen as modifications or extensions of the liberal original.[1]

Liberalism created "the individual." A principal aim of its advocates was to free humans from the restrictions and obligations of handed-down institutions. Defenders of the old regime, not too surprisingly, offered their critique pointing to some alarming consequences of the new arrangement. Their critique, later called the mass society theory, holds that the new liberal arrangements disrupt or break down traditional social groupings, leaving individuals isolated, anxious, and powerless. Manipulative demagogues then make appeals to the "vulnerable" masses, offering them plausible but unrealistic solutions. Moved by the demagoguery, the gullible masses then overthrow the established regimes. Dictatorship, death, and destruction follow. The accounts are embellished with examples drawn from ancient Greece and Rome; the French Revolution is cited as the archetypical modern case.

Commenting on the same societies and recognizing some of the same problems, the pluralist theory sees a solution to the problems of isolation, anxiety, and powerlessness through the creation of voluntary associations of formally organized groups. Making use of liberal freedoms of speech, press, and assembly, individuals sharing a given concern could form associations and work together for their goals, thereby gaining power or influence they would not have as individuals. Put differently, this allows some degree of representation, some channels of influence that would not exist either in the old regime or in "the mass society." A wide and diverse range of associations results, this bringing about a dispersion of power. The pluralist theory challenged the claims of Marxism and its many variants and also those of the mass society theory.

The early formulations of liberalism focused on individuals and on social arrangements allowing them free choices. Economic liberalism focused on the choices of individual entrepreneurs who headed small firms, the thousands of retail outlets, or manufacturing establishments. But that reality changed in the course of the nineteenth and twentieth centuries. Economies of scale, growing capital requirements, and need for expert services meant that large units became more frequent, or in some versions became the typical or dominant experience. Responding to this new development, some commentators formulated another major social theory, the theory of bureaucracy.

As opposed to the image of liberal society with its "new realm of freedom," this new theory sees individuals, to an ever-greater degree, working in giant organizations, their behavior controlled by bureaucratic rules. Within those establishments, the "rule of the expert" replaces the individualism and freedom championed in liberal theory and practice. The bureaucratic tendency appears in both private and public affairs. It also appears within voluntary associations. To be effective, those organizations also must be large, have substantial resources, and have expert direction. Among other things, this position largely erased the distinction between free and authoritarian regimes. Both, it was argued, would be forced to institute expert rule and the bureaucratic form.

Our knowledge of social theories, even of those in the active repertory, is ordinarily rather limited. Educated citizens will have picked up a sketchy understanding of the frequently used theories in the course of growing up. Liberalism, for example, is the common sense of economically advanced capitalist societies. We pick up bits and pieces of the framework in early family training, in schools, and from the mass media. One might gain a more detailed understanding of the theory at a university, possibly in a course on political philosophy or one on social theory. Few people would ever be thoroughly informed about the theory itself, about its logic, its variant forms, and the shifts of emphasis.

Even more problematic, very few people would be informed about the impacts and consequences of liberal practice. To learn how liberalism actually worked—in Britain, France, Italy, or the United States—a specialized history course would be required, perhaps one in economic history. Did the enlarged trade territories that came with the Prussian Customs Union or the later European Union increase the wealth of the affected nations? How much difference, if any, was made by the reform? Should we extend the practice, instituting it elsewhere? Apart from a small number of specialists, most of them economic historians, few people are likely to have more than a passing knowledge of the answers to those questions.

Similar problems appear with respect to other major social theories; for example, with Marxism in its many variants, or with the mass society theory. Educated citizens frequently refer to these theories, using elements of the vocabulary and vouching for many of the major conclusions. But few informed citizens could provide serious documentation for any claim about the thought and behavior of "the bourgeoisie" or "the masses." Although the theories provide the organizing principles for much of our thought, discussion, and practice, the evidential basis for many of those widely accepted conclusions, as will be seen, is limited and in some cases is mistaken.

All social theories are subject to what might be termed "the problem of drift." A theory is formulated, disseminated, widely used, and modified with changed circumstances. It may then for a time lose its attraction and fall into abeyance. But then, still later, it is revived, perhaps with a slightly different focus, possibly with a new vocabulary. At any given point in that history, opinions would vary as to the theory's utility. For some, it might be passé; for others, it might be valuable and still useful.

The erratic relationship between a given theory and "relevant evidence" contributes to the drift. Given the necessary division of intellectual labor, it sometimes happens that a theory is treated as viable in one specialization but at the same time is rejected by another. Max Weber's Protestant Ethic thesis is routinely commended by sociologists and by many in the humanities. Economic historians, specialists whose works deal with the sources of economic growth, rarely assign any importance to the Weber thesis or to the famous ethic. Michel Foucault constructed a fictional history of "the prison," one assigning considerable importance to Jeremy Bentham's panopticon design. The work is routinely commended by a faithful band of followers, most of them in the humanities. None of them appear to be aware of a simple fact known to most penologists; namely, that the structure was "never built."[2] Not knowing that a central proposition of a given theory has been rejected, the framework may still be treated as viable, useful, accurate, and appropriate. As will be seen, that is the case with respect to the theory of the mass society.

A social psychological element also contributes to these discontinuities. Scholars, academics, and researchers have an interest in producing new materials, new findings, and new insights. After a decade or so of work on a given paradigm, the possibilities for new and significant contributions is ordinarily exhausted or, at best, rather limited. At that point, accordingly, there is an incentive to reach out for and to develop other frameworks. The previous "dominant paradigm" will come to be judged as no longer interesting and, accordingly, is dropped from discussion.

In the late 1950s and early 1960s community power structures were actively researched and discussed. Two sharply divided positions emerged. The reputational method associated with Floyd Hunter concluded that "power" was held by a small and cohesive elite. The decisional method associated with Robert Dahl concluded that power was widely dispersed, all groups having some bases for influence. In the language of the period, it was a struggle between the "elitists" and the "pluralists."[3]

The entire effort came to an abrupt end. The themes researched have been left largely untouched for a quarter of a century.[4] The once hotly disputed theoretical issues have also been abandoned. It is not as if "power" had disappeared from American communities. The problem is that the subject itself is no longer "approved" within the most likely research community. One of the basic assumptions of normal science is that knowledge is cumulative. With continuous research effort and with regular sifting and winnowing, a better understanding will be achieved. But that has not been the case with the study of power.

The pluralist theory was actively discussed and researched, in political science and sociology, in the 1950s and 1960s. But the theory, its themes, and its research agenda were subsequently retired from the active repertory and researchers in those fields turned to other concerns. In the 1990s some pluralist themes reappeared but were now discussed with a different vocabulary. The concern was now with social capital, civic culture, and civil society. The problem again is one of truncated development and a lack of continuity. The opportunity for cumulation was passed up as the theory and findings of one era effectively disappeared.

None of the three theories considered here is "on the cutting edge" in current social science literatures. The mass society theory, as noted, has long since been rejected by serious social science. It does, however, regularly recur in mass media treatments of "contemporary society." It is also a staple in the humanities. Pluralism was once a major theory in the social sciences. Subsequently eclipsed, it is now best described as "on the back burner." But many of the themes, as indicated, have appeared in a new guise. Max Weber's discussion of bureaucracy is not central in contemporary organizational studies. Most specialists would argue, justifiably, that the field has gone far beyond Weber's original. But Weber's argument, which might be called "bureaucratic determinism," is still present and widely discussed in popular sociology and in the humanities.

Given the problem of drift, it is appropriate that we undertake an inventory of the theories in question. This work will lay out the major propositions of each of the three theories. It will then review and bring evidence to bear on those claims. And it will provide some conclusions. It is essentially a stocktaking effort. We are asking, What is useful and what is not in the theories under review? The basic questions are as follows: What stands up? What does not? And what remains to be investigated?

NOTES

1. For a discussion of liberalism and assessment of Marxist responses, see the companion volume to the present work, Richard F. Hamilton, *Marxism, Revisionism, and Leninism: Explication, Assessment, and Commentary* (Westport, Conn.: Praeger, 2000).

2. Both the Weber and Foucault cases are reviewed and documented in Richard F. Hamilton, *The Social Misconstruction of Reality: Validity and Verification in the Scholarly Community* (New Haven: Yale University Press, 1996), chs. 3 and 6.

3. Floyd Hunter, *Community Power Structure* (Chapel Hill: University of North Carolina Press, 1953); Robert A. Dahl, *Who Governs? Democracy and Power in an American City* (New Haven: Yale University Press, 1961); G. William Domhoff, *Who Really Rules? New Haven and Community Power Reexamined* (Santa Monica, Calif.: Goodyear, 1978); Nelson Polsby, *Community Power and Political Theory: A Further Look at the Problem of Evidence and Inference*, 2d ed. (New Haven: Yale University Press, 1980).

4. Yali Peng, "Intellectual Fads in Political Science: The Cases of Political Socialization and Community Power Studies," *PS: Political Science & Politics* 27 (1994): 100–108.

CHAPTER 1

Mass Society

The mass society theory, in all of its various formulations, is based on a sweeping general claim about "the modern world," one announcing a "breakdown of community." These formulations argue the collapse of the stable, cohesive, and supportive communities found in the days of yore. In modern times, as a consequence, one finds rootlessness, fragmentation, breakdown, individuation, isolation, powerlessness, and widespread anxiety.

The original formulations of this position, those of the nineteenth century, were put forth by conservatives, persons identified with or defending the old regime.[1] These were critiques of the liberal theory or, more precisely, of liberal practice. The basic aim of the liberals was to free individuals from the restraints of traditional institutions. That aim was to be achieved by dismantling the "irrational" arrangements of the old regime. Liberals, understandably, were enthusiastic about the achievement—free men could do things, accomplish things, create things that were impossible under the old arrangement. The collective benefits, they argued, were (or would be) enormous. The conservative critics agreed about some aspects of the history; for example, about the general process of individuation. They, however, called it fragmentation or "decline of community." They, understandably, provided very different assessments of the consequences. At its simplest, the liberals argued an immense range of benefits coming with the transformation, a conclusion signaled, for example, in Adam Smith's title, *The Wealth of Nations*. The mass society theorists agreed with the basic diagnosis but drew strikingly opposite conclusions pointing to a wide and alarming range of personal and social costs.

The modern world begins, supposedly, with an enormous uprooting of populations. Ever greater numbers are forced to move from small and stable communities into large cities. In place of the strong, intimate, personal supports found in the small community, large cities are characterized by fleeting, impersonal contacts. The family is now smaller. The isolated nuclear family—father, mother, and dependent children—is now the rule, replacing the extended family of farm and village. The urban neighborhoods are less personal. The frequent moves required in urban locales make deep, long-lasting friendships difficult, if not impossible. As opposed to the support and solidarity of the village, instrumental and competitive relationships are typical in large cities and this too makes sustained social ties problematic. In the mass society people are "atomized." The human condition is one of isolation and loneliness. The claims put forth in this tradition are typically unidirectional—the prediction is "more and more." There is ever more uprooting, more isolation, more anxiety, and more societal breakdown.

The nineteenth-century versions of this theory focused on the insidious role of demagogues. In those accounts, traditional rulers, monarchs, the aristocracy, and the upper classes did their best to govern fundamentally unstable societies. But from time to time demagogues arose out of the masses, men who played on the fears and anxieties of an uneducated, poorly informed, and gullible populace. The plans or programs offered by the demagogues were said to involve "easy solutions." But those plans, basically, were unrealistic or manipulative, providing no solutions at all. The demagogues brought revolution, which was followed by disorder, destruction, and death. The traditional patterns of rule were disrupted; the experienced and well-meaning leaders were displaced, either killed or driven into exile. The efforts of the demagogues made an already desperate situation worse.

Conservative commentators pointed to the French Revolution as the archetypical case, with Robespierre and his associates as the irresponsible demagogues. Mass society theorists also pointed to the experience of ancient Greece and Rome. There too the demagogues had done their worst, overthrowing the Athenian democracy and bringing an end to the Roman republic. The republic was succeeded by a series of emperors and praetorians, men who, with rare exception, showed various combinations of incompetence, irresponsibility, and viciousness.

The lesson of the mass society theory, in brief, was that if the masses overthrew the traditional leaders, things would be much worse. The "successes" of liberalism, the destruction of traditional social structures, the elimination of stable communities, and the resulting individualism (also called egoism) could only worsen an already precarious situation. The theory, accordingly, counseled acceptance or acquiescence.

It is easy to see such claims as ideological, as pretense, as justifications for old-regime privilege. Such claims were (and are) given short shrift in the liberal dramaturgy and, still later, in the dramaturgy of the left. In those accounts, the old regime is portrayed as powerful. The rulers, after all, have vast wealth and influence; they control the police and the ultimate force, the army.

Later liberal and left accounts appearing in the twentieth century would assign considerable importance to the rulers' control of the press and other media.

In private discussions, however, the leaders of the old regime reported a sense of powerlessness. Their hold on power, they felt, was tenuous; they stood on the edge of the abyss. Chateaubriand, the French ambassador to Britain, congratulated Lord Liverpool, the British prime minister, on the stability of his nation's institutions. Liverpool pointed to the metropolis outside his windows and replied, "What can be stable with these enormous cities? One insurrection in London and all is lost." The French Revolution itself proved the flimsiness of "established" rule. Later, in 1830, the restored monarchy in France collapsed after only a week of fighting in the capital. In 1848 Louis Philippe's regime fell after only two days of struggle. A month later the Prussian king and queen, effectively prisoners of the revolution, were forced to do obeisance to the fallen insurgents. The queen's comment: "Only the guillotine is missing." More than a century later the historian J. R. Jones summarized the later British experience:

The apparently massive strength and predominant influence of conservatism in the last seventy-five years have led historians to miss the fact that, during long periods of this time, many conservatives felt that they were irretrievably on the defensive, faced not with just electoral defeat but also doomed to become a permanent and shrinking minority, exercising a dwindling influence on the mind and life of the nation.[2]

Early in the twentieth century, in a different strand of development, sociologists in Europe and North America developed an extensive literature that argued the loss-of-community thesis. Among the Europeans, we have Ferdinand Tönnies and Georg Simmel. The latter's essay, "The Metropolis and Mental Life," had considerable influence in North America, especially in the development of sociology at the University of Chicago. The Chicago school was founded by Robert Ezra Park, who had studied under Simmel. Park's essay, "The City: Suggestions for Investigation of Human Behavior in the Urban Environment," provided the agenda for generations of sociologists. Another central work in the Chicago tradition was Louis Wirth's 1938 article, "Urbanism as a Way of Life." The city, Wirth wrote, is

characterized by secondary rather than primary contacts. The contacts of the city may indeed be face to face, but they are nevertheless impersonal, superficial, transitory, and segmental. . . . Our acquaintances tend to stand in a relationship of utility to us. . . . [Each] is overwhelmingly regarded as a means for the achievement of our own ends. Whereas the individual gains, on the one hand, a certain degree of emancipation or freedom from the personal and emotional controls of intimate groups, he loses, on the other hand, the spontaneous self-expression, the morale, and the sense of participation that comes with living in an integrated society. This constitutes essentially the state of *anomie*, or the social void, to which Durkheim alludes.[3]

Writing almost a half-century after Wirth, sociologist Barrett A. Lee and his coworkers—in an important challenge to those claims—commented on this tradition as follows:

Few themes in the literature of the social sciences have commanded more sustained attention than that of the decline of community. . . . In its basic version, the thesis exhibits a decidedly antiurban bias, stressing the invidious contrast between the integrated small-town resident and the disaffiliated city dweller. As human settlements increase in scale during societal modernization, individuals are presumably uprooted from their web of "gemeinschaft" relationships and cast socially and psychologically adrift in a "sea of strangers." One alleged consequence of the modernization process is an attenuation of local sentiments and ties. Just as the urban setting reduces allegiance to the family and other primary groups, so does it weaken attachment to the neighborhood. Conventional wisdom asserts unequivocally that [quoting Park] "in the city environment the neighborhood tends to lose much of the significance which it possessed in simpler and more primitive forms of society."[4]

The sociologists do not appear to have had any clear political orientation. Their work was value-neutral, pointing to what they took as a basic fact about modern societies without proposing any specific remedies.

Later in the twentieth century a new version of the mass society theory was formulated. This may be termed the left variant. All three versions of the theory, right, neutral, and left, agree on the basics, the underlying root causes of the modern condition, all agreeing on the decline of community. But the right and left differ sharply in their portraits of the rulers, the elites, the upper classes, and the bourgeoisie. In the rightist version, the rulers face a serious threat from below, from the demagogues and their mass followings. Their control is said to be very tenuous. In the left version, the rulers are portrayed as skillful controllers of the society. Their success depends on the adept use of the mass media.

The bourgeoisie, the ruling class, or its executive agency, the "power elite," is said to control the mass media of communication—the press, magazines, motion pictures, radio, and television—using them for their purposes. Much news and commentary is said to be self-serving. It is essentially ideological, material designed to justify and defend "the status quo." The entertainment provided is diversionary in character, intended to distract people from their real problems. Advertising in the media serves the same purposes: distraction, creation of artificial needs, and provision of false solutions. The bourgeoisie, it is said, owns and controls the media. With their vast resources, they are able to hire specialists of all kinds—market researchers, media consultants, psychologists, and so forth—to aid them in this manipulative effort. The near-helpless audience (as ever, atomized, powerless, and anxious) is psychologically disposed to accept the "nostrums" provided.

Elements of this position appeared in the writings of the Italian Marxist, Antonio Gramsci, with his concept of ideological hegemony. Some writers in

the "Frankfurt school," most notably Herbert Marcuse, also argued this position. It appeared also in the work of C. Wright Mills, in his influential book,
The Power Elite. Many others have offered variants of this position.[5]

The left mass society theory provides a third "revision" of the Marxist
framework; that is, after those of Bernstein and Lenin. It is the third major
attempt to explain the absence of the proletarian revolution.[6] Marx and Engels
assigned no great importance to the mass media. They occasionally referred
to items in the "bourgeois press," adding sardonic comments about its "paid
lackeys." But newspaper accounts were treated as of little importance. They
could not stop or reverse the "wheel of history." But in this third revision, the
bourgeoisie had found the means to halt the "inevitable" course. The controllers of the media were able to penetrate the minds of the masses and could
determine the content of their outlooks. The masses were said to be drugged
or, to use a favored term, they were "narcotized."

The mass society position appears in still another setting: within the mass
media itself. In the 1950s, in the Eisenhower era, the mass media were unambiguously affirmative about "society" and its major institutions. Families were
happy and wholesome; the nation's leaders, at all levels, were honorable and
upstanding. In the late 1960s media content changed dramatically. Programs
now made use of the mass society portrait and the themes of social dissolution. Families, neighborhoods, and cities were now "falling apart." Many
exposés, in books, magazines, motion pictures, and television, in the news
and in "investigative reports," told tales of cunning manipulation. Unlike the
right and left versions of the mass society theory, these critics do not appear
to have any clear political program. They appear, rather, to be driven by an
interest in "exposure." No evident plan, directive, or call for action seems to
be involved. Many of the participants appear to be modern-day liberals, not
socialists or Marxists. This position will be referred to as the left-liberal variant of the mass society theory.[7]

The mass society theory has had a peculiar episodic history, a coming and
going in attention. It had a wave of popularity in the 1940s when Karl
Mannheim, Emil Lederer, Hannah Arendt, and Sigmund Neumann, all German exile-scholars, attempted to explain the major events of the age.[8] A sociologist, William Kornhauser presented an empirically based synthesis in 1959,
but this effort, on balance, had little impact.[9] In the 1960s a wave of "left" mass
society theorizing appeared, beginning with Herbert Marcuse's influential work,
One Dimensional Man. In 1970 Charles Reich's *The Greening of America*
appeared, a book destined to have, for several years, an enormous influence.
His depiction of the nation is entirely within the mass society framework:

America is one vast, terrifying anti-community. The great organizations to which most
people give their working day, and the apartments and suburbs to which they return at
night are equally places of loneliness and isolation. Modern living has obliterated
place, locality, and neighborhood. . . . The family, the most basic social system, has

been ruthlessly stripped of its functional essentials. Friendship has been coated over with a layer of impenetrable artificiality.[10]

Few research-oriented social scientists have given the mass society theory much credence in the last couple of decades, this for very good reason: Virtually all of the major claims of the theory have been controverted by an overwhelming body of evidence. Many academics in other fields, however, continue to argue its merit. It is a favorite of specialists in the literary sciences. The theory, as noted, is also a favorite of journalists, of social affairs commentators, of writers, dramatists, and poets.[11]

This paradoxical result requires some explanation. The depictions of "the human condition" in contemporary accounts have a distinctive bifurcated character. The work produced by research-oriented scholars ordinarily has a very limited audience, most of it appearing in limited-circulation journals for small groups of specialists. Those specialists rarely attempt to bring their findings to the attention of larger audiences. Attempts to correct misinformation conveyed by the mass media are also infrequent. The producers of mass media content show an opposite neglect: They rarely contact academic specialists to inquire about the lessons found in the latest research. Some examples of this bifurcation will be reviewed later in this chapter.

Those who argue and defend mass society claims, on the whole, have an enormous audience. Writing in 1956, Daniel Bell, the noted sociologist, stated that apart from Marxism, the mass society theory was probably the most influential social theory in the Western world. Four decades later, that conclusion is still valid. These intellectual productions reach millions of susceptible members of the upper and upper-middle classes, most especially those referred to as the "intelligentsia."[12]

The mass society theory proves well-nigh indestructible. It continues to have wide and enthusiastic support in some circles, regardless of any and all countering evidence. Some people know the relevant evidence but engage in various "theory-saving" efforts, essentially ad hoc dismissals of fact. Some people, of course, simply do not know the available evidence, this stemming from the compartmentalization of academia. Some academics do not make the effort required to find out what is happening elsewhere. Others appear to be indifferent to evidence. Personal psychology or dispositions may also be operating. Some people appear to have a psychological "fixation": They are "driven" to a negative reading of the human condition.[13]

THE PREMODERN EXPERIENCE

The mass society theory, in most formulations, begins with the division of human experience into two sharply contrasting epochs. It is the distinction of traditional and modern societies, or, in other words, of arrangements "before" and "after" the recent transition. Before, human communities were rooted; people had a place and had identities based on a rooted communal existence. After, we have uprooting, dissolution of community, and continuous movement.

Gerhart Lenski and Jean Lenski, in their overview of human existence from the earliest beginnings to the present, provide a strikingly different conclusion: "For the first 4 million years or more of hominid history, our ancestors all lived in hunting and gathering societies. This was the only type of society in existence throughout this period. Only in the last 10,000 to 12,000 years—the last one-fourth of 1 percent of hominid history—have other types of societies evolved."[14] Hunters and gatherers are, of course, migratory populations. Their condition differed from the mass society in that entire communities were moving, not isolated individuals. Those populations would have no fixed roots and little sense of place as bases for their identities. Only in the last ten to twelve millennia did other possibilities appear and become dominant, the two principal ones being horticultural and agricultural societies.

These societies would be more rooted than those of the hunters and gatherers. It would be a mistake, however, to see these forms as sharply distinguished from the contemporary experience. Steven Hochstadt has provided a sweeping review of migration in preindustrial Germany. He reports high levels of movement, levels exceeding those found in the twentieth century. "In all probability," he concludes, "German urban communities in the centuries before industrialization housed a more mobile population than they do now." Writing of the village experience, he concludes that "outmigration reached 40%–50% in the seventeenth century and 35% in the eighteenth." Hochstadt's summary conclusion reads, "Migration is a necessary element in all historical forms of material life, nomadic, agrarian, and industrial. Thus it cannot be said to be uniquely 'caused' by a certain state in the development of economic life."[15]

Conservative mass society theorists and contemporary left liberal social critics both make regular use of what might be termed good-old-days hypotheses. We do have some evidence on the quality of life in those "old days," evidence that is routinely overlooked in those formulations. Hochstadt, describing villages in seventeenth-century Germany, reports that from "one-third to one-half of all children died before reaching the age of 20." A study of Sweden's demography in the late eighteenth century gives roughly comparable death rates. It adds another figure—the "life expectancy" of marriages. Couples pledging to stay together "till death do us part" were agreeing to a relationship that would last, on average, about fifteen years. In the typical experience, one of the partners would not live to see their oldest child as a young adult.[16]

Those findings indicate the falsity of another aspect of the good-old-days portraiture. Extended families, those having "three generations under one roof," are often said to have been the typical form. In fact, however, such families were rare and when present were of brief duration. The average age at first marriage was high and death came early. And that means most families would have had only two generations present and many of those, obviously, would have been incomplete, "broken" by death as opposed to by divorce. The possibility of frequent three-generation families occurs only in the late twentieth century, with marriage occurring at a younger age and with significant increases of life expectancies.[17]

ON THE RECENT EXPERIENCE

The mass society claims about contemporary life involve what might be termed "bad new days" hypotheses. The principal claims, in most formulations of this position, come in broad, sweeping, categorical form. The initial formulations here follow that procedure. Later we will consider some appropriate modifications and specifications.

1. Modern societies are characterized by an absence of close personal connections. The typical condition of persons living in such societies is isolation.
2. Most formulations provide a before–after comparison, with connectedness in the old days, isolation in the new days. The modern era has seen a unidirectional "downward" tendency.
3. Most people in those modern societies are said to be unhappy and dissatisfied with their own lives and with life in their communities.
4. The trends, in most readings, are said to be negative—things are getting worse. Given the presumed trends, the expressions of unhappiness or dissatisfaction, accordingly, would show a steady increase.
5. Some accounts make an appropriate specification. Rather than the sweeping characterization—modern society is mass society—a differentiated formulation is sometimes offered: The pathologies of modern life are found in the urban context. Connectedness is said to decline across the continuum as one moves from the villages and towns to the metropolis.
6. Reports of unhappiness, dissatisfaction, and isolation accordingly will increase with the size of community. Most discussions of social involvement assign considerable importance to the community-size factor. One is not, presumably, talking of 5- or 10-point percentage differences.

Most formulations of the mass society thesis provide an incomplete test of the basic claims: They argue that the lack of social connections, the isolation, and the resulting anxieties are due to the factors indicated (urbanization, competitiveness, high mobility, industrialization, etc.). Put differently, the causal factors giving rise to the mass society count for a lot. Any other factors count for little or nothing. Most mass society accounts neglect an obvious requirement; namely, consideration of the *ceteris paribus* assumption. Three alternatives will be explored here:

7. Race or race-related penalties might have some impact on the levels of unhappiness, satisfaction, and trust found in the large cities. The black population is very disproportionately concentrated in those settings.

8. Social connections vary systematically with marital status. At its simplest, this means that married persons connect disproportionately with family members and relatives; single, separated, and divorced persons connect disproportionately with friends. Persons in the latter categories are more likely to be located in large cities, a fact which, in part at least, is linked to life-cycle factors (as opposed to the "urban condition").

9. Social connections vary systematically by age. People do different things as they pass from young-adult to senior-citizen status. Different options are open to them, and some options, effectively, are definitively closed. One's siblings and cousins are, on the whole, located within a narrow spectrum of age cohorts, the majority being within a ten- or fifteen-year span. Most friends are also found within a narrow age range. In some measure then, the extent of one's connectedness will be determined by age. Persons who survive to their mid-seventies, with rare exception, will have lost all relatives of the previous generation. They will also have lost roughly half of their siblings, cousins, and friends. Some of the isolation and loneliness present in "modern society," in short, is best seen as a "fact of life."

A REVIEW OF EVIDENCE

The first of these claims might be described as the "isolation and loneliness" theme. Beginning in 1972, the National Opinion Research Center (NORC) has conducted annual national surveys that contain a wide range of questions on basic social facts and issues. These are referred to as the General Social Surveys (GSS). Questions are asked about social ties, specifically about the frequency of social contacts. Each survey provides a cross-sectional portrait of the U.S. adult population. These surveys allow assessment of the claims of isolation and involvement and also those about the trends.[18]

The key question reads, "Would you use this card and tell me which answer comes closest to how often you do the following things. Spend a social evening with: your parents, a brother or sister, relatives, someone who lives in your neighborhood, friends who live outside the neighborhood?" In addition, people were asked about the frequency of visits to a bar or tavern? Seven degrees of frequency were offered, ranging from "almost every day" to "never." Appropriate exclusions were made where no such relative was available; that is, for respondents whose parents had died or those without siblings. These questions set a demanding standard; that is, spending a social evening with people. A wide range of more limited contacts were thus excluded, such as casual conversations in the neighborhood or at work, lunch meetings, church or voluntary association contacts (these linkages, however, were picked up with other questions and will be reviewed in the next chapter). Because of that demanding requirement, the results that follow dealing with family and friendship contacts understate the extent of social connections. Some people might not frequent bars or taverns but might spend time at city or country clubs. Because it is a different kind of connection, and to simplify the discussion, visits to bars or taverns are not reported in the following tables.[19] For an initial overview, the results from four GSS surveys, those from 1990 to 1994 (there was no survey in 1992), have been merged (Table 1.1).

Overall, the results show considerable amounts of social connectedness in the five areas reported, as measured by the "social evening" standard. Some lack of contact also appears, most often with respect to neighbors, with three-tenths reporting never having that kind of evening. No sweeping categorical judgment seems appropriate. American society is not overwhelmingly "social." In no case does a majority report frequent or "dense" contacts. At the same time, however, no majority reports isolation or a general absence of contact. Apart from the neighborly contacts, most responses fall toward the social end of the continuum. Approximately three-tenths of the respondents report at least once-a-week contact with parents. The opposite case, no contact at all, is reported by one-seventh of the respondents, and another tenth report meeting only once a year.

The social tendency is most pronounced with respect to contact with relatives. It is less strong with respect to contacts with siblings and friends and is least so with neighbors. Roughly one-sixth of the respondents appear to be either without friends or to have very attenuated friendship relationships, to that extent apparently confirming the mass society prediction. But, against that experience, almost a quarter reported regular weekly contacts with friends and another fifth indicated contacts several times a month.[20]

This evidence, in summary, does not support the first of the basic mass society claims—that people in the mass society are isolated. Most report some involvement, ranging from middling to much, as the typical experience. One should, in addition, consider the possibility of combinations. Thirty percent of the respondents reported no contact with neighbors, but two-fifths of those "unneighborly" respondents reported seeing their parents at least several times a month; half of them reported the same level of contact with relatives; and two-fifths reported seeing friends that often. The options could overlap. A brother or other relative could also be a friend. That "someone" in the neighborhood could be a sister or other relative.

The GSS questions allow direct inquiry as to the extent of isolation. The basic question is, How many respondents report *no* contact at all? Put differently, how many report "never" in response to all five relationships presented in Table 1.1? The answer, for the GSS merged samples, 1990–1994, is 1.3 percent. Even with a more relaxed standard, those saying never, or about once a year, or several times a year, isolation amounts to only 7.3 percent of the total (N = 3,481). The basic conclusion is that extreme isolation in the contemporary United States is very rare.[21]

Table 1.1
Frequency of Social Evenings (NORC-GSS: 1990–1994 Merge)

	Type of Contact				
	Parents	**Siblings**	**Relatives**	**Neighbors**	**Friends**
Frequency of Contact					
Almost everyday	9 %	6 %	8 %	5 %	3 %
Once or twice a week	20	14	26	17	20
Several times a month	14	13	19	12	20
About once a month	14	15	17	14	23
Several times a year	19	25	19	12	18
About once a year	11	17	7	9	7
Never	14	11	4	30	10
N =	(2,584)	(3,202)	(4,988)	(4,981)	(4,986)
No such relatives	27 %	9 %			
N =	(3,515)	(3,510)			

One should ask about the appropriate standard or reference point. It is conceivable that the hunters and gatherers might have reported weekly or daily contacts with respect to all of these GSS questions (apart from the bar visits and friends outside the neighborhood). But for a modern society the expectation of daily contact would be unrealistic. In agrarian and industrial societies, at all times and places, some people will have little or no contact with parents, this reflecting unfortunate interpersonal experiences. Some of that separation might be due to geography: Long-distance migration breaks up families. Some of it might be due to poverty, the costs of visits being prohibitive. At all times, some people will choose an isolated existence. Some people are not sociable, preferring instead quiet evenings with a book, or working on a stamp collection, or watching television. Some of that minority isolation, in other words, is due to interpersonal difficulties, to some psychological factors unrelated to the social factors characteristic of the mass society. Again, consideration should be given to the *ceteris paribus* assumption, to the possibility that other things are not equal. The basic question is, How much of that minority isolation is due to the mass society and how much to other factors?

THE TRENDS FROM THE 1970s TO THE 1990s

The mass society theory predicts a steady loss of social connections. This, the second of the delineated claims, may be tested with the GSS questions, which cover more than two decades of experience. To simplify the large quantity of information, the studies have been merged into five periods, the early and late 1970s, the early and late 1980s, and the early 1990s. Arithmetic means have been calculated for each kind of contact. A 6 was given for daily contact, a 5 for visits once or twice a week, and so on down to a 0 for no contact. A score of 3.00 would mean the average frequency of visits was about once a month.

In four of the five areas the prediction of decline is not supported (Table 1.2). Some fluctuations appear with respect to contacts with parents, siblings, and relatives, but on balance the levels in the early 1990s are very close to those of the 1970s. In one area, contact with neighbors, evidence consonant with the mass society prediction does appear, in that a fair-sized and significant decline is registered. That might stem from the corrosiveness of modern society, or again it might be due to some other factors. The increase in women's employment would reduce the amount of time available for such contacts. Contacts with friends showed some minor fluctuations, but on balance the best conclusion is "no change."

Table 1.2
Sociability Trends (NORC-GSS: Five Merges)

	Average Number of Contacts with[a]				
	Parents[b]	Siblings[b]	Relatives	Neighbors	Friends
Year					
1972-1974	N/A[c]	N/A[c]	3.62	2.93	2.97
1975-1978	2.98	2.66	3.56	2.73	2.95
1980-1984	3.12	2.75	3.47	2.63	3.05
1985-1989	2.99	2.66	3.49	2.54	3.00
1990-1994	2.96	2.65	3.50	2.40	3.08

[a]Arithmetic means. Scoring as follows: almost every day = 6; once or twice a week = 5; several times a month = 4; about once a month = 3; several times a year = 2; about once a year = 1; never = 0.

[b]Those with parents and/or siblings.

[c]N/A = not asked.

PERSONAL REACTIONS: HAPPINESS AND SATISFACTION

The third of the basic claims focuses on reported reactions. People in the mass society presumably recognize their plight and, accordingly, would express their feelings of isolation, their resulting anxieties, and their sense of desperation. Majorities should report those sentiments. With "things" getting worse, the fourth prediction is that reports of happiness and/or satisfaction should show declines.

The GSS question on general happiness has been asked for more than two decades. It reads, "Taken all together, how would you say things are these days—would you say that you are very happy, pretty happy, or not too happy?" The results, shown in Table 1.3, indicate, first, that most people, the majority,

Table 1.3
General Happiness and Marital Happiness: 1972–1994 (NORC-GSS: Five Merges)

	Very Happy	Pretty Happy	Not Too Happy	Total
General Happiness				
1972-1974	35 %	51 %	14 %	4,586
1975-1978	34	54	14	6,028
1980-1984	33	54	12	6,091
1985-1989	32	57	13	7,408
1990-1994	31	58	11	7,443
Marital Happiness				
1973-1974[a]	69 %	29 %	3 %	2,131
1975-1978	66	31	3	3,887
1980-1984	65	32	3	3,549
1985-1989	62	36	3	4,101
1990-1994	62	35	3	3,906

Note: Figures do not add to 100 percent due to rounding.
[a]Not asked in 1972.

describe themselves as "pretty happy." Most of the rest, approximately a third of the total, say they are "very happy." Extreme distress, the response antici- pated by the mass society theorists, is reported by approximately one-eighth of the respondents.[22]

If things were getting worse, that should be reflected in these responses. The findings show a very slight change, a 4-percent decline in the "very happy" responses over the two-decade period. The middling "pretty happy" category shows a 7-percent increase, while the "not too happy" choice shows a modest decline. The majority choices go very much against the mass society claims. The small changes in the distributions provide no compelling support for the "getting worse" claims. As always, one must put the *ceteris paribus* question: Is the unhappiness of the not-too-happy eighth due to the circumstances of the mass society? Or is it due to something else: the death of a loved one, illness, poverty, losses associated with age, or a concern with troubles else- where in the nation or in the world?

The GSS also inquired about marital happiness: "Taking things all together, how would you describe your marriage? Would you say that your marriage is very happy, pretty happy, or not too happy?" Over the last two decades, be- tween three-fifths and two-thirds of the marrieds have described their mar- riages as "very happy." Most of the rest, approximately a third, report the relationship as "pretty happy." The "not-too-happy" choice is minuscule, at 3 percent at all times (in the individual studies the range is 2 and 4 percent). A modest negative trend is indicated, with the percentage saying "very happy" falling by 7 percentage points. The corresponding increase appears in the "pretty happy" column (Table 1.3).[23]

Those results focus on the currently married and thus include answers from a segment, 23 percent of the total, who have been divorced (at least once). That segment matches the "first-marriage" majority in their reports of marital happiness.[24] The two facts, high levels of marital breakup and high levels of reported marital happiness, are not contradictory. A large number of marriages, the most problematic ones, did break up, a development made possible by the general easing of divorce laws in the 1950s and 1960s.[25] For most, the marital breakup was followed by a second marriage, one that was found, presumably, to be more rewarding. The exclusive focus on "marital breakup" is obviously one-sided. It is akin to an account of a cyclical process—economic fluctua- tions, for example—which reported only the "downside."

One staple item in the repertory of mass society claims is the notion of increasing marital breakdown. For a couple of decades public discussion was framed by two presumed facts: the "soaring" divorce rate and "half of today's marriages ending in divorce." The divorce rate in the United States increased in the 1960s and 1970s to all-time high levels. But then, beginning in the early 1980s, the rate began to decline. The changing rates and the constant 50-percent divorce "conclusion" are incompatible. With the divorce rates ris- ing and then declining, the predictions with respect to marital breakup should change accordingly.[26]

The current levels of marital stability and breakup may be obtained from the GSS. Three studies, in 1993, 1994, and 1996, were merged to increase the number of cases. All persons reporting ever being married, including the widowed, were considered for this purpose. Current marital status and marital history were then examined by cohort. Among those fifty to fifty-nine years of age, 49 percent reported no prior divorce (N = 942). Another 23 percent had remarried following a divorce. Twenty-eight percent were either separated or divorced at the time of the interview. Similar results, of 47, 21, and 31 percent, respectively, were found in the forty- to forty-nine-year-old cohort. Some family specialists argue that a response bias is operating and that the incidence of divorce is underreported. Some respondents do not accurately report their previous marital histories.[27]

It is not "in the cards" that younger cohorts will repeat the experience of those older segments. People are now marrying at a later age, both of the partners thus having greater self-knowledge when making the decision. That suggests the down trend in divorce is likely to continue. Put differently, increased marital stability seems likely.

One GSS question asked about the composition of the parental family when the respondent was sixteen years old. The responses allow a portrait of family structures across much of the twentieth century. Those who were seventy or older in 1990 would have been born in 1920 or earlier (and have reached age sixteen in 1936 or earlier). Those who were twenty-nine or younger were born in 1961 or later. Sizable majorities in all age categories report intact families at age sixteen. For the five over-thirty categories, approximately three of four report unbroken families. A modest change in the pattern appears among those eighteen to twenty-nine. For them, approximately two-thirds reported intact families. The transition from "old days" to "new days" brought a decline in intact families of approximately 10 percentage points. That translates into two increases of roughly 5 percentage points, the first for stepparent families, the second for "mom only" families (Table 1.4).

The sources of the family breakup vary considerably by age. In the seventy-plus category the death of one or both parents was the principal cause. In the younger cohorts divorce was the principal cause, the relationship being strongly inverse with age. One may summarize as follows: In the oldest cohort, roughly one-quarter of all families were broken when the respondent was sixteen; in the youngest cohort, roughly 33 percent were broken at that age. In the oldest category, two-thirds of the breakups were the result of a death. In the youngest, two-thirds were the result of a divorce. For assessment of the "good-old" versus the "bad-new" days one must ask whether death or divorce would be most harmful for the surviving family members.

The GSS also asked for assessments of family life. The question in this case asked about the satisfaction experienced: "For each area of life I am going to name, tell me the number that shows how much *satisfaction* you get from that area—your family life." A card was presented containing seven numbered categories ranging from "a very great deal" to "none." The distri-

Table 1.4
Family Structure at Age Sixteen by Age of Respondent (NORC-GSS: 1988–1991 Merge)

	Age					
	18-29	30-39	40-49	50-59	60-69	70 or more
Living with:						
Both parents	67 %	78 %	77 %	76 %	77 %	77 %
Step parent(s)	11	5	7	6	5	4
Mom only	16	13	10	13	10	10
Other Arrangements	6	6	5	5	8	9
N =	(1,248)	(1,366)	(1,038)	(612)	(719)	(770)
Of those not with biological parents at age 16, family broken by:[a]						
Death	20 %	30 %	37 %	49 %	59 %	76 %
Divorce	70	52	49	38	27	15
N =	(423)	(322)	(241)	(168)	(179)	(189)

[a]Columns do not add to 100 percent. Remainder sums all other causes.

bution of responses over the last two decades is indicated in Table 1.5. At all points, roughly two-fifths of the respondents reported "a very great deal" of satisfaction and another third chose "a great deal." No decline was indicated, the level of reported satisfaction remaining high and constant. Much attention has been given in the mass media to dysfunctional or problem families. In this data, the combination of the three low-satisfaction categories (some, little, or none) shows the frequencies to be small, ranging from 6 to 8 percent.[28]

Another question in this series asked about the amount of satisfaction gained from "the city or place you live in" (also in Table 1.5). At all points, roughly half of the respondents reported high levels of satisfaction, either "a very great deal" or "a great deal." A modest negative change is indicated: Those reporting "a very great deal" of satisfaction declined some five points. Most of the change involved a shift to the adjacent category, to "a great deal." The combination of three low-satisfaction categories shows a smallish minority at all points, amounting to roughly one in seven respondents.[29] Only 2 percent said "none"; that is, no satisfaction at all.

Table 1.5
Family and Community Satisfaction: 1973–1994 (NORC-GSS: Five Merges)

	A Very Great Deal	A Great Deal	Quite A Bit	A Fair Amount	Some, A Little, None	Total
Satisfaction from Family Life						
1973-1974	43 %	32 %	10 %	8 %	7 %	2,973
1975-1978	41	35	11	7	6	6,009
1980-1984	44	32	11	7	7	6,110
1985-1989	41	34	11	7	8	4,921
1990-1994	41	34	10	8	7	3,465
Satisfaction from City or Place You Live In						
1973-1974	22 %	25 %	17 %	23 %	13 %	2,985
1975-1978	19	29	17	21	14	6,026
1980-1984	19	30	18	20	14	6,120
1985-1989	18	29	19	21	14	4,930
1990-1994	17	31	19	20	14	3,477

Note: Figures do not add to 100 percent due to rounding.

These findings are not exceptional; they do not "stand alone." An extremely detailed investigation of these questions was reported in the work of Angus Campbell, Philip E. Converse, and Willard L. Rodgers. They conducted a comprehensive national survey in 1971, and their major publication was entitled *The Quality of American Life*. It is probably the best work produced to date on these and many other related questions. At one point in the survey respondents were asked about their satisfaction with fifteen aspects of their lives. Here too, a card with numbered options was presented. The choice of 1 meant "completely dissatisfied," and of 7 meant "completely satisfied." The distributions were presented, and for sake of economy, arithmetic means were calculated.

The highest level of reported satisfaction was with marriage, the mean being 6.27. Next came family life (5.92), health (5.78), neighborhood (5.76), and friendships (5.74). The community ("city or county") was further down on the list, in ninth place (5.60). Those results, obviously, are generally comparable to the findings of the GSS. Those assessments involving social relationships (leaving aside health) are highly positive, just the opposite of the mass society expectations. Three percent of the total said they were "completely dissatisfied" with their neighborhood. One percent said the same of their family life. Less than half of a percent reported complete dissatisfaction with their marriage.[30]

A provisional summary is in order: Most people report extensive and positive family relationships. The same holds for friendships. The levels of involvement, in short, are generally high. A third of those questioned describe themselves as "very happy," while the majority report they are "pretty happy." High levels of marital happiness are reported, along with high levels of satisfaction with family life. The reports of satisfaction with the community are also generally positive, although understandably these are not as favorable as those involving closer ties.

Popular accounts routinely assume that isolated persons are unhappy and desperate, and willing to do almost anything to escape that condition. Some people, however, choose isolation. Some people wish to live alone, preferring to work as shepherds, night watchmen, or lighthouse keepers. For some at least, the equation of loneliness with desperation might be unwarranted or at minimum an untested hypothesis. Earlier, we sorted out a group of isolates, that 7.3 percent of the population who reported, at best, contacts several times a year in at least one of the five areas of inquiry. Asked about personal happiness, 28 percent of them said "very happy," 56 percent said "pretty happy," and 16 percent said "not too happy" (N = 253). The comparable figures among the other 93 percent were 31, 59, and 10, respectively (N = 3,233).[31]

URBANISM AS A WAY OF LIFE

Modern society is, of course, "urban society." That expression suggests a predominance of large cities and dense population settlements. One prominent sociologist, Robert Wuthnow, describes the condition and historical tendency as follows:

The villages and farming communities where most people lived at the start of the twentieth century have become virtually extinct. A century ago, nearly three-quarters of the American population lived in small towns and in rural areas. Today, fewer than one-quarter reside in these locales. Nationally, the vast majority of people live in metropolitan areas. If the South is excluded these areas now include more than 80 percent of the population. The composition of urban areas has also changed dramatically over the past century. At one time, urban neighborhoods—reinforced by a common ethnic heritage, language, customs, local shops, and schools—provided community, but these, too, mostly have been lost. People now live anonymous lives in suburban housing developments or in high-rise apartment buildings.[32]

One may easily assess Wuthnow's initial claim: The 1990 U.S. Census showed approximately three-quarters of the resident population living in an "urban place." Although easily ascertained, few nonspecialists know the meaning of that term. The census definition of "urban" is "residence in an incorporated community with 2,500 or more persons."[33] Bucolic villages—Chittenango, New York, Crooksville, Ohio, and Cresco, Iowa—by that definition contain urban populations.

The question of urban dominance obviously requires closer examination. In 1990 the state of Ohio, an urban and industrial state, the seventh largest in the nation, had a population of 10,847,000. The largest cities at that point were Columbus (632,910), Cleveland (505,616), and Cincinnati (364,040). (The respective figures for 1980 were 564,826, 573,822, and 385,457; all Ohio cities except Columbus lost population in the 1980s.) The three cities combined, clearly, make up only a small part, one-seventh, of the state's total. The combined population of the state's ten largest cities came to 2,579,586, 23.8 percent of the total. The tenth largest city was Lorain, with 71,245 inhabitants. Another quarter, approximately, of the state's population lived outside the ten largest cities but within the counties containing those cities. The two segments combined, the ten large cities plus their county populations, contained 52.5 percent of the state's population (up from 48.7 percent in 1980, with most of the gain, clearly, in suburbia).

Three conclusions follow: Approximately one-quarter of the state's population lived in the ten largest cities. Another quarter lived in the immediately surrounding suburbs, in the nine counties containing those cities. And, just under half of the state's population lived in counties whose largest community was smaller than Lorain.[34]

The Census Bureau has developed other definitions, one focusing on metropolitan areas. In this case, the definition was changed from size of incorporated units to one emphasizing economic interdependence. The procedure begins with central cities and adds entire counties that show the requisite links to the core city. By that procedure, a large portion of the nation's population is classified as "metropolitan." But that does not mean densely populated living arrangements with those conventional "urban" correlates. Some examples, again from the Ohio experience, indicate the problem.

The Cleveland Consolidated Metropolitan Statistical Area (CMSA) includes the city's county, Cuyahoga, plus five others. Those other counties contain three of the state's ten largest cities (Akron, Parma, and Lorain). The Cincinnati CMSA contains eight other counties in addition to its own, Hamilton. Two of those counties are located in Kentucky and one is in Indiana. Columbus, the state's largest city, is located in Franklin County. The MSA includes six other counties. A person driving through the six would see many small towns, many farms, and much open country. The "metropolitan area" definition, in short, reclassifies small town and rural settings, removing them from "rural" America and declaring them to be urban. That redefinition, which occurs within the Bureau of the Census, has no impact on the social patterns of the communities involved. Boone County, Kentucky, and Licking County, Ohio, do not become impersonal and their citizens do not become isolated as a result of the Census classification.[35]

The same problem appears with respect to "urban growth." Most depictions of mass society have urban growth occurring exclusively through migration: "Uprooted" persons leave the countryside and move to the city. But growth (or decline) may stem from any of three sources: migration, natural increase, and annexation. In the latter case, the city "reaches out" and incorporates populations in outlying territories. But no changes in social relations follow. There is no sudden loss of connectedness. One striking instance of this kind of urban growth occurred in a single day, April 17, 1920, with the creation of Greater Berlin. The city annexed seven independent towns, some fifty-nine smaller communities, and twenty-seven country estates. It was now thirteen times its former size. The new metropolis included numerous lakes, waterways, forests, and other green spaces. Its population jumped from 2 to 4 million in the course of a single night, possibly the most rapid urban growth in the entire modern period.[36] At minimum, one must make an obvious specification: How much of the urban growth is due to migration? How much is due to natural increase? How much is due to annexation?

To test our fifth hypothesis, the assumed impersonality of the cities (or of the metropolis), the Survey Research Center's (SRC) Belt Code will be used. Respondents were divided into those living in Standard Metropolitan Statistical Areas (SMSAs) and those living elsewhere. The SMSA populations were divided into four categories: persons living in the twelve largest central cities (New York, Los Angeles, Chicago, etc.), those in the next eighty-eight smaller cities, those in suburbs of the twelve largest cities, and those in suburbs of the next eighty-eight cities. The nonmetropolitan population was divided by the size of the county's largest town (whether it was more or less than 10,000 persons). To maximize the number of cases for analysis, we merged four GSS studies, those of 1988, 1989, 1990, and 1991, all based on the 1980 census.[37]

The nation's population at that point fell into two roughly equal segments, one-half living in the SMSAs, one-half living in the nonmetropolitan counties (top line of Table 1.6). The twelve largest central cities, those figuring so prominently in discussions of "urban America," contain only 8 percent of the total population. Adding the next category, the eighty-eight smaller central cities, yields a "big city" population amounting to 20 percent of the total. More people, 28 percent of the total, live in the suburbs of those central cities. Beginning around 1950, many American cities, especially those in the northeast, were turned "inside out," the centers being emptied and the suburbs showing considerable growth.

The largest single category of the six in the SRC Belt Code is a nonmetropolitan segment, those in counties having a town of 10,000 or more. In most instances, that town would be the county seat. Three-eighths of the American population live in these counties. Finally, we have the rural counties, those with no large town; they contain approximately one-eighth of the nation's population. More people reside in those rural counties than in the twelve largest cities.

The insistent equation of "modern society" and "urban" is obviously very misleading. It provides an erroneous conception of the typical experience. The twelve largest cities taken together form a small part of the total and, for

Table 1.6
Size of Community and Sociability (NORC-GSS: 1988–1991 Merge)

	Metropolitan Areas				Nonmetropolitan Areas	
	Central Cities		Suburbs		Counties	
	12 Largest	Next 88	12 Largest	Next 88	Largest Town 10,000 or More	No Town of 10,000 or More
Percent Across = 99 N = 5,907	8	12	11	17	38	13
Contacts with Relatives						
At least 1-2 a week	34 %	34 %	32 %	33 %	36 %	39 %
Several times a month	18	20	19	19	18	16
About once a month	11	13	17	19	15	16
Several times a year	18	21	23	19	19	19
About once a year	12	8	6	6	7	6
Never	7	4	3	4	5	5
N =	(291)	(497)	(447)	(688)	(1,483)	(524)
Contacts with Neighbors						
At least 1-2 a week	28 %	24 %	21 %	22 %	24 %	24 %
Several times a month	12	12	12	11	10	12
About once a month	17	10	13	15	15	18
Several times a year	10	11	16	12	12	13
About once a year	5	11	10	9	9	8
Never	28	33	29	32	30	26
N =	(291)	(497)	(445)	(687)	(1,480)	(523)
Contacts with Friends						
At least 1-2 a week	29 %	24 %	21 %	21 %	22 %	17 %
Several times a month	20	22	20	21	19	15
About once a month	20	23	24	26	23	23
Several times a year	14	16	23	17	17	19
About once a year	4	6	6	5	7	11
Never	14	8	7	10	11	16
N =	(291)	(499)	(448)	(687)	(1,483)	(524)

better or worse, it is a declining part. Suburbs range from the small and bu-colic to the large and cluttered. In most instances, however, they are not densely populated communities. In much of the popular literature, suburbia has been portrayed as having warm and friendly relationships, and if anything, the problem would be an excess of involvement. If we were to choose a midpoint, a community to represent the modal or typical experience, the one-hundredth largest city, along with its suburbs, might be appropriate. In 1990 that was Newport News, Virginia, with a population of 171,000.[38]

The patterns of sociability reported within the six community categories are shown in Table 1.6. Reading across the top row for each kind of contact allows a quick overview of the results. Frequent visiting with relatives, at least once or twice a week, shows little variation across the six categories. The differences between the categories are all small, at best a few points. The pattern of neighborhood visiting is also not that anticipated in most discussions of the subject. The large cities actually showed slightly more visiting with neighbors than any of the other categories. Frequent visits with friends outside the neighborhood also occurred most often in the large cities, again by a small margin. In the extreme size categories, we have 29 and 17 percent, respectively, visiting once or twice a week; the equivalent amount reporting "never" visiting are 14 and 16 percent, respectively. The findings with respect to parental contacts and those with siblings also do not support the standard mass society depiction of "the modern condition." As opposed to the expected strong relationship of impersonality increasing with size, the basic result shows a rough constancy of pattern in all six categories. The differences, on the whole, are small and irregular. Two slight reversals appear; in opposition to the mass society claims, contacts with neighbors and friends are most frequent in the large cities.

Given the importance of the large cities in the mass society theory, a more detailed examination of the twelve largest is appropriate. The following figures contrast the very frequent (several times or more per month) with the infrequent contacts (once a year or never). For visits with relatives, the respective figures are 52 and 19 percent; for neighborly visits, 40 and 33 percent; and for visits with friends, 49 and 18 percent. In all three comparisons, social involvement is far more frequent than isolation.

This evidence provides a serious challenge to the basic mass society claims. The dual claims—the impersonal city versus the friendly towns and villages—receive no serious support in this evidence on contacts with relatives, neighbors, friends outside the neighborhood, parents, and siblings.[39]

Findings of this sort are not new. They provide still another confirmation of results reported in many previous studies. Nearly a half-century ago, three sociologists, Joel Smith, William H. Form, and Gregory P. Stone, investigated friendship patterns in the middle-size city of Lansing, Michigan. Respondents were asked for the names and addresses of their three best friends. Only 15 percent could not name three best friends. Only 4.5 percent (N = 573) reported no friends. A quarter of a century ago, Melvin Seeman published a study entitled "The Urban Alienations: Some Dubious Theses from Marx to Marcuse." With data from the United States, France, and Sweden, he tested for "the lack of community in urban society." His conclusion was that "the evidence provokes serious doubt about the established wisdom."[40]

Population density figured prominently in many discussions of urban problems. It was the crowding that gave rise to the distinctive impersonality. In

many American cities, however, particularly those of the Rust Belt, population densities have declined dramatically. Detroit's territory was almost constant
in the period from 1970 to 1990 (in 1990 it was 138.7 square miles). The population density in those twenty years fell from 10,953 to 7,410 persons per square
mile. San Diego expanded slightly in that same period, going from 316.9 to 324
square miles. Its density increased, from 2,199 to 3,428, but was still less than
half the Detroit figure. Phoenix engaged in an exuberant annexation of desert
lands (247.9 to 419.9 square miles). Its density, however, was effectively unchanged, 2,346 in 1970 and 2,342 in 1990.[41] Population density, it will be
noted, has largely disappeared from discussions of urban problems.

One other finding should be noted: In recent decades the migration pattern
has reversed. The dominant tendency for some years now has been one of
migration to nonmetropolitan areas.[42]

THE URBAN MALAISE

The principal lesson of the previous pages is that the predicted differences
between city and countryside, the dramatic loss of social ties in the city, is not
supported. This section will report on the sixth claim, the personal reactions,
evaluations, or assessments of life as experienced in the different community
contexts.

A useful first view of this subject may be gained from the reports on personal happiness. Overall, as seen earlier, about three out of ten respondents
describe themselves as "very happy." The big-city dwellers are slightly less
likely to give this response, the level being lowest in the twelve largest cities
(25 percent), and in the next eighty-eight (27 percent). Majorities everywhere
described themselves as "pretty happy." The "not too happy" responses are
more frequent in the cities, the numbers for the twelve and eighty-eight cities,
respectively, being 15 and 12 percent (Table 1.7). This comparison, in short,
shows modest support for the mass society position.

The reports on marital happiness show no clear variation by size or type of
community. In all contexts, as seen, majorities of the marrieds reported a "very
happy" relationship. The best case for the urban disorganization and distress hypothesis appears in the "not so happy" category: 7 percent in the twelve largest
cities and 5 percent in the eighty-eight, versus 2 and 3 percent elsewhere.

Some other findings show stronger and more consistent support for the
received hypotheses. Asked how much satisfaction they get from "the city or
place you live in," roughly half of those living in the suburbs and nonmetropolitan counties said either "a very great deal" or "a great deal." The positive
responses were less frequent in the eighty-eight cities (41 percent), and still
less in the twelve (35 percent). Asked about the satisfaction received from
"your family life," the percentages in the large cities were again somewhat
lower. Sizable majorities in all settings, not surprisingly, reported high satisfaction with their friendships. Some differences by community size appear,
but they are small and irregular. The difference between the largest cities and

Table 1.7
Size of Community and Various Outlooks (NORC-GSS: 1988–1991 Merge)

	Metropolitan Areas				Nonmetropolitan Areas	
	Central Cities		Suburbs		Counties	
	12 Largest	Next 88	12 Largest	Next 88	Largest Town 10,000 or More	No Town of 10,000 or More
Happiness – General						
Very happy	25 %	27 %	35 %	36 %	35 %	31 %
Pretty happy	60	61	54	56	57	61
Not so happy	15	12	11	9	9	8
N =	(453)	(728)	(669)	(1,006)	(2,231)	(770)
Marital Happiness						
Very happy	60 %	58 %	65 %	63 %	64 %	61 %
Pretty happy	33	37	33	35	34	37
Not so happy	7	5	2	2	3	2
N =	(153)	(323)	(346)	(560)	(1,302)	(467)
Satisfaction	Those saying "Very great deal" or "Great deal"					
City or place living in	35 %	41 %	45 %	51 %	49 %	51 %
N =	(311)	(494)	(456)	(674)	(1,496)	(503)
Family	64 %	69 %	77 %	76 %	78 %	78 %
N =	(310)	(492)	(456)	(673)	(1,497)	(502)
Friendship	67 %	67 %	63 %	70 %	72 %	72 %
N =	(310)	(494)	(456)	(673)	(1,498)	(502)
Trust or Suspicion						
People would take advantage	49 %	45 %	30 %	29 %	36 %	33 %
N =	(305)	(487)	(454)	(670)	(1,498)	(496)
People look out for themselves	49 %	45 %	43 %	41 %	46 %	37 %
N =	(304)	(490)	(449)	(670)	(1,494)	(502)
Can't be too careful	68 %	62 %	51 %	51 %	56 %	56 %
N =	(308)	(494)	(457)	(457)	(1,496)	(504)

smallest counties amounts to 5 percentage points. The lowest level of satisfaction, by a few points, appears in the suburbs of the twelve largest cities.

A three-question series asked about the character of interpersonal relationships, whether "people would try to be fair" (versus "would take advantage"), whether they would "try to be helpful" (versus "look out for themselves"), and whether "most people can be trusted" (versus "can't be too careful"). All three involve interpersonal trust versus fear or suspicion. For all three questions, the greatest trust was registered in the suburbs and nonmetropolitan counties. The populations in the eighty-eight cities were somewhat less trusting. The lowest levels of trust appeared in the twelve largest cities. The differences in trust between the extreme categories, the twelve largest cities and the smaller counties, amount to 19, 15, and 14 percent, respectively. The difference with respect to satisfaction with city or place is 16 percent. These are the largest differences found in the eight comparisons. These four items constitute the "best case" for the mass society argument. The support in the remaining comparisons is modest, involving still smaller percentage differences.[43]

VALUE DIFFERENCES

Differences of 15 to 20 percentage points appear with respect to cultural values. The cities, not too surprisingly, are more liberal and the rural counties more traditional. A fair-sized minority of city dwellers favor making divorce laws easier; a sizable majority of the rural county population would make them more restrictive (from the GSS merge, 1988–1991, data not shown). One of the largest differences involves the liberal position on premarital sex, with "not wrong at all" being much more frequent in the large cities. The nation as a whole is very traditional with respect to extramarital sex, with 78 percent saying it is "always wrong." The "swinger's option," that it is not wrong at all, was chosen by 8 percent in the twelve largest cities and by only 1 percent in the rural counties. Slightly more liberalism was found with respect to homosexuality, with only 70 percent of adult Americans declaring it "always wrong." The liberal option was chosen by roughly one in four in the metropolitan cities and suburbs, but by only 6 percent in the rural counties.

The insistent emphasis on the negative features of big-city life is one-sided, neglecting some obvious advantages. From the Middle Ages on, it was recognized that *Stadtluft macht frei*—city air makes one free. Contemporary populations recognize that too. Small communities, regardless of context, whether villages, small workplaces, or small colleges, are basically monocultural, providing little room for "deviant" individuals or minorities. Those who cannot abide the dominant tendency recognize the obvious option: moving to a larger community. The urban condition, its size and variety, makes possible a freedom of outlook and of association that is not available in the small towns or villages. In this case, it should be noted, the city is not a punitive setting, but one that liberates. Some people choose it for this very reason: "free spirits" move to the city to gain those benefits. There is a little-noted correlate: Culturally conservative persons migrate to the small towns to find a milieu consonant with their values.[44]

OTHER FACTORS

Some of these modest confirmations of the mass society position might be deceptive. One should, as always, consider the possibility that something else might be operating. One of the strongest confirmations of a mass society theme appeared with respect to "satisfaction with city." That could stem from the inherent costs of city life, or it could be due to some other related factor. One obvious possibility, our seventh proposition, is that the result is due to the costs or penalties associated with race. Black populations are located, very disproportionately, in the large cities. They form 39 percent and 24 percent, respectively, of the total population in the twelve and next eighty-eight largest cities. They form less than 10 percent in the four other contexts (GSS 1988–1991 merge). Put differently, that means 51 percent of the black population is located in the 100 largest cities, as against 16 percent of whites. Blacks in all contexts are less likely to report they are "very happy." And blacks in all contexts, not too surprisingly, report less satisfaction with their communities. They are also much less likely than whites to say that "most people would try to be fair." Overall, 62 percent of blacks felt that "most people would try to take advantage," as against only 32 percent of whites.

Part of the original modest difference in community satisfaction is due to race and race-related penalties. A small "city-size effect" remains among the white populations, with the big-city segments (the twelve and the eighty-eight) still less likely to report themselves "very happy" and reporting less satisfaction from their communities. The difference between the extreme categories in sensed fairness, 19 percentage points overall (shown in Table 1.7), is reduced to 11 points among whites (Table 1.8).

A different relationship appears within the black population. The levels of reported happiness are low in all contexts, with little variation by location. The least satisfaction with the community is reported in the twelve cities and their suburbs; most satisfaction is reported in the small counties. In striking contrast to the pattern among whites, with majorities everywhere expecting people to be fair, among blacks only one in three share that optimism. The expectation of fairness is lowest in the small counties, running at only 22 percent.

The persistent attention given to the presumed impersonality and isolation of the large cities overlooks another important consideration. Patterns of sociability vary with marital status. The large cities have more never-married persons than the other categories. Just over one-third of the large-city dwellers are single, as opposed to one-sixth in the large counties and only one-eighth in the small counties. Separated persons are also more frequent, by a small margin, in the twelve largest cities (Table 1.9). Only a minority of the large-city populations are married, roughly one-third in the twelve cities and 44 percent in the eighty-

Table 1.8
Race and Various Outlooks (NORC-GSS: 1988–1991 Merge)

	Metropolitan Areas				Nonmetropolitan Areas	
	Central Cities		Suburbs		Counties	
	12 Largest	Next 88	12 Largest	Next 88	Largest Town 10,000 or More	No Town of 10,000 or More
Happiness			Those saying "Very happy"			
Whites	27 %	30 %	37 %	36 %	36 %	32 %
N =	(242)	(521)	(574)	(923)	(1,959)	(709)
Blacks	21 %	19 %	24 %	24 %	25 %	23 %
N =	(178)	(178)	(62)	(54)	(173)	(52)
Satisfaction with city or place living in			Those saying "Very great deal" or "Great deal"			
Whites	39 %	43 %	46 %	53 %	61 %	53 %
N =	(166)	(350)	(389)	(613)	(1,311)	(463)
Blacks	29 %	37 %	27 %	32 %	37 %	42 %
N =	(118)	(124)	(48)	(38)	(118)	(33)
Trust in people			Those saying "People would try to be fair"			
Whites	54 %	57 %	68 %	66 %	62 %	65 %
N =	(164)	(344)	(387)	(612)	(1,314)	(457)
Blacks	30 %	34 %	35 %	33 %	31 %	22 %
N =	(118)	(123)	(48)	(36)	(117)	(32)

eight. Elsewhere, in the suburbs and nonmetropolitan counties, majorities are married. The divorced are distributed more or less equally across community types, although slightly less frequent in the small counties. The widowed also appear more or less equally across community types, but are slightly more frequent in the twelve largest cities and in the small counties.

A couple of age-old "facts of life" are associated with marital status. The first is that single persons tend to go out a lot and married persons tend to be home-bodies. Single persons are much more likely to have contacts with neighbors and with friends. They are also more likely to spend time in bars (Table 1.10). There is little difference in the extent of contacts with relatives, those links being strong for all five segments (the specific patterns would, of course, change sig-

Table 1.9
Size of Community and Marital Status (NORC-GSS: 1988–1991 Merge)

| | Metropolitan Areas | | | | Nonmetropolitan Areas | |
| | Central Cities | | Suburbs | | Counties | |
Marital Status	12 Largest	Next 88	12 Largest	Next 88	Largest Town 10,000 or More	No Town of 10,000 or More
Never Married	36 %	25 %	23 %	19 %	18 %	13 %
Married	34	44	52	55	58	61
Separated	6	5	3	2	3	3
Divorced	11	15	14	13	11	9
Widowed	13	11	9	11	10	15
N =	(459)	(734)	(674)	(1,014)	(2,252)	(773)

nificantly over the life cycle). Singles have more frequent contact with parents and siblings, but that has an easy explanation: Many of them are still living in the parental household.[45] Separated and divorced persons, understandably, revert to the "never-married" pattern, again picking up contacts with neighbors, friends, and relatives. The widowed have relatively strong contacts with relatives and neighbors. All other contacts, however, are attenuated.

The differences in marital status across the six categories of community might affect the previous results. They might, for example, hide some evidence supporting the mass society claims. A limited control, however, shows this is not the case. Examination of the sociability patterns of the combined married and widowed, both of them low-involvement segments, shows no serious variation by community category. And the same no-serious-difference result appears among the combined high-involvement segments of single, separated, and divorced (Table 1.11). The community-size factor in this case counts for nothing, contrary to the mass society claim. The routinely neglected marital-status factor, in all categories of community, counts for much.[46]

The patterns of sociability are, to some degree, set or influenced by still another everyday "fact of life." Most people marry and have children and, as just seen, they then reduce the frequency of contacts with friends and neighbors. It is, effectively, a zero-sum game. Children ultimately marry and leave the home, thus opening up new (or revived) options, those with friends and neighbors. With advancing age, two things happen: Some contacts diminish in fre-

Table 1.10
Marital Status and Sociability (NORC-GSS: 1988–1991 Merge)

| | Marital Status | | | | |
	Never Married	Married	Separated	Divorced	Widowed
Contacts with Relatives					
At least 1-2 a week	36 %	33 %	41 %	37 %	40 %
Several times a month	17	21	17	15	15
About once a month	16	16	15	14	11
Several times a year	20	20	16	19	18
About once a year	8	7	5	6	6
Never	4	3	6	7	9
N =	(782)	(2,105)	(130)	(488)	(424)
Contacts with Neighbors					
At least 1-2 a week	37 %	17 %	27 %	24 %	34 %
Several times a month	12	11	9	12	9
About once a month	10	18	18	13	9
Several times a year	8	15	11	9	8
About once a year	6	11	6	8	5
Never	27	28	29	35	36
N =	(784)	(2,099)	(128)	(488)	(423)
Contacts with Friends					
At least 1-2 a week	43 %	14 %	27 %	27 %	16 %
Several times a month	23	18	18	21	17
About once a month	17	27	19	25	18
Several times a year	8	22	15	14	19
About once a year	3	8	9	4	8
Never	6	10	12	10	23
N =	(784)	(2,105)	(130)	(489)	(423)
Going to Bars or Taverns					
At least 1-2 a week	29 %	5 %	12 %	14 %	3 %
Several times a month	13	4	11	7	1
About once a month	14	9	12	12	4
Several times a year	11	11	11	14	5
About once a year	9	14	12	13	5
Never	35	57	43	40	83
N =	(782)	(2,104)	(130)	(488)	(424)

quency as age peers die—including siblings, relatives, friends, and neighbors—and efforts to form new contacts are also reduced due to diminished strength and capacity. A general withdrawal, usually called disengagement, occurs with increasing age. Other things equal, some withdrawal is "in the cards." That process

Table 1.11
Sociability by Size of Community and Marital Status (NORC-GSS: 1988–1991 Merge)

	Metropolitan Areas				Nonmetropolitan Areas	
	Central Cities		Suburbs		Counties	
	12 Largest	Next 88	12 Largest	Next 88	Largest Town 10,000 or More	No Town of 10,000 or More
Marital Status			Frequent contact with friends[a]			
Married or widowed	17 %	18 %	12 %	13 %	16 %	12 %
N =	(134)	(275)	(265)	(445)	(1012)	(397)
Single, separated, or divorced	38 %	32 %	34 %	37 %	37 %	33 %
N =	(157)	(223)	(183)	(242)	(471)	(127)
			Frequent contact with neighbors[a]			
Married or widowed	24 %	19 %	18 %	18 %	20 %	22 %
N =	(134)	(274)	(264)	(445)	(1009)	(396)
Single, separated, or divorced	32 %	32 %	26 %	30 %	33 %	32 %
N =	(157)	(222)	(181)	(242)	(471)	(127)

[a]Amounts are for people saying "almost daily" and "several times a week," combined.

is likely to be accompanied by an increasing sense of isolation, loneliness, and, probably, powerlessness. Those feelings, it should be noted, are routine correlates of aging; they are not products of the mass society.

Age-related disengagement may be seen clearly in the GSS evidence (Table 1.12). The pattern, unexpectedly, is most pronounced in the case of contacts with parents. All of the respondents answering this question had at least one living parent. For both marital-status segments, there are very sharp declines in the percentages reporting frequent contact. Some disengagement from siblings is also indicated. All persons answering this question had living brothers and/or sisters. A marked reversal appears late in life among the single, separated, and divorced. One possible explanation is that without children of

Table 1.12
Age and Sociability by Marital Status (NORC-GSS: 1988–1991 Merge)

| | Average Number of Contacts with[a] | | | | |
	Parents[b]	Siblings[b]	Relatives	Neighbors	Friends
Married and Widowed					
Age					
18-29	3.47	3.27	3.99	2.41	3.37
30-39	3.12	2.71	3.55	2.32	2.99
40-49	2.75	2.41	3.36	2.04	2.73
50-59	2.40	2.29	3.40	2.14	2.58
60 or more	1.18	2.15	3.39	2.48	2.36
Singles, Separated, and Divorced					
Age					
18-29	3.77	3.53	3.82	3.22	4.02
30-39	3.16	2.99	3.54	2.43	3.69
40-49	2.96	2.53	3.28	2.37	3.41
50-59	2.53	2.17	3.04	1.93	2.70
60 or more	1.00	2.48	3.01	2.46	2.58

[a]Arithmetic means. Scoring as follows: almost every day = 6; once or twice a week = 5; several times a month = 4; about once a month = 3; several times a year = 2; about once a year = 1; never = 0.

[b]Those with parents and/or siblings.

their own, many of them reach out to their closest surviving relatives. This becomes easier on the occasion of retirement.

A somewhat different pattern appears in regard to contacts with relatives. Basically, the frequency declines somewhat through to middle age and is stable from then on. A majority maintains family connections at all points in their careers, seeing relatives at least once a month. Some disengagement also appears. Among the married and widowed, the "never" category (not shown in Table 1.12) increases from 2 to 7 percent across the age span. Many of these persons would have no or few offspring, a fact that determines subsequent opportunities. In the combined "singles" category, the increase is from 2 to 19 percent.

Still another pattern appears with respect to contacts with neighbors. For both marital segments there is some attenuation through to middle age followed by a modest increase, a reengagement, among the elderly. Older persons are more likely to be "settled." Household moves fall off dramatically with increasing age. Visits with neighbors are low-cost activities, and those contacts are easily formed and easily maintained.

Contacts with friends outside of the neighborhood dwindle with age for both marital segments. Both segments show regular increases of the "never" response from 7 to 21 percent for the married/widowed and 3 to 21 percent for the others. Two factors are probably operating: the number of friends ineluctably declines, and for those suffering the infirmities of age the costs of such visits steadily increase.

Earlier we sorted out the extreme isolates, those who replied "never," "about once a year," or, at best, "several times a year" to the five questions about the frequency of social contacts. Overall, 7.3 percent of the respondents indicated that extreme pattern. That self-reported isolation varies with age, going from 1 percent among those in their twenties to approximately one in eight among those fifty and over. Some of the elderly, those living in senior citizens' homes, would not be represented in the samples (which do not include institutional populations). Many persons who moved to such homes would have shifted from an isolated existence to one with frequent daily contacts.

The isolation that accompanies age might well cause feelings of powerlessness. Given the correlated disengagement, however, neither condition is likely to lead to insurgency or disruption of the political system. The persons affected by those "facts of life" are unlikely candidates for the ever-threatening demagogue. Television viewing increases considerably among the elderly, but that is not likely to generate the pathologies of consumerism. Much of the advertising addressing their specific needs deals with the merits of pain-killing medicines.

One might anticipate that a decline in happiness and satisfaction would be associated with the normal age-related infirmities and personal losses. But that was not the case. The relationships between age and self-reported happiness, marital happiness, and family satisfaction are flat, essentially the same across all of the categories. The relationship between age and satisfaction with the community is both strong and positive. Among those eighteen to twenty-nine years of age, 34 percent (N = 657) reported a "great deal" or a "very great deal" of community satisfaction. Among those seventy and over, 64 percent (N = 464) chose those response categories.[47]

Finally, still another "fact of life," a demographic factor, would have a decisive impact on patterns of sociability. A person born into a large family, one with many brothers and sisters, is likely, ultimately, to have many nephews and nieces. If that same large family were well endowed with aunts and uncles, its members would also be likely to have a generous supply of cousins. When, later in life, the National Opinion Research Center's interviewer appeared, that individual would be in a position to report, other things equal, extensive contacts with relatives. If that individual married a person from a similar family background, the chances for kinship "envelopment" would be doubled. Many of one's closest friends might also be kinsmen, persons chosen from among that large mass of relatives. Other things equal, that couple would probably have an above-average number of children of their own, and many grandchildren.

The opposite experience would occur in the case of the only child born of parents who themselves were only children. That only child, obviously, would have no aunts, uncles, or cousins. If that person married an only child of only-children parents, and they in turn produced a single child, that child would have no close relatives apart from the parents. By force of familial circumstances, the only social contacts (or networks) available would be of a nonkin variety, the friends or neighbors. The density of contacts with friends and neighbors, in short, would vary inversely with the size of one's family.

UPROOTED MASSES

Some uprooting does occur. But the conventional formulations require critical attention and some specification. Some people "leave the land" and move to larger communities. Much of the movement to the city, however, occurs in a communal context. Many people move with or follow other family members who preceded them. Since many other people from the home communities have moved or are moving following the same routes, some social networks are either there, in place on arrival, or are carried along in the course of the migration. The mass society theorists assume that individual migration is the typical form. Most studies indicate that community-to-community migration—"chain" migration—is the most frequent form.[48]

The focus on uprooting, moreover, neglects an obvious subsequent process, namely that of rerooting. People who move to the city do not remain hopelessly isolated for the rest of their lives. They make contacts, find new friends, and gradually build up social networks. The single-minded focus on uprooting is another instance of one-sided thinking. Again only the initial phase of a two-phase process is reported and discussed.

The GSS studies allowed some investigation of this question. Respondents who were living in nonmetropolitan counties at age sixteen (classified according to the SRC Belt Code; see note 44) were found at the time of interview either in metropolitan cities or in the suburbs of those cities (both segments therefore migrants to the city), or in the original nonmetropolitan category. The three groups showed no serious differences in the frequency of neighborhood visiting or in contacts with friends outside the neighborhood. A serious deficit appeared, not surprisingly, in the contacts with parents. Eleven percent of those living in the 100 largest cities (N = 196) reported frequent contact, as against 34 percent (N = 1,102) of those still living in the counties. A smaller deficit appears with respect to contacts with siblings and relatives. Similar deficits were also associated with the opposite "flow," that is, among the city-to-county migrants (GSS merge, 1988–1991).

A final observation: The movement "off the land" is a unique episode, one that, in the United States, peaked in the 1940s. For the last half-century, the number of persons involved in that uprooting movement has steadily declined. With less than 2 percent of the population still "on the farm," little further movement of that variety is possible. For all practical purposes, that episode has ended.[49]

Mass society presentations, as noted, typically depict trends with no turn-around. The various pathologies are always "increasing," the expectation always "more and more." But it is a rare tendency that does not attenuate and at some point turn around. Could society continue to fall apart on all measures? Could divorce rates or crime rates soar without limit? We, so it is said, are an increasingly mobile population. More and more of us are forced to move, following the opportunities imposed by impersonal market processes. Could mobility increase without some limiting costs? Again, there is an evident failure to think through implications.

Mobility is strongly age related. Almost everyone in the late teens or early twenties moves out of the parental household. Among young adults moves occur frequently. For some, a smallish minority, the college years normally entail much moving. For most people, college and noncollege alike, those are years of poor-paying beginning jobs. But with skill acquisition and better pay comes better housing and more attractive neighborhoods. Over time, in short, most people "settle down." Evidence from the U.S. Census Current Population Surveys shows the strong age relationship (Table 1.13). In 1996–1997, roughly one-sixth of the population reported a change of residence. Among young adults, those twenty to twenty-four, almost one-third moved. Among those sixty-five and over, less than 5 percent did so.[50]

Most of these changes of residence involve short distances. More than three-fifths of them occur within the county and thus are not likely to produce any serious disruption of interpersonal relationships. Since the average age of the American population has been increasing since 1960, we should expect a corresponding overall decline in mobility. That has in fact been the case (see Table 1.13).[51]

Everything reported in the previous paragraphs might be counted as the routine correlates of demographic and life-cycle facts. But the "concerned" mass society theorist, always sounding the alarm, misses all of this. Two other routine facts are missed. In a period when large birth cohorts were coming of age, as when the baby boomers began leaving home in the late 1960s, the nation as a whole would experience high mobility. By the 1990s the boomers would have settled down. And the much smaller 1970s cohorts would now be

Table 1.13
Residential Mobility (One Year Moves)

<u>A. By Age - 1996-1997</u>

Total (1 year and over)	16.0 %
20 - 24 years	32.1
25 - 29 years	31.5
30 - 44 years	16.5
45 - 64 years	8.7
65 - 74 years	4.5
75 years and over	4.9

<u>B. All Ages</u>

1950-1951	21.2 %	1975-1976	17.7
1955-1956	21.1	1980-1981	17.2
1960-1961	20.6	1985-1986	18.6
1965-1966	19.8	1990-1991	17.0
1970-1971	18.7	1995-1996	16.3

Sources: U.S. Bureau of the Census, *Current Population Reports*, series P-20, no. 510 (Washington, D.C.: U.S. Government Printing Office, 1998); and U.S. Bureau of the Census, "Table A-1. Annual Geographical Mobility Rates, by Type of Movement: 1947–1997," 23 July 1998, available <http://www.census.gov/population/socdemo/migration/tab-a-1.txt>.

leaving home in the 1990s. Both facts would mean low mobility. Another "fact of life" is that women marry at a younger age than men, a difference of roughly two years. In 1996–1997 that meant that women in the twenty to twenty-four age category were more mobile than the equivalent men, the respective percentages being 34.9 and 29.3. The opposite pattern is found in the two next-older categories. Another such fact: In the early 1980s the nation experienced serious inflation and very high interest rates. Those high charges forced many people to postpone their intended moves. When interest rates fell in the mid-1980s, the postponed demand brought a sharp increase in mobility (as may be seen in Table 1.13).

CONCLUSIONS

An assessment of hypotheses may yield one of four possible results:

1. Confirmation. Evidence supports the original claim.
2. Rejection (or disconfirmation). Evidence does not support the original.
3. Mixed results. The original claim might be contingent (that is, supported only in given circumstances), or the factual claim might be confirmed but the causal implication either questioned or rejected.
4. Uncertainty. The available evidence does not allow an empirically based conclusion. Evidence might be lacking entirely, or it might be of such poor quality as to make the drawing of conclusions inappropriate.

The evidence reviewed here allows the following conclusions with respect to the eight propositions spelled out earlier.

First, the claim that modern societies are characterized by an absence of close personal connections is rejected. The evidence presented here does not support that claim. Most people report extensive social involvement. Very few indicate isolated lives.

Second, there is no significant support for the claim of deteriorating social relations over time. This claim, accordingly, is also rejected. The evidence from the General Social Surveys, covering the last two decades, shows stability in most measures. Only with respect to neighborhood contacts is a decline registered. Contacts with friends outside the neighborhood showed little change.

Third, we have the claims of pervasive unhappiness and general dissatisfaction with "modern life." These are rejected. In their self-reports, most people indicate they are either "very happy" or, more frequently, "pretty happy." A small minority, at all points, say they are "not too happy." The other measures of happiness and satisfaction yielded similar results; that is, generally positive reports.

Fourth, the claim that unhappiness and dissatisfaction would show a steady increase is rejected. Slight declines in general happiness, marital happiness, and satisfaction with community were found. Basically, this meant a shift of some 5 percent from the most positive category to the next most positive. Negative judgments were infrequent at all points; the levels of discontent were both low and constant.

Fifth, we have the appropriate specification; namely, the focus on the urban "malaise." The claim is that the anticipated pathologies will be found at the urban end of the community-size continuum. This is rejected. The patterns of social involvement do not vary systematically by type of community; the metropolitan cities are little different from the rural counties. For all of the emphasis on the United States as an urban society, only a small minority live in the giant cities and the percentage doing so is declining.

Sixth, some measures of happiness and satisfactions vary as anticipated in this theory; that is, they decline in the larger communities. But the differences are small, and, in part, are linked to another factor: race. The best conclusion is "mixed," at best very modest support.

The seventh, eighth, and ninth claims are not routinely part of the mass society repertory. They focus on various "facts of life," ones regularly neglected by mass society theorists. The regular neglect of these factors means that the critics of modern society routinely overlook the *ceteris paribus* requirement.

The seventh claim is that happiness, satisfaction with community, and interpersonal trust vary substantially by race, and black populations are disproportionately located within the large cities. This is confirmed. Part of the original result, the modest confirmation of the sixth proposition, stems from the penalties of race.

Eighth, sociability patterns vary with marital status. This is confirmed. The social relations of married persons are concentrated within the family; those of single, separated, and divorced persons involve considerable "outreach" to neighbors and friends. Outside the large cities, the majority of adults are married. In the 100 largest cities, only a minority (roughly two-fifths) are married. A control for marital status shows no special impact of urban life.

Ninth, sociability patterns vary with age. Over the years, one will lose social ties as relatives and friends die. With physical capacity waning, the ability to form new ties also declines. This is confirmed. The tendency is modest. Some increase in isolation appears in the older age categories. The majority, however, retain social ties, in part because younger relatives, children, and grandchildren take the place of one's age peers.

Some of these conclusions are summarized, in a more economical statistical form, in the Appendix. That discussion reviews both the direction of impacts and the relative weights of the factors discussed.

Some words of caution are needed. The social connections and personal assessments reported here cover only a limited recent segment of the modern era. The processes focused on by mass society theorists—industrialization, urbanization, individuation, and so forth—emerged and developed over more than two centuries. The General Social Surveys cover only three decades of recent experience in the United States. It is possible that those decades are atypical or that these findings miss "the larger picture." It is possible that social relations were seriously disrupted at other times and in other places and that for those contexts the theory was both accurate and appropriate. Were one to argue that option, some specification would be necessary. The most obvious need is for answers to two basic questions: When did that corrosive, fragmented (or anomic) mass society end? And, what circumstances brought about the transformation?

ON THE SOCIOLOGY OF KNOWLEDGE

The survey results presented here are based on high-quality representative samples of the American adult population. Those findings, as seen, are not consonant with the arguments of the mass society position. The responses provided by the American population run counter to all those sweeping claims about loss of connection, isolation, anxiety, and desperation.

Results of this kind, as seen earlier, are not new. Similar findings were reported decades ago in the serious research literature. The question arises: Why the disparities? Why does the notion of "breakdown" have such resonance in popular literature, in the humanities, and on the fringes of the social sciences? Those questions merely restate one posed in 1959 by Scott Greer and Ella Kube: "In conclusion we may ask why, in view of the data reported, so many writers have emphasized the isolation and anomie of the urban individual, his reliance upon secondary relationships, and his loss of community. Why has the urbanite been pictured as a lost individual, a particle in a social 'dust heap'?"[52]

Findings of the sort reported here, although easily accessible, rarely appear in popular sources, in newspapers, in news magazines, or television news, or in public affairs programs. A sharp disparity exists between these generally positive findings and the more frequent negative ones found in journalistic accounts, in popular public affairs literature, or in popular sociology. Readers, listeners, or viewers are regularly told of the all-pervasive loneliness found in modern society, but few people in those audiences are ever told about the evidence on which the claims are based. An Associated Press report, for example, opened with the following statement: "If you're feeling loneliness, you're not alone. Loneliness is more common today than the common cold, according to Ann Clark, a psychologist who teaches at the United States International University [in San Diego]. 'A recent survey found that more than half of those questioned had experienced severe loneliness within the past week,' Clark said." Shortly thereafter, the Gallup organization asked, "How often do you ever feel lonely?" The responses were distributed as follows: frequently, 10 percent; sometimes, 26 percent; seldom, 40 percent; and never, 23 percent.[53]

In 1970 Philip Slater, a sociologist, published a book entitled *The Pursuit of Loneliness: American Culture at the Breaking Point*. The work, from the title onward, makes use of the mass society framework. Although few of the book's assertions were backed by evidence, it was nevertheless very well received. A revised edition appeared in 1976 and a third followed in 1990. Many of the questions addressed by Slater were investigated by Angus Campbell and his associates in *The Quality of American Life*. At one point those researchers used semantic differential scales. Respondents were presented with paired opposite terms and asked to locate themselves, basically to describe their lives, on a seven-point scale. Of special relevance for Slater's theme is the "lonely–friendly" pair. Three percent chose 1, the "lonely" extreme. Almost half, 49 percent, chose 7, the "friendly" extreme. Twenty-one percent located at 6 and another 11 percent at 5.[54]

One explanation for the disparity, a first possibility, might be described as technical. The universities, institutions charged with the generation and transmission of knowledge, have divided their ever-more complicated tasks among a wide range of fields or specialties. One result of this division of academic labor is that the professors in one department may not be aware of findings generated elsewhere, especially those of a distant field. Due to this compartmentalization, those critics of modern society may never have come across the countering research literature.

This problem, departmental provincialism, is a persistent and recurring one. Many professors, as noted earlier, vouch for Max Weber's Protestant ethic thesis but know little or nothing of either religious or economic history. Many who vouch for the work of Sigmund Freud show no awareness of the devastating critiques that have appeared in recent years. Dozens of reviewers approved Michel Foucault's account of "the birth of the prison," indicating no awareness of the actual history. There is a pattern to this approval: Acceptance of those claims increases with distance from the relevant expertise. Psychologists, on the whole, are very critical of Freud's accomplishments. At some remove, however, as in the humanities, his work is widely approved.[55]

A different kind of compartmentalization problem appears in the reviewing process. The "informed public" would ordinarily learn of new works through reviews and comment in newspapers, in general circulation magazines, or in "high-quality" journals of comment and opinion. The reception of some leading works in the mass society tradition provides some instructive lessons.

Slater's *Pursuit of Loneliness*, as noted, provides a dismal portrait of contemporary American society. But, as was also noted, the presentation is largely dataless, essentially one of assertion without evidence. The book, nevertheless, received favorable notice in two leading news magazines, first in *Newsweek*, then in *Time*: "Perceptive and provocative when analyzing American do-it-yourselfism and even the much-prized American family as devices that ensure further loneliness and isolation."[56] Shortly thereafter, Edgar Z. Friedenberg, in a long and enthusiastic review, announced,

If I had to select a single book by which to tell a stranger what life in this country has become and why, it would be this one. . . . Reading *The Pursuit of Loneliness* provides almost physical relief from the agonies of life in America. . . . The book accounts for the real horrors . . . but it also notes explicitly the small, nasty evils which . . . are ubiquitous and account for far more of the distress, frustration, and ultimately the terror of daily life.[57]

Kenneth Keniston reviewed it for the *New York Times Book Review*, describing it as "brilliant, sweeping . . . an insightful, well-written, and thought-provoking book." Two specialized journals, the *Library Journal* and *Choice*, perform an important mediating (or "gatekeeping") function, giving guidance to libraries with limited budgets. The *Library Journal* described Slater's book as an "exciting, sometimes startling set of analyses highly recommended to general collections." *Choice* provided its usual paragraph-long summary, ending with this statement: "The book is already popular and should be in demand among socially conscious undergraduates and their contemporaries."[58]

Some reviews appeared in academic journals. One of the earliest, by Gordon Halpern in the *Annals of the American Academy*, provided a straightforward description of the book's contents, beginning with, "A crisis is rapidly approaching for American society." Halpern indicated some doubts about several of Slater's hyperbolic judgments, whether, for example, his prediction of a choice limited to "either acceptance of the new culture or 'living under a fascist regime' is not, in fact, exaggerated." In the last sentences, however, the work was commended as "extremely interesting, thought-provoking reading. Slater's ideas are worth listening to."[59]

The field of sociology, the most likely producer of that relevant literature, has three leading journals. In order of prestige, these are the *American Sociological Review*, the *American Journal of Sociology*, and *Social Forces*. Charles Winick's review in the *American Sociological Review* provided a summary of the book's contents, indicating no skepticism about any of its claims. His summary reads, "Moderates who still belong to the old culture may have a choice, perhaps in the next decade, of either participating in expansion of the new culture or helping to usher in facism [*sic*]. One of the most extraordinary features of this extraordinary book is its power to convince one that such a choice may have to be made in the near future." The *American Journal of Sociology* contained a review by Bennett Berger. It signaled serious grounds for doubt. Pointing to the diversity of the American population and to the diversity of trends, he noted that "by generalizing from any one or a few of them one can plausibly argue just about anything one wishes—particularly if one discounts the relevance of attitude and other survey data." Berger found some "tidbits" that made the book "very worthwhile reading," this yielding his "mixed response." His last sentence refers to the peculiarities of the era, "these days of verbal overkill." Irwin Deutscher's review in *Social Forces* was severely critical. Pointing to serious problems in the handling of evidence, he describes the work as "a magnificent polemic" dressed up with "a low level of scholarship."[60]

The critical responses, it will be noted, are sharply differentiated. The reviews seen by the attentive public contained very positive assessments. Those seen by the small audiences of specialists in academic journals were divided, some pointing to serious difficulties. The general public would not have learned anything of those criticisms. With some system, it appears, the lessons provided by those knowledgeable experts had been avoided. This points to a second explanation for the problem signaled by Greer and Kube; namely, a failure of editorial judgment.

A third explanation appears in one of Berger's comments in his point about discounting the importance of evidence. Some commentators fail or refuse to consider the implications of readily available evidence. Data avoidance or what might be called the evidence-aversion problem appears also in the next example. Two years after Slater's book, Vance Packard, a writer of popular exposés, argued the "falling apart" position in a book entitled *A Nation of Strangers*. Packard's thesis appears in a brief introductory statement: "Personal isolation is becoming a major social fact of our time. A great many people are disturbed by the feeling that they are rootless or increasingly anonymous, that they are living in a continually changing environment where there is little sense of community."[61]

Packard's work differs from most writings in this tradition in that some documentation was provided—three appendixes and seven pages of notes—but that effort proved to be more appearance than reality. Many of the references are to secondary literature, to newspaper and magazine reports, and some are to other exposés, to Packard's *The Naked Society*, Slater's *Pursuit of Loneliness*, and Alvin Toffler's *Future Shock*. Some original studies, some government reports, and some sociological researches are cited. But the question posed earlier—How representative was the selection?—must also be considered. The answer is, not very. A small part of the large research literature on social connectedness was cited earlier in this chapter, much of it appearing prior to the publication of Packard's account. None of the earlier works cited, those from the 1950s and 1960s, are referred to by Packard.[62] In this case, the answer to the Greer and Kube query is easy: Packard systematically avoided the research literature that contained findings going against his main theme. Put differently, the answer to their query is that Packard shows extreme bias in the reporting of the relevant literature.

The critical reception of Packard's book parallels the treatment of Slater's work. Harriet Van Horne, a columnist for the *New York Post*, discussed it in *Saturday Review*. Accepting all of its major claims, she declared it to be "an important book, one that should be read by personnel directors, corporation presidents, and community leaders" and, most of all, by anyone contemplating a move. "With every move, it seems, you lose a little of yourself." Granville Hicks, the noted literary critic, reviewed it for the *New York Times Book Review*, and said Packard "does a reasonably thorough and reliable job." He made some objection to the author's style, to the use of jargon and sentences "to be marveled at," but in the end judged it "a useful book." In a later note, a *Times* editor commended the book and reported that except for the style Hicks "liked it." The work was highly recommended in the *Library Journal*: "Well worth reading because of the fresh material it presents . . . and its lively and highly readable style." A strong dissent appeared in the *New Republic*, where Peter Michelson described the conclusions as "obvious and superficial" and the methodology as "simplistic and anachronistic."[63]

The specialists agreed with the latter judgment. The first of these critiques, the work of Herbert Gans, appeared in *Psychology Today*, a journal that attempts to bring expert knowledge to a wider public. A wide range of problems were indicated, one of these, understandably, being that of data avoidance: Packard provides "hair-raising anecdotes" about loneliness and pathology but "all the reliable studies of communities . . . indicate that rates of loneliness and pathology are very low and that satisfaction is great." The critiques in the three leading sociology journals were also very negative. A brief deprecating ten-line note in *Social Forces* referred readers to Gans's critique. The *American Journal of Sociology* arranged a review symposium in which three specialists provided eleven pages of comment on *A Nation of Strangers*. The comments by Amos H. Hawley were very negative, focusing on erratic sampling procedures, odd-lot illustration problems, failure to establish causal connections, misinterpretations, and so forth. Claude Fischer was also very negative. He lists six "logical fallacies and semantic smoke screens in the argument." Another concern, a major one, was data avoidance; in particular, Packard's use of quotations from "pop social scientists . . . while simultaneously ignoring mounds of sound scientific research." The third panelist, Brian J. L. Barry, also commented on Packard's "failure to consider accumulating contrary evidence to his basic hypothesis that high mobility leads unremittingly to social malaise." Because of the growing volume of book production, in 1971 the *American Sociological Review* stopped publishing reviews. Thereafter reviews appeared in a separate journal entitled *Contemporary Sociology*. The latter did not review Packard's work.[64]

Questions of timing and sequence should also be noted. The approving reviews in popular sources appeared just after the book's publication. The initial reviews of Packard's work, as seen, came in August and September 1972. The disapproving academic reviews came later, those in the sociology journals appearing in June and July 1973. A significant time lag occurs before the "experts" are heard from. Even then that expert opinion was not heeded. A subsequent *New York Times* comment, from February 1974, ignored the assessments of Gans, Hawley, Fischer, and Berry. Only the judgment of their reviewer, Granville Hicks, that he liked it, was reported. The *Book Review* audience was never informed of the criticisms.

The work of Angus Campbell and colleagues, *The Quality of American Life*, as noted, is a serious scholarly volume. Because of its detail and complexity, it would not ordinarily be recommended for popular consumption. The *Book Review Index* lists twenty-two reviews of Slater's work and thirty of Packard's. The Campbell and colleagues work received a total of eight reviews, one in *Science*, the rest in specialized academic journals. Several appeared in political science journals, the home field of the lead authors. Two of the leading sociology journals reviewed the book. The reviews were generally approving. They provided descriptions of methods and findings. They noted the preliminary character of the work, a point stressed by the authors.

They also commented on methodological and theoretical problems, pointing to alternative strategies and research directions.[65]

Campbell's *Sense of Well-Being in America*, the follow-up study, was written for a popular audience. This book, described by one reviewer as "eminently readable," analyzes five national surveys covering the years 1957 to 1978. It was recommended by the *Library Journal* and *Choice*. The *Book Review Index* lists a total of thirteen reviews spread over four years. Only one review appeared in a "popular" source, a dismissive three-paragraph account by Charles Kaiser in the *New York Times Book Review*. The rest were in specialized academic journals, principally in those of political science and sociology.[66]

The lessons are clear: Two seriously flawed popular works promulgating mass society themes received wide and approving attention in reviews addressed to the well-educated public. Two serious works reporting high-quality research, evidence challenging those themes, received little attention in the major public outlets. The popular works were also reviewed in the scholarly journals where the judgments were generally negative. The reactions, in short, are sharply bifurcated. One set of gatekeepers provided generous approbation for the mass society portraiture; the other set, on the whole, reported disapproval. The informed public, it will be noted, would not be aware of those dissenting views. Given their "conditioning" by approving gatekeepers, it seems likely that the "informed public" would come to share that dismal viewpoint; namely, that things are falling apart.

The subsequent treatment of these books provides some other instructive lessons. One measure of recognition is provided by the number of citations a work receives. Slater's *Pursuit of Loneliness* received much attention in the 1970s but later disappeared from view. Packard's *Nation of Strangers* had a very short "active life." Campbell and colleagues' *Quality of American Life* has received considerable attention over the years. More than eighty citations were listed in the 1990 *Social Sciences Citation Index*, and some sixty in 1994. Some compartmentalization, a different variety, appeared in this connection. None of those citations appeared in the three leading sociology journals. Campbell's follow-up study, *The Sense of Well-Being in America*, was cited thirty-three times in 1990 and twenty times in 1994. Only two of those were in the leading sociology journals. Sociologists, it appears, either do not know of these leading studies or for reasons unknown have dropped them from discussion.[67]

In a 1992 publication, thirty-three years after Greer and Kube posed their question, Robert Wuthnow, the sociologist quoted earlier, reviewed the standard mass society claims. His initial conclusion was that "the social fabric has not unraveled nearly to the extent that many critics have suggested." That qualified statement is followed by his main argument; namely, that small support groups have taken the place of the traditional social ties that in fact have now disappeared. These support groups "may help us adapt to the emotional pressures of living in a diverse, individualistic society, but . . . cannot truly replace the traditional communities that we have lost." A passing reference, in a note, is made to Fischer's work, but otherwise the "lost community" thesis appears intact and is treated as a valid depiction. Again, the extensive evidence on the subject has not been reported to the reader.[68]

Wuthnow comments as follows about attitudes toward neighbors: "Instead of feeling a common bond with our neighbors, we fear them." The accompanying note refers the reader to a "major study" based on "hundreds of qualitative interviews." A cautionary sentence is added: "It is, however, written for a popular audience and many of its claims would require further substantiation."[69]

Some U.S. government agencies conduct annual national surveys that focus on housing and neighborhood quality. These surveys involve tens of thousands of interviews, the sample sizes running at about 55,000. In the 1970s and early 1980s respondents were asked for an "overall opinion of [the] neighborhood." Given four response categories, approximately one-third said "excellent," and approximately one-half said "good." The percentages saying "poor" varied between 2 and 3 percent. No trend was indicated. A different question was used in the surveys from 1985 to 1995, opinions now being indicated by a one-to-ten choice, with ten being the best or highest level of satisfaction. At all points some seven-tenths of the respondents chose options eight, nine, or ten. The most frequent choice, at all points, was ten. These results cast considerable doubt on Wuthnow's claim of an all-pervasive fear of "our neighbors." Here again we have an example of the bifurcated treatment of findings. The negative judgment based on "soft" qualitative evidence is reported; the well-documented positive conclusion goes unmentioned.[70]

Mass society presentations are selective in still other ways. The relationships discussed and reviewed here, following those standard treatments, are all located outside the workplace. The implicit assumption is that work is conducted in large and impersonal settings. But most employed persons give rather positive reports about their coworkers. On the impersonal–friendly dimension, they lean very much in the latter direction.[71] Religious settings are also routinely neglected in mass society accounts. Roughly three-fifths of the American adult population report attending services at least once a week. Another quarter report attending one, two, or three times a month (GSS 1988–1991 merge). As will be seen in the next chapter, many people are also involved in voluntary associations.

The American people, on the whole, as judged by their self-reports, lead satisfactory lives. At the same time, they are regularly exposed to print and audiovisual sources reporting that the quality of human life in the United States is poor and getting worse. This might be a case of media manipulation. If so, however, it must differ substantially from the conventional portraits of media influence. The immediate producers of these pessimistic accounts are intellectuals, reporters, commentators, and investigative journalists. Most of them are salaried employees, working for various media organizations. They might be responding to the demands of their employers. In contrast to other business leaders, the media elite tend to be liberal and "critical" in outlook. One investigation of the attitudes of the "creative people," those who produce media content, found them to be true believers. In their view, the generally negative portraits they produced depicted the way things actually are.[72]

An important sampling problem appears in this connection. Much of our national and international news is disseminated by organizations located in two of the twelve largest cities, New York and Washington. Virtually all prime-time entertainment originates with organizations based in Los Angeles. Prime-time programs, whether crime stories or sitcoms, are based, overwhelmingly, in the largest cities, most in New York, Los Angeles, and Chicago. Few "shows" pay attention to Philadelphia, Houston, San Diego, or Phoenix. On occasion, sitcoms have been based in smaller cities, Minneapolis, Columbus, or Cincinnati, but even there one saw very little of those cities. In recent experience, the suburbs rarely appear as settings of prime-time programs. This selectivity means that attention is continually focused on a very small part of the nation's life. New York, Los Angeles, Chicago, and the other occasional large-city settings contain less than 8 percent of the nation's population (as seen in Table 1.6). With only occasional exceptions, such as *The Waltons*, *Little House on the Prairie*, *Dr. Quinn, Medicine Woman*, and *Northern Exposure*, the rest of the nation scarcely appears. The standard portrayals of "our society" provide support for the easy generalizations about the mass society. They show, unambiguously, that "we" are an urban society. The activities of big-city police departments, of big-city lawyers, and of big-city hospitals demonstrate, again and again, that "we" live in a society that is "falling apart."

Another kind of sampling bias is evident in much of the mass media content. Even within the large cities, as seen, many people report general happiness, happy marriages, much contact with family and friends, and so on. But a happy marriage and rewarding family life do not provide "useful" material for prime-time programming. Conflict is the basic stuff of "interesting" or "exciting" drama. This was clear from at least the time of Thespis, who placed an actor, the protagonist (the first struggler, or first combatant), in opposition to the chorus. Whether on the stage, in television, or in motion pictures, the prime need is dysfunctional relationships: murder for the police stories, serious conflict for the law offices (whether defenders or prosecutors), and serious trauma, preferably multiple cases, for the big-city hospitals. From one perspective the result is, or might be, a "good show." From another, it is flagrant sampling bias. That might be acceptable if the audience recognized these productions as make-believe.

But some educated persons deny the fiction involved and argue the typicality of the presentation: The drama is a metaphor, a representation of a pervasive problem in our society. The invocation of the familiar expression, "it is a metaphor for" bypasses the central empirical question, that of frequency. For the willing (or gullible) audience one simply declares the massive dimensions of the problem.

The mass society position, as outlined here, is in need of serious revision. The influenced "masses" appear to be located largely within the upper and upper-middle classes (but are not coterminous with those classes). An element of manipulation is operating, in that media gatekeepers, with some system, exclude or denigrate evidence challenging the basic position and commend instead the truths offered by "soft" social science. The "controls," however, are not entirely external, some of the support for the reading being self-induced. Those trained in the verities of the mass society worldview agree to the rejection of readily available evidence. Faced with recalcitrant evidence they engage in either denial or reinterpretation, in a "recoding" of the evidence: Yes, there is much social contact, but we know those relationships to be of a "superficial" character. In another line of argument, those happy and/or satisfied citizens are said to be mistaken in their assessments, the "saving" claim here being that of "false consciousness." Americans say they are happy, that they have happy marriages, good families, many friends, are satisfied with their community, and so forth, but we, the knowledgeable few, know they are *really* unhappy. It is not at all clear why educated and informed citizens choose to engage in this kind of behavior.

Seen from the perspective of normal science, two imperatives follow for those persons making the false-consciousness argument. First, there is the need for full disclosure. One should report the contrary evidence; namely, that the population itself reports high levels of social involvement and makes generally positive assessments of their lives and circumstances, and that few negative trends are indicated. One should note also that even those trends might have other causes, ones not linked to the mass society. Second, one should report the research method used in reaching those opposite conclusions. The basic question is this: How does the critic of the mass society know all these things? How does he or she know about the typical condition and personal reactions of millions of individuals? Survey research organizations give a lot of attention to the problem of sampling, to finding and interviewing representative cross-sections of large populations. What kind of sample does the mass society theorist have? How many persons were contacted? And how representative was the selection?

The mass society formulations, as seen, portray "our society" as filled with ever-worsening pathologies. The tale is one long history of decline and loss. The evidence reviewed and presented here challenges that portrayal on all points, faulting that depiction on questions of both extent and tendency. There can be no question as to the existence of serious problems and, in some areas, of serious losses. The most visible loss, perhaps, is the transformation of the flourishing industrial cities of the 1950s into the Rust Belt cities of the 1980s. One can point to real problems of crime, poverty, and homelessness. There are problems involving urban ghettos, inadequate schools, and an underclass.

To address social problems, three kinds of effort are needed. The first is to ascertain the dimensions: What is the extent of the problem? The second task is to discover the sources of the problem. And the third is to develop solutions, to spell out some viable plans.

Most formulations of the mass society position make no serious effort to discover the extent of the problems delineated. The mode, typically, is declarative. The questions of quality are "solved" by declaration: The problems are announced as "large" and "growing." Most such formulations involve what might be called a magnification bias. The problems are all-pervasive.

The typical mass society analysis provides no serious discussion or investigation of the second need, locating the causes of the pathologies. As with the treatment of extent, the formulations are sweeping, general, giving only a "broad brush" portrait. One points to "large" causes—industrialization, urbanization, fragmentation, and anomie—without any attempt at specification or investigation. Again, the declarationist mode is typical.

For all of the expressed concern, contemporary mass society formulations rarely provide solutions. How could we reduce the widespread anxiety that supposedly typifies "our society?" How might we reduce the fear of "our" neighbors? The "hard-hitting" critiques rarely provide solutions. There appear to be no feasible plans.

The magnification bias, the insistent hyperbolic usage, might well have immobilizing effects. Concerned citizens might easily conclude that "society's" problems are "too big." If anonymity, isolation, and loneliness are all-pervasive, if they are inherent features of modern society, the lesson, it would appear, is that there are no solutions.

NOTES

1. The leading nineteenth-century proponents of this position were Louis de Bonald, Joseph de Maistre, and, from a different perspective, Gustave Le Bon. An influential twentieth-century writer in this tradition was José Ortega y Gasset, in his *Revolt of the Masses* (New York: Norton, 1940). For a useful critique, see Neil McInnes, "Ortega and the Myth of the Mass," *The National Interest* 44 (Summer 1996): 78–88. See also the work of Robert A. Nisbet, *The Quest for Community: A Study in the Ethics of Order and Freedom* (New York: Oxford University Press, 1953); reissued as *Community and Power* (New York: Oxford University Press, 1962); and Robert N. Bellah, Richard Madsen, William Sullivan, Ann Swidler, and Steven M. Tipton, *Habits of the Heart: Individualism and Commitment in American Life* (Berkeley and Los Angeles: University of California Press, 1985). See also Andrew M. Greeley's review of this work in *Sociology and Social Research* 70 (1985): 114. For a collection of articles and chapters arguing these themes, see Eric and Mary Josephson, eds., *Man Alone: Alienation in Modern Society* (New York: Dell, 1962). Many of these critiques focus on the large cities, on the metropolis, as the source of the problem. For Germany, see Klaus Bergmann, *Agrarromantik und Großstadtfeindschaft* (Meisenheim: Anton Hain, 1970); and Andrew Lees, "Critics of Urban Society in Germany, 1854–1914," *Journal of the History of Ideas* 40 (1979): 61–83. An important figure there was Wilhelm Heinrich Riehl. Brief discussions of his work may be found in Bergmann, Lees, and also George L. Mosse, *The Crisis of German Ideology* (New York: Grosset

and Dunlap, 1964), 19–24. For discussion of the American experience, see Morton and Lucia White, *The Intellectual versus the City from Thomas Jefferson to Frank Lloyd Wright* (Cambridge: Harvard University Press and MIT Press, 1962). For a sweeping comparative view, see Andrew Lees, *Cities Perceived: Urban Society in European and American Thought, 1820–1940* (New York: Columbia University Press, 1985). Two useful comprehensive book-length reviews of this position are Salvador Giner, *Mass Society* (London: Martin Robertson, 1976); and Sandor Halebsky, *Mass Society and Political Conflict: Toward a Reconstruction of Theory* (Cambridge: Cambridge University Press, 1976). I have discussed and critiqued the mass society theory on several occasions. For comments, evidence, and further references see Richard F. Hamilton, *Class and Politics in the United States* (New York: Wiley, 1972), 46–49, 516–517; *Restraining Myths* (New York: Sage, Halsted, Wiley, 1975), 13–16, 206–208, 268–270; *Who Voted for Hitler?* (Princeton: Princeton University Press, 1982), 64–65, 433–437; and, with James D. Wright, *The State of the Masses* (New York: Aldine, 1986), Ch. 4 and pp. 375–376.

2. Liverpool is quoted in Val Lorwin, "Working Class Politics and Economic Development in Western Europe," *American Historical Review* 63 (1958): 341. On the Prussian events, see Veit Valentin, *Geschichte der deutschen Revolution von 1848–1849*. Vol. 1 (1930; reprint, Cologne: Kiepenheuer & Witsch, 1977), 446. See also J. R. Jones, "England," in *The European Right: A Historical Profile*, ed. Hans Rogger and Eugen Weber (Berkeley and Los Angeles: University of California Press, 1966), 29–30; and M. S. Anderson, *The Ascendancy of Europe 1815–1914*, 2d ed. (London: Longman, 1985), 64–67.

3. On the European sociologists, see Halebsky, *Mass Society*, 25–35, and Giner, *Mass Society*, Chs. 5 and 6. The Simmel, Park, and Wirth essays are reprinted in Richard Sennett, ed., *Classic Essays on the Culture of Cities* (New York: Appleton–Century–Crofts, 1969). The passage from Wirth's article appears there on p. 153. Durkheim's position differs from that of the others mentioned. He saw a change from "mechanical solidarity" in the small communities to "organic solidarity" in the new larger society. He argued a change in the form of interpersonal connections, as opposed to an unambiguous "loss" of social ties. For later expositions of the mass society position, see Arnold M. Rose, *Theory and Method in the Social Sciences* (Westport, Conn.: Greenwood, 1974), Ch. 2, and Leon Bramson, *The Political Context of Sociology* (Princeton: Princeton University Press, 1961).

4. Barrett A. Lee, R. S. Oropesa, Barbara J. Metch, and Avery M. Guest, "Testing the Decline-of-Community Thesis: Neighborhood Organizations in Seattle, 1929 and 1979," *American Journal of Sociology* 89 (1984): 1161–1162. For a more extensive overview, see Claude S. Fischer, "'Urbanism as a Way of Life': A Review and an Agenda," *Sociological Methods and Research* 1 (1972): 187–242. Lee et al., and Fischer have provided empirically based critiques of the decline thesis (see note 40).

5. On Gramsci and bourgeois cultural hegemony, see Martin Clark, *Antonio Gramsci and the Revolution That Failed* (New Haven: Yale University Press, 1977), 2, 225. For comment and criticism, see Axel van den Berg, *The Immanent Utopia: From Marxism on the State to the State of Marxism* (Princeton: Princeton University Press, 1988), 145–150. The left (or "critical") mass society theory appears in Herbert Marcuse, *One Dimensional Man: Studies in the Ideology of Advanced Industrial Society* (Boston: Beacon, 1964), Introduction, Ch. 1; C. Wright Mills, *The Power Elite* (New York: Oxford University Press, 1957), Ch. 13; and, among others, Vance Packard, *The Hid-*

den Persuaders (New York: David McKay, 1957); Herbert Schiller, *Mass Communication and American Empire* (New York: Augustus Kelley, 1969), *The Mind Managers* (Boston: Beacon, 1973), and *Communication and Cultural Domination* (New York: Pantheon, 1978); Robert Cirino, *Don't Blame the People* (New York: Vintage, 1972); and David Paletz and Robert Entman, *Media Power Politics* (New York: Free Press, 1981). For a recent statement, see Michael Parenti, *Democracy for the Few*, 6th ed. (New York: St. Martin's Press, 1994), Ch. 9. For a critique of this position, see Edward Shils, "Daydreams and Nightmares: Reflections on the Criticism of Mass Culture," *Sewanee Review* 65 (1959): 586–608. The essay appears also in Shils, *The Intellectuals and the Powers and Other Essays* (Chicago: University of Chicago Press, 1972).

6. For exposition and assessment of Marxism and the first two "revisions," see Richard F. Hamilton, *Marxism, Revisionism, and Leninism: Explication, Assessment, and Commentary* (Westport, Conn.: Praeger, 2000).

7. For the transformation of the media in the 1960s, see David Halberstam, *The Powers That Be* (New York: Knopf, 1979); S. Robert Lichter, Stanley Rothman, Linda S. Lichter, *The Media Elite: America's New Powerbrokers* (Bethesda, Md.: Adler & Adler, 1986). On the changed treatment of family relations, see Lynette Friedrich Cofer and Robin Smith Jacobvitz, "The Loss of Moral Turf: Mass Media and Family Values," in *Rebuilding the Nest: A New Commitment to the American Family*, ed. David Blankenhorn, Steven Bayme, and Jean Bethke Elshtain (Milwaukee: Family Service America, 1990). The relations of government and press during the Vietnam War contributed greatly to this transformation, especially with the publication of the Pentagon Papers. On this, see David Rudenstine, *The Day the Presses Stopped: A History of the Pentagon Papers Case* (Berkeley and Los Angeles: University of California Press, 1996). The Watergate events, of course, also contributed. For that, see Carl Bernstein and Bob Woodward, *All the President's Men* (New York: Simon & Schuster, 1974).

8. Karl Mannheim, *Man and Society in an Age of Reconstruction: Studies in Modern Social Structure* (New York: Harcourt, Brace, 1940); Emil Lederer, *The State of the Masses: The Threat of the Classless Society* (New York: Norton, 1940); Hannah Arendt, *The Origins of Totalitarianism* (New York: Harcourt, Brace, 1951); Sigmund Neumann, *Permanent Revolution: The Total State in a World at War* (New York: Harper, 1942), Ch. 4.

9. William Kornhauser, *The Politics of Mass Society* (Glencoe, Ill.: Free Press, 1959). For a later statement, see Kornhauser's "Mass Society," in the *International Encyclopedia of the Social Sciences*, vol. 10 (New York: Macmillan/Free Press, 1968), 58–64.

10. Charles A. Reich, *The Greening of America* (New York: Random House, 1970). For a review and assessment, see Hamilton and Wright, *State of the Masses*, 3–11. Our conclusion: "Reich's procedures are best described as the method of free fantasy, a method that makes anything possible. At best, it is a generalization based on the atypical experiences of an absurdly biased sample" (pp. 54–55).

11. John Carey, *The Intellectuals and the Masses: Pride and Prejudice Among the Literary Intelligentsia, 1880–1939* (London: Faber and Faber, 1992).

12. Daniel Bell, "America as a Mass Society: A Critique," in his *End of Ideology: On the Exhaustion of Political Ideas in the Fifties* (New York: Collier, 1961), 21. Giner writes, "As we have seen, one of the labels that our civilization most frequently received is that of 'mass society.'" *Mass Society*, 246.

13. Some research on the psychological orientations is reported in Lichter et al., *Media Elite*. For a review of the social factors involved in persistent misreadings of evidence see, Richard F. Hamilton, *The Social Misconstruction of Reality: Validity and Verification in the Scholarly Community* (New Haven: Yale University Press, 1996), Chs. 7 and 8.

14. Gerhard Lenski, Jean Lenski, and Patrick Nolan, *Human Societies: An Introduction to Macrosociology*, 6th ed. (New York: McGraw-Hill, 1991), 87.

15. Steve Hochstadt, "Migration in Preindustrial Germany," *Central European History* 15 (1983): 209, 217. See also Hochstadt's "Migration and Industrialization in Germany: 1815–1977," *Social Science History* 5 (1981): 445–468, "The Socioeconomic Determinants of Increasing Mobility in Nineteenth-Century Germany," in *European Migrants: Global and Local Perspectives*, ed. Dirk Hoerder and Leslie Page Moch (Boston: Northeastern University Press, 1995), and *Mobility and Modernity: Migration in Germany, 1820–1990* (Ann Arbor: University of Michigan Press, 1999). Also of some relevance in this connection are Sidney M. Greenfield, "Industrialization and the Family in Sociological Theory," *American Journal of Sociology* 67 (1961): 312–322; Frank F. Furstenberg, Jr., "Industrialization and the American Family: A Look Backward," *American Sociological Review* 31 (1966): 326–337.

16. Hochstadt, "Migration in Preindustrial Germany," 209. For Sweden, see Teresa Sullivan, "Longer Lives and Life-Long Relations: A Life Table Exegesis," *Concilium* 12 (January 1979): 15–25 (specifically 20–21). I wish to thank Andrew Greeley, both for bringing this finding to my attention and for the basic formulation.

17. Marion J. Levy, Jr., "Aspects of the Analysis of Family Structure," in *Aspects of the Analysis of Family Structure*, ed. Ansley J. Coale (Princeton: Princeton University Press, 1965). Horace Miner's study of a Quebec community in the mid-1930s contains some relevant evidence on this point. He traced the life cycle and inheritance pattern of St. Denis families over three generations. In a forty-year span, the period beginning with the marriage of the first couple, that household would have had "three generations under one roof" for, roughly, two brief six-year episodes. The oldest children in the second and third generations would have been under that roof simultaneously with a grandparent and, possibly, might have had some recollection of the experience. St. Denis had large families at that point, the average was ten, and on average only seven survived to adulthood. Four or five of the surviving seven would have had no three-generation experience. See his *St. Denis: A French-Canadian Parish* (Chicago: University of Chicago Press, 1939), 85.

18. These surveys are based on national cross-sectional samples of the adult (eighteen and over), noninstitutional U.S. population. They are all multistage area samples. The earliest studies, those of 1972 through 1974, were modified probability samples, allowing a quota element at the block level. The 1975 and 1976 studies were transitional, half full probability and half block quota. From 1977 onward the studies have been based on full probability samples. For further details, see James A. Davis and Tom W. Smith, *General Social Surveys, 1972–1993: Cumulative Codebook* (Chicago: National Opinion Research Center, 1993), 811–822.

19. Approximately half of the respondents say they never go to bars or taverns. There is a strong age relationship. The patterns were examined, but for the sake of economy, except where something of interest appeared, the results are not reported here. For an earlier account of the "barflies," see Hamilton and Wright, *State of the Masses*, 100–105.

20. The question asks about social evenings with friends living outside the neighborhood. People answering rarely or never could possibly have friends living in the

neighborhood. Investigation of this subgroup, however, showed a pronounced general tendency toward isolation. The percentages reporting never having contact with parents, siblings, relatives, and neighbors were, respectively, 38, 32, 17, and 56 (these figures should be compared with those in the bottom line of Table 1.1). There is an easy alternative explanation: The 10 percent reporting "never" having contact with friends outside the neighborhood were elderly. Fifty percent of them were sixty or over (N = 484).

21. That base figure includes those without parents and without siblings. For another useful overview of the friendship–isolation question, see Linda De Stefano, "Pressures of Modern Life Bring Increased Importance to Friendship," *Gallup Poll Monthly* 294 (March 1990): 24–33. Some people wish to avoid human contact and, accordingly, choose to live in inaccessible locations. They would be underrepresented in even the best-quality survey or poll.

22. The "happiness" question was used earlier, in 1957, in an important survey of adult Americans and in an equally important follow-up study in 1976. The levels of reported happiness at both points are approximately the same as those shown in Table 1.3. On the basis of this and several other measures, the authors gave emphasis to a principal finding, that *"American well-being generally has remained constant from 1957 to 1976."* See Joseph Veroff, Elizabeth Douvan, and Richard A. Kulka, *The Inner American: A Self-Portrait from 1957 to 1976* (New York: Basic Books, 1981), Ch. 2. For the responses to the happiness question, see p. 56; the quotation is from p. 57. Comparable results appear in the European Values Study, a project based on surveys in ten European nations in 1990. The question in this case allowed four responses: "Taking all things together, would you say you are . . . very happy, quite happy, not very happy, or not at all happy?" Overall, 25 percent of those responding said "very happy" and 64 percent said "quite happy." The most frequent reports of "malaise" were found in Portugal, where a quarter of the respondents chose "not very" or "not at all happy." From European Values Study Group, "1990 Values Survey, Tabulated Results" (Allensbach/Bodensee, Federal Republic of Germany: Institut für Demoskopie, n.d.).

23. The slight decline in reported marital happiness was first reported by Norval D. Glenn, "The Recent Trend in Marital Success in the United States," *Journal of Marriage and the Family* 53 (1991): 261–270. See also Stacy J. Rogers and Paul R. Amato, "Is Marital Quality Declining? The Evidence from Two Generations," *Social Forces* 75 (1997): 1089–1100.

24. On the happiness of first and second marriages, see Elizabeth Vemer, Marilyn Coleman, Lawrence H. Ganong, and Harris Cooper, "Marital Satisfaction in Remarriage: A Meta-Analysis," *Journal of Marriage and the Family* 51 (1989): 713–725; Marilyn Coleman and Lawrence H. Ganong, "Remarriage and Stepfamily Research in the 1980s: Increased Interest in an Old Family Form," *Journal of Marriage and the Family* 52 (1990): 925–940. For reports from 1957–1976, see Veroff, Douvan, and Kulkar, *Inner American*, Ch. 4. For research and discussion of marriage and marital satisfaction, see Norval D. Glenn, "Values, Attitudes, and the State of American Marriage," in *Promises to Keep: Decline and Renewal of Marriage in America*, ed. David Popenoe, Jean Bethke Elshtain, and David Blankenhorn (Lanham, Md.: Rowman and Littlefield, 1997).

25. Dorothy M. Stetson and Gerald C. Wright, Jr., "The Effects of Laws on Divorce in American States," *Journal of Marriage and the Family* 37 (1975): 537–547. A later article by the same authors finds "no-fault" divorce laws had little effect on the incidence of marital breakup. See Gerald C. Wright, Jr. and Dorothy M. Stetson, "The

Impact of No-Fault Divorce Law Reform on Divorce in American States," *Journal of Marriage and the Family* 40 (1978): 575–580. Liberals, not too surprisingly, are the principal advocates of liberalized divorce laws. With divorce easier, again not surprisingly, divorce rates rise. Neglecting their own contribution to this result, some left-liberal critics point to the rising rates as evidence of social "decay," and as support for their critique of the mass society.

26. A series showing divorces per 1,000 of population begins at 3.5 in 1970 and rises to the peak years, 5.3 in 1979, 5.2 in 1980, and 5.3 in 1981. Since then the rate declined to 4.4 in 1995. From U.S. Bureau of the Census, *Statistical Abstract of the United States: 1988* (Washington, D.C.: U.S. Government Printing Office, 1988), 83; *Statistical Abstract: 1998*, 111. Another series gives the divorce rate per 1,000 married women fifteen years and older. This puts the peak in 1979, at 22.8 per 1,000, followed by a decline to 19.8 in 1995 (same sources).

27. For the higher estimates, see S. H. Preston and J. McDonald, "The Incidence of Divorce Within Cohorts of American Marriages Contracted Since the Civil War," *Demography* 16 (1979): 1–26; Teresa Castro Martin and Larry L. Bumpass, "Recent Trends in Marital Disruption," *Demography* 26 (1989): 37–51. Some sense of the complications may be found in Diane Colasanto and James Shriver, "Mirror of America: Middle-Aged Face Marital Crisis," *Gallup Report* 284 (May 1989): 34–38. Three studies providing some challenge to the insistent claims about the decline of the family are Mary Jo Bane, *Here to Stay: American Families in the Twentieth Century* (New York: Basic Books, 1976); Theodore Caplow, Howard M. Bahr, Bruce A. Chadwick, Reuben Hill, and Margaret Holmes Williamson, *Middletown Families: Fifty Years of Change and Continuity* (Minneapolis: University of Minnesota Press, 1982); David Popenoe, *Disturbing the Nest: Family Change and Decline in Modern Societies* (New York: de Gruyter, 1988). Two useful collections of articles and commentary are Blankenhorn, Baymer, and Elshtain, *Rebuilding the Nest*, and Popenoe, Elshtain, and Blankenhorn, *Promises to Keep.* An important overview and commentary appears in Norval D. Glenn, "A Critique of Twenty Family and Marriage and the Family Textbooks," *Family Relations* 46 (1997): 197–208. There were three replies and a subsequent comment by Glenn (pp. 208–226).

28. The percentage is small, but the absolute number, of course, is large. In 1990 there were approximately 178 million persons in the United States of age twenty or older. Five percent reporting low satisfaction from their "family life" means approximately 9 million persons. Two separate and distinct questions are at issue here, the typical experience and the incidence of self-reported dissatisfaction. Based on U.S. Bureau of the Census, *Statistical Abstract: 1998*, 21.

29. Following the procedure of the previous note, the 14 percent reporting little or no satisfaction from the community means roughly 25 million persons. Those responses might reflect experience with declining communities but, as always, one should consider other possibilities. People with single-minded life concerns, with work, or a hobby, or with religion, might live in high-quality communities but could, appropriately, report little or no satisfaction from those settings. That alternative was investigated but was not supported. Those reporting little community satisfaction also reported little happiness, low levels of marital happiness, very limited family satisfaction, and very low job satisfaction.

30. Angus Campbell, Philip E. Converse, Willard L. Rodgers, *The Quality of American Life: Perceptions, Evaluations, and Satisfactions* (New York: Russell Sage Foun-

dation, 1976), 63. For the record, the lowest levels of satisfaction reported were for standard of living, 5.31; amount of education, 4.69; and savings, 4.27. Dissatisfaction with savings shows a strong inverse relation with age; young people have little money in the bank. For a follow-up study, also of very high quality, see Angus Campbell, *The Sense of Well-Being in America: Recent Patterns and Trends* (New York: McGraw-Hill, 1981). For additional evidence on sociability and satisfaction or dissatisfaction based on those surveys, see Hamilton and Wright, *State of the Masses*, Ch. 4.

31. For an earlier report on friendship networks, satisfactions, and isolation, see Hamilton and Wright, *State of the Masses*, 167–172.

32. Robert Wuthnow, *Sharing the Journey: Support Groups and America's New Quest for Community* (New York: Free Press, 1994), 33–34. Data in Table 1.6 allow an assessment of Wuthnow's claim about the "anonymous lives" of people living in the suburbs. He presents no evidence with respect to high-rise apartment buildings.

33. On the definition of "urban place," see U.S. Bureau of the Census, *Statistical Abstract: 1998*, 4 (there are several other components to that definition that involve Census designation of populations as urban). See also Donald C. Dahmann and Laarni T. Dacquel, "Residents of Farms and Rural Areas: 1990," *Current Population Reports*, series P-20, Population Characteristics no. 457 (Washington, D.C.: U.S. Bureau of the Census, 1992).

34. U.S. Department of Commerce, *1990 Census of Population and Housing. Housing Unit Counts—Ohio*, 1990 CPH-2-37 (Washington, D.C.: U.S. Government Printing Office, 1993). The 1990 census found 75.2 percent of the U.S. population to be urban. The figure for Ohio was 74.1 percent. From U.S. Bureau of the Census, *Statistical Abstract: 1998*, 46. Similar results were found for Indiana. The capital city, Indianapolis, was the state's largest, with 731,327 persons in 1990. The second city, Fort Wayne, had 173,072. The top ten contained 28.6 percent of the state's total population. The surrounding nine counties contained another 15.6 percent. A majority of the state's population, 55.8 percent, lived in a county whose largest city was smaller than Terre Haute, with 57,483 persons. U.S. Department of Commerce, *1990 Population and Housing—Indiana*, vol. 16, p. 52.

35. The definitions of "metropolitan areas" are complex and changing. William C. Flanagan, *Urban Sociology: Images and Structure*, 2d ed. (Boston: Allyn and Bacon, 1995), 199–200, a current urban sociology text, reports that in 1950 the Census Bureau began to enumerate metropolitan populations by employing the Standard Metropolitan Statistical Area (SMSA) as a unit of measure. This measure counted all cities or twin cities with populations of 50,000 or more, including the population of the surrounding county or counties that were considered to be "socially or economically integrated" with the central urban area. Since the measure was standardized for all such cities and surrounding counties, it was bound occasionally to include some fairly nonurban territory; open country, farmland, and even barren desert were incorporated in a number of cases." For more detail, see U.S. Bureau of the Census, *Geographic Areas Reference Manual* (Washington, D.C.: U.S. Government Printing Office, 1994). Note 1 reads, "The collective term used for Federal metropolitan areas has varied over time, beginning with *standard metropolitan area (SMA)* in 1950, changing to *standard metropolitan statistical area (SMSA)* in 1959, to *metropolitan statistical area (MSA)* in 1983, and to *metropolitan area (MA)* in 1990." In addition, there are Consolidated Metropolitan Statistical Areas, Primary Metropolitan Statistical Areas, and New England County Metropolitan Areas.

36. See Hamilton, *Who Voted*, 64–65. Most accounts focus on the large cities and their annexation of surrounding territory. But smaller communities also engage in this kind of "outreach." Between 1960 and 1990 Athens, Ohio (1990 population, 21,265), increased its territory from 4.7 to 6.8 square miles. Ironton (1990 population, 12,751), the seat of Lawrence county, went from 0.4 to 4.1 square miles in the same period.

37. I would have preferred working within the framework provided by the 1990 census, but when this chapter was written only three GSS surveys are available and in several instances appropriate questions were not asked, thus reducing the number of cases. The twelve largest cities in 1980 were New York, Chicago, Los Angeles, Philadelphia, Houston, Detroit, Dallas, San Diego, Phoenix, Baltimore, San Antonio, and Indianapolis. An analysis of trends of social involvements and satisfactions within the framework of the SRC Belt Code is effectively impossible. The series covers three census periods. The original survey was based on the 1970 census and appropriate changes were made after the censuses of 1980 and 1990. Three of the largest cities of 1970, Milwaukee, Washington, and Cleveland (and the suburbs), dropped from the top twelve to the next-eighty-eight category in the 1980 census. A fourth, Indianapolis, fell off the top twelve list in the 1990 census. Milwaukee, Washington, and Cleveland experienced steady population losses in this twenty-year span. Indianapolis had a small loss in the 1970s and a small gain in the 1980s. The four Rust Belt cities that fell from the original top twelve were later replaced by four Sun Belt cities, San Diego, Phoenix, San Antonio, and San Jose. The latter cities registered significant population gains, some through migration but much of it also through annexation. San Diego added 172 square miles to its territory between 1970 and 1990. In that same period most of the older Rust Belt cities had near constant boundaries. Milwaukee gained just over one square mile. Washington, D.C., had no change. See U.S. Bureau of the Census, *Statistical Abstract: 1972*, 21–23; *1984*, 28–30; and *1992*, 35–37. Changes would have occurred also in the other SRC Belt Code categories. Some of the original eighty-eight cities would have fallen below the 100 mark and have been replaced by newcomers. Suburbs of both the gainers and losers would also have been relocated accordingly. Some of the rural counties would have moved into the large-county category, either by virtue of population growth in the county seat or through annexation. The principal consequence, obviously, is that much uncontrolled variance would be present in any trend data based on the SRC Belt Code. The comparisons of the largest twelve cities, to borrow the familiar image, would involve eight apples and four oranges. Eight of the cities are present in that category in all samples. The four cities that fell from the top twelve rank were located at the bottom of the 1970 list; that is, in positions eight through twelve, which means their contribution to the overall result would be relatively small. The new "oranges," however, have somewhat greater impact, with San Diego in sixth position and Phoenix in eighth. An immense amount of work would be needed to reconstitute the data so as to compare the same legal entities; that is, the same cities and counties. To reconstitute constant boundaries for the cities, large, medium, and small, would be virtually impossible. For further information, see James A. Davis and Tom W. Smith, *General Social Surveys, 1972–1993: Cumulative Codebook* (Chicago: National Opinion Research Center, 1993), 906, 1022.

38. Still another portrait of urbanism may be had through a straightforward use of size categories. The 1990 census reported a total population of 248.7 million. One-quarter, 24.8 percent of that total, was located in unincorporated places. Another 11.3 percent lived in incorporated places with less than 10,000 persons, and another 8.2 percent lived in communities with 10,000 to 24,999 persons. That means the "typical

American," the median case, would be found in the next category—places with 25,000 to 49,999 persons. Many persons in that category, of course, would be living in Standard Metropolitan Areas, but their immediate circumstances would probably not match the portrayals found in those alarming depictions of "the urban condition." From U.S. Bureau of the Census, *Statistical Abstract: 1998*, recalculated from tables on p. 46.

39. For many Americans living on farms, everyday life was extremely isolated. A medical doctor practicing on the frontier described the "loneliness of the North Dakota prairie" as "a great breeder of anxiety and worry. Sometimes it seemed like the more remote the farm, the more likely you were to find a mentally distressed patient waiting for you." Richard Critchfield, *Those Days: An American Album* (Garden City, N.Y.: Anchor/Doubleday, 1968), 213. Ole Rölvaag's novel, *Giants in the Earth* (New York: Harper, 1929), depicts the same problem.

40. The two works cited are Joel Smith, William H. Form, and Gregory P. Stone, "Local Intimacy in a Middle-Sized City," *American Journal of Sociology* 60 (1954): 276–284; and Melvin Seeman, "The Urban Alienations: Some Dubious Theses from Marx to Marcuse," *Journal of Personality and Social Psychology* 19 (1971): 135–143. Smith, Form, and Stone cite several studies of neighboring and primary groups that go back even farther. Many other studies demonstrated that the principal mass society claims were "dubious theses." The following represent only a small sample from a larger literature: Scott Greer, "Urbanism Reconsidered: A Comparative Study of Local Areas in a Metropolis," *American Sociological Review* 21 (1956): 19–25; Wendell Bell and Marion D. Boat, "Urban Neighborhoods and Informal Social Relations," *American Journal of Sociology* 62 (1957): 391–398; Michael Young and Peter Willmott, *Family and Kinship in East London* (London: Routledge & Kegan Paul, 1957); Burt N. Adams, *Kinship in an Urban Setting* (Chicago: Markham, 1968); Dale Rogers Marshall, "Who Participates in What? A Bibliographic Essay on Individual Participation in Urban Areas," *Urban Affairs Quarterly* 4 (1968): 201–223; Scott Greer and Ella Kube, "Urbanism and Social Structure: A Los Angeles Study," in *Community Structure and Analysis*, ed. Marvin B. Sussman (New York: Crowell, 1959), Ch. 4; and William H. Key, "Rural–Urban Social Participation," in *Urbanism in World Perspective*, ed. Sylvia F. Fava (New York: Crowell, 1968). For an overview of these and other similar studies, see Halebsky, *Mass Society*, 73–92. In the 1950s Juan Linz reviewed some German surveys dealing with these questions. His conclusion was that "much of the guesswork about 'alienated' city life is at least doubtful." See his "Social Bases of West German Politics" (Ph.D. diss., Columbia University, 1959), 367. For more recent evidence, see Claude S. Fischer, *To Dwell Among Friends: Personal Networks in Town and City* (Chicago: University of Chicago Press, 1981); *The Urban Experience*, 2d ed. (San Diego: Harcourt Brace Jovanovich, 1984); and "Ambivalent Communities: How Americans Understand Their Localities," in *America at Century's End*, ed. Alan Wolfe (Berkeley and Los Angeles: University of California Press, 1991), Ch. 4. See also Lee et al., "Testing the Decline-of-Community Thesis." All of the works cited here contain many references to other studies. For a review of more recent studies, see Flanagan, *Urban Sociology*, 68–80. Several of these studies were summarized for a wider audience by Carin Rubenstein, "The Folks Next Door Aren't Strangers After All," *New York Times*, 7 January 1993, sec. C, p. 1.

41. U.S. Bureau of the Census, *Statistical Abstract: 1972, 1984*, and *1992*.

42. On the movement from the metropolitan regions, see Glenn V. Fuguitt, "The Nonmetropolitan Population Turnaround," *Annual Review of Sociology* 11 (1985): 259–280; Calvin Beale and Kenneth M. Johnson, "The Rural Rebound Revisited," *Ameri-*

can Demographics 17 (July 1995): 46–49; and Kenneth M. Johnson and Calvin L. Beale, "The Rural Rebound," *Wilson Quarterly* 22 (Spring 1998): 16–27.

43. Asked whether life was "exciting," "routine," or "dull," the responses showed little variation by the size or kind of community. Rural-county respondents, by a small 4-point margin, were more likely than the big-city dwellers to say "routine." Unexpectedly perhaps, the suburbanites were most likely to report that life was "exciting." Race proved to be a relevant factor. White respondents were more likely to report their lives as "exciting"; blacks were more likely to say "routine" or "dull." These results are based on the GSS merge, 1988–1991.

44. Hamilton, *Class and Politics*, 257. The GSS asked the location of respondents when they were age sixteen, classifying them according to the SRC Belt Code. Three-tenths of those raised in metropolitan regions had migrated "to the country"; that is, were living in nonmetropolitan counties when interviewed (GSS merge, 1988–1991). Those city-to-country migrants were somewhat more conservative with respect to sexual permissiveness and to liberalizing divorce laws than those who remained in the cities.

45. Among singles, 39 percent (N = 698) report frequent parental contact; among the marrieds, only 25 percent (N = 1,643) do so. Among those age eighteen to twenty-nine the respective figures are 44 percent (N = 467) and 36 percent (N = 311).

46. Married and widowed respondents in the rural counties report greater contact with their parents than those in all other communities, the respective percentages of frequent contact being 31 (N = 268) and 23 (N = 1,483). The other three categories—single, separated, and divorced respondents in those counties—have, by far, the highest percentage of frequent parental contacts: 48 percent (N = 103) versus 34 percent (N = 1,030) in the five other settings (GSS merge, 1988–1991). In those rural counties, that combination—single status and "marital breakdown"—proved to be uniquely linked to strong intergenerational ties.

47. This is based on the GSS merge for the 1990–1994 studies (to match the results contained in Tables 1.5 and 1.6). For some earlier results, see Hamilton and Wright, *State of the Masses*, 209–214. Those results, based on the "Quality of American Life" study, 1971, found age to be positively related with marital and family satisfaction.

48. For overviews of Italian migration patterns, see John S. MacDonald and Leatrice D. MacDonald, "Chain Migration, Ethnic Neighborhood Formation and Social Networks," *Milbank Memorial Fund Quarterly* 42 (1964): 82–97; and Walter Firey, *Land Use in Central Boston* (Cambridge: Harvard University Press, 1947), Ch. 5. In 1848 the Carnegie family left Dunfermline (Scotland) and traveled to New York, then over the Erie Canal to Buffalo, across Lake Erie to Cleveland, then with canals to Pittsburgh, ending up in Allegheny, a suburb there. This was no random choice: Margaret Carnegie's two sisters lived there. One of them, Annie, was a widow who owned a house. The family lived with her until they were established. See Joseph Frazier Wall, *Andrew Carnegie* (Pittsburgh: University of Pittsburgh Press, 1979), 74–79. A similar experience is reported in William Form, *On the Shoulders of Immigrants: A Family Portrait* (Columbus, Ohio: North Star Press, 1999), 147–151, 237–240.

49. The ending of the episode is indicated in surveys that ask about social origins. The 1952 National Election Study, for example, found half of the older working-class respondents, those fifty-five and over, reporting farm origins. Among those age twenty-five to thirty-four, only 30 percent did so. By 1964 the respective percentages were 42 and 20. See Hamilton, *Class and Politics*, 310. The recent GSS surveys (1988–1991 merge) show a continuation of the trend. Among respondents seventy years and older, 46 percent

(N = 442) report farm origins. Among those age eighteen to twenty-nine, the figure is 8 percent (N = 651). Two other largely overlooked possibilities should be mentioned. Some people give up farming but do not leave the land, choosing instead to commute to jobs elsewhere. And some give up farming and sell their property for urban development. Almost all urban territory, it should be remembered, was once farmland.

50. Another series showing moves in a five-year period, 1980 to 1985, found that 39.9 percent had changed residence in that time. The highest mobility, 70.4 percent, occurred among those age twenty-five to twenty-nine; the lowest, 16.2 percent, was among those sixty-five and over. From U.S. Bureau of the Census, *Statistical Abstract: 1987*, 25.

51. For evidence on the decline of mobility in twentieth-century Germany, see Hochstadt, *Mobility and Modernity*, Ch. 6. Hochstadt's evidence is set against a generous supply of assertions by eminent authorities who declare high and increasing mobility as "the fact."

52. Greer and Kube, "Urbanism and Social Structure," 111. In a similar vein, in his 1968 review, Marshall, "Who Participates," 202, wrote:

The studies of urban participation reviewed here should be central to an understanding of urban society. . . . [Those studies] indicate that urban society is characterized by a high degree of participation and organization but that the patterns are exceedingly diverse and complex. Thus, the conclusion drawn is that research must no longer focus on debates about whether or not there is organization; rather it must attempt to delineate the diverse patterns of participation which do exist, and the complex implications of these patterns.

53. "Only the Lonely Can End Loneliness," *Columbus Dispatch*, 30 November 1987, p. 3B. No information was provided about that survey; a letter to Clark (27 January 1988) did not produce any further information. For the Gallup findings, see DeStefano, "Pressures of Modern Life," 31.

54. Philip E. Slater, *The Pursuit of Loneliness: American Culture at the Breaking Point* (Boston: Beacon, 1970). The revised second edition, from 1976, was also with Beacon. The third edition (Beacon, 1990), a reprint of the second, has a new introduction by Todd Gitlin. For the evidence, see Campbell, Converse, and Rodgers, *Quality of American Life*, 38. Slater's original reports that modern man experiences "ineffable boredom" and "fearsome ennui" (p. 19). Those statements appear unchanged in the subsequent editions (pp. 25–26, 29). The Campbell, Converse, and Rodgers study included "boring" and "interesting" as a set of their semantic differential paired terms. Two percent described their lives as boring (a1) while 36 percent indicated their lives were interesting (a7). Another three-eighths of the respondents chose 6 or 5; that is, leaning heavily to the "interesting" extreme.

55. On Weber and Foucault, see Hamilton, *Social Misconstruction*, Chs. 3, 6. For discussion of Freud, see Frederick Crews, Harold Blum, Marcia Cavell, Morris Eagle, and Freda Crews, *The Memory Wars: Freud's Legacy in Dispute* (New York: New York Review of Books, 1995); and Frederick Crews, ed., *Unauthorized Freud: Doubters Confront Legend* (New York: Viking, 1998). For a comprehensive review, see Malcolm Macmillan, *Freud Evaluated: The Completed Arc* (Cambridge: MIT Press, 1997). In 1977–1978, Freud was the second most-cited twentieth-century author in the *Arts and Humanities Citation Index*. On this point, see Allan Megill, "The Reception of Foucault by Historians," *Journal of the History of Ideas* 48 (1987): 139–140. The point about the academic division of labor is not intended as support for a roman-

tic (that is, utopian) critique, that we should "abolish the division of labor" and return to some fictive wholeness. The academic enterprise is complex; a division of labor and specialization are unavoidable necessities. The appropriate solution, borrowing from the military experience, is to "guard the flanks." That means one should find out what is happening in those other fields; some reconnaissance is necessary. Although interdisciplinary efforts are routinely commended, departmental provincialism is the more frequent reality.

56. Robert A. Gross, "Self-Deceived Society," *Newsweek*, 18 May 1970, pp. 114–116; author unknown, "America: Going, Going, Gone?" *Time*, 1 June 1970, pp. 86–87.

57. Edgar Z. Friedenberg, "National Self-Abuse," *New York Review of Books*, 4 June 1970, pp. 36–38.

58. Kenneth Keniston, "Three Books That Suggest a Radical Critique of Modern America," *New York Times Book Review*, 6 September 1970, pp. 3, 20; George Adelman, untitled review of Slater, *Library Journal* 95 (March 1970): 881–882; unknown author, untitled review of Slater, *Choice* 7 (November 1970): 1268.

59. Gordon Halpern, untitled review of Slater, *Annals of the American Academy* 392 (Novermber 1970): 227–228.

60. Charles Winick, *American Sociological Review* 36 (1971): 766; Bennett M. Berger, *American Journal of Sociology* 77 (1971): 143–146; and Irwin Deutscher, *Social Forces* 49 (1971) :642–643. All three reviews in *American Sociological Review, American Journal of Sociology*, and *Social Forces* have no titles.

61. Vance Packard, *A Nation of Strangers* (New York: David McKay, 1971), ix. One might argue a unique "period effect." A range of like-minded works appeared in those years of "uprising." The most notable, perhaps, are Theodore Roszak, *The Making of a Counter-Culture* (Garden City, N.Y.: Doubleday, 1969); Reich, *Greening of America*, 1970; Slater, *Pursuit of Loneliness*, 1970; and Alvin Toffler, *Future Shock* (New York: Random House, 1970). For discussion and criticism, see Hamilton and Wright, *State of the Masses*, Chs. 1 and 2. A quarter of a century later, Reich was still arguing the same themes and using the same "broad brush" methods. See his *Opposing the System* (New York: Crown, 1995).

62. See note 40. Packard, *A Nation of Strangers*, has only one reference to the countering sociological evidence, on p. 188. A "few sociologists," he reports, "led by Eugene Litwak of the University of Michigan, argued that [the breakup of primary ties following on mobility] was not necessarily so." A half page is given to a summary of Litwak's conclusions. Packard says nothing about the merit of those findings, only that "this position is viewed skeptically by some." Litwak's conclusions, it should be noted, were based on large systematic surveys (as opposed to a position that was merely "argued"). Packard shows no comparable hesitancy with respect to assertions supporting his reading of things. Philip Slater, for example, "in observing that our society is already one of the most mobile ever known, predicts: 'We will become increasingly a nation of itinerants, moving continually on an irregular . . . circuit of jobs'" (p. 13). See Eugene Litwak, "Geographic Mobility and Extended Family Cohesion," *American Sociological Review* 25 (1960): 285–394; Eugene Litwak and Ivan Szelenyi, "Primary Group Structures and Their Functions: Kin, Neighbors, and Friends," *American Sociological Review* 34 (1969): 465–481; Philip Fellin and Eugene Litwak, "Neighborhood Cohesion Under Conditions of Mobility," *American Sociological Review* 28 (1963): 364–376.

63. Harriet Van Horne, "The Moving Van Land," *Saturday Review*, 55 (1972): 71–72; Granville Hicks, "Rootless Americans," *New York Times Book Review*, 10 September 1972, pp. 3, 50; unknown author, untitled review of Packard, *New York Times Book Review*, 10 February 1974, p. 26; Harry Frumerman, untitled review of Packard, *Library Journal* 97 (August 1972): 2629–2630; Peter Michelson, "Where Did the Neighborhood Go?" *New Republic*, 7 October 1972, pp. 25–27.

64. Herbert J. Gans, "Stimulus/Response: Vance Packard Misperceives the Way Most American Movers Live," *Psychology Today* 4 (September 1972): 20–27. Some additional comments appear in the December 1972 issue, pp. 5–6; *Social Forces* 51 (1973): 522. For the Hawley, Fischer, and Berry symposium, see *American Journal of Sociology* 79 (1973): 165–175. Various authors, "Input," *Psychology Today* 6 (December 1972): 5–6. Two reviews in *Social Forces* and *American Journal of Sociology* have no titles.

65. Charles Y. Glock, "The Sense of Well-Being: Developing Measures," *Science*, 1 October 1976, pp. 52–54; Andrew A. Beveridge, *Political Science Quarterly* 91 (1976): 529–531; Wesley D. Clark, *Annals of the American Academy* 428 (November 1976): 170; Richard M. Cohn, *Contemporary Sociology* 6 (1977): 489–490; and Robert Boguslaw, *Social Forces* 56 (1977): 283–285. The rest of the four reviews in *Political Science Quarterly, Annals of American Academy, Contemporary Sociology*, and *Social Forces* have no titles.

66. The *American Journal of Sociology* did not review either *The Quality of American Life* or *Sense of Well-Being in America*. Edgar Z. Friedenberg reviewed the latter in the *American Journal of Orthopsychiatry* 52 (1982): 559. Edgar Z. Friedenberg's review of Campbell in *American Journal of Orthopsychiatry* has no title. Except for the *New York Times*, his was the most negative review: "I think it unlikely that a sense of well-being can be assessed by a simple questionnaire procedure." Charles Kaiser, untitled review of Campbell, *New York Times Book Review*, 10 October 1980, pp. 16, 18.

67. The 1997 *Citation Index* reports two citations of Packard and three of Slater. There were some seventy citations of *The Quality of American Life*, and seventeen of *The Sense of Well Being in America*. As before, few of these appeared in sociology journals. There were, for example, none in the *American Sociological Review* and none in the *American Journal of Sociology*.

68. Wuthnow, *Sharing the Journey*, 12, 16, 33–34.

69. Ibid., 424, note 9. The major study is Paul Leinberger and Bruce Tucker, *The New Individualists: The Generation After the Organization Man* (New York: HarperCollins, 1991).

70. For the neighborhood satisfaction data, see U.S. Bureau of the Census, *Annual Housing Survey of the United States*, Current Housing Reports, series H-150, part B, nos. 77, 79, 81, 83; *American Housing Survey for the United States*, Current Housing Reports, series H-150, nos. 85, 87, 89, 91, 93, 95.

71. See Hamilton and Wright, *State of the Masses*, 250. See also Chapter 3 in this book for more evidence on this point.

72. Ben Stein, *The View from Sunset Boulevard* (New York: Basic Books, 1979). See also Allen H. Barton, "Consensus and Conflict Among American Leaders," *Public Opinion Quarterly* 38 (1974–1975): 507–530; and Lichter, Rothman, and Lidoter, *Media Elite*.

CHAPTER 2

Pluralism

A BRIEF HISTORY OF THE CONCEPT

Pluralism is a theory about the organization of political power.[1] The central argument is that "power" is somehow divided.[2] The pluralist theory stands in opposition to arguments of unitary power, that all power rests with a monarch (literally, a single ruler), or with a dictator, or a class, such as the bourgeoisie, or with a small cohesive elite, as in the mass society theory. The pluralist argument, basically, holds that power cannot be completely centralized in large complex societies. To some degree, decision making must be dispersed. Quite apart from the empirical question, that of possibility, there is also a normative argument; namely, that it is advantageous for all concerned that power be dispersed.

The key question is this: How is that power divided? One may think of the options as involving points along a continuum. We have, first of all, the single center of power, as for example in the case of the so-called absolute monarch. Charles V, the powerful Holy Roman Emperor, ruled over a large sprawling empire that included Spain, much of the newly discovered Americas, the United Netherlands, Austria, and the Kingdom of the Two Sicilies. But his power, his ability to know what was happening, let alone direct and control operations, was severely limited.[3]

The "means of administration" improved considerably by the twentieth century. Adolf Hitler and his police agencies, the Gestapo, the SS, and the Security Service, had much greater oversight and control than was possible in any previous century. Even there, some dispersion, some delegation of power, was to be seen. The twelve-year Reich has been described, appropriately, as a feudal system, with the various ministries and police agencies ruled by the "barons," each struggling for influence and rewards.[4]

The dispersion of powers to ruthless competing barons within a murderous regime is one extreme. The dispersion of powers in a democratic system, with an established rule of law, an independent judiciary, and rights of speech, assembly, and appeal for most people, is a much-preferred alternative. The central pluralist assumption, the fact that may be seen in any complex society, is *some* dispersion of power. That fact ought to be the beginning point for any serious empirical analysis.

In 1748 Montesquieu reported on the division of powers within the English government, within the monarchical regime. There was a separation of legislative and executive functions and the emergence of an independent judiciary. Some economic historians have pointed to a greater degree of pluralism within the Dutch and English governments in the eighteenth century. Businessmen had more access to or presence in those governments, and that in turn meant those nations developed superior economic policies with considerable payoff. The obvious points of comparison are Spain and Portugal. Although beginning with considerable advantages, the economic policies of those "absolute" monarchies proved disastrous.[5]

Elected legislative bodies appeared and developed throughout the nineteenth century. Some powers, particularly those of the purse, of taxation, were reserved for those legislatures. Suffrage initially was very restricted, in Europe typically to some well-off 5 or 10 percent of the adult male population. That meant some power to aristocrats, businessmen, lawyers, and also to some intellectuals. It meant, in short, a modest if restricted dispersion of power among privileged groups.

Later in the century one found middling levels of participation, with suffrage again limited by income and property requirements and also, in all cases, restricted only to males. The extensions came gradually in Britain in a series of steps over a century. They came suddenly in France and Germany. The outcomes, understandably, were quite different. The former might be described as generally successful, the latter as problematic.

The most important extensions of suffrage came in the twentieth century, basically in the aftermath of the two world wars. These extensions, ultimately, brought "universal" suffrage. No suffrage arrangement, it should be noted, is universal. Noncitizens are excluded in most settings; incarcerated felons and institutionalized mental patients are also excluded. Most countries have some residency requirements. Suffrage is restricted to adults, but there is no constancy about that definition. In Germany the state of Lower Saxony extended the suffrage to sixteen-year-olds in 1996.[6]

The extension of suffrage, of the right to participate in the selection of legislators and, in presidential systems, to choose the chief executive, is obviously an important dispersion of power. Securing the right to vote was no easy achievement. It required major social struggles, which, in most cases, extended over more than a century. From an early point, however, some commentators, right, left, and center, questioned the significance of the achievement. Conservative mass society opponents predicted the appearance of demagogues and gullible masses. At a later point, Marxists denounced elections as a sham, as an exercise organized by the bourgeoisie and allowing no serious influence for the masses. Some concerned liberals argued that a single vote, one from among millions, was close to no power at all. Early on, Edmund Burke, the eminent conservative thinker, argued the normative case. Periodic voting gave individuals some power of review. But between elections, incumbents should be free to make their own choices. Because they were more informed, Burke argued, they should not be bound by the judgments of the electorate.[7]

Some commentators recognized and addressed the problem. An effective democracy required opportunities for public influence between elections. The vote itself was a very limited communication, indicating only a preference for one candidate or party over another. Opportunities for more detailed or specific expressions of public sentiment were needed. Some commentators saw a solution in a new institutional development: voluntary associations. Those agencies would serve the important purpose of mediating between the masses and the government. One of the first analyses arguing this position was that of Alexis de Tocqueville, in his *De la Démocratie en Amerique* (1835). The work is one long brilliant analysis of the world's first modern democracy. His conclusions, put forward as general propositions, would have implications for all the other democracies that, he argued, would surely follow. His work made continuous comparisons with the experience elsewhere, but most insistently with that of aristocratic France.[8]

Out of his wealth of insights, later commentators have focused on his discussion of voluntary associations in a chapter entitled, "Of the Use Which the Americans Make of Public Associations in Civil Life." His most cited statement reads as follows:

Americans of all ages, all conditions, and all dispositions constantly form associations. . . . They have not only commercial and manufacturing companies, in which all take part, but associations of a thousand other kinds, religious, moral, serious, futile, general or restricted, enormous or diminutive. The Americans make associations to give entertainments, to found seminaries, to build inns, to construct churches, to diffuse books, to send missionaries to the antipodes; in this manner they found hospitals, prisons, and schools. If it is proposed to inculcate some truth or to foster some feeling by the encouragement of a great example, they form a society. Wherever at the head of some new undertaking you see the government in France, or a man of rank in England, in the United States you will be sure to find an association.[9]

Tocqueville assigned considerable importance to those associations: "Nothing, in my opinion, is more deserving of our attention than the intellectual and moral associations of America." The chapter ends with this statement: "If men are to remain civilized or to become so, the art of associating together must grow and improve in the same ratio in which the equality of conditions is increased." These associations were essentially small communities, each with its own government, each serving as a training ground for leadership. The United States (or any subsequent democracy) would, in these settings, be training a large "staff" of leaders. As a consequence, he argued, democracies would have exceptional capacities; they would be capable of achievements not possible in other regimes. The efforts of the French official or the English man of rank enervate the society; their efforts stand in the way of the wider mobilization of leaders.[10]

Tocqueville moved then to a closely related question: How do people who share an interest find one another? In a society of some tens of millions, perhaps a thousand are numismatists. How would they come together to form an association? Tocqueville's next chapter, "Of the Relation Between Public Associations and the Newspapers," addresses that question:

In democratic countries it frequently happens that a great number of men who wish or who want to combine cannot accomplish it because they are very insignificant and lost amid the crowd, they cannot see and do not know where to find one another. A newspaper then takes up the notion or the feeling that had occurred simultaneously, but singly, to each of them . . . and these wandering minds . . . at length meet and unite.

The relationship, he argues, is reciprocal: "There is a necessary connection between public associations and newspapers: newspapers make associations, and associations make newspapers."[11]

Most discussions of democratic pluralism still focus, in one way or another, on voluntary associations. Government policy, it is argued, is the product of "inputs" by the voluntary associations (also called pressure groups). To understand the policy choices, one must examine the demands made by associations A, B, C, D, and so on. One correlate, it is argued, is that the leaders of the contending organizations will learn the "arts of compromise." They have to negotiate compromise solutions. Group A would gain something, but its leaders would have to make concessions so that Group B would gain some benefit. Such compromise was part of the normal give and take of democratic politics. Large numbers of leaders skilled in the arts of compromise would enhance the possibilities for peaceful social change. Tocqueville wrote that political associations may "be considered as large free schools, where all the members of the community go to learn the general theory of association."[12]

The pluralist theory flourished in the social sciences and in the public media in the 1950s and early 1960s.[13] There was a triumphalist note in much of that discussion, the pluralist "fact" being presented as a definitive answer to the Marxism championed in the Second World by the Soviet Union, the East European satellite states, and China. The linkage to the Cold War was unmistakable. In another related theme, pluralism was joined to a "secular" (that is, non-Marxist) revisionism. The coming of the middle-class majority and appearance of the affluent and politically moderate workers meant the definitive rejection of the key Marxist prediction. Not too surprisingly, with the revival of the left later in the 1960s, pluralism came to be a prime theoretical target.

In some pluralist discussions of the 1950s, "the state" was treated as an independent arbitrator, as a neutral referee adjudicating the conflicting claims "from below." That reading ultimately brought an appropriate course correction, one which "brought the state back in." The initial digression was a mistake, one quickly admitted by most contributors to the discussion. Some others claimed they had never left the state out of their analyses. One could easily grant the critic's point: Yes, of course, the state was an active partner in the working out of policy compromises. It too was involved in the give and take. Its members, ministers, department heads, and civil servants were also practicing the arts of compromise.

The course correction also involved a mistake: The agency discussed was "the state," as opposed to political regimes, governments, ministries, or persons. The problem is one of reification: The state does not act. It was Bismarck who decided, or Puttkammer, the minster of the interior, who initiated, who favored a given solution to the problem. Governments or individuals were not and are not neutral decision makers. They would, of course, favor organizations and initiatives consonant with their policies. A right liberal government would ordinarily favor employers' associations, say by supporting "right to work" laws. A left liberal government would ordinarily favor unions, say by guarantees of collective bargaining. Both would be operating within the framework of a given state.[14]

It is useful to see the pluralist argument in relationship to both the liberal and mass society theories. Liberalism, traditionally, focused on individuals, on their (presumed) isolated actions, on their individual calculations of advantage, and so forth. And, as such, it was easy and appropriate to conclude that individuals are "powerless," most especially in a large and complex society. Those individuals would only gain power if they joined together, if they organized as a pressure group for collective representation of their interests. Central to Tocqueville's argument and to the later pluralist variants is the assumption of aggregation, that people sharing interests would find one another and would create a more powerful instrument; namely, an association. The central innovation in this viewpoint is the focus on those intermediate organizations, those standing between the masses and the government. Those organizations are seen as small communities, as settings allowing closer contact, direction, and control by the members.

Pluralism, as delineated here, depends on prior liberal victories. The basic freedoms are necessary prerequisites to the development of associations. Without those freedoms, there would be no freedom for discussion, no aggregation of interests, and no associations. This conclusion is so commonsensical that it does not even appear in most discussions of pluralism. Freedom of speech, press, and assembly were anchored in the U.S. Constitution.[15] This allowed the early formation of associations, the development that Tocqueville and many others found so remarkable. The United States also had a significant early extension of suffrage. Even before the Age of Jackson, almost all adult white males had the right to vote. And, accordingly, one saw the emergence of the first mass parties of the modern era.[16]

Many accounts of "American exceptionalism" place emphasis on the "absence of a feudal past." Those formulations point to what was not present, neglecting the positive side of the lesson; namely, what was there. As a new nation, one reaching out to settle thinly populated areas, very little de facto central government presence was possible. The limited administrative outreach, from Washington or from state capitals, meant that government, what there was of it, was necessarily local and broadly participatory.

In many areas the first task faced was to "make the land safe for settlement." That meant defeating and removing the previous occupants. A key agency in this effort was the militia, an organization that enlisted all ablebodied adult white males. Although not initially a voluntary association, after the victory it typically developed free and easy clublike ways and, more important, provided the basis for the first political party of the territory. Many of the victorious officers turned to political careers in addition to managing their newly acquired real estate holdings. The votes and efforts of their former comrades-in-arms helped them to gain state and national offices. Andrew Jackson provides an obvious example of this kind of career. William Henry Harrison led regular army forces, but his later political efforts were also aided by militia units. The election of officers was customary in the militia. Abraham Lincoln was elected by his company during the Black Hawk War, that being his first electoral victory. The military affairs of the continental European nations in this period, in striking contrast, were conducted by professional armies with no noticeable participatory characteristics. In contrast to the militias, those armies trained men in obedience and, presumably, generated attitudes of deference.[17]

The absence of a feudal past means no centuries-old arrangement of land-holding linked to an aristocratic class structure. The land-holding arrangements in the United States were all new or of recent vintage. Those holdings, in part at least, were linked to the previous military experience. The soldiers, in the Revolution and in the War of 1812, were paid with land, in both cases allocated by rank.[18] All social arrangements in this new society necessarily differed from those of Europe's old regimes. In the feudal arrangement the lord of the manor would ordinarily oversee the dispensation of justice. On the American frontier, "justice" was a hastily extemporized collective affair.[19]

The basic freedoms contained in the American Constitution appeared in France in three separate episodes, in the First, Second, and Third Republics. The First Republic collapsed into Jacobin totalitarianism, then into Napoleonic authoritarianism. The Second Republic, in 1848, again brought an instant declaration of rights. The explosion of voluntary associations and newspapers allows a very precise before-and-after comparison. The experiment, on the whole, was not very successful. Louis Napoleon Bonaparte's *coup d'état* in December 1851 brought another authoritarian regime. Not until the 1880s, in the Third Republic, were most basic rights secured for more than a brief period. Serious restrictions on freedom of association continued until 1901.[20]

The difference between an open society, as in the United States, and the closed practice of the European continent may be seen in another comparison. The old regime, obviously, did not allow freedom of association. If some concerned—or enlightened—citizens wished to get together, if they sought to aggregate their individual interests, that effort had to be secret or underground. In many contexts the secret organization was the Free Masons.[21] The Marxian practice also depended on the liberal achievement. It assumes a general aggregation of working-class interests. The formation of trade unions and the workers' party were greatly facilitated by free speech, press, and assembly. Without those freedoms, the revolutionary effort would have had to be underground, like that of the Masons. The "wheel of history," in that case, would presumably have moved at a much slower pace.

THE ASSUMPTIONS OF PLURALISM

The following are seven basic assumptions of pluralism:

1. A democratic society will be characterized by a widespread, general involvement in voluntary associations. The argument, essentially, is that most adult citizens are represented in associations. This formulation, it will be noted, alters Tocqueville's original, which, literally, placed the stress on Americans. The key underlying question is one of the author's intentions. Was Tocqueville's argument intended to be cultural or systemic? Was he arguing some unique propensity of Americans? Or was he arguing a characteristic expected of all democracies? His introduction indicates the latter. There, on the opening page, he points up his general aims: "The democracy which governs the American communities appears to be rapidly rising into power in Europe. . . . It is evident to all alike that a great democratic revolution is going on among us." Later, he describes his intention: "My wish has been to find [in America] instruction by which we may ourselves profit."[22]

2. Reflecting the diversity of individual interests, people will join several associations. The expectation, in short, is that multiple memberships will be typical. Membership in a single organization could lead to intolerance, with like-minded individuals showing exceptional dedication to some exclusive purpose. Involvement in several associations broadens one and forces recognition of other competing views.

3. The growth of affluence and extension of education will bring an increase in associational memberships.

4. Newspapers will facilitate the aggregation of interests. In a later period one must expand the repertory of means to include magazines, radio, television, and mail solicitation.

5. The voluntary associations are internally democratic. They will, accordingly, accurately express member interests.

6. People are viewed as rational individuals making unconstrained choices. As in liberalism, a high degree of rationality is assumed. Knowing their own self-inter-

est, people will choose an association (or will form an association) to aid in achieving that interest.

7. Voluntary associations train leaders in the arts of compromise. Put differently, participation in decision making generates moderate attitudes.

ASSESSMENT

The first of these propositions argues widespread involvement in voluntary associations. It is the argument of "America as a nation of joiners." Tocqueville's original statement is unequivocal: Americans of all ages and all conditions joined associations. Some ninety years later, Charles and Mary Beard seconded that conclusion, adding another claim about the frequency. They state that the "tendency of Americans to unite with their fellows for varied purposes—a tendency noted a hundred years earlier by de Tocqueville— now became a general mania. . . . It was a rare American who was not a member of four or five societies."[23]

A decade or so after the Beards's confident judgment the first public opinion polls addressing this question appeared. Those early studies, based on local rather than national surveys, found substantial minorities having no voluntary association membership. The largest segment of joiners had only a single affiliation.[24] In 1953 the first national survey, by the National Opinion Research Center, asked about families having members in voluntary associations. It found 52 percent reporting positively. A 1954 Gallup study found 55 percent of adult respondents reporting one or more memberships. A 1955 NORC study found 46 percent in at least one association. The 1950s studies, in short, found approximately half of the adult population to be members. In 1960 a NORC study found 57 percent responding positively. It was easy to assume a favorable trend. With growing affluence and increasing education, more joining seemed the obvious consequence. A major study done in 1989 found 79 percent reporting organizational involvement. In the 1990s the General Social Surveys found two-thirds of adult Americans reporting one or more memberships (see Table 2.1). Another study from the early 1990s, the World Values Survey, reported 82 percent belonging to at least one group.[25]

Several methodological problems must be addressed at this point. One could count all memberships equally, including those in churches. But church memberships have ordinarily been treated differently. Following a consensus established now for a half-century, these involvements have been excluded from most pluralist analyses. Church memberships, it was argued, were not entirely voluntary, with children having being brought in as infants and the connection later sustained through strong parental influences. Membership in church-affiliated organizations, however, have usually been counted as voluntary involvements. Memberships in those associations, as will be seen, are by far the most frequent affiliation of adult Americans. But that finding is not accurate, a significant bias having been established. Tom W. Smith reports an analysis of the 1987 GSS that found "54% of those saying they belonged to church-affiliated groups belonged only to the church/congregation as a whole." Many respondents, obviously, did not make the distinction intended by the researchers. One could exclude the church-affiliated groups entirely, as Smith did in one series. That reduced the overall level of affiliation by approximately 10 percentage points (in the 1974 GSS, the unadjusted figure was 74.7 percent; with church-affiliated groups excluded, it was 63.9 percent). In the tables contained here, those groups have been retained. One should, as a rule-of-thumb procedure, discount the church-affiliated percentages by half.[26]

Union membership is a condition of employment in closed or union shops. Unions differ from most associations in that many countries have given them special legislative sanction. To avoid the "free rider" problem, the law obliges employees to join an established union. Thus, for many, this association might not be voluntary. Some analyses, accordingly, give two figures: membership totals with and without the union connection.[27]

Following a second longstanding consensus, pluralists have focused on instrumental organizations, those that somehow attempt to influence government policies. Many organizations, it is argued, are expressive in character, having no significant political goals. That would be the case with leisure-time groups of all kinds: for coin collectors, stamp collectors, bird watchers, garden clubs, Bible discussion groups, sport groups, and choral societies. Excluding those would leave only a minority as members of instrumental associations. As a limited test, the church-related and sports associations were excluded from the count of memberships in the merged GSS data from the early 1990s. The result was that 58 percent had no affiliation with the remaining organizations and 24 percent had only a single membership. Only 7 percent had three or more memberships, and some of those would have been in other expressive organizations. Almond and Verba put an appropriate question, asking respondents if any organization they belonged to was "in any way concerned with governmental, political, or public affairs; for instance, do they take stands on or discuss public issues or try to influence governmental decisions?" Only about one in four of all respondents responded positively to that question. Only a minority of the members, 42 percent of the total, saw at least one of their organizations as political.[28]

This discussion, it will be noted, is categorical in form, as if associations were either instrumental or expressive. But mixed cases are easily possible. Political organizations on occasion retreat from their instrumental goals to become social clubs, basically a group of old-timers getting together for drinks and conversation. And the adoration society, usually devoted to prayer, might make political interventions; for example, with regard to abortion. Segregated institutions lost their legal status through the efforts of an instrumental voluntary association, the National Association for the Advancement of Colored People. The civil rights movement, the massive effort to undo de facto segregation, was largely church based, led by members of the clergy. One of the most important institutional changes of the modern era, in short, was driven by expressive associations.

Serious questions have been raised about these longstanding conventions: the exclusion of religious bodies, the denominations, and the instrumental–expressive distinction. The questions, basically, are concerned with utility. One possibility is that the ready acceptance of those conventions has been disadvantageous. It may have hindered our understanding of important social processes. These issues will be discussed at greater length later in this chapter.

The pluralist theory assumes direct involvement. But some associations provide little or no room for participation. In some instances members pay dues and in exchange receive some services, but the transaction occurs without any meetings, discussion, consultation, or elections. In some cases the opportunities for involvement are necessarily rather limited. The sheer size of the organization and the time constraints (many members on the road working irregular hours) limit involvement for the 1.6 million members of the International Brotherhood of Teamsters union, once the nation's largest labor organization. The American Association of Retired Persons, the world's largest secular organization, twenty times the size of the Teamsters, had a membership of 32 million in 1999.

Question wordings and placement pose another difficulty. A single question or a pair (number and kinds) will ordinarily yield lower proportions of members. This was the case with the Wright and Hyman study, in which the question also contained a significant restriction: "Do you happen to belong to any groups or organizations in the community here?" It appeared as the second-to-last item on a questionnaire containing 136 questions. A detailed set of questions, the most often-used procedure, will ordinarily stimulate memory and enlarge the number of memberships reported.

Researchers and commentators must recognize those problems and do what they can to solve them, but precise or definitive solutions seem unlikely. Should union memberships be counted or not? Plausible arguments may be made for both options. And how should one handle the instrumental–expressive distinction with all of its complications? It follows that the precise number of memberships, or the exact percentage, whether 35, 52, or 60 percent, cannot be easily ascertained. One should not abandon the search for precision. One might, however, reconsider the importance of that specific focus.

The NORC General Social Surveys have adopted the following procedure. The interviewer states, "Now we would like to know something about the groups or organizations to which individuals belong. Here is a list of various organizations. Could you tell me whether or not you are a member of each type?" Respondents are presented with a card listing sixteen types of association. The options listed are fraternal groups; service clubs; veterans' groups; political clubs; labor unions; sports groups; youth groups; school service groups; hobby or garden clubs; school fraternities or sororities; nationality groups; farm organizations; literary, art, discussion, or study groups; professional or academic societies; church-affiliated groups; and, a residual category, any other groups. The interviewer is instructed to read each item and to "code one for each." The most recent studies show approximately three in ten with no membership, one-quarter with a single involvement, one-sixth with two, and roughly one-quarter with three or more (see Table 2.1). The "code one" restriction, clearly, yields some undercount.[29]

The Tocqueville–Beard emphasis—all Americans as joiners—is clearly mistaken in both fact and importance. For more than a half-century now the available evidence has shown that many Americans, a significant minority, are not joiners.[30] These studies show a minority, just under half, with multiple memberships.

Table 2.1
Voluntary Association Memberships: 1974–1994 (NORC-GSS: Four Merges)

	1974[a]	1975-1979	1980-1984	1985-1989	1990-1994
Number of Memberships					
None	25 %	28 %	31 %	30 %	31 %
One	26	28	25	25	24
Two	19	17	18	18	17
Three or more	30	27	26	27	28
Average	1.94	1.78	1.74	1.77	1.80
N =	(1,481)	(4,547)	(4,520)	(4,951)	(3,474)
Type of Association[b]					
Church-affiliated	42 %	38 %	34 %	35 %	34 %
Sports groups	18	19	20	20	19
Professional or academic	13	13	15	16	17
School service groups	18	14	12	13	15
Hobby or garden clubs	10	9	9	9	11
Labor unions	17	16	14	12	11
Service clubs	9	9	10	10	10
Literary, art, discussion or study groups	9	9	9	9	10

[a]Only one study from the early 1970s, that of 1974, contained the membership questions.
[b]Incomplete listing. This is only those ≥ 10 percent in the 1990s.

Given the basic finding in regard to frequency, the key question becomes that of the pattern. Who are the joiners? What are their characteristics? The basic answer is that membership varies directly with class level. The fre-

Table 2.2
Socioeconomic Status and Multiple Memberships: Males and Females (NORC-GSS: 1990–1994 Merge)

	Males	(N)	Females	(N)
Occupation (Full-Time Employed)	Percent with 3 or More Memberships			
Managerial, Executive	40 %	(159)	41 %	(97)
Professional	54	(139)	51	(156)
Technical	32	(37)	28	(36)
Sales	42	(98)	26	(82)
Clerical	40	(63)	20	(235)
Crafts	19	(168)	27	(26)
Laborers	17	(180)	13	(82)
Service	23	(60)	17	(93)
Education				
Sixteen years or more	51	(400)	50	(417)
Thirteen to fifteen years	31	(367)	33	(491)
Twelve years	25	(396)	16	(663)
Eleven years or less	13	(312)	12	(419)
Family Income				
$40,000 or more	46	(513)	39	(515)
$25,000 to $39,999	27	(319)	28	(367)
$12,500 to $24,999	25	(318)	23	(432)
Less than $12,500	14	(210)	14	(453)

quency of joining increases substantially with occupational level, education, and income (Table 2.2). That finding appeared with the first of the empirical studies and has been sustained, without exception, in all subsequent investigations. One must consider the implications of that finding.

Recognition of the two basic findings, that not all join and that joining is strongly class related, led to a revision of the pluralist theory in its 1950s efflorescence. Some writers argued an extended-representation claim, that the trade unions, for example, represented members and nonmembers alike. While always possible, the claim should be recognized as an untested hypothesis. A union might include such representation as part of its task, but it might not. It might see its task narrowly, as the defense of a job monopoly. Another option argues the potential that the nonmembers could form (or join) an organization if a serious need arose. Freedom of association guaranteed the possibility; the growing real incomes made possible an opportunity not previously available. One saving argument was that not joining meant satisfaction. It meant that no serious problem existed. That too, it should be noted, was inference, or, another expression for the same thing, untested hypothesis.

Still another reading was provided by a leading political scientist, Robert Dahl, who offered a series of propositions. He wrote, "Many different kinds of resources for influencing officials are available to different citizens," and, realistically, added that "With few exceptions, these resources are unequally distributed." Another proposition stated that "individuals best off in their access to one kind of resource are often badly off with respect to many other resources." Rich persons and/or those holding high positions in corporate hierarchies have many resources at their disposal, but they are very poorly supplied with respect to one key resource: votes. But the "often badly off" qualifier seems unlikely. Apart from votes, well-off populations are more amply endowed with all other resources. Dahl's final proposition holds, "Virtually no one, and certainly no group of more than a few individuals, is entirely lacking in some influence resources."[31]

This reading shifts from an exclusive focus on voluntary associations, supplementing the initial argument with a consideration of other instrumentalities that might give some power to the general populace. One can easily agree that other sources of influence need consideration. But the no-one-entirely-lacking proviso seems "overextended," an attempt to save the broad-based pluralistic imagery. Homeless men sleeping under the bridges and along the river, to be sure, are not entirely lacking sources of influences. But the combined weight of their influence vis-à-vis almost any other group of comparable size must be very limited.

The second assumption, that of multiple memberships, holds that people will join several associations. It is obvious, given what has been reported thus far, that multiple memberships continue to be a minority experience. The General Social Surveys of 1990–1994 found one-sixth of the adult population reporting two memberships and only 28 percent with three or more association involvements (Table 2.1). That, of course, includes both instrumental and expressive associations. The most frequent memberships at that point were probably expressive in character, these being church-affiliated groups, 34 percent (considerably overreported, it will be remembered), and sports groups, 19 percent.

The point may be put more forcefully. The Beards's original statement is obviously in need of correction. It should read, "It is a rare American who is a member of four or five societies." In the 1990s, 8 percent reported four memberships, 4 percent reported five, and 5 percent indicated six or more. The 17 percent with four or more memberships possess 49 percent of all memberships. If organizational involvements were the decisive instrumentality, that would mean a significant concentration of power in the hands of that one-sixth of the adult population.[32]

Many of the 1950s formulations made generous assumptions about the ease of joining or, alternatively, about the ease of organizing for the representation of interests. But such formulations lack realism, neglecting a rather basic consideration: Memberships cost money. The more memberships, the greater the cost. And the greater the involvement, the greater the cost. Those "facts of life," those "obvious" realities, are regularly overlooked.[33]

The third assumption focuses on the anticipated trend, the expectation of increased joining. For the period from 1970 to the 1990s, we have had three different assertions or findings. Baumgartner and Walker argue, largely by logic and inference, that the upward trend has continued; that is to say, more and more joining through to the 1990s. A countering statement, by Robert Putnam, based on some evidence, reports that joining has declined, that there has been a loss of involvement. A third position, put forth by Tom W. Smith and based on the GSS series, argues no significant change. Everett C. Ladd has presented a large collection of evidence challenging Putnam's claim.[34]

The GSS series shows a slight decline in association memberships in the 1970s. The percentages reporting three or more memberships fell from 30 in 1974 to 27 in the late 1970s, but thereafter little change is evident. The best conclusion to be drawn from this evidence is stability over the last two decades. These data continue Smith's series and, not too surprisingly, sustain his earlier conclusion; that is, no significant change (see Table 2.1). These results clearly go against the earlier expectation of steadily increasing affiliation, and the recent argument, the claimed "loss of social capital."[35]

An examination of the types of organizations joined provides some further lessons (also in Table 2.1). The most frequent kind of membership reported, at all points and by a considerable margin, is church-related groups. In most cases, presumably, these are expressive associations. The second most frequent kind, sports associations, is also expressive. In the 1990s two varieties of instrumental associations follow in the ranking: professional or academic and school service groups. The two principal "losers" over the two-decade period are the church-related groups and the labor unions. The church-related memberships declined early on, in the 1974–1984 period. The fall in union membership continued over the entire period. Membership in unions, the organizations that figured so prominently in the 1950s discussions of pluralism, has fallen to the level of the hobby or garden clubs. Membership in fraternal and veterans' organizations declined (not shown in Table 2.1). Membership in political clubs (also not shown in Table 2.1) was constant at 4 percent throughout the period.

Some other factors affecting association involvement deserve attention. Membership, on the whole, is age related, with such ties increasing to mid-life, peaking at forty to forty-nine, then tapering off with more advanced age. The basic pattern, clearly, is an inverted U.[36] Other things equal, that means the overall level of joining should change depending on the size of the cohorts in the mid-life years. The overall rate should move upward when the baby-boomers, those born between 1946 and 1964, reach middle age. The 1946 cohort, the "leading edge" of the boomers, would have been forty years old in 1986. The overall rate should accordingly have increased in the following years. A very modest increase is indicated in Table 2.1, but one would have expected much more in the 1990s.

Not shown in Table 2.1 is a fragment of relevant evidence: In the early 1990s, the younger and middle-aged categories showed less involvement than the equivalent cohorts in the late 1970s. The decline was greatest among those in their forties, with the percentage having three or more memberships falling from 37 to 26. Older respondents, those sixty and above, actually increased their involvement by a few percentage points in the same period. The decline of memberships in the younger cohorts might stem from the increased involvement of women in the labor force.

Age affects the specific kinds of membership in several ways, reflecting diverse age-related life events. Memberships in sports organizations vary inversely with age (Table 2.3). Memberships in church groups vary positively with age. Some of the positive relationships with age appear to be due to period effects. An obvious correlate of a declining farm sector is a decline of memberships in farm organizations, especially among the younger cohorts. Fraternal organizations have lost popularity among the young. Given the history of military involvements since the early 1940s, it is not surprising that membership in veterans organizations has a strong positive relationship with age. Memberships in school organizations have an inverted-U pattern, with the frequencies greatest for those in their thirties and forties. Memberships in professional organizations and labor unions, also not surprisingly, have an inverted-U pattern. Some organizations, finally, show no clear relationship with age. This fourth pattern is found with respect to hobby, literary, and nationality groups.

One might anticipate a disaffiliation in the older age groups. But the GSS results show a differentiated result. Some linkages attenuate, this being clear with professional organizations, labor unions, school service groups, and, most obviously, sports organizations. Some linkages increased with age, this

Table 2.3
Age and Memberships (NORC-GSS: 1990–1994 Merge)

	Age					
	18-29	30-39	40-49	50-59	60-69	70 or more
Number of Memberships						
None	36 %	32 %	26 %	31 %	26 %	30 %
One	23	22	20	26	30	28
Two	16	16	20	17	18	18
Three or More	24	30	34	27	27	24
Average	1.59	1.80	2.02	1.84	1.84	1.68
N =	(657)	(897)	(654)	(404)	(394)	(463)
Type of Association						
Church-affiliated	25 %	31 %	34 %	39 %	42 %	42 %
Sports groups	26	23	23	15	11	8
Professional or academic	16	20	23	19	12	8
School service groups	14	21	22	11	7	3
Hobby or garden clubs	12	10	12	9	15	12
Labor unions	6	13	13	12	12	8
Service clubs	8	9	12	13	9	12
Literary, art, discussion or study groups	10	8	11	11	10	11

being the case with church-affiliated groups. In others, the previous levels were maintained as seen with hobby or garden clubs, general service organizations, and the literary and art organizations. Most of these are obviously expressive agencies. Membership in these associations increased among the elderly between the late 1970s and early 1990s (not shown in Table 2.3). Membership in political organizations, 4 percent overall, also varied positively with age, rising to 7 percent among those seventy and over.

The instances where membership increases with age probably reflect both longer life expectancies and correlated improvements in the health and well-being of the elderly. Early retirement became more frequent in this period, bringing considerable increases in leisure time. One possible use of that time, obviously, was organizational activity, an opportunity not available for most people in any previous generation. Most persons in the elderly cohorts, moreover, report satisfaction with their financial circumstances, suggesting that many of them are able to pay the costs of such involvement. This circumstance also, as a typical experience, would be markedly different from the lives of any previous generation.[37]

In the earlier analyses it was routinely assumed that the falloff of memberships in the older cohorts was due to the infirmities of age, presumably leading to an inevitable withdrawal. An important analysis by Stephen J. Cutler, however, has shown two processes to be operating. Older cohorts have less education than those in the middle years, and the poorly educated respondents show the early disaffiliation. The better-educated and better-off segments among the elderly maintained their organizational involvements into their seventies, successfully postponing any age-related disaffiliation.[38]

In the previous chapter we saw that being married had a distinctive impact on the patterns of sociability. Basically, the marrieds tended to be homebodies. The singles, separateds, and divorceds, in contrast, spent much time visiting with friends and neighbors. It seemed likely that a similar pattern would appear with respect to association memberships. The results in this case, however, proved much more complicated.

For this purpose, single persons (those never married) were compared with married persons within three broad age categories (Table 2.4). The most consistent finding appears with respect to church-related associations. In all three age categories, the marrieds are much more likely than singles to be involved with religious associations. Among the young males, both single and married, membership in sports organizations far exceeds the involvement with church-related associations. This is the only segment in which a reversal of the predominance of the church-related associations occurs. Among the young, the singles have equal or in most cases higher levels of involvement in all of the other eight kinds of organization. Although the differences in some instances are small, the consistency of the pattern is striking. The young singles are also more likely to have multiple group memberships.

Most of those differences disappear among the middle aged. The marrieds, as indicated, tend to join religious associations. They also, not surprisingly, are much more likely to be involved in school service associations. (It is easy to read "school service" as referring to Parent–Teacher Associations, but the reverse pattern among the young suggests that it also includes university-based associations of all kinds, such as student government or alumni organizations.) The singles are slightly more likely to be involved in literary associations, and, by a considerable margin, in an all-embracing "other" category. Otherwise, the basic result for the middle aged is one of no difference.

Table 2.4
Memberships by Age and Marital Status (NORC-GSS: 1990–1994 Merge)

	Age					
	18-29		30-49		50 or more	
	Single[a]	Married	Single[a]	Married	Single[a]	Married
Number of Memberships						
None	35 %	38 %	32 %	27 %	46 %	25 %
One	22	25	25	20	21	27
Two	15	18	15	19	13	19
Three or More	28	19	28	35	21	29
Average	1.75	1.41	1.75	2.01	1.38	1.95
N =	(373)	(241)	(236)	(945)	(68)	(687)
Type of Association						
Church-affiliated	23 %	30 %	23 %	37 %	22 %	42 %
Sports groups	27	24	22	24	2	12
Professional or academic	19	13	23	22	19	15
School service groups	17	10	11	26	3	9
Hobby or garden clubs	12	10	13	12	7	12
Labor unions	7	6	13	13	13	13
Service clubs	9	8	10	10	7	13
Literary, art, discussion or study groups	14	5	13	9	9	11

[a]"Single" columns include those never married only.

Among the older respondents, those fifty and over, a distinctive third pattern appears. Nearly half of these singles have no association involvements, while the marrieds report many connections, including many multiple memberships. More often than not, here it is the marrieds who have the edge in the wide range of secular associations.

An exploration of the sources of these patterns would take us far afield. The pattern found among the young suggests that persons with religious commitments tend to marry earlier than those with more secular orientations. The young singles, as may be seen from the base numbers, are a large collectivity and doubtlessly rather diverse. Many of them, probably, would be university students, many of them either learning or reinforcing secular orientations. Most of them, of course, eventually marry, thus changing the composition of the equivalent middle-aged segment. The oldest singles, on the whole, appear to be notably uninvolved, lacking both marital ties and association linkages. They appear to be distinctively passive and/or recessive in their behavior. It is unfortunate that the subareas of sociology, marriage and family, religion, and politics do not explore the implications of these "boundary-line" issues. Regardless of the causes, the differences in political direction and in "leverage" of the segments, would remain. Young singles, for example, would be represented, disproportionately, through secular organizations; young marrieds would exert their influence, disproportionately, in religious organizations.[39]

Another factor deserving attention is the size or character of the community. The noted urban sociologist, Louis Wirth, operating within the mass society tradition, offered this bold statement: "Reduced to a stage of virtual impotence as an individual, the urbanite is bound to exert himself by joining with others of similar interests into groups organized to obtain his ends. This results in the enormous multiplication of voluntary organizations directed toward as great a variety of objectives as there are human needs and interests."[40]

For this purpose, as in the previous chapter, the SRC Belt Code was used. The differences in the extent of joining are small in all comparisons (Table 2.5). The twelve largest central cities are the most "anomic," with 43 percent reporting no voluntary associational ties. Those cities, however, are only marginally different from the small counties (those with no town of 10,000 or more), where 36 percent report no affiliation. The greatest involvement, by small margins, was found in the suburbs of the eighty-eight cities and in the large counties (nonmetropolitan with towns of more than 10,000). Wirth's confident judgment, in short, provides no serious guidance for the 1990s reality.

More striking perhaps are the differences in the patterns of involvement. Church-affiliated involvements are first in all settings, although in the twelve largest cities the percentage is lower than elsewhere. Those large cities have a unique pattern of involvement. Sports organizations generate less interest there (which is striking given the low average age of adult city dwellers). Professional associations have a strong presence in suburban communities, the level of joining being roughly equal to that of sports associations. Those living in small counties show limited interest in sport, professional, school, and literary associations. The small counties have strong representation in veterans organizations and in fraternal associations (not shown in Table 2.5).

One conclusion from the foregoing is that the overall level of membership in the United States is affected by several diverse factors, some of them likely to increase involvement, some likely to have the opposite effect. If one as-

Table 2.5
Voluntary Association Memberships by Size of Community (NORC-GSS: 1988–1991 Merge)

	Metropolitan Areas				Nonmetropolitan Areas	
	SMSAs		Suburbs		Counties	
	12 Largest	Next 88	12 Largest	Next 88	Largest Town 10,000 or more	No Town of 10,000 or less
Number of Memberships						
None	43 %	31 %	32 %	28 %	28 %	36 %
One	24	25	25	23	26	23
Two	11	22	17	19	19	17
Three or More	23	23	27	31	27	24
Average	1.41	1.62	1.78	1.88	1.84	1.59
N =	(310)	(492)	(459)	(675)	(1,499)	(505)
Type of Association						
Church-affiliated	24 %	35 %	27 %	34 %	37 %	34 %
Sports clubs	15	18	20	23	22	14
Professional or academic	15	15	20	22	15	9
School service groups	8	15	14	15	14	11
Hobby or garden clubs	8	10	10	12	11	10
Labor unions	15	11	13	12	12	11
Service clubs	8	9	9	11	10	10
Literary, art, discussion or study groups	9	9	12	10	9	5

sumed, as was often done in the 1950s, that increased education, increased affluence, and the shift to white-collar employment were the decisive factors, a steady increase in membership and greater dispersion of power would be expected. But that, as seen, has not been the case.

No serious change in total voluntary association memberships has appeared in recent years. Some changes have occurred, but rather than a general societal tendency, a more differentiated account seems appropriate. Two types of involvement have declined, those in church-related associations and unions. Professional associations, in contrast, show a modest growth. Some growth of membership also appears in the older cohorts. The differentiated account should consider cohort size, the age factor, and unique historical contributions. Several other factors, marital status and city size, appear to have some unsuspected effects.

The decline in joining by the middle-aged segments might stem from the increased participation of women in the labor force. The decline appears among both men and women. Full-time work for wives could bring a reduction in the after-work participation of both marriage partners. Exploration with the GSS merge 1975–1979 showed that housewives have the lowest levels of association involvement (and for them school associations figure prominently). Both the full-time employed women and the housewives in GSS 1990–1994 showed less involvement than the equivalent categories in the late 1970s.

The presence of children is another largely neglected fact-of-life consideration. Among married women, membership in hobby, political, and professional groups declines as the number of children increases, while membership in school associations varies positively. The growth and decline in the latter affiliations closely follow changes in average family size. All of the exploration reported here, which is of course very preliminary, was done with an appropriate age control.

The fourth proposition holds that newspapers (or in a later period, the mass media) facilitate the aggregation of interests. This hypothesis has not been put to systematic test. Although a central part of Tocqueville's argument, this claim has, on the whole, been neglected in subsequent discussions of pluralism. Those discussions, accordingly, make an untenable assumption about the ease with which individuals sharing interests would find one other. They effectively beg the question of mechanism; that is, how the concerned individual finds the appropriate organization or how individuals sharing a given concern would come together to form an organization.

Tocqueville, it should be noted, was making a sweeping and untenable assumption about the character of newspapers. He was assuming unbiased treatments of the events of the day. In one respect, the American press of the 1830s (and for many subsequent decades) was just the opposite; many accounts report heavy partisan bias. From the end of the Civil War through to the 1964 election, a substantial majority of American newspapers were Republican. A majority of the Democratic newspapers were conservative in outlook and most of them were located in the South. That partisanship would pose serious difficulties for any other political direction.[41]

Discussions of newspaper bias typically focus on the treatment of factual material, indicating a "slant," or an "angle," some distortion or misrepresentation, or, in the extreme case, the outright lie. The effect of such treatments would be cognitive (distorted understanding) and possibly behavioral (voting for the recommended party). Such treatments would also, presumably, have an impact on the formation and growth of associations, favoring some and discouraging others. While most accounts of bias focus on slanted or distorted news, another even more decisive option is available. One could blank out opposing views; that is, give them no attention whatsoever. David Halberstam has provided an account of such extreme bias involving the *Los Angeles Times*. Over three generations, he reports, the newspaper was "devoid of fairness and justice."

[Norman Chandler] was publishing in the tradition of his father and grandfather, and publishing for his peers, the big boys in the California Club, the conservative anti-labor barons of Southern California. The friends of the Chandlers were written about as they wished; their enemies were deprived of space, or attacked. The *Times* sanitized and laundered the operations of a rich anti-labor establishment and its politicians; it repeatedly used red scares to crush any kind of social-welfare legislation. It gave its enemies no space and no voice.

It was intensely, virulently partisan. The *Times* was not an organ of the Republican Party of Southern California, it *was* the Republican Party. It chose the candidates for the party; if anything the Republican Party was an organ of the *Times*.[42]

Ultimately, some enlightened family members prevailed and, in 1958, it was announced that the paper would be fair. In the 1960 presidential election, in a major departure, the paper reported on both Nixon and Kennedy. A grandson, Otis Chandler, took over at that point and completed the transformation, making it into a quality newspaper.

The transformation of the *Times* was part of a nationwide change, the political usage and direct controls of the media yielding to more open or permissive procedures allowing greater freedom or autonomy to reporters and commentators. The transformation began with a competitive struggle between the media for advertiser dollars. Initially the struggle was between the mass-circulation magazines and television, but it spilled over and affected other media. The magazines that had celebrated the affluence and moderate politics of the 1950s, *The Saturday Evening Post, Life, Look*, and, to a lesser extent, *Collier's*, sought out and published "controversial" content as their economic circumstances worsened.[43]

A major move toward newspaper concentration and chain ownership occurred between 1950 and 1990, with the percentage of group-owned papers increasing from 24 to 75. Some critics emphasize the controls by an ever-smaller number of capitalists, members of "the power elite."[44] Many commentators, especially those of the "critical" persuasion, do not recognize the possible diversity of motive; that is, between political influence and profit seeking. In the nineteenth century newspapers tended to be party linked or commercial. The latter, often called the "penny press," aimed for large circulation and advertising dollars. The penny press, emphasizing crime and scandal, tended to avoid politics, since a partisan emphasis could hurt circulation. Many critics do not make this distinction, seeing the media, in its entirety, as engaged in a defense of "the system" (or of "the status quo"). If interested in profits, the imposition of a political line could be damaging. Some chains, accordingly, allow individual papers to continue their previous traditions, their concern being profitability, not political influence. The shift from individual (or family) ownership to a chain brings another important change: The chief executive will be a manager, frequently someone from outside the community. The manager might not be part of the local power structure and thus not subject to the same set of loyalties and influences as the previous owner.

The *New York Herald Tribune* was once an important and influential newspaper, one closely linked to the so-called Eastern Establishment. But in the post–World War II years, its owners made a series of management errors, among them failing to invest and upgrade its capital plant. That choice ultimately brought about its demise. Those moderate Republicans, Eastern elites, then had to make do with the *New York Times*. In its years of decline, the *Herald Tribune* became more permissive, allowing content not previously seen in its pages. The so-called New Journalism began there with the writing of Tom Wolfe and Jimmy Breslin, who reported on, respectively, "top dog" and "underdog" foibles. The *Tribune* developed an "insistent hunger for flair." One staff member said there was "a willingness to be a little outrageous." Richard Kluger reports that the paper was willing "to take chances because [it] had nothing to lose by doing so; not to was to hasten its oblivion."[45]

The more permissive reporting began, in the early 1960s, with accounts of the civil rights struggle. Most subsequent histories of that movement indicate the decisive role of media coverage in generating public approval, membership in supportive associations, and financial contributions. Theodore White reviewed the television treatment of Bull Connor's police (and police dogs) in the Birmingham riots of April 1963. CBS was trying to recapture its audience lead from NBC at that time and Birmingham gave them a major opportunity. White, who was with CBS at that point, writes that they would "have done anything, within the ethics of television, to outdo NBC." In 1955–1956, in the course of the Montgomery bus boycott, a dynamite bomb destroyed the front of the leader's house. The subsequent media coverage made that leader, Martin Luther King, a national figure. At a later point, King and 100 other leaders of the boycott were arrested. The "photograph of him with a numbered plaque hanging from his neck captured national and international attention. Statements in support of the boycott, as well as cash contributions, poured in from all over the world."[46]

That struggle was followed by the "uprising" in the universities and by the widespread opposition to the Vietnam War. By the 1980s the nation's mass media were more open than at any time in its history. That would mean, following Tocqueville's prediction, that a wider range of opinion was represented and, accordingly, a wider range of associations developed.[47]

Implicit in Tocqueville's formulation is an assumption of unbiased reporting, as if all interests and associations were receiving appropriate and fair attention. The news, in that view, consists of reports on the entirety of the day's major events. But a wider range of reports is not the same as a cross-section. Basically, the new arrangement brings a different set of determinants. The imperious demands of the publisher were replaced by the "needs" of working journalists. Two significant biases appear at this point, first, the need for "hot," "exciting," or "controversial" material (as opposed to everyday routines, dominant tendencies, etc.) and second, the need for simplicity (as opposed to detail and complication). The report of a controversial story in television news programs ordinarily involves interviews with representatives of associations having polar opposite positions on the issue. That means the polar positions will be systematically overrepresented in "the news" and that all other positions, "centrist" positions, ones necessarily more complex, will be underrepresented. In general, the polar positions fit the need for simplicity and slogan-like summary, as in the familiar pro-life versus pro-choice polarity, or the gun control versus National Rifle Association opposition. Associations, understandably, welcome the opportunity to air their views; it gives them a free advertisement. As opposed to the passive imagery, "the press" merely "reflecting" the day's events, many associations initiate the effort, actively competing for attention.[48]

Contextual factors play a role in the competition of associations. In a "dialectical process," one association advertises its services pointing to the need to counter the threat posed by its opposition. Stressing the growth of conservatism in the Reagan years, the American Civil Liberties Union (ACLU) nearly doubled its membership. The organization was transformed in this period. At the beginning of the 1980s it had virtually no computers. With the growth of memberships and funding, the ACLU's state affiliates were linked to a central computer for coordination of comparable cases. The organization's executive director said the influx of donations "accelerated the transition of the ACLU from a kind of mom-and-pop grocery into a conglomerate." The Planned Parenthood Federation of America tripled its operating budget in the Reagan years, topping $300 million in 1989. It had 600 clinics at the beginning of the decade; by 1989, it had 850. The organization's vice president for communications said the "growth resulted directly from the Reagan Administration's threat to reproductive rights." Amnesty International tripled its membership between 1985 and 1989, reaching nearly 400,000. Its budget, $3 million in 1981, rose to about $23 million in 1989. Its executive director credited American policy in Latin America for part of the surge: "People give to Amnesty because they see us as an antidote to the foreign policy."[49]

The environmental organization, Greenpeace, was founded in 1971 by a group of Canadians protesting U.S. nuclear testing in Alaska. In the mid-1970s it had some 20,000 members. In 1995 it had 3.1 million members, a budget of $145 million, forty-three offices in thirty countries, a staff of 1,200, and, as part of their capital equipment, "four vessels, a helicopter, hundreds of dinghies, and the latest communications equipment." Its greatest strength, according to one account, is its ability to draw on tens of thousands of volunteers. The largest increase in members followed the destruction of *The Rainbow Warrior*, when French intelligence agents blew up the Greenpeace ship and killed a photographer. The subsequent wave of public sympathy enabled the organization to expand into Eastern Europe and Latin America.[50]

The dialectical struggle was evident again in two subsequent episodes. With the advent of the Clinton presidency in 1993, the Reagan–Bush "threat" was removed and, according to one account, "some people believed there was less need to support environmental causes." One presumed result was that the combined membership in five leading environmental groups fell, from a peak of 2.4 million in 1990 to 2.1 million in 1994. Another account reports that after Clinton's election liberal groups "fell on hard times financially . . . while conservative groups enjoyed a boon. The Sierra Club laid off workers after the environment-friendly administration took office, while the Christian Coalition claimed its membership doubled thanks to the Clintons." The subsequent Republican congressional victory in November 1994 led to renewed growth of liberal advocacy groups and optimistic expectations for others. The National Organization for Women reported that in the weeks following the election they "collected five times the usual level of gifts over $500, and 10,000 new members" joined up. The director of the Advocacy Institute, an organization which "trains and nurtures liberal interest groups," saw a "silver lining in this disaster [in that] the ability to alarm and motivate contributors has grown enormously."[51]

The fifth proposition holds that the voluntary associations are internally democratic. The argument seems plausible. One would expect, at minimum, a strong tendency in that direction. As small communities, it should be easy for members to contact and influence their leaders. If not representative, if not following the will of the constituents, the members could replace the unresponsive leaders or, in the extreme case, they could quit and form a new and more responsive association. Many commentators have proceeded on the basis of the logical case (as opposed to direct investigation) and, accordingly, have assumed a close correspondence between member wishes and leaders' initiatives. They have, in short, taken voluntary association pronouncements as a substitute for public opinion polls.

Some ninety years ago the internal-democracy argument was subjected to serious criticism in a major monographic study by Robert Michels entitled *Political Parties*. His argument is based, for the most part, on an analysis of the German Social Democratic Party, at that time the world's largest socialist party. The rule of August Bebel, Wilhelm Liebknecht, and the other party leaders faced no serious challenge "from below." The party that promised "a new realm of freedom" in fact brought another kind of domination (*Herrschaft*). Michels's argument might be formulated as follows: To be effective, to have power or influence, requires a large organization. A large organization, in turn, must have trained, specialized leaders, persons capable of managing that sizable enterprise. Those leaders will have (or will acquire) an expertise far superior to that of its untutored members, thus allowing them to check any insurgency. They will also have (or would soon develop) interests different from those of the membership. One prime interest would be to maintain their positions as leaders of the association, positions that carry with them a range of important benefits: salary, expense money, prestige, more attractive work, and so on. Michels stated his position forcefully as an iron law, which, in the English translation, reads as follows: "He who says organization says oligarchy." That translation, however, is not accurate. The original reads "*sagt Tendenz zur Oligarchie*"—"says tendency to oligarchy."[52]

The key phrase in the exposition is "interests different from" those of the members. The interests of "the bourgeoisie" might, conceivably, be diametrically opposed to those of "the proletariat." The interests of the organizational oligarchs would rarely be directly opposed to those of the members, not in the extreme sense of a polar (or dialectical) confrontation. The dominating interest for many organizational leaders would be an enhanced living standard. Their well-being would depend on having a large dues-paying membership and on other contributions (to be discussed later). The oligarchs would be in a position to set their own salaries and benefits. Their interest, accordingly, would be to maximize the organization's "working capital." That would require at least the appearance of representation. It would also, as will be seen, lead to a range of other kinds of initiatives.

Michels's arguments have been most thoroughly studied in connection with labor unions, this being a frequent topic in the social sciences beginning in the 1950s. His principal conclusion—oligarchy—has been regularly confirmed. Although well documented, there has been a persistent refusal to reckon with the conclusion. Michels's work and findings largely disappeared from the academic realm in the 1960s. The conclusion and its implications, in short, have not received the attention they deserve.

Many social scientists know a striking exception to Michels's law in the case of the International Typographers Union, studied by Lipset, Trow, and Coleman. This organization had some very exceptional characteristics, beginning with small shops, concentrated location, and a membership with unusual literary skills. The democracy, the longstanding two-party competition described and analyzed in this important work, it should be noted, subsequently disappeared. The union thus became a "conforming" case; in other words, another confirmation of the iron law. A study by Richard Freeman and James Medoff appears to challenge Michels's argument. They conclude, "There is a great deal of democracy, defined as access to a union's voice-making machinery, particularly at the local union level." The studies they cite show much leadership turnover in small locals providing modest remuneration. Turnover in the national unions, however, was less frequent, with a U.S. Department of Labor study reporting 20 percent in a two-year period from 1971 to 1973. Among those instances of turnover, most were due to retirement, resignation, or death of the incumbent. In three instances the retiring president was replaced by the union's secretary-treasurer (i.e., another member of the oligarchy). Only six of thirty-six turnovers came about through electoral defeat.[53]

The sixth assumption argues a rational choice: Well-informed citizens choose associations to maximize their goals (either representation and/or subsequent benefits). Implicit in the argument is a straightforward means-end relationship.

In 1965, Mancur Olson provided an important critique of this pluralist assumption. His argument goes as follows: A small organization, if successful in its effort, could achieve some tangible benefits from a government and could possibly bring some large "return" for each of the members. But, being small, the probability of its achieving significant benefits would also be small. To achieve such benefits, an organization must be strong; that is, must have many members. But in that case any benefits gained must be divided among, potentially, millions of members, and the individual share would again be small. Either way, the lesson is that individual membership is not economically rational. Put differently, the investment of money, time, and effort is not likely to bring a commensurate (let alone an enhanced) return. Olson's conclusion is that people join organizations for other reasons: for nontangible returns, or because of compulsion, or for peripheral benefits not signaled as the organization's main offering.[54]

People join expressive organizations for the benefit of their feelings, rather than for the hope of material rewards. A patriotic organization celebrates the goodness of the nation or defends its interests, but for most members there is no concrete payoff. Many people are in labor unions because of compulsion: The law of the land requires it as a prerequisite or condition of employment. Olson cites the American Farm Bureau Federation to illustrate the importance of peripheral benefits. Among other things, the federation owns insurance companies that offer relatively low-cost automobile insurance. To gain that benefit, one must join the federation. It is the peripheral benefit that explains a paradoxical result: In Illinois at one point the number of members exceeded the number of farmers in the state. The same dynamic appears in the nation's largest association, the American Association of Retired Persons. The AARP is a giant conglomerate offering a vast range of services. Put differently, grassroots "representation" is a small part of the enterprise.[55]

The narrowly conceived rational-choice assumption requires some modification. Members may well be acting rationally in the cases just reviewed, but for many the rationales involved are not likely to be those conventionally invoked, those linked to the organization's manifest purposes. The Farm Bureau may look like an agency representing the interests of farmers; that is, a conventional pressure group. But for many participants the salient motives do not fit within that framework. For some of its leaders the principal immediate aims are member growth and a large treasury. For some of the members the salient concern is the peripheral service, cheap insurance.

The seventh assumption, that association involvement brings training in the "arts of compromise," is largely unresearched. The phrase itself points up the difficulty. What does it mean? And a closely related question is, How would those "arts" be measured? There is clearly a need for further thought.

One might consider, first of all, the question of organizational technique, the skills involved in running a meeting, managing committees, writing reports, and getting elected or named to office. Much of that would, of course, be learned "on the job." Some of that knowledge would have been gained earlier, in the course of primary socialization: Parents with those skills would teach them to their children. Given the standard relationship of membership with socioeconomic status, that intergenerational transfer of skills would occur, very disproportionately, in high-status families, again in the upper and upper-middle classes. Some would have been taught in schools, in civics courses, in student government, and so forth. Again, it seems likely that this training would be strongly class related.[56]

Second, the arts-of-compromise expression involves a disguised normative judgment. Those arts, as practiced, are being treated as a "good thing." Their use is for the public good: All groups presumably win in the compromises. Put differently, the avoidance of conflict benefits everyone. But that usage begs an important empirical question. If the arts are practiced for the benefit of organizational oligarchs, the a priori assumption of beneficence might not be justified.

The fact of oligarchic control, of leaders with interests separate from those of the membership, points to the need for consideration of other analytic possibilities. Those leaders will have an incentive to distort the information they provide so as to maximize the organization's resources. They will be motivated to exaggerate the seriousness of the problems they deal with. They will ordinarily exaggerate the size of the resources needed to handle those problems. They will exaggerate the size and capacities of their own organization, thus dramatizing its unique ability to provide the necessary solutions. With rare exceptions, one would be dealing with magnification biases.[57]

Put differently, organization oligarchs will engage in manipulation. They will use techniques not found among "the arts of compromise." A definition is useful: Manipulation is the selective provision of information intended to

move people to choices they would not make otherwise. The account dramatizing an imminent crisis would, presumably, lead people to join the association, to contribute private funds, and to support enhanced expenditure of public
funds. If the "crisis" were portrayed differently, as a modest one or as no
problem at all, the responses would of course be very different.

CONCLUSIONS

The following conclusions appear warranted with respect to the seven pluralist assumptions.

First, the assumption of a widespread general involvement in voluntary
associations is confirmed, but in need of specification. The General Social
Surveys indicate that approximately two-thirds of the U.S. adult population
are members of at least one organization. That summary conclusion, however, requires some qualification. The pluralist theory, from Tocqueville to
the present, focuses on instrumental associations, ones that in some way attempt to exert power. The most frequent memberships, however, are in religious groups and sports associations, both probably with strong expressive
concerns. When those two types of organization were excluded from the count,
less than a majority were members.

Second, the assumption of multiple memberships as the typical experience
is rejected. Overall, in the early 1990s one-third had no affiliation and another one-quarter had only a single membership. Again, precise measurement is difficult. A restriction to instrumental associations would strikingly
reduce the size of the minority with multiple memberships.

Third, the positive trend of increased aggregate joining coming with increased affluence and education is rejected. Real per capita expenditures increased throughout this period, as did the levels of formal educational
accomplishment.[58] At the same time, however, the aggregate level of joining
fell off by a few percentage points and then remained constant from the early
1980s. Some other factors appear to be countering the affluence–education
impacts. Age and life-cycle events appear to be involved.

Fourth, the media role and the aggregation of interests is uncertain. No
systematic studies of media impacts, of the effects on joining, appear to have
been done. Available materials do not allow a precise test. This claim was
discussed with illustrative cases as opposed to systematic evidence. The argument seems plausible, but greater specification, consideration of a wider
range of media, and more precise testing, preferably with longitudinal studies, is needed.

Fifth, the assumption of internal democracy is rejected. This assumption
was rejected in an early monographic study, Robert Michels's *Political Parties*. Some reconsideration is needed. One should ask about the "degree" of
democracy or, put differently, about the extent of responsiveness. Here too,
one would face serious measurement problems. At minimum, one should rec-

ognize that the a priori assumption of internal democracy begs the question. In any given case, the hypothesis ought to be put to the test and justified.

Sixth, the assumption of rationality is uncertain. No precise test was undertaken here. That would, in any case, be a difficult task. Here too, as with the fourth assumption, the discussion was based on a handful of examples, and again some reconsideration is needed. Following Mancur Olson's argument, one must ask a prior question: Which rationale? The organization is officially dedicated to the representation of farmers and their interests. But many members are not farmers and many members are apparently rationally seeking another goal. If an organization were driven by the peripheral concerns, the focus on its manifest purpose—representation—would be mistaken. Again, it is important that questions not be begged.

Seventh, whether association involvements train in the arts of compromise and generate moderate attitudes and behaviors is uncertain. There appears to be no systematic study of this assumption. The evidence reviewed here is again illustrative, based on an assortment of cases. This assumption also appears open to question, at least as a generalization. Other options ought to be indicated and explored. The knowledge of organizational techniques might easily serve the interests of oligarchs. In the extreme case, the oligarchs' use of "the arts" could be both immoderate and uncompromising; that is, for defense of their interests. Single-interest advocacy groups might also use organizational techniques in immoderate ways; that is, for the mobilization of conflict.

DISCUSSION

Several research problems remain open. More work should be done on the personal, social, and economic causes of membership. More work is needed on the alleged effects of involvement in associations; that is, the effects on members' attitudes and behaviors. More attention should be given the presumed representational function of associations; that is, the extent to which they do reflect members' interests and concerns.

David Horton Smith has provided an important critique of voluntary association research. Some fifty years ago, as noted, a consensus was developed that excluded church memberships from most tabulations and analyses of association involvements. The original argument was that many or most church ties were not voluntary. Smith cites evidence challenging that assumption. Church involvements, moreover, were said to be expressive, a second consensus, and therefore not really relevant to the pluralist argument. But given the murkiness of the instrumental–expressive distinction and the ease of shifting from one to the other focus, that consensus should also be reconsidered. Counting church memberships would change dramatically the basic frequencies reported in the literature. The possible impacts and influence on "civil society" might also be sizable. In any event, there is no evident justification for ignoring church ties, a procedure that assumes the influence to be negligible. Smith shows that the findings from the two relevant academic specialties, the sociology of religion and the sociology of associations, have little overlap. The findings in one field are rarely cited in the publications of the other.[59]

Another important question has been neglected in most discussions of pluralism, that of the character of needs, wants, or concerns. It has been taken for granted that people generally have a wide range of pressing unsatisfied needs. Rather than assuming the general character of needs, however, one ought to undertake investigation. In the 1970s the National Election Studies asked respondents the following question: "We like to have people tell us, in their own words, what sort of problems they have to deal with in their daily lives, can you tell me what some of the problems are that you face these days in your own life?" In 1972 and 1976 approximately one-sixth of the respondents reported no problem. As one person put it, "everything's okay." For those respondents, there would be no obvious need for any instrumental organizational involvement. If involved, one might expect a preference for expressive associations.[60]

Roughly two-fifths of those who did report problems signaled some economic difficulty. For most people at that time the problem was inflation. At a considerable remove came reports of problems with health, government, family, self (life situation), time pressures, job problems, crime, and personal safety. None of these were mentioned by as much as 10 percent of the respondents. Each of those categories moreover includes a wide range of specific difficulties. Those involving government included, for example, inadequacies of community services, transport, garbage, snow removal, fire protection, schools, police, and welfare workers. For many of those problems, the choice of an "organizational weapon" is neither obvious nor plausible.

A second prior question has also been bypassed in most discussions of pluralism: the choice of means. Rather than assuming that an association is the obvious choice, this question also should be researched. One investigation, based on a national sample, found the following distribution: "Active in at least one organization involved in community problems," 32 percent; "Have ever contacted a state or national government official about some issue or problem," 18 percent; "Have ever formed a group or organization to attempt to solve some local community problem," 14 percent.[61] Some problems might be addressed through personal networks with the help of relatives or friends. Some problems, those associated with health and age, for example, might have no evident collective solution.

When considering the uses of a theory, one must address the question of "coverage." The basic question is, Where does it apply? Tocqueville and Beard saw the pluralist theory as having application to the entire society. Everyone was (or soon would be) in organizations and thus participating in the exercise of power. But from the time of the first surveys it was clear that this reading of things had a limited application. The major claims apply largely to rather privileged minorities of the population, those best described as the upper and upper-middle classes. The pluralist efflorescence of the 1950s attempted, as indicated, to extend the theory to the entire society principally through various "elastic" usages and through assumptions of beneficent trends.[62] But those efforts by and large proved unjustified and hence were unrealistic. Where other classes organized, the associations were generally oligarchic; that is, allowing limited grassroots influence. This was (and is) most clearly evident in the case of labor unions, small business groups, and farm organizations.

A realistic pluralist theory ought to recognize the strong and persistent class-related tendency. That fact ought to be built into the basic formulation of the theory. One should recognize the simple facts of life: Organizational activity costs money—membership fees, special assessments, and out-of-pocket contributions, plus the costs of getting to and from meetings. The greater the involvement, the more money needed. Without money involvement is limited, as in the case of marginal farmers, the traditional working class, and the poor.

There is also the "dynamic" consideration. Economic downswings, other things equal, depress organized activity. The increase of economic grievances is ordinarily linked to a decline in the strength of organizations representing the aggrieved, because the money required to support their activity is dramatically reduced. Marx and Engels routinely predicted that the working-class revolution would come with the next economic downswing. But that is the nonexistent case; the revolutions of the twentieth century are linked to wars, not to depressions.[63]

Time is another resource needed for active involvement in associations. As with money, some people have it and some do not. The "leisure classes" would have greater freedom for such activity. Professionals have more opportunities than heavily committed corporate executives who put in long hours.[64] Any persons "freed" for such purposes would have better opportunities. Lawyers in large law firms are given time off for activities that might aid their collective purposes. Some jobs, in contrast, effectively deny such involvement. Persons on shift work, especially those on the second shift, would be excluded from most organizational activities. Many business and service clubs have noon lunch meetings. The proprietors of small shops, those with at best one or two employees, are not free to attend, since much of their business is conducted at that time. Long-distance truckers would also find it difficult to attend meetings.

Another fact of life is regularly overlooked. High-level executives work long hours, somewhere between sixty and eighty per week. In the ordinary workday they would also have some commuting time and family time. Those executives report many organizational memberships, in voluntary associations, on boards of directors, and on boards of trustees. But much of that must be membership without involvement. Put differently, it means they are likely to be absentee members.

A closely related consideration also deserves attention; namely, the quality of one's free time. Physically demanding labor discourages leisure-time involvement. With other things equal (such as a forty-hour workweek), clerical and sales employees would be distinctly advantaged while construction workers, auto workers, and punch press operators would be disadvantaged. The former might be wide awake, alert, and ready for evenings of meetings, discussion, and committee work. The latter, ordinarily, would not be "ready," fatigue being an obvious problem. Here too, as with the money question, intellectuals appear to be curiously inhibited. Discussions of involvement and participation rarely consider this simple fact of life: How hard is the work?[65]

Any factor that brings people together in the course of everyday life will favor organization. It is easier to organize a thousand workers in a large plant than the same number dispersed in twenty smaller shops. Other things equal, it is easier to organize a given number of persons in cities than the same number scattered in villages or the countryside. People who share work and living space, a two-fold congregation, are easier to organize. Those employed in a company town, for example, share the problems posed by a given employer and can easily discuss their grievances after work. The rule here is that congregation favors association; dispersion inhibits it. One should add a corollary: Organizations with dispersed members will tend to be nonparticipatory and oligarchic.

With respect to the size of community, one additional factor needs consideration, one other way in which "other things" are not equal. Small communities of all kinds operate with an informal antidivisiveness rule. Contentious issues have long-term effects, with families and friends at odds for decades thereafter (a fact easily appreciated following strikes in small towns or company towns). Knowing this, people in small communities, both elites and masses, go to considerable lengths to contain or limit contention. Small communities of all kinds (villages, workshops, colleges) operate with such rules and, as a result, are basically monocultural or single-identity settings. That means the voluntary associations found in small communities are likely to be expressive in character, as opposed to instrumental.[66]

The focus on voluntary association experience as decisive for the development of skills and outlooks, as noted, needs more attention. Some of that training is likely to come through intergenerational transmission. Given the striking overrepresentation of the upper and upper-middle classes in associations, it follows that their children will be exceptionally advantaged as a result of routine primary (i.e., familial) socialization. This too is a simple fact of life, one that could hardly be otherwise.

Some organizational skills are developed in everyday life through on-the-job experience. Some jobs require the generation of information and the writing of reports, efforts that would make for adept committee work elsewhere. Persons who manage meetings on the job could easily transfer those skills elsewhere. Persons in occupations that require public speaking will have an advantage over most others. In this respect, other things equal, preachers and professors will be considerably advantaged when compared to plumbers and punch press operators. Even with a limited control, restricting consideration to otherwise advantaged professionals, preachers and professors would ordinarily be more at ease in public speaking than doctors, dentists, or journalists.

The lesson, in short, is that there ought to be a clear and explicit recognition of what might be termed the limits of the possible. In some cases, guided by the general or extended theory, some practitioners initiated policies that went "beyond those limits." That experience, understandably, allows a test of the present argument. Recognizing that the poor were left out of this ordinary exercise of power, the 1960s antipoverty program mandated a policy of "maximum feasible participation." The outcome, as formulated in one famous assessment, was "maximum feasible misunderstanding."[67] In that period of pluralist exuberance, the Ford Foundation funded and supported an effort to decentralize New York City's school system. It too was part of a general program of "empowerment." The result, as became clear some years later, was the rule of oligarchs. Various entrepreneurs had discovered the opportunity for patronage and personal enrichment.[68]

The empowerment of poor communities had an unanticipated consequence, one that effectively undercut the aim of these programs. The programs' executors sought out and rewarded local citizens who showed leadership abilities. Those rewards in turn enabled the beneficiaries to leave the communities they were supposed to aid, a process referred to as "creaming." The loss of leadership left those communities with less power than before and thus more dependent on interventions "from above." A similar process was observed three score years earlier by Robert Michels, who wrote that "the involuntary task of the socialist party [is] to remove from the proletariat, to deproletarianize, some of the most capable and best informed of its members."[69]

The fifth proposition, the assumption of internal democracy, requires reformulation. As stated, the claim (or hypothesis) calls for a yes or no, for a confirmed or rejected judgment. If rejected, a positive alternative hypothesis is needed. The suggested alternative is that some associations are disguised business organizations. Put differently, they are enterprises intended to generate income for their "owners." The proprietors, understandably, show little enthusiasm for internal democracy.

The drive for income and personal benefits appears dramatically in an unexpected context in the case of some socialist leaders. August Bebel and Wilhelm Liebknecht were in the "socialism business," an enterprise that brought them very handsome returns.[70] Other entrepreneurs are in the trade union business, one "labor leader" generating an annual income in the mid-1980s of $530,000 plus expenses.[71] The proposition holds also for various philanthropic organizations soliciting funds for the cure of major diseases.[72] These are all, of course, "non-profit" organizations. They do not function as ordinary enterprises, attempting to maximize returns on invested capital. In lieu of capital, these organizations are sustained by membership dues and by contributions. The "returns" to the managers in these cases would be salaries and benefits, ordinarily set by boards of trustees, persons who in most cases were chosen by the oligarchs themselves.

The concern with income maximization gives rise to a little-noted characteristic found in some voluntary associations; namely, elasticity in the definition of the eligible membership. A study of small business organizations discovered that they did not define a key term: small. That reluctance allowed them to secure the support of sizable enterprises, some with more than 1,000 employees, some actually from the top "giants" of the nation. The American Association of Retired Persons is not restricted to the retired, but allows nonretired persons from age fifty to join. The American Farm Bureau Federation, as noted, had a membership in one state that exceeded the number of farmers. That "outreach" depends on a generous definition of the underlying population, of those claimed for representation. The more ample the definition, the greater the opportunity for dues revenues.[73]

The "democratizing" assumption found in many discussions of pluralism holds that the involvement begins with the member. Sensing some need, some problem, the concerned citizen either seeks out the appropriate organization or, if not available, joins with others to form one. But another option has been recognized; namely, that the organization itself initiates and sustains the involvement. Some organizations make use of a sales staff for this purpose. These persons are employed on a commission basis to generate membership. The organization, in effect, creates (or magnifies) the demand. In addition to hired staff, one may also make use of direct mail solicitation. These procedures obviously go far beyond those anticipated in Tocqueville's original.[74]

Dues payments would ordinarily be the principal source of income for any association. Another possible source, however, is grants or contributions. For special projects, members could be asked for "one-time" assessments. The giant firms that are members of small-business associations provide large grants, ones well above any dues requirement. Support could also be solicited from private foundations that shared the association's interests and concerns. Still another income source, one rarely recognized, is local, state, and national government. The executive branch of any government consists of a multitude of agencies, each with its own budget, some part of which is discretionary. Those agencies provide financial assistance to advocacy groups that support its purposes.[75]

Those concerns for the larger constituency mean that the original representational assumption is misleading. The focus on the "small democracy" consisting of leaders and a narrowly defined clientele does not reflect the actual dynamics of many organizations. The leaders, the oligarchs, have incentives to reach beyond the narrow clientele (for example, beyond the small businesses, the mom-and-pop grocery stores) to those other clients. The big-business grant provides additional income for the small-business organization. In exchange, the latter will provide representation for those interests. It will take public positions favored by the giant firms thus, for public relations purposes, giving an appearance of broad public support for (or against) a given issue. In such cases, it will be noted, the reflective assumption (the organizational pronouncement as opinion poll) is neither accurate nor appropriate.[76]

That diversity of motives has serious implications for the basic pluralist imagery. The key assumption, the voluntary association as "mediating" agency, must be modified. The diverse motives present among both leaders and followers means that the associations may diverge considerably from their announced purposes. Baumgartner and Walker state the point as follows: "Many of the prominent organizations engaged in lobbying in Washington, despite their fancy letterheads listing dozens of prominent citizens as members, have only the most tenuous connections with those they claim to represent. . . . Many groups are little more than figments of public relations."[77]

The principal implication of this discussion is that an association's pronouncement on any given issue should not be taken at face value as a reflection of underlying member sentiment. Those issue positions may reflect other determinants. There is an easy test of the democratizing assumption: One should inquire if the association has polled its members. If so, one should examine the sample characteristics, question formulations, response rates, and so on.[78]

A cautionary note: Categorical formulations, while having the advantage of convenience, are often impediments to serious thinking. The paired opposites—associations "are democratic" or "are oligarchic"—is a prime example. The rejection of the former, the argument that member sentiments ineluctably force responsiveness, does not establish the polar opposite position that associations reflect exclusively the interests of oligarchs. At minimum, one ought to consider partitive formulations, the degrees to which associations reflect those interests. Mutuality is also a possibility: The association may serve both leader and member interests, as in the case of the auto insurance.

Pluralism should not be treated as a static theory. Since the realities of organizational life change, the theory ought to be altered to reflect those changes. Tocqueville focused on the role of newspapers. A wide range of mass media made their appearance in the twentieth century. And a wide range of techniques—commissioned sales forces, direct mail solicitation, fringe benefit offerings, and so forth—have made both more and larger organizations possible. The increase in the number of funding organizations, both private foundations and government agencies, has aided that process of growth. The increase in the number of "think tanks" has provided a wealth of backup information for many efforts of advocacy.[79]

The growth of large organizations without strong member involvement means an overall enhancement of oligarchy, of leadership free to proceed with considerable autonomy. Many of those organizations would be single-purpose advocacy groups, ones not particularly disposed to compromise. Such groups, moreover, would ordinarily be more interested in "results" than in either representation of member wishes or the accuracy of information provided. Rather than aiding "the democratic process" their impacts could easily be detrimental.

In January 1993 an extensive campaign was undertaken to alert people to an alarming fact: Super Bowl Sunday "is the single worst day for domestic violence in the USA. There is an increase of as much as 40% in the volume handled by domestic violence shelters on this day." This effort began with the Women's Action Coalition (WAC) of Los Angeles and Fairness and Accuracy in Reporting (FAIR). The passage appeared in an e-mail message transmitted by a sociology graduate student who had it from the Progressive Sociology Network that in turn had it from the Progressive Economists Network. FAIR called on NBC, the network carrying the game, to provide two cautionary public service announcements on domestic violence during the game. Anna Quindlen, an op-ed writer for the *New York Times*, it was reported, "wrote a fine editorial . . . supporting this effort." NBC did respond to this campaign, giving time for a spot announcement provided by FAIR.

Subsequently, it was discovered that no study correlating Super Bowl viewing and domestic violence existed. The single relevant study was based on "emergency room admissions for reasons of assault" in the northeast region of the State of Virginia over a two-year period. It tracked "only the outcomes of the Washington Redskins football team." The authors found a statistically significant increase in admissions of women after the Redskins won games. It also found a similar increase in admissions of men after Redskin losses (this finding was not mentioned by FAIR). A second test, based on data from the largest hospital in Norfolk, Virginia, did not confirm those findings. No "40-percent" figure was given in the article.[80]

The Christian Coalition "led the charge of the religious right in national and local politics" for much of the 1990s. Toward the end of the decade, it floundered and some disaffected former leaders revealed some details of its operation. The coalition, those leaders reported, "distorted the size of its base by keeping thousands of names of dead people, wrong addresses and duplicates on its list of supporters; printed millions of voter guides that the coalition leaders expected would never be distributed, and hired temporary workers to look busy in the mail room and phone banks to impress reporters and camera crews."[81]

These observations raise questions about the underlying beneficent assumption of pluralism, that association involvement per se is a "good thing." The suggestion here is that the new technologies have changed the character of public life in such a way as to require reconsideration of that assumption. Voluntary associations can generate a large membership. They might be democratic, providing direct and accurate representation for the members. Or, operating with a "revolving" membership, one enlisted by the sales staff or through direct mail advertising, an organization might proceed with considerable independence, replacing disaffected members with a steady supply of new recruits. The use of peripheral benefits provides another source of independence: Members joining for the cheap insurance may well be indifferent to the organization's efforts of advocacy.

In those famous (or infamous) "old days," many newspaper and magazine publishers used their properties for direct personal advantage, arrogantly and ruthlessly favoring their preferred parties and/or interests. The relaxation of controls that came in the 1960s made possible a new institutional arrangement, one that allowed relatively free reporting of a wider range of associations, parties, and positions. Following Tocqueville, that made possible new and different aggregations of interests.

If the reporting were "objective," as in providing a comprehensive account of the day's "news," that in itself would be a significant change. Some commentators, however, have argued a new source of bias. They claim, with some evidence, that liberal journalists favor "news" that supports their political values.[82] If so, the shift from "old days" to "new days" would have brought an important change in the principle guiding news selection. The framework imposed by conservative and (usually) Republican publishers would have been replaced by a more diffuse arrangement, one guided generally by liberal principles. Greater autonomy (or power) has been accorded to working journalists. And greater power (or access) has been given to "outside" advocacy groups. The previous arrangement was clear, unambiguous, and authoritarian: The publisher gave orders or informally signaled the direction.[83] The new decentralized arrangement depends more on small-group dynamics (discussions among working journalists) and allows interventions by outside agencies. The Superbowl business began simply enough with a press conference by a "concerned" advocacy group.

Useful pluralism, the realistic variant of the theory, should focus on divisions within the ranks of the privileged, those of the upper and upper-middle classes. The modern world began with divisions within the ruling classes of the monarchic–aristocratic regimes. The key struggles were Tories versus Whigs, monarchists versus the *frondeurs*. With the appearance of a "modern" opposition in the eighteenth century with the champions of the Enlightenment, the predecessors of the later liberals, it was a struggle of the old regime versus the new, but with both sets of contenders highly placed.

The image of narrowly based classes, ones held together by "obvious" class interests, is mistaken. The principal aggregations of interest in the modern era, from the outset, involved divisions within "the ruling class." Beaumarchais wrote his play, *The Marriage of Figaro*, a highly incendiary work, in 1787. Marie Antoinette and several other supportive members of the court arranged for a reading at Versailles. Louis XVI recognized the threat and forbade its public presentation. Through astute diplomacy, Beaumarchais ultimately succeeded in having the play performed in France. Mozart set the play to music and, with permission of the Emperor, it was performed in Vienna and was enthusiastically received.[84]

Much of the history of the nineteenth century is regularly misread as a result of the imposition of class-based readings. The political struggles in Britain throughout that century were based on divisions within upper- and upper-middle-class ranks. The masses were not enfranchised, and hence were not represented in Parliament, even after the Third Reform Act (1884). The most famous insurgency of the century, that of the Chartists, was easily defused, in 1848 no less, and those working-class demands were postponed with little difficulty. The major reforms were the product of party struggle, not class struggle. The Liberals, it will be noted, were in power in Britain throughout much of the nineteenth century. That means they had gained a majority among the well-off classes. A similar development may be seen in France. In the last episode of the Orleanist regime the liberals had a majority in the parliament, under very restricted suffrage. It was the agitation of liberal intellectuals for suffrage reform that led to the collapse of the regime.[85]

The recurring efforts to portray American politics as class based also flounder. The Adams–Jackson struggle as a clash of old (or established) elites versus the hero of the masses has long been proven inadequate. The actual history involved one set of elites against another set, each with a distinctive coalition of mass support. In one way or another, that arrangement has persisted to the present.[86] The appropriate image, therefore, is one involving diverse aggregations of elites at the top of the society and diverse masses reacting to their various offerings. One is dealing with a "pluralism of elites." The principal repertory of mass reactions would be voting, ratifying or rejecting the elite offerings, or apathy and indifference. On occasion—the exceptional experience—persons or groups succeed in mobilizing the masses or, more precisely, some small parts of that collectivity. Most of those aggregations are short lived. Those with longer life tend to be oligarchic; that is, they are led by persons who either originally or from the moment of success would ordinarily be classified as privileged.

The pluralist theory faces still another serious difficulty; namely, a virtual principle of indeterminacy. The theory is most useful for after-the-fact explanation, for post hoc reconstruction of processes and outcomes. It would have required exceptional insight, prior to the event, to foresee the alliance of Beaumarchais and Marie Antoinette against Louis XVI. Who would have predicted Emperor Joseph's permission for Mozart's *Figaro*? Or who would have recognized the reason for it, to aid Joseph's struggle against an obstreperous aristocracy? Who would have anticipated the coalition of prointervention forces in the United States in 1898 that led to the Spanish–American War? Or, an example from recent experience, given the conventional positions, who would have expected a quiet alliance of some concerned feminists and pro-gun advocates?[87]

In summary, the pluralist theory proves useful and appropriate for describing organizational and political dynamics located, for the most part, within the ranks of privileged classes. It provides little useful insight into the behavior of other classes of the society: the lower-middle class, the working class, or the "underclass." For those classes, some other theory seems more appropriate.

The themes discussed in this chapter were central ones for the social sciences of the 1950s and early 1960s, most especially in sociology and political science. With the rise of radicalism in the universities in the late 1960s, pluralism fell into disfavor. This moderate or gradualist argument, one with an almost doctrinal status, came to be seen as a heresy, a transparent ideology obscuring the "real" power relationships. In the "advanced capitalist" nations Marxism then gained its greatest university-based following in the entire modern era. A quarter of a century later, Marxism is still present and commended in the textbooks, most obviously in sociology.

Pluralism, in striking contrast, has not made a comeback, at least not in its 1950s version, with mediating voluntary associations as the key to democracy. Many pluralist themes have resurfaced, but in most instances it is with a new vocabulary, new terms of analysis, and often with a changed focus. In sociology attention has shifted from associations to social movements. The focus is no longer on individual grievances and the aggregation of interests. The new approach, called "resource mobilization," emphasizes the enabling conditions. It focuses on the contributions (money, time, effort) provided by various groups, many of them well-endowed, contributions that make possible and facilitate new collective efforts.[88]

Some theorists have focused on corporatism, on the linkage of associations and government agencies. As already seen, joint efforts of this sort are a significant current development. Much of the theoretical effort has focused on a tripartite linkage, on the cooperative efforts of business, unions, and government.[89]

Other theorists have changed the focus and terminology to concentrate on "social capital." This enlarges the range of social connections to include many kinds of social ties, not just formal associations. While having some justification, the extended focus makes assessment of claims—density of involvement, trends, and influence—much more difficult.[90]

Still another approach, one with a much longer intellectual history, draws on political philosophy and focuses on "civil society." Here, typically, one finds very sweeping portraits, the subject matter including all social involvements that are not integral to "the state." Much of the work in this tradition, regrettably, is characterized by murky formulations that make empirical assessment difficult.[91]

From the perspective of still another theory, pluralism and its recent variants are of no special importance at all. The affairs of this world, it is claimed, are more and more dominated by bureaucratic organizations directed by technical experts. These theorists point to the growth of big government and giant private firms. Following Robert Michels, even leisure-time activities, it is said, are more and more dominated by unyielding bureaucracies. This theoretical development is the subject of our next chapter.

NOTES

1. For an earlier discussion, evidence, and references on the subject, see Richard F. Hamilton, *Class and Politics in the United States* (New York: Wiley, 1972), 34–46. See also Francis W. Coker, "Pluralism," *Encyclopedia of the Social Sciences*, vol. 12 (New York: Macmillan, 1937), 170–174; Henry S. Kariel, "Pluralism," *International Encyclopedia of the Social Sciences*, vol. 12 (New York: Macmillan/Free Press, 1968), 164–169. Signaling a shift in interest or topicality, a later encyclopedia contains no entry under pluralism, the listings going directly from Phenomenology to Police in *The Encyclopedia of Sociology* (New York: Macmillan, 1992).

2. The use of the quotation marks is to signify that power is not a thing such as gold, diamonds, water, or oil reserves, something that with relative ease can be divided and possessed. Power is inherently social; that is, based on social relationships. At its simplest, it involves someone who gives an order and someone else who obeys, who accepts and carries out the command. Reworking Max Weber's definition, power refers to the realization of an individual or collective intention "in a communal action even against the resistance of others." On the definition, see *From Max Weber: Essays in Sociology*, trans. and ed. H. H. Gerth and C. Wright Mills (London: Routledge & Kegan Paul, 1948), 180. On the two-sidedness of power relationships and the importance of consent, see Chester I. Barnard, *The Functions of the Executive* (Cambridge: Harvard University Press, 1938), Ch. 12.

3. For an overview, see J. H. Elliott, *Imperial Spain, 1469–1716* (1963; reprint, London: Penguin, 1990), Ch. 5.

4. Robert Koehl, "Feudal Aspects of National Socialism," *American Political Science Review* 54 (1960): 921–933; Edward Peterson, *The Limits of Hitler's Power* (Princeton: Princeton University Press, 1969).

5. Baron de Montesquieu, *The Spirit of the Laws*, book XI, trans. Thomas Nugent (New York: Hafner, 1949). See also the critical comments of the editor, Franz Neumann, on pp. li–lix. On the organization and management of the European economies, see Rondo Cameron, *A Concise Economic History of the World: From Paleolithic Times to the Present*, 2d ed. (New York: Oxford University Press, 1993), 120–143, 153–161.

6. On the extension of suffrage, see Stein Rokkan, *Citizens Elections Parties: Approaches to the Comparative Study of the Processes of Development* (New York: David McKay, 1970), Part II.

7. For a brief statement, see Alfred Cobban, *Edmund Burke and the Revolt Against the Eighteenth Century* (1929; reprint, London: Allen & Unwin, 1960), 59–72; or, for more detail, G. E. Weare, *Edmund Burke's Connection with Bristol, from 1774 till 1780: With a Prefatory Memoir of Burke* (Bristol: William Bennett, 1894). See also Edmund Burke, *Reflections on the Revolution in France*, ed. Conor Cruise O'Brien (1790; reprint, Harmondsworth: Penguin, 1969). Max Weber, more than a century later, shared Burke's position, see p. 126.

8. Alexis de Tocqueville, *De la Démocratie en Amérique*, vol. 1 (Paris: Charles Gosselin, 1835). The references here are to *Democracy in America*, Henry Reeve text, rev. Francis Bowen (New York: Knopf, 1963). The initial discussion of associations appears in Vol. 1, pp. 191–198. The key chapters are contained in Vol. 2, Book II, Chs. 5 and 6. The second volume was published in 1840. For discussions of the key agency, see D. B. Robertson, ed., *Voluntary Associations: A Study of Groups in Free Societies* (Richmond, Va.: John Knox Press, 1966); David L. Sills, "Voluntary Associations,"

International Encyclopedia of the Social Sciences, vol. 16, pp. 362–379; Constance Smith and Anne Freedman, *Voluntary Associations: Perspectives on the Literature* (Cambridge: Harvard University Press, 1972); Aida K. Tomeh, "Formal Voluntary Organizations: Participation, Correlates, and Interrelationships," *Sociological Inquiry* 43 (1973): 89–122; David Horton Smith and Jon Van Til, eds., *International Perspectives on Voluntary Action Research* (Washington, D.C.: University Press of America, 1983); David Knoke, *Organizing for Collective Action: The Political Economies of Associations* (New York: Aldine, 1990); and Sidney Verba, Kay Lehman Schlozman, and Henry E. Brady, *Voice and Equality: Civic Voluntarism in American Politics* (Cambridge: Harvard University Press, 1995).

9. Tocqueville, *Democracy*, vol. 2, p. 106.

10. Ibid., vol. 2, pp. 106, 110; see also vol. 1, pp. 85–97, 249–253.

11. Ibid., vol. 2, pp. 111–112.

12. Ibid., vol. 2, pp. 115–120. The quotation is from p. 116.

13. For commentaries pro and con, see Hamilton, *Class and Politics*, 65–66, note 21. See also, for discussions by sociologists, Seymour Martin Lipset, *Political Man: The Social Bases of Politics* (Garden City, N.Y.: Doubleday, 1960); Arnold Rose, *The Power Structure* (New York: Oxford University Press, 1967); William A. Gamson, *The Strategy of Social Protest* (Homewood, Ill.: Dorsey, 1975); G. William Domhoff, *The Higher Circles: The Governing Class in America* (New York: Random House, 1970), Ch. 9; and G. William Domhoff, *Who Rules America Now?* rev. ed. (Prospect Heights, Ill.: Waveland Press, 1997), 203–210. For discussions by political scientists, see Arthur F. Bentley, *The Process of Government* (Chicago: University of Chicago Press, 1908); David B. Truman, *The Governmental Process: Political Interests and Public Opinion* (New York: Knopf, 1951); Earl Latham, *The Group Basis of Politics* (Ithaca: Cornell University Press, 1952); E. E. Schattschneider, *The Semisovereign People: A Realist's View of Democracy in America* (New York: Holt, Rinehart & Winston, 1960); Gabriel A. Almond and Sidney Verba, *The Civic Culture: Political Attitudes and Democracy in Five Nations* (Princeton: Princeton University Press, 1963), esp. Ch. 11; Robert A. Dahl, *Pluralist Democracy in the United States: Conflict and Consent* (Chicago: Rand McNally, 1967), *Dilemmas of Pluralist Democracy: Autonomy vs. Control* (New Haven: Yale University Press, 1982), *Democracy and Its Critics* (New Haven: Yale University Press, 1989), esp. Part 5; William E. Connolly, ed., *The Bias of Pluralism* (New York: Atherton, 1969); Theodore J. Lowi, *The End of Liberalism: Ideology, Policy, and the Crisis of Public Authority* (New York: Norton, 1969); and Nelson W. Polsby, *Community Power and Political Theory: A Further Look at the Problem of Evidence and Inference*, 2d ed. (New Haven: Yale University Press, 1980).

14. See Theda Skocpol, "Bringing the State Back In: Strategies of Analysis in Current Research," in *Bringing the State Back In*, ed. Peter B. Evans, Dietrich Rueschemeyer, and Theda Skocpol (New York: Cambridge University Press, 1985), Ch. 1. For a response, see Gabriel A. Almond, "The Return to the State," *American Political Science Review* 82 (1988): 853–874; and Eric A. Nordlinger, Theodore J. Lowi, and Sergio Fabbrini, "The Return to the State: Critiques," *American Political Science Review* 82 (1988): 875–901. See also G. William Domhoff, *State Autonomy or Class Dominance? Case Studies on Policy Making in America* (New York: Aldine de Gruyter, 1996), esp. Chs. 3 and 5. Bismarck's dismissal in 1890 did not alter the German state. The direction and quality of decision making, however, changed dramatically with his successors. Between 1928 and 1933 the German state had five

chancellors—Müller, Brüning, Papen, Schleicher, and Hitler—all with strikingly different policies. On March 23, 1933, Hitler's government achieved passage of the Enabling Law, which gave his party dictatorial powers, definitively changing the character of the state. For an important thought-provoking treatment of some aspects of this history, see Henry Ashby Turner, Jr., *Hitler's Thirty Days to Power* (Reading, Mass.: Addison-Wesley, 1996).

15. The entire question is covered in the few brief lines of the First Amendment: "Congress shall make no law respecting an establishment of religion, or prohibiting the free exercise thereof; or abridging the freedom of speech, or of the press; or the right of the people peaceably to assemble, and to petition the Government for a redress of grievances." A widespread misconception exists about the content of that amendment, many people having been led to believe it provides a *guarantee* of those freedoms. As may be seen, however, it does nothing of the kind. The amendment is jurisdictional: It says Congress shall not legislate in those areas, but says nothing about other governments. Connecticut, Massachusetts, and New Hampshire made use of this opportunity and did establish religions; that is, gave them privileged positions. The separation came only in the 1830s. See Evarts B. Greene, *Religion and the State: The Making and Testing of an American Tradition* (New York: New York University Press, 1941), 84–93.

16. On the extension of voting rights, see Chilton Williamson, *American Suffrage: From Property to Democracy, 1760–1860* (Princeton: Princeton University Press, 1960).

17. For an overview, see Walter Millis, *Arms and Men: A Study of American Military History* (New York: Putnam, 1956), esp. Ch. 1. In 1824 Andrew Jackson received 97 percent of the votes cast in Tennessee and 80 percent of those cast in Alabama, which he had opened for settlement. See Lee Benson, "Research Problems in American Political Historiography," in *Common Frontiers in the Social Sciences*, ed. Mirra Komarovsky (Glencoe, Ill.: Free Press, 1957), 146–155. On Lincoln and the militia, see David Herbert Donald, *Lincoln* (London: Jonathan Cape, 1995), 44–45. On the importance of the American militia, see John Shy, *A People Numerous and Armed: Reflections on the Military Struggle for American Independence* (New York: Oxford University Press, 1976), 216–224; and Charles Royster, *A Revolutionary People at War: The Continental Army and American Character, 1775–1783* (Chapel Hill: University of North Carolina Press, 1979), 36–43, 320–330.

18. On the wars and landholdings, see Benjamin Horace Hibbard, *A History of the Public Land Policies* (1924; reprint, Madison: University of Wisconsin Press, 1965), Ch. 7; and James W. Oberly, *Sixty Million Acres: American Veterans and the Public Lands Before the Civil War* (Kent, Ohio: Kent State University Press, 1990). Some gigantic land grants, those of the Hudson valley for example, created conditions similar to the large estates of England, with tenants and rents, but those arrangements were not quietly accepted. See Irving Marks, *Agrarian Conflicts in Colonial New York, 1711–1775* (New York: Columbia University Press, 1940); and Robert E. Shalhope, *Bennington and the Green Mountain Boys: The Emergence of Liberal Democracy in Vermont, 1760–1850* (Baltimore: Johns Hopkins University Press, 1996). The Revolution brought a new landed elite. Ethan Allen was brigadier general of the state militia and an unofficial advisor to the governor. His brother, Ira Allen, was Vermont's treasurer and surveyor general. Ira "was particularly adept at manipulating the laws of the state to his own economic benefit. . . . [He] took advantage of his office as surveyor general by taking his salary in land, amassing by war's end more than one hundred thousand acres" (Shalhope, *Bennington*, 182–183).

19. For a brief account of the administration of justice in Britain early in the nineteenth century, see Norman McCord, *British History 1815–1906* (New York: Oxford University Press, 1991), 67–69. Tocqueville was impressed by the American practice: "During my stay in the United States I witnessed the spontaneous formation of committees in a county for the pursuit and prosecution of a man who had committed a great crime" (Tocqueville, *Democracy*, vol. 1, p. 95).

20. For a brilliant, detailed account of the 1848 democratization and its consequences, see Peter Amann, *Revolution and Mass Democracy: The Paris Club Movement in 1848* (Princeton: Princeton University Press, 1975). Tocqueville was present in Paris at that point as an observer and participant. See his *Recollections* (Garden City, N.Y.: Doubleday, 1970). For a useful overview of the French experience, see Arnold M. Rose, *Theory and Method in the Social Sciences* (Westport, Conn.: Greenwood Press, 1974), Ch. 4. The Napoleonic *Code Civile* prohibited, except by government authorization, "any associations of more than twenty persons with the intention of meeting every day or on certain specified days in order to occupy themselves with religious, literary, political or other matters." That legislation, Rose reports on p. 80, remained in force until 1901 and, except for occupational groups, stifled the development of associations at a time when other countries were gaining experience and building a tradition. Another difference from the Anglo-American experience is noted by Rose on p. 74: "Most associations in France are registered with the police." For a brief but useful comparative overview of the right of assembly, see Harold J. Laski, "Freedom of Association," *Encyclopedia of the Social Sciences*, vol. 3 (New York: Macmillan, 1937), pp. 447–450. See also David Zeldin, "Voluntary Action in Britain," in *Voluntary Action Research: 1974*, ed. David Horton Smith (Lexington, Mass.: Lexington Books, 1974), Ch. 14.

21. See Margaret C. Jacob, *Living the Enlightenment: Freemasonry and Politics in 18th Century Europe* (New York: Oxford University Press, 1991); and A. Ramos Oliveira, *Politics, Economics and Men of Modern Spain* (London: Gollancz, 1946), 42–46. Oliveira, on p. 27, provides this summary statement: "The history of Spanish Liberalism throughout its eventful life was, to an incalculable extent, the history of secret societies and, in particular, of Freemasonry."

22. Tocqueville, *Democracy*, vol. 1, pp. 3, 14.

23. Charles and Mary Beard, *The Rise of American Civilization*, vol 2 (New York: Macmillan, 1927), 730–731. Other commentators made similar observations. See, for example, James Bryce, *The American Commonwealth*, new ed., vol. 2 (New York: Macmillan, 1910), 281–283: "Associations are created, extended, and worked in the United States more quickly and effectively than in any other country." Max Weber also remarked on this tendency, describing the United States as the "association-land par excellence," as quoted in James E. Curtis, "Voluntary Association Joining: A Cross-National Comparative Note," *American Sociological Review* 36 (1971): 872–880. A journalistic account from the early 1950s declared, "Except for the few intellectuals who don't believe in 'joining,' and the very, very poor who can't afford to, practically all adult Americans belong to some club or other." See Floyd Dotson, "Patterns of Voluntary Association Among Urban Working-Class Families," *American Sociological Review* 16 (1951): 687–693. In a 1960 publication several leading academic authors declared, "The industrial society . . . is pluralistic, with a great variety of associations and groups and of large-scale operations; the individual is attached to a variety of such groups and organizations." See Clark Kerr, John T. Dunlop, Frederick H. Harbison, and Charles A. Myers, *Industrialism and Industrial Man* (New York: Oxford University Press, 1964), 26.

24. One of the first of these studies, of employed New York City residents in 1934–1935, was Mirra Komarovsky, "The Voluntary Associations of Urban Dwellers," *American Sociological Review* 11 (1946): 686–698. She cited ten earlier studies, nine of them of small cities or towns. For a summary report on the findings of these early studies, see John C. Scott, "Membership and Participation in Voluntary Associations," *American Sociological Review* 22 (1957): 315–326, esp. pp. 317–318.

25. See Hamilton, *Class and Politics*, 36–37. The principal studies are Charles R. Wright and Herbert H. Hyman, "Voluntary Association Memberships of American Adults: Evidence from National Sample Surveys," *American Sociological Review* 23 (1958): 284–294, and "Trends in Voluntary Association Memberships of American Adults: Replication Based on Secondary Analysis of National Sample Surveys," *American Sociological Review* 36 (1971): 191–206; and Murray Hausknecht, *The Joiners* (New York: Bedminster, 1962), 15–16. The comparative study is Almond and Verba, *Civic Culture*, Ch. 11. For a later overview, see David Knoke, "Associations and Interest Groups," *Annual Review of Sociology* 12 (1986): 1–21. The major survey from 1989 is Verba, Schlozman, and Brady, *Voice and Equality*, 62. The World Values Survey result is reported in Everett C. Ladd, "Civic Participation and American Democracy," *The Public Perspective* 7 (June–July 1996): 10. One study from the early 1960s found 80 percent joining and a majority with multiple memberships. See Nicholas Babchuk and Alan Booth, "Voluntary Association Membership: A Longitudinal Analysis," *American Sociological Review* 34 (1969): 31–45. This high level of reported involvement may stem from the inclusive questions used. Poker, bridge, and other card clubs, and bowling teams, together with Parent–Teacher Associations were the most common memberships. This study sampled the adult population of the state of Nebraska. One national study found some regional variation in membership levels, with the Midwest being above average. See Hamilton, *Class and Politics*, 68. Another early study from the 1950s also found exceptionally high levels of involvement in four diverse San Francisco census tracts (including two of low economic status). See Wendell Bell and Maryanne T. Force, "Urban Neighborhood Types and Participation in Formal Associations," *American Sociological Review* 21 (1956): 25–34. The article does not give the question wording used. An early study by Herbert Goldhamer, based on a sample of Chicago residents, found 70 percent of the men were members of organizations. See his "Some Factors Affecting Participation in Voluntary Associations" (Ph.D. diss., University of Chicago, 1942). A Detroit study found 80 percent of the men were members. See Morris Axelrod, "A Study of Formal and Informal Group Participation in a Large Urban Community" (Ph.D. diss., University of Michigan, 1953). Both of these studies are reported in Bell and Force, "Urban Neighborhood Types." For a brief summary of Axelrod's findings, see his "Urban Structure and Social Participation," *American Sociological Review* 21 (1956): 13–18. The overall level of membership, for men and women, was 63 percent. Thirty-one percent reported only a single membership. The level of participation in those associations, on the whole, was very low.

26. For further consideration and evidence on the problems discussed here, see Frank R. Baumgartner and Jack L. Walker, "Survey Research and Membership in Voluntary Associations," *American Journal of Political Science* 32 (1988): 908–928; and Tom W. Smith, "Trends in Voluntary Group Membership: Comments on Baumgartner and Walker," *American Journal of Political Science* 34 (1990): 646–661, and a reply on pp. 662–670. For the bias in reports of church-affiliated groups, see Smith, "Trends," 654, note 11, and Baumgartner and Walker, "Reply," 667.

27. On the unions and their activities, see J. David Greenstone, *Labor in American Politics* (New York: Knopf, 1969); Richard B. Freeman and James L. Medoff, *What Do Unions Do?* (New York: Basic Books, 1984); Michael Goldfield, *The Decline of Organized Labor in the United States* (Chicago: University of Chicago Press, 1987); Daniel B. Cornfield, *Becoming a Mighty Voice: Conflict and Change in the United Furniture Workers of America* (New York: Russell Sage, 1989); William H. Form, *Segmented Labor, Fractured Politics: Labor Politics in American Life* (New York: Plenum, 1995); and Max Green, *Epitaph for American Labor: How Union Leaders Lost Touch with America* (Washington, D.C.: AEI Press, 1996).

28. Almond and Verba, *Civic Culture*, 305–307. See also Verba, Schlozman, and Brady, *Voice and Equality*, 62–65, who found 48 percent in organizations seen as taking political stands. On the instrumental–expressive distinction, see Hamilton, *Class and Politics*, 37–38.

29. The General Social Survey follows the procedure developed in Sidney Verba and Norman H. Nie, *Participation in America: Political Democracy and Social Equality* (New York: Harper & Row, 1972), 176–181. The GSS made one significant change, adding "Church-affiliated groups" to the list. Some important modifications appear in Verba, Schlozman, and Brady, *Voice and Equality*, 59–61, 91–93.

30. Some authors have focused on the Americans-as-joiners theme, thus making a cultural interpretation of Tocqueville. Curtis, "Voluntary Association Joining," found that Canadians, in 1968, had a higher level of joining than Americans. In a later study, he and his colleagues found the U.S. level equaled or surpassed in Canada, Australia, the Netherlands, Northern Ireland, Norway, and Sweden. See James E. Curtis, Edward G. Grabb, and Douglas E. Baer, "Voluntary Association Membership in Fifteen Countries: A Comparative Analysis," *American Sociological Review* 57 (1992): 139–152. The lowest overall levels of reported membership were in Italy, France, and Spain. Verba, Schlozman, and Brady, *Voice and Equality*, 81, report results from a 1981 Gallup study of twelve nations. The United States led all the others in joining (at 76%), the next contenders being Northern Ireland (66%), Denmark (62%), and the Netherlands (62%). No figures were given for Canada or Australia. The lowest levels of joining, by far, appeared in Spain (31%), Japan (29%), France (27%), and Italy (26%). The cultural argument is explored further in Edward G. Grabb and James E. Curtis, "Voluntary Association Activity in English Canada, French Canada, and the United States: A Multivariate Analysis," *Canadian Journal of Sociology* 17 (1992): 371–388. This article focuses on the arguments in Seymour Martin Lipset, *The First New Nation* (New York: Basic Books, 1963), and *Continental Divide: The Values and Institutions of Canada and the United States* (New York: Routledge, 1990).

31. Robert A. Dahl, *Who Governs? Democracy and Power in an American City* (New Haven: Yale University Press, 1961), 228. Another important contribution dealing with the same themes and the same city is G. William Domhoff, *Who Really Rules? New Haven and Community Power Reexamined* (Santa Monica, Calif.: Goodyear, 1978).

32. See also Scott, "Membership and Participation," 315–326. His detailed study is based on a survey in Bennington, Vermont. He found a majority, 64 percent, with at least one membership. Some 15 percent held four or more memberships. They held 50 percent of the total.

33. Scott's study is a notable exception to this general indifference to "the money question." Annual membership expenditures in 1947 ranged from less than $5 to $75 or more. One-fifth of the joiners paid almost four-fifths of the total membership costs.

Also of interest is that 16 percent of the members held all of the officerships; 14 percent held all of the committeeships. See ibid., 318–319.

34. Robert D. Putnam, "The Strange Disappearance of Civic America," *The American Prospect* 24 (1996): 34–48, "Bowling Alone: America's Declining Social Capital," *Journal of Democracy* (6 January 1995): 65–78, and "Tuning In, Tuning Out: The Strange Disappearance of Social Capital in America," *PS: Political Science and Politics* 24 (1995): 664–683. See also, Baumgartner and Walker, "Survey Research"; Smith, "Trends"; Everett C. Ladd, "Civic Participation," 1–22, and *The Ladd Report* (New York: Free Press, 1999); and Pamela Paxton, "Is Social Capital Declining in the United States? A Multiple Indicator Assessment," *American Journal of Sociology* 105 (1999): 88–128.

35. The merges of several studies might conceivably hide something. The detailed exploration showed the highest mean number of memberships, 1.94, in the 1974 study. The means edged downward in the 1970s, reaching a low of 1.59 in 1980. The next study, from 1983, found a relatively high figure of 1.86. From 1984 to 1994 the means fluctuated, but remained generally at a high level. Apart from one outlier (1.69 in 1991), the range was 1.75 to 1.87. The 1974 study had a quota sample component at the block level which, conceivably, might account for the difference vis-à-vis the later studies. The 1975 study had a split-half sample, half quota, half full probability. An exploration showed no difference between the two halves in either the number of memberships or the types joined.

36. The curvilinear pattern may be seen also in data for six countries in Curtis, "Voluntary Associat'on Joining," 877 (from the Almond–Verba study).

37. On the financial satisfaction of the elderly, see Richard F. Hamilton and James D. Wright, *The State of the Masses* (New York: Aldine, 1986), 210–211. The General Social Surveys show the same pattern. In the early 1990s, 22 percent of persons age eighteen to twenty-nine reported they were "pretty well" satisfied with their financial situation. The positive assessments increased linearly in the older cohorts, reaching 48 percent among those eighty and over. Similar patterns appeared in the four other GSS merges. After 1964—after the baby boom—the family size declined, which would ordinarily mean a commensurate increase of the empty-nest period for husbands and wives. One reasonable expectation, accordingly, is that leisure-time involvement will continue to increase in the first decade of the new millennium.

38. Stephen J. Cutler, "Age Differences in Voluntary Association Memberships," *Social Forces* 55 (1976): 43–56. On the income question, overall there is a curvilinear pattern, with total family income declining in the older age categories. But per capita income continues to increase. See Richard F. Hamilton, *Marxism, Revisionism, and Leninism: Explication, Assessment, and Commentary* (Westport, Conn.: Praeger, 2000), Ch. 3. One cannot cover all relevant factors in this brief overview. Life-cycle position, which is not a precise equivalent to age, also deserves attention. See Marvin B. Sussman, "Activity Patterns of Post-Parental Couples and Their Relationship to Family Continuity," *Marriage and Family Living* 17 (1955): 338–341; Joseph Harry, "Family Localism and Social Participation," *American Journal of Sociology* 75 (1970): 821–827; and David Knoke and Randall Thomson, "Voluntary Association Membership Trends and the Family Life Cycle," *Social Forces* 56 (1977): 48–65. Gender, not unexpectedly, is another factor influencing membership choices. Men are much more likely to be involved in sports, fraternal, labor union, and veterans' organizations. Women are much more likely to be involved in church and school organizations. The differences are small or nonexistent for some organizations, such as hobby, service, and political groups.

39. Although religion is "learned in the family," the academic specialties—the sociology of religion and family sociology—show little overlap. On this point, see Darwin L. Thomas and Marie Cornwall, "Religion and Family in the 1980s: Discovery and Development," *Journal of Marriage and the Family* 52 (1990): 983–992. See also Ross M. Stolzenberg, Mary Blair-Loy, and Linda J. Waite, "Religious Participation in Early Adulthood: Age and Family Life Cycle Effects on Church Membership," *American Sociological Review* 60 (1995): 84–103. Divorced persons are less involved than the married; separated persons are the least involved of all. The average number of memberships for married, divorced, and separated persons of age thirty to forty-nine, respectively, are 2.01, 1.74, and 1.47. For those of age fifty or more, the figures are 1.95, 1.55, and 1.22 (GSS merge, 1990–1994). The findings summarized here were confirmed with GSS data from 1984–1989, the pattern among the young being even more pronounced. Union membership shows no difference by marital status in any of the age segments. This linkage, of course, is not voluntary in the same way as the other memberships. This pattern was also found in GSS 1984–1989.

40. Louis Wirth, "Urbanism as a Way of Life," in *Classic Essays on the Culture of Cities*, ed. Richard Sennett (New York: Appleton–Century–Crofts, 1969), 162.

41. On the character of the American press in the nineteenth century, see Frank Luther Mott, *American Journalism: A History, 1690–1960*, 3d ed. (New York: Macmillan, 1962), Ch. 9. See also Michael Emery, Edwin Emery, and Nancy L. Roberts, *The Press and America: An Interpretive History of the Mass Media*, 8th ed. (Boston: Allyn and Bacon, 1996). The Republican candidates received a majority of daily newspaper endorsements in all elections from 1932 to 1960. The Republican advantage was even greater in terms of circulation, reaching 80 percent in 1952. The 1964 election brought a striking reversal of the historic pattern. Lyndon Johnson gained a plurality of the endorsements, 42 percent (those newspapers having 62 percent of the circulation). Ronald Reagan received only a plurality in 1980. Bush received an even smaller plurality, 31 percent in 1988. In 1992, in a second reversal, Clinton received a modest plurality, 18 percent. The new trend was noncommitment, at 42 percent in 1980, 55 percent in 1988, and 67 percent in 1992. See Harold W. Stanley and Richard G. Niemi, *Vital Statistics on American Politics*, 5th ed. (Washington, D.C.: CQ Press, 1995), 71–73. The patterns of endorsement are very loosely correlated with the actual results, no "powerful" media impacts being apparent. In 1948, 65 percent of the nation's daily newspapers endorsed Thomas E. Dewey, the Republican candidate. That understates his advantage, since those newspapers had 79 percent of total daily circulation. Harry Truman was endorsed by 15 percent of the newspapers, which had only 10 percent of the circulation. Despite the serious disadvantage in press support, Truman won the election.

42. David Halberstam, *The Powers That Be* (New York: Knopf, 1979), 116–117. Another instance of "old school" practice appears in the case of *The Repository*, the leading newspaper of Canton, Ohio. Until 1996, over the course of 177 years, it had never endorsed a Democrat for president. Clayton G. Horn was the editor for four decades through to the 1970s. In the 1950s he "banned the name of the Democratic Mayor, Charles Babcock, from the paper, referring to him as 'a city official.'" For more detail, see Michael Winerip, "At 'President McKinley's Paper,' the Editors Take Endorsements Seriously," *New York Times*, 2 November 1996, sec. 1, p. 7.

43. For the transformation of the *Los Angeles Times*, see Halberstam, *The Powers*, Ch. 8. That work also deals with the changes at CBS, *Time*, the *Washington Post*, and

the *New York Times*. For another account of the change at the *New York Times*, see Gay Talese, *The Kingdom and the Power* (New York: New American Library, 1969). For brief treatments of the changes, see Michael J. Robinson, "Television and American Politics: 1956–1976," *The Public Interest* 48 (Summer 1977): 3–39; Stanley Rothman, "The Mass Media in Post-Industrial America," in *The Third Century: America as a Post-Industrial Society*, ed. Seymour Martin Lipset (Stanford: Hoover Institution Press, 1979), Ch. 15; Robert Lerner and Stanley Rothman, "The Media, the Polity, and Public Opinion," in *Political Behavior Annual*, vol. 1 (Boulder, Colo.: Westview Press, 1986). For the changes in motion pictures, see Michael Medved, *Hollywood vs. America: Popular Culture and the War on Traditional Values* (New York: HarperCollins, 1992), Chs. 17 and 18, esp. pp. 282–285. For more detail, see S. Robert Lichter, Stanley Rothman, and Linda S. Lichter, *The Media Elite: America's New Powerbrokers* (Bethesda, Md.: Adler & Adler, 1986); Jeremy Tunstall, *Communications Deregulation: The Unleashing of America's Communications Industry* (New York: Blackwell, 1986); and Joel Smith, *Understanding the Media: A Sociology of Mass Communication* (Cresskill, N.J.: Hampton, 1995), Ch. 6.

44. For a review of newspaper history, see Mott, *American Journalism*, and, for the recent concentration, David Pearce Demers, *The Menace of the Corporate Newspaper: Fact or Fiction?* (Ames: Iowa State University Press, 1996), Ch. 2. Demers, on p. 314, reports "that chain and large newspapers are more vigorous editorially and that large newspapers place much more emphasis on product quality" (see especially Chs. 8, 9, and 10). For the argument of corporate control, see Edward S. Herman and Robert W. McChesney, *The Global Media: The New Missionaries of Corporate Capitalism* (London: Cassell, 1997).

45. For this history, see Richard Kluger, *The Paper: The Life and Death of the New York Herald Tribune* (New York: Knopf, 1986), 672–674, 726–727. For accounts of similar dynamics in other contexts, see Milton Moskowitz, "Who Killed Colliers?" *Nation*, 5 January 1957, 3–5; Norman Cousins, "The Death of 'Look,'" *Saturday Review*, 7 October 1971, 26–27; and, for the collapse of the *Saturday Evening Post*, see Otto Friedrich, *Decline and Fall: The Struggle for Power at a Great American Magazine* (London: Michael Joseph, 1972).

46. Theodore White, *In Search of History: A Personal Adventure* (New York: Warner, 1978), 506–507. See also Lincoln Sitkoff, *The Struggle for Black Equality: 1954–1992*, rev. ed. (New York: Hill and Wang, 1993), 47–49. For the media treatment of the Selma events of March 1965, see p. 176.

47. On the new social movements, see Donald Von Eschen, Jerome Kirk, and Maurice Pinard, "The Organizational Substructure of Disorderly Politics," *Social Forces* 49 (1971): 529–544; J. Craig Jenkins and Craig M. Eckert, "Channeling Black Insurgency: Elite Patronage and Professional Social Movement Organizations in the Development of the Black Movement," *American Sociological Review* 51 (1986): 812–829; J. Craig Jenkins, "Interpreting the Stormy 1960s: Three Theories in Search of a Political Age," *Research in Political Sociology* 3 (1987): 269–303; and Todd Gitlin, *The Whole World Is Watching: Mass Media in the Making and Unmaking of the New Left* (Berkeley and Los Angeles: University of California Press, 1980). See also John D. McCarthy and Mayer N. Zald, "Resource Mobilization and Social Movements: A Partial Theory," *American Journal of Sociology* 82 (1977): 1212–1241. They write on pp. 1229–1330, "Much publicity is dependent upon [an organization's] ability to induce the media to give free attention. . . . By staging events which will possibly be

'newsworthy,' by attending to the needs of news organizations, and by cultivating representatives of the media, [organizations] may manipulate media coverage of their activities more or less successfully."

48. As need arises, journalists reach out to the advocacy groups. Many advocates, understandably, seek to establish and maintain their contacts with media personnel. For a review of the approaches used by various pressure groups, see Kay Lehman Schlozman and John T. Tierney, *Organized Interests and American Democracy* (New York: Harper & Row, 1986), 178–184. Advocacy groups may also use oppositional tactics: boycotts, legal measures, or, for radio and television outlets, a threat to licensing renewal. These tactics are detailed in Kathryn C. Montgomery, *Target: Prime Time: Advocacy Groups and the Struggle Over Entertainment Television* (New York: Oxford University Press, 1989). The media, she indicates, have developed countering tactics.

49. "Liberal Causes Cash in on a Rash of Conservatism," *New York Times*, 29 October 1989, sec. 3, p. 13. In one instance, ACLU growth was unintended. In the fall of 1988 President George Bush attacked his opponent, Michael Dukakis, describing him as a "card-carrying member" of the organization. One apparent effect was the addition of 60,000 members. On the ACLU, see Richard E. Morgan, *The "Rights Industry" in Our Time* (New York: Basic Books, 1984); and William A. Donohue, *The Politics of the American Civil Liberties Union* (New Brunswick, N.J.: Transaction Books, 1985), and *Twilight of Liberty: The Legacy of the ACLU* (New Brunswick, N.J.: Transaction Books, 1994).

50. "Liberal Causes," *New York Times*, and Marlise Simons, "For Greenpeace Guerillas, Environmentalism Is Again a Growth Industry," *New York Times*, 8 July 1995, sec. 1, p. 3.

51. Keith Schneider, "Big Environment Hits a Recession," *New York Times*, 1 January 1995, sec. 3, p. 4; Neil A. Lewis, "Groups Plan to Exploit G.O.P. Rise," *New York Times*, 28 November 1994, sec. A, p. 15; and, on the same theme, Scott McCartney, "How Newt Gingrich Helps Raise Millions for Liberal Causes," *Wall Street Journal*, 28 November 1994, A1.

52. Robert Michels, *Political Parties: A Sociological Study of the Oligarchical Tendencies of Modern Democracy*, trans. Eden Paul and Cedar Paul [1915] (1911; reprint, Glencoe, Ill.: Free Press, 1958). For accounts of the man and his work, see Juan J. Linz, "Michels," *International Encyclopedia of the Social Sciences*, vol. 10, pp. 265–272; and Seymour Martin Lipset, *Revolution and Counterrevolution: Change and Persistence in Social Structures* (New York: Basic Books, 1968), Ch. 12. Lipset, on p. 417, describes Michels's work as "one of the twentieth century's most influential books." For a critical study, see Philip J. Cook, "Robert Michels's Political Parties in Perspective," *Journal of Politics* 33 (1971): 773–796. Cook points up the translation error in the English edition. Michels's argument, it will be noted, closely parallels the sweeping claim of bureaucratization put forward by Max Weber, the subject of the next chapter.

53. Seymour Martin Lipset, Martin A. Trow, and James S. Coleman, *Union Democracy* (1956; reprint, Garden City, N.Y.: Anchor Books, 1962); Herman Benson, "The Fight for Union Democracy," in *Unions in Transition: Entering the Second Century*, ed. Seymour Martin Lipset (San Francisco: ICS Press, 1986), Ch. 13; Kay Stratton, "Union Democracy in the International Typographical Union: Thirty Years Later," *Journal of Labor Research* 10 (1989): 119–134; Freeman and Medoff, *What Do Unions Do?* Ch. 14 (quotation from p. 220); and U.S. Department of Labor, *Directory of National Unions and Employee Associations, 1973* (Washington, D.C.: U.S. Govern-

ment Printing Office, 1973), 62. A subsequent study based on a larger sample, one restricted to well-paid officeholders, reported the "primacy of age as a determining force in national union office turnover," also effectively a confirmation of the iron law. See Marcus H. Sandver, "Officer Turnover in National Unions: A Time Series Analysis," *Bulletin of Business Research* 53 (January 1978): 6–7. Turnover in office is more frequent in small union locals, basically in units where the rewards of office are modest. See Leon Applebaum, "Officer Turnover and Salary Structures in Local Unions," *Industrial and Labor Relations Review* 19 (1966): 224–230; and Leon Applebaum and Harry R. Blaine, "Compensation and Turnover of Union Officers," *Industrial Relations* 14 (1973): 156–157. Philip M. Marcus focused on "responsiveness" to the membership (as opposed to turnover), in his "Union Conventions and Executive Boards: A Formal Analysis of Organizational Structure," *American Sociological Review* 31 (1966): 61–70. The study, however, contains no direct measure of responsiveness, the entire case being based on inference. Two important alternative hypotheses appear, without further discussion, in a late footnote on p. 70; namely, that union presidents "have almost complete control over conventions [and that they] select and control committees." David Kwavnick describes an example of the extreme case, a union whose policies went directly against its own members' interests, in his "Pressure-Group Demands and Organizational Objectives: The CNTU, the Lapalme Affair, and National Bargaining Units," *Canadian Journal of Political Science* 6 (1973): 582–601. For other reviews of trade union experience, see Cornfield, *Becoming a Mighty Voice*, 13–18. An iron law would apply to all organizations. For a detailed analysis of private corporations, with the managers ordinarily dominating the outside directors, the elected representatives of the stockholders, see Myles L. Mace, *Directors: Myth and Reality* (Boston: Harvard Business School Press, 1986). For an analysis of the iron law in still another context, see Paul M. Harrison, *Authority and Power in the Free Church Tradition: A Social Case Study of the American Baptist Convention* (Princeton: Princeton University Press, 1959).

54. Mancur Olson, *The Logic of Collective Action: Public Goods and the Theory of Groups* (Cambridge: Harvard University Press, 1965), Ch. 1. For further discussion, references, and evidence on the motives for political action, see Verba, Schlozman, and Brady, *Voice and Equality*, Chs. 4 and 5.

55. On the Farm Bureau, see Olson, *Logic of Collective Action*, 148–159. In 1994 the AARP took in more from insurance fees ($164.9 million) than from dues ($145.7 million). It also had $47.3 million in advertising revenue. The largest part of their $343.5 million in expenses went for publications ($100 million), followed by "member services and acquisition" ($73.7 million). Lobbying and research ($35.1 million) was obviously only a small part of their effort, roughly 10 percent of the total. More was given for "activities and administration" ($42.2 million) than for lobbying. See Milt Freudenheim, "A.A.R.P. Will License Its Name to Managed Health Care Plans," *New York Times*, 29 April 1996, sec. A, p. 1.

56. Michael Hanks and Bruce K. Eckland, "Adult Voluntary Associations and Adolescent Socialization," *Sociological Quarterly* 19 (1978): 481–490; and Michael Hanks, "Youth, Voluntary Associations and Political Socialization," *Social Forces* 60 (1981): 211–223; Robert W. Hodge and Donald J. Treiman, "Social Participation and Social Status," *American Sociological Review* 33 (1968): 722–740; and Edgar Litt, "Civic Education, Community Norms, and Political Indoctrination," *American Sociological Review* 28 (1963): 69–75. It is easy to assume that class per se is the decisive factor,

that a person born and raised in a given class will benefit or be penalized by virtue of that class position. Hodge and Treiman offer an important specification on p. 722: "Membership appears to be at least as strongly influenced by parent's level of participation in such organizations as by respondent's socioeconomic status."

57. Sometime in the 1980s Oprah Winfrey predicted that one-fifth of all heterosexuals would be "dead of AIDS" by 1990. Gene Antonio, author of *The AIDS Cover-UP?* predicted that as many as 64 million people in the United States would be infected with HIV by 1990. The book had claimed sales of 300,000. From Michael Fumento, "AIDS So Far," *Commentary* 92 (December 1991): 46. For more, see Fumento, *The Myth of Heterosexual AIDS* (New York: Basic Books, 1990), Ch. 1.

58. For the evidence on per capita expenditures, see Hamilton, *Marxism*, 121.

59. David Horton Smith, "Churches Are Generally Ignored in Contemporary Voluntary Action Research: Causes and Consequences," *Review of Religious Research* 24 (1983): 295–303. Also see Thomas and Cornwall, "Religion and Family." Another example of compartmentalization should be noted: This chapter has a sociological focus. It raises questions about the determinants of involvement and about the interpersonal effects of that involvement. The actual exercise of power, the processes of influencing, appears in another literature, that of political science. See, for example, Schlozman and Tierney, *Organized Interests*, Chs. 7–14.

60. See Hamilton and Wright, *State of the Masses*, 124–139. Chapters 3 and 5 review evidence on goals and concerns and on satisfactions and dissatisfactions.

61. On the choice of means, see Verba and Nie, *Participation in America*, 31 and, for more, Chs. 3 and 4.

62. A later example of such elastic usage appears in Rose, *Theory and Method*, Ch. 3.

63. See Hamilton, *Marxism*, Ch. 2. For many social scientists, money is a taboo subject. Analyses of revolutions, for example, rarely consider the money costs and the financing questions. For an unusually frank and open discussion of the importance of money, see Alexander Solzhenitsyn's fictionalized account, *Lenin in Zurich*, trans. H. T. Willetts (New York: Farrar, Straus and Giroux, 1976), 14–17, 73, 120, and elsewhere.

64. As shown in Table 2.2, professionals lead in associational involvements, outdoing managers by a fair-sized margin. The managers are better paid, both the men and women outdoing equivalent professionals by some $4,000 per year in the 1990s. But the professionals have a shorter average workweek. Overall, male professionals have three more hours of free time than the managers; female professionals have six more hours per week. This is based on the merged GSS studies, 1990–1994.

65. A West German survey presented respondents with a series of statements about their free time. One of these read, "I am physically rather exhausted, my work is physically very demanding" ("Bin ich köperlich ziemlich fertig, meine Arbeit strength köperlich sehr an"). A majority of farm laborers and farmers agreed with the statement, along with a sizable minority of workers, the respective percentages being 63, 57, and 44. Among salaried white-collar workers, 16 percent agreed; among civil servants, 10 percent. Elisabeth Noelle and Erich Peter Neumann, eds., *Jahrbuch der Öffentlichen Meinung, 1958–1964* (Allensbach: Verlag für Demoskopie, 1965), 386.

66. Small-town dwellers are less likely to talk politics and, on a wide range of questions, more likely to say "don't know" or give no response. For discussion and evidence, see Hamilton, *Class and Politics*, 259–267. A selective factor also operates; nonconformists are likely to leave the small-community settings, moving off to larger and more open communities.

67. For the history and the outcomes, see Daniel P. Moynihan, *Maximum Feasible Misunderstanding: Community Action in the War on Poverty* (New York: Free Press, 1970), esp. Ch. 7. For a brief review of relevant studies, see Russell L. Curtis, Jr. and Louis A. Zurcher, Jr., "Voluntary Associations and the Social Integration of the Poor," *Social Problems* 18 (1971): 339–357. For more detail, See Louis A. Zurcher, Jr., *Poverty Warriors: The Human Experience of Planned Social Intervention* (Austin: University of Texas Press, 1970); and Louis A. Zurcher, Jr. and Charles M. Bonjean, eds., *Planned Social Intervention: An Interdisciplinary Anthology* (Scranton, Pa.: Chandler, 1970).

68. For an overview, see John R. Everett, "The Decentralization Fiasco and Our Ghetto Schools," *Atlantic*, December 1968, 71–73. For more detail, see Martin Mayer, *The Teachers' Strike: New York, 1968* (New York: Harper & Row, 1969). For the later effects, see Matthew Purdy, "Web of Patronage in Schools Grips Those Who Can Undo It," *New York Times*, 14 May 1996, sec. A, p. 1. The Ford Foundation was very much involved in the "war on poverty," there too supporting the "empowerment" efforts. See Moynihan, *Maximum Feasible Misunderstanding*, xxii–xxv, xxiv, 34–36, 40–43.

69. On creaming, see Curtis and Zurcher, "Voluntary Associations," 347. See also the summary judgments contained in Moynihan, *Maximum Feasible Misunderstanding*, 130, 149. Moynihan writes on p. 137, "The major immediate beneficiaries of these programs have been non-poor persons who have been afforded the opportunity of executive, technical and professional positions in the program." Elections were held among the poor to choose representatives for community-action-program governing boards. The turnout figures indicate very limited interest: 4.2 percent in Cleveland, 2.7 percent in Philadelphia, and 0.7 percent in Los Angeles. Smaller communities "sometimes got larger turnouts," but even these were very low. The Michels quotation is from *Political Parties*, 294.

70. Prior to the Anti-Socialist Law (1878), Wilhelm Liebknecht's earnings "soared to about six times that of the average worker he represented." In 1885, when that repressive law was still in force, his "various literary, editorial, and agitational enterprises earned him an incredible 7,000 marks a year." That income put him "among the highest-paid people in the nation." From Raymond H. Dominick, *Wilhelm Liebknecht and the Founding of the German Social Democratic Party* (Chapel Hill: University of North Carolina Press, 1982), 262–263, 331. August Bebel's income, Dominick reports on p. 385, easily exceeded 10,000 marks a year. In the late 1880s he purchased "a handsome estate" in Switzerland. The three-storied house, called the "Villa Julie," was a lake-front property facing the Zürichersee. See also William Harvey Maehl, *August Bebel: Shadow Emperor of the German Workers* (Philadelphia: American Philosophical Society, 1980), 361. Ferdinand Lassalle, the leader of the other principal branch of German socialism, was known to have been a wealthy man. One biographer reports on the extent of that wealth: "Among over 5 million heads of Prussian households (1855), not more than 1,500 had more income than Lassalle." See Richard W. Reichard, *Crippled from Birth: German Social Democracy 1844–1870* (Ames: Iowa State University Press, 1969), 139.

71. Jackie Presser, at one time the president of the International Brotherhood of Teamsters, received four salaries in 1984 that totaled $530,000. He was the nation's highest-paid union official. Presser received $228,500 as president of the 1.9-million-member union (plus $45,000 for expenses). In addition, he was "paid a salary of

$224,000 by Local 507, $59,500 as president of Teamsters Joint Council 41, and $18,100 as president of the Ohio Conference of Teamsters." The second most highly paid labor official was Harold Friedman, one of the Teamster's seventeen international vice presidents, a close associate of Presser's. He derived his salary (and expense money) from four posts in the Teamsters plus a fifth position as president of "a Cleveland local of the Bakery, Confectionary and Tobacco Workers union." "Teamster Leader Was Paid $530,000," from the *New York Times*, 2 May 1985, sec. A, p. 22. On Presser, see Kenneth C. Crowe, *Collision: How the Rank and File Took Back the Teamsters* (New York: Scribner, 1993); and F. C. Duke Zeller, *Devil's Pact: Inside the World of the Teamster's Union* (Secaucus, N.J.: Carol, 1996).

72. James T. Bennett and Thomas J. DiLorenzo, *Unhealthy Charities: Hazardous to Your Health and Wealth* (New York: Basic Books, 1994). For an earlier study of this topic, see Richard Carter, *The Gentle Legions* (New York: Doubleday, 1961). Also of interest in this connection is Robert N. Proctor's analysis of the "social construction of ignorance." See his *Cancer Wars: How Politics Shapes What We Know and Don't Know About Cancer* (New York: Basic Books, 1995). For still another context, see Michael Maren, *The Road to Hell: The Ravaging Effects of Foreign Aid and International Charity* (New York: Free Press, 1997).

73. Richard F. Hamilton, *Restraining Myths* (New York: Sage, Halsted, Wiley, 1975), Ch. 7, esp. pp. 245–246.

74. Ibid. Much of the information reported there comes from Harmon Zeigler, *The Politics of Small Business* (Washington, D.C.: Public Affairs Press, 1961). See also R. Kenneth Godwin and Robert Cameron Mitchell, "The Implications of Direct Mail for Political Organizations," *Social Science Quarterly* 65 (1984): 829–839. For a study of sponsored organizations, see Richard P. Taub, George P. Surgeon, Sara Lindholm, Phyllis Betts Otti, and Amy Bridges, "Urban Voluntary Associations, Locality Based and Externally Induced," *American Journal of Sociology* 83 (1977): 425–442.

75. For a comprehensive account, see James T. Bennett and Thomas J. DiLorenzo, *Destroying Democracy: How Government Funds Partisan Politics* (Washington, D.C.: Cato Institute, 1985).

76. The major small-business organizations in the United States routinely take conservative positions on most issues, thus providing support for a standard claim about "petty bourgeois" attitudes. An investigation of survey responses found small-business owners to be generally liberal in outlook, little different from manual workers. For the contrast of attitudes and organizational pronouncements, see Hamilton, *Restraining Myths*, Chs. 2 and 7.

77. Baumgartner and Walker, "Survey Research," 908.

78. The disparity in procedures—the double standard—is striking. Many intellectuals and the informed public bring immense suspicion and skepticism to the discussion of public opinion polls. But faced with the pronouncement of associations speaking "on behalf of" a vast membership, the skepticism, that intense "methodological" concern, vanishes. See Hamilton, *Restraining Myths*, 249–250.

79. On the activities of the policy-oriented research centers, see Domhoff, *Higher Circles*, Chs. 5, 6; G. William Domhoff, *The Powers That Be: Processes of Ruling Class Domination in America* (New York: Vintage, 1978), Ch. 3; James Allen Smith, *The Idea Brokers: Think Tanks and the Rise of the New Policy Elite* (New York: Free Press, 1991); and David M. Ricci, *The Transformation of American Politics: The New Washington and the Rise of Think Tanks* (New Haven: Yale University Press, 1993).

The passage of a major welfare reform measure in 1996 was followed by a mobilization of the think tanks, right and left, to generate evidence on the impacts. See John Harwood, "Think Tanks Battle to Judge the Impact of Welfare Overhaul," *Wall Street Journal*, 30 January 1997, p. A1. Three book-length accounts describing the rise of conservative research organizations are John S. Saloma III, *Ominous Politics: The New Conservative Labyrinth* (New York: Hill and Wang, 1984); Sidney Blumenthal, *The Rise of the Counter-Establishment: From Conservative Ideology to Political Power* (New York: Times Books, 1986); and Joseph G. Peschek, *Policy-Planning Organizations: Elite Agendas and America's Rightward Turn* (Philadelphia: Temple University Press, 1987).

80. See Garland F. White, Janet Katz, and Kathryn E. Scarborough, "The Impact of Professional Football Games Upon Violent Assaults on Women," *Violence and Victims* 7 (1992): 157–171. For an after-the-fact review, see Janet E. Katz and Garland F. White, "Engaging the Media: A Case Study of the Politics of Crime and the Media," *Social Justice* 20, no. 3–4 (1993): 57–68. The episode, understandably, received considerable media attention. An outstanding account, one that had much impact, is Ken Ringle, "Debunking the 'Day of Dread' for Women," the *Washington Post*, 31 January 1993, sec. A, pp. 1, 16. Others appeared in "Author: Abuse Study Misquoted," (author unknown), *USA Today*, 1 February 1993, p. 7C; Alan M. Dershowitz, "The Myth of the Super Bowl and Battered Women," the *Los Angeles Times*, 7 February 1993, sec. M, p. 5; Robin Abcarian, "Final Score: Women Often Lose on Big Game Days," the *Los Angeles Times*, 14 February 1993, sec. E, pp. 1, 5; and "Review & Outlook: Football's Day of Dread," the *Wall Street Journal*, 5 February 1993, sec. A, p. 10. None of these subsequent accounts reported the parallel finding, the correlation of increased violence against males. For another instructive case study, see the following: H. Bruce Franklin, *M.I.A. or Mythmaking in America* (New York: Lawrence Hill Books, 1992); Susan Katz Keating, *Prisoners of Hope: Exploiting the POW/MIA Myth in America* (New York: Random House, 1994); Malcolm McConnell, *Inside Hanoi's Secret Archives: Solving the MIA Mystery* (New York: Simon & Schuster, 1995).

81. Laurie Goodstein, "Coalition's Woes May Hinder Goals of Christian Right," *New York Times*, 2 August 1999, sec. A, p. 1.

82. On the liberalism of media elites, see Allen H. Barton, "Consensus and Conflict Among American Leaders," *Public Opinion Quarterly* 38 (1974–1975): 507–530; S. Robert Lichter, Stanley Rothman, and Linda S. Lichter, *The Media Elite: America's New Powerbrokers* (Bethesda, Md.: Adler & Adler, 1986); and Robert Lerner, Althea K. Nagai, and Stanley Rothman, *American Elites* (New Haven: Yale University Press, 1996). For evidence on the values of journalists, see Leo Rosten, *The Washington Correspondents* (New York: Harcourt, Brace, 1937); Stephen Hess, *The Washington Reporters* (Washington, D.C.: Brookings, 1981); S. Robert Lichter, Linda S. Lichter, and Stanley Rothman, *Prime Time: How TV Portrays American Culture* (Washington, D.C.: Regnery, 1994); and Montgomery, *Target: Prime Time*. For a somewhat different image based on a cross-section of journalists (not just those of the elite press), see David H. Weaver and G. Cleveland Wilhoit, *The American Journalist: A Portrait of U.S. Newspapermen and Their Work* (Bloomington: Indiana University Press, 1986). For a challenge to the Lichters and Rothman, see Herbert J. Gans, "Are U.S. Journalists Dangerously Liberal?" *Columbia Journalism Review* 24 (November–December 1985): 29–33. Gans argues that journalists' "personal political beliefs are irrelevant, or virtually so, to the way they covered the news," and provides a range of sources including his *Deciding What's News* (New York: Pantheon, 1979). Schlozman

and Tierney, *Organized Interests*, 179, report that business organizations "perceive an antibusiness bias in the news media—an unwillingness to treat the business viewpoint objectively or to give the business community equal access for the presentation of its views."

83. The presentation here is necessarily much oversimplified, suggesting the polar extremes: direct orders from publisher and/or editor versus journalistic autonomy (or relative autonomy). Even under the "old regime," before relaxation, many media organizations avoided direct orders, instead depending on gentler controls involving what was called "sensing policy." Editors provided clues as to what was desired, such as placement of or "spiking" (submergence) of stories, and journalists responded; that is, conformed. The key account of this procedure is Warren Breed, "Social Control in the Newsroom: A Functional Analysis," *Social Forces* 33 (1955): 326–335. For a wide range of examples showing the diversity of controls and the erratic record of "success," see Kluger, *The Paper*, 462, 480–481, 487, 493, 512, 538–539, 540, 558, 583–584, 586, 587, 589, 597, 598–599, 628, 632, 635–636, 665, 684, 693, 695, 707. Some of the diversity and complication also appears in Friedrich, *Decline and Fall*.

84. On Beaumarchais, see Hamilton, *Marxism*, 14–15.

85. On the Chartists, see McCord, *British History*, 146–152; on 1848 in France, see Richard F. Hamilton, *The Bourgeois Epoch: Marx and Engels on Britain, France, and Germany* (Chapel Hill: University of North Carolina Press, 1991), Ch. 3.

86. On the divided elites and their constituencies, see Lee Benson, *The Concept of Jacksonian Democracy: New York State as a Test Case* (Princeton: Princeton University Press, 1961); Edward Pessen, *Jacksonian America: Society, Personality, and Politics*, rev. ed. (Homewood, Ill.: Dorsey, 1978), Ch. 11; and Hamilton, *Class and Politics*. As opposed to the frequent focus on classes, strata, and horizontal lines of cleavage, this reading of the history points to the importance of vertical divisions, what the Dutch call *verzuiling*. Some additional evidence on this point may be found in Hamilton, *Marxism*, Ch. 3.

87. See Don B. Kates, Jr., ed., *Restricting Handguns: The Liberal Skeptics Speak Out* (Croton-on-Hudson, N.Y.: North River Press, 1979), esp. Section 5, by Carol Ruth Silver and Kates, "Self-Defense, Handgun Ownership, and the Independence of Women in a Violent, Sexist Society"; and David B. Kopel, ed., *Guns: Who Should Have Them?* (Amherst, N.Y.: Prometheus), 1995), esp. Ch. 1, by Mary Zeiss Stange, "Arms and the Woman: A Feminist Reappraisal." Those concerned feminists appear to have evidence on their side showing that the availability of hand guns reduces violence against women.

88. The key work in this tradition is John D. McCarthy and Mayer N. Zald, *The Trend of Social Movements in America: Professionalization and Resource Mobilization* (Morristown, N.J.: General Learning Press, 1973). They write that their view "does not necessarily deny the existence of grievances. It stresses the structural conditions that facilitate the expression of grievances." In subsequent work, the approaches have been treated as opposites, grievances being given very little attention. The literature in this tradition is extensive. For overviews, see John D. McCarthy and Mayer N. Zald, "Resource Mobilization and Social Movements: A Partial Theory," *American Journal of Sociology* 82 (1977): 1212–1241; John D. McCarthy and Mayer N. Zald, "Social Movements," in *The Handbook of Sociology*, ed. Neil Smelser (Newbury Park, Calif.: Sage, 1988); and Doug McAdam, John D. McCarthy, and Mayer N. Zald, eds., *Comparative Perspectives on Social Movements: Political Opportunities, Mobilizing Structures, and Cultural Framings* (Cambridge: Cambridge University Press, 1996).

89. For overviews, see Philippe C. Schmitter and Gerhard Lehmbruch, eds., *Trends Towards Corporatist Intermediation* (Beverly Hills, Calif.: Sage, 1979); and Suzanne Berger, *Organizing Interests in Western Europe: Pluralism, Corporatism, and the Transformation of Politics* (New York: Cambridge University Press, 1981).

90. See Putnam, "Strange Disappearance," "Bowling Alone," and "Tuning In, Tuning Out," and his *Making Democracy Work: Civic Traditions in Modern Italy* (Princeton: Princeton University Press, 1993). For a summary overview, see Bob Edwards, ed., "Social Capital, Civil Society, and Contemporary Democracy," *American Behavioral Scientist* 40, no. 5 (special issue) (1997); and Paxton, "Is Social Capital Declining." For some skeptical comments about the usefulness of the concept, see Alejandro Portes, "Social Capital: Its Origins and Applications in Modern Sociology," *Annual Review of Sociology* 24 (1998): 1–24.

91. John Keane, ed., *Civil Society and the State: New European Perspectives* (London: Verso, 1988); and John A. Hall, ed., *Civil Society: Theory, History, Comparison* (Cambridge: Polity Press, 1995). See also Krishan Kumar, "Civil Society: An Inquiry into the Usefulness of an Historical Term," *British Journal of Sociology* 44 (1993): 375–395, with a comment by Christopher Bryant, same issue, pp. 397–401, and a response by Kumar, same journal, 45 (1994): 127–131; Larry Diamond, "Rethinking Civil Society: Toward Democratic Consolidation," *Journal of Democracy* 5 (1994): 4–17; and Michael W. Foley and Bob Edwards, "The Paradox of Civil Society," *Journal of Democracy* 7 (1996): 38–52.

CHAPTER 3

Bureaucracy

THE CONCEPT AND ITS HISTORY

The bureaucratization argument is easily summarized: Modern societies, to
an ever increasing degree, are dominated by large, hierarchical, formally organized agencies. Work and leisure, to an ever greater extent, are contained
within and directed by those agencies. Those bureaucracies, it is said, control
and direct the lives of contemporary populations. Those organizations are
viewed as constraining and punitive; they restrict freedom and spontaneity.

The most influential statement of this position is the work of Max Weber,
the eminent German sociologist. In a chapter entitled "Bureaucracy," its characteristics are spelled out over several pages.[1] The first of these is "fixed and
official jurisdictional areas . . . ordered by rules . . . by laws or administrative
regulations." Those jurisdictional areas are arranged in "a firmly ordered system of super- and subordination in which there is a supervision of the lower
offices by the higher ones. . . . With the full development of the bureaucratic
type, the office hierarchy is monocratically organized." The modern bureaucracy "usually presupposes thorough and expert training. This increasingly
holds for the modern executive and employee of private enterprises, in the
same manner as it holds for the state official." The management of the office
"follows general rules, which are more or less stable, more or less exhaustive,
and which can be learned. Knowledge of these rules represents a special technical learning which the officials possess."[2]

The second section of Weber's chapter deals with the position of the official within the modern or fully developed bureaucracy. There is, first, "the
requirement of a firmly prescribed course of training [with] special examinations which are prerequisites of employment." The "pure type" of official,
Weber states, "is *appointed* by a superior authority" on the basis of demon-

strated technical expertise. An elected official is "not a purely bureaucratic figure." In this connection, however, Weber points to an appearance–reality disparity. "Of course," he indicates, "the formal existence of an election does not by itself mean that no appointment hides behind the election—in the state, especially, appointment by party chiefs. . . . Once firmly organized, the parties can turn a formally free election into the mere acclamation of a candidate designated by the party chief." The "formally free election," he declares, is ordinarily "a fight, conducted according to definite rules, for votes in favor of one or two designated candidates."[3]

This dismal portrait of democracy, it should be noted, was no passing fancy for Weber. It is inherent in the logic of his theoretical system. The parties will bureaucratize. They will become mass organizations; they will develop hierarchies that will be ruled by experts who will make expert appointments. The "people's choice" is between two (or possibly more) candidates chosen by the party chiefs. Weber's "realism" in this respect was consonant with and supported by the findings of Robert Michels's *Political Parties*, reviewed in Chapter 2.

Weber's outlook was manifested subsequently in his attitude toward Germany's new democracy, the Weimar republic. In conversation with General Ludendorff, he declared, "In a democracy the people choose a leader in whom they trust. Then the chosen leader says, 'Now shut up and obey me.' People and party are then no longer free to interfere in his business." Ludendorff replied, "I could like such democracy." Weber added, "Later the people can sit in judgment. If the leader has made mistakes—to the gallows with him!"[4] His "ideal" is clearly plebiscitory as opposed to participatory democracy.

Weber argues further that "the position of the official is held for life, at least in public bureaucracies; and this is increasingly the case for all similar structures." The training, expertise, and knowledge acquired will benefit the agency, presumably until retirement. A notion of "career" is also assumed, specifically that the official will move "within the hierarchical order . . . from the lower, less important, and lower paid to the higher positions."[5]

Bureaucratic organization differs from previous forms in that office holding is conceived of as a "vocation" or, put differently, according to Weber, "the position of the official is in the nature of a duty." The office is no longer treated as a personal possession, one "to be exploited for rents or emoluments, as was normally the case during the Middle Ages and frequently up to the threshold of recent times. . . . Entrance into an office, including one in the private economy, is considered an acceptance of a specific obligation of faithful management in return for a secure existence." The affairs of the organization, in this reading, will be conducted according to calculable rules; that is, "without regard for persons." It is in this sense that the bureaucracy is described, appropriately, as "impersonal."[6]

Weber has presented a theory of history, specifically of modern history, which stands in sharp contrast to Marx's and Engels's summary depiction of "all hitherto existing society" at the beginning of the *Manifesto*. Weber's single-sentence equivalent would read, "The history of the modern world is a history of the extension of bureaucracy." In contrast to Marx's and Engels's economic determinism and class struggle, Weber's is a theory of bureaucratic determinism, of the irreversible domination of this form of organization in human affairs.

The underlying causal factor, the determining consideration forcing the extension of this form of organization, is efficiency. Because of its importance, an extensive quotation is appropriate:

The decisive reason for the advance of bureaucratic organization has always been its purely technical superiority over any other form of organization. The fully developed bureaucratic mechanism compares with other organizations exactly as does the machine with the non-mechanical modes of production.

Precision, speed, unambiguity, knowledge of the files, continuity, discretion, unity, strict subordination, reduction of friction and of material and personal costs—these are raised to the optimum point in the strictly bureaucratic administration, and especially in its monocratic form.[7]

The logic of the case is spelled out in several long paragraphs. A large bureaucratic army would be "technically superior" to the private regiments that preceded it. A bureaucratic department of taxation is superior to the earlier personal regime, that of the tax farmers, the buying of offices, and the exploitation of an office for personal gain. One might have doubts about the efficiency of workman's compensation departments or of the Social Security Administration, but the test of the claim would be to find the viable alternative, the nonbureaucratic form that could more efficiently adjudicate cases and supply compensation. Weber put the issue as follows: "As compared with all collegiate, honorific, and avocational forms of administration, trained bureaucracy is superior on all [of the previously listed] points."[8]

A case study of Prussia may help in the assessment of this bold claim. It also helps in considering the relative merits of the Marxian and Weberian arguments. If a Marxist living in 1740 were commenting on the prospects for the various European nations, it is unlikely that Prussia would figure prominently in that analysis. The nation was small, economically backward, and thinly populated. Its principal economic base was agriculture, most involving poor sandy soil with limited yields. The nation had no significant mineral resources. Its principal resources were social: It had a well-developed bureaucratic army and some advanced agencies of government, principally in taxation and police. With that army, King Frederick II, who ruled from 1740 to 1786, defeated a major power, Austria, and gained Silesia. Later, in 1815, after Napoleon's defeat, Prussia was given Westphalia. Two more agricultural regions had been added to the nation. From the Marxian perspective, the most that could be anticipated was increased agricultural production, the soil in both of the new territories being superior to that of Brandenburg or its eastern possession, Prussia. In the nineteenth century both of those territories proved to have significant mineral deposits, coal being the most important. Westphalia contained the Ruhr region, the leading center of German industry. Silesia became the second industrial center.

It was the bureaucratic instrument that made Prussia a significant European power that allowed the acquisition of those territories. Those episodes made possible one of the decisive events of the nineteenth century, the unification of Germany with Prussian dominance. Max Weber, the son of a prominent Prussian legislator, had an intimate knowledge of that history. It is no accident—borrowing a standard Marxian cliché—that Weber assigned decisive importance to the bureaucratic form. The argument may be summarized as follows: Without the bureaucratic instrument (army and administration), Prussia would never have been a major European power. And if not a power, "Germany" would never have been unified under Prussian dominance. Silesia would have remained a part of Austria. Westphalian industry might, conceivably, have been located within a loose confederation of German states, or within a confederation under Austrian dominance.[9]

Weber's account of bureaucracy was intended primarily as an analytical statement, as a depiction of a given organizational form and an explanation for why it was gaining dominance. On occasion, however, Weber also provides an evaluation. Unlike the Marx–Engels statement, which portrays "history" leading to a new epoch that would be unquestionably better, Weber had serious doubts about the desirability of the bureaucratic tendency. The final pages of Weber's *Protestant Ethic and the Spirit of Capitalism* have often been linked with the bureaucratic argument, although, strictly speaking, they deal with a separate but related concern. "The Puritan wanted to work in a calling," he wrote, but "we are forced to do so." Puritan asceticism, it seems, "did its part in building the tremendous cosmos of the modern economic order [one] now bound to the technical and economic conditions of machine production which today determine the lives of all the individuals who are born into this mechanism." This modern cosmos, he declared, has "become an iron cage."[10]

The image of modern life as an iron cage is frequently invoked by academics, especially by those of the literary persuasion. That image, it should be noted, is usually taken out of context when applied to bureaucracy. In Weber, the subject is clearly material goods. Richard Baxter, the Puritan theologian, wrote that the concern for external goods should lie on the shoulders of the "saint like a light cloak, which can be thrown aside at any moment." But Weber declares, "fate decreed that the cloak should become an iron cage." The point is elaborated in the subsequent paragraph: "Material goods have gained an increasing and finally an inexorable power over the lives of men as at no previous period in history."[11]

Although ordinarily treated as an unwanted imposition, Weber in fact sees the growth of bureaucracy as, in great measure, stemming from that irrational interest in material goods. Those "born into this mechanism," those now living in the iron cage, have done so through their own choices. Weber is more than willing to admit that those are blind choices. The irrational driving sense of duty of the Puritans has been transformed into this new irrational "pursuit of wealth [which, now] stripped of its religious and ethical meaning, tends to become associated with purely mundane passions." Weber's attitude toward this "modern" development is intensely negative. Perhaps "new prophets will arise, or there will be a great rebirth of old ideas and ideals," he wrote. The alternative is "mechanized petrification, embellished with a sort of convulsive self-importance." His contempt for this contemporary stage of "cultural development" is expressed as follows: "Specialists without spirit, sensualists without heart; this nullity imagines that it has attained a level of civilization never before achieved."[12]

These formulations apply especially to the developments of Western Europe and the United States. But in an important extension, in a speech given in July 1918, Weber argued that socialism was merely an extension of the bureaucratic advance. Rather than providing "a new realm of freedom," socialism would constitute the extreme case, the all-encompassing bureaucracy. Gerth and Mills summarize Weber's argument as follows:

Socialization of the means of production would merely subject an as yet relatively autonomous economic life to the bureaucratic management of the state. The state would indeed become total, and Weber, hating bureaucracy as a shackle upon the liberal individual, felt that socialism would thus lead to a further serfdom. "For the time being," he wrote, "the dictatorship of the official and not that of the worker is on the march."[13]

Weber's critique of socialism has been largely neglected in scholarly accounts. The practice, it will be noted, has been peculiarly one-sided: Weber's argument about bureaucracy has been used to critique Western or capitalist societies.

It is worth noting that, again, as with the mass society theory, we have a then-versus-now comparison, an argument of good old days versus bad new ones. Freedom, choice, and spontaneity are being claimed for those old days. The new days are characterized by soul-destroying constraints, by some ultimate "domination." Gerth and Mills provide a convenient summary of the argument:

Weber thus identifies bureaucracy with rationality, and the process of rationalization with mechanism, depersonalization, and oppressive routine. Rationality, in this context, is seen as adverse to personal freedom. Accordingly, Weber is a nostalgic liberal, feeling himself on the defensive. He deplores the type of man that the mechanization and the routine of bureaucracy selects and forms. The narrowed professional, publicly certified and examined, and ready for tenure and career. His craving for security is balanced by his moderate ambitions and he is rewarded by the honor of official status. This type of man Weber deplored as a petty routine creature, lacking in heroism, human spontaneity, and inventiveness.[14]

A contemporary statement of the bureaucratization argument appears in an introductory sociology text written by Neil Smelser, a sociologist of considerable eminence, the author or editor of many books attesting to a vast historical and comparative knowledge. A heading in the textbook provides the summary conclusion: "The Future: More Bureaucracy." The text declares that "the end is not yet in sight." No data are offered to support this central claim. Commenting on the implications, Smelser reports that "we will continue to feel ambivalent about bureaucracy because of its impersonality, its frustrations, and its intrusion into our lives."[15]

THE PROPOSITIONS

The principal arguments are summarized in the following propositions:

1. Bureaucracies are large and growing. Most people work in giant offices or shops employing thousands of persons. The typical (or average) workplace is becoming ever larger.

2. Bureaucracies are impersonal. Because of the large size of the typical establishment and the emphasis placed on formal rules, it follows that work relationships are impersonal.

3. Bureaucracies are intrusive. The intent of these agencies is control, the coordination of persons and resources. It follows that bureaucracies are limiting; they frustrate personal impulses and reduce individual freedom.

4. Bureaucracies tend toward monocratic rule. The fully developed bureaucracy, Weber argues, will have a single center of power; the organization is controlled and directed "from the top."

5. Bureaucracies will be directed by technically trained experts. The rule of amateurs (those with unique personal gifts), or of inheritors (whether monarchs or the offspring of business leaders), or those ruling through personal connections (through a party machine, as with political bosses) will more and more yield to rule by the experts.

ASSESSMENT

The first proposition holds that bureaucracy is both large and growing. Two separate claims are contained here, one declaring the present extent, the other announcing the continuing tendency. Considering the longer term, say from the seventeenth century to the present, there can be little doubt as to overall growth of this organizational form. Governments, even the largest of them, those of Spain, France, or England, were small. Most government employees were in the military, the police, or tax collection agencies. The controls exercised by those agencies, as judged by modern standards, were very limited. There were few large firms in the private sector. Most of those were in shipbuilding, most of them in the Netherlands and England. There were some giant mixed government–private agencies, the most notable being the Dutch East India Company and the English trading companies. The Dutch company, founded in 1602, was by mid-century "the world's greatest trading corporation [and] the dominant European maritime power in southeast Asia. Its fleet numbering some six thousand ships . . . was manned by perhaps 48,000 sailors."[16] Evidence on size and growth prior to the twentieth century is limited. It follows that documentation must be spotty and the conclusions based largely on plausible inference.

The twin arguments, large size and continued growth, appear frequently in the late twentieth century. A sociological work arguing this claim, published in 1979, opens with this statement: "The workplace today is a vastly changed place from the ships and offices of seventy-five or a hundred years ago. Then nearly all employees worked for small firms, while today large numbers toil for the giant corporations."[17] This portrait of giantism, like Weber's and Smelser's, was not accompanied by supporting evidence, although evidence on the point was readily available. National samples of the U.S. economically active population (those in the civilian labor force) are readily available, and respondents have been asked, among other things, about the size of their workplace (how many persons were employed there).[18] The frequency distributions for three studies, from 1973, 1977, and 1996, are shown in Table 3.1.

The most striking finding is that the typical workplace is small. Approximately half of the respondents worked in settings with fewer than fifty coworkers. Roughly five times as many persons were employed in those small establishments as in the giant units of 2,000 or more. Or, making another comparison, more people were employed in the smallest units, those with less than ten persons, than in units with 500 or more employees. For rule-of-thumb purposes, one can focus on that median experience, on the fifty-person cutting line. A unit with less than fifty persons would probably have, at best, three layers of hierarchy; basically, an owner or manager, a small number of supervisors, and the line employees. That hardly accords with the equation of modern life with giant bureaucracies. These "snapshots" show that the typical experience had been seriously misrepresented.

The three studies ask about the "location where you work," what specialists call an establishment. Another term that might appear in this connection is the notion of a firm or enterprise. Many persons working in the smaller establishments of Table 3.1 were employees of giant firms. General Motors (GM) is a giant firm with, in 1995, a total of 745,000 employees employed in 316 locations in 171 cities within the United States. The company also oper-

Table 3.1
Size of Enterprise (Persons in Civilian Labor Force)

	1973	1977	1996
Size of Unit			
1 to 9	26 %	24 %	27 %
10 to 49	23	27	23
50 to 99	10	11	12
100 to 499	20	19	20
500 to 999	7	6	6
1,000 to 1,999	4	5	4
2,000 or more	10	9	8
N =	(2,076)	(2,239)	(1,965)

Sources: Robert P. Quinn, Thomas W. Mangione, and Stanley E. Seashore, *Quality of Employment Survey, 1972–1973*, and *Quality of Employment Survey, 1977: Cross-Section* [computer files] (Ann Arbor, Mich.: Institute for Social Research, 1975 and 1979), variable 73 for 1973 and variable 100 for 1977 data; James A. Davis and Tom W. Smith, *General Social Surveys, 1972–1996*: [Cumulative] [computer file] (Chicago: National Opinion Research Center, 1997), variable LOCALNUM.

Note: In *Quality of Employment Survey*, the question was asked with a card saying, "About how many people work at the location where you work—I mean all types of workers in all areas and departments?" In *General Social Survey*, the question was, "About how many people work at the location where you work? (Count part-time as well as full-time employees in all areas, departments, and buildings)."

ates in 20 locations in Canada and in 51 establishments elsewhere in the world. The tabulation based on firms would count General Motors as one giant enterprise. The tabulation based on establishments, as with the 1996 General Social Survey, breaks up the large firm and yields a much smaller average experience. General Motors dealers—moreover, those selling the Chevrolets, Pontiacs, Oldsmobiles, and Cadillacs—are not directly employed by the firm. They are franchise establishments run by independent proprietors. In 1995 there were approximately 8,800 General Motors vehicle dealers in the United States, 1,000 in Canada and Mexico, and approximately 5,500 outlets overseas. Most would be relatively small, most of them probably having fewer than fifty employees.

A further cautionary note: One thinks of General Motors as an automobile manufacturer with giant assembly plants as its principal units. But only 8 percent of the 316 establishments were vehicle assembly plants. Moody's describes the operation as follows:

Of [the 316,] 25 are engaged in the final assembly of GM cars and trucks, 30 are service parts operations responsible for distribution or warehousing; 20 are associated with Electronic Data Systems Corporation as large information processing centers and offices; 31 major plants, offices, and research facilities relate to the operations of Hughes Electronics Corporation; and the remainder are offices or involved primarily in the testing of vehicles or the manufacture of automotive components and power products.[19]

One must also consider some other complications. In recent decades the fast-food enterprises—McDonald's, Kentucky Fried Chicken, Wendy's, Rax, and others—have shown very rapid growth. McDonald's is a large firm. But the outlets, the local establishments, are typically rather small; most of them, like the automobile dealerships, are franchise units.[20] Most of the employees would be found, in Table 3.1, in the small units. The basic question is this: Should those employees be counted as members of a giant bureaucracy or as members of a small shop?

Given the popular depictions, it would be easy to conclude that the bureaucratic rules of General Motors would be all-pervasive, that they would cover all 316 establishments. That inference, however, would be mistaken. Early on in the development of the firm, which grew through the acquisition of other producers, it was recognized that the extension of central control was not practical. It would be difficult to implement and to oversee, and, more important, it would be extremely costly. The result was a delegation of powers, with the creation of a "federal" organization. The relatively autonomous subordinate units of General Motors were referred to as divisions. To some degree, each worked out its own policies, developed its own rules, and made its own purchases (even competing against other GM divisions). The ultimate rule for General Motors and other firms following this procedure was performance as measured by year-end profitability or, as it came to be known, by the "bottom line." The logic of the divisional policy was reinforced in a later period with the coming of other developments; diversification, the acquisition of different product lines, and the development of conglomerates and multinationals.[21]

It would be pointless—a bootless effort, as Thorstein Veblen might put it—for the firm to impose central control, rules, oversight, and so forth on those very diverse units. The bottom line procedure was cheaper, more effective, and more in line with the ultimate goal of profitability. An important lesson follows: One central Weberian notion, monocratic rule, is mistaken. It is not "the rule," and not the tendency.[22]

In 1984 Mark Granovetter published an important article dealing with the issues of size and trends. His account focused primarily on the size of establishments. One major conclusion is signaled in the title: "Small Is Bountiful."

Another statement deserves special emphasis: "This paper gives the first systematic empirical account of the evolution of workplace size." Granovetter's analysis focuses on persons in private employment, thus excluding the approximately one-sixth employed in "government"; that is, somewhere in public service. His initial focus, understandably, provides a breakdown by industry. Data for 1981 showed the largest average number of persons per establishment was in manufacturing (59.5), followed by mining (29.9), and then transportation and public utilities (24.4). Services such as finance, insurance and real estate, and retail trade were all smallish, at 11.4, 11.1, and 10.6, respectively. Construction was smallest of all, at 8.1. A principal lesson with respect to manufacturing establishments is that "at *no* point in the twentieth century have more than one in three manufacturing workers been employed in establishments of more than 1000 workers."[23]

As for the trend, Granovetter's series shows a growth in the size of manufacturing establishments through to 1967, at which point one in three employees worked in an establishment with 1,000 or more persons. His figures then show a reversal. From 1967 to 1977 the percentage employed in the giant establishments declined, from 32.8 to 27.5, just the opposite of the more-and-more assertions. That decline continued in subsequent years, the 1996 figure being 20.6 percent.[24] Put differently, roughly four-fifths of those in manufacturing worked in units of less than 1,000 (Table 3.2).

Findings are reported for three other sectors showing considerable absolute growth; retail trade, wholesale trade, and the heterogeneous service category. Granovetter reports little change in the establishment size for the first two in the period 1939 to 1977. He summarized as follows:

In retail trade, the proportion of the workforce in very small (under 20) establishments has declined strongly since 1939, but there has been little change in the proportion in stores with less than 100 employees. This is not surprising if we keep in mind that a store with 100 employees is already a sizable operation. The size distribution in wholesale trade shows no consistent trend over this period, while that in services shows a fairly steady tendency for workers to be in larger establishments.[25]

Comparable figures extending those series through to 1996 show a small increase in large-establishment employment in retail trade, with roughly one in four working in units of 100 or more. The wholesale series indicates a continuous modest increase of employment in large establishments. In the service sector, the increased employment in large establishments (100 or more employees) was dramatic, going from one-sixth in 1948 to approximately one-half in the recent experience (Table 3.3).[26] We have, clearly, a differentiated result: a decline in "typical" establishment size in manufacturing and some increases in the other sectors. One should not overlook the different measures. Large in manufacturing means 1,000 or more; elsewhere it means 100 or more.

Granovetter also provided an overall summary showing the pattern from 1960 to 1981. The result was a slight decline in large-establishment employ-

Table 3.2
Percentage of Employees in U.S. Manufacturing Establishments of Various Sizes

Year	Less than 20	Less than 100	1,000 or more
1967	5.6 %	23.2 %	32.4 %
1972	6.2	24.8	28.7
1977	6.5	25.3	27.5
1982	7.9	28.4	25.2
1987	8.2	29.5	23.7
1993	8.3	29.7	21.7
1996	8.2	29.9	20.6

Sources: 1967–1977 from Mark Granovetter, "Small Is Bountiful: Labor Markets and Establishment Size," *American Sociological Review* 49 (1984): 326; 1982 and 1987 from U.S. Bureau of the Census, *Census of Manufactures* (Washington, D.C.: U.S. Government Printing Office, respective years); and 1993 and 1996 from U.S. Department of Commerce, *County Business Patterns* (Washington, D.C.: U.S. Government Printing Office, respective years).

ment, the percentages falling from 21.6 in 1960 to 18.7 in 1981. The decline of large-establishment employment continued in subsequent years, falling to 12.8 percent in 1996 (Table 3.4).[27]

The focus on establishments is one of several possible measures of size. The usage here is based on convenience and availability. Granovetter provides some figures for both establishments and firms. In 1977, 27.5 percent of those employed in manufacturing were in *establishments* of 1,000 or more; 65.7 percent of them were employed in *firms* of equivalent size. At the same time, approximately two-thirds of those in retail businesses were in firms with less than 1,000. Roughly four-fifths of those in selected service industries were in firms with less than 1,000.

A report by Steve Lohr on employment in giant firms, the *Fortune* 500, indicates a decline from 16 million in 1979 to 12 million in 1991. At the latter point, not quite one in ten persons in the civilian labor force was directly employed in a giant firm. Lohr's article, it should be noted, links the decline to subcontracting ("outsourcing").[28]

One could focus on firms, adding all those employed in franchise dealerships and also those in firms engaged in outsourcing. That procedure would yield substantial support for the giantism thesis. That might suggest sweeping controls, but that would be an inference as opposed to actual investigation. The basic question is this: Does the specific work setting make a difference? One

Table 3.3
Percentage of Employees in Retail, Wholesale, and Service Establishments of Various Sizes

	Retail		Wholesale		Services	
Year	Less than 20	Less than 100	Less than 20	Less than 100	Less than 20	Less than 100
1939	63.8 %	85.0 %	44.4 %	83.0 %	55.6 %	NA
1948	58.3	82.4	37.6	NA	55.5	83.5 %
1954	56.0	83.0	41.9	81.5	47.4	76.1
1958	55.6	83.7	43.7	83.2	50.6	77.5
1963	53.4	83.4	45.0	84.1	48.2	75.2
1967	48.8	82.4	41.6	81.4	43.6	71.7
1972	46.3	82.5	NA	NA	42.3	71.7
1977	42.7	81.9	40.6[a]	79.6[a]	40.0	68.1
1982	35.6	74.4	39.5[a]	78.8[a]	37.1	64.8
1987	35.4	76.8	36.6[a]	75.0[a]	27.7	50.1
1992	34.7	76.0	36.2[b]	74.0[b]	22.6	45.1
1996[a]	32.6	73.8	34.2	72.3	25.4	49.4

Sources: 1939–1977, Mark Granovetter, "Small Is Bountiful: Labor Markets and Establish-ment Size," *American Sociological Review* 49 (1984): 326; U.S. Department of Commerce, *Census of Wholesale Trade* (Washington, D.C.: U.S. Government Printing Office, various years); *Census of Retail Trade* (Washington, D.C.: U.S. Government Printing Office, various years); *Census of Service Industries* (Washington, D.C.: U.S. Government Printing Office, various years); and *County Business Patterns* (Washington, D.C.: U.S. Government Printing Office, various years).

[a]Figures are from *County Business Patterns*.

[b]Figures are for 1993.

test would involve comparison of employees in four settings: small shops owned by independent entrepreneurs, small shops owned by the large corpo-ration, small franchise units linked to a large corporation, and small firms engaged in outsourcing. The key question is if the quality of work differs significantly in those settings. If so, in what ways? I have not found any study that has undertaken this task.

Table 3.4
Percentage of Employees in Establishments of Various Sizes

Year	Less than 20	Less than 100	1,000 or more
1960	23.9 %	48.0 %	21.6 %
1969	21.6	46.5	21.5
1974	23.0	47.7	19.5
1981	23.2	49.0	18.7
1988	23.7	51.0	15.4
1989	23.5	50.7	15.3
1990	23.9	51.3	15.2
1991	25.6	53.8	14.0
1993	26.5	55.7	12.5
1995	26.0	55.4	11.8
1996	25.6	54.6	12.8

Sources: Figures for 1960–1981 from Mark Granovetter, "Small Is Bountiful: Labor Markets and Establishment Size," *American Sociological Review* 49 (1984): 327; U.S. Bureau of Labor Statistics, *Employment and Wages* (Washington, D.C.: U.S. Government Printing Office, various years); and figures for 1996 from U.S. Department of Commerce, *County Business Patterns 1996* (Washington, D.C.: U.S. Government Printing Office, 1998), Table 1b.

Granovetter's account, as noted, deals with nongovernmental units, excluding approximately one-sixth of the labor force. That experience should also be studied and the claims assessed. Again, one must deal with the cliché problem. Much discussion, especially in the popular realm, focuses on "the growth of big government." Explicitly or implicitly, the focus is also on "oppressive" or "intrusive" government. A first point: Use of the singular is inappropriate, since we have a variety of such agencies: national, state, county, township, and municipal governments, school governments, and special purpose governments (such as the Cook Country Mosquito Abatement District). It follows that a differentiated portrait is needed. Some information on the numbers, on the basic frequencies, is appropriate.

The expression "big government" ordinarily refers to the federal government or, as often expressed, to the government "in Washington." There can be little doubt as to the growth of that government in the course of this century.

At the turn of the century, at the time of McKinley's presidency, that government consisted of roughly 240,000 persons, eight-tenths of 1 percent of civilian employment. The numbers and the percentages moved upward in the subsequent decades. The number had increased tenfold by 1960, and the percentage had risen to 3.4. The number of civilian employees increased again, to just under 3 million in 1970 (which included some 33,000 temporary census workers). At that point they formed 3.6 percent of the total (Table 3.5).

In 1997 the federal government had 2,816,000 civilian employees. Without the census temporaries, the number was below that of 1970. Given the growth of the civilian labor force in this period, it is clear that the federal government's share of the total declined. The percentages for 1970 and 1995 were 3.6 and 2.2, respectively. By this measure, the growth of "big government" ended with the 1970 peak. The federal government has been declining in relative size for nearly three decades.[29]

The previous paragraphs deal exclusively with civilian employment in the federal government. To those numbers one should add active-duty military personnel, all of whom would be employed by the Department of Defense. In 1960 and 1970 the personnel on active military duty exceeded the total civilian federal government employment. Those on active duty increased dramatically over the course of the Korean War, moving from 1,460,000 in 1950 to 3,636,000 in 1952. The number fell in subsequent years, to 2,475,000 in 1960, and rose again over the course of the Vietnam War, reaching a second high, 3,546,000 in 1968. The number on active duty then fell off sharply to just over 2 million in 1976, and remained at that level to 1990. With the ending of the Cold War, the number declined once again, falling to 1,056,000 in 1996. The latter figure, it will be noted, is well below that of 1950.

Military service differs significantly from work in other public or private bureaucracies. The patterns of growth and decline are markedly different from those of most civilian activities. For many, the involvement would be nonvoluntary and short term, that being especially the case for draftees in the period from 1948 to 1973. Civilian employment in the federal government, as seen in Table 3.5, peaked in 1970. Recalculating that line to include military personnel yields a total labor force in 1970 of 85,836,000, with total federal government employment at 6,062,000 or 7.1 percent. For 1997 the equivalent figures are 137,736,000, 4,255,000, and 3.1 percent. The last quarter-century, in short, has seen a dramatic decline in the size of the federal government.[30]

The insistent focus on the federal government is seriously misleading. The other governments, taken together, are much larger than "the feds," accounting for 85 percent of total government employment in 1995. The states have more employees than the federal government. And local governments (all varieties) have more employees than the states. The largest category of all is school districts, which in 1992 employed 5,134,000 of the 18,745,000 total government employment.[31] This form of government "intrusion," called compulsory education, has been with us for some time. For the most part, that intrusion has been approved by substantial majorities of the citizenry.

Table 3.5
Federal Government Civilian Employment: 1901–1995

Year	Total Civilian Labor Force (1,000s)	Civilian Employment in Federal Government	Government as Percent of Total
1901	29,153	239,476	0.8
1910	36,709	388,708	1.1
1920	41,340	655,265	1.6
1930	48,523	601,319	1.2
1940	55,640	1,042,420	1.9
1950	62,208	1,960,708	3.2
1960	69,628	2,398,704	3.4
1970	82,771	2,997,000	3.6
1980	106,940	2,987,000	2.8
1990	125,840	3,233,000	2.7
1997	136,297	2,816,000	2.2

Sources: For 1901–1960, U.S. Bureau of the Census, *Historical Statistics of the United States, 1975* (Washington, D.C.: U.S. Government Printing Office, 1975), 126, 127, 1,102; for 1970–1997, U.S. Bureau of the Census, *Statistical Abstract of the United States, 1998* (Washington, D.C.: U.S. Government Printing Office, 1998), Tables 560 and 644.

Discussions of federal government intrusiveness typically lack specification. The entire government is portrayed as involved in those "bad things," somehow or other "invading" our lives, restricting our freedom, limiting our privacy, and so on. Again, some detail and some numbers prove useful. The overwhelming majority of federal civilian employees, not surprisingly, work in the executive branch. The majority of the latter work in fourteen executive departments (State, Treasury, Defense, Justice, etc.); the rest are in some forty-plus independent agencies; for example, the Farm Credit Administration, the Federal Communications Commission, the Federal Election Commission, the Arms Control and Disarmament Agency, the American Battle Monuments Commission, and the Smithsonian Institution.

For most of the post–World War II period, the Department of Defense (DOD) was the federal government's largest employer of civilian labor. In 1997 it had 749,461 employees. That number, it should be noted, is down almost 28 percent from the 1990 level. The members of the armed forces must be added to DOD employment figures. The total was 2,188,023 in 1997, down by 889,834 from 3,077,857 in 1990.

The second largest federal government employer is now an independent agency, the U.S. Postal Service. In 1995, with 845,393 employees, it overtook the Department of Defense as the largest employer of civilians. The third largest agency is Veterans Affairs (formerly the Veterans Administration), with 263,904. Fourth on this list is Treasury (155,951), fifth is Agriculture (113,321), and sixth is the Social Security Administration (66,850). The latter was separated from the Health and Human Services Department in the previous year.[32]

The Postal Service intrudes on our lives—reaching as far as our mailboxes—some six days a week. It is not clear whether Defense ought to be counted as an intrusion. A significant element of compulsion disappeared in the early 1970s with the ending of the draft. Veterans Affairs is basically a welfare agency, providing services for former members of the armed forces. Treasury does intrude into most people's lives, not a happy occasion for many, but most people would probably agree that taxation is a necessary activity. The Department of Agriculture undertakes agricultural research, transmits information through its extension agents, administers price support programs, and also administers the food stamp program. The Social Security Administration intrudes in many lives, sending monthly checks, but few people would view the provision of retirement income as a bad thing.

Personnel figures give one indication of government size. A somewhat different picture appears when considering government expenditure. One summary overview gives federal outlays in a handful of summary categories, the leaders being national defense, human resources, and net interest. In the period from 1964 to 1970, defense expenditures were easily "number one." The percentage share in that period ran in the mid-forties. In all those years—Vietnam War years, it will be remembered—the share for human resources moved steadily upward, from 29.8 to 38.5 percent. In 1971, the relationship reversed, with the defense and human resources percentages at 37.5 and 43.7, respectively. The predominance of human resources expenditures has continued to the present, the principal change being in the extent of the imbalance. The 1998 percentages were defense, 16.2, and human resources, 62.5. The latter percentage meant $1.033 trillion. In order of magnitude, this came under the following headings: Social Security; income security (various other transfer payments); Medicare; health (an omnibus category); education, training, employment, and social services; and finally, veterans' benefits and services.[33]

The image of a large, growing, and intrusive federal government appears to be off on all accounts. Overall, seen in terms of employment, the U.S. federal government is not large.[34] And it is not growing. Seen in terms of functions and expenditure, most people would not see its principal efforts as a bad thing, as intrusive or punitive. Most of the government's activity involves provision of income, payment for medical and other services, national defense, and the delivery of mail. The federal government also includes a wide range of regulatory agencies. Their size and impacts will be discussed later in this chapter.

Another of the big-government clichés focuses on location: The government "in Washington" is the source of the problem. Only 7 percent of federal government employees work in the District of Columbia. Some, to be sure, work in immediately adjacent areas of Virginia and Maryland, but even with generous estimates it is clear that some five of six federal employees are employed elsewhere, widely scattered across the nation. It would be more appropriate perhaps, more in keeping with the underlying spirit of the argument, to emphasize that dispersion: "They are everywhere."[35]

State governments have grown slightly faster than other nonfederal governments. The number of persons so employed, as indicated, far exceeds the number of civilians in the federal government. The largest single item of state expenditure is for public welfare. Education comes next, the bulk of that expenditure being for higher education. In third place comes insurance trust expenditures. Again, this does not add up to a picture of oppressive government.[36]

The second proposition holds that bureaucracies are impersonal. The argument needs specification: In what sense impersonal? Bureaucracies are supposed to treat clients impersonally, in the sense that no special favor will be given (contracts to friends, better terms for relatives, etc.). In liberal societies operating under the rule of law bureaucracies are also supposed to treat employees in an impersonal manner, meaning that no special favor will be given to family members, friends, coworkers, communal groups, and so forth. Such favor has occurred, especially in former times, but presently, in its "fully developed form" (a favorite Weber expression), such favoritism is ordinarily illegal and accordingly subject to penalties.

At the same time, nothing about the organizational form forbids friendly treatment of clients. Many organizations, especially in the private sector, encourage or even require such treatment. There is nothing inherent in the basic arrangement, moreover, that prevents friendly relationships among the employees. Many organizations take much time and effort to foster warm interpersonal ties, for the simple and obvious reason that it makes everyday life more pleasant. The enhanced morale, presumably, has beneficial impacts for the organization: greater loyalty, less turnover, reduced training costs, and greater productivity.

This aspect of the critique of bureaucracy has long since been recognized as, to say the least, dubious. From the time of the first serious studies of such organizations, generally positive assessments of interpersonal relationships have been reported, both those with supervisors and with coworkers. The supposed problematic character of social relations in large organizations, it will be noted, could be easily demonstrated. Self-reports by employees in organizations of various sizes, small to large, should unambiguously attest to that conclusion. But that, on the whole, has not been the case.[37]

The 1972–1973 Quality of Employment Survey allows exploration of the correlates of size. Unfortunately, as noted previously, it does not allow one to

distinguish between independent firms and the branches of a large corporation. It does allow exploration of the relationship between size of the unit and
the reports of participants about work in those settings. If conditions in the
1,000-plus units were definitively "bad," that should be evident in the comparisons with those working in middling or small shops.

Popular critiques of the large workplace routinely overlook two basic facts
of life: Large shops ordinarily pay more than small ones, and they provide
better fringe benefits. Other things equal, that should motivate people to choose
large-shop employment. Both pay and benefits are generally reported to be
better in the larger units (Table 3.6).[38] One could, to be sure, enjoy the income
and the benefits but still find the work unsatisfactory. In 1914, in the archetypical case, Henry Ford hired assembly-line workers for $5 a day, a "fabu-
lous" wage at that time. But that would not affect the quality of the work
itself, which, supposedly, was not at all attractive.

Asked directly about job satisfaction, majorities in all settings reported
some degree of satisfaction (that is, little outright dissatisfaction). The highest levels of satisfaction were found in the smallest units, but overall the differences are small. Employees in the large and giant units were not dissatisfied
(or "alienated"), but merely less positive and more likely to report they were
"somewhat satisfied."

A summary judgment on the merits of the current job is provided by the
following question: "Knowing what you know now, if you had to decide all
over again whether to take the job you now have, what would you decide?
Would you decide without any hesitation to take the same job?" Sizable majorities in all settings said they would choose the same job. Those in the smaller
units were slightly more likely to prefer the same job, but the pattern is erratic
and the differences are very small. The difference between the two extremes
is a matter of only 5 percentage points.

The relationships with coworkers are important aspects of work, and are
typically assumed to be better in small or nonbureaucratic settings. That assumption is generally confirmed; the highest percentage reporting friendly
coworkers is found in the smallest establishments, those of nine or less. That
said, an important qualification must be entered. Close to half of those in the
giant units, those of 2,000 or more, responded "very true" to the statement
about friendly coworkers. That does not mean impersonal relationships for
the others. Most of the others chose the "somewhat true" option. Only small
minorities gave negative responses on this point.

A similar pattern was found in the judgments about supervisors. Friendly
supervisors, seven in ten, were reported in the smallest shops. The positive
reports fell off somewhat in the larger units. But even in the large and giant
ones, roughly half said "very true" to the statement about friendly supervisors, and most of the rest said "somewhat true." Roughly one in seven gave
negative judgments that could support the argument of impersonality.

A pair of qualifying conditions should be noted. Social relationships in small
shops are regularly found to be very positive. That could mean the social circum-

Table 3.6
Job Characteristics by Size of Unit

	Size of Unit						
	1 to 9	10 to 49	50 to 99	100 to 499	500 to 999	1,000 to 1,999	2,000 and over
Pay is good							
Very true of my job	31 %	38 %	36 %	38 %	36 %	53 %	55 %
N =	(332)	(452)	(194)	(399)	(135)	(89)	(213)
Fringe benefits are good							
Very true of my job	28 %	41 %	39 %	50 %	44 %	51 %	66 %
N =	(324)	(452)	(189)	(395)	(131)	(89)	(213)
Job satisfaction							
Very satisfied	55 %	49 %	45 %	51 %	49 %	43 %	41 %
Somewhat satisfied	33	43	42	37	42	46	45
N =	(340)	(460)	(194)	(403)	(137)	(89)	(213)
Take the same job?							
Without hesitation	73 %	73 %	63 %	71 %	67 %	65 %	68 %
N =	(338)	(459)	(193)	(401)	(136)	(89)	(213)
Coworkers are friendly							
Very true	67 %	62 %	52 %	63 %	66 %	46 %	49 %
Somewhat true	24	29	37	31	28	46	46
N =	(325)	(452)	(194)	(397)	(134)	(89)	(213)
Supervisors are friendly							
Very true	70 %	62 %	61 %	57 %	50 %	45 %	55 %
Somewhat true	21	28	28	28	31	35	28
N =	(319)	(450)	(193)	(397)	(134)	(89)	(213)

Source: Robert P. Quinn, Thomas W. Mangione, and Stanley E. Seashore, *Quality of Employment Survey, 1972–1973* [computer file] (Ann Arbor, Mich.: Institute for Social Research, Social Science Archive, 1975), variables 5, 72, 73, 634, 642, 654, 658, 659, and 661.

Note: Wage and salary workers only; excludes the self-employed.

stances in small shops are inherently positive, warm, and supportive, a "proof" of the small-community idyll. But there is another easy alternative: Persons who for one reason or another do not fit in would have a strong incentive to leave, effectively being driven to seek employment elsewhere. This is to suggest that selection is involved; the twofold process, exclusion of nonconformists and "dropping out," would leave a very cohesive community.[39]

Large units, as seen, provide high earnings and a range of fringe benefits that, on the whole, would discourage exits. Most also have a seniority system that provides a measure of job security. If somehow "locked into" a given department and forced to remain with an unpleasant work group the work might conceivably be very "alienating." But many large firms, especially those with union-sponsored work rules, require posting of job openings, with skill and seniority being key criteria for selection (friends and family members might also provide information about openings). Those procedures allow escape from an unpleasant work group and a shift to another office or department that is more congenial without ever leaving the "giant bureaucracy." The bureaucratic rules in this case make possible the choice of amicable working relationships.[40]

Findings showing the "personal" character of the large workplace are routine in serious organizational studies. Similarly, the findings of high levels of work satisfaction and the absence of support for the bureaucracy-means-alienation thesis are also commonplace results. The best case against the large units would be the modest difference, the finding of somewhat less work satisfaction than elsewhere. Those findings, however, rarely appear in sociology textbooks or in the work of self-described critical intellectuals.[41]

The third proposition holds that bureaucracies are intrusive, that they diminish the lives of their members. Employment in bureaucracies leads to a unique "deformation," to the "bureaucratic personality." A classic presentation of this theme appears in Robert K. Merton's article (later a chapter), "Bureaucratic Structure and Personality," first published in 1940. The argument, basically, is a punitive one: Bureaucracy distorts the personalities of those working in them, making them "smaller," less flexible, and less capable. A discussion of "overconformity" and of the type, "the bureaucratic personality," follows. The work contains no compelling research to support those assertions.[42]

Three decades later Melvin Kohn published a commentary on the subject and presented some relevant evidence. He began by observing that, surprisingly, "there has been little empirical study of how bureaucracy affects those who spend their working hours in its employ." He summarized his research as follows: "There is a small but consistent tendency for men who work in bureaucratic organizations to be more intellectually flexible, more open to new experience, and more self-directed in their values than are men who work in nonbureaucratic organizations." He also offered some explanations: Bureaucracies draw on a more educated workforce, they offer "far greater job protections," they provide somewhat higher income, and they have substantively more complex work.[43]

A review of the treatment of Merton's and Kohn's contributions in the literature yields an instructive lesson. The *Social Science Citation Index* gives some indication of the attention paid to works in (and around) the social sciences. From 1990 to 1996 Merton's dataless article was cited twenty-six times; Kohn's empirically based response was cited seven times. The problem may also be seen in Smelser's textbook. University students reading that work are told that bureaucracy is large, growing, and punitive. No reference is made to Granovetter or Kohn.[44]

The punitiveness argument appears in another context. The large bureaucratic enterprise allows an ever finer division of labor. The tasks are now smaller, more repetitive, ever less challenging, and dull. This too, as was seen, is not supported by evidence, at least as far as self-reports are concerned. This line of argument was revived in Harry Braverman's influential work first, published in 1974. Among the flurry of "workplace rebellion" writings that appeared in the early 1970s, it alone has survived and remains in print a quarter of a century later. Although still used in university-level courses, a comprehensive review of studies on the topic indicates that Braverman's principal argument, the "degradation of skills," was not supported.[45]

The accounts of skill degradation are typically embellished with references to Frederick W. Taylor, to Taylorism, and to his "scientific management" procedures involving further division of labor, time-studied tasks, and piecework incentive arrangements. Those accounts have it that Taylorism is typical of or distinctive to "capitalism." It is also said to be growing, an ever more pervasive aspect of "work under capitalism." One review cited by William H. Form reported that "workers occupied a small place in [Taylor's] total system. He devoted less attention to time and motion studies and wage systems than to reorganizing managerial planning." Form also reports that "in no country did [Taylorism] become widespread." Few major corporations in the United States implemented his procedures; it spread to only a few industries in Britain. Although "the exact impact of Taylorism on skills is unknown," Form concludes, "it probably had only a marginal impact on the substance of skills."[46]

Form is mistaken about one detail. Taylor's methods were widely used in the Soviet Union, where from the mid-1930s to the mid-1950s more than three-quarters of Soviet industrial workers were engaged in incentive piecework. V. I. Lenin was an enthusiastic supporter of scientific management procedures. This fact, not too surprisingly, goes unmentioned in the critiques of work "under capitalism."[47]

Those critiques of capitalism are one-sided in still another way: They do not discuss alternatives. The critique typically comes with an unexplored and hence unassessed alternative. Work under capitalism, with its division of labor and dull routines, is hateful. Work, presumably, would be more attractive with some other organization of "the labor process," as, for example, in socialist economies. The implication that "things would be better" (i.e., work more charming), however, is typically not explored. If one "ended" the division of labor, the likely consequences should be indicated: lowered productivity, higher prices, and increased poverty.[48]

The supposedly sophisticated critiques fail to reckon with some everyday facts of life. Put differently, they are marked by persistent reality avoidance. One simple fact of life is that a week contains 168 hours. If employed full time, and if that means a forty-hour workweek, 24 percent of the week would be taken up by work. Some allowance should also be made for commuting. If this is ten hours (two hours per working day), a very high estimate, another 6 percent would be added to the total. Eight hours of sleep, fifty-six hours, would take another third of the week. That leaves sixty-two hours, 37 percent of the total, for all other activities: meals, family time, leisure, or a combination of these, and so on. Most of that free time would be spent in nonbureaucratic settings.

Another consideration, another fact of modern life, involves the length of one's worklife. Labor-force involvement has changed in several respects in the last half-century. One dramatic change has been the appearance of early retirement. In 1947 close to half of the employed male population over age sixty-five was still employed. In 1995 only one-sixth continued working beyond that age. One-third of men ages fifty-five to sixty-four in 1995 were no longer in the labor force.[49] On retirement, most people would have some contact with a couple of other bureaucracies, those supplying pension income and medical care benefits. Apart from that limited involvement, however, given increased life expectancies, most recent retirees are engaged in what is probably the largest episode of unconstrained mass leisure in the history of the world.

A second and even more dramatic change has been the sizable increase of women's labor-force participation. The percentage of women in the labor force (of those sixteen an over) increased from 31.8 in 1947 to 59.5 in 1997. For many, that would mean leaving nonbureaucratic employment—housework—for work elsewhere, some of it, clearly a small part, in large bureaucratic enterprises. In this case, however, the "critical" standard is often reversed: Employment outside the home is now frequently defined positively; it is a liberating experience.[50] There are, to be sure, other factors involved. Many housewives in the labor force face a "double-bind," in that the housework remains an insistent task, although, more and more, husbands are sharing those burdens. Some of that labor-force involvement, it should be noted, is part time. Women's participation, moreover, falls off after age thirty-five to forty-four. Among women fifty-five to sixty-four, half are not gainfully employed. Among those over sixty-five, only one in twelve remain in the labor force. Most of those older women are also participating in that largest episode of mass leisure.

The fourth proposition, drawn from Weber's original, is the argument of a tendency toward monocratic rule. As already seen, this proposition needs some qualification. The dominant arrangement within industry involves some delegation of power; that is, the divisional form. The explanation, put simply, is that the monocratic form with a single control center is impossible. No center can assemble and digest the information needed for the effective direction of a large, diverse, multitask enterprise. The effective solution has been decentralization with a performance-based control mechanism (as opposed to the extension of rules from a single center, collection of performance reports, and assessment at the same center). Franchise systems, as indicated, provide a variation on this pattern.

Another important specification was provided a half-century ago by Alvin Gouldner in an important study entitled *Patterns of Industrial Bureaucracy*. The firm he studied had three separate and distinct sets of bureaucratic rules. Some were generated by management, some by the union (called "representative" rules), and some by outside agencies. The latter rules, such as the "no smoking" signs, were there to conform to the requirements of insurers. But, Gouldner pointed out, management and workers both ignored the latter signs. His term, accordingly, was "mock bureaucracy." In subsequent decades, rules from outside would appear with much greater frequency. The penalties attached for their violation also increased significantly. Those rules, in short, could no longer be ignored.[51]

Gouldner's study points to a pluralistic arrangement of power. Management rules might conceivably be viewed as constraining or punitive, as designed to maximize performance (i.e., work) by participants. But the other two are protective, aiming to defend employee or client interests. Union rules protect against excessive demands (e.g., speedup), provide job guarantees, protect against arbitrary authority, and so forth. The outside rules, provided by government agencies, also provide protections: against unemployment, injury, discrimination, and so forth. Government rules guarantee the right to organize unions. Government agencies also supervise union elections and work to guarantee fair outcomes.

These commonplace observations again indicate the inadequacy of the sweeping critiques of "bureaucracy." Those critiques provide a highly selective review of evidence, thus yielding the picture of alienating and punitive bureaucracy. No serious intellectual purpose is served by such one-sided depictions. A realistic account would point up the obvious fact: A problematic bureaucracy may be countered by another bureaucracy. Arbitrary managerial authority may be countered by union authority. And arbitrary union authority may be countered by National Labor Relations Board supervision or by the courts. Those possibilities do not represent ideal solutions; they are merely better than the principal alternative. Constrained power, in short, is ordinarily preferable to the unconstrained variety. Much of the growth of bureaucracy is stimulated by that sensed need for constraint. Regulatory agencies are created for the express purpose of intrusion, to oversee and control irresponsible behaviors.

The fifth proposition holds that bureaucracies, more and more, will be directed by technically trained experts. This argument requires little discussion, since, on the whole, it has been amply supported. A century ago most business leaders were trained "on the job." Some self-made men made no secret of their contempt for school learning. That practice has been replaced by recruitment of university graduates and, increasingly, of those having advanced degrees in business administration, law, economics and finance, engineering, and, on occasion, the natural sciences.[52]

Governments have also shifted from personal rule, from coterie or patronage-based arrangements, to the recruitment of professionals. Max Weber described the process as follows: "In large states everywhere modern democracy is becoming a bureaucratised democracy. And it must be so; for it is replacing the aristocratic or other titular officials by a paid civil service. . . . It is the same within the parties too. This is inevitable."[53] France instituted sweeping measures under Napoleon. Prussia and other German states responded with similar reforms requiring university-based legal training, examinations, and extensive on-job training for a wide range of government appointments. The United States was a late developer in this respect, with the first step toward a professional civil service coming with the Pendleton Act of 1883. Initially, only one-tenth of the federal employees were affected. At the turn of the century only a minority, some 40 percent, were covered. Civil service reform came slowly, and fitfully, in state and local governments.[54]

In most countries the highest positions in government remain "political," with the occupants ordinarily chosen by the elected government, an arrangement reflecting the basic concept of democratic rule. Those are not civil service positions; they are not held for life. Following the Weberian logic, however, even here one would expect to find a concern for technocratic principles; that is, for expert rule.

Because they are rarely reviewed, we lose sight of or are ignorant of the prebureaucratic arrangements and of the rule of the dilettantes or amateurs. Grover Cleveland's secretary of state, Walter Gresham, died in office. A few weeks later Cleveland appointed his attorney general, Richard Olney, as Gresham's replacement. One writer described Olney as "a man of action, who had won wide approval among the comfortable classes for his ruthless advice to Cleveland to break the railroad strike on the ground that the United States mail must go through. He knew nothing about foreign affairs when he became Secretary of State but he was not at all averse to learning quickly and dangerously." Senator Henry Cabot Lodge approved of the choice: Cleveland "could not do better. Olney is a gentleman, a man of training and education, and a very able lawyer." Elihu Root's first appointment in the federal government, in July 1899, was as secretary of war. At that point, a biographer notes, he "knew almost nothing about the army." William Howard Taft chose Philander C. Knox, a corporate lawyer, to be his secretary of state. One source reports that "he had no experience in foreign affairs." Four years later, Woodrow

Wilson, the nation's first university-trained political expert, the holder of a Ph.D. in political science, chose William Jennings Bryan, also not known for his competence in foreign affairs, to be his secretary of state. The choice in this case was purely political: The leader of his party's populist faction had to be rewarded. Bryan saw the foreign service as an opportunity for patronage and appointed the party's faithful to positions throughout the world. Some of the consequences, in Santo Domingo for example, were disastrous.[55]

The bureaucratic tendency, the shift toward an expert civil service, is evident in the American experience. The process, however, proved unexpectedly slow and erratic. Some other factors operate to counter the incentives for efficient administration. Put differently, they impede the movement toward the fully developed bureaucratic form. The most important of those factors appear to be personal, the need for trusted associates, and political, the need to reward members of one's party.

CONCLUSIONS

The following conclusions with respect to the initial propositions appear to be warranted.

The first proposition holds that bureaucracies, both private and public, are large and growing. In this case a mixed judgment is required. On the size question, yes, many workplaces, both private and public, are large. The giant private firms in the major First World nations in the second half of the twentieth century are among the largest ever seen in human history. The governments of the Soviet Union and of China in this period, both having vast socialized sectors, were even larger when seen in terms of the number of lives affected or in terms of the proportion of the population employed in a single national enterprise. Although many private firms in the United States are large, it was also seen that most employed persons do not work in large or giant establishments. Approximately half work in small units employing fewer than fifty persons. Most of the rest are found in middle-sized units, those with 50 to 499 employees.

As for the trend, the prediction of growing bureaucracy is rejected. The recent experience in the United States has been one of declining size. Although not researched here, it seems likely that declines would have occurred elsewhere in the First World, with parallel shifts from large-unit extraction and manufacturing industries to smaller-unit service firms. With the growth of private-sector activities in China and widespread privatization elsewhere in former Communist nations, the size of the typical workplace may well be declining there also.

The second proposition claimed impersonality as the typical experience. This claim has long since been rejected, with most studies finding congenial and supportive social relations to be the typical experience. The persistence of the claim appears to stem from two factors: a failure (or refusal) to deal with the available evidence, and a semantic argument, an inappropriate use of a key term. The basic plan of most modern (or "fully developed") bureaucracies assumes impersonality in the sense that no special favor will be shown clients or employees. The old-style political machine was highly personal in that the boss would reward friends and supporters while penalizing opponents. Modern bureaucratic rules seek to avoid that kind of personalism. But equality of treatment, as indicated, does not prevent the appearance of friendly relationships in everyday life.

The third proposition argues intrusiveness: Bureaucracies dominate more and more aspects of our lives. This is rejected. Most employed persons, as indicated, do not work in large or giant establishments. With a shorter work week, longer vacations, earlier retirement, and longer lives, most people have more free time than ever before in the modern era; that is, time that is not constrained or determined by any bureaucracy. Some studies, moreover, indicate that work in bureaucracies in some ways is more "liberating" than work in other contexts.

The fourth proposition asserts the monocratic tendency. This too has been rejected. A single center cannot know, monitor, and direct the multifarious operations of any large organization. The operational imperative for firms has been the divisional form, a delegation of direct day-to-day supervision to the subordinate units, a procedure also found within universities. Moreover, as opposed to the single, all-controlling agency, one major development of the nineteenth and twentieth centuries has been the development of counter-organization, most notably in the form of voluntary associations and government regulatory agencies.[56]

The fifth proposition argues the rule by experts. This reflects a supposedly imperative demand for expert rule. This prediction, as seen, has been generally supported. Both private and public bureaucracies over the last two centuries have shifted away from personal arrangements and the use of amateurs. Both have required and sought out technically trained personnel.

Two qualifications, however, have been signaled involving the rate of change and the extent. The development came early in some countries, as in France and the German states. Elsewhere, bureaucratization came slowly, notably in Britain and the United States. Some positions are untouched by those imperatives or, put differently, some space for purely personal (or party) choices remains. The principal impediment to the demand for expertise is a countering imperative, a personal factor, the demand for trust or loyalty among the members of leadership groups (whether in government or private firms). In democratic societies, moreover, party-related needs also carry some weight.

The competing demands, personal and political needs and those of objective administration, are often presented as sharply opposed. In practice, however, it is likely that leaders would prefer staff members who were both loyal and competent. One might wish that the deserving party faithful would also have the requisite expertise. But competence is always in short supply. Most of those with the requisite knowledge and abilities would be otherwise occupied and not disposed to take on what in any case would be a short-term appointment.

The "hard-hitting" discussions, those "critical" depictions of bureaucracy, are very misleading. Most people work in medium-size and small establishments, not in large bureaucracies. The latter units are not growing, with just the opposite being the case. Bureaucratic work is not ultimately punitive or "alienating." Most of those involved in large bureaucracies provide generally positive assessments of their work experience. Most bureaucracies are not intrusive; that is, doing nasty things that somehow reduce the quality of life. And finally, early retirement from the labor force means a substantial increase in leisure time not encumbered by bureaucratic rules and regulations.

The critique of "big government" is curiously misplaced. The focus on the federal government, as seen, is mistaken, since state and local governments, collectively, are much larger. The claimed growth of the federal government is mistaken. The claim of intrusiveness is also open to some question, at least as a sweeping generalization. Many of the services provided are likely to be viewed positively, most especially those involving pensions and medical benefits.

The sweeping critique of bureaucracy also shows an unwillingness to make appropriate specifications. The federal government grew considerably in the 1960s, most of that growth involving the welfare state; arrangements to deliver income and medical benefits. Regulatory agencies, typically, are small, both in regard to staff and budget. They do make regular and insistent intrusions. Most of those agencies, however, would also be viewed favorably, at least in principle. One might consider the implications of the most extreme alternative: dissolution of the Arms Control and Disarmament Agency, the Consumer Product Safety Commission, the Environmental Protection Agency, the Equal Employment Opportunity Commission, the Federal Election Commission, or the Securities and Exchange Commission. The work of most such agencies is likely to be viewed with favor.[57]

Many people have raised serious objections to the actual performance of those government agencies, both those of the welfare state and the regulatory agencies. Many of the concerns are entirely justified. In most instances, however, the objections involve what might be called "design flaws" as opposed to questions of principle. The activities of a given agency, for example, did not produce the results intended, or the unintended side effects proved costly, or there were problems with implementation ("the law's delay, the insolence of office").

The solutions to those problems in most instances are bureaucratic. They typically involve rewriting the law or the administrative regulations (or both), or undertaking some new efforts in the recruitment and training of personnel. Successful solutions would ordinarily require a detailed knowledge of the agency and its operations. A thorough knowledge of the agency's effectiveness would be needed; that is, evaluation studies of its performance. In addition to that basic social science research, legal skills would be needed for any changes in the law and/or regulations. Successful interventions, in short, require a wide range of technical knowledge, knowledge acquired through professional training and on-the-job experience.

What are the likely consequences of the relentlessly negative portrayal of "bureaucracy"? One possibility is that the blind (or unthinking) antibureaucratic critique ultimately worsens the quality of life. The arguments are directed principally to university students. Later in life the principal recipients would be the "informed" or "educated" public. Those most likely to be influenced would be the "sensitive," especially those who are "socially concerned." Many people giving credence to those lessons would be led to avoid careers in the bureaucracies. That self-selection would remove the "sensitive" from the settings in which they might otherwise design and work for intelligent reforms. Their choices would leave those organizations to be managed, presumably, by persons lacking that sensitivity, persons concerned only with their own careers, or worse, concerned only with the "bottom line." To the extent that the sensitive critics remove themselves from bureaucratic careers, they would also be unfitting themselves for the work of reform. Their recommendations, as a consequence, would always be poorly informed and thus, ultimately, inexpert.

All in all, it is a curious performance. We have "scientific" intellectuals who, neglecting the findings of their own science, put forward a patently contrary-to-fact portrait of the modern world. A "world-historical" argument is presented, and generously commended, to university students and to many others. The centerpiece of the argument is a trend statement: the growth of bureaucracy, more and more of it. But with rare exception, no supporting evidence is provided, no data showing that continued growth. This "truth" has, with only rare exception, been taken as self-evident. Not until Granovetter's 1984 article, the first of its kind, was this dogma challenged. And even then, as seen, it has been neglected in much of the subsequent "critical" commentary.

The condemnation of the "condition of modern man" is relentless. It is peculiar in that the pretense of realism is combined with a ready acceptance of romantic fantasies about premodern life. Gerth and Mills point to Max Weber's use of Schiller's phrase, the "disenchantment of the world" (*die Entzauberung der Welt*): "The extent and direction of 'rationalization,'" they write, "is thus measured negatively in terms of the degree to which magical elements of thought are displaced." Toward the end of the *Protestant Ethic*, it will be remembered, Weber saw "new prophets" as one alternative to the current tendencies, or another option, "a great rebirth of old ideas and ideals," which were not specified. "Old ideals" might not be all that beneficial for the contemporary world. At minimum, some thought is required.[58]

Any serious account of trends, of the modern tendency, needs some consideration of a base point, some portrait of how things were. But in the arguments of Weber and other antimodernists the contrasting base point has, at best, only a shadowy presence. All we have is the quiet implication that the conditions of life "then" were somehow better. But most premoderns lived in dank cottages with dirt floors. They lived miserable lives, suffering helplessly in the face of crop failure and pestilence. For most premoderns, life was short and its quality poor. It is possible that the prophets served the people well, but one should not prejudge such matters. Some of those prophecies brought disaster.[59]

Weber's argument here is a curious one. For reasons that are not clear, he is predicting "good things" from an entire category of human beings, from the "prophets." And from another category, rational bureaucratic experts, he is anticipating bad things (or at minimum, something markedly less attractive). Traditional religions have long recognized the difficulty. Anyone can make claims; anyone can announce a new truth. Religious leaders have spent much time and effort on this matter, attempting to sort out the true from the false prophets. It is puzzling: Why should Weber, this eminently modern man, vouch for the wisdom of the "prophets"? Why should he bypass the obvious difficulties?

Commenting on a large literature, Richard Scott, a leading specialist in the field of organizations, reports that Weber's model of bureaucracy has been superseded by more complex and better-supported formulations. Weber's analysis, one shared also by economists' analyses of the firm, "viewed organizations as unified actors organized around specific goals set by entrepreneurs or chief executives." From an early point it was recognized that that image ignored "the reality of organizational behavior." But finding the "intentionally simplified view of the firm" to be a useful "heuristic fiction," the model, Scott writes, "survived into the 1950s as an 'ideal-type' characterization, capturing the distinctive features of a generic form without pretending to be complete or 'accurate.'" The "reigning theoretical models of single-purpose organizations," he adds, "were slow to change despite accumulating empirical evidence of the diversity of participants' interests." Scott reviews subsequent developments in organizational theory, the first and most fundamental being the transition from Weber's "unified" imagery to "multiple actor models." This change was seen in Alvin Gouldner's work in his depiction of three types of bureaucracy within a single firm. That revision points to the existence of diverse agents within organizations and to consequent power struggles.[60]

Scott describes the intellectual history as follows:

Organizational historians have observed how organizational forms that once appeared to march relentlessly toward ever more centralized and unitary structures began in the early decades of this century to alter their course and move in the direction of devising more decentralized, often multidivisional, structures. Now, perhaps, at the end of this century, we are seeing another major shift as key corporations increasingly downscale, contract-out, and seek to develop various loose alliances and more horizontal linkages with one another. . . . The hegemony of the unified, hierarchical, one-form-fits-all model appears to be broken.[61]

That is an appropriate summary of the specialized literature. But in university-level social science textbooks, in humanities courses, and in much of the mass media, the single-form imagery, that of a pervasive, expanding, and oppressive bureaucracy, continues to reign.

NOTES

1. Max Weber, *From Max Weber: Essays in Sociology*, ed. and trans. H. H. Gerth and C. Wright Mills (London: Routledge & Kegan Paul, 1948), Ch. 8. Another version, a revision of the Gerth–Mills translation, may be found in Max Weber, *Economy and Society: An Outline of Interpretive Sociology*, vol. 3, ed. Guenther Roth and Claus Wittich (New York: Bedminster Press, 1968), 956–1005. For the original, see Weber, *Wirtschaft und Gesellschaft: Grundriss der verstehenden Soziologie*, 4th ed., ed. Johannes Winckelmann (Tübingen: J.C.B. Mohr–Paul Siebeck, 1956), part III, Ch. 4.

2. Weber, *From Max Weber*, 196–198. Some commentators have raised a definitional question involving coverage or extent. Are all employees, including routine clerical employees and blue-collar workers, members of the bureaucracy? Or does the term apply only to those with that "special technical" training, essentially the managers and, possibly, the professionals? In this chapter I proceed with the former understanding. Most discussions of bureaucracy assert comprehensive impacts. Few make use of partitive expressions.

3. Ibid., 198–200.

4. Ibid., 41–42. The original report of this conversation appears in Marianne Weber, *Max Weber: Ein Lebensbild* (1926; reprint, Heidelberg: Lambert Schneider, 1950), 700–703.

5. Weber, *From Max Weber*, 202–203.

6. Ibid., 198–199, 215.

7. Ibid., 214.

8. No discussion of bureaucracy would be complete without a consideration of the typical inefficiencies, of the pathologies. On this theme, see Victor A. Thompson, *Modern Organization* (New York: Knopf, 1961), Ch. 8; Peter M. Blau and Marshall W. Meyer, *Bureaucracy in Modern Society*, 3d ed. (New York: Random House, 1987), Ch. 7; and Harry Cohen, *The Demonics of Bureaucracy: Problems of Change in a Government Agency* (Ames: Iowa State University Press, 1965). See also the important article/chapter by Robert K. Merton, "Bureaucratic Structure and Personality," *Social Forces* 17 (1940): 560–568.

9. This brief sketch necessarily simplifies a complex history. The presence of a bureaucracy itself would not have been sufficient to explain the rise of Prussia. Some weight must be given to Frederick's intelligence, determination, and charismatic presence on the battlefield. For a brief overview, see Gerhard Ritter, *Frederick the Great: A Historical Profile*, trans. Peter Paret (Berkeley and Los Angeles: University of California Press, 1968). For more detail, see Robert B. Asprey, *Frederick the Great: The Magnificent Enigma* (New York: Ticknor & Fields, 1986). On the Prussian bureaucracy, see Ernest Barker, *The Development of Public Services in Western Europe, 1660–*

1930 (London: Oxford University Press, 1944); and Hans Rosenberg, *Bureaucracy, Aristocracy and Autocracy: The Prussian Experience, 1660–1815* (1958; reprint, Boston: Beacon Press, 1966). Some consideration should also be given to the significance of tax revenues. The economic determinism of Marxism focuses almost exclusively on capitalists and their profits, thus overlooking the importance of public finance. The taxes gained by Prussia from Silesia and Westphalia made possible a much larger army and a stronger state.

10. Max Weber, *The Protestant Ethic and the Spirit of Capitalism*, trans. Talcott Parsons (New York: Scribner's, 1930), 181. A minor detail: The original reads *stahlhartes Gehäuse*, which would make it a steel cage or shell. For a critique of the work, see Richard F. Hamilton, *The Social Misconstruction of Reality: Validity and Verification in the Scholarly Community* (New Haven: Yale University Press, 1996), Ch. 3. For an extended discussion, see Arthur Mitzman, *The Iron Cage: An Historical Interpretation of Max Weber* (New York: Knopf, 1970).

11. Weber, *Protestant Ethic*, 181.

12. Ibid., 182. The last passage appears as a quotation in the original, although no source is given. That pursuit of wealth, according to Weber, has reached its highest development in the United States. The fugitive character of Weber's documentation, a persistent problem in this work, may be seen in the accompanying note 115. It contains a hearsay statement about a single American businessman, "the leading dry-goods man of an Ohio city."

13. Weber, *From Max Weber*, 49–50. The speech was published as "Der Sozialismus" in Weber's *Gesammelte Aufsätze zur Soziologie und Sozialpolitik* (Tübingen: J.C.B. Mohr–Paul Siebeck, 1924), 492–518. For an English translation, see J.E.T. Eldridge, ed., *Max Weber: The Interpretation of Social Reality* (New York: Scribner's, 1971), 191–219, esp. p. 209.

14. Weber, *From Max Weber*, 50. This brief summary, published in 1948, anticipates the major themes that were to appear in C. Wright Mills, *White Collar: The American Middle Classes* (New York: Oxford University Press, 1951). For other passages indicating Weber's ultimate disdain for the bureaucratic tendency, see Mitzman, *Iron Cage*, 177–178, 184, 232, 259–260. He wrote of the coming "inescapable universal bureaucratization," calling it "that bondage of the future."

15. Neil Smelser, *Sociology*, 5th ed. (Englewood Cliffs, N.J.: Prentice Hall, 1995), 124.

16. Leonard Thompson, *A History of South Africa*, rev. ed. (New Haven: Yale University Press, 1995), 33. For more detail, see C. R. Boxer, *The Dutch Seaborne Empire* (1965; reprint, London: Penguin, 1990). For the diverse English efforts, see Robert Brenner, "The Social Basis of English Commercial Expansion, 1550–1650," *Journal of Economic History* 32 (1972): 361–384. For a popular history of a key firm, see John Keay, *The Honourable Company: A History of the English East India Company* (New York: Macmillan, 1991).

17. Richard Edwards, *Contested Terrain: The Transformation of the Workplace in the Twentieth Century* (New York: Basic Books, 1979), vii.

18. Robert P. Quinn, Thomas W. Mangione, and Stanley E. Seashore, *Quality of Employment Survey, 1972–1973*, and *Quality of Employment Survey, 1977: Cross-Section* [computer files] (Ann Arbor, Mich.: Institute for Social Research, 1975 and 1979), variable 73 for 1973 and variable 100 for 1977 data; James A. Davis and Tom W. Smith, *General Social Surveys, 1972–1996*: [Cumulative file] [computer file] (Chicago: National Opinion Research Center, 1997), variable LOCALNUM. Some impreci-

sion is likely in the upper reaches of these distributions. Persons working in small shops could provide precise and accurate statements. Persons working in large establishments might not know the precise number (e.g., whether 1,900 or 2,100 employees).

19. *Moody's Industrial Manual: 1996* (New York: Moody's Investors Services, 1996), 1087–1098. The quotation in the previous paragraph is also from *Moody's*, p. 1088.

20. Thomas S. Dicke, *Franchising in America: The Development of a Business Method, 1840–1980* (Chapel Hill: University of North Carolina Press, 1992). On the fast-food chains, see Stan Luxenberg, *Roadside Empires* (New York: Viking, 1985).

21. See Alfred D. Chandler, Jr., *Strategy and Structure: Chapters in the History of the Industrial Enterprise* (Cambridge: MIT Press, 1962); and Chandler, ed., *Giant Enterprise: Ford, General Motors, and the Automobile Industry: Sources and Readings* (New York: Harcourt, Brace & World, 1964). For a popular account, see Ed Cray, *Chrome Colossus: General Motors and Its Times* (New York: McGraw-Hill, 1980), 191–192. The details of the divisional arrangement are, understandably, rather complex and are constantly changing. For "bits and pieces" on the theme, see Cray, *Chrome Colossus*, 197–198, 294, 317, 324, 331–332, 377–378, 406, 448–449. For more detail plus some appropriate references, see Neil Fligstein, "The Spread of the Multidivisional Form Among Large Firms, 1919–1979," *American Sociological Review* 50 (1985): 377–391. Conglomerates are generally larger than the ordinary giant firm, the entrepreneurs having crossed industry boundaries in search of acquisitions. But this form proved a mistake, coordination being difficult and the returns not commensurate with the investment. As a consequence it has fallen into disfavor. See Gerald F. Davis, Kristina A. Kiekmann, and Catherine H. Tinsley, "The Decline and Fall of the Conglomerate Firm in the 1980s: The Deinstitutionalization of an Organizational Form," *American Sociological Review* 59 (1994): 547–570.

22. Apart from the appropriate specialists, few academics are likely to know these aspects of American corporate history. But a parallel tendency is easily observed within the universities themselves, where a similar process, de facto decentralization, may be seen. Academics themselves, within the departments, make many of the key decisions; most obviously, those of hiring, promotion, and salary. All of those decisions, to be sure, must be approved by boards of trustees, but in most instances that is a formality. With the growth of conglomerates in the mass media, many publishing "houses" came to be owned by major corporations. One might assume that the managers of those corporations would police or otherwise guarantee acceptable content in the books published, but a detailed investigation found no such attempts. The managers judged the subordinate units in terms of their profitability. See Lewis A. Coser, Charles Kadushin, and Walter W. Powell, *Books: The Culture and Commerce of Publishing* (New York: Basic Books, 1982), 180–182.

23. Mark Granovetter, "Small Is Bountiful: Labor Markets and Establishment Size," *American Sociological Review* 49 (1984): 323–334.

24. Ibid., 326, Table 2; U.S. Bureau of the Census, *Statistical Abstract of the United States: 1996* (Washington, D.C.: U.S. Government Printing Office, 1996), Table 840.

25. Granovetter, "Small Is Bountiful," 326.

26. Ibid., 326, Table 2; U.S. Bureau of the Census, *Statistical Abstract: 1996*, Table 840.

27. Granovetter, "Small Is Bountiful," 327, Table 5; U.S. Bureau of the Census, *Statistical Abstract: 1996*, Table 838. This series is based on the U.S. Bureau of the

Census, *County Business Patterns* (Washington, D.C.: U.S. Government Printing Office, various years). It "excludes government employees, railroad employees, self-employed persons, etc." Some comparable figures for Germany appear in W. L. Guttsman, *The German Social Democratic Party, 1875–1933* (London: George Allen & Unwin, 1981), 24–27. Just over 45 percent of the industrial labor force in 1882 was employed in enterprises with one to five persons, and fewer than 5 percent were in units of 1,000 or more. Some growth in the typical size occurred in the following decades, but in 1907 fewer than 10 percent were employed in the giant units. In 1925 fewer than 20 percent were employed there. Even at that late point, more persons were employed in units of one to five. Most of the growth in this period occurred in mid-size units, those of 11 to 50, 51 to 200, and 201 to 1,000.

28. Steve Lohr, "Fewer Ties Are Bonding Workers to Corporations," *New York Times*, 14 August 1992, sec. A, p. 1. Lohr gives his sources, without any specifics, as Bureau of Labor Statistics and *Fortune* magazine. General Motors, as indicated, had 745,000 employees in 1995. At the end of 1998 the total was reported as 594,000. In 1995 the firm was operating in 316 locations in the United States, but in only 291 in 1998. Outsourcing is one possibility, but reorganization is another. Giant firms are not constant entities. They are continuously acquiring, merging, and divesting. In June 1995 GM sold its assets of the National Car Rental System to an organization that agreed to continue the employment of its 6,400 employees and to continue the purchase of GM vehicles. A series of complicated transactions involved the components of the former Hughes Corporation. Electronic Data Systems was split off from GM in June 1966. See *Moody's Industrial Manual, 1999* (New York: Mergent, 1999), 3421–3423.

29. U.S. Bureau of the Census, *Statistical Abstract: 1996*, Table 532.

30. The figures are from Department of Defense, Statistical Information Analysis Division, *DOD Active Duty Military Personnel Strength Levels*, available <http://web1.whs.osd.mil/mmid/military/trends.htm>.

31. U.S. Bureau of the Census, *Statistical Abstract: 1998*, Table 530, and *1996*, Table 501. The regular emphasis on federal government growth is seriously misleading. In the period from 1980 to 1992 state governments were the growth leaders, increasing by 22.4 percent, followed by the counties (21.6 percent), and then the school districts (20.4 percent). Some federal government growth occurred in that period, specifically during the Reagan and Bush presidencies. It amounted to 5.1 percent.

32. U.S. Bureau of the Census, *Statistical Abstract: 1998*, Tables 559, 571.

33. U.S. Office of Management and Budget, *Historical Tables,* Section 3, 17 December 1999, available <W3.access.gpo.gov/usbudget/fy2000/pdf/hist.pdf>.

34. One sketchy presentation gives "government employment as a percent of spending." Sweden and Denmark were high with, respectively, 32.4 and 31.3 percent. They were followed by France, 24.3 percent; Britain, 19.3 percent; Germany, 14.9 percent; and the United States, 14.5 percent. Lowest by far of the seven countries listed was Japan, at 5.9 percent. Japan, of course, has a very small defense establishment, a modest welfare state, and little state-owned enterprise. These figures appear in "On the Payrolls of Big Government," *New York Times*, 11 October 1995, sec. A, p. 13, and came from the Organization of Economic Cooperation and Development (no further information provided). Another presentation gives generally comparable results. The measure used was the number of state employees per 1,000 of the population. In 1980 Sweden and Denmark were both high with, respectively, 156.3 and 128.8. The United States had a middle position (77.9) in this twelve-nation comparison. Japan was again

low at 33.6. From "Wer leistet sich wieviel staatsdiener?" *Frankfurter Allgemeine Zeitung*, 7 April 1983. Their figures came from the Institut der deutschen Wirtschaft in Cologne.

35. U.S. Bureau of the Census, *Statistical Abstract: 1998*, Table 562. Those figures do not include persons employed by the Central Intelligence Agency, the Defense Intelligence Agency, or the National Security Agency. For discussion of these agencies, see Jeffrey Richelson, *The U.S. Intelligence Community*, 2d ed. (New York: HarperBusiness, 1989).

36. U.S. Bureau of the Census, *Statistical Abstract: 1998*, Table 500.

37. An early study by F. J. Roethlisberger and W. J. Dickson found cohesive work groups, ones that successfully countered demands for heightened productivity. See their *Management and the Worker* (Cambridge: Harvard University Press, 1947). For a comprehensive review of studies through to the early 1960s, see Delbert C. Miller and William H. Form, *Industrial Sociology: The Sociology of Work Organizations*, 2d ed. (New York: Harper & Row, 1964), Ch. 7. A study of workers in what was once the world's largest textile mill, one which at its peak employed some 17,000 persons, found family and work to be very closely linked. One respondent reported, "My brothers and sisters and I would go down to the mill together. We'd work together all day and come back home together. We were never separated when we were living at home." See Tamara K. Hareven and Randolph Langenbach, *Amoskeag: Life and Work in an American Factory-City* (New York: Pantheon Books, 1978), 10, 242. Although presumed to be a powerful determinant of satisfactions, size of workplace has not been a favored variable in American social science. For an important review and investigation, see Juan J. Linz, "The Social Bases of West German Politics" (Ph.D. diss., Columbia University, 1959), Ch. 11. Some of his findings deserve wider circulation. The percentage who preferred to work in the same establishment varied directly with size: 34 percent for those in plants under 10, and 56 percent among those in plants of 1,000 or more (p. 409). Work satisfaction showed no variation by size of plant (p. 410). See also Richard F. Hamilton, *Affluence and the French Worker in the Fourth Republic* (Princeton: Princeton University Press, 1967), Ch. 10.

38. Frederic M. Sherer found the income differential increasing over time. See his "Industrial Structure, Scale Economies, and Worker Alienation," in *Essays on Industrial Organization in Honor of Joe S. Bain*, ed. Robert T. Masson and P. David Qualls (Cambridge: Ballinger, 1976), Ch. 6. See also Ross M. Stolzenberg, "Bringing the Boss Back In: Employer Size, Employee Schooling, and Socioeconomic Achievement," *American Sociological Review* 43 (1978): 813–828. Table 3.6 is based on wage and salaried workers only. It excludes the self-employed, most of whom are located in smaller units. The latter were more positive about the pay and the fringe benefits and indicated greater job satisfaction. The responses of white- and blue-collar workers were examined separately. The latter were generally less positive, but the differences were small; the patterns shown in Table 3.6 appeared in both segments.

39. One should consider another hypothesis, another fact-of-life consideration: The amount of noise in the workplace increases with the size of establishment. The heavy machinery, the stamping machines, drill presses, punch presses, the assembly of vehicles, and so on are typically found in large units. The obvious correlate is that the greater the noise, the smaller the opportunity for friendly interaction. Samuel Gompers and his coworkers worked at a table and rolled tobacco leaves into cigars allowing easy interaction throughout the entire day. But that attractive arrangement is not pos-

sible for those at the punch presses, at the looms, or, in automobile factories, for those on the line.

40. The same result could be achieved informally, through intentional kin-based recruitment, an arrangement favored by both management and the workers. Many instances of this appear in Hareven and Langenbach, *Amoskeag*, beginning with p. 20.

41. Many of these questions are reviewed, with evidence, in Richard F. Hamilton and James D. Wright, *The State of the Masses* (New York: Aldine, 1986), Ch. 6. Although running contrary to intellectuals' prejudices, some workers, a minority, like routine work; some like work "on the line" (p. 257).

42. See Merton, "Bureaucratic Structure." It was republished, with minor changes, in Robert K. Merton, Ailsa P. Gray, Barbara Hockey, and Hanan C. Selvin, eds., *Reader in Bureaucracy* (Glencoe, Ill.: Free Press, 1952), 361–371; and in Merton's *Social Theory and Social Structure*, rev. and enl. ed. (Glencoe, Ill.: Free Press, 1957), Ch. VI.

43. Melvin L. Kohn, "Bureaucratic Man: A Portrait and an Interpretation," *American Sociological Review* 36 (1971): 461–474. Two earlier studies cited by Kohn challenged the standard hypothesis. Peter M. Blau, in 1955, "found that the job securities provided to the employees of a government bureaucracy generate favorable attitudes toward change" (Kohn, p. 462). The reference is to Blau, *The Dynamics of Bureaucracy: A Study of Interpersonal Relations in Two Government Agencies* (Chicago: University of Chicago Press, 1955), 183–200. A second study cited also provided little support for the original claim. See Charles M. Bonjean and Michael D. Grimes, "Bureaucracy and Alienation: A Dimensional Approach," *Social Forces* 48 (1970): 365–373. For a later discussion and a review of later studies, see James Q. Wilson, *Bureaucracy: What Government Agencies Do and Why They Do It* (New York: Basic Books, 1989), 69–70. This work provides a brilliant compendious overview. Wilson's comments on Weber's position and on the need for correction appear in the Preface, pp. ix–x.

44. Kohn's article received more citations, relatively, in the 1970s; that is, shortly after publication. From 1974 to 1980 Merton's article/chapter was cited forty-three times; Kohn's work received twenty-nine citations. Granovetter's article averaged five citations per year in the early 1990s. There were two in 1995 and three in 1996.

45. Harry Braverman, *Labor and Monopoly Capital: The Degradation of Work in the Twentieth Century* (New York: Monthly Review Press, 1974). The work was still in print in 1999. For the review of evidence on the subject, see William H. Form, "On the Degradation of Skills," *Annual Review of Sociology* 12 (1987): 29–47.

46. Form, "Degradation of Skills," 40.

47. For a discussion and references, see Hamilton and Wright, *State of the Masses*, 70–71. Braverman, *Labor and Monopoly Capital*, 12–13, spells out "the Soviet connection," but the Soviet experience disappears entirely from his subsequent discussion. At one point he rejects the term "bureaucratization" as "an evasive and unfortunate use of Weberian terminology." The use of these control mechanisms, he wrote on p. 120, "is better understood as the specific product of the capitalist organization of work, and reflects not primarily scale but social antagonisms." On the man and his work, see Robert Kanigel, *The One Best Way: Frederick Winslow Taylor and the Enigma of Efficiency* (New York: Viking, 1997). Lenin, Trotsky, and Stalin were all enthusiastic supporters of Taylorism (see pp. 525–526).

48. For a study of automobile manufacturing that abandoned "the line" in favor of more individual or craftsmanlike conditions, see Arthur S. Weinberg, "Six American

Workers Assess Job Redesign at Saab–Scandia," *Monthly Labor Review* 98 (1975): 52–54. The six American automobile workers spent a month working in the Saab–Scandia plant in Sweden. They liked the leisurely pace and the job rotation, but did not see how the company "could function economically at this slow pace." One "obvious" economic truth may be seen in this experience: The Saab costs more than cars produced on the line. For discussion of this case and other similar attempts, see Hamilton and Wright, *State of the Masses*, 268–272.

49. On the changes in the labor force, see U.S. Bureau of the Census, *Statistical Abstract: 1993*, Tables 621 and 622, *1996*, Table 617. A slight reversal of this trend appeared in the 1990s. Between 1990 and 1997 labor-force participation of men sixty-five and above increased, going from 16.3 to 17.1 percent. See U.S. Bureau of the Census, *Statistical Abstract: 1998*, Table 645. These sources also provided the information for women's employment reported in the following paragraph. For the earlier figures, see U.S. Bureau of the Census, *Historical Statistics of the United States: Colonial Times to 1970* (Washington, D.C.: U.S. Government Printing Office, 1975), part 1, pp. 131–132.

50. Myra M. Ferree, "Working Class Jobs: Housework and Paid Work as Sources of Satisfaction," *Social Problems* 23 (1976): 431–441. Her study, based on a small sample of women in the Boston area, found the working wives to be "happier and more satisfied with their lives." A subsequent study by James D. Wright, based on six national surveys, found no support for those claims. See his "Are Working Women *Really* More Satisfied? Evidence from Several National Surveys," *Journal of Marriage and the Family* 40 (1978): 301–313. In subsequent social science literature, Ferree's work has been cited more frequently than Wright's. Between 1981 and 1990 the number of citations were, respectively, fifty-one and forty-one (based on the *Social Science Citation Index*).

51. Alvin W. Gouldner, *Patterns of Industrial Bureaucracy* (Glencoe, Ill.: Free Press, 1954).

52. W. Lloyd Warner and James C. Abegglen, *Big Business Leaders in America* (New York: Harper, 1955); Jay M. Gould, *The Technical Elite* (New York: Augustus M. Kelley, 1966). See also Myles L. Mace, *Directors: Myth and Reality* (Boston: Harvard Business School Press, 1986), esp. Ch. 8. Family members, the inheritors, are typically amateurs, persons with power but lacking in technical expertise. They are, Mace indicates, basically an annoyance, an impediment to efficient operation of the firm.

53. From Eldridge, *Max Weber*, 195–197.

54. See Barker, *Development of Public Services*; Robert D. Putnam, *The Comparative Study of Political Elites* (Englewood Cliffs, N.J.: Prentice Hall, 1976); and Joel D. Aberbach, Robert D. Putnam, and Bert A. Rockman, *Bureaucrats and Politicians in Western Democracies* (Cambridge: Harvard University Press, 1981). See also Putnam's "Elite Transformation in Advanced Industrial Societies: An Empirical Assessment of the Theory of Technocracy," *Comparative Political Studies* 10 (1977): 383–412. For a compendious review of the Canadian experience, see John Porter, *The Vertical Mosaic: An Analysis of Social Class and Power in Canada* (Toronto: University of Toronto Press, 1965). Weber anticipated a very rapid movement. There is, however, some question about the rate of change. A half-century later, a study of 171 American cities found one-sixth of them had no civil service coverage. Another quarter covered only policemen and firemen. See Raymond E. Wolfinger and John Osgood

Field, "Political Ethos and the Structure of City Government," *American Political Science Review* 60 (1966): 306–326, Table 4.

55. On Olney, see Karl Schriftgiesser, *The Gentleman from Massachusetts: Henry Cabot Lodge* (Boston: Little, Brown, 1945), 137; then, Richard W. Leopold, *Elihu Root and the Conservative Tradition* (Boston: Houghton Mifflin, 1954), 24. For Knox, see Charles Vevier, *The United Sates and China, 1906–1913: A Study of Finance and Diplomacy* (New Brunswick, N.J.: Rutgers University Press, 1955), 89. Vevier adds, "Unlike Hay and Root, Knox had no intention of overworking himself in office, and Taft got the impression that his Secretary of State was lazy." On Bryan and the Caribbean disasters, see Arthur S. Link, *Woodrow Wilson and the Progressive Era, 1910–1917* (New York: Harper Torchbooks, 1963), 93–102.

56. A political scientist, Thomas R. Dye, argues monocratic rule. Large economic institutions, industrial corporations, banks, utilities, insurance companies, and investment banks, he writes, "decide what will be produced, how much it will cost, how many people will be employed, and what their wages will be . . . how much money will be available for capital investment, what interest rates will be charged." His review is selective (or one-sided), neglecting all countering organizations, all that might challenge the monolith. Those large institutions, presumably, are not constrained by unions or by government regulation. There is no mention of market constraints. See his *Who's Running America? The Clinton Years*, 6th ed. (Englewood Cliffs, N.J.: Prentice Hall, 1995), 14.

57. The Food and Drug Administration was created under a law "passed at Theodore Roosevelt's behest in 1906." But the law had serious "limitations and loopholes." Through to the 1930s, entrepreneurs could with impunity concoct and sell all kinds of nostrums, some with serious detrimental effects, some even lethal. A bill addressing those problems was introduced in the Senate during Franklin Roosevelt's first hundred days. But it was then stalled for five years, opposition coming from quacks, food producers, and newspaper publishers (who benefited from patent medicine advertisements). A watered-down measure was finally passed in June 1938. For brief histories of this episode, see Arthur M. Schlesinger, Jr., *The Coming of the New Deal* (Boston: Houghton Mifflin, 1938), 355–359; and Kenneth S. Davis, *FDR, the New Deal Years 1933–1937: A History* (New York: Random House, 1986), 472–474, 485–486. Public pressure for reform measures was generated by publication of a best-selling exposé, Arthur Kallet and F. J. Schlink, *100,000,000 Guinea Pigs: Dangers in Everyday Foods, Drugs and Cosmetics* (New York: Vanguard, 1932). The history, of course, did not end with the new law. The seesaw struggle of interests continues to the present day. For some sense of the complexities, see Robert N. Proctor, *Cancer Wars: How Politics Shapes What We Know and Don't Know About Cancer* (New York: Basic Books, 1995).

58. Weber, *From Max Weber*, 51. Their translation does not do justice to the original: *Entzauberung* means "the removal of magic from." That "rationalization," presumably, is removing magic from "our" lives. Also see Weber, *Protestant Ethic*, 182.

59. For an instructive case study of a prophecy and its disastrous effects, see Thompson, *History of South Africa*, 78–79. For another example, see Michael C. Meyer and William L. Sherman, *The Course of Mexican History*, 5th ed. (New York: Oxford University Press, 1995), 41, 103, 113.

60. W. Richard Scott, "The Evolution of Organization Theory," in *Studies in Organizational Sociology: Essays in Honor of Charles K. Warriner*, ed. Gale Miller (Green-

wich, Conn.: JAI Press, 1991), 54; and Gouldner, *Patterns of Industrial Bureaucracy*.
   61. Ibid., 60. For more detailed discussion, see W. Richard Scott, *Organizations: Rational, Natural, and Open Systems*, 3d ed. (Englewood Cliffs, N.J.: Prentice Hall, 1992), and *Institutions and Organizations* (Thousand Oaks, Calif.: Sage, 1995). As indicated, the literature on the subject is enormous. Other compendious reviews are Andrew H. Van de Ven and William F. Joyce, eds., *Perspectives on Organization Design and Behavior* (New York: Wiley, 1981); Ronald G. Corwin, *The Organization–Society Nexus: A Critical Review of Models and Metaphors* (New York: Greenwood Press, 1987); and Walter W. Powell and Paul J. DiMaggio, eds., *The New Institutionalism in Organizational Analysis* (Chicago: University of Chicago Press, 1991).

CHAPTER 4

Social Theories and Social Research

THE MAJOR SOCIAL THEORIES: AN OVERVIEW

Major social theories, although diverse in their emphases and conclusions, share two common focal concerns: the institutional (or structural) and the social psychological. The term "institution" (or social structure), as used here, refers to relatively fixed social arrangements such as, for example, families, schools, workplaces, churches, local communities, governments, and so forth.[1] Social psychology refers to the training or socialization of individuals living within those structures. The family is a major institution in all societies. Among other things, families play a key role in the training of children, teaching "the values of the society."

Many formulations of such sociological "truths" are static. One must recognize, however, the ever-changing character of institutions; older ones being transformed, new ones being created. Some of the social psychological formulations are categorical, not addressing questions of degree. One must recognize the "imperfections" of any training and ask about the rates of success or failure. Families do teach children, but they do not all teach the same values. And they teach with varying degrees of insistence and with differing success. Finally, one must recognize the many other factors operating. Families in 1750 would have had little competition in the training of their children. In the 1990s, schools, peer groups, and mass media provided many competing alternatives.

The three theories assessed in this work make use of various combinations of institutional and social psychological elements and provide a diverse range of predictions. Several basic questions were posed in the introduction to this work: What is useful and what is not in the theories under review? What stands up and what does not? And what remains to be investigated?

The mass society theory portrays a society that is falling apart, its communal institutions crumbling. The social psychological consequence is that individuals in that society are distressed, anxious to find "a way out." For this theory, the answer to the "what is useful" question is, very little (see the summary on pp. 42–43). Most of the propositions delineated were rejected. The best case for the theory involved small overall declines in general happiness, marital happiness, and community satisfaction, involving attenuation rather than shifts to outright unhappiness or dissatisfaction. Greater dissatisfaction was indicated, by small to middling margins, with life in the largest cities. But even this confirming evidence is open to question, the result being linked to other factors: race, marital status, and age. Sorting out of these factors should be high on the research agenda; that is, on the list of things to be investigated.

The mass society account is largely contrary to fact. Put more directly, it is a fiction. Most migration is collective; it is serial or chain migration, people moving with or following other people they know. Most migration involves short-distance moves; most migrants are never very far from their roots. Cities do grow through the addition of migrants, but they also grow through annexation, a process that does not disturb established social ties. The typical mass society account, moreover, is truncated, providing an incomplete narrative. Migrants arrive in the city, they are isolated and lonely, and they remain that way for the rest of their lives. Those lonely people, presumably, have no capacity for friendship; they are unable to organize themselves to overcome their powerlessness.

It is curious that such an implausible logic should have gained such currency, especially among self-announced critical intellectuals. Here too, as with the rudiments of the Marxist fiction, the view has been sustained despite the availability of substantial contrary evidence showing extensive social involvement. That evidence also shows that existing social ties are generally assessed positively. One possibility, of course, is that the proponents of the mass society view do not know that evidence, never having taken the trouble to inquire. Another possibility is the recourse to permissive epistemologies. The critical analyst declares the inadequacy of the survey research procedures. And, without indicating the alternative research method, the critic simply declares the superior truth. Respondents say they are happy or satisfied with their friendships, but the analyst knows those judgments to be false. The relationships are declared to be empty or shallow. They hide an underlying alienation.

The mass society theory has had an episodic history, a coming and going within the universities, where, borrowing an expression from Nietzsche, one sees a *retour éternel*.[2] In television news and commentary, in many magazines, and in the daily press, mass society formulations are much more frequent, a near-constant presence. The users (or better, perhaps, the proponents or advocates) of this theory advance its claims, as seen, despite the ready availability of much contrary evidence. One key problem remaining for investigation, therefore, is to account for its remarkable persistence.

More may be said for pluralism, for the argument of an aggregation of interests in voluntary associations, than for the mass society theory. Those associations, it is said, would give people some degree of control over their lives. With some power or influence, their assessments of life, community, and society would be generally positive.

As opposed to the earlier versions of the theory, those seeing "everyone" in many associations, differentiated readings prove appropriate (see pp. 95–96 for the summary). Most persons, a majority, are in organizations, but only a minority is found in instrumental associations, those seeking to exercise power. A smaller minority has multiple memberships. Some people, in short, are members of instrumental organizations, some are involved, some learn the lessons, and some gain various benefits. But some, effectively, are "out of it." Given the findings, the focus of the theory must be changed. The key question becomes this: In what contexts do the pluralist claims apply?

The pluralist arguments best describe a minority, perhaps a fifth to a third of the population, most of whom would be upper or upper-middle class. Some others are members of large and powerful organizations, but ones that simultaneously are oligarchic in character and thus provide little opportunity for participation or for member control of the leaders. And some people, of course, have no organizational involvements. The pluralist theory, in short, is useful for analysis of some aspects of some people's lives, principally for those in the upper and upper-middle classes. For the rest, some other theory is needed.

The theory of bureaucracy sees large formal organizations gaining ever-greater dominance in modern life, an experience said to be alienating. Five propositions on this theme were spelled out and assessed (see pp. 149–151). The first involved the questions of extent and growth. Our review of evidence from the United States shows that most people work in small and middling establishments. The average size of the workplace has been declining now for some two decades. The second, third, and fourth propositions, the claims of impersonality, intrusiveness, and monocratic rule, were rejected.

The fifth claim, the argument of expert rule, was generally supported. The only qualifications noted involved timing, the rate of the change, and the continuing role of personal factors. For any work group, whether a presidential cabinet, a legislative body, a personnel office, or one on the shop floor, congeniality and trust (or loyalty) are constant requirements. It is difficult to work under any other circumstances.

As with the pluralist theory, some delimiting conclusions prove appropriate with respect to the theory of bureaucracy. As opposed to the claim of an all-pervasive domination, the evidence reviewed here also shows the need for differentiated formulations. Some people work in large bureaucratic organizations, but that is a minority and a declining one. Despite the insistent portrait of bureaucracy as punitive, the judgments made by those directly involved are, on the whole, generally positive. Much of modern life, moreover, is spent outside of the organization, in leisure-time pursuits or in retirement. As with the mass society portraiture, the argument of bureaucratic omnipresence is also largely fictional. Its claims, as seen, have been asserted despite the ready availability of important contrary evidence.

Other social theories also make use of institutional and social psychological assumptions. A previous volume reviewed and assessed Marxism and its two principal variants, the reformist and revolutionary arguments, in much the same way as was done here.[3] All three positions focus on the institutional development and dynamics of modern capitalism. All three predict a set of ineluctable consequences leading to the arrival of "socialism." Marxism predicts the development of sharply opposing classes, each with a distinctive consciousness, the outcome being a proletarian revolution that overthrows capitalism. That revolution was said to be imminent. It would come with the next economic crisis or, if not then, in the course of the immediately following crisis.

That revolution did not occur within the predicted time span and, accordingly, for those concerned, it was necessary to explain the delay and, still anticipating the triumph of the proletariat, to show how the changed conditions would bring about the transformation to socialism. Bernstein and Lenin provided reformist and revolutionary readings of the epochal change. The former pointed to the economic success of capitalism, to the improvement of workers' conditions, and to the consequent development of moderate or reformist demands. Socialism, he argued, would arrive through an "evolutionary" route, through electoral victories. It would be democratic socialism.

The Leninist variant argued the postponed revolution. Capitalism had saved itself, temporarily, through overseas colonial investment that brought in "superprofits." With exploitation and the class struggle "exported," the revolution would occur first in the colonies. With their liberation and the denial of the superprofits, exploitation would return home and the revolution, the final conflict, would follow.

The six theories, those reviewed here and in the previous work, do not have final, definitive, or "canonical" formulations. They are always in flux, all appearing in new forms with new variations and emphases. This "short list" of theories, moreover, is not intended to be exclusive, as if they were the only important social theories of the modern age. The modern world begins with the Enlightenment, with a theory or worldview that, in the nineteenth century, came to be called liberalism. That theory effectively provides the background for the six positions reviewed and assessed in this and the previous volume. Marxism and the mass society theories were arguments against or critiques of the operations of liberalism. Pluralism provided some remedy to the individualizing tendencies that accompanied the liberal development. In the earliest formulation, liberalism focused on individuals, on their free judgments and choices. But later in the modern era large firms and ever-larger governments appeared, effectively submerging the individual in the giant enterprise. The liberal theory accordingly has also gone through many variations and has seen many different emphases. It too is "very much with us."

These theories are not separate and exclusive. Depicting the same societies, it is understandable that some areas of agreement would be found and that some judgments would be shared. Some mass society elements, for example, appear in the original statement of Marxism. Capitalism, it was said, uprooted the villagers and forced the creation of great cities with their appalling conditions. But in contrast to the conservative mass society view, with the insistent stress on "losses," Marx and Engels saw the move as a step ahead. The new circumstance rescued people from "the idiocy of rural life" and made possible both a new consciousness and a new political organization.

The assessment of the six theories found few elements worth retaining. The principal prediction of the Marxian theory, imminent proletarian revolution, was not sustained. The revisionist variant predicted the coming of socialism through the electoral route. But that prediction, on the whole, also has not been sustained. Only in a few cases did Socialist (or Social Democratic, or Labor) parties gain majorities. And even when in power, the implementation of the program was limited and, typically, problematic. One fact attesting to that conclusion is the performance of contemporary social democratic parties. At the present time, in the year 2000, almost all European governments are headed by social democrats. But, since the Mitterand experience in France following the 1981 election, none of them have moved to "socialize the means of production." The Leninist variant, which predicts a working-class "revolution" after the victories of colonial national liberation struggles, has clearly not been sustained.

The most that can be said for Marxism is that some attitudes and behaviors do vary with class, although the impact is nowhere as strong as predicted. Workers, on the whole, are somewhat more likely to have left-liberal political outlooks and to favor social democratic parties than are middle-class populations. "Left-liberal" here means support for the welfare state, basically for a comprehensive "safety net." These are tendencies as opposed to categorical differences. Since there are significant numbers of both "Tory workers" and middle-class left-liberals, the class differences tend to be rather small, but also persistent; that is, not diminishing.[4]

The pluralist theory provides useful observations for analysis of some better-off segments of the society. The theory of bureaucracy offers some elements for analysis of a major institutional development. But with respect to both voluntary associations and bureaucracy, there is a need for partitive formulations, for consideration of the question of extent: How many people are touched by them? And, equally important, there is a need for consideration of the social psychological impacts: How are those touched by these institutions affected by them?

INSTITUTIONS AND THEIR IMPACTS

Another try at the development of an appropriate social theory will be made in the following pages. They contain, first, a sketch of modern institutional developments; second, a sketch of the likely social psychological responses; and third, some observations with regard to methods, specifically on the need to link theories and research.

The first task is to review the history and development of social institutions over the last two or three centuries. This review will cover only a small segment of human experience, that of Western societies: those of Europe, much of North and South America, plus a few other related settlements.[5]

It is appropriate that we begin with the universal institution; that is, with the family. This institution typically consists of husband, wife, and dependent children. The family typically provides its members with affection and sustenance (food, shelter, and clothing). It is the socially approved setting for the procreation and training of children.

Through to at least the nineteenth century, most families lived in small communities that provided a minimum of order and also, when possible, guaranteed some minimum of welfare. Under the old regime, governance of those communities was typically in the hands of a major property owner, the local aristocrat. Where the farmers were independent, typically in the hill country, some limited arrangements for self-government were found. Most families were also linked to a church. Throughout most of Western history, communities typically had a single church and most people in those communities, accordingly, shared the same basic beliefs.

Arrangements for governance of larger territories developed over several centuries, the procedures generally being referred to as the polity. The arrangements typically operated on national, regional, and local levels, each with diverse powers and degrees of independence. Given the limited "means of administration," even the so-called absolute monarchs had to delegate power, most obviously to the aristocrats who managed the smaller communities. The national government, typically, had little impact on everyday life. The most insistent government presence, for most families, would have been the tax collector. Until well into the twentieth century those taxes went primarily for the costs of monarchy itself (food, clothing, shelter, office space, etc.), and for the army, police, and tax collection, basically for ministries of war, interior, and finance. Until the seventeenth century armies were small and the involvement accordingly limited, basically to some tens of thousands of professional soldiers.

Well into the nineteenth century most people spent their entire lives in small communities, and there the family, clearly, was the central institution determining the conditions of their existence. Those families were simultaneously economic units. In an agrarian society, most families worked a piece of land and themselves produced most of life's necessities. Children were assigned obligatory tasks at an early age: feeding livestock, collecting eggs, cleaning stables, cutting firewood, plus an assortment of household tasks. Later came planting, hoeing, pruning, harvesting, and so forth. Parents were present at almost all times, supervising and directing their activities. When children went about in the community, to the store, or on errands, or even at play, they would continue to be under the supervision of adults, many of them kinsfolk, who would not hesitate to intervene, either to correct or to report misbehavior.

The third institution, the church, would provide direction—"moral authority"—for all members of the community. Many of the values taught by the family originated with the church. Those values, typically, would be shared, taught, and reinforced by all three institutions—by the family, the community, and the church. A church commandment, "Honor thy father and thy mother," gave powerful support to the authority of the traditional family.[6]

Until late in the nineteenth century those villages would have been almost completely cut off from the outside world. Given the general poverty and minimal literacy, few newspapers, magazines, or books would ever appear there. Only a few local notables and possibly a clergyman would be able to read those publications. News of that outside world would arrive irregularly, in bits and pieces, and would be "filtered" by those same notables.

There would be no place in those villages for adolescent "peer groups." The notions of "teenagers" and an independent "youth culture" would not appear until well into the twentieth century. The notion of a "counterculture" would have been difficult to explain. A compelling logic governed people's lives. With economic disaster, hunger, and possible starvation always imminent, independent or free-spirited behavior could easily threaten a family's existence. Everyday life was dominated by a set of imperative demands, by things that simply "had to be done." Put differently, there was very little room for personal freedom, spontaneity, or creativity.

Given the preeminent position of families in that arrangement it is not surprising that many early sociology texts put forth an unqualified declaration that the family socialized children in the values of the society. That training proceeded, presumably, with exceptional efficiency, a point indicated in the usage, with the terms "family," "values," and "society" being treated as nonproblematic. That presumed efficiency is indicated in another usage, in the frequent references to "common" or "shared" values, to an untroubled "consensus."

Since this depiction of premodern society obviously simplifies, some words of caution are needed. A prime need, in all analysis, is for information on frequencies. How many people in these communities lived in intact nuclear families? How frequent were other living arrangements? Premodern communities in Western societies were characterized by late marriage. One insistent procedural rule was that couples wishing to marry had to be able to provide for a family. Those unable to provide had to postpone marriage or reject it entirely. The late marriage pattern taken in conjunction with another fact, short life expectancy, meant that broken families were a frequent occurrence. The surviving spouse might remarry, the children living with a stepparent. In many cases children were given out to other families.[7]

We have some evidence on the frequency of the various family forms in previous centuries, but we have virtually no evidence on values, on the extent of the presumed consensus.[8] And obviously we have no serious evidence on satisfactions or dissatisfactions. Extensive inquiry with polls and surveys would not occur until the mid-twentieth century. A wide consensus on values is probable in the earlier experience, but that judgment is based on inference, not evidence. We also have no serious evidence on the claims about the family satisfying the needs for affection. That too is unsupported inference.

Some intellectuals, those steeped in the romantic tradition, idealize those traditional communities, writing of the warmth, the extensive social supports, and the social harmony found there. All those benefits, reportedly, were "lost" in the later urban, industrial society. Those depictions, however, involve gross distortion. They omit many important characteristics of premodern experience, beginning with low and irregular crop yields, inadequate nutrition, stunted growth, physical disabilities, and short life. A late or early frost, a hailstorm, or an insect infestation would bring crop failures and widespread hunger. With hunger came the related problem of susceptibility to infectious disease, about which one could do nothing. The paintings showing families harvesting on a warm autumn day, or those depicting the woodcutters at work in the forest, or those of rustic peasant cottages, do not show smallpox or tuberculosis. And they do not communicate some other facts of life: rotten teeth, bad breath, and unwashed bodies.[9]

In the nineteenth century Western societies created an important new institution, a public school system, one destined to have enormous effects. The development came earlier in Western Europe; later in Eastern Europe. The effort began with modest requirements, children being removed from the family, generally at ages six through ten, for a relatively short school year. The requirement was gradually extended to five, six, and more years. In the twentieth century, beginning in the United States, some years of high school were added.

The new arrangement postponed children's entry into the labor force. Rather than working under the direction of parents in a family-owned enterprise, or working under the direction of owners, foremen, and skilled workers in an outside firm, daily contact was now with teachers and classroom peers. Schools and teachers became more important than ever before in human history. The obvious correlate was that parental influence, while still important, would be reduced.[10]

In the early stages of this development the lessons taught in the schools were broadly consonant with local community values. In the British and American experience local notables chose teachers on the basis of technical competence and appropriate outlooks and behavior. At the opposite extreme, the French government developed a national school system with plans and programs directed from Paris. Teachers, eventually, were trained in professional schools directed by the Ministry of Education. Reading, writing, and arithmetic, to be sure, would be constants everywhere. But in matters of culture or ideological orientation, markedly different content appeared in the centralized systems, which, typically, were developed with some larger purpose in mind. In France the schools came to teach secular, enlightenment, liberal values. A church–state struggle over control of the schools ensued, one of the most serious conflicts of the nineteenth and twentieth centuries. In the local communities, typically, the parish priest and the schoolteacher fought out the cultural wars, attempting to win over pupils and their families.[11]

The development of educational institutions required the training of tens of thousands, then later hundreds of thousands of teachers. In most economically advanced nations, teacher ultimately became the largest single occupational category among a 10,000-plus total of jobs. Teachers would ultimately touch all persons in the nation, for five or six days a week over four, eight, and, later, ten or twelve years. The potential influence, obviously, would be enormous. The statement that the family teaches the values of the society, accordingly, requires alteration to include consideration of the schools as a socializing agency. There would, as noted, be some variation in the impacts depending on the degree of centralization or decentralization. In the French case, with a nationwide system devoted to a *mission civilisatrice*, the educational institution would be a major means of mass communication. This institution would probably be even more powerful than those later agencies, the mass media, that figure so prominently in the work of the mass society theorists.

Public schooling extended literacy to ever-larger proportions of the general population. Basic literacy in certain countries increased from 10 percent to 80 percent of the adult population in the course of the nineteenth century.[12] The extension of literacy was a necessary precondition for the appearance and growth of the first medium of mass communication, one based on printed materials. The publishing industry ultimately would have several component parts: books (texts and trade), newspapers, and magazines. Since those media have different uses, it is important to consider them separately and in rough sequence of their appearance.

The growth of schools brings with it, like night following the day, a corresponding growth of textbooks. They must be written, manufactured, sold, and from time to time revised. Those interested in the outlooks of any population from the nineteenth century onward should review the history and contents of those schoolbooks. For American social historians, this effort should begin with the McGuffey readers. From 1836 to about 1920, "more than half the school children of America . . . learned to read from the *McGuffey Readers* [and] during that time over 122 million copies were sold." Those copies were used many times over, hence some multiplier is appropriate, some suggesting five, others going to twice that.[13]

A major extension of educational opportunity came in the twentieth century. The percentage of Americans aged twenty-five and over who graduated high school went from 13.5 percent in 1910 to 82.8 percent in 1998. The textbook industry probably grew even more than those figures would suggest given the increasingly diverse offerings and more frequent editions. The later expansion of higher education, with college graduates increasing from 2.7 percent of the population in 1910 to 24.4 percent in 1998, meant still another significant area of textbook growth.[14]

Four lessons should be noted in this connection. The first is that educational institutions and the media are not separate and independent agencies, but rather are closely linked. Schoolteachers nowadays have some role in the selection of textbooks, their input having grown considerably with a general decentralization of decision making. Professors, with only rare exceptions, choose the textbooks used in their courses. Two categories of intellectuals, in short, are important decision makers in the determination of this mass media content.

The second lesson involves impacts or influence. Schools and universities combine both personal and impersonal influences. Students are influenced, presumably, by the regular personal contacts with teachers or professors. Outside of class, students would also be influenced, again presumably, by the content of the assigned texts. Educational institutions, in short, typically involve two mutually reinforcing channels of communication. In this respect the influence differs from the single-channel impersonal influence typical of the other means of mass communication: magazines, movies, television, and so forth.

Third, many intellectuals misrepresent their own position, activity, and possible impacts. Many discussions of the mass media, especially those provided by "critical" intellectuals, pay no attention to textbooks but instead focus on other media. Those other media, moreover, are routinely said to have nefarious effects. It is not at all clear why textbooks should be excluded from those analyses. And it is not clear why, implicitly at least, textbooks are assumed to have beneficial effects. One should not prejudge the outcomes. A textbook with a "message," one intended to change values, might generate hostility and rejection. The tendentious text might generate contempt rather than a change in values.

The fourth lesson is that the direct influence of teachers and/or professors ends when the student leaves school. At that point job requirements gain considerably in importance, and later those of a new family. For most people, the last reading of Dickens, Dostoevsky, or Proust would occur in some last course taken at a university. Students majoring in fields dominated by leftist or liberal professors would begin learning new and different lessons effectively with the completion of their last examinations.[15]

The mass literacy provided by the schools made possible the growth of a second print medium, trade books; everything from literature to cook books. In the former category we would have the works of Walter Scott, Charles Dickens, Victor Hugo, and many others through to the present with Stephen King, Danielle Steel, and J. K. Rowling on the current best-seller lists.

Here too, new opportunities were created for persons with intellectual interests. Freelance writers, independent entrepreneurs producing cultural goods for sale in a free market, could now generate substantial fortunes. This brought another new channel for intellectual influence, although, to be sure, the lessons varied considerably. Some writers were conservative, Walter Scott, for example, with his dreamy tales of medieval knights and their exploits. For others, Lord Byron, for example, the new medium allowed the propagation of a new, critical program. Victor Hugo recognized the possibility. For him, "Romanticism is . . . nothing more than liberalism in literature." Previously taboo subject matter, lines of commentary, and criticism now became available in distant provinces and in the villages, in settings that until then had been at best insular or at worst closed.

The schools and textbooks, in combination, created and imposed an important new cultural fact. All European nations once had a wide array of dialects and spellings. The new institutions brought a new standard, the "King's English," or a language called "French," or throughout much of central Europe, one called "*hoch Deutsch.*" Across large territories school children now read the same language and were instructed by unyielding teachers who insisted on "proper" pronunciation and usage. In what was to become Germany, most children became bilingual, speaking a dialect at home and high German in school.

For better or worse, this intellectual input contributed everywhere to the formation of national consciousness and to the development or strengthening of nation states. Some of the new texts created, for the first time in the modern era, "national memories." School children would have read nationalist lessons in the textbooks. In many instances the message would have been reinforced by patriotic schoolteachers. The combined influence of texts and teachers made possible the major nation-building efforts of the nineteenth century in Germany, Italy, and later of the Balkan nations.

The creation of mass literacy made possible two other mass media: newspapers and magazines. In both cases the new media brought more employment opportunities for intellectuals, for salaried journalists and freelance contributors. As with books, the quality of these publications ranged from high to low, from the serious to the frivolous. Many contemporary intellectuals emphasize the restraints or "controls" under which these writers operated. Controls exist at all times and places. As opposed to the simple freedom-versus-tyranny dichotomy, the real world involves "more-or-less" choices. For most economically advanced nations, those generally following liberal plans, the reality was greater freedom.

The nineteenth-century educational institutions made possible, directly and indirectly, more opportunities for intellectual careers than ever before in human history. Among those employed in journalism in the nineteenth century were Karl Marx, Friedrich Engels, and Wilhelm Liebknecht. Censorship was a de facto restraint, but it was a problem that could be circumvented by adept intellectuals. The direct critique of present-day tyranny was impossible, but if the drama were set in ancient Babylon, as in Verdi's *Nabucco*, the chorus could sing of its yearning for freedom and all audiences understood the message. That anthem was taken over without change and became an important cultural artifact of Italian unification.[16] Many critical works, Marx's *Das Kapital*, for example, faced no problems from the censor.

Public libraries as we know them depend on both the educational institutions and the print media, the former creating the requisite literacy, the latter producing the products to be housed and distributed. Begun for all practical purposes in the nineteenth century, libraries provide subsidies (largely from public monies) for publishers and, indirectly, for authors. They make published materials available to a sizable audience, one extending far beyond the direct purchasers. They also directly employ several hundred thousand persons interested in cultural goods.

This combination, the education–media complex, initially provided employment for thousands, later for hundreds of thousands, and ultimately, at the end of the twentieth century, for millions of persons: teachers, authors, journalists, professors, and so on. The U.S. Bureau of Labor Statistics reported, in 1997, 4,798,000 teachers, 869,000 professors, 257,000 editors and reporters, 217,000 librarians, and 137,000 authors in the civilian labor force.[17]

Those five categories together form only a small part of the nation's labor force, less than 5 percent of the total. Collectively, however, they would have much more influence than the numbers might suggest. Their occupations involve communication (or facilitating it) with much of the rest of the nation's population. No other segment of the population has that kind of access. Plumbers, electricians, assembly-line workers, secretaries, engineers, and businessmen typically work with, at best, rather small groups in the performance of their tasks. Some communication is involved, but none of it is as extensive as that associated with the classroom or with books, newspapers, magazines, or television. An important implication follows: To understand modern society, to understand the outlook of the masses in that society, one must understand the operations and impacts of this education–media complex.

Few intellectuals put forth this lesson: Intellectuals themselves are highly influential. A favored opposite position is that intellectuals are alienated and powerless. Their creative impulses are thwarted by the constraints of an oppressive society, or, in another version, by the constraints imposed by business, by the corporations, or by the power elite.

One author, Ben Bagdikian, has reported the existence of a "new communications cartel," an extraordinary concentration of media in a few hands. "At issue," he writes, "is the possession of power to surround almost every man, woman, and child in the country with controlled images and words, to socialize each new generation of Americans, to alter the political agenda of the country. And with that power comes the ability to exert influence that in many ways are greater than that of schools, religion, parents, and even government itself." Each of the dominant firms, he reports, "has adopted a strategy of creating its own closed system of control over every step in the national media process, from creation of content to its delivery, no content—news, entertainment, or other public messages—will reach the public unless a handful of corporate decision-makers decide that it will." That close control is intended to serve the interests of the owners. "With minor exceptions," Bagdikian claims, "they share highly conservative political and economic values. Most also own interests in other industries—defense, consumer products and services—and have shown little hesitation in using their control of the news to support the fortunes of their other subsidiaries."[18]

It is an alarming portrait. "They" are gaining ever-greater control over our lives and consciousness. The control, it will be noted, is twofold, affecting the producers, all the employees in the media, and the consumers, all those paying attention to those productions. That depiction would be consonant with the claims of two major theoretical positions some people might have learned in college, those of Marxism (several renditions thereof) and the mass society theory. But the depiction in this case is based on inference, on a plausible logic, rather than on actual evidence.

On two key points, the argument is mistaken. Media managers, on the whole, are liberal in outlook. And one major study showed that they made no effort to control the ideological content of their publications. In fact, they proved remarkably indifferent to the question of content. Their interest was profitability, or, as expressed in the vernacular, their concern was the "bottom line." Bagdikian's work makes no reference to those studies. If his claims about the new "cartel" were valid, his work would never have been published. Its manifest success indicates that the book's major claims are mistaken.[19]

One of the most important institutional developments of the last 150 or so years was industrialization. The term refers to the transformation of the economy whereby most of the production of goods and services was shifted from farms and small shops to factories and offices. The family was significantly changed as a result of industrialization. Much of the productive effort once undertaken within families, on farms and in small shops, was shifted to other locations. That meant some family members were now removed from the household for long hours of work elsewhere. The most important change involved the father, a person once described, appropriately, as the main earner, the breadwinner, or as the head of the house. For much of the nineteenth century and well into the twentieth, full-time employment meant six ten-hour days, sixty hours of work plus some hours of travel time. Other family members would also spend some part of their lives outside the home. The extension of schooling removed children from the home for ever-longer periods. On leaving school, boys and girls would enter the labor force, increasingly in jobs away from home. With marriage, women would typically enter a new household and another full-time occupation, the tasks of household management.

This institutional change "set the stage for" the development and influence of the Marxian theory. The masses, it was said, "lost" their previous independence. Farmers and small shopkeepers, members of the petty bourgeoisie, were now forced into the proletariat. Removed from the confining conditions of rural life, now living in great cities, these workers developed a new collective consciousness. They would quickly recognize their exploitation by the owners. They would then organize and, in a revolutionary action, overthrow the entire system. A new realm of freedom would follow.

The principal hypothesis of the Marxian theory is that class position would have a significant impact on the consciousness of the workers and on their behavior. The previous sources of consciousness—the family, the small communities, and the churches—would decline in importance. These influences would be replaced by this powerful new determinant. It was part of a general process of secularization that accompanied the development of capitalism. The new circumstance would erode the traditional bases of consciousness, operating with presumed irresistible force. This declaration of weight, of strength or importance, justified the main prediction: Those developments would "inevitably" lead to revolution.

While a plausible logic, one that sustained socialists (and one that frightened capitalists) for decades, it eventually proved so problematic as to need serious repair. The revisions provided by Bernstein and Lenin also involved the assignment of weights to the presumed "decisive" factors. Again, importance was declared and defended with plausible logic rather than through investigation and presentation of pertinent evidence.[20]

It is useful to consider an equally plausible alternative logic, one that begins with the likely consequences of six ten-hour days of work. A first implication, one that is easy and obvious, is physical exhaustion. Manual work in the nineteenth century was much more onerous than work in the late twentieth century. A much larger part of the effort involved toting and hauling, tasks later performed by conveyor belts, moving assembly lines, and fork-lift trucks. A "breadwinner" would rise early, have a quick breakfast, then walk to work, the distance ranging from perhaps a few hundred yards to several miles. The ten hours of work would be interrupted by a brief lunch break. At the end of the shift the worker would return home, wash up, and have supper. Then, perhaps, he would read a poor-quality newspaper and, exhausted, would soon doze off. Both the father and mother would turn in early, maybe around ten in the evening. On Sunday everyone would sleep in. Where a religious influence existed, the family would attend church and perhaps socialize a bit with friends and neighbors. On Sunday the family had the "big meal." Sunday afternoon and evening allowed some family time. It was, effectively, the only time in the week available for this purpose.[21]

The tasks performed by housewives in those families would include shopping, preparation of meals, washing and repair of clothes, cleaning house, and care of dependent children. The demands, for both husbands and wives, were relentless. There was no letup, no summer vacation, no retirement at age sixty-five. Moreover, there was only a very limited welfare state to help when catastrophe struck. The industrial accident that incapacitated the breadwinner, or the tuberculosis, malaria, or appendicitis that carried away either parent, required some hasty rearrangements to carry the survivors through.

The conventional terms of analysis seriously misrepresent one aspect of the family relationships. The father, the so-called head of the house, was absent from the household during most of the family's waking hours. During most of those waking hours the mother would be the de facto head of the household. The statement that the family socializes the children is misleading, since it was mothers who provided most of that training. During the working day their direction was pivotal for both girls and boys. Among other things, appropriate gender behavior, how girls and boys should behave, was taught largely by mothers.[22]

The mother also, in many cases, had de facto control over household finances. The weekly earnings were turned over to her on Saturday evening. She made most of the purchases for the family, buying groceries, clothing, and paying the rent. It would have been pointless for the main earner to have retained those sums, carrying the money to the mines, steel mills, or construction sites.

How, one may ask, would socialism fit in this picture? Again, it is useful to begin with some basic facts of life. For most factory workers the job provided no opportunity at all for discussion of common concerns; that is, for the development of a "class consciousness." The noise levels in most factories prevent any serious discussion. The only occasions for such discussion would be during the brief lunch break or while traveling to or from work. One might see an opportunity at union meetings, or at meetings of the socialist party. Twentieth-century studies of union involvement show attendance to be very limited. It would take an unusual level of commitment for a worker, after ten hours of work, to either stay after hours for a meeting or to go out somewhere for a meeting at, say, 7:30 in the evening. The most likely possibility is that it rarely happened, exhaustion deterring that choice. Another possibility is that the worker who did attend would doze off in the course of the meeting. The same expectations would apply to meetings of a socialist party. Perhaps the meetings would take place on Sunday. If so, the head of the house might experience both personal conflict (a need for rest versus political action) and interpersonal conflict (obligations to the family versus those to the party).

Still another point needs consideration: The socialists promised a solution for the problems facing the breadwinners, but socialism offered nothing for the problems facing housewives. Union or socialist activities were a problem for those families. At minimum, the father might be taken away from the family for an evening or a Sunday afternoon. Much worse, union activity could lead to loss of a job and subsequent blacklisting. And still worse, armed struggle "on the barricades" could bring serious injury, loss of life, or subsequent imprisonment, all of which would provide wives and dependent children with strong incentives to oppose any participation.[23]

Urbanization brought another major transformation in the handed-down social arrangements. This refers to the growth of cities stemming from migration (people seeking better jobs), improved life expectancies, and annexation of surrounding territories. The process, as indicated in Chapter 1, was a gradual one, extending over many generations. Moreover, as opposed to categorical either/or thinking, even the current reality is rather complicated. Many people, as seen, still live in rural counties dominated by a small town, the county seat.

The shift from village to city brought with it a wide range of new social arrangements. Cities ultimately developed many specialized agencies not ordinarily found in the villages. These included independent governments (that is, separate from the dominant notables or families governing in the villages). The governments developed several specialized agencies, among them police, fire, water, and sanitation. Primary and later secondary education, originally under the direction of this government, was later managed by a separate elected school board.

Political parties and voluntary associations should also be added to the list of new nineteenth-century institutional innovations. The liberal parties were the first of the newcomers. Their presence stimulated some organization of conservative counterparts, basically of aristocratic parties defending old-regime arrangements. Socialist parties made their appearance and, here and there, also some religious parties. Later, in the twentieth century, the Communists split off from the Socialists. Fascist parties were active from roughly 1920 to 1945. All this was made possible by a general democratization of governing arrangements. Without some extension of the basic freedoms of speech, press, and association, none of this would have been possible.

The major social theories reviewed in this chapter give little or no consideration to another important social institution. The military, the largest component of which is ordinarily the modern mass army, is routinely overlooked. The omission effectively declares its unimportance. Throughout most of Western European history armies were small and depended on recruitment of volunteers or, when in need, through the use of more forceful methods, such as dragooning, impressment, or conscription. The "military revolution" of the seventeenth century considerably enlarged the European armies and brought several other associated changes.[24] Mass armies, those imposing an obligation on eligible males, first appeared with the French Revolution and continued with much greater insistence into the Napoleonic period, the arrangement being adopted both by revolutionary and counterrevolutionary regimes. The major powers reverted to the smaller, more select, and less costly army after 1815. Various international tensions in the decades before 1914 led the major powers to again expand their mass armies, the obligation for eligible males normally being two or three years plus a decade or more of reserve service.[25]

The obligation had implications for some of the other institutions. It postponed marriage for two or more years and, in the normal case, postponed the birth of the first child (and all subsequent children). The men taken for service were removed from the civilian labor force, postponing the learning of skills and the practice of civilian occupations. The lessons of socialism would presumably be postponed for that period, during which time, perhaps, the recruits learned the lessons of nationalism.

The military differs from other institutions in that the experience is both selective and episodic, which means that any analysis must be differentiated. Although military obligations are often referred to as "universal," that is never the case. All military organizations screen out and reject those lacking basic intellectual and physical qualifications. Although not widely discussed, cost is also a factor. Some might have wished to train the entire eligible male population, but budgetary constraints would not allow that luxury. Democratic and authoritarian regimes differed in their preferences. Republican France sought wide recruitment. Authoritarian Prussia operated with a constitutional limit on the size of the peacetime army, a restriction welcomed by the nation's military leaders. It allowed them to select trainees on the basis of presumed loyalty, rejecting the politically unreliable working-class children. Britain and its colonies had no peacetime military obligation, nor did the United States, hence those considerations basically do not apply there.

Those in the military might see only peacetime service, or they might see combat. Those in the Prussian army between 1864 and 1871 might have fought in three brief wars. Those in the German army from 1871 to 1913 would have fought no European wars. Those in the service in 1914, if they survived, would have experienced four years of very intense combat. The point, clearly, is that the things learned in the course of a military career would differ considerably depending on the events of the period.

The social sciences, as indicated, pay little attention to military institutions. It is another largely unrecognized residue of the liberal heritage. One consequence is that the social sciences have little to say with respect to any "socialization" the military experience might provide. That neglect carries with it an implicit conclusion that the military counts for nothing in the formation of outlooks and behavior. Combat experience creates unique attitudes among some of the participants, attitudes then carried over into civilian life. The activities of war-trained paramilitary forces in Italy and Germany were decisive for the subsequent Fascist and Nazi takeovers. Paramilitary units in the American South after the Civil War did much to end Reconstruction.[26]

By the middle of the twentieth century most economically advanced nations had extended the range of the mass media, adding audiovisual means of communication to the repertory discussed earlier. In sequence of development, this means motion pictures, radio, and television. The range of offerings increased dramatically later in the century, with cable, cassettes, CDs, the Internet, and many other possibilities. This meant still more sources of information, still more possible agents of socialization. By the 1990s the range of options available to provide information along with new or alternative values was the largest ever in the world's history.

Two other institutional offerings have appeared in the course of the century, two massive "industries" as judged in terms of public participation and the gross revenues involved. These are the various activities appearing under the heading of "sport" and those under the heading of "tourism." In several countries sport is larger than steel and auto, fields once referred to as "basic industries." One recent review describes travel and tourism as "the largest industry in the world."[27]

The possible impacts of these two industries would be hard to assess. Sport might amount to little more than a major diversion. The time spent on wins, losses, rankings, point spreads, and so forth is time taken away from other things, from politics, economics, and social affairs generally. Tourism might be "broadening"; that is, providing insight and understanding not obtained otherwise. Or it might be simply another diversion: The travelers saw many things but learned little of their significance.

SOME SUMMARY OBSERVATIONS

An adequate social theory should begin with consideration of a society's major institutions. That analysis should review the history and development of those institutions. It should also be comparative, considering the national differences and the variations associated with timing and sequence. The theory should also be revised, as necessary, when those institutions change and new ones appear.

Second, that adequate social theory should reflect current research and analysis of social psychological responses. The people living within those major institutions are presumably affected by them. Rather than making a priori judgments about impacts, these too are matters for investigation. Some socialization, some kinds and degrees of influence, would presumably occur within each one of those contexts. The basic questions, then, are as follows: What kind of impact? How strong is the impact? And how lasting? Another key question is that of relative weight: How much influence? How much impact is made by family, school, church, mass media, and the workplace?

That systematic review of social psychologies should produce an adequate "mapping" of mass outlooks and preferences. There is a need also for consideration of activity, of efforts to maintain or change things, to bring realities into accord with those preferences. Hence, a third area of theoretical concern should be with the exercise of influence, with efforts affecting outcomes. For this purpose, some realistic variant of the pluralist theory seems most appropriate.

A fourth concern, one signaled throughout this work, is the need to link theoretical and research efforts. Until roughly the mid-twentieth century, a direct investigation of "consciousness" and of mass political activity (or inactivity) posed serious difficulties. One had to go by plausible logic, aided perhaps by a scatter of visible evidence: strike activity, for example, or the growth of membership in unions or in political parties, or the votes for those parties. Some central questions, however, could not be resolved with that evidence. For example, on a key issue, did a vote for a socialist party signify support for its revolutionary aims? Or was it a vote for the "immediate" program; that is, for the reformist plans of the party? Or was it a vote for both?

The development of representative cross-sectional public opinion surveys, particularly with their enormous growth in the years following World War II, allowed direct investigation of these questions. If class position were decisive, that would be indicated in the first serious survey and in all of those that came after. If family training and religion counted for little or nothing, that too would be indicated in that first survey.

That first survey would provide a "snapshot," one taken decades after the industrialization process first began. A picture taken at that time should show class holding an eminent position, especially in comparison to the traditional influences of family training and religion. Given the predicted "dynamic," snapshots taken at later points should show class growing in importance and the other two declining. The evidence gained from surveys has not sustained any of those predictions. That evidence showed class having some effect in the directions anticipated, but that factor was distinctly secondary to both family training and religion.[28]

The declarations of the centrality of class, the resurgence of Marxism that began in the late 1960s, paid little attention to evidence that was readily available at the time. In subsequent decades, with evidence going so heavily against the declarations of weight and those of the trend, it became necessary, for those attached to the theory, to discount or dismiss scientific procedures. The same problem faces the advocates of the mass society theory. The argument of community breakdown, of consequent isolation and widespread anxiety, is also challenged by a wealth of contrary evidence. To sustain the contrary-to-fact conclusions, permissive epistemologies were developed and propagated that stress a repertory of genres, opaque texts, situated perspectives, and a need for "interpretation."[29]

An adequate social theory requires, initially at least, a willingness to accept and explore a larger range of options. Before settling on a favored institution and declaring its importance, one should review the repertory of institutions. Consideration of the range of institutions does mean greater complexity, especially as opposed to the one-sided emphasis on some favorite. If after investigation it appears that institutions A, D, and R have the greatest impact, that they are most decisive in predicting some key social changes, it is then appropriate to give them a central place in the resulting theory. If the social sciences do not systematically explore those institutions, their development, and their interrelationships, they cannot properly address—let alone research—those key social changes.[30]

Systematic social analysis, the construction of appropriate theories based on continuous and advancing investigation, runs up against a recurrent problem. Many people, intellectuals among them, show a "stickiness" in their mental processes, a reluctance to give up the old frameworks. There is, as seen, a regular imposition of views or outlooks developed, in some instances, more than a century earlier. Put differently, there is a refusal of innovation when new ideas are appropriate. It is a separate issue, separate from the task of developing adequate social theories, but there is some need to consider the sources of that reluctance.[31] Why do "advanced" intellectuals dwell on ancient theories? Why the fixation? Intellectuals regularly present themselves as bold, innovative, and critical thinkers. But in many instances their behavior belies the claims.

NOTES

1. The terms "institution" and "structure" (or social structure) are widely used in sociology, but with little evident consensus as to their meaning. Some writers purport to have the definitive usage; some claim a definitive list of the "institutions." I see no good reason for accepting their judgments. The terms institution, structure, and social arrangement will be used interchangeably throughout this chapter.

2. See, for example, Lawrence M. Friedman, *The Horizontal Society* (New Haven: Yale University Press, 1999).

3. Richard F. Hamilton, *Marxism, Revisionism, and Leninism: Explication, Assessment, and Commentary* (Westport, Conn.: Praeger, 2000).

4. For literature on this topic and recent evidence, see Jeff Manza, Michael Hout, and Clem Brooks, "Class Voting in Capitalist Democracies Since World War II: Dealignment, Realignment, or Trendless Fluctuation?" *Annual Review of Sociology* 21 (1995): 137–162; and Clem Brooks and Jeff Manza "Class Politics and Political Change in the United States, 1952–1992," *Social Forces* 76 (1997): 379–408. For comprehensive overviews, see Geoffrey Evans, ed., *The End of Class Politics? Class Voting in Comparative Context* (New York: Oxford University Press, 1999); and Jeff Manza and Clem Brooks, *Social Cleavages and Political Change: Voter Alignments and U.S. Party Coalitions* (New York: Oxford University Press, 1999).

5. For a sweeping overview of institutional arrangements that covers all societies, see Gerhard Lenski, Jean Lenski, and Patrick Nolan, *Human Societies: An Introduction to Macrosociology*, 6th ed. (New York: McGraw-Hill, 1991). Agrarian and industrial societies, those to be considered here, are discussed in Chapters 7 and 9–15. For an outstanding comprehensive review of European experience, see M. S. Anderson, *The Ascendancy of Europe 1815–1914*, 2d ed. (London: Longman, 1985).

6. For a portrait of these dynamics in one traditional community from the mid-1930s, see Horace Miner, *St. Denis: A French-Canadian Parish* (Chicago: University of Chicago Press, 1939).

7. In 1829 Charles Sherman, an Ohio State Supreme Court justice, died, probably of typhoid, leaving his wife Elizabeth and their eight children still at home "very poor." The oldest child, William, a nine-year-old, "fell to the charge of" Thomas Ewing, a neighbor who lived two doors up the street. The mother kept the three youngest children, but the others, William wrote in his memoirs, "were scattered." Michael

Fellman, *Citizen Sherman: A Life of William Tecumseh Sherman* (New York: Random House, 1995), 4–7.

8. Peter Laslett, *The World We Have Lost Further Explored*, 3d rev. ed. of *The World We Have Lost* [1965] (London: Methuen, 1983); Peter Laslett, Richard Wall, Jean Robin, and Peter Laslett, eds., *Family Forms in Historic Europe* (Cambridge: Cambridge University Press, 1983). See also, for an extended review and commentary, Jack Goody, "Comparing Family Systems in Europe and Asia: Are There Different Sets of Rules?" *Population and Development Review* 22, no. 1 (1996): 1–20.

9. The human sciences, the literary, historical, and social science sources, are remarkably indifferent to such matters. One striking exception to that "rule" is provided by George Orwell, *The Road to Wigan Pier* (New York: Harcourt, Brace & World, 1958), 96–97. Few twenty-year-olds in that mining community, he reported, had a full set of teeth; many of those remaining were in bad shape. It is a curious oversight, as if there were a tooth taboo. How many motion picture depictions of the "good old days" show rotten teeth?

10. For a brief account, see Anderson, *Ascendancy*, 170–171; for more detail, see Robert Ulich, *The Education of Nations: A Comparison in Historical Perspective* (Cambridge: Harvard University Press, 1967); and Robert S. and Helen Merrell Lynd, *Middletown: A Study in American Culture* (New York: Harcourt, Brace, 1929), Chs. 13–16.

11. This brief account necessarily simplifies. Most countries operated with dual arrangements; that is, with both secular and church-related schools. As schools became more costly, the former became, by far, the dominant component. On the schools, see Antoine Prost, *L'Enseignement en France, 1800–1967* (Paris: Armand Colin, 1968); and Eugen Weber, *Peasants into Frenchmen: The Modernization of Rural France 1870–1914* (Stanford: Stanford University Press, 1976), Ch. 18. On Germany, see Karl A. Scheunes, *Schooling and Society: The Politics of Education in Prussia and Bavaria 1850–1900* (Oxford: Berg, 1989); and Marjorie Lamberti, *State, Society, and the Elementary School in Imperial Germany* (New York: Oxford University Press, 1989). All Western European nations experienced struggles, major or minor, over the schools. For an account of the events in Belgium, see Neal Ascherson, *The King Incorporated: Leopold II in the Age of Trusts* (Garden City, N.Y.: Doubleday, 1964), Ch. 15. For some comparable struggles in one important American setting, see Diane Ravitch, *The Great School Wars: New York City, 1805–1973: A History of the Public Schools as Battlefield of Social Change* (New York: Basic Books, 1974).

12. Carlo M. Cipolla, *Literacy and Development in the West* (Baltimore: Penguin Books, 1969).

13. Gerry Bohning, "The McGuffey Eclectic Readers: 1836–1986," *The Reading Teacher* 40 (1986): 263–269. For more detail and text samples, see John H. Westerhoff III, *McGuffey and His Readers: Piety, Morality, and Education in Nineteenth-Century America* (Nashville: Abingdon, 1978).

14. National Center for Educational Statistics, *Digest of Education Statistics, 1997*, available <http://nces.ed.gov/pubs/digest97/d97t008.html>; and U.S. Bureau of the Census, 10 December 1998, available <http://www.census.gov:80/population/socdemo/education/tablea-01.txt>.

15. Richard F. Hamilton and Lowell L. Hargens, "The Politics of the Professors: Self-Identifications, 1969–1984," *Social Forces* 71 (1993): 603–627.

16. For a more extended discussion, see John Bokina, *Opera and Politics* (New Haven: Yale University Press, 1997). The lessons of liberty, of the opposition to tyr-

anny, appear in Beethoven's opera *Fidelio*. The same themes, combined with lessons of national liberation, are found in Rossini's operas, *Wilhelm Tell, The Siege of Corinth*, and *Moses and Pharoah*.

17. U.S. Bureau of the Census, *Statistical Abstract of the United States, 1998* (Washington, D.C.: U.S. Government Printing Office, 1998), 417, Table 672.

18. Ben Bagdikian, *The Media Monopoly*, 5th ed. (Boston: Beacon, 1997), ix–xi. Similar views are contained in Thomas R. Dye, *Who's Running America? The Clinton Years*, 6th ed. (Englewood Cliffs, N.J.: Prentice Hall, 1995), Ch. 4. The many editions of both books means they have sold well or, in other words, that there is a market for this kind of content. That market is created by the decisions of some professors who deemed the works to be meritorious and worth the attention of students. It also means that two commercial publishers responded to that demand.

19. The major study is Lewis A. Coser, Charles Kadushin, and Walter W. Powell, *Books: The Culture and Commerce of Publishing* (New York: Basic Books, 1982), 31–33, 180–181. The editors, they report on p. 113, "tend overwhelmingly to be liberals." For evidence on the liberal tendencies, see also Allen H. Barton, "Consensus and Conflict Among American Leaders," *Public Opinion Quarterly* 38 (1974–1975): 507–530; S. Robert Lichter, Stanley Rothman, and Linda S. Lichter, *The Media Elite: America's New Powerbrokers* (Bethesda, Md.: Adler & Adler, 1986); and Robert Lerner, Althea K. Nagai, and Stanley Rothman, *American Elites* (New Haven: Yale University Press, 1996). The latter, on p. 50, reports the self-identified ideologies—conservative, moderate, or liberal—of twelve elite groups. Only two showed conservative majorities, the military (77 percent) and business (63 percent). Television, movie, and media elites all showed liberal majorities, the percentages being 75, 67, and 55, respectively.

20. See Hamilton, *Marxism*, for review and assessment of these arguments. Some parallels to this procedure appear in much of contemporary sociology, with many writers focusing on the class–race–gender trinity and pointing to manifest inequalities. Some sociologists add ethnicity to the basic list. As with class, much of the work on race, gender, and ethnicity is based on assertion as opposed to evidence, with commentators simply declaring importance. Much of that literature, moreover, assumes a constancy of oppression, failing to recognize or denying obvious changes. For well-documented studies of change in one of those areas, see Richard D. Alba, *Italian Americans: Into the Twilight of Ethnicity* (Englewood Cliffs, N.J.: Prentice Hall, 1985), and *Ethnic Identity: The Transformation of White America* (New Haven: Yale University Press, 1990).

21. For more detail, see Lynd and Lynd, *Middletown*, part 1, entitled "Getting a Living." On the workday and workweek, see pp. 53–56.

22. Marion J. Levy, Jr., *Our Mother-Tempers* (Berkeley and Los Angeles: University of California Press, 1989).

23. The points made here are based on inference, not evidence. Mark Traugott was generous in provision of guidance on this question (in a letter of 25 May 1999). See his *Armies of the Poor: Determinants of Working-Class Participation in the Parisian Insurrection of June 1848* (Princeton: Princeton University Press, 1985); and also David Barry, *Women and Political Insurgency: France in the Mid-Nineteenth Century* (New York: St. Martin's Press, 1996).

24. Geoffrey Parker, *The Military Revolution: Military Innovation and the Rise of the West, 1500–1800*, 2d ed. (Cambridge: Cambridge University Press, 1996); Will-

iam H. McNeill, *The Pursuit of Power: Technology, Armed Force, and Society Since* A.D. *1000* (Chicago: University of Chicago Press, 1982).

25. Anderson, *Ascendancy*, Ch. 6; David G. Herrmann, *The Arming of Europe and the Making of the First World War* (Princeton: Princeton University Press, 1996); and David Stevenson, *Armaments and the Coming of War: Europe, 1904–1914* (Oxford: Clarendon, 1996).

26. For Germany, Italy, and the American South, see Richard F. Hamilton, *Who Voted for Hitler?* (Princeton: Princeton University Press, 1982), 335–351, 445, 454–462. See also Richard F. Hamilton and James D. Wright, "The Support for 'Hard Line' Foreign Policy," in Richard F. Hamilton, *Restraining Myths: Critical Studies of U.S. Social Structure and Politics* (New York: Sage, Halsted, Wiley, 1975); and Adam Clymer, "Sharp Divergence Found in Views of Military and Civilians," *New York Times*, 9 September 1999, sec. A, p. 20. This article reports findings from a large survey of military leaders and prominent civilians, both with and without military experience.

27. See "Survey: Travel and Tourism," *The Economist*, 10 January 1998, 46.

28. Richard Rose, ed., *Electoral Behavior: A Comparative Handbook* (New York: Free Press, 1974), 17; Ronald Inglehart, *The Silent Revolution: Changing Values and Political Styles Among Western Publics* (Princeton: Princeton University Press, 1977), 246–249. See also Jeff Manza and Clem Brooks, "The Religious Factor in U.S. Presidential Elections, 1960–1992," *American Journal of Sociology* 103 (1997): 38–81; and their *Social Cleavages and Political Change*. Some fifty-plus years of comment on the rise of Nazism attests to the importance of ungrounded theoretical preferences. German election results showed, unambiguously, the importance of the "religious factor": Protestants and Catholics had markedly different tendencies. Those same results did not provide any clear evidence of lower-middle-class preferences. Nevertheless, with rare exceptions, subsequent commentators neglected the easily documented fact, religion, and based their analyses on the never-established lower-middle-class hypothesis. For a review of this pathology, see Richard F. Hamilton, *Social Misconstruction of Reality: Validity and Verification in the Scholarly Community* (New Haven: Yale University Press, 1996), Chs. 4 and 5. For further evidence on the relative importance of class and religion, see Sidney Verba, Kay Lehman Schlozman, and Henry E. Brady, *Voice and Equality: Civic Voluntarism in American Politics* (Cambridge: Harvard University Press, 1995); and Jeff Manza and Clem Brooks, *Social Cleavages and Political Change*.

29. On these new directions, see Mario Bunge, *Social Science Under Debate: A Philosophical Perspective* (Toronto: University of Toronto Press, 1998), 93–99, and "In Praise of Intolerance to Charlatanism in Academia," *Annals of the New York Academy of Sciences* 775 (1996): 96–115. See also P. R. Gross and N. Levitt, *Higher Superstition: The Academic Left and Its Quarrels with Science* (Baltimore: Johns Hopkins University Press, 1994).

30. Critical thinkers should routinely give consideration to alternative hypotheses, alternatives to the season's favorite arguments. But that is clearly not the general tendency, with many self-declared critics instead "running with the pack." For an important article addressing the problem, see T. C. Chamberlin, "The Method of Multiple Working Hypotheses," *Science* 148 (1965): 754–759. Originally publishing the article in 1890, *Science* has reprinted it on four subsequent occasions.

31. For discussion of this problem, see Hamilton, *Social Misconstruction*, Chs. 7, 8.

Sociability and Satisfaction:
A Multiple Regression Analysis

Young Ho Kim

To complement the assessment of mass society theory, we conducted some statistical analyses using the GSS data merged from 1990 through 1994. While an ordered logistic regression using maximum likelihood (ML) estimations would be more statistically appropriate for our dependent variables (i.e., measured on ordinal scales), we report here the results of multivariate regression analyses using ordinary least squares (OLS) estimations. We decided to do so because the results of both regression analyses were virtually identical, and the results of OLS regression are usually more familiar and relatively easier to interpret.

Table A.1 summarizes the variables included in our regression models. Since all the variables are already described in detail in the main text, no additional explanation is necessary, except the codings of SOCFRND and SOCCOM, and a treatment of population size (LOGSIZE). The GSS coded the responses of both SOCFRND and SOCCOM into 1 through 7. While those seven categories on an ordinal scale are quite close to a continuous measurement in social sciences, we attempted to make them more compatible with an interval scale. Although somewhat arbitrary, we transformed each response into its roughly equivalent number of days a year. Since one year has 365 days, four categories like "almost everyday," "once a month," "once a year," and "never" would be obvious: 365, 12, 1, and 0, respectively. To the remaining three responses—"several a year," "several a month," and "1–2 a week"—we assigned the closest estimations.

For the population-size variable, because of its broad range and skewedness, we used a logarithm. Our sample ranges from 1,000 through a little more than 7.3 million, with most of the cases highly concentrated on the lower end. Following a customary treatment of such variables, we logged it to make the

Table A.1
Summary of Variables

Variable	Description	Coding		
Dependent Variables				
SOCFRND	Number of social evenings with friends	Never	→	0
		Once a year	→	1
		Several a year	→	6
		Once a month	→	12
SOCCOM	Number of social evenings with neighbors	Several a month	→	60
		1-2 a week	→	100
		almost everyday	→	365
SATCITY	Satisfaction with city (place you live)	None	→	0
		A little	→	1
		Some	→	2
		Fairly	→	3
		Quite a bit	→	4
		Great deal	→	5
		Very great deal	→	6
Independent Variables				
MARITAL	Marital status	Married and widowed	→	0
		Single, separated, and divorced	→	1
RACE	Race	Black	→	0
		White	→	1
AGE	Age	18 - 89 (90 years and over → 89)		
LOGSIZE	Common log of population size of places			
SRCBELT	SRC belt code	Metropolitan areas	→	0
		Nonmetropolitan areas	→	1

distribution closer to a normal curve. We used a common logarithm (a log of base 10) instead of a natural logarithm for convenience of interpretation. A unit change in common logarithm implies a digit change. A unit change in LOGSIZE, for example, would mean changes from 10 to 100, and from 100 to 1000, and so forth, in population size.

We tested six regression models (Table A.2). For each of three dependent variables, we attempted to measure and compare the relative impacts of two sets of independent variables. A main difference between two sets of inde-

Table A.2
Sociability and Satisfaction: OLS Regression Analyses

Dependent Variables	Independent Variables	Unstandardized Coefficient (B)	Standardized Coefficients (Beta)	Standard Error	Sig. T	R^2
SOCFRND	MARITAL	28.687	0.207	2.080	.000	0.092
	RACE	3.042	0.015	2.935	.300	
	AGE	- 0.613	- 0.162	0.056	.000	
	LOGSIZE	1.881	0.026	1.082	.082	
SOCFRND	MARITAL	28.855	0.208	2.035	.000	0.092
	RACE	2.719	0.014	2.812	.333	
	AGE	- 0.616	- 0.164	0.055	.000	
	SRCBELT	- 3.068	- 0.023	1.869	.101	
SOCCOM	MARITAL	21.664	0.127	2.651	.000	0.038
	RACE	- 16.062	- 0.065	3.714	.000	
	AGE	- 3.226	- 0.689	0.401	.000	
	AGESQUARE	0.032	0.714	0.004	.000	
	LOGSIZE	- 3.437	- 0.038	1.369	.012	
SOCCOM	MARITAL	21.824	0.127	2.623	.000	0.039
	RACE	- 15.184	- 0.061	3.600	.000	
	AGE	- 3.296	- 0.699	0.396	.000	
	AGESQUARE	0.033	0.718	0.004	.000	
	SRCBELT	6.582	0.040	2.390	.006	
SATCITY	MARITAL	- 0.248	- 0.081	0.057	.000	0.059
	RACE	0.410	0.094	0.057	.000	
	AGE	0.013	0.155	0.002	.000	
	LOGSIZE	- 0.078	- 0.049	0.029	.007	
SATCITY	MARITAL	- 0.249	- 0.081	0.056	.000	0.059
	RACE	0.463	0.106	0.075	.000	
	AGE	0.013	0.160	0.001	.000	
	SRCBELT	0.103	0.035	0.050	.040	

pendent variables is the fourth variable of each set, LOGSIZE and SRCBELT. They are alternate measures of urbanization.

The results in Table A.2 confirm the arguments made in the text. Basically, they show that marital status, race, and age affect people's sociability and satisfaction with their community more than urbanization.

Overall, marital status has the largest impact on people's sociability with friends. Age has the strongest impact on sociability with neighbors. The effects of population size, SRC belt code, and race on the frequencies of social contacts with friends are not statistically significant (as underlined in Table A.2).

While the impacts of all five independent variables on social contacts with neighbors are statistically significant (i.e., their significance levels are all within an acceptable range of less than 0.05), population size and SRC belt code have the least influence. We added a squared term for age (AGESQUARE), because, as mentioned in the text, the relationship between age and sociability with neighbors is curvilinear, with people's contacts with neighbors increasing somewhat in their later years.

The magnitudes of impact of five independent variables on people's satisfaction with their community, shown as unstandardized coefficients (B), are all statistically significant. In their relative strength, however, population size and SRC belt code again have the least impact in each model.

One more notable thing is the amount of variation in each of the dependent variables explained by the independent variables (R^2). Although we included some factors other than urbanization in our models, R^2 values of our models are still not very high. This means that many other factors are affecting people's sociability and satisfaction with their living places. It is further evidence of the mass society theory's inadequacy.

Bibliography

Aberbach, Joel D., Robert D. Putnam, and Bert A. Rockman. *Bureaucrats and Politicians in Western Democracies*. Cambridge: Harvard University Press, 1981.

Adams, Burt N. *Kinship in an Urban Setting*. Chicago: Markham, 1968.

Alba, Richard D. *Italian Americans: Into the Twilight of Ethnicity*. Englewood Cliffs, N.J.: Prentice Hall, 1985.

————. *Ethnic Identity: The Transformation of White America*. New Haven: Yale University Press, 1990.

Almond, Gabriel A. "The Return to the State." *American Political Science Review* 82 (1988): 853–874.

Almond, Gabriel A., and Sidney Verba. *The Civic Culture: Political Attitudes and Democracy in Five Nations*. Princeton: Princeton University Press, 1963.

Amann, Peter. *Revolution and Mass Democracy: The Paris Club Movement in 1848*. Princeton: Princeton University Press, 1975.

Anderson, M. S. *The Ascendancy of Europe 1815–1914*. 2d ed. London: Longman, 1985.

Antonio, Gene. *The AIDS Cover-Up? The Real and Alarming Facts About AIDS*. San Francisco: Ignatius Press, 1986.

Applebaum, Leon. "Officer Turnover and Salary Structures in Local Unions." *Industrial and Labor Relations Review* 19 (1966): 224–230.

Applebaum, Leon, and Harry R. Blaine. "Compensation and Turnover of Union Officers." *Industrial Relations* 14 (1973): 156–157.

Arendt, Hannah. *The Origins of Totalitarianism*. New York: Harcourt, Brace, 1951.

Ascherson, Neal. *The King Incorporated: Leopold II in the Age of Trusts*. Garden City, N.Y.: Doubleday, 1964.

Asprey, Robert B. *Frederick the Great: The Magnificent Enigma*. New York: Ticknor & Fields, 1986.

Axelrod, Morris. "A Study of Formal and Informal Group Participation in a Large Urban Community." Ph.D. diss., University of Michigan, 1953.

———. "Urban Structure and Social Participation." *American Sociological Review* 21 (1956): 13–18.

Babchuk, Nicholas, and Alan Booth. "Voluntary Association Membership: A Longitudinal Analysis." *American Sociological Review* 34 (1969): 31–45.

Bagdikian, Ben. *The Media Monopoly.* 5th ed. Boston: Beacon, 1997.

Bane, Mary Jo. *Here to Stay: American Families in the Twentieth Century.* New York: Basic Books, 1976.

Barker, Ernest. *The Development of Public Services in Western Europe, 1660–1930.* London: Oxford University Press, 1944.

Barnard, Chester I. *The Functions of the Executive.* Cambridge: Harvard University Press, 1938.

Barry, David. *Women and Political Insurgency: France in the Mid-Nineteenth Century.* New York: St. Martin's Press, 1996.

Barton, Allen H. "Consensus and Conflict Among American Leaders." *Public Opinion Quarterly* 38 (1974–1975): 507–530.

Baumgartner, Frank R., and Jack L. Walker. "Survey Research and Membership in Voluntary Associations." *American Journal of Political Science* 32 (1988): 908–928.

———. "Reply to Smith." *American Journal of Political Science* 34 (1990): 662–670.

Beale, Calvin, and Kenneth M. Johnson. "The Rural Rebound Revisited." *American Demographics* 17 (July 1995): 46–49.

Beard, Charles, and Mary Beard. *The Rise of American Civilization.* New York: Macmillan, 1927.

Bell, Daniel. *End of Ideology: On the Exhaustion of Political Ideas in the Fifties.* New York: Collier, 1961.

Bell, Wendell, and Marion D. Boat. "Urban Neighborhoods and Informal Social Relations." *American Journal of Sociology* 62 (1957): 391–398.

Bell, Wendell, and Maryanne T. Force. "Urban Neighborhood Types and Participation in Formal Associations." *American Sociological Review* 21 (1956): 25–34.

Bellah, Robert N., Richard Madsen, William Sullivan, Ann Swidler, and Steven M. Tipton. *Habits of the Heart: Individualism and Commitment in American Life.* Berkeley and Los Angeles: University of California Press, 1985.

Bennett, James T., and Thomas J. DiLorenzo. *Destroying Democracy: How Government Funds Partisan Politics.* Washington, D.C.: Cato Institute, 1985.

———. *Unhealthy Charities: Hazardous to Your Health and Wealth.* New York: Basic Books, 1994.

Benson, Lee. "Research Problems in American Political Historiography." In *Common Frontiers in the Social Sciences,* edited by Mirra Komarovsky. Glencoe, Ill.: Free Press, 1957.

———. *The Concept of Jacksonian Democracy: New York State as a Test Case.* Princeton: Princeton University Press, 1961.

Bentley, Arthur F. *The Process of Government.* Chicago: University of Chicago Press, 1908.

Berger, Suzanne. *Organizing Interests in Western Europe: Pluralism, Corporatism, and the Transformation of Politics.* New York: Cambridge University Press, 1981.

Bergmann, Klaus. *Agrarromantik und Großstadtfeindschaft.* Meisenheim: Anton Hain, 1970.

Bernstein, Carl, and Bob Woodward. *All the President's Men.* New York: Simon & Schuster, 1974.

Blankenhorn, David, Steven Bayme, and Jean Bethke Elshtain, eds. *Rebuilding the Nest: A New Commitment to the American Family.* Milwaukee: Family Service America, 1990.

Blau, Peter M. *The Dynamics of Bureaucracy: A Study of Interpersonal Relations in Two Government Agencies.* Chicago: University of Chicago Press, 1955.

Blau, Peter M., and Marshall W. Meyer. *Bureaucracy in Modern Society.* 3d ed. New York: Random House, 1987.

Blumenthal, Sidney. *The Rise of the Counter-Establishment: From Conservative Ideology to Political Power.* New York: Times Books, 1986.

Bohning, Gerry. "The McGuffey Eclectic Readers: 1836–1986." *The Reading Teacher* 40 (1986): 263–269.

Bokina, John. *Opera and Politics.* New Haven: Yale University Press, 1997.

Bonjean, Charles M., and Michael D. Grimes. "Bureaucracy and Alienation: A Dimensional Approach." *Social Forces* 48 (1970): 365–373.

Boxer, C. R. *The Dutch Seaborne Empire.* 1965. Reprint, London: Penguin, 1990.

Bramson, Leon. *The Political Context of Sociology.* Princeton: Princeton University Press, 1961.

Braverman, Harry. *Labor and Monopoly Capital: The Degradation of Work in the Twentieth Century.* New York: Monthly Review Press, 1974.

Breed, Warren. "Social Control in the Newsroom: A Functional Analysis." *Social Forces* 33 (1955): 326–335.

Brenner, Robert. "The Social Basis of English Commercial Expansion, 1550–1650." *Journal of Economic History* 32 (1972): 361–384.

Brooks, Clem, and Jeff Manza. "Class Politics and Political Change in the United States, 1952–1992." *Social Forces* 76 (1997): 379–408.

Bryant, Christopher. "Social Self-Organization, Civility and Sociology: A Comment on Kumar's 'Civil Society.'" *British Journal of Sociology* 44 (1993): 397–401.

Bryce, James. *The American Commonwealth.* New ed. New York: Macmillan, 1910.

Burke, Edmund. *Reflections on the Revolution in France.* Edited by Conor Cruise O'Brien. 1790. Reprint, Harmondsworth: Penguin, 1969.

Bunge, Mario. "In Praise of Intolerance to Charlatanism in Academia." *Annals of the New York Academy of Sciences* 775 (1996): 96–115.

———. *Social Science Under Debate: A Philosophical Perspective.* Toronto: University of Toronto Press, 1998.

Cameron, Rondo. *A Concise Economic History of the World: From Paleolithic Times to the Present.* 2d ed. New York: Oxford University Press, 1993.

Campbell, Angus. *The Sense of Well-Being in America: Recent Patterns and Trends.* New York: McGraw-Hill, 1981.

Campbell, Angus, Philip E. Converse, and Willard L. Rodgers. *The Quality of American Life: Perceptions, Evaluations, and Satisfactions.* New York: Russell Sage Foundation, 1976.

Caplow, Theodore, Howard M. Bahr, Bruce A. Chadwick, Reuben Hill, and Margaret Holmes Williamson. *Middletown Families: Fifty Years of Change and Continuity.* Minneapolis: University of Minnesota Press, 1982.

Carey, John. *The Intellectuals and the Masses: Pride and Prejudice Among the Literary Intelligentsia, 1880–1939.* London: Faber and Faber, 1992.

Carter, Richard. *The Gentle Legions*. New York: Doubleday, 1961.

Chandler, Alfred D., Jr. *Strategy and Structure: Chapters in the History of the Industrial Enterprise*. Cambridge: MIT Press, 1962.

————, ed. *Giant Enterprise: Ford, General Motors, and the Automobile Industry: Sources and Readings*. New York: Harcourt, Brace & World, 1964.

Cipolla, Carlo M. *Literacy and Development in the West*. Baltimore: Penguin Books, 1969.

Cirino, Robert. *Don't Blame the People*. New York: Vintage, 1972.

Clark, Martin. *Antonio Gramsci and the Revolution That Failed*. New Haven: Yale University Press, 1977.

Clymer, Adam. "Sharp Divergence Found in Views of Military and Civilians." *New York Times*, 9 September 1999, sec. A, p. 20.

Cobban, Alfred. *Edmund Burke and the Revolt Against the Eighteenth Century*. 1929. Reprint, London: Allen & Unwin, 1960.

Cofer, Lynette Friedrich, and Robin Smith Jacobvitz. "The Loss of Moral Turf: Mass Media and Family Values." In *Rebuilding the Nest: A New Commitment to the American Family*, edited by David Blankenhorn, Steven Bayme, and Jean Bethke Elshtain. Milwaukee: Family Service America, 1990.

Cohen, Harry. *The Demonics of Bureaucracy: Problems of Change in a Government Agency*. Ames: Iowa State University Press, 1965.

Coker, Francis W. "Pluralism." *Encyclopedia of the Social Sciences*. Vol. 12. New York: Macmillan, 1937.

Colasanto, Diane, and James Shriver. "Mirror of America: Middle-Aged Face Marital Crisis." *Gallup Report* 284 (May 1989): 34–38.

Coleman, Marilyn, and Lawrence H. Ganong. "Remarriage and Stepfamily Research in the 1980s: Increased Interest in an Old Family Form." *Journal of Marriage and the Family* 52 (1990): 925–940.

Connolly, William E., ed. *The Bias of Pluralism*. New York: Atherton, 1969.

Cook, Philip J. "Robert Michels's Political Parties in Perspective." *Journal of Politics* 33 (1971): 773–796.

Cornfield, Daniel B. *Becoming a Mighty Voice: Conflict and Change in the United Furniture Workers of America*. New York: Russell Sage, 1989.

Corwin, Ronald G. *The Organization–Society Nexus: A Critical Review of Models and Metaphors*. New York: Greenwood Press, 1987.

Coser, Lewis A., Charles Kadushin, and Walter W. Powell. *Books: The Culture and Commerce of Publishing*. New York: Basic Books, 1982.

Cousins, Norman. "The Death of 'Look.'" *Saturday Review*, 7 October 1971, 26–27.

Cray, Ed. *Chrome Colossus: General Motors and Its Times*. New York: McGraw-Hill, 1980.

Crews, Frederick, ed. *Unauthorized Freud: Doubters Confront Legend*. New York: Viking, 1998.

Crews, Frederick, Harold Blum, Marcia Cavell, Morris Eagle, and Freda Crews. *The Memory Wars: Freud's Legacy in Dispute*. New York: New York Review of Books, 1995.

Critchfield, Richard. *Those Days: An American Album*. Garden City, N.Y.: Anchor/ Doubleday, 1968.

Crowe, Kenneth C. *Collision: How the Rank and File Took Back the Teamsters*. New York: Scribner, 1993.

Curtis, James E. "Voluntary Association Joining: A Cross-National Comparative Note." *American Sociological Review* 36 (1971): 872–880.

Curtis, James E., Edward G. Grabb, and Douglas E. Baer. "Voluntary Association Membership in Fifteen Countries: A Comparative Analysis." *American Sociological Review* 57 (1992): 139–152.

Curtis, Russell L., Jr., and Louis A. Zurcher, Jr. "Voluntary Associations and the Social Integration of the Poor." *Social Problems* 18 (1971): 339–357.

Cutler, Stephen J. "Age Differences in Voluntary Association Memberships." *Social Forces* 55 (1976): 43–56.

Dahl, Robert A. *Who Governs? Democracy and Power in an American City*. New Haven: Yale University Press, 1961.

———. *Pluralist Democracy in the United States: Conflict and Consent*. Chicago: Rand McNally, 1967.

———. *Dilemmas of Pluralist Democracy: Autonomy vs. Control*. New Haven: Yale University Press, 1982.

———. *Democracy and Its Critics*. New Haven: Yale University Press, 1989.

Dahmann, Donald C., and Laarni T. Dacquel. "Residents of Farms and Rural Areas: 1990." *Current Population Reports*. Series P-20, Population Characteristics no. 457. Washington, D.C.: U.S. Bureau of the Census, 1992.

Davis, Gerald F., Kristina A. Kiekmann, and Catherine H. Tinsley. "The Decline and Fall of the Conglomerate Firm in the 1980s: The Deinstitutionalization of an Organizational Form." *American Sociological Review* 59 (1994): 547–570.

Davis, James A., and Tom W. Smith. *General Social Surveys, 1972–1993: Cumulative Codebook*. Chicago: National Opinion Research Center, 1993.

Davis, Kenneth S. *FDR, the New Deal Years 1933–1937: A History*. New York: Random House, 1986.

Demers, David Pearce. *The Menace of the Corporate Newspaper: Fact or Fiction?* Ames: Iowa State University Press, 1996.

De Stefano, Linda. "Pressures of Modern Life Bring Increased Importance to Friendship." *Gallup Poll Monthly* 294 (March 1990): 24–33.

Diamond, Larry. "Rethinking Civil Society: Toward Democratic Consolidation." *Journal of Democracy* 5 (1994): 4–17.

Dicke, Thomas S. *Franchising in America: The Development of a Business Method, 1840–1980*. Chapel Hill: University of North Carolina Press, 1992.

Domhoff, G. William. *The Higher Circles: The Governing Class in America*. New York: Random House, 1970.

———. *Who Really Rules? New Haven and Community Power Reexamined*. Santa Monica, Calif.: Goodyear, 1978.

———. *State Autonomy or Class Dominance? Case Studies on Policy Making in America*. New York: Aldine de Gruyter, 1996.

———. *Who Rules America Now?* Rev. ed. Prospect Heights, Ill.: Waveland Press, 1997.

Dominick, Raymond H. *Wilhelm Liebknecht and the Founding of the German Social Democratic Party*. Chapel Hill: University of North Carolina Press, 1982.

Donald, David Herbert. *Lincoln*. London: Jonathan Cape, 1995.

Donohue, William A. *The Politics of the American Civil Liberties Union*. New Brunswick, N.J.: Transaction Books, 1985.

————. *Twilight of Liberty: The Legacy of the ACLU*. New Brunswick, N.J.: Transaction Books, 1994.

Dotson, Floyd. "Patterns of Voluntary Association Among Urban Working-Class Families." *American Sociological Review* 16 (1951): 687–693.

Dye, Thomas R. *Who's Running America? The Clinton Years*. 6th ed. Englewood Cliffs, N.J.: Prentice Hall, 1995.

Edwards, Bob, ed. "Social Capital, Civil Society, and Contemporary Democracy." *American Behavioral Scientist* 40, no. 5 (special issue) (1997).

Edwards, Richard. *Contested Terrain: The Transformation of the Workplace in the Twentieth Century*. New York: Basic Books, 1979.

Eldridge, J.E.T., ed. *Max Weber: The Interpretation of Social Reality*. New York: Scribner's, 1971.

Elliott, J. H. *Imperial Spain, 1469–1716*. 1963. Reprint, London: Penguin, 1990.

Emery, Michael, Edwin Emery, and Nancy L. Roberts. *The Press and America: An Interpretive History of the Mass Media*. 8th ed. Boston: Allyn and Bacon, 1996.

Eschen, Donald Von, Jerome Kirk, and Maurice Pinard. "The Organizational Substructure of Disorderly Politics." *Social Forces* 49 (1971): 529–544.

Everett, John R. "The Decentralization Fiasco and Our Ghetto Schools." *Atlantic*, December 1968, 71–73.

Fellin, Philip, and Eugene Litwak, "Neighborhood Cohesion Under Conditions of Mobility." *American Sociological Review* 28 (1963): 364–376.

Fellman, Michael. *Citizen Sherman: A Life of William Tecumseh Sherman*. New York: Random House, 1995.

Ferree, Myra M. "Working Class Jobs: Housework and Paid Work as Sources of Satisfaction." *Social Problems* 23 (1976): 431–441.

Firey, Walter. *Land Use in Central Boston*. Cambridge: Harvard University Press, 1947.

Fischer, Claude S. "'Urbanism as a Way of Life': A Review and an Agenda." *Sociological Methods and Research* 1 (1972): 187–242.

————. *To Dwell Among Friends: Personal Networks in Town and City*. Chicago: University of Chicago Press, 1981.

————. *The Urban Experience*. 2d ed. San Diego: Harcourt Brace Jovanovich, 1984.

————. "Ambivalent Communities: How Americans Understand Their Localities." In *America at Century's End*, edited by Alan Wolfe. Berkeley and Los Angeles: University of California Press, 1991.

Flanagan, William C. *Urban Sociology: Images and Structure*. 2d ed. Boston: Allyn and Bacon, 1995.

Fligstein, Neil. "The Spread of the Multidivisional Form Among Large Firms, 1919–1979." *American Sociological Review* 50 (1985): 377–391.

Foley, Michael W., and Bob Edwards. "The Paradox of Civil Society." *Journal of Democracy* 7 (1996): 38–52.

Form, William H. "On the Degradation of Skills." *Annual Review of Sociology* 12 (1987): 29–47.

————. *Segmented Labor, Fractured Politics: Labor Politics in American Life*. New York: Plenum, 1995.

————. *On the Shoulders of Immigrants: A Family Portrait*. Columbus, Ohio: North Star Press, 1999.

Franklin, H. Bruce. *M.I.A. or Mythmaking in America*. New York: Lawrence Hill Books, 1992.

Freeman, Richard B., and James L. Medoff. *What Do Unions Do?* New York: Basic Books, 1984.

Freudenheim, Milt. "A.A.R.P. Will License Its Name to Managed Health Care Plans." *New York Times*, 29 April 1996, sec. A, p. 1.

Friedrich, Otto. *Decline and Fall: The Struggle for Power at a Great American Magazine*. London: Michael Joseph, 1972.

Fuguitt, Glenn V. "The Nonmetropolitan Population Turnaround." *Annual Review of Sociology* 11 (1985): 259–280.

Fumento, Michael. *The Myth of Heterosexual AIDS*. New York: Basic Books, 1990.

———. "AIDS So Far." *Commentary* 92 (December 1991): 46–49.

Furstenberg, Frank F., Jr. "Industrialization and the American Family: A Look Backward." *American Sociological Review* 31 (1966): 326–337.

Gamson, William A. *The Strategy of Social Protest*. Homewood, Ill.: Dorsey, 1975.

Gans, Herbert J. "Stimulus/Response: Vance Packard Misperceives the Way Most American Movers Live." *Psychology Today* 4 (September 1972): 20–27.

———. *Deciding What's News*. New York: Pantheon, 1979.

———. "Are U.S. Journalists Dangerously Liberal?" *Columbia Journalism Review* 24 (November–December 1985): 29–33.

Giner, Salvador. *Mass Society*. London: Martin Robertson, 1976.

Gitlin, Todd. *The Whole World Is Watching: Mass Media in the Making and Unmaking of the New Left*. Berkeley and Los Angeles: University of California Press, 1980.

Glenn, Norval D. "The Recent Trend in Marital Success in the United States." *Journal of Marriage and the Family* 53 (1991): 261–270.

———. "A Critique of Twenty Family and Marriage and the Family Textbooks." *Family Relations* 46 (1997): 197–208.

———. "Values, Attitudes, and the State of American Marriage." In *Promises to Keep: Decline and Renewal of Marriage in America*, edited by David Popenoe, Jean Bethke Elshtain, and David Blankenhorn. Lanham, Md.: Rowman and Littlefield, 1997.

Godwin, R. Kenneth, and Robert Cameron Mitchell. "The Implications of Direct Mail for Political Organizations." *Social Science Quarterly* 65 (1984): 829–839.

Goldfield, Michael. *The Decline of Organized Labor in the United States*. Chicago: University of Chicago Press, 1987.

Goldhamer, Herbert. "Some Factors Affecting Participation in Voluntary Associations." Ph.D. diss., University of Chicago, 1942.

Goodstein, Laurie. "Coalition's Woes May Hinder Goals of Christian Right." *New York Times*, 2 August 1999, sec. A, p. 1.

Goody, Jack. "Comparing Family Systems in Europe and Asia: Are There Different Sets of Rules?" *Population and Development Review* 22, no. 1 (1996): 1–20.

Gould, Jay M. *The Technical Elite*. New York: Augustus M. Kelley, 1966.

Gouldner, Alvin W. *Patterns of Industrial Bureaucracy*. Glencoe, Ill.: Free Press, 1954.

Grabb, Edward G., and James E. Curtis. "Voluntary Association Activity in English Canada, French Canada, and the United States: A Multivariate Analysis." *Canadian Journal of Sociology* 17 (1992): 371–388.

Granovetter, Mark. "Small Is Bountiful: Labor Markets and Establishment Size." *American Sociological Review* 49 (1984): 323–334.

Greeley, Andrew M. "Book Review: Habit of Heart." *Sociology and Social Research* 70 (1985): 114.

Green, Max. *Epitaph for American Labor: How Union Leaders Lost Touch with America*. Washington, D.C.: AEI Press, 1996.

Greene, Evarts B. *Religion and the State: The Making and Testing of an American Tradition*. New York: New York University Press, 1941.

Greenfield, Sidney M. "Industrialization and the Family in Sociological Theory." *American Journal of Sociology* 67 (1961): 312–322.

Greenstone, J. David. *Labor in American Politics*. New York: Knopf, 1969.

Greer, Scott. "Urbanism Reconsidered: A Comparative Study of Local Areas in a Metropolis." *American Sociological Review* 21 (1956): 19–25.

Greer, Scott, and Ella Kube, "Urbanism and Social Structure: A Los Angeles Study." In *Community Structure and Analysis*, edited by Marvin B. Sussman. New York: Crowell, 1959.

Gross, P. R., and N. Levitt. *Higher Superstition: The Academic Left and Its Quarrels with Science*. Baltimore: Johns Hopkins University Press, 1994.

Guttman, W. L. *The German Social Democratic Party, 1875–1933*. London: George Allen & Unwin, 1981.

Halberstam, David. *The Powers That Be*. New York: Knopf, 1979.

Halebsky, Sandor. *Mass Society and Political Conflict: Toward a Reconstruction of Theory*. Cambridge: Cambridge University Press, 1976.

Hall, John A., ed. *Civil Society: Theory, History, Comparison*. Cambridge: Polity Press, 1995.

Halpern, Gordon. Untitled, review of Slater. *Annals of the American Academy* 392 (November 1970): 227–228.

Hamilton, Richard F. *Affluence and the French Worker in the Fourth Republic*. Princeton: Princeton University Press, 1967.

———. *Class and Politics in the United States*. New York: Wiley, 1972.

———. *Restraining Myths: Critical Studies of U.S. Social Structure and Politics*. New York: Sage, Halsted, Wiley, 1975.

———. *Who Voted for Hitler?* Princeton: Princeton University Press, 1982.

———. *The Bourgeois Epoch: Marx and Engels on Britain, France, and Germany*. Chapel Hill: University of North Carolina Press, 1991.

———. *The Social Misconstruction of Reality: Validity and Verification in the Scholarly Community*. New Haven: Yale University Press, 1996.

———. *Marxism, Revisionism, and Leninism: Explication, Assessment, and Commentary*. Westport, Conn.: Praeger, 2000.

Hamilton, Richard F., and Lowell L. Hargens. "The Politics of the Professors: Self-Identifications, 1969–1984." *Social Forces* 71 (1993): 603–627.

Hamilton, Richard F., and James D. Wright. *The State of the Masses*. New York: Aldine, 1986.

Hanks, Michael. "Youth, Voluntary Associations and Political Socialization." *Social Forces* 60 (1981): 211–223.

Hanks, Michael, and Bruce K. Eckland. "Adult Voluntary Associations and Adolescent Socialization." *Sociological Quarterly* 19 (1978): 481–490.

Hareven, Tamara K., and Randolph Langenbach. *Amoskeag: Life and Work in an American Factory-City*. New York: Pantheon Books, 1978.

Harrison, Paul M. *Authority and Power in the Free Church Tradition: A Social Case Study of the American Baptist Convention*. Princeton: Princeton University Press, 1959.

Harry, Joseph. "Family Localism and Social Participation." *American Journal of Sociology* 75 (1970): 821–827.

Harwood, John. "Think Tanks Battle to Judge the Impact of Welfare Overhaul." *Wall Street Journal*, 30 January 1997, A1.

Hausknecht, Murray. *The Joiners*. New York: Bedminster, 1962.

Herrmann, David G. *The Arming of Europe and the Making of the First World War*. Princeton: Princeton University Press, 1996.

Hess, Stephen. *The Washington Reporters*. Washington, D.C.: Brookings, 1981.

Hibbard, Benjamin Horace. *A History of the Public Land Policies*. 1924. Reprint, Madison: University of Wisconsin Press, 1965.

Hochstadt, Steve. "Migration and Industrialization in Germany: 1815–1977." *Social Science History* 5 (1981): 445–468.

———. "Migration in Preindustrial Germany." *Central European History* 15 (1983): 195–224.

———. "The Socioeconomic Determinants of Increasing Mobility in Nineteenth-Century Germany." In *European Migrants: Global and Local Perspectives*, edited by Dirk Hoerder and Leslie Page Moch. Boston: Northeastern University Press, 1995.

———. *Mobility and Modernity: Migration in Germany, 1820–1990*. Ann Arbor: University of Michigan Press, 1999.

Hodge, Robert W., and Donald J. Treiman. "Social Participation and Social Status." *American Sociological Review* 33 (1968): 722–740.

Hunter, Floyd. *Community Power Structure*. Chapel Hill: University of North Carolina Press, 1953.

Inglehart, Ronald. *The Silent Revolution: Changing Values and Political Styles Among Western Publics*. Princeton: Princeton University Press, 1977.

Jacob, Margaret C. *Living the Enlightenment: Freemasonry and Politics in 18th Century Europe*. New York: Oxford University Press, 1991.

Jenkins, J. Craig. "Interpreting the Stormy 1960s: Three Theories in Search of a Political Age." *Research in Political Sociology* 3 (1987): 269–303.

Jenkins, J. Craig, and Craig M. Eckert. "Channeling Black Insurgency: Elite Patronage and Professional Social Movement Organizations in the Development of the Black Movement." *American Sociological Review* 51 (1986): 812–829.

Johnson, Kenneth M., and Calvin L. Beale. "The Rural Rebound." *Wilson Quarterly* 22 (Spring 1998): 16–27.

Jones, J. R. "England." In *The European Right: A Historical Profile*, edited by Hans Rogger and Eugen Weber. Berkeley and Los Angeles: University of California Press, 1966.

Josephson, Eric, and Mary Josephson, eds. *Man Alone: Alienation in Modern Society*. New York: Dell, 1962.

Kallet, Arthur, and F. J. Schlink. *100,000,000 Guinea Pigs: Dangers in Everyday Foods, Drugs and Cosmetics*. New York: Vanguard, 1932.

Kanigel, Robert. *The One Best Way: Frederick Winslow Taylor and the Enigma of Efficiency*. New York: Viking, 1997.

Kariel, Henry S. "Pluralism." *International Encyclopedia of the Social Sciences*. Vol. 12. New York: Macmillan/Free Press, 1968.

Kates, Don B., Jr., ed. *Restricting Handguns: The Liberal Skeptics Speak Out*. Croton-on-Hudson, N.Y.: North River Press, 1979.

Katz, Janet E., and Garland F. White. "Engaging the Media: A Case Study of the Politics of Crime and the Media." *Social Justice* 20, no. 3–4 (1993): 57–68.

Keane, John, ed. *Civil Society and the State: New European Perspectives*. London: Verso, 1988.

Keating, Susan Katz. *Prisoners of Hope: Exploiting the POW/MIA Myth in America*. New York: Random House, 1994.

Keay, John. *The Honourable Company: A History of the English East India Company*. New York: Macmillan, 1991.

Kerr, Clark, John T. Dunlop, Frederick H. Harbison, and Charles A. Myers. *Industrialism and Industrial Man*. New York: Oxford University Press, 1964.

Key, William H. "Rural–Urban Social Participation." In *Urbanism in World Perspective*, edited by Sylvia F. Fava. New York: Crowell, 1968.

Kluger, Richard. *The Paper: The Life and Death of the New York Herald Tribune*. New York: Knopf, 1986.

Knoke, David. "Associations and Interest Groups." *Annual Review of Sociology* 12 (1986): 1–21.

———. *Organizing for Collective Action: The Political Economies of Associations*. New York: Aldine, 1990.

Knoke, David, and Randall Thomson. "Voluntary Association Membership Trends and the Family Life Cycle." *Social Forces* 56 (1977): 48–65.

Koehl, Robert. "Feudal Aspects of National Socialism." *American Political Science Review* 54 (1960): 921–933.

Kohn, Melvin L. "Bureaucratic Man: A Portrait and an Interpretation." *American Sociological Review* 36 (1971): 461–474.

Komarovsky, Mirra. "The Voluntary Associations of Urban Dwellers." *American Sociological Review* 11 (1946): 686–698.

Kornhauser, William. *The Politics of Mass Society*. Glencoe, Ill.: Free Press, 1959.

———. "Mass Society." In *International Encyclopedia of the Social Sciences*. Vol. 10. New York: Macmillan/Free Press, 1968.

Kumar, Krishan. "Civil Society: An Inquiry into the Usefulness of an Historical Term." *British Journal of Sociology* 44 (1993): 375–395.

———. "Civil Society Again: A Reply to Christopher Bryant's 'Social Self-Organization, Civility and Sociology.'" *British Journal of Sociology* 45 (1994): 127–131.

Kwavnick, David. "Pressure-Group Demands and Organizational Objectives: The CNTU, the Lapalme Affair, and National Bargaining Units." *Canadian Journal of Political Science* 6 (1973): 582–601.

Ladd, Everett C. "Civic Participation and American Democracy." *The Public Perspective* 7 (June–July 1996): 1–22.

———. *The Ladd Report*. New York: Free Press, 1999.

Lamberti, Marjorie. *State, Society, and the Elementary School in Imperial Germany*. New York: Oxford University Press, 1989.

Laski, Harold J. "Freedom of Association." *Encyclopedia of the Social Sciences*. Vol. III. New York: Macmillan, 1937.

Laslett, Peter. *The World We Have Lost Further Explored*. 3d rev. ed. of *The World We Have Lost* [1965]. London: Methuen, 1983.

Laslett, Peter, Richard Wall, Jean Robin, and Peter Laslett, eds. *Family Forms in Historic Europe*. Cambridge: Cambridge University Press, 1983.

Latham, Earl. *The Group Basis of Politics*. Ithaca: Cornell University Press, 1952.

Lederer, Emil. *The State of the Masses: The Threat of the Classless Society*. New York: Norton, 1940.

Lee, Barrett A., R. S. Oropesa, Barbara J. Metch, and Avery M. Guest. "Testing the Decline-of-Community Thesis: Neighborhood Organizations in Seattle, 1929 and 1979." *American Journal of Sociology* 89 (1984): 1161–1188.

Lees, Andrew. "Critics of Urban Society in Germany, 1854–1914." *Journal of the History of Ideas* 40 (1979): 61–83.

———. *Cities Perceived: Urban Society in European and American Thought, 1820–1940*. New York: Columbia University Press, 1985.

Leinberger, Paul, and Bruce Tucker. *The New Individualists: The Generation After the Organization Man*. New York: HarperCollins, 1991.

Lenski, Gerhard, Jean Lenski, and Patrick Nolan. *Human Societies: An Introduction to Macrosociology*. 6th ed. New York: McGraw-Hill, 1991.

Leopold, Richard W. *Elihu Root and the Conservative Tradition*. Boston: Houghton Mifflin, 1954.

Lerner, Robert, Althea K. Nagai, and Stanley Rothman. *American Elites*. New Haven: Yale University Press, 1996.

Lerner, Robert, and Stanley Rothman. "The Media, the Polity, and Public Opinion." In *Political Behavior Annual*, Vol. 1. Boulder, Colo.: Westview Press, 1986.

Levy, Marion J., Jr. "Aspects of the Analysis of Family Structure." In *Aspects of the Analysis of Family Structure*, edited by Ansley J. Coale. Princeton: Princeton University Press, 1965.

———. *Our Mother-Tempers*. Berkeley and Los Angeles: University of California Press, 1989.

Lewis, Neil A. "Groups Plan to Exploit G.O.P. Rise." *New York Times*, 28 November 1994, sec. A, p. 15.

"Liberal Causes Cash in on a Rash of Conservatism." *New York Times*, 29 October 1989, sec. 3, p. 13.

Lichter, S. Robert, Linda S. Lichter, and Stanley Rothman. *Prime Time: How TV Portrays American Culture*. Washington, D.C.: Regnery, 1994.

Lichter, S. Robert, Stanley Rothman, and Linda S. Lichter. *The Media Elite: America's New Powerbrokers*. Bethesda, Md.: Adler & Adler, 1986.

Link, Arthur S. *Woodrow Wilson and the Progressive Era, 1910–1917*. New York: Harper Torchbooks, 1963.

Linz, Juan. "The Social Bases of West German Politics." Ph.D. diss., Columbia University, 1959.

———. "Michels." *International Encyclopedia of the Social Sciences*. Vol. 10. New York: Macmillan/Free Press, 1968.

Lipset, Seymour Martin. *Political Man: The Social Bases of Politics*. Garden City, N.Y.: Doubleday, 1960.

———. *The First New Nation*. New York: Basic Books, 1963.

———. *Revolution and Counterrevolution: Change and Persistence in Social Structures*. New York: Basic Books, 1968.

———. *Continental Divide: The Values and Institutions of Canada and the United States*. New York: Routledge, 1990.

Lipset, Seymour Martin, Martin A. Trow, and James S. Coleman. *Union Democracy*. 1956. Reprint, Garden City, N.Y.: Anchor Books, 1962.

Litt, Edgar. "Civic Education, Community Norms, and Political Indoctrination." *American Sociological Review* 28 (1963): 69–75.

Litwak, Eugene. "Geographic Mobility and Extended Family Cohesion." *American Sociological Review* 25 (1960): 285–394.

Litwak, Eugene, and Ivan Szelenyi, "Primary Group Structures and Their Functions: Kin, Neighbors, and Friends." *American Sociological Review* 34 (1969): 465–481.

Lohr, Steve. "Fewer Ties Are Bonding Workers to Corporations." *New York Times*, 14 August 1992, sec. A, p. 1.

Lorwin, Val. "Working Class Politics and Economic Development in Western Europe." *American Historical Review* 63 (1958): 341.

Lowi, Theodore J. *The End of Liberalism: Ideology, Policy, and the Crisis of Public Authority*. New York: Norton, 1969.

Luxenberg, Stan. *Roadside Empires*. New York: Viking, 1985.

Lynd, Robert S., and Helen Merrell Lynd. *Middletown: A Study in American Culture*. New York: Harcourt, Brace, 1929.

MacDonald, John S., and Leatrice D. MacDonald. "Chain Migration, Ethnic Neighborhood Formation and Social Networks." *Milbank Memorial Fund Quarterly* 42 (1964): 82–97.

Mace, Myles L. *Directors: Myth and Reality*. Boston: Harvard Business School Press, 1986.

Macmillan, Malcolm. *Freud Evaluated: The Completed Arc*. Cambridge: MIT Press, 1997.

Maehl, William Harvey. *August Bebel: Shadow Emperor of the German Workers*. Philadelphia: American Philosophical Society, 1980.

Mannheim, Karl. *Man and Society in an Age of Reconstruction: Studies in Modern Social Structure*. New York: Harcourt, Brace, 1940.

Manza, Jeff, and Clem Brooks. *Social Cleavages and Political Change: Voter Alignments and U.S. Party Coalitions*. New York: Oxford University Press, 1999.

———. "The Religious Factor in U.S. Presidential Elections, 1960–1992." *American Journal of Sociology* 103 (1997): 38–81.

Manza, Jeff, Michael Hout, and Clem Brooks. "Class Voting in Capitalist Democracies Since World War II: Dealignment, Realignment, or Trendless Fluctuation?" *Annual Review of Sociology* 21 (1995): 137–162.

Marcus, Philip M. "Union Conventions and Executive Boards: A Formal Analysis of Organizational Structure." *American Sociological Review* 31 (1966): 61–70.

Marcuse, Herbert. *One Dimensional Man: Studies in the Ideology of Advanced Industrial Society*. Boston: Beacon, 1964.

Maren, Michael. *The Road to Hell: The Ravaging Effects of Foreign Aid and International Charity*. New York: Free Press, 1997.

Marks, Irving. *Agrarian Conflicts in Colonial New York, 1711–1775*. New York: Columbia University Press, 1940.

Marshall, Dale Rogers. "Who Participates in What? A Bibliographic Essay on Individual Participation in Urban Areas." *Urban Affairs Quarterly* 4 (1968): 201–223.

Martin, Teresa Castro, and Larry L. Bumpass. "Recent Trends in Marital Disruption." *Demography* 26 (1989): 37–51.

Mayer, Martin. *The Teachers' Strike: New York, 1968*. New York: Harper & Row, 1969.

McAdam, Doug, John D. McCarthy, and Mayer N. Zald, eds. *Comparative Perspectives on Social Movements: Political Opportunities, Mobilizing Structures, and Cultural Framings*. Cambridge: Cambridge University Press, 1996.

McCarthy, John D., and Mayer N. Zald. *The Trend of Social Movements in America: Professionalization and Resource Mobilization*. Morristown, N.J.: General Learning Press, 1973.

———. "Resource Mobilization and Social Movements: A Partial Theory." *American Journal of Sociology* 82 (1977): 1212–1241.

———. "Social Movements." In *The Handbook of Sociology*, edited by Neil Smelser. Newbury Park, Calif.: Sage, 1988.

McCartney, Scott. "How Newt Gingrich Helps Raise Millions for Liberal Causes." *Wall Street Journal*, 28 November 1994, A1.

McConnell, Malcolm. *Inside Hanoi's Secret Archives: Solving the MIA Mystery*. New York: Simon & Schuster, 1995.

McCord, Norman. *British History 1815–1906*. New York: Oxford University Press, 1991.

McInnes, Neil. "Ortega and the Myth of the Mass." *The National Interest* 44 (Summer 1996): 78–88.

McNeill, William H. *The Pursuit of Power: Technology, Armed Force, and Society Since A.D. 1000*. Chicago: University of Chicago Press, 1982.

Medved, Michael. *Hollywood vs. America: Popular Culture and the War on Traditional Values*. New York: HarperCollins, 1992.

Megill, Allan. "The Reception of Foucault by Historians." *Journal of the History of Ideas* 48 (1987): 139–140.

Merton, Robert K. "Bureaucratic Structure and Personality." *Social Forces* 17 (1940): 560–568.

———. *Social Theory and Social Structure*. Rev. and enl. ed. Glencoe, Ill.: Free Press, 1957.

Merton, Robert K., Ailsa P. Gray, Barbara Hockey, and Hanan C. Selvin, eds. *Reader in Bureaucracy*. Glencoe, Ill.: Free Press, 1952.

Meyer, Michael C., and William L. Sherman. *The Course of Mexican History*. 5th ed. New York: Oxford University Press, 1995.

Michels, Robert. *Political Parties: A Sociological Study of the Oligarchical Tendencies of Modern Democracy*. 1911. Reprint, translated [1915] by Eden Paul and Cedar Paul. Glencoe, Ill.: Free Press, 1958.

Miller, Delbert C., and William H. Form. *Industrial Sociology: The Sociology of Work Organizations*. 2d ed. New York: Harper & Row, 1964.

Millis, Walter. *Arms and Men: A Study of American Military History*. New York: Putnam, 1956.

Mills, C. Wright. *White Collar: The American Middle Classes*. New York: Oxford University Press, 1951.

———. *The Power Elite*. New York: Oxford University Press, 1957.

Miner, Horace. *St. Denis: A French-Canadian Parish*. Chicago: University of Chicago Press, 1939.

Mitzman, Arthur. *The Iron Cage: An Historical Interpretation of Max Weber*. New York: Knopf, 1970.

Montesquieu, Baron de. *The Spirit of the Laws*. Translated by Thomas Nugent. New York: Hafner, 1949.

Montgomery, Kathryn C. *Target: Prime Time: Advocacy Groups and the Struggle Over Entertainment Television*. New York: Oxford University Press, 1989.

Moody's Industrial Manual: 1996. New York: Moody's Investors Services, 1996.

Moody's Industrial Manual: 1999. New York: Mergent, 1999.

Morgan, Richard E. *The "Rights Industry" in Our Time.* New York: Basic Books, 1984.

Moskowitz, Milton. "Who Killed Colliers?" *Nation*, 5 January 1957, 3–5.

Mosse, George L. *The Crisis of German Ideology.* New York: Grosset and Dunlap, 1964.

Mott, Frank Luther. *American Journalism: A History, 1690–1960.* 3d ed. New York: Macmillan, 1962.

Moynihan, Daniel P. *Maximum Feasible Misunderstanding: Community Action in the War on Poverty.* New York: Free Press, 1970.

National Center for Educational Statistics. *Digest of Education Statistics.* 1997. Available <http://nces.ed.gov/pubs/digest97/d97t008.html>.

Neumann, Sigmund. *Permanent Revolution: The Total State in a World at War.* New York: Harper, 1942.

Nisbet, Robert A. *The Quest for Community: A Study in the Ethics of Order and Freedom.* New York: Oxford University Press, 1953; reissued as *Community and Power.* New York: Oxford University Press, 1962.

Noelle, Elisabeth, and Erich Peter Neumann, eds. *Jahrbuch der Öffentlichen Meinung, 1958–1964.* Allensbach: Verlag für Demoskopie, 1965.

Nordlinger, Eric A., Theodore J. Lowi, and Sergio Fabbrini. "The Return to the State: Critiques." *American Political Science Review* 82 (1988): 875–901.

Oberly, James W. *Sixty Million Acres: American Veterans and the Public Lands Before the Civil War.* Kent, Ohio: Kent State University Press, 1990.

Oliveira, A. Ramos. *Politics, Economics and Men of Modern Spain.* London: Gollancz, 1946.

Olson, Mancur. *The Logic of Collective Action: Public Goods and the Theory of Groups.* Cambridge: Harvard University Press, 1965.

"On the Payrolls of Big Government." *New York Times*, 11 October 1995, sec. A, p. 13.

"Only the Lonely Can End Loneliness." *Columbus Dispatch*, 30 November 1987, 3B.

Ortega y Gasset, José. *Revolt of the Masses.* New York: Norton, 1940.

Orwell, George. *The Road to Wigan Pier.* New York: Harcourt, Brace & World, 1958.

Packard, Vance. *The Hidden Persuaders.* New York: David McKay, 1957.

———. *A Nation of Strangers.* New York: David McKay, 1971.

Paletz, David, and Robert Entman. *Media Power Politics.* New York: Free Press, 1981.

Parenti, Michael. *Democracy for the Few.* 6th ed. New York: St. Martin's Press, 1994.

Parker, Geoffrey. *The Military Revolution: Military Innovation and the Rise of the West, 1500–1800.* 2d ed. Cambridge: Cambridge University Press, 1996.

Paxton, Pamela. "Is Social Capital Declining in the United States? A Multiple Indicator Assessment." *American Journal of Sociology* 105 (1999): 88–128.

Peng, Yali. "Intellectual Fads in Political Science: The Cases of Political Socialization and Community Power Studies." *PS: Political Science & Politics* 27 (1994): 100–108.

Peschek, Joseph G. *Policy-Planning Organizations: Elite Agendas and America's Rightward Turn.* Philadelphia: Temple University Press, 1987.

Pessen, Edward. *Jacksonian America: Society, Personality, and Politics.* Rev. ed. Homewood, Ill.: Dorsey, 1978.

Peterson, Edward. *The Limits of Hitler's Power.* Princeton: Princeton University Press, 1969.

Polsby, Nelson W. *Community Power and Political Theory: A Further Look at the Problem of Evidence and Inference.* 2d ed. New Haven: Yale University Press, 1980.

Popenoe, David. *Disturbing the Nest: Family Change and Decline in Modern Societies.* New York: de Gruyter, 1988.

Popenoe, David, Jean Bethke Elshtain, and David Blankenhorn, eds. *Promises to Keep: Decline and Renewal of Marriage in America.* Lanham, Md.: Rowman and Littlefield, 1996.

Porter, John. *The Vertical Mosaic: An Analysis of Social Class and Power in Canada.* Toronto: University of Toronto Press, 1965.

Portes, Alejandro. "Social Capital: Its Origins and Applications in Modern Sociology." *Annual Review of Sociology* 24 (1998): 1–24.

Powell, Walter W., and Paul J. DiMaggio, eds. *The New Institutionalism in Organizational Analysis.* Chicago: University of Chicago Press, 1991.

Preston, S. H., and J. McDonald. "The Incidence of Divorce Within Cohorts of American Marriages Contracted Since the Civil War." *Demography* 16 (1979): 1–26.

Proctor, Robert N. *Cancer Wars: How Politics Shapes What We Know and Don't Know About Cancer.* New York: Basic Books, 1995.

Prost, Antoine. *L'Enseignement en France, 1800–1967.* Paris: Armand Colin, 1968.

Purdy, Matthew. "Web of Patronage in Schools Grips Those Who Can Undo It." *New York Times*, 14 May 1996, sec. A, p. 1.

Putnam, Robert D. *The Comparative Study of Political Elites.* Englewood Cliffs, N.J.: Prentice Hall, 1976.

———. "Elite Transformation in Advanced Industrial Societies: An Empirical Assessment of the Theory of Technocracy." *Comparative Political Studies* 10 (1977): 383–412.

———. *Making Democracy Work: Civic Traditions in Modern Italy.* Princeton: Princeton University Press, 1993.

———. "Bowling Alone: America's Declining Social Capital." *Journal of Democracy* 6 (January 1995): 65–78.

———. "Tuning In, Tuning Out: The Strange Disappearance of Social Capital in America." *PS: Political Science and Politics* 24 (1995): 664–683.

———. "The Strange Disappearance of Civic America." *The American Prospect* 24 (1996): 34–48.

Ravitch, Diane. *The Great School Wars: New York City, 1805–1973: A History of the Public Schools as Battlefield of Social Change.* New York: Basic Books, 1974.

Reich, Charles A. *The Greening of America.* New York: Random House, 1970.

———. *Opposing the System.* New York: Crown, 1995.

Reichard, Richard W. *Crippled from Birth: German Social Democracy 1844–1870.* Ames: Iowa State University Press, 1969.

Ricci, David M. *The Transformation of American Politics: The New Washington and the Rise of Think Tanks.* New Haven: Yale University Press, 1993.

Richelson, Jeffrey. *The U.S. Intelligence Community.* 2d ed. New York: HarperBusiness, 1989.

Ringle, Ken. "Debunking the 'Day of Dread' for Women." *Washington Post*, 31 January 1993, A1, A16.

Ritter, Gerhard. *Frederick the Great: A Historical Profile*, translated by Peter Paret. Berkeley and Los Angeles: University of California Press, 1968.

Robertson, D. B., ed. *Voluntary Associations: A Study of Groups in Free Societies.* Richmond, Va.: John Knox Press, 1966.

Robinson, Michael J. "Television and American Politics: 1956–1976." *The Public Interest* 48 (Summer 1977): 3–39.

Roethlisberger, F. J., and W. J. Dickson. *Management and the Worker.* Cambridge: Harvard University Press, 1947.

Rogers, Stacy J., and Paul R. Amato. "Is Marital Quality Declining? The Evidence from Two Generations." *Social Forces* 75 (1997): 1089–1100.

Rokkan, Stein. *Citizens Elections Parties: Approaches to the Comparative Study of the Processes of Development.* New York: David McKay, 1970.

Rölvaag, Ole. *Giants in the Earth.* New York: Harper, 1929.

Rose, Arnold M. *The Power Structure.* New York: Oxford University Press, 1967.

———. *Theory and Method in the Social Sciences.* Westport, Conn.: Greenwood Press, 1974.

Rose, Richard, ed. *Electoral Behavior: A Comparative Handbook.* New York: Free Press, 1974.

Rosenberg, Hans. *Bureaucracy, Aristocracy and Autocracy: The Prussian Experience, 1660–1815.* 1958. Reprint, Boston: Beacon Press, 1966.

Rosten, Leo. *The Washington Correspondents.* New York: Harcourt, Brace, 1937.

Roszak, Theodore. *The Making of a Counter-Culture.* Garden City, N.Y.: Doubleday, 1969.

Rothman, Stanley. "The Mass Media in Post-Industrial America." In *The Third Century: America as a Post-Industrial Society,* edited by Seymour Martin Lipset. Stanford: Hoover Institution Press, 1979.

Royster, Charles. *A Revolutionary People at War: The Continental Army and American Character, 1775–1783.* Chapel Hill: University of North Carolina Press, 1979.

Rubenstein, Carin. "The Folks Next Door Aren't Strangers After All." *New York Times,* 7 January 1993, sec. C, p. 1.

Rudenstine, David. *The Day the Presses Stopped: A History of the Pentagon Papers Case.* Berkeley and Los Angeles: University of California Press, 1996.

Saloma, John S., III. *Ominous Politics: The New Conservative Labyrinth.* New York: Hill and Wang, 1984.

Sandver, Marcus H. "Officer Turnover in National Unions: A Time Series Analysis." *Bulletin of Business Research* 53 (January 1978): 6–7.

Schattschneider, E. E. *The Semisovereign People: A Realist's View of Democracy in America.* New York: Holt, Rinehart & Winston, 1960.

Scheunes, Karl A. *Schooling and Society: The Politics of Education in Prussia and Bavaria 1850–1900.* Oxford: Berg, 1989.

Schiller, Herbert. *Mass Communication and American Empire.* New York: Augustus Kelley, 1969.

———. *The Mind Managers.* Boston: Beacon, 1973.

———. *Communication and Cultural Domination.* New York: Pantheon, 1978.

Schlesinger, Arthur M., Jr. *The Coming of the New Deal.* Boston: Houghton Mifflin, 1938.

Schlozman, Kay Lehman, and John T. Tierney. *Organized Interests and American Democracy.* New York: Harper & Row, 1986.

Schmitter, Philippe C., and Gerhard Lehmbruch, eds. *Trends Towards Corporatist Intermediation.* Beverly Hills, Calif.: Sage, 1979.

Schneider, Keith. "Big Environment Hits a Recession." *New York Times,* 1 January 1995, sec. 3, p. 4.

Schriftgiesser, Karl. *The Gentleman from Massachusetts: Henry Cabot Lodge*. Boston: Little, Brown, 1945.

Scott, John C., Jr. "Membership and Participation in Voluntary Associations." *American Sociological Review* 22 (1957): 315–326.

Scott, W. Richard. "The Evolution of Organization Theory." In *Studies in Organizational Sociology: Essays in Honor of Charles K. Warriner*, edited by Gale Miller. Greenwich, Conn.: JAI Press, 1991.

———. *Organizations: Rational, Natural, and Open Systems*. 3d ed. Englewood Cliffs, N.J.: Prentice Hall, 1992.

———. *Institutions and Organizations*. Thousand Oaks, Calif.: Sage, 1995.

Seeman, Melvin. "The Urban Alienations: Some Dubious Theses from Marx to Marcuse." *Journal of Personality and Social Psychology* 19 (1971): 135–143.

Sennett, Richard, ed. *Classic Essays on the Culture of Cities*. New York: Appleton–Century–Crofts, 1969.

Shalhope, Robert E. *Bennington and the Green Mountain Boys: The Emergence of Liberal Democracy in Vermont, 1760–1850*. Baltimore: Johns Hopkins University Press, 1996.

Sherer, Frederic M. "Industrial Structure, Scale Economies, and Worker Alienation." In *Essays on Industrial Organization in Honor of Joe S. Bain*, edited by Robert T. Masson and P. David Qualls. Cambridge: Ballinger, 1976.

Shils, Edward. "Daydreams and Nightmares: Reflections on the Criticism of Mass Culture." *Sewanee Review* 65 (1959): 586–608.

———. *The Intellectuals and the Powers and Other Essays*. Chicago: University of Chicago Press, 1972.

Shy, John. *A People Numerous and Armed: Reflections on the Military Struggle for American Independence*. New York: Oxford University Press, 1976.

Sills, David L. "Voluntary Associations." *International Encyclopedia of the Social Sciences*. Vol. 16. New York: Macmillan, 1968.

Silver, Carol Ruth, and Don B. Kates. "Self-Defense, Handgun Ownership, and the Independence of Women in a Violent, Sexist Society." In *Restricting Handguns: The Liberal Skeptics Speak Out*, edited by Don B. Kates, Jr. Croton-on-Hudson, N.Y.: North River Press, 1979.

Simons, Marlise. "For Greenpeace Guerillas, Environmentalism Is Again a Growth Industry." *New York Times*, international edition, 8 July 1995, sec. 1, p. 3.

Sitkoff, Lincoln. *The Struggle for Black Equality: 1954–1992*. Rev. ed. New York: Hill and Wang, 1993.

Skocpol, Theda. "Bringing the State Back In: Strategies of Analysis in Current Research." In *Bringing the State Back In*, edited by Peter B. Evans, Dietrich Rueschemeyer, and Theda Skocpol. New York: Cambridge University Press, 1985.

Slater, Philip E. *The Pursuit of Loneliness: American Culture at the Breaking Point*. Boston: Beacon, 1970.

Smelser, Neil. *Sociology*. 5th ed. Englewood Cliffs, N.J.: Prentice Hall, 1995.

Smith, Constance, and Anne Freedman. *Voluntary Associations: Perspectives on the Literature*. Cambridge: Harvard University Press, 1972.

Smith, David Horton. "Churches Are Generally Ignored in Contemporary Voluntary Action Research: Causes and Consequences." *Review of Religious Research* 24 (1983): 295–303.

Smith, David Horton, and Jon Van Til, eds. *International Perspectives on Voluntary Action Research*. Washington, D.C.: University Press of America, 1983.

Smith, James Allen. *The Idea Brokers: Think Tanks and the Rise of the New Policy Elite.* New York: Free Press, 1991.

Smith, Joel. *Understanding the Media: A Sociology of Mass Communication.* Cresskill, N.J.: Hampton, 1995.

Smith, Joel, William H. Form, and Gregory P. Stone. "Local Intimacy in a Middle-Sized City." *American Journal of Sociology* 60 (1954): 276–284.

Smith, Tom W. "Trends in Voluntary Group Membership: Comments on Baumgartner and Walker." *American Journal of Political Science* 34 (1990): 646–661.

Solzhenitsyn, Alexander. *Lenin in Zurich.* Translated by H. T. Willetts. New York: Farrar, Straus and Giroux, 1976.

Stange, Mary Zeiss. "Arms and the Woman: A Feminist Reappraisal." In *Guns: Who Should Have Them?* edited by David B. Kopel. Amherst, N.Y.: Prometheus, 1995.

Stanley, Harold W., and Richard G. Niemi. *Vital Statistics on American Politics.* 5th ed. Washington, D.C.: CQ Press, 1995.

Stein, Ben. *The View from Sunset Boulevard.* New York: Basic Books, 1979.

Stetson, Dorothy M., and Gerald C. Wright, Jr. "The Effects of Laws on Divorce in American States." *Journal of Marriage and the Family* 37 (1975): 537–547.

Stevenson, David. *Armaments and the Coming of War: Europe, 1904–1914.* Oxford: Clarendon, 1996.

Stolzenberg, Ross M. "Bringing the Boss Back In: Employer Size, Employee Schooling, and Socioeconomic Achievement." *American Sociological Review* 43 (1978): 813–828.

Stolzenberg, Ross M., Mary Blair-Loy, and Linda J. Waite. "Religious Participation in Early Adulthood: Age and Family Life Cycle Effects on Church Membership." *American Sociological Review* 60 (1995): 84–103.

Stratton, Kay. "Union Democracy in the International Typographical Union: Thirty Years Later." *Journal of Labor Research* 10 (1989): 119–134.

Sullivan, Teresa. "Longer Lives and Life-Long Relations: A Life Table Exegesis." *Concilium* 12 (January 1979): 15–25.

"Survey: Travel and Tourism." *The Economist,* 10 January 1998, 46.

Sussman, Marvin B. "Activity Patterns of Post-Parental Couples and Their Relationship to Family Continuity." *Marriage and Family Living* 17 (1955): 338–341.

Talese, Gay. *The Kingdom and the Power.* New York: New American Library, 1969.

Taub, Richard P., George P. Surgeon, Sara Lindholm, Phyllis Betts Otti, and Amy Bridges. "Urban Voluntary Associations, Locality Based and Externally Induced." *American Journal of Sociology* 83 (1977): 425–442.

Thomas, Darwin L., and Marie Cornwall. "Religion and Family in the 1980s: Discovery and Development." *Journal of Marriage and the Family* 52 (1990): 983–992.

Thompson, Leonard. *A History of South Africa.* Rev. ed. New Haven: Yale University Press, 1995.

Thompson, Victor A. *Modern Organization.* New York: Knopf, 1961.

Tocqueville, Alexis de. *De la Démocratie en Amérique.* Vol. 1. Paris: Charles Gosselin, 1835.

———. *Democracy in America.* Revised by Francis Bowen. New York: Knopf, 1963.

———. *Recollections.* Garden City, N.Y.: Doubleday, 1970.

Toffler, Alvin. *Future Shock.* New York: Random House, 1970.

Tomeh, Aida K. "Formal Voluntary Organizations: Participation, Correlates, and Interrelationships." *Sociological Inquiry* 43 (1973): 89–122.

Traugott, Mark. *Armies of the Poor: Determinants of Working-Class Participation in the Parisian Insurrection of June 1848*. Princeton: Princeton University Press, 1985.

Truman, David B. *The Governmental Process: Political Interests and Public Opinion*. New York: Knopf, 1951.

Tunstall, Jeremy. *Communications Deregulation: The Unleashing of America's Communications Industry*. New York: Blackwell, 1986.

Turner, Henry Ashby, Jr. *Hitler's Thirty Days to Power*. Reading, Mass.: Addison-Wesley, 1996.

Ulich, Robert. *The Education of Nations: A Comparison in Historical Perspective*. Cambridge: Harvard University Press, 1967.

U.S. Bureau of the Census. *Historical Statistics of the United States: Colonial Times to 1970*. Washington, D.C.: U.S. Government Printing Office, 1975.

―――. *American Housing Survey for the United States*. Current Housing Reports, series H-150, nos. 85, 87, 89, 91, 93, and 95.

―――. *Annual Housing Survey for the United States*. Current Housing Reports, series H-150, part B, nos. 77, 79, 81, and 83.

―――. *County Business Patterns*. Washington, D.C.: Government Printing Office, 1998.

―――. *Geographic Areas Reference Manual*. Washington, D.C.: U.S. Government Printing Office, 1994.

―――. *Statistical Abstract of the United States*. Washington, D.C.: U.S. Government Printing Office, various years.

―――. 1998 10 December. Available <http://www.census.gov:80/population/socdemo/education/table-a-01.txt>.

U.S. Department of Commerce. *1990 Census of Population and Housing. Housing Unit Counts–Ohio*. 1990 CPH-2-37. Washington, D.C.: U.S. Government Printing Office, 1993.

U.S. Department of Labor. *Directory of National Unions and Employee Associations, 1973*. Washington, D.C.: U.S. Government Printing Office, 1973.

Valentin, Veit. *Geschichte der deutschen Revolution von 1848–1849*. Vol. I. 1930. Reprint, Cologne: Kiepenheuer & Witsch, 1977.

van den Berg, Axel. *The Immanent Utopia: From Marxism on the State to the State of Marxism*. Princeton: Princeton University Press, 1988.

Van de Ven, Andrew H., and William F. Joyce, eds. *Perspectives on Organization Design and Behavior*. New York: Wiley, 1981.

Vemer, Elizabeth, Marilyn Coleman, Lawrence H. Ganong, and Harris Cooper. "Marital Satisfaction in Remarriage: A Meta-Analysis." *Journal of Marriage and the Family* 51 (1989): 713–725.

Verba, Sidney, and Norman H. Nie. *Participation in America: Political Democracy and Social Equality*. New York: Harper & Row, 1972.

Verba, Sidney, Kay Lehman Schlozman, and Henry E. Brady. *Voice and Equality: Civic Voluntarism in American Politics*. Cambridge: Harvard University Press, 1995.

Veroff, Joseph, Elizabeth Douvan, and Richard A. Kulka. *The Inner American: A Self-Portrait from 1957 to 1976*. New York: Basic Books, 1981.

Vevier, Charles. *The United Sates and China, 1906–1913: A Study of Finance and Diplomacy*. New Brunswick, N.J.: Rutgers University Press, 1955.

Wall, Joseph Frazier. *Andrew Carnegie*. Pittsburgh: University of Pittsburgh Press, 1979.

Warner, W. Lloyd, and James C. Abegglen. *Big Business Leaders in America*. New York: Harper, 1955.

Weare, G. E. *Edmund Burke's Connection with Bristol, from 1774 till 1780: With a Prefatory Memoir of Burke*. Bristol: William Bennett, 1894.

Weaver, David H., and G. Cleveland Wilhoit. *The American Journalist: A Portrait of U.S. Newspapermen and Their Work*. Bloomington: Indiana University Press, 1986.

Weber, Eugen. *Peasants into Frenchmen: The Modernization of Rural France 1870–1914*. Stanford: Stanford University Press, 1976.

Weber, Marianne. *Max Weber: Ein Lebensbild*. 1926. Reprint, Heidelberg: Lambert Schneider, 1950.

Weber, Max. *Gesammelte Aufsätze zur Soziologie und Sozialpolitik*. Tübingen: J.C.B. Mohr–Paul Siebeck, 1924.

———. *The Protestant Ethic and the Spirit of Capitalism*. Translated by Talcott Parsons. New York: Scribner's, 1930.

———. *From Max Weber: Essays in Sociology*. Edited and translated by H. H. Gerth and C. Wright Mills. London: Routledge & Kegan Paul, 1948.

———. *Wirtschaft und Gesellschaft: Grundriss der verstehenden Soziologie*, 4th ed. Edited by Johannes Winckelmann. Tübingen: J.C.B. Mohr–Paul Siebeck, 1956.

———. *Economy and Society: An Outline of Interpretive Sociology*. Vol. 3. Edited by Guenther Roth and Claus Wittich. New York: Bedminster Press, 1968.

Weinberg, Arthur S. "Six American Workers Assess Job Redesign at Saab–Scandia." *Monthly Labor Review* 98 (1975): 52–54.

Westerhoff, John H., III. *McGuffey and His Readers: Piety, Morality, and Education in Nineteenth-Century America*. Nashville: Abingdon, 1978.

White, Garland F., Janet Katz, and Kathryn E. Scarborough. "The Impact of Professional Football Games Upon Violent Assaults on Women." *Violence and Victims* 7 (1992): 157–171.

White, Morton, and Lucia White. *The Intellectual versus the City from Thomas Jefferson to Frank Lloyd Wright*. Cambridge: Harvard University Press and MIT Press, 1962.

White, Theodore. *In Search of History: A Personal Adventure*. New York: Warner, 1978.

Williamson, Chilton. *American Suffrage: From Property to Democracy, 1760–1860*. Princeton: Princeton University Press, 1960.

Wilson, James Q. *Bureaucracy: What Government Agencies Do and Why They Do It*. New York: Basic Books, 1989.

Winerip, Michael. "At 'President McKinley's Paper,' the Editors Take Endorsements Seriously." *New York Times*, 2 November 1996, sec. 1, p. 7.

Winick, Charles. Untitled, review of Slater. *American Sociological Review* 36 (1971): 766.

Wirth, Louis. "Urbanism as a Way of Life." In *Classic Essays on the Culture of Cities*, edited by Richard Sennett. New York: Appleton–Century–Crofts, 1969.

Wolfinger, Raymond E., and John Osgood Field. "Political Ethos and the Structure of City Government." *American Political Science Review* 60 (1966): 306–326.

Wright, Charles R., and Herbert H. Hyman. "Voluntary Association Memberships of American Adults: Evidence from National Sample Surveys." *American Sociological Review* 23 (1958): 284–294.

————. "Trends in Voluntary Association Memberships of American Adults: Replication Based on Secondary Analysis of National Sample Surveys." *American Sociological Review* 36 (1971): 191–206.

Wright, Gerald C., Jr. and Dorothy M. Stetson. "The Impact of No-Fault Divorce Law Reform on Divorce in American States." *Journal of Marriage and the Family* 40 (1978): 575–580.

Wright, James D. "Are Working Women *Really* More Satisfied? Evidence from Several National Surveys." *Journal of Marriage and the Family* 40 (1978): 301–313.

Wuthnow, Robert. *Sharing the Journey: Support Groups and America's New Quest for Community*. New York: Free Press, 1994.

Young, Michael, and Peter Willmott. *Family and Kinship in East London*. London: Routledge & Kegan Paul, 1957.

Zeigler, Harmon. *The Politics of Small Business*. Washington, D.C.: Public Affairs Press, 1961.

Zeldin, David. "Voluntary Action in Britain." In *Voluntary Action Research: 1974*, edited by David Horton Smith. Lexington, Mass.: Lexington Books, 1974.

Zeller, F. C. Duke. *Devil's Pact: Inside the World of the Teamster's Union*. Secaucus, N.J.: Carol, 1996.

Zurcher, Louis A., Jr. *Poverty Warriors: The Human Experience of Planned Social Intervention*. Austin: University of Texas Press, 1970.

Zurcher, Louis A., Jr., and Charles M. Bonjean, eds. *Planned Social Intervention: An Interdisciplinary Anthology*. Scranton, Pa.: Chandler, 1970.

Index

ABOUT THE AUTHOR

Richard F. Hamilton, a specialist in political and historical sociology, is a Professor Emeritus at The Ohio State University. He is now a research associate at the University's Mershon Center. His eight previous books have brought evidence to bear on a wide range of theories and hypotheses focused on the experience of the United States, Germany, France, and Britain. His previous book, *Marxism, Revisionism, and Leninism* (Praeger, 2000), is a companion to this volume.

CANADA'S CHANGING FAMILIES: CHALLENGES TO PUBLIC POLICY

Maureen Baker, Ph.D. Guest Editor

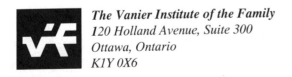

The Vanier Institute of the Family
120 Holland Avenue, Suite 300
Ottawa, Ontario
K1Y 0X6

Canadian Cataloguing In Publication Data

Main entry under title:

Canada's changing families : challenges to public policy

Issued also in French under title: Les politiques gouvernementales face aux familles en transition.
Includes bibliographical references.
ISBN 0-919520-51-0

1. Family policy—Canada. 2. Family—Social aspects—Canada.
I. Baker, Maureen. II. Vanier Institute of the Family.

HQ560.C34 1994   362.82'0971   C94-900016-7

The Vanier Institute of the Family
ii

CANADA'S CHANGING FAMILIES: CHALLENGES TO PUBLIC POLICY

Maureen Baker, Ph.D. Guest Editor
McGill University School of Social Work

Céline Le Bourdais
_Institut national de la recherche
scientifique (INRS) - Urbanisation_

Linda Duxbury
Carleton University

Jane Fulton
University of Ottawa

Christopher Higgins
University of Western Ontario

Frédéric Lesemann
Université de Montréal

Nicole Marcil-Gratton
Université de Montréal

Terrence R. Morrison
Athabasca University

Roger Nicol
Université de Montréal

Julien D. Payne
University of Ottawa

Sherri Torjman
Caledon Institute of Social Policy

Brian Wharf
University of Victoria

The Vanier Institute of the Family

iii

FOREWORD

In North America, the individual citizen has been the primary concern and beneficiary of most government action with respect to the development of social and economic policy. There are, however, limits to which the interests of individuals can be advanced without an adequate recognition of the commitments that bind them together with others in the family relationships that they almost universally declare to be most important to them. It is customary for policymakers to fashion policies for women, for children, for men, for seniors. Yet, the question remains: how can the best interests of children be served without due acknowledgement that they are a son or daughter, a brother or sister, a grandson or granddaughter? How can the interests of women be served if our policies and practices fail to acknowledge that the vast majority of women are daughters, wives, and mothers? The need for coherent family support demands that the policies and programs oriented toward the individual citizen now be complemented by those oriented toward strengthening the emotional commitments, relationships of material interdependence and patterns of familial interaction that characterize the lives of practically all citizens.

In recent years, governments at all levels have struggled, often on the basis of inadequate knowledge, to respond to the implications of family diversity and the changing patterns of family formation and functioning. Family-supportive policies have tended to evolve in a piecemeal fashion in response to single issues like child care, domestic violence, childhood poverty and reproductive technologies. Typically, each such pressing issue has been approached as though it were discrete from others and dealt with by a government bureaucracy oriented more to the differentiated functions of public administration than to the integrated functioning of families.

Within the life span of a single generation, Canadians have witnessed a revolution in their patterns of family living. Today, it is estimated that close to one-half of all children born in the last two decades will have seen their parents separate or divorce before they reach twenty years of age. The once typical male breadwinner family of the 1950s has been displaced by the two-wage-earner family as normative, both statistically and culturally. Adults have chosen to bear fewer children than at any time in the past so that families are typically smaller and children, with the exception of the increasing number who are growing up within blended families, have fewer siblings and relatives than those of previous generations. There have been notable increases in the rates of cohabitation and it is no longer possible to assume that love and marriage necessarily go together. The number of children growing up in poverty is tragically high and the costs of such neglect will be borne by them as individuals and by the larger society as the consequences of their poorer health, diminished educational achievements and lack of social integration unfold. In recent years, it has become apparent that too many families are far from safe havens and that women, children and the elderly have been subject to abuse and violence at the hands of their loved ones. And now we face the extraordinary challenges posed by new reproductive technologies that carry with them the potential to redefine the future of our families, our culture and our society.

These dramatic changes in the patterns of family formation and functioning point clearly to the need for a forward-looking, progressive and coherent set of public policies and programs to better support the families of today. The need for family policies that both acknowledge the new realities of family life and that affirm enduring values is evident.

Canada's Changing Families: Challenges to Public Policy is being published by the Vanier Institute of the Family during the International Year of the Family. It is intended to inform and stimulate public discussion and debate that may guide us toward more coherent policy responses to the evolving needs of Canada's families.

The Vanier Institute of the Family has been exceptionally fortunate in being able to count on the experience and expertise of Professor Maureen Baker who has served as Guest Editor in the planning and production of this anthology. Her past work is well-respected by Canadian researchers, legislators and public policy analysts. Her dedication to this project, which she has managed with great skill, is a reflection not only of her commitment to sound scholarship but also to Canada's families.

The researchers, scholars and public policy experts who graciously accepted our invitation to contribute to this book deserve special thanks. They have, each in their own way, used this opportunity to consolidate years of research and reflection in order to identify the most important trends and central issues to which Canadians will be forced to respond in the years to come.

This project could not have been undertaken without the financial support and encouragement of the Donner Canadian Foundation, which has sponsored the Vanier Institute's Programme of Applied Family Policy Studies. The advice of Mr. Robert Couchman, past-President of the Foundation, and Ms. Gail Sinclair, former Senior Programme Officer with the Foundation, proved especially valuable and has been much appreciated.

The overall Programme of Applied Family Policy Studies has also benefitted from the involvement of the Vanier Institute's Board of Directors as well as the members of a Project Advisory Committee appointed by the Board. For their thoughtful advice and encouragement, special thanks are due to Dr. Rosemary Ommer, Program Chairperson of the Board and Chair of the Advisory Committee, and her Advisory Committee colleagues: Mr. Eric Johansen, Mme Nicole Marcil-Gratton, Dr. Susan McDaniel, Mrs. Marilyn Peers and Mr. George Thomson.

Finally, no publication such as this would ever see the light of day were it not for the work of people like Anne Mason, VIF's Project Coordinator; Michelle Greig-Murray, VIF's Secretary; and our translators, Loraine Desjardins-Pariseault, Toyi Soglo and Ernest Wiltshire. To each, I express sincere thanks.

Robert Glossop, Ph.D.
Director of Programs

CONTENTS

CHAPTER ONE

Thinking About Families: Trends and Policies

Maureen Baker

INTRODUCTION

Over the past three decades, major changes have occurred in family life, providing new challenges for family members, employers, service providers and policy makers. With 1994 designated as International Year of the Family by the United Nations, we hope to gain a better understanding of the changing nature of family relationships, how they are influenced by social and economic trends, and ways of strengthening policies and programs to support family life.

This book is intended to stimulate discussion of social issues and policy initiatives relating to families. Although the focus is on Canada, an attempt has been made to compare Canadian trends and policy initiatives with those in other jurisdictions. The central question of the book is how can public programs and policies be made more sensitive to and supportive of family life.

A number of policy issues and initiatives will be raised and discussed in this book. Each policy issue will be placed within a historical, socioeconomic and political context, outlining the recent trends affecting policy decisions. Before providing an outline of each chapter, it is important to understand how researchers and policymakers have defined "family" and "family policy", ideologies behind family policies, and what changes have taken place in Canadian families over the past few decades.

Defining Family and Family Policy

Many different definitions of "family" have been used for purposes of research, census-taking, social policy and the delivery of social benefits. Most include single parents and couples sharing a home, regardless of their marital status, but not all definitions include same-sex couples. Most definitions include parents and their children, while some also involve couples who do not have children. Others extend the definition of family to grandparents, aunts, uncles and cousins.

The most prevalent definition used in Canadian research and policy making is Statistics Canada's "census family." This unit includes married couples with or without never-married children (and cohabiting couples who have lived together for longer than one year), or a single parent living together with never-married children. As with any definition, some social scientists and cultural groups feel that this particular definition is too narrow and does not encompass fully the group which most people consider to be their family, either through blood relationships, adoption, legal marriage, or feelings of closeness. Yet a common definition must be agreed upon when taking a census, initiating a social policy or designing any research project.

The Canadian government also uses the term "household" in gathering statistics relating to family and personal life. By household, they are referring to people sharing a dwelling, whether or not they are related by blood, adoption or marriage. For example, a boarder might be part of the household, but not necessarily part of the family.

Although the "census family" will be a prevalent definition in this book, the term "families" in the plural will be used to indicate that there are many family structures and acceptable definitions. Any variation from the Statistics Canada definition of census family will be indicated by the use of qualifying words such as one-parent family or remarried families. Without these qualifying words, the term "family" will refer to cohabiting/married couples, with or without dependent children, rather than other relatives included in an extended family.

All social and economic policies influence families in some way, but the term "family policy" usually refers specifically to the pursuit and attainment of collective goals and values in addressing problems of families in relation to society (Zimmerman, 1992). Family policy is often more broadly defined to include aspects of social or economic policies indirectly influencing families, such as educational practices, tax concessions, labour market policies and social services. In this book, family policy is defined in this broader sense, focusing on the implicit and explicit ideas about the government's role in family life inherent in programs related to marriage and divorce, procreation, childbearing and childrearing, education, and the care of dependents.

Families, the State and Society

Social scientists have used the term "state" to refer not only to government departments and their policies, but also to government-funded agencies which implement and enforce these policies. This would encompass the child welfare agencies, social services, the criminal justice system and the public schools. There are many reasons why the state would be interested in people's private lives. Information on marriages, births and deaths needs to be collected in order to plan and provide public services and facilities. Marriages and births are recorded and regulated to ensure that dependents are supported, to help prevent potential birth defects through inbreeding, to assist individuals to preserve private property, to minimize social conflict, and to protect the community. The state monitors childrearing practices and interpersonal relations between family members in order to protect vulnerable members and to maintain social order.

In North America, laws and practices assume that families are responsible for many services which are invaluable to the state. Although adults want children for their own personal reasons, the state needs them to reproduce the taxpayers, consumers and labour force members of the nation. Families help define and enforce at what age a person is allowed to engage in a sexual relationship and with whom, and what degree of closeness is too close for a sexual liaison. The state needs parents to socialize or discipline children to be law-abiding citizens, to fit into educational systems and labour force requirements, to perpetuate the culture, and to establish permanent relationships and reproduce the next generation.

Many critics have argued, however, that state involvement in family life varies for different income and cultural groups, and tends to be more interventionist for visible minorities and for those on social assistance. Furthermore, involvement is not always based on informed policy about how people actually live or why they live this way. Instead, programs and policies are often based on preconceived notions about the preferred structure of families, the role of women in families, the responsibilities of parents toward their children, and the reasons behind the need for social assistance. These ideas permeate our culture but change over time with economic and social trends.

Throughout this century, "the family" has been viewed as the basic unit of economic, physical and emotional support. North American governments have only stepped in to intervene when a child has been neglected or abused or when there are insufficient financial resources. According to current family law both parents are responsible for the care and support of their children, even after divorce, and spouses are expected to assist each other during marriage. Family members are required to register their marriages, births, and deaths; pay their taxes; feed and clothe their children; send their children to school; complete their census forms; and generally be law-abiding and peaceful. As long as these obligations are fulfilled, the state's direct involvement in family life is minimal.

Ideologies Behind Family Policies

Although many changes have occurred in family life throughout the last century, an understanding of these changes has not always been reflected in social policies. In many programs and policies created over the years, the homogeneity or uniform nature of families has been overemphasized, implying that most people live in nuclear family units consisting of breadwinner/father and homemaker/mother, legally married and living with their two or three children. Recent statistics from the Canadian government indicate that this family model is no longer dominant. For example, lone-parent families accounted for 20% of families with children in 1991, and 17% of children live with just one parent (Lindsay, 1992: 9, 12).

In addition, most mothers are now employed or looking for paid work. Although lone-parent mothers used to have a higher rate of employment than mothers in two-parent families, this situation is now reversed. In families with children under 16 years old, 64.6% of mothers in two-parent families were employed in 1991, compared to 52.2% of female lone parents (Ibid:23). In families with children between 6 and 15 years, 70.3% of mothers in two-parent families were employed compared to 62.2% of lone-parent mothers. This lower rate of employment for lone-parent mothers suggests that many are unemployed but looking for work, studying, or living on welfare. In addition, there appears to be a generational difference in work patterns as younger wives and mothers are more likely to be employed than those who are older.

Another trend away from the 'traditional' single-earner nuclear family is that a growing percentage of couples are not legally married. Twelve percent of all people in couple unions were living common-law in 1990, although this figure reached 82% for 15 to 19 year olds and 50% for 20 to 24 years olds (Stout, 1991:19). Yet governments and social scientists still talk about "the family" as though there were few variations in structure and as though any variation from the nuclear family model were unusual or "deviant."

The existence and maintenance of bias in discussing and studying family life have been thoroughly discussed by sociologist Margrit Eichler, who identified and analyzed four biases in the professional and scholarly family literature. She referred to these as the monolithic bias, the conservative bias, the sexist bias and the microstructural bias (Eichler, 1988). Eichler argued that the academic portrayal of family life in North America has focused on the experiences of middle-class white families comprised of two married parents living together, as well as the perceptions and social concerns of male family researchers (Eichler, 1988).

Policy makers often bring to their jobs assumptions about the way families live, and these ideas are not always representative of the broad range of lifestyles prevalent in modern society. Also, because their advisors have often come from similar gender, cultural and socioeconomic backgrounds and receive their training in specialized fields such as law or economics, they do not always reflect the thinking of everyday people or even the wider range of the social sciences (Baker, 1990b). These factors help to perpetuate the transmission of biases and myths in policy making. Although it was feminist social scientists who first articulated their concerns about these biases, now most researchers and some policy makers are trying to present a more balanced and realistic portrayal of family life.

Regardless of their view of the world, most researchers and social service workers now agree that families are not "havens from the harsh world" as they were once portrayed. The distinction between the so-called "private world of family" and the "public world of work" is now criticized as inaccurate. There is also a recognition that such a distinction has negative consequences in policy-making. For example, this view has allowed governments to assume that domestic services are provided willingly at home for no pay and that workers leave family responsibilities at home when they enter the workplace. Therefore, employees do not need child care services, flexible hours or special leave for family responsibilities. Until recently, this false dichotomy has also enabled the state and community to turn a blind eye to family violence. In fact, some researchers and activists argue that viewing family life as "private" and outside the realm of government regulation has encouraged social policies which have disadvantaged women and children (Ursel, 1992).

Policymakers can no longer assume that what takes place at home is of no relevance to the community or to governments. As a society and as community members, we are becoming more concerned about the physical and emotional safety of women, children and the elderly in their homes. Educators continue to try to counteract some of the more negative influences of their students' family lives. Similarly, there is an understanding of the important connection between domestic responsibilities and employment status, and that parents with dependent children, especially mothers, require assistance in resolving the inevitable conflicts between employment demands and family life.

The field of family policy is not without controversy. An attempt to create a more explicit and cohesive family policy arises from two separate traditions. One tradition is based on the realization that families are changing, with more two-income and lone-parent families, that parents make an important contribution to society in having children and that they increasingly need social support to combine more effectively family life with earning a living. The other tradition assumes that "the family" is deteriorating and attempts must be made to legislate supports to help the traditional nuclear family maintain its position against the intrusion of alternative lifestyles. In both cases, there has been a new emphasis placed on strengthening families. Yet those who applaud new family forms are suspicious of the call for "a family policy" because they fear that it could represent a conservative agenda opposing greater equality for women, gays, and "families of choice." Creating social policies which bring together these two opposing viewpoints and deal adequately with the multidimensional aspects of family life is indeed a challenge.

Several major trends have influenced family policy in Canada over the past few decades.

Changing Family Trends

Especially since World War Two, the structure of family life has changed in western industrialized countries, including Canada. Before any discussion of family policies, there needs to be an understanding of these trends, as new policies usually are initiated by people lobbying governments to ameliorate what they perceive to be "problems" caused by rapid social change. Several important socioeconomic and demographic changes have taken place which have direct implications for social policies.

1. Birthrates Have Been Declining

Since the late 1800s, birthrates have been falling in most industrialized countries, and Canada is no exception. In the period 1851 to 1861, for example, the crude birthrate in Canada (or the number of births per 1,000 population) was 45. Although there was an increase after the Second World War (the Post-War Baby Boom), the crude birthrate falling to 14.4 by 1987 before rising slightly to 15.2 in 1990 and then falling again to 14.9 in 1991.

There are many reasons why birthrates tend to decline with industrialization. As societies industrialize, manufacturing, office and service jobs are created in towns and cities, and people tend to migrate to these towns in search of work. The cost of housing and food are usually higher in urban compared to rural areas, however, and industrialization also creates the need for new technical skills and literacy, requiring a more educated labour force. Parents need to keep their children in school to better enable them to find work, and compulsory education laws often follow (Gaffield, 1990). As such, children become economic liabilities rather than assets. As the cost of living rises and one wage is no longer enough to support a family, both husbands and wives enter the paid work force. Unless other relatives are able to care for the children, child care becomes a problematic and expensive issue.

Having fewer children is often the only way couples can reduce conflicts between earning a living and raising a family. As a result, public demand for birth control tends to increase, contraceptive technology expands, and family planning becomes more widespread and socially acceptable. Ideologies supporting a more public role for women often emerge, and birthrates continue to decline. Although this pattern has been prevalent in many industrialized countries, there are, of course, cultural variations within as well as between countries in the use of contraception, birthrates and the participation of mothers in the paid labour force.

The consequences of declining birthrates are not necessarily the same for women, families and society. From a woman's perspective, fewer children may mean higher quality care for each existing child, more time and opportunity to participate in the labour force or self-development activities, and a higher standard of living (Eichler, 1988:312). For families, fewer children could mean a higher per capita income, less time over the life course devoted to child care activities, easier residential mobility and, logistically, an easier and less costly divorce. From the state's viewpoint, falling birthrates lead to an aging population, which may increase concerns about how to fund future social programs with a shrinking labour force contributing to the tax base of the nation. In addition, governments may be concerned about the rising cost of medical care which has been disproportionately costly for the "old elderly". Rapidly declining birthrates among cultural minorities could be seen as leading to decreasing power within the entire nation or region. In addition, some economists have warned about declining economic productivity and prosperity with lower birthrates. In other words, declining birthrates have been interpreted differently by various groups (Baker, 1993b).

Crude birthrates are not very accurate measures because they are influenced by the average age as well as the ratio of men to women in the population. In addition, in any one year, the crude birthrate can be affected by high unemployment and a slow economy. The more accurate measure is the total fertility rate, which is the average number of children a woman is likely to have in her lifetime. The same trend is apparent for this measure, however. In 1921, a woman had on average 3.5 children (Ram, 1990:82) compared to 1.8 in 1990 (Dumas, 1992:46). Fertility rates are also calculated for different age categories, called "age-specific fertility rates", as they are quite different for older or younger women. Many of today's young women are delaying childbirth until they finish their education, find steady work, and build up some savings. It also appears as though an increasing percentage of couples are not having any children (between 15% and 20%), either through choice or infertility problems, although it is difficult to determine this percentage more accurately until the postwar baby boom generation reaches the end of their childbearing years.

2. Rising Life Expectancy At Birth

Throughout this century, life expectancies at birth have gradually increased. For example, in 1931 the average life expectancy of a Canadian male was 60.0 years while it was 62.1 for females. By 1990, this had changed to about 74 for men and 81 for women (Dumas, 1992:60). There are several reasons for this rise in life expectancy. In the early part of the century, infant mortality rates and maternal death rates declined in response to improved sanitation, diet, housing and health services, including the invention of antibiotics and inoculations for use against contagious diseases. In addition, occupational health and safety regulations have prevented some work-related deaths, and medical breakthroughs have prolonged life for accident victims and people with acute and degenerative illnesses.

Rising life expectancies have led to several other social trends and policy changes. Fewer infant deaths, for example, contribute to a lowerbirth rate as families no longer need to have more children than they want in order to ensure that some live to adulthood. Rising life expectancy also means the potential for longer marriages, more generations per family, and more grandparents seeing their grandchildren mature. However, longer life expectancy may also result in divorce becoming more prevalent. In the last century, some unhappy marriages continued because of feelings of duty, absence of the concept of "free will", or dissolution of the marriage through early death.

As the average age of Canada's population increases, the greater proportion of elderly people makes it necessary to plan for different kinds of housing, health and social services, and expanded pension costs. Organizations catering to elderly persons will be competing for the same scarce resources as organizations serving children and youth.

3. *More People Are Living Together Outside Marriage*

In comparison with previous decades, more Canadians are now living together without being legally married. In 1990, Statistics Canada reported that 12% of all couples were in common-law relationships compared to 6 percent in 1981 (Stout, 1991:18). Quebec had the highest percentage of residents aged fifteen and over living in common-law relationships (13%), while New Brunswick had the lowest (5%). Given that most common-law partners are relatively young, it is not surprising that the vast majority have never been legally married.

From 1984-90, the proportion of Canadians aged eighteen to sixty-four who had ever lived common-law nearly doubled, but among those aged forty to forty-nine, the proportion almost tripled. More than half the women and 43% of the men who lived common-law in 1986 were younger than age thirty. Since 1984 the median age of common-law partners has continued to rise (Stout, 1991:19).

Statistics Canada's Family History Survey of 1984 found that 63% of first common-law unions end in marriage, while 35% end in separation and 2% with the death of one of the partners. For this reason, some have referred to the trend of living together before marriage as a new courtship pattern or trial marriage. On the other hand, a few people see cohabitation as an alternative to legal marriage, especially if they are separated but not divorced. Some feel that the government has no right to meddle in people's personal or sexual lives. Others feel that legal marriage involves rigid gender roles and expectations of behaviour that they may want to avoid.

Common-law relationships in Canada used to be considered as temporary arrangements that could be seen as trial marriages. Now they are becoming more like legal marriages. Yet statistically, common-law relationships still differ from legal marriage in that their duration is shorter and their fertility rates are lower. Furthermore, marriages that are preceded by cohabitation have slightly higher rates of dissolution (Burch and Madan, 1986; Beaujot, 1990). However, the 1991 census has shown that these relationships are becoming more prevalent, especially in Quebec. Furthermore, 42% of these relationships in Canada include children, either born to the common-law partners or brought into the family from other unions. These trends are very similar to many European countries, where the distinction between legal marriage and cohabitation is becoming blurred both legally and socially.

4. *More Mothers Are Working For Pay*

- In 1941, about 4.5% of married women were working in the labour force (Baker, 1990a:8).
- By 1992, this had risen to 61.4% (Statistics Canada, Feb. 1992:B8).

In the 1960s, women's labour force participation was influenced by marriage, the employment status and income of husbands, and the presence of children. If they were married, women were less likely to be working outside the home, unless their husbands were unemployed, sporadically employed or low earners. Similarly, the presence of preschool children and the absence of non-family child care services also kept mothers out of the labour force. Now, younger women are more likely than older women to be in the labour force regardless of marriage or the presence of children. Canadian government statistics, for example, indicate that:

- about three quarters of mothers with children under 12 are now working for pay, compared to 35% of all women aged 45 and over.
- In addition, married women are as likely, or more likely, to be working for pay as separated, divorced or widowed women (Ibid).

There are five major reasons for the increasing presence of mothers in the paid labour force. The first is the need for two incomes in the family because of the relative decline of individual wages in comparison with the cost of living. Second, changes in the structure of the labour force have made it more difficult for women to move in and out of the labour force in order to bear and raise children, the way they used to in the 1950s. Now they are more likely to retain their jobs and take a temporary maternity leave, if they are lucky enough to have a full-time permanent position. Third, laws relating to maternity and parental leave and benefits have been amended to allow women to retain their employment positions after giving birth. Fourth, improvements in birth control have enabled couples to plan women's pregnancies to fit in with educational and work requirements. The fifth reason for the increasing presence of mothers in the labour force relates to changing gender roles. As women gained more formal education since the 1960s, they raised their expectations about using this education to work for pay in order to support themselves or contribute to the family income.

The implications of the participation of married women in the labour force are many. In the last century, when married men and fathers left the home/farm due to industrialization in order to find work, their authority gradually diminished as family "heads". In addition, the patriarchal family or the family in which men have more legal authority than women has further declined now that most wives and mothers are working for pay. When men are no longer sole breadwinners, wives often increase their decision-making power within the marriage (Hobson, 1990). Changes are also taking place in the division of labour within the home as women spend more time at paid employment. Most research still indicates, however, that women continue to spend more time than men at family caregiving and housework, and also retain responsibility for these tasks (Le Bourdais, Hamel and Bernard, 1987; Marshall, 1990; Baines, Evans and Neysmith, 1991). Laws and social policies are beginning to change in recognition of these transitions in family and economic roles.

5. The Percentage Of Lone-Parent Families Has Been Rising

From 1961 to 1991, lone-parent families as a percentage of all families with children increased from 11% to 20% (Lindsay, 1992:15). Separation and divorce is the major reason for rising rates of one-parent families, while a second reason is the increase in births outside marriage.

a. Separation and Divorce

Throughout this century, and especially since the late 1960s, rates of separation and divorce have risen in Canada, but also in many industrialized countries. In 1921, for example, the divorce rate per 100,000 population in Canada was 6.4. By 1987, the rate had risen to 355.1 before falling slightly to 308.1 in 1988 and 294 in 1990 (Lindsay, 1992:11).

There are many reasons for rising separation and divorce rates. The growing separation of religion and the state has encouraged people to view marriage as a contract which can be broken under certain circumstances, just like business contracts. In addition, growing individualism, including the idea that people deserve happiness in their personal relationships, has discouraged couples from staying together out of duty or concern for family reputation. Furthermore, the logistics of divorce may be easier with fewer children per family. In addition, now that more women are working for pay and can at least partially support themselves, divorce may be more economically feasible for both men and women in unhappy marriages. Finally, divorce laws were liberalized in Canada in 1968 and 1985, and these reforms eased the process of divorce and thereby further contributed to rising divorce rates.

Most divorced people remarry, and about 3/4 of men and 2/3 of women remarry after divorce (Adams and Nagnur, 1990:144). Research indicates, however, that lone parents have higher remarriage rates than those without children. For example, a recent Statistics Canada publication based on 1984 data indicates that 77% of female lone parents who were separated/divorced remarried after being on their own for an average of 5.6 years. Interestingly, 97.4% of female lone parents who had been single and never-married married after an average of 4.4 years as a lone parent (Lindsay, 1992:18). Men are more likely than women to remarry after divorce, but remarriage rates have been declining for both men and women as cohabitation has become more socially acceptable.

Although the personal and family consequences of divorce can be at least temporarily devastating for some while energizing for others, the policy implications of higher rates of separation, divorce and one-parent families are very consequential. After divorce and support laws in Canada and the United States were reformed, divorce rates increased rapidly and growing numbers of children now live in households with just one parent. On the assumption that most women were at least partially self-supporting, the new laws removed some of the legal protection for the economic support of women and children (Weitzman, 1985; Drakich, 1988). Furthermore, even when the courts ordered non-custodial parents to pay support to former spouses and to their children, a majority failed to pay. Private enforcement procedures have proven ineffective (Galarneau, 1992). Consequently, the numbers of separated and divorced women and their children living on public assistance has grown with rising rates of marriage dissolution. Today, one of the major family policy issues in countries with private child support enforcement procedures is how to retrieve more of this money from non-custodial parents.

b. Rise in Births Outside Marriage

In addition to the creation of one-parent families though separation and divorce, a growing percentage of births are occurring outside marriage. In Canada, however, many of these children are born to couples who are living in permanent but non-marital relationships. As an example of the rise in births outside marriage, only 11% of female lone parents and 4% of male lone parents were never-married in 1981 compared to 20% and 8% in 1991 (Lindsay, 1992:11). In Quebec, 33% of all children were born outside of legal marriage in 1988 (Marcil-Gratton, 1989).

There are several reasons for an increase in births outside marriage. As society has become more secularized, attitudes have changed about the state's right to be involved in personal life. Sexual attitudes and practices have become more liberal since the 1950s, especially within unmarried but "committed" relationships. Legislative changes to protect women and children have made legal marriage and cohabitation, as well as the rights of children born inside and outside of marriage, very similar. These changes were made in response to demands for legal reform, but may have discouraged people from legally marrying before bearing children.

In 1968, about 70% of unmarried mothers in Ontario had their children placed for adoption. By 1977, this figure declined to about 12% (Eichler, 1983:281). Since that time, the percentage of unmarried mothers across North America who allow their children to be adopted has dwindled (although reliable statistics are not available). More women are able to support themselves and their children financially either through paid employment or improved social welfare benefits. Also, attitudes towards sex and illegitimacy have contributed to a change in the former trend to give up a baby for adoption. In addition, many mothers have made a deliberate choice to reproduce outside marriage and many are involved in permanent but non-marital relationships.

Although birthrates have declined since the 1960s for adolescents as well as for women from other age groups, additional social services are often required for young mothers. Especially those who are still adolescents and who may have interrupted their education to give birth and consequently have few job skills, little experience, and few employment opportunities. In order to become self-supporting, many of these mothers will require special education and training programs, child care services, and improved social benefits.

Increasing numbers of one-parent families have meant higher government expenditures to support women and children without adequate incomes. According to Statistics Canada data, 61% of single parent mothers were living below the poverty line in 1990 (Lindsay, 1992:35), with very little support from the non-custodial parent. Consequently, policies relating to child custody after divorce, awarding support and enforcing support have been questioned. Despite the principle of equality enshrined in family law, women who were formerly homemakers often need government assistance in job training, finding work or obtaining higher wages. In addition, there is a growing demand for more generous maternity and parental benefits and public child care services to assist all parents to better combine work and family life.

Changing Trends

In summary, families are changing in Canada along with changes in the structure of the economy, the labour force, laws, and social attitudes. Life expectancies at birth are increasing, especially for women, and birthrates are declining. Both families and households are becoming smaller, and two-income families are now in the majority. Childbearing tends to be completed earlier than several generations ago, although many middle-class women are delaying first births until after their education is completed. In addition, families are becoming less permanent units with rising rates of separation, divorce and recoupling.

Although the popularity of legal marriage has been declining recently, the percentage living as couples has been relatively stable since 1981 (Dumas, 1992:25). Most people eventually marry and most who divorce remarry. Furthermore, people are still closely tied to their extended family even when they live far apart.

Chapter Overview

In Chapter Two, Julien Payne begins by discussing the social and economic trends affecting marriage and divorce laws in Canada and raises some questions about the implications of these trends for family policy. He then outlines the ways in which Canadian family law has evolved during the past twenty-five years, noting the division of powers between provincial and federal governments. Some specific legal issues pertaining to such issues as childbirth, reproductive technologies and adoption are then addressed, but Payne focuses on the economic and parenting consequences of separation and divorce. Some suggestions leading to a more constructive and humane solution to the human and socioeconomic problems associated with separation and divorce are discussed towards the end of the chapter.

In Chapter Three, Linda Duxbury and Christopher Higgins discuss families in a changing economy, reviewing economic and social trends leading to the rise in two-income families, fewer children, more working mothers, the need for public child care and fewer older women available for voluntary work. The focus is on the restructuring made necessary by two-income families, especially with respect to the care of dependent children and frail elderly persons. Duxbury and Higgins address the recent policy responses to the needs of two-income families, sole-support mothers and those providing home care for disabled elderly persons and children. They argue that we cannot afford, socially or financially, to continue to expect employees to resolve their work/family conflicts on their own. Workers who have difficulty balancing work and family are more likely to quit their jobs, be less productive, arrive late, be absent from work, and suffer poorer physical and mental health. Unless governments and employers provide more assistance to these employees, "there will be no capable workers to carry on."

In Chapter Four, Terrence Morrison discusses education, schooling and today's families. He begins with a discussion of four major societal changes influencing learning and education: increasing specialization, the weakening of social ties, more pronounced cultural and social diversity, and the emergence of an instrumental outlook. Morrison argues that given these changes, education and formal schooling must be transformed to reintegrate learning and make it more relevant to the everyday life and work of families.

In Chapter Five, Brian Wharf provides a profile of the services which typically exist in Canadian communities to respond to the needs of families in crisis. He then argues that while all families experience crises, the kinds and extent of assistance to which one is entitled to prevent or cope with crises depends largely on one's social position and status. Rich white families deal with their crises through a variety of measures including boarding schools, live-in housekeepers and nannies, vacations, summer camps, and psychiatrists. The middle classes enjoy a few of these buffers from crisis, but the poor and particularly female-headed families and members of minority groups have to rely on state and voluntary provisions, such as social assistance, the child welfare system, transition houses and food banks. Wharf examines the adequacy and effectiveness of these programs, given the stigma of being poor, non-white and female. He questions whether services which are by current definitions selective and targeted can be transformed into programs for the social development of all people.

In Chapter Six, Sherri Torjman begins her discussion of family income security by talking in general terms about how the state has provided income security for its people. She outlines the social security programs available in Canada, focusing on programs for families with children. Trends in the financing of income security are discussed generally, especially the shifting of responsibility from the federal government to provincial governments to communities and families themselves. Poverty is viewed as resulting from a failed income security system, and the long-term costs and consequences of poverty are discussed. Torjman compares Canada's income security system with those of other jurisdictions, and argues that Canada is less generous than other industrialized countries except the United States. Recent changes in taxes and social programs, combined with high unemployment rates, have weakened federal support for families.

In Chapter Seven, Jane Fulton begins her discussion of families and health by broadening the definition of health to include quality of life. She outlines the principles behind Canada' health care system and the system's historic orientation to acute care in hospitals and physician-provided services. Recent issues relating to the allocation of scarce resources provide the backdrop to her discussion of new reproductive technologies, long-term care of the elderly, and rising costs related to an aging population. She outlines the relationship between poverty and high rates of illness and premature death. In anticipating the future, Fulton identifies the need to change the focus of our health care system away from sickness toward improving the quality of life for Canadians in all communities and from families in all economic circumstances.

In Chapter Eight, Céline Le Bourdais and Nicole Marcil-Gratton discuss a proactive approach to family policy by outlining recent policy developments in Quebec. They place these policies within a historical, cultural and socioeconomic context, discuss the principles behind these policies, and show how Quebec's policies differ from those of other Canadian jurisdictions. Special attention is placed on the newborn allowance, child care, housing allowances, and the administrative structure of family policy in Quebec.

In Chapter Nine, Canada's policy initiatives are compared to those of other industrialized nations. Frédéric Lesemann and Roger Nicol discuss three models of family policy, best illustrated by France, Sweden, and Great Britain/United States, showing the different philosophical basis of each. While France provides considerable public support to parents through universal child allowances, state-run child care services and support for parents who care for their children at home, the English-speaking countries tend to see child-rearing and care of elderly dependents as a private matter. By contrast, Sweden has offered government support to assist parents to fully participate in the work force, providing generous parental leave, subsidized day care and employment equity for women. Nevertheless, there has been a trend throughout industrialized countries to target more social and family benefits to middle- and lower-income families and to families deemed to be "at risk". Lesemann concludes that unless we acknowledge the contribution all parents make to society, the quality of life will decline and social cohesiveness will deteriorate in the future.

In the last chapter, Maureen Baker summarizes the policy initiatives introduced in previous chapters and attempts to assess the effectiveness of different types of policies. The central question of the last chapter is why certain other countries have been more successful in reducing child and family poverty or in eliminating work/family conflicts than Canada. In answering this difficult question, various political constraints in policy formulation are outlined, including the structure of government, international economic forces, prevailing political sentiments, the force of interest groups, and changing demographic trends. In asking whether or not Canada needs more explicit family policies, Baker argues that a stronger commitment needs to be made to protecting the social and economic environments of children, and to encouraging equality among family members, while at the same time respecting the variety of family structures and lifestyles.

CHAPTER TWO

Family Law in Canada

Julien D. Payne

Changing Social and Economic Trends Affecting Canadian Family Law

Canadian family law has been historically linked to the status of marriage. The formation of marriage, the consequences of marriage, and the annulment or dissolution of marriage have long been regarded as subject to state regulation and outside the control of the individual. "Marriage" has been judicially defined as "a voluntary union for life of one man and one woman to the exclusion of all others." Although this definition has been challenged under section 15 of the *Canadian Charter of Rights and Freedoms* as contravening the equality rights of same-sex cohabitants, the outcome of this challenge must await a definitive ruling by the Supreme Court of Canada. If the challenge is upheld, the implications for the future of Canadian family law could be immense.

Federal divorce laws reflect the nuclear family. Even the rights and responsibilities of members of the extended family, such as grandparents, aunts and uncles, receive scant attention. Although provincial legislation deals with more diverse aspects of family dysfunction, its traditional emphasis on the breakdown of the nuclear family is still predominant.

Recent years have witnessed changing family structures in Canada. High divorce and remarriage rates, increases in common-law and same-sex relationships, the two-income family, the changing needs of the labour force, cultural diversity, and the ageing of the population all present new challenges for Canada. Contemporary family policy issues include the following:

- How can the economic interests of women and children be protected in the event of marriage breakdown or divorce?

- How can parental ties be preserved notwithstanding separation and divorce?

- Is a national child care program feasible or desirable?

- How should Canada respond to declining birthrates? Are financial incentives for parenthood, such as those adopted in Quebec, a solution? Does the answer lie in increased immigration?

- How should Canada address the problem of the ageing of its population? What will be its impact on health care, residential care, or family care for the aged?

- Should new reproductive technologies be outlawed or regulated?

- How should law and society respond to domestic violence?

- To what extent should Canadian law recognize rights and responsibilities between unmarried cohabitants of the opposite sex or of the same sex?

- How should Canadian family law be administered? By traditional courts? By Unified Family Courts? By Administrative Tribunals? By Governmental or Community Agencies? What do innovative processes, such as mediation and arbitration, offer as alternative means of resolving family disputes? Should they be subsidized by the state?

- To what extent should Canadians be entitled to regulate the legal consequences of family breakdown by marriage contracts, cohabitation agreements or separation agreements?

- How should Canadian law respond to native families with their own cultural identity and heritage? Does the answer lie in new substantive laws or in delegating decision-making authority to the native communities? Do immigrant families require special recognition?

Many of the above issues fall outside the scope of this analysis, which will concentrate on separation and divorce. Within these terms of reference, the following information is important for future policy- and lawmakers:

- The vast majority of Canadians will marry at least once during their lifetime. Projections suggest that 28 percent of all marriages will end in divorce but 75 percent of all divorcees will marry again or form permanent cohabitational relationships. Marriages that end in divorce have an average duration of 12.5 years and the median is 10.7 years (Canada, Department of Justice, 1990:35 and 41; Vanier Institute of the Family, 1992A:9).

- Two-income families are the norm in Canada. The number of married women in the Canadian labour force has increased over the last 20 years from 35 percent to over 61 percent (Vanier Institute of the Family, 1992A:13; Statistics Canada, February 1992:8). Separated and divorced women who are incapable of achieving economic self-sufficiency in the labour force are likely to live in poverty unless they remarry or form a new permanent marriage-like relationship (Canadian Research Institute for Law and the Family, 1989:51-74).

- Three generational families living under the same roof represent approximately 6 percent of all families. With an ever-increasing ageing population, this statistic may increase dramatically over the next 20 years (Vanier Institute of the Family, 1992C:11).

- Approximately 12 percent of all adults live in common-law relationships with members of the opposite sex. More than 50 percent of them are between the ages of 20 and 35 and have never been married (Vanier Institute of the Family, 1992A).

- One out of every six children in Canada lives in poverty. Associated with poverty are poorer health, lower educational achievements and emotional and behavioural problems.

- Single-parent households represent 20 percent of all Canadian families with children (Lindsay, 1992:9). More than 75 percent of these households are headed by women. Separation and divorce result in single parenthood more frequently than death. When children are living with their mother in a single-parent household, they are five times more likely to live in poverty than children who are living with two parents. It is not true, however, that children in poverty are more frequently living in a single-parent household. Two-parent families with children represent the largest group of families living in poverty.

- More than one million children have encountered the divorce of their parents during the last 25 years. In 74 percent of all divorce cases, mothers obtain sole custody of the children. Approximately one in eight fathers (13 percent) receive sole custody of their children. Some form of joint custody arrangement exist in 11 percent of all divorces, and third-party custody arrangements are found in less than one per cent of all divorces (Millar, 1991:86).

- More than 50 percent of the children of divorce will live in a family unit with their custodial parent's new partner. Ten percent of these children will encounter a second family breakdown and will live in two or more reconstituted families.

- The high rate of default in the payment of court-ordered spousal and child support is rarely related to inability to pay. Even when payments are made in full, they generally provide only a standard of living at the poverty level.

- In the 1950s, six out of ten immigrants were European. Today, one out of two immigrants is from Asia, the Caribbean, Africa and Central America. More than 20 percent of Canadians have a cultural heritage that is neither English nor French (Vanier Institute of the Family, 1992A:11).

Canadian family law faces an uncertain future as it grapples with diverse family structures and cultural norms and the problems of dysfunctional families. Given the above information, it might be thought that the state should assume greater responsibility for ensuring the economic well-being of family members, both old and young, regardless of whether or not the family relationship has broken down. This prospect seems remote in the face of huge federal and provincial deficits. Ironically, as certain advocacy groups call for a state-subsidized national child care program, provincial governments are calling for family members to assume additional responsibilities for the care and support of ageing parents.

The Evolution of Canadian Family Law During the Past Twenty-Five Years

Canadian family law has focused on the pathology of family relationships. It concentrates on the rights and obligations of family members when their relationships become dysfunctional or break down completely.

The primary sources of family law in Canada are found in federal and provincial statutes. Federal legislation regulates divorce whereas provincial legislation regulates the rights and duties of family members independently of divorce. Appreciation of the underlying principles of Canadian family law can probably best be achieved by an overview of major legal developments that have occurred during the last 25 years.

The actual or prospective role of the law in regulating, molding and sustaining family relationships has been a neglected field of research in Canada. Federal and provincial statutory reforms have been piecemeal and have lacked a coherent vision of family policies. The predominant legal trend has been towards the assertion of individual rights and liberties rather than the assertion of any family right. Consequently, the rights of members of the extended family, such as grandparents, aunts, uncles, and ex-in-laws are often ignored as the law focuses on husbands, wives and children. Family law statutes reflect the philosophy that state intervention is an intrusion upon privacy that can only be justified by serious family dysfunction or breakdown.

Since 1968, Canadian family law has undergone radical changes. It began with divorce reform. Before 1968, adultery constituted the sole ground for divorce, except in Nova Scotia where matrimonial cruelty constituted an alternative ground for relief. In Quebec and Newfoundland, divorce was only available by private Act of Parliament prior to the introduction of judicial divorce in 1968. With the enactment of the first comprehensive federal *Divorce Act* in 1968, several no-fault divorce grounds were introduced in addition to an extended list of offence grounds. The *Divorce Act* of 1968 also broke new ground by establishing formal legal equality of support rights and obligations between divorcing men and women. Divorcing husbands became legally entitled to sue their wives for support for the first time in Canadian history. Although the *Divorce Act, 1985* has since amended the law relating to the criteria for divorce, spousal support, child support, custody and access, the radical breakthroughs occurred with the *Divorce Act* of 1968 which laid the groundwork for future federal and provincial statutory changes.

Before 1968, the support of divorcing or divorced spouses was regulated by provincial statutes that imposed a unilateral obligation on a "guilty" husband to maintain his "innocent" wife in the event of a breakdown of their marriage ensuing from his commission of a matrimonial offence. The same principles applied to spousal support claims brought independently of divorce. During the 1970s and 1980s, most provinces enacted legislation eliminating the offence concept as the foundation of spousal support rights and obligations, although spousal misconduct is not always totally excluded from judicial consideration in the determination of the right to, amount or duration of spousal support on marriage breakdown. In addition, following the precedent established by the federal *Divorce Act* of 1968, the right to spousal support on marriage breakdown in the absence of divorce is no longer confined to wives, under provincial legislation; a financially dependent spouse of either gender may look to his or her marital partner for financial support on the breakdown of their marriage. The governing consideration is no longer gender-based but turns upon the reasonable needs of the claimant and the ability of his or her spouse to pay. Each spouse is expected to strive for financial self-sufficiency to the extent that this is practicable. Thus, marriage is no longer perceived as creating an automatic right to lifelong financial support for a dependent spouse in the event of marriage breakdown. The promotion of self-sufficiency by lawyers and the courts is warranted in short-term marriages where transitional spousal support arrangements will permit full reintegration into the labour force. Longer term marriages, where one spouse, almost invariably the wife and mother, has sacrificed her employment potential and future earning capacity for the benefit of her husband and their children, warrant different treatment. Short-term transitional spousal support orders are singularly inappropriate for displaced homemaking spouses of long-standing. Unfortunately, many courts have in the past asserted the notion of self-sufficiency to the prejudice of wives and mothers who sacrificed their economic well-being for the welfare of the family. Whether the recent more enlightened approach of the Supreme Court of Canada in the Moge case will ameliorate the situation is yet to be seen as courts grapple with the contemporary notion of "compensatory support."

These changes in the right to divorce and the right to spousal support on divorce or marriage breakdown were accompanied by equally fundamental changes in provincial statutes governing the division of property on marriage breakdown or divorce. Separated and divorced wives no longer find themselves in the prejudicial position in which Irene Murdoch found herself in the mid-1970s, when the Supreme Court of Canada denied her any interest in a ranch held in her husband's name, notwithstanding that she had worked alongside her husband in the fields. Although the Supreme Court of Canada subsequently abandoned the Murdoch decision in favour of a more enlightened approach, the inequities of the Murdoch case triggered provincial legislation that provides for property sharing on marriage breakdown that is no longer dependent on who owns the property or who purchased it.

A qualified concept of "children's rights" has also evolved. Former legal distinctions drawn between legitimate and illegitimate children have been eliminated. Where the state threatens to remove a child from the family, a court may order that the child be represented by an independent lawyer. Many provincial child protection statutes expressly endorse principles of family autonomy and minimal state intervention consistent with the best interests of the child. Rules of evidence have been relaxed so as to protect the interests of children who appear as witnesses in criminal prosecutions for sexual assault or child abuse. In contested custody proceedings, an independent assessment may be ordered by the court to determine the needs of the children and the respective abilities of the parents to accommodate those needs.

Many new legal procedures have been introduced to facilitate family dispute resolution. Mandatory financial and property statements are now prepared by the spouses to provide information that will expedite the settlement or adjudication of support and property disputes. Pre-trial conferences have been devised to reduce or eliminate contentious issues. The discretionary jurisdiction of the court over the costs of litigation is being exercised so as to promote the consensual resolution of issues. The consolidation of issues in a single court proceeding has been facilitated by statutory changes and by amendments to provincial rules of court. The use of mediation as an alternative or supplement to litigation has been endorsed by the federal *Divorce Act, 1985* and by several provincial statutes. In a few urban centres, Unified Family Courts have been established with comprehensive and exclusive jurisdiction over family law matters and with access to support services that can deflect the need for hostile negotiations or costly litigation. There still remains, however, considerable room for improvement in the development of alternative processes to litigation that will aid in the constructive resolution of family conflict.

Legal Aspects of Childbirth, Reproductive Technologies and Adoption

Not too many years ago, only legitimate children received full protection under the law. Child support, custody, access, and succession rights were affected by whether the child was legitimate or illegitimate. Today, provincial legislation in Canada has substantially abolished the status of illegitimacy and its detrimental legal consequences. Any residual statutory discrimination against illegitimate children is unlikely to survive legal challenge under the equality provisions of section 15 of the *Canadian Charter of Rights and Freedoms*.

The focus of attention has thus shifted from birth or conception in lawful wedlock to proof of paternity. Several provinces have enacted legislation establishing presumptions of paternity where, for example, the mother is married to or cohabiting with a man at the time of probable conception or where a man has acknowledged the child as his or has been registered as the father on the child's birth certificate. In cases of disputed paternity, blood tests may be ordered by a court to establish parenthood. New technology has developed whereby HLA blood tests offer a high degree of positive proof of paternity in all cases, rather than simply excluding possible paternity in some cases as was the case in the past. DNA fingerprinting, which has been used primarily in criminal prosecutions, may ultimately provide foolproof evidence of paternity in family disputes.

Although the issue of paternity may be critical in some cases, legal rights and obligations as between parent and child are no longer confined to natural or biological parents. For example, a person who stands in the place of a parent to his or her spouse's children may be ordered by a court to contribute to the support of those children, at least to the extent that the natural parents are unable to discharge that obligation. This is true under federal divorce legislation as well as under statutes in most Canadian provinces.

Provincial and federal laws have not yet come to grips with new reproductive technologies. The legal implications of artificial human insemination and surrogate parenting arrangements are largely unresolved, although provincial and federal commissions have examined this controversial subject. The danger that women may be exploited by the commercialization of surrogate parenting arrangements has caused several foreign jurisdictions, including England, New South Wales, Australia, and New York State, to declare surrogate parenting contracts unenforceable in the courts. This empowers their courts to disregard the terms of any such contract insofar as it is inconsistent with the best interests of the child. The commercial exploitation of surrogate parenting by the creation or operation of agencies to recruit women for surrogate pregnancy or to make arrangements for persons wishing to use a surrogate parent has been made a criminal offence in England.

In 1985, the Ontario Law Reform Commission took a different view of surrogate parenting arrangements. It recommended that surrogacy contracts should not be declared void or unenforceable. Instead, they should be enforceable, subject to a discretionary jurisdiction in the courts to vary the terms of the contract. This approach evoked strong criticism on the basis that, instead of empowering women, it subordinated their judgments to the unfettered discretion of the judiciary.

A somewhat less controversial means of transferring parental rights and duties between natural parents and third parties is the process of adoption. Even in this context, however, controversy is not unknown. Indeed, some native communities in Canada have complained of the "cultural genocide" associated with "residential schools" and the placement of native children with adoptive parents of a different race and culture in faraway places, including the United States. Transracial and transnational adoptions arranged by provincially established child welfare authorities, which have been unrepresentative of the native culture, stand in marked contrast to the long-established practice of customary adoptions in Inuit and Indian communities. Customary native adoptions have provided an informal means of promoting family survival in remote northern communities. They are unfettered by formal requirements and reflect simple consensual arrangements made between the natural and adoptive parents. With the notable exception of customary native adoptions, which have received judicial recognition by Canadian courts, adoption is now a creature of provincial statutes that dates back only to the late 19th and early 20th century.

As a statutory process, adoption requires a court order; an agreement between the affected parties is insufficient to constitute a legal adoption. The statutory process of adoption is subject to express restrictions and designated formal procedures. Its effect is to extinguish the parental relationship existing between a child and his or her natural parents and to substitute a legally-created parental relationship between the child and the adoptive parents.

Statutorily-authorized adoptions in Canada take several forms. Children "in need of protection" who have been permanently removed from their natural parents by provincial child welfare authorities, such as Children's Aid Societies, may be placed with adoptive parents. Almost two thirds of all adoptions in Canada fall into this category. The number of annual adoption placements by provincial child welfare authorities has decreased during the last ten years from some 4,500 to approximately 1,750 (Vanier Institute of the Family, 1992B:4, citing Daly and Sobol study undertaken on behalf of the Royal Commission on New Reproductive Technologies). These placements usually involve so-called "hard to place" children. Prospective adoptive parents can expect to join a six-year waiting list, assuming that the waiting list in their community is not already closed. Not surprisingly, many of them look to the alternative of private adoption. The number of private adoptions in Canada has remained constant during the last decade, with annual placements averaging 1100 or so. Private adoptions currently represent over one third of all adoptions in Canada. Private adoptions may be arranged through agencies or persons who have been provincially licensed to arrange for adoptions. Alternatively, they may result from direct placements which often involve relatives or a stepparent.

Traditionally, adoption placements arranged through child welfare authorities have been shrouded in secrecy. The natural and adoptive parents are unknown to each other and the natural parent's rights are completely displaced by those of the adoptive parent. The adoption records are "sealed." Even when the adopted child attains adulthood, he or she has very limited access to information concerning his or her natural parents, although several provinces have established adoption registries to enable the adopted child to re-establish contact with the natural parents, if all parties are agreeable. In contrast to "closed" adoptions involving provincial child welfare authorities, intra-familial and stepparental private adoptions are "open" and contact between the child and the natural parent may be preserved or even nurtured. Private adoptions, which are non-familial, and which usually involve the intervention of provincially-licensed persons or agencies, may be either "open" or "closed." The extent to which private adoptions involve an exchange of information on a continuing basis or the preservation of a meaningful relationship between the child and the natural parent largely depends upon the wishes of the natural and adoptive parents, the practices of the placement agency, and the degree of freedom accorded by the applicable legislation, which varies significantly between the provinces.

The insufficiency of Canadian children available for adoption, which may be attributable to lower birthrates, the availability of contraception and abortion, and the increased social acceptability of unmarried mothers raising their own children, has led to an increase in international adoptions. Particularly noteworthy in this respect is the adoption of Romanian orphans by Canadian adoptive parents.

Parenting Rights on Family Breakdown or Divorce

When the parents of a young child are living in a stable family relationship, they are jointly responsible for making day-to-day as well as long-term decisions that affect the child's upbringing. They will decide such important matters as where the child will live; the school that the child will attend; the religious upbringing, if any, of the child; and appropriate dental, medical or surgical treatment. They may be called upon to consent to their child's marriage or to his or her application for a separate passport. They may also assume responsibility for the administration of property owned by the child. If a child is living with a single unmarried parent, the aforementioned powers will be exercisable by that parent.

If cohabiting or married parents separate or divorce, as the case may be, the role of each parent must be redefined. To use the language of the law, issues of "custody" of and "access" to any child must be determined. If these issues arise on divorce, the federal *Divorce Act, 1985* constitutes the governing legislation. If they arise independently of divorce, they are regulated by provincial statutes, which differ among the provinces. Generally speaking, however, custody and access disputes are determined by reference to "the best interests of the child" under both federal and provincial legislation, regardless of the language of the particular statute deemed applicable. The outcome of any custody or access dispute is unlikely to be affected, therefore, by whether the dispute is regulated by federal divorce legislation or by provincial statutory provisions. Since it is impractical to provide a detailed review of the diverse provincial statutes dealing with custody and access, the following analysis will focus on the federal divorce legislation.

The terms "custody" and "access" are technical concepts used to define parenting rights under the *Divorce Act, 1985*. "Custody" is defined to include "care, upbringing and any other incident of custody." Access is defined as the right to visit, although a divorcing or divorced spouse with access privileges is also entitled to make inquiries and receive information concerning the health, education, or welfare of the child. These inquiries may be directed to the parent with custody or to a third party, such as a teacher or doctor.

Parenting arrangements, whether agreed upon by divorcing or divorced spouses or ordered by a court, usually grant "sole custody" of the children to one spouse while conferring "reasonable" or "generous" access privileges on the other spouse. In the ordinary course of events, access involves the children staying with the non-custodial parent every other weekend and from three to six weeks during the summer holidays. Other school vacations and special days are often shared equally between the parents from year to year. Mid-week contact between the child and the non-custodial parent is also common, as is reasonable telephone contact.

In the absence of specific directions to the contrary, a divorced parent with sole custody of the children exercises parental control over and ultimate responsibility for major decisions concerning the care, upbringing and education of the children. The non-custodial parent with access privileges loses rights and privileges that he or she previously enjoyed as a joint legal guardian of the children. Although it is open to the non-custodial parent to challenge decisions of the custodial parent by recourse to the courts, the financial and psychological costs of engaging in litigation are often too burdensome to provide a realistic means of resolving disputes. Consequently, non-custodial parents with access privileges may feel that they have been relegated to passive bystanders if the custodial parent fails to encourage their active involvement in diverse aspects of the children's upbringing. Indeed, many non-custodial fathers who fail to pay court-ordered child support seek to justify their failure by complaining that they have been transformed from parents into mere debtors who have no right to make any input into the upbringing of the children whom they have been ordered to support.

Parents who wish to avoid conflict should develop a specific parenting plan on separation or divorce. There are relatively few separated or divorced parents who cannot make some positive contributions to the upbringing of their children in addition to the provision of financial support. Sound parenting plans shift the focus away from blame and can prevent hostile negotiations and acrimonious litigation. They enable parents to put the best interests of the children ahead of selfish concerns.

Separation and divorce are intended to sever the ties between the couple. They were never intended to destroy bonds between parents and children. Unfortunately, all too often, separation and divorce do produce this result. The reason often lies in the improper processing of the divorce – not only the legal divorce, but also the "emotional" divorce. Many separating and divorcing couples need assistance to put their personal hostilities aside so that they can develop plans to ensure the future well-being of their children. Contemporary wisdom among professional groups, including psychiatrists, psychologists, family therapists, social workers, lawyers and judges, stipulates that the growth and development of children of separated or divorced parents is best assured by preserving a positive relationship between the children and both of their parents. For separated and divorced parents, this may be difficult to achieve because the emotional dynamics associated with the breakdown of interpersonal relationships impede effective communication and rational settlements.

The importance of preserving meaningful contact between children of the marriage and both of their divorcing parents is expressly acknowledged in sections 16 and 17 of the *Divorce Act, 1985*. These sections provide that, in making a custody or access order, "the court shall give effect to the principle that a child of the marriage should have as much contact with each spouse as is consistent with the best interests of the child and, for that purpose, take into consideration the willingness of the person for whom custody is sought to facilitate such contact." Some women's groups are apprehensive that this so-called "friendly parent" rule may force women into joint custody or unsupervised access arrangements in situations involving spousal and child abuse. Courts must be careful to ensure that the "maximum contact" principle is wisely applied so as to avoid prejudice to the physical, sexual or emotional well-being of mothers and children.

The Divorce Act, 1985 empowers courts to grant custody and access orders to "any one or more persons." In approximately 11 percent of all divorce cases, some form of joint custody arrangement is reached (Millar, 1991:86). This may result from spousal agreement or a court order. The term "joint custody," though frequently used by lawyers and courts, is imprecise. It can cover a wide variety of situations. The expression "joint legal custody" is sometimes used to signify that divorced parents will continue to share the responsibility for making major decisions affecting their children, even though the children live primarily with one parent, usually their mother. With joint legal custody arrangements, neither parent has exclusive responsibility for deciding all matters relating to the children's health, education or welfare. The expression "joint physical custody" is used to signify that the child will spend a substantial amount of time living with each parent. Cases that attract public attention usually involve 50:50 time-sharing arrangements between the parents. The children may spend three and one-half days per week with each parent, or spend alternating weeks, months or years with each parent. More often than not, however, the time sharing ratio is not equal, although the child resides with each parent for a substantial amount of time.

Judicial attitudes towards joint custody have ranged from strong aversion to qualified support. Although judges do not normally interfere with consensual arrangements for joint custody, most courts are disinclined to order joint custody if either parent objects to any such arrangement. The preponderance of judicial authority in Canada asserts that joint custody should not be ordered where there is substantial spousal hostility and the parents are unwilling or unable to co-operate in decision-making that affects the upbringing of their children. A different judicial approach may be adopted if shared parenting arrangements have been working well for some time after separation and one of the parents seeks to change those arrangements. Separated or divorced parents who have already established successful shared parenting arrangements through mediation or a negotiated settlement are expected to make every effort to preserve those arrangements. Compelling reasons must exist before courts will interfere by granting an order for sole custody in these circumstances.

A court may grant an order for joint custody as between the divorcing parents or as between either or both parents and any third parties, such as grandparents or other relatives. Third party orders, whether for joint or sole custody, are rare and are found in less than one percent of all divorce cases (Millar, 1991: 86). There is some indication, however, that grandparents are beginning to demand, and receive, greater recognition than has been accorded to them in the past, with respect to the exercise of access privileges.

The *Divorce Act, 1985* identifies the "best interests of the child" as the sole criterion for resolving custody and access disputes. It further provides that the best interests of the child are to be determined by reference to the "condition, means, needs and other circumstances" of the child. These statutory criteria are elusive and offer little guidance to parents, lawyers and courts in their efforts to resolve parenting disputes. Lawyers and courts have adopted the following three basic assumptions as to the best interests of a child in custody disputes. Firstly, a young child should be in the custody of the parent who has assumed the primary caretaking responsibilities for that child. With rare exceptions, this test points to the mother as the preferred sole custodian. Secondly, siblings should be kept together; granting custody of one child to the mother and of another child to the father should be avoided unless the circumstances are exceptional. Thirdly, existing custody arrangements should not normally be disturbed when the children are living in a stable and healthy environment following the separation of their parents.

Twenty-five years ago, spousal misconduct, such as adultery, cruelty or desertion, had a major impact on custody disputes that went to court. The "guilty" spouse would be denied custody. It would be granted to the "innocent" spouse. The *Divorce Act, 1985* endorses a different perspective. It provides that the court shall not take into consideration the past conduct of any person unless that conduct "is relevant to the ability of that person to act as a parent of the child." Spousal guilt or innocence is thus perceived as artificial and inappropriate to a determination of the best interests of the child. Canadian judges have frequently acknowledged that custody and access orders must not seek to impose a penalty for spousal misconduct or confer a benefit on an unimpeachable spouse. In the words of a justice of the Supreme Court of Canada, "a spouse who is well nigh impossible as a spouse may nevertheless be a wonderful parent." It would be naive, however, to assume that all lawyers and judges agree with this statement by focusing on parenting ability to the exclusion of spousal misconduct. Indeed, some judges believe that spousal fault before separation provides valuable insight into a spouse's character and responsibility as a parent. Whether spousal misconduct is perceived as relevant or irrelevant to "the ability of that person to act as a parent" will ultimately depend on the attitudes and perspective of the presiding judge. Consequently, the possibility of bitterly contested custody battles is not eliminated by the provisions of the *Divorce Act, 1985* which purport to establish the "best interests of the child" as the sole criterion to the exclusion of spousal misconduct. For the most part, however, protracted acrimonious negotiations and litigation can be avoided if lawyers and judges act responsibly.

Some disputes can be avoided by the formulation of a well-conceived parenting plan by either or both parents. Mediation, whereby a neutral third party seeks to assist separated or divorce parents in reaching consensual parenting arrangements, may also provide a means of avoiding or resolving disputes. Mediation is not a panacea, however, and feminist critics have pointed out its limitations where gender power imbalance militates against the use of mediation by wives and mothers. If disputing parents cannot or will not agree on workable parenting arrangements, a judge may order an independent assessment of the family to be carried out by a qualified professional person or agency in the social or health sciences. The purpose of the assessment is to determine the child's needs in terms of appropriate parenting arrangements and the respective ability of each parent to accommodate these needs. Although the report of the independent assessor can be challenged in any subsequent litigation, judges usually endorse the findings of the assessor, even though the ultimate responsibility for making a decision lies with the judge who must take account of all the relevant evidence.

The notion that fighting over children, whether in or out of court, can provide a therapeutic catharsis for all or any members of the family is generally condemned by professionals in all disciplines. Embittered negotiations or protracted litigation between warring parents, championed by aggressive legal gladiators, cannot heal the inevitable wounds of separation or divorce. Indeed, they re-open the wounds and allow them to fester long after the legal conflict has been terminated. The infection usually spreads to the children and impairs the prospect of positive child bonds being preserved with the absent parent. In addition, such improper processing of the parenting consequences of separation and divorce may undermine the ability of the children to develop positive interpersonal relationships in their adulthood.

Law and the courts have a limited role to play but should not be at the forefront of endeavours to promote constructive solutions to the parenting crises of separation and divorce. Practising lawyers and judges are increasingly recognizing the important role that mediators can play in the resolution of parenting disputes. The strength of mediation lies not only in the flexibility of the parenting arrangements that may be thereby achieved but also in the emphasis that the mediation process places on family breakdown as a multi-faceted problem wherein the interests of all members of the fragmented family must be addressed in order to promote co-operative parenting after separation or divorce. The best interests of a child cannot be segregated from the best interests of the fragmented family. Effective parenting cannot be mandated but can be encouraged through education and counselling. The law must allow families more self-determination in resolving the parenting consequences of separation and divorce. If third party intervention is necessary, it should, whenever possible, be facilitative rather than coercive. It should promote an understanding of the emotional trauma of separation and divorce and empower parents to jointly accept responsibility for the growth and development of their children. There should be a realistic appraisal of the options that may accommodate the interests of all affected family members, including the members of any extended or reconstituted families. The pursuit of this goal must be unfettered by technical legal concepts, definitions or procedures that impede a comprehensive evaluation of practical alternatives.

Spousal and Child Support Under Provincial and Federal Legislation

Separated spouses may seek spousal or child support under provincial legislation or under federal divorce legislation. Unmarried cohabitants of the opposite sex may also be entitled to seek "spousal" support as well as child support under provincial legislation. Provincial statutes differ widely from each other in their specific provisions respecting spousal and child support. Their language also differs substantially from that in the *Divorce Act, 1985* which regulates spousal and child support on divorce. Provincial legislation in Alberta and the Northwest Territories adheres to the traditional offence concept which has always required the commission of a matrimonial offence as a condition precedent to an application to the courts for spousal and child support. Other provinces and territories have abandoned the offence concept in favour of a needs and ability to pay approach in which spousal misconduct is largely irrelevant. Several provinces, including New Brunswick, Newfoundland, Nova Scotia, Ontario and Prince Edward Island provide a detailed statutory list of factors that the courts must take into account in determining the right to, duration and amount of spousal and child support. The shortcomings of an unrefined list of designated factors, which leads to unbridled judicial discretion, have been tempered in Newfoundland, Ontario, and Saskatchewan by the articulation of specific objectives for support orders.

Differences between provincial statutes and federal divorce legislation are primarily differences of form rather than substance, whether the courts are dealing with conduct or any other factor. As stated previously, formal legal equality exists between separated and divorced spouses of either sex insofar as support rights and obligations are concerned under both provincial and federal legislation. A husband in need has just as much right to seek spousal support from his financially independent wife as she has if their financial situation is reversed. In reality, very few divorced husbands obtain spousal support from their wives. This is probably attributable to the following circumstances:

- Most divorcing husbands have full-time employment.
- Men earn higher incomes than women.
- Dependent children usually live with their mother after divorce.

More surprisingly, relatively few divorced wives receive spousal support. In this age of supposed equality, lawyers and courts often unrealistically expect homemaking wives and mothers with young children to become financially self-sufficient if their marriage breaks down. Less than twenty percent of all divorcing wives receive long-term periodic spousal support after divorce (Canada, Department of Justice, 1990:75). The correlation that exists between poverty and parenting after divorce is aggravated by the general policy of setting off spousal and child support payments against social assistance entitlements, subject only to an extremely modest reserve in certain provinces. Consequently, separated and divorced women who stayed at home to raise children are the new poor in Canada. They are usually untrained for the labour force and can never regain the lost years when they were unemployed and had no opportunity to build a career or contribute to a pension plan. A recent federal study concluded that women who are out of the labour force for more than ten years sacrifice more than $80,000 in lost future income potential that can never be recaptured when they enter or return to the labour force (Canada, Department of Justice and Status of Women, 1992:1).

Subsection 15(5) of the *Divorce Act, 1985* defines "factors" that a court must consider in determining the right to, amount and duration of spousal and child support. It provides that "the court shall take into consideration the condition, needs, means and other circumstances of each spouse and of any child of the marriage for whom support is sought, including: (a) the length of time the spouses cohabited; (b) the functions performed by the spouses during cohabitation; and (c) any order, agreement or arrangement relating to support of the spouse or child." These criteria confer a virtually unfettered discretion on the court to have regard to any facts that the trial judge considers relevant, with the exception of matrimonial misconduct.

Subsection 15(6) of the *Divorce Act, 1985* stipulates that, in making an order for support, "the court shall not take into consideration any misconduct of a spouse in relation to the marriage." As is the case with custody disputes, however, spousal misconduct may be irrelevant in law but image is still a fact of life for judges, who have feelings and attitudes just like other human beings.

Subsection 15(7) of the *Divorce Act, 1985* provides guidelines as to how judges should exercise their discretion in granting spousal support. Subsection 15(7) defines four objectives of spousal support orders. They are as follows:

(i) to recognize any economic advantages or disadvantages arising from the marriage or its breakdown;

(ii) to apportion between the spouses any financial consequences arising from child care;

(iii) to relieve any economic hardship arising from the marriage breakdown; and

(iv) insofar as practicable, to promote the economic self-sufficiency of each spouse within a reasonable period of time.

Legislative endorsement of four policy objectives manifests the realization that economic variables of marriage breakdown and divorce do not lend themselves to the application of any single objective. Long-term marriages that ultimately break down often leave in their wake a condition of financial dependence because wives have assumed the role of full-time homemakers. The legitimate objectives of spousal support in such cases rarely coincide with the objectives that should be pursued with respect to short-term childless marriages. Periodic spousal support will ordinarily be denied to a young spouse who has no children and whose economic status was not materially affected by a marriage of short duration. At most, a modest lump sum may be ordered to compensate for any economic loss sustained. Childless marriages cannot be treated in the same way as marriages with dependent children. The short duration of a marriage is no bar to periodic spousal support where a dependent spouse is unable to take full-time employment by reason of parental responsibilities. A wife and mother who is unable to find employment that will generate a reasonable income cannot be reproached if she elects to take full-time care of her child until admission to kindergarten or school. The two-income family cannot be equated with the one-income family. A "clean break" accommodated by an order for lump sum in lieu of periodic spousal support may provide a workable and desirable solution for a wealthy couple, for the two-income family and for childless marriages of short duration. Rehabilitative orders by way of periodic spousal support for a fixed term may be appropriate where there is a present incapacity to pay a lump sum and the dependent spouse can reasonably be expected to enter or re-enter the labour force within the foreseeable future. Continuing periodic spousal support orders may provide the only practical solution for dependent spouses who cannot be expected to achieve a reasonable level of economic self-sufficiency. There are no fixed rules, however, whereby particular types of order are tied to the specific objectives sought to be achieved. In the final analysis, the court must determine the most appropriate kind of order having regard to the attendant circumstances of the case, including the present and prospective financial well-being of both the spouses and their dependent children.

Although the objectives of spousal support, as defined in the *Divorce Act, 1985*, provide a legal foundation for fair and reasonable spousal support orders on divorce, they must be applied in light of the economic realities facing Canadians who divorce and thereafter enter into new family obligations. Compensating a homemaking wife for her years of service in the home or for raising the children after spousal separation is a legitimate objective of spousal support orders but may be financially impractical unless the court is dealing with a husband who is a well-established professional or businessman. It is far more problematic when the husband is an employee in receipt of a modest income, who is likely to remarry and assume additional family support obligations. That is not to say that the criteria defined in the *Divorce Act, 1985* are unsound. It is simply to recognize that they must be applied in light of the practicalities of each particular case.

Provincial statutory support regimes, as well as the *Divorce Act, 1985*, impose an obligation on parents to support their children. Although the statutory definitions of "parent" and "child" take a variety of forms, it is common for child support obligations to be owed not only by the natural parents but also by any person "who stands in the place of a parent" towards a child. The child support obligations of natural or adoptive parents legally outweigh the obligation of a person who stands in the place of a parent to his partner's children but it is often impractical to apply a principle of primary and secondary obligations if the natural parent has moved out of the province where the children live.

Six provincial and territorial statutes expressly confine child support rights to unmarried children under the age of majority. Four provinces empower their courts to order support for children over the age of majority in circumstances involving disability or post-secondary education. Pursuant to the *Divorce Act, 1985*, a divorcing or divorced spouse may be ordered to pay support in respect of an adult child who is unable to achieve self-sufficiency by reason of "illness, disability or other cause." Child support is frequently granted under the *Divorce Act, 1985* to provide an adult child with post-secondary education but will not normally be ordered beyond the first undergraduate degree or diploma.

Provincial statutes, like the *Divorce Act, 1985*, identify specific factors that the court shall take into consideration in determining the right to and amount of child support. In the final analysis, however, needs and ability to pay are the legal foundation of child support rights and obligations. The *Divorce Act, 1985* provides that orders for child support should (i) recognize that the spouses have a joint financial obligation to support their children, and (ii) that obligation should be apportioned between the spouses in accordance with their respective abilities to contribute to the financial support of the children.

The Supreme Court of Canada has asserted that the legal principles regulating spousal support and those regulating child support must be kept separate and distinct. Although courts have frequently stated that the costs of a child's upbringing should be considered in assessing child support and expert opinion of such costs has been admitted in isolated cases, specific evidence of child-connected expenses is usually lacking. In some cases, courts have applied an arbitrary yardstick to segregate personal and child-connected expenses in the absence of specific evidence. It has been suggested that one third of a custodial parent's expenses represents basic household costs that continue with or without children, that a further one third represents the personal expenses of the custodial parent, and that the final one third represents child-connected costs.

The drawing of distinctions between spousal and child support may contribute to the economic crisis that many custodial mothers and children face on marriage breakdown by reason of the low incidence of spousal support and the modest amounts of child support that are customarily ordered. Judicial rhetoric that children must come first is loudly proclaimed but rarely applied. It is inevitable, of course, that many children will suffer financial setbacks when their parents separate. Two households cannot live as cheaply as one when the family income remains the same.

Although few Canadians can afford the luxury of supporting two families at a comfortable level on one income, separated and divorced husbands and fathers can afford to pay larger amounts of spousal or child support without facing poverty. Empirical data in Canada indicate that a divorced custodial parent is unlikely to receive more than twenty per cent of the net income of the paying spouse and parent as spousal and/or child support (Canada, Department of Justice, 1990:vi and 83-85). It should not surprise us, therefore, that single mothers and their children represent a disproportionate percentage of the poverty classes. This societal problem is not confined to Canada and has led to the development of "child support guidelines" in England, Australia and the United States. These guidelines quantify an exact amount of child support by reference to fixed schedules. Federal, provincial and territorial authorities are currently examining the feasibility and desirability of implementing quantitative "child support guidelines" in Canada. Fixed schedules for the quantification of child support could promote (i) simple and inexpensive administrative procedures for assessing the amount of child support; (ii) consistency of amounts in comparable family situations; and (iii) higher child support payments that more realistically reflect the actual costs of raising a child. Even if quantitative guidelines are implemented, they are not a panacea. Piecemeal reforms that provide more child support, without financial viability for the caretaking parent, will still result in poverty for both parent and child. Furthermore, quantitative child support guidelines provide no relief for displaced homemaking wives whose children have already left home.

If the financial plight of separated and divorced women is to be resolved, fair laws regulating spousal and child support rights and obligations are not sufficient. They must be buttressed by cohesive socioeconomic programs that guarantee income security for all disadvantaged Canadians, including the economic victims of separation or divorce. Although today's problem is one of spousal and child support, tomorrow's will include the support of elderly and infirm parents. People are living longer. Canada's population is growing older. Today's children will have to carry the burden for tomorrow's elderly. One in six children in Canada is now living in poverty. How can these children be realistically expected to contribute towards the future costs generated by an ageing population? The state must invest in these children now in order for dividends to be reaped in the future. This is true whether poor children are the innocent victims of separation and divorce or are being raised in a low-income two parent family.

Concluding Observations

The following observations will refer to married couples but are often equally applicable to unmarried cohabitants who have lived together for some years. For many Canadians, separation or divorce trigger three crises: (i) an emotional crisis; (ii) a financial crisis; (iii) a parenting crisis.

The emotional crisis is experienced not only by the couple but also by their children. The human dynamics of separation and divorce pass through various phases, namely, denial, hostility, and depression, to ultimate acceptance of the death of the marriage. The processing of the "emotional divorce" by the couple rarely takes less than one year. The reaction of children to parental separation and divorce is also traumatic and can be aggravated by their parents' mismanagement of their own emotional divorce. If persistent conflict or poverty is triggered by parental separation, the children's well-being can be threatened to the point where it affects their ability to develop stable relationships when they reach adulthood.

When family dysfunction results in separation, couples often precipitously resort to the legal system for instant solutions to their problems. Very few people are aware of other resources in the community that provide counselling, therapy, and mediation services to deal with family dysfunction. Separating and divorcing couples should be advised of these resources, both public and private, that can facilitate the handling of the emotional turbulence and the development of sound financial and parenting plans that will respect the interests of all affected parties.

The limitations of the adversarial legal process in addressing the emotional, economic and parenting consequences of separation and divorce must be more openly acknowledged. Good parenting cannot be judicially decreed. Nor can well-intentioned legislative principles guarantee economic security on separation or divorce.

Notwithstanding the emergence of the two-income family during the past twenty-five years, many separated and divorced mothers and their children still face poverty. Defining the economic problem is, of course, much easier than finding a solution. Equitable property sharing is already provided for spouses by provincial legislation and for unmarried cohabitants by judicial rulings. In a few instances, greater economic justice for separated and divorced spouses might be accommodated by deviation from the norm of equal and immediate sharing of property, if the spouses are financially unequal by reason of child care responsibilities assumed during the marriage or on its breakdown. For the vast majority of couples, their accumulated property cannot provide long-term economic security, regardless of how it is divided.

A second partial solution to the economic hardship sustained by divorced wives, mothers and children would be to increase the amount of spousal or child support on separation or divorce. Long-term substantial increases are impractical, however, for many divorced husbands and fathers who remarry or assume additional family obligations. Nor does the answer lie in any simplistic legal principle asserting the priority of first family support obligations. Although divorced husbands and fathers can, and should, pay more than the parsimonious amounts currently paid, additional steps must be taken in order to alleviate the poverty of divorced wives, mothers and children.

With increasing numbers of sequential marriages, solutions to the financial crisis of marriage breakdown must be sought not only within the parameters of family law but also in social and economic policies that promote the financial viability of all persons in need, including the economic victims of marriage breakdown. The war on the feminization of poverty must be won by innovative and coherent socioeconomic policies that ensure pay equity and equal opportunities for women in the labour force and that provide a guaranteed minimum income for all financially disadvantaged Canadians. Opportunities for paid employment in the home, rather than the office or factory, the development of concrete programs for job sharing, and the feasibility of establishing child care or nursery facilities in schools or places of employment must be more closely examined. The relationship between support payments, social assistance, and earned income must also be rationalized if a reasonable level of income security is to be guaranteed to women and children on marriage breakdown. Joint federal and provincial efforts must be made to co-ordinate the diverse systems of income security for family members. Otherwise, faced with the projection that one third of all married Canadians will divorce at least once and the fact that the median duration of dissolved marriages is 10.7 years, Canadian family law will remain ineffective in its attempt to alleviate poverty on divorce.

Whereas the economic crisis of separation and divorce requires the implementation of substantive programs, the parenting crisis is largely a problem of process. It is time to abandon the technical legal terminology of "custody" and "access" with its inherent uncertainties and its emphasis on parental rights rather than parental responsibilities. Formal legal agreements and court orders should be drafted in language that parents and children can understand. They should be comprehensive and comprehensible. Abandonment of the legal jargon of "custody," "joint custody" and "access" would not merely constitute a linguistic change. It would foster a functional approach to parenting after separation and divorce that would underline the fact that "parents are forever" except in circumstances where the children are demonstrably at risk.

Some people favour the implementation of a statutory presumption of joint custody. Other people favour a statutory presumption whereby custody would be granted to the parent who had previously assumed primary caretaking responsibilities for the child. Either of these presumptions would necessarily be provisional, rather than conclusive. They would open the door to rebuttal evidence that would emphasize misconduct rather than the potential contributions of each parent to the growth and development of their child. Presumptions produce a negative perspective whereas what is needed is a positive approach based on past family history and future parenting plans that can accommodate the different contributions that each parent can make to the upbringing of their children. We hardly serve our children well when the law insists on detailed financial statements to determine economic disputes on separation or divorce but requires no detailed information respecting the personality, character and attributes of the children and the ability of each of the parents to contribute to their future upbringing. There seems no reason whatsoever why divorcing parents should not be required to submit a detailed plan concerning their prospective parenting privileges and responsibilities before they are allowed to litigate parenting disputes. The voluntary use of parenting plans should also be encouraged as a means of avoiding hostile negotiations and litigation. We must look beyond legal solutions. The law is already discouraging litigation as a means of resolving parenting disputes. Voluntary mediation and mandatory independent assessments have evolved and may provide a foundation for innovative processes for the avoidance and resolution of not only parenting disputes but also economic disputes arising on separation or divorce.

Although the day may come when community-based centres will provide a multi-disciplinary approach to the resolution of the multi-faceted crises of marriage breakdown, that development lies in the future. In the meantime, the various professions and federal and provincial governmental agencies, including departments as diverse as Employment, Finance, Revenue Canada, Health and Welfare, and Justice, which are directly or indirectly involved in the "systemic management" of the human process of marriage breakdown, must recognize their own limitations and foster improved lines of communication in the search for more constructive and comprehensive solutions to the human and socioeconomic problems associated with separation and divorce.

CHAPTER THREE

Families in the Economy

Linda Duxbury
Christopher Higgins

Substantial changes in the composition of the Canadian work force are creating a new emphasis on the balance between work and family life. There are now more: (1) dual-income families, (2) working heads of single-parent families, (3) working women of all ages, (4) working mothers, particularly mothers of young children, (5) men with direct responsibility for family care, and (6) workers caring for elderly parents or relatives (Galinsky, Friedman, and Hernandez, 1991; Edmonds, Cote-O'Hara and MacKenzie, 1990; Statistics Canada, 1993a). In many families it has become an economic necessity to have both partners work outside the home. Estimates suggest that approximately forty percent of Canadian families would drop below the poverty line if both parents did not work (BNA, 1989; Statistics Canada, 1993a).

Women in the Labour Force

One of the most significant changes in the Canadian labour market over the last 25 to 30 years has been the dramatic increase in the participation of women in the labour force. Women have demonstrated their interest in and commitment to lifelong careers rather than intermittent jobs by: (1) delaying marriage (median age of women at first marriage, 23.6, is now higher than ever previously recorded), (2) deferring childbearing (median age of professional women at birth of first child was 31 in 1992), and (3) returning to work after the birth of their child (69% of mothers of children under 6 were in the labour force in 1991) (Mattis, 1990; Schwartz, 1991; Statistics Canada, 1993a).

Among Western democracies, Canada ranks first in dependence on women in the work force (Schwartz, 1991). The 1991 census indicates that 68% of all women with children at home were in the labour force. This was an increase from 61% in the 1986 census and 52% in the 1981 census. Eighty percent of the women currently in the workforce are in the childbearing years and 80% of these employees are expected to have children during their work life (Statistics Canada, 1993a; Galinsky, 1989). The number of working women with young children aged six and under has also increased substantially over the years. The participation rate for this group was 49% in 1981 but increased to 69% in 1991 (Statistics Canada, 1993a). High levels of divorce have contributed to an increase in the number of single-parent families in the labour force. In 1991, 69% of single parents participated in the labour force, up from 63% in 1981.

The Demise of the "Traditional" Family

The traditional family with "Mom" at home and "Dad" at work has changed. In 1961, only 20% of all two-parent families reported that both spouses worked outside the home. In 1981 this had increased to almost 40%. By 1991, 65% of husband and wife families were dual-income. Only 13% fit the traditional male breadwinner model (Ontario Women's Directorate, 1991).

The increase in the number of working mothers has made the old models of coordinating work and family life inappropriate for a majority of the labour force (Lee and Kanungo, 1984). Families with working mothers and fathers must devise new ways of meeting the increased demands of work and family life (Lee and Kanungo, 1984). Employers must develop new ways to manage their work force. The new reality has had a marked effect on what the family requires of each family member and on what employers can expect from employees. "Caring for elder parents, children or both is not new. Combining it with a career is" (BNA, 1988:7).

Consequences of These Changes

One major consequence of the change in work force demographics has been the increased incidence of work-family conflict in Canadian families. Work-family conflict occurs when an individual has to perform multiple roles such as worker, spouse and parent (Greenhaus and Beutell, 1985). Each of these roles imposes demands on their incumbents requiring time, energy and commitment. The cumulative demands of multiple roles can result in role strain of two types: overload and interference. Overload exists when the total demands on time and energy associated with the prescribed activities of multiple roles are too great to perform the roles adequately or comfortably. Interference occurs when conflicting demands make it difficult to fulfil the requirements of multiple roles.

Impact on Employers: The inability to balance work and family demands has been linked to reduced work performance, increased absenteeism, higher turnover, poor morale, increased work conflict and inequities in workloads. A number of work-related problems have been found to be more common among employees with dependent and/or elder-care responsibilities including increased lateness, unscheduled days off, emergency hours off, absenteeism, excessive use of the telephone, decreased productivity, missed meetings, lower quality of work, lower morale and job satisfaction (BNA, 1988). Recent estimates suggest that at least one quarter of the human resource challenges faced by Canadian organizations are the result of employees having to manage dual responsibilities at home and at work (Galinsky, Friedman and Hernandez, 1991).

Impact on Individuals and Families: Conflict between work and family demands is also a problem for employees. It is linked to marital problems, impaired parenting, reduced life satisfaction, and an increased incidence of stress-related illnesses (Greenhaus and Beutell, 1985; Voydanoff, 1987; Pleck, 1985; Higgins, Duxbury and Lee, 1993). The Conference Board (MacBride-King and Paris, 1989) indicated that 80% of Canadian employees experience some degree of stress or anxiety related to attempting to balance the conflicting demands of work and family. Not surprisingly, the greatest work-family conflict was experienced by employees with children at home.

Higgins, Duxbury and Lee (1993) examined the extent to which 22,000 Canadian employees were able to balance work and family. Their data indicated the following:

- forty percent of working mothers and 25% of working fathers are experiencing high levels of work-family conflict;
- half of parents surveyed report high levels of difficulty in managing their family time;
- fifty percent of working mothers and 36% of working fathers report high levels of stress;
- forty percent of working mothers and 25% of working fathers report high levels of depressed mood;
- less than half of the parents surveyed are highly satisfied with their present lifestyle.

Impact on Working Women: Research indicates that working mothers have more difficulties balancing work and family demands than fathers (Piotrkowski, Rapoport, and Rapoport, 1987; Gupta and Jenkins, 1985; Higgins, Duxbury and Lee, 1993). Factors contributing to this include: responsibility for child care; increased household maintenance demands (the "second shift"); socio-cultural expectations that young children will suffer if their mothers are working (the "motherhood mandate"); and socio-cultural expectations that women should be the primary parent.

Problems Encountered in the 1990s by Employees with Family Responsibilities

1. Child Care

Galinsky and Stein (1990) note four sources of stress concerning child care: (1) it is difficult to find, (2) some child-care arrangements are more satisfactory than others, (3) parents are often forced to put together a patchwork system of care that tends to fall apart, and (4) child care is expensive and strains many low income families. The National Child-Care Study (Lero et al., 1992) indicates that finding child care is one of the most problematic aspects of being a working parent.

Available data indicate that the supply of high-quality affordable child care in Canada does not meet the demand, especially for infant and after-school care. Estimates indicate that 75% of mothers and 57% of fathers have trouble finding child care of any kind (BNA, 1989).

Most parents in need of child-care services turn to informal, unlicensed, private arrangements (Burke et al., 1991). In 1988, informal arrangements accounted for 68% of non-parental child care compared with just 8% for day-care centres. The existing evidence suggests that about 50% of those not using licensed day care would do so if provided the opportunity. These parents have not, however, been able to find licensed day-care openings which fit their requirements (i.e., price, age of child). The most severe shortages appear to be licensed infant day care centres (only 5.4% of children served) and after-school day care for children between the ages of 6 and 12 (5.6% of children served) (Health and Welfare, 1991).

While most children are looked after by someone outside the family, relatives are often called upon by many parents to assist with child care. This was particularly so in families with low incomes. In 1988, 43% of children in families with incomes of $50,000 or less were cared for by a relative, compared with 29% of children in families with incomes over $50,000 (Burke et al., 1991).

It is becoming increasingly clear that quality child-care programs are not only necessary in preschool years but also through early adolescence. Surveys in local communities indicate that as many as 25% of school-aged children have no adult supervision after school (BNA, 1989). Parents of adolescents do not need to monitor their children as closely, but nevertheless need to arrange for some kind of supervision during non-school hours.

Research indicates that having difficulties with child-care arrangements and having latch key children are strong predictors of absenteeism from work and decreased work productivity (Fernandez, 1986). The breakdown of child-care arrangements has also been linked to increased stress, decreased mental health, more stress-related health problems and lower marital satisfaction (Galinsky, 1989; Higgins, Duxbury and Lee, 1993).

Most children in need of care stayed with one care arrangement throughout the year. However, in 1988, over 800,000 children moved to a new caregiver at least once during the year (Burke et al., 1991). This was cited as one of the main difficulties encountered by working parents.

Overall, child care remains predominantly a women's issue. Women are more likely to be responsible for locating child care, to work at maintaining the child-care package, and to stay home when a child is sick. Consequently, women experience more stress in relation to child care than men (Hughes and Galinsky, 1988; Duxbury et al., 1992).

2. Elder Care

Dependent care is not just a question of care for children. Concern over elder-care responsibilities is now increasing. Elder care is defined as providing some type of assistance with the daily living activities for an elderly relative who is chronically ill, frail or disabled. The number of workers with adult caregiver responsibilities is growing rapidly as the parents of baby boomers enter their 60s, 70s and 80s. Estimates suggest that in 1991 approximately one quarter of employees over 40 had elder-care responsibilities.

Since the recent growth in the female work force involves comparatively younger women whose parents are not yet old enough to require daily assistance, society has yet to feel the full effects of elder-care problems. The 1991 Canadian census estimated that one in ten Canadians currently has elder-care responsibilities. This figure is expected to increase to one in four in the next decade as the proportion of society comprised of the elderly increases dramatically. Data indicate that the number of people over age 80 is growing rapidly and is expected to double in 20 years (BNA, 1989). Statistics Canada estimates that by 2036, 25% of the Canadian population will be over 65, versus 12% in 1991 (Gauthier, 1991:16).

The trend toward women delaying childbearing until they are established in their career suggests that dependent care (both children and elderly) may become more of an issue in the next decade as a greater number of families find themselves caring for young children and elderly parents – the so-called "sandwich generation."

According to the Bureau of National Affairs (1988), 80% of the care needed by the elderly is provided by the family. Of those family members helping elders, most are female spouses or middle-aged daughters or daughters-in-law. Grocery shopping, transportation and housework are the types of help given most frequently by care providers (BNA, 1989) and these tasks take 10 to 20 hours per week (BNA, 1989). Little direct outside support is presently in place for those with elder-care responsibilities.

"Elder care can be the equivalent of taking on a second job for those who work outside the home (BNA, 1989)." Increasingly, more workers are caring for their elderly relatives or loved ones, and the stress in doing so is similar to that felt by working parents who must arrange child care. Corporations need to understand that elder care, like all other personal concerns, affects employees' ability to function at work. As in the case of child care, studies show that productivity suffers when people try to balance work and the care of parents. Tardiness, unscheduled days off, emergency days or hours off, absenteeism and frequent telephone use are workplace problems associated with elder-care responsibilities (BNA, 1989).

Elder care is further complicated by distance as elderly parents often live in different communities. Family members who provide "indirect" care such as frequent visits, phone calls and general management of the elder's affairs from afar have been found to experience tremendous feelings of guilt and increased stress (BNA, 1988). Research suggests that the majority of people who provide elder care have had to make lifestyle changes since becoming care providers including spending less time with their own family, paying less attention to their own health, and taking fewer vacations (BNA, 1989). Although only about 10% of elder-care givers had to quit their jobs to care for an elder relative, between 20 and 40% had to rearrange work schedules, reduce their work hours or take unpaid time off. As the baby-boom generation moves towards middle age, and their parents toward old age, employees with such conflicts (often mature employees with substantial work demands) will increase in number.

3. Time and Timing of Paid Employment

Keeping a home and raising children or caring for an elderly dependent, as anyone who has ever done it knows, is a full-time job. The increasing rarity of the full-time homemaker has done more to reduce everyone's leisure time than any other factor. If both mother and father are working, someone still has to find time to make lunch, attend doctor appointments, shop for groceries and cook. The inability to manage one's family time has been linked to greater role overload, stress, physical and mental health problems, higher levels of work-family conflict, and reduced performance of both family and work responsibilities (Duxbury et al., 1992). Both time in paid employment and timing of paid employment have an impact on an employee's ability to balance work and family.

Time Spent in Paid Employment: Time at work is the cornerstone around which the other daily activities must be made to fit. As a fixed commodity, time allocated to employment is necessarily unavailable for other activities, including time with the family. Thus, time spent at work offers an important and concrete measure of one dimension of employment that affects individuals and their families.

Twenty years ago, experts were predicting that by 1985, people would work just 23 hours a week and retire at age 38. Ten years ago, the consensus was that new technology and innovation would be a panacea, providing a four-day work week and more leisure. Today, each of these predictions is laughable. Data collected by Higgins, Duxbury and Lee (1993) indicate that in 1991 the average Canadian white-collar employee worked approximately 45 hours a week at the office. On top of this, over a third of the employees surveyed spent several additional hours performing job-related work at home on both work- and nonworkdays. Sixteen percent of the employees surveyed spent more than 60 hours per week in work.

Today's employees are working long hours and devoting a large portion of their day (both in the office and at home) to work-related activities. When one combines this with the knowledge that total hours spent at work each week is the most reliable predictor of role overload, family strain, stress and work-family conflict, it is not surprising that a significant portion of the Canadian work force is experiencing problems. In support of this contention, a recent report by Statistics Canada (1993b) estimated that stress-related disorders due to overwork costs Canadian businesses $12 billion per year.

Timing of Paid Employment: The dilemma facing working parents resides neither in the family, nor in the workplace, but rather in the combination of the two. Evidence is mounting that the timing, scheduling and location of work may be more important to the family than the actual number of hours worked. For example, a survey conducted by the Canadian Mental Health Association (1984) reported that most Canadians perceive that their job's rigid time and location demands conflict with their responsibilities and interests off the job (e.g., family and community).

Higgins, Duxbury and Lee (1993) found that approximately two thirds of Canadian employees have virtually no work-time flexibility. This lack of flexibility causes problems for employees with conflicting family demands since: (1) excessive work hours limit time with one's family; (2) the work day either starts too early or ends too late, restricting quality time with the family; and (3) work schedules often do not mesh with child-care arrangements and other family activities.

The lack of fit between an employee's work schedule and needed services is a further source of stress and tension. Workers, particularly those who are subject to strict time policies, have trouble getting to the doctor, dentist and bank. Teacher conferences, athletics and school performances, which usually take place during the workday, also cause problems for working parents.

4. Organizational Climate

Research by Lee et al. (1992) suggests that the existence of family benefits and programs to support working parents do not always guarantee their use. Having family-friendly policies is one matter, but how these policies are interpreted and implemented, and thus their effectiveness, depends upon attitudes held by an employee's immediate supervisor (Galinsky, 1989; Duxbury et al., 1992; Lee et al., 1992).

In many organizations, however, the supervisor may not have much power. He or she may want to give a parent permission to stay at home with an acutely ill child, but is prevented from doing so because of company policy. Experiencing a non-supportive work/family culture is linked to poor outcomes in mental and physical well-being. In fact, a non-supportive work environment seems to be one of the most powerful predictors of work-family conflict and stress (Galinsky and Stein, 1990).

Supporting Families in the Economy

Although there is increasing recognition of the problems faced by working parents and employees with elder-care responsibilities, only preliminary efforts have been directed at implementing policies that help these employees cope with work and family demands. Demographic changes have outpaced political, social and organizational structures and practices. The majority of Canadian employees today are feeling the burden of combining work and dependent care in a climate that has been unresponsive to the realities of work and family life. Many individuals have adapted by using vacation time, changing their work schedule with a colleague, using their own personal leave time to handle family emergencies, calling in sick, taking an unpaid leave of absence, setting priorities and dividing tasks within the family (BNA, 1988; Lee et al., 1992).

The majority of employees interviewed by Lee et al., (1992) reported: (1) that they were already using all their personal and family resources to balance work and family, and (2) that any further improvement in their work and family situation would require a change in the workplace or the community (Lee et al., 1992). Other research suggests that the majority of today's working parents are unhappy with the lack of support provided by business and government alike (Galinsky, Friedman and Hernandez, 1991).

Organizational Response to Work and Family Issues

To date, the majority of firms have not responded to the changing needs of an increasingly diverse work force. Despite the oft-expressed interest in supporting families, the actual practices of most companies lag behind. As a result, families (especially female workers) have had to cope with the mounting stress of balancing work and family demands in the absence of organizational support.

According to Friedman (1987) there are several reasons for corporate inaction on work and family issues. First, in a time of cost-cutting, restructuring and downsizing, many companies view family concerns as something that should be addressed in better economic times. The recession has also meant that many organizations have not had to address work and family issues because they have occurred in the context of a labour surplus. Employees who perceive that they can be easily replaced are competing for jobs, and are often willing to make sacrifices such as working long hours and overtime to ensure job security.

Second, many companies still do not see the connection between work and family issues and the bottom line. The lack of information on flexible work arrangements, child and dependent-care options, as well as the lack of documented evidence that such involvement will have a positive impact on the bottom line, deters many employers from implementing family benefits. Unless management understands why family benefits and flexible work arrangements make sense from a business standpoint, many managers will be reluctant to support them.

Third, the majority of corporate decision makers are from the diminishing "traditional family." Without personal experience or employees' input, management remains unaware of the problems and their impact on performance and employees. The film "Walking the Tightrope", produced by the U.S. Bureau of National Affairs, ends with the statement that "this country will see a surge in the development of work and family initiatives when the CEO is pregnant (Galinksy, 1989)."

Perhaps the greatest obstacle to company activity, however, is the absence of employee demands. The workplace does not yet have an environment that is conducive to speaking up about work and family problems ("the conspiracy of silence," Schwartz, 1991). Many employees fear reprisals or dismissal if they bring work and family concerns to the attention of those higher in the organization.

Government Response to Work and Family Issues

The government, as legislators and policy makers, have reacted cautiously to the changing workplace. The various child-care subsidies available in most major Canadian cities do not adequately address the work and family needs of employees, particularly low-income workers. The only benefits most Canadians receive from the government to help them balance work and family come during the period immediately before and after the birth of a child or through provisions in the income tax system. The Federal government provides maternity and parental benefits under Unemployment Insurance with up to 57% replacement of previous wages. Some provinces, such as Quebec, provide much more leave time (see Chapter Eight). Furthermore, tax deductions for employees with child-care expenses are allowed and have recently been raised to $5,000 per pre-school child.

A study done by the U.S. Government (BNA, 1989) suggests that many Americans feel that their government is out of touch. Over 80% of those surveyed said that the federal government does not pay enough attention to child care and other family concerns (BNA, 1989). The survey concluded (BNA, 1989:5): "Many politicians have talked a lot about family but few have made the crucial issues, child care, job security, family leave and flexibility a legislative priority." It is likely that many Canadians share this view with their neighbours to the South.

What Could Organizations Do to Assist Working Families?

Some corporations are recognizing that they can no longer afford to ignore the reality that their employees face a very different reality from that of 20 or 30 years ago when the norms of workplace behaviour and expectations were set. Corporations are finally beginning to establish programs and policies to accommodate the needs of employees with responsibilities for child and elder care. For example, it is not uncommon for organizations to top up maternity benefits provided by government to 80 to 100% of earnings.

Friedman (1987) notes that the corporate response to employees' family needs has gone through two phases. The first was the M&M phase: No mess, no fuss (low cost, low risk solutions that served many employees). This second was related to the Jane Fonda phrase: No pain, no gain (a more significant commitment to family concerns).

Any company that addresses work and family issues faces a number of challenges (Friedman, 1987). Should they develop a new service or revise an older benefit? Should the solutions be extensive, serving a large number of employees with a small amount of help, or intensive, helping a few in a more meaningful way? Should they respond to the old or the young? Should the justification be a bottom line concern or a matter of social responsibility? Will companies respond better to government carrots or sticks? (Friedman, 1987).

A number of creative practices designed to accommodate the needs of working couples are being implemented in companies across Canada and the United States. The following are reviewed below: (1) Dependent-care programs, (2) Flexible work arrangements, (3) Supportive organizational climate, and (4) Supervisor support.

It is important to remember, however, when considering these solutions, that the primary concern of most employees with family responsibilities is the availability of a job with good security and adequate pay (Lee et al., 1992). This is the essential foundation for sustaining stable family life. If private business and government fail to deliver on these counts, all other concerns about responsiveness are largely irrelevant (Kingston, 1990).

1. Dependent-Care Programs

Dependent care, including children, elderly, and people with disabilities, is a business issue for the obvious reason that employees cannot come to work unless their dependents are cared for. Study after study shows that working parents have trouble arranging child care and that those with the most problems also experience the most frequent work disruptions and the greatest absenteeism. Moreover, the lack of child care is still a major barrier to the entry of women into the labour force (Rogers and Rogers, 1989).

Child care needs vary greatly and many companies have a limited ability to address them. Interest in child care is great and employees often focus on the issue of on-site care. Unfortunately, companies that get involved with child-care centres find themselves making difficult trade-offs as a result of the high costs. If they do not subsidize the cost of care how do they justify providing this considerable benefit to only high income employees. If they do provide subsidies, how do they justify giving this benefit to one group of parents while other parents buy child care outside the company and other employees receive no comparable benefit.

Research suggests that an effective corporate dependent-care program might include some (or all) of the following (Rogers and Rogers, 1989; Galinsky, Friedman and Hernandez, 1991):

1. Help in finding existing dependent care and efforts to increase the supply of care in the community, especially care for sick children (i.e., training day-care providers to take care of employees' children in their homes, sick-child day care for care of children too ill to go to their regular care provider);
2. financial assistance for child or elder care, especially for lower income employees (i.e., dependent-care options in a flexible benefits plan, subsidies or vouchers which can be redeemed by employees at the day-care site of their choice);
3. involvement with schools, and other community organizations to promote programs for school-aged children whose parents work;
4. support for child-care or adult-care centres in locations convenient to company employees (not necessarily on site);
5. efforts to move government policies (provincial and federal) towards greater investment in children and care of the frail elderly;
6. flexible or cafeteria style benefit packages which allow employees to choose among several work and family benefit programs or to set aside money for child care or elder care in a tax-free account;
7. alternative work schedules, allowing employees to choose a work schedule that best helps them balance work and family responsibilities;

8. supply a building where the organization takes the lead with respect to increasing services, particularly the development of new family day-care homes, after-school programs, "hot" or "warm lines" (telephone services for children who are home alone), and safe homes (places for latch-key children to turn to if they are in need of help);

9. respite care (employer can help pay for care services for the frail elderly so that the caregiver can get a break from his or her duties).

At present the most common way for companies to address dependent-care issues is through referral and resource services. Although these programs can be very helpful, a number of limitations have been identified including the fact that by themselves they have little impact on affordability, quality of care or supply of care where market conditions are highly unfavourable. From the employees' point of view, one of the most frequently requested supports is personal-leave days. Employees dislike being forced to lie when their children or elderly dependents are sick; they want these days off to be legitimate (Galinsky and Stein, 1990).

2. Flexible Work Arrangements

As organizations are required to "do more with less" in order to survive, it is clear that reducing time spent working is not an option for most employers and employees. There is, however, nothing inherently magical about the five-day, forty-hour work week. In fact, this traditional work schedule is based on organizational policies that are outdated and out of touch with current employee demographics and needs. These policies operate on what Kanter (1977) calls the "myth of separate worlds" – a critically flawed assumption that assumes that employees can easily separate the demands of work and family.

Higgins, Duxbury and Lee (1993) suggest that the lack of control over when and where one works causes more problems than the number of hours spent in work. This implies that the provision of greater work-time and work-location flexibility will enable employees to minimize the potential negative effects involved with conflicting work and family demands.

Organizations can increase work flexibility with respect to the pattern of hours worked per day, the pattern of days worked per week or the work location. The following flexible work arrangements, which are available to a limited extent in Canadian organizations, have been linked to improved employee attitudes and morale, an increased ability to balance work and family demands, improved recruitment, higher retention, increased productivity, lower absenteeism and heightened commitment to the organization (Higgins, Duxbury and Lee, 1993):

1. Flextime – A schedule that allows varying starting and quitting times. Workers must maintain a core schedule, however, such as 10:00 a.m. to 3:00 p.m.;

2. Compressed Work Week – A full week's work completed in fewer than five days;

3. Regular Part-time Work – Less than full-time work that includes job security and benefits;

4. Job Sharing – Two people voluntarily sharing one job with prorated salary and benefits;

5. Leave of Absence – Paid or unpaid time away from the job without loss of employment rights;

6. Telework – Employees working off-site, often linked to a main office by a computer;

7. Work Sharing – An alternative to layoffs in which all or part of a workforce temporarily reduces hours and pay. In some U.S. States, workers may receive unemployment compensation while their hours are shortened.

Despite the fact that increasing numbers of employees want flexible work arrangements, "resistance is strong and obstacles are many. Upper management is reluctant to introduce change; unions are reluctant to negotiate some arrangements (i.e., telework, part-time work); supervisors find it difficult to manage workers on flexible arrangements; and employees who cannot participate are often resentful of those who can (BNA, 1989:24)."

Higgins, Duxbury and Lee (1993) have indicated that about 60% of women with children at home want to work part-time temporarily. A number of factors have, however, discouraged women from reducing their status to part-time, including: they cannot afford the loss of pay and other benefits, managers at all levels and unions show resistance to part-time work, and there is a stigma attached to part-time work for career mothers (the "Mommy track").

3. Supportive Organizational Climate

Galinsky and Stein (1990) identify eight factors that are features of organizations that are more responsive to work and family issues. They are: (1) work and family is a legitimate issue of the organization, relevant to its mission; (2) work and family efforts have the support of a powerful executive; (3) someone is officially in charge of work and family issues and initiatives; (4) different functional areas are considered together (i.e., benefits, personnel policies, training are seen as a whole, each contributing to the overall work and family effort); (5) work and family policies are assessed and reviewed regularly; (6) there is an emphasis on flexibility and evaluation of employees on what they produce, not the hours they put in; (7) the organizational culture is recognized as central to work and family solutions; and (8) supportive policies are seen as essential in the recruitment, retention and motivation of employees.

4. Supervisor Support

Research has clearly demonstrated that work and family policies are ineffective if supervisors do not support them (Galinsky and Stein, 1990; Duxbury, Higgins and Lee, 1992; Higgins, Duxbury and Lee, 1993). Formal policies alone are insufficient to ensure that employed parents are able to satisfy the role demands of work and family. Without the understanding of their supervisors, many employed parents do not feel comfortable in making use of family-related policies.

Research by Galinsky and Stein (1990) suggests that the relationship with the supervisor is one of the most powerful predictors of work and family problems. Supervisor support lowers stress; lack of supervisor support increases stress. Galinsky and Stein (1990) found that supervisor support occurs when supervisors: (1) feel that handling family issues, especially as they affect the job performance, is a legitimate part of the role; (2) are knowledgeable about company policies that apply to family issues; (3) are flexible when work and family problems arise; and (4) handle employees' work and family problems fairly and without favouritism. Having a supportive supervisor has been found to be roughly equivalent to having a supportive spouse in its effects on stress (National Council of Jewish Women, 1988).

A number of progressive organizations are responding to this issue by providing training to supervisors. This training focuses on sensitizing managers to work-family issues in order that supervisors behave in a manner that facilitates employees using the benefits to which they are entitled.

What Could Governments Do to Assist Working Families?

The concern with the impact of work-place policies on families is not misdirected. What is misdirected is the expectation that Canadians should leave the responsibility for work and family issues to private companies. As noted by Aldous (1990), we cannot leave, to a few progressive business leaders, the problems of easing the well-documented conflicts between fulfilling job requirements and caring for family members. The historical record on the provision of worker benefits indicates that social responsibility has never promoted much business policy (Kingston, 1990). Few businesses see it in their self-interest to institute family benefits as there is little evidence that it affects the bottom line. The implication of this history is that the future of the responsive work place probably depends on government intervention.

Advocates of the responsive workplace who see demography as their saviour (i.e., organizations will be motivated by labour shortages to introduce family benefits) may be ill-advised to place their hopes on a "market" solution. That solution will be inherently unequal. "Just as higher pay tends to go to those with greater human capital, so will the rewards of family-oriented benefits. The predictable result is that those with greatest need will receive the least (Kingston, 1990:450)." Work and family problems are more intractable for the lower paid employees. In fact, women with low pay cannot afford to take advantage of unpaid family benefits programs or part-time work options even when they are available.

Government action requiring businesses to implement family benefits and providing them with subsidies or tax incentives to fund them is warranted. Governments could develop a base of community services upon which companies can build. They could help those in greatest need by providing tax breaks for low-income parents. They could make day care a national issue, although the federal/provincial jurisdictional problems may make this an intractable solution. Governments could also pass legislation establishing minimum standards to ensure child care of acceptable quality. Providing tax credits to companies who assist in child care and tax breaks to parents who wish to stay home with their children would be another possible response. Finally, government should become a model employer itself and set an example for the private sector.

Affordable, high quality child care, in particular, is an issue that the government should address. One quarter of mothers of pre-schoolers, who are not in the paid workforce, say they would work if they had access to safe and affordable child care (BNA, 1989). Business can only play a limited role in such issues as child care for working mothers. "Companies can be innovative and experiment but I don't believe corporate day care answers the needs of two million children under 5." (Aldous, 1990:362).

A business case can be made suggesting that it is in the government's best interests to offer child-care tax credits to Canadian corporations who provide day-care assistance. In the U.S., 89% of the tax revenue the government gives up through child-care tax credits was returned in the form of work-related taxes paid by working mothers (BNA, 1989). Child-care tax credits facilitated 730,000 mothers to re-enter the labour market in 1989. These mothers produced $3.5 billion in taxes on their income and increased the nation's GNP by $8.4 billion (BNA, 1989).

Conclusions

The choice to have a family is complex, yet one study shows that two thirds of women under 40 who have reached the upper levels in Canadian corporations and institutions are childless, while virtually all men in leadership positions are fathers (Schwartz, 1991). If organizations and governments continue to send the message to women that a demanding work life is incompatible with a satisfying family life, we are in danger of creating a society where more and more leaders have traded family for career success. The price of business success should not be disinterest in the family. Nor should the price of having a family be the abandonment of professional ambition.

What, then, is the cost of continuing to operate in the traditional fashion now practised by organizations? While both the potential costs and benefits of new policies are admittedly unclear, the price of not changing is hardly obscure. Workers who have difficulties balancing work and family demands are more likely to quit their jobs, be less productive, arrive late, be absent from work, and suffer poorer physical and mental health. Working parents, in particular, need flexibility in working hours and working days in order to attend to sick children, family crises, and gaps in child-care arrangements.

If human resource policies are not made more responsive, employees at all levels will continue to bear the major brunt of work and family conflict. Our nation's ability to compete is threatened by inadequate investment in our most important resource: people (Galinsky, 1989:1). "The business of Canada is families, and especially the children they nurture. If we skimp on their welfare, there will be no capable workers to carry on (Aldous, 1990:365)."

CHAPTER FOUR

Towards Authentic Learning: Reconnecting Families and Education

Terrence R. Morrison

The Modern Problem

The shifting relationship between education and the family, and its expression throughout the life cycle, is deeply embedded in the larger transformations underway in our society. More particularly, current attitudes toward the family and education are coloured, not only by social changes, but also by how people define, perceive and understand these changes. Far too often, we are confronted with a perceptual minefield in relation to change; a tendency to quickly categorize change and, on the basis of this categorization, to shift quickly to faultfinding and blame. Parents and other taxpayers blame teachers and schools for supposedly not meeting the educational needs of the young. Teachers and educators return the favour and blame parents and families for abandoning their primary caring responsibilities. Governments find themselves caught in between and are madly searching for a cost-effective policy of appeasement. As for the young, they are tragically emerging as mere pawns in this game of blame.

While the combatants pay lip service to the needs or motivation of the young, there always seems to be a "larger issue" at stake in the debate; whether that be fiscal debt, a need to be competitive or working conditions. Well, there is a larger issue at stake in the relationship between families and education, and that issue is learning, how it occurs and its vast untapped potential. And that is the subject of this chapter. Learning is a pre-eminently shared experience and, for that reason, it provides the optimal basis for forging a much-needed new partnership between education and the family.

Separate Spheres

By way of illustration, consider four of the broad transformations which have unfolded during this century. First, activities, groups, institutions and roles that once were unified or fused have become disentangled and specialized. (Selznick, 1993:1-35). We have separated production and consumption, household and paid work, church and state, religion and community, ownership and management, education and parenting, and law and morality.

The family, in particular, has been caught in the vortex of this drive toward distinctiveness and specialization. Its historic role in the education and socialization of the young, for example, has been hived off and professionalized, to the point where the role of the school, as standing in loco parentis, now means not only in place of the parent, but in replacement of the parent. The family, at one time an integrator of social relationships, now struggles to find its identity in a world of disconnected spheres of activity (Berger & Berger, 1983:2-23). And in that struggle to find or reassert its uniqueness, the family, paradoxically, is in danger of becoming just another separate sphere of life.

Weakened Ties

A second transformation is a weakening of social ties. Many words and concepts have been used to describe the fallout of this process — excessive individualism, atomization and self-indulgence to name just a few (Taylor, 1989; and Wolfe, 1993). Modern life tends to loosen the intimate connections of shared experience and its associated feeling of inter-reliance. The general trend appears to be a movement toward a more fragmented social life in which individualism reigns.

As an integral facet of our concentration on the individual, we have spent the last three decades discussing and arguing for rights — this was necessary and overdue. It is now time to turn to responsibility and our communal willingness to deliver on the rights we agree exist (Friedman, 1990; and Morgan, 1984). If a child has a right to read, then we must outline our responsibilities in this matter. If a child has the right to grow up not being malnourished, then we must confront the responsibilities which follow. Responsibilities convert rights into action and they are, by definition, collective. A responsibilities agenda in public policy and social relationships, moreover, is not a defense against further societal change. In fact, it can be the basis for a true transformation in society. Newly proposed rights, for example the right to universally accessible and high-quality day care, require for their implementation an imaginative reconstruction of work in our society. So too, delivering fully on existing rights, such as the right to read, demands a parallel transformation in our concepts and institutions of learning. When linked to rights, it is responsibilities which drive change. In the words of Ronald Dworkin, professor of jurisprudence at Oxford University, "it matters as much that we live up to our freedom as that we have it" (Dworkin, 1993:239).

Diversity

One of the earlier fears associated with modernization was that it would lead to cultural homogenization. This line of thinking reached its zenith with a series of bold forecasts that, with the collapse of communism, the world would be witnessing the "end of history" and the triumph of Western-capitalist culture (Fukuyama, 1992).

What is most striking about the waning years of this century, however, is that we are witnessing a worldwide outbreak of cultural diversity: from the boiling over of historical group resentments, through the emergence of newly discovered cultural traditions, to claims from several quarters for a myriad of cultural rights. Sociologist Elise Boulding speaks, for example, of the 10,000 societies residing inside 168 nation states (Cleveland, 1993:25-48). Moreover, through mass migrations and differential rates of procreation, societies are being born in which "everyone is a minority." With these tendencies come what Daniel Patrick Moynihan has described as the new and uncertain politics of pandemonium (Moynihan, 1993).

Accommodating and allowing for the expression of diversity has become a central issue in curricular development at all levels of education. In schools there has been a multiculturalization of the curriculum, from the preservation of heritage languages to group cultural studies of various kinds and shapes. Cultural legitimacy and the standing of one's group in society seems to be increasingly determined on the basis of whether one's perspective is embedded in the curriculum of schools. This has led, quite expectedly, to a counter-criticism: that excessive curricular diversity fragments learning and is responsible for a turning away from the "basics," whatever they are (DeSousa, 1991; Graff, 1993). Absolutism clashes with relativism in the daily life of classrooms, at all levels of education, mirroring the basic uncertainty of modern life. To that degree, schools reflect the society of which they are a part. They are not, as some maintain, divorced from reality. The reality is that if there is a problem, it is with the real world not with the schools for reflecting it.

The family again finds itself in the vortex of the swirling pressures of cultural diversity. The very existence of a multiplicity of familial forms and lifestyles, and the debates which surround their place in the crafting of family policy, is testimony to this pressure. The family is also a breeding ground for the concept of the value of each person as an individual. At the same time, the family is "wired" to the larger world and, through the power of modern telecommunications, it is a receptor of new knowledge about the commonalities of global existence. Through the family run three of the most central and paradoxical themes of our time: the reality of group diversity; the struggle for individual rights apart from those of the group; and the awareness of the need for a global identity which transcends both group and individual rights.

Instrumental Outlook

A fourth transformation in modern society is the emergence to prominence of what can be called an instrumental outlook. Within such a world view, everything and everyone is defined and converted into a tool, a means for the achievement of something else. We have become a strategic society in which life is reduced to tactics in a zero sum game. The emergence of the strategic society has particular salience for the relationship between families and education. A case in point is the current focus upon, indeed obsession with, what is called competitiveness. According to this view, unless our society, in the face of foreign trade rivals, increases its competitiveness, it will suffer economic decline and all that comes with such a prospect (Reich, 1991; Thurow, 1992; Government of Canada, 1992).

While various factors are cited for our presumed lack of competitiveness — poor quality in product manufacturing, stilted and bureaucratic organizations, lack of customer focus, fiscal deficits, too much or too little state involvement — critics apparently agree that a core source of the problem rests with the educational system (Wirth, 1993). The curriculum of schools, it is argued, must be reformed, moved either back in time to the "basics" or forward to the "new skills" of the knowledge economy.

The new competitiveness critique of schools, and indirectly of parents and children, sees children as our society's strategic resource. Increasingly, policymakers and other leaders in our society view children as capital, little economic warriors to be filled with skills and other ammunition and sent out to do battle with their youthful counterparts in Japan and Germany (Louv, 1991). They are the "instruments" for our future strategic advantage. Anyone who stands in the way, particularly teachers, must be made to feel "accountable" for their failure to deliver and be retrained themselves. Parents, for their part, are not unmoved by this competitiveness ideology, for many of them are involved in their own strategy for positioning their families and children for maximum educational advantage. Witness, in this regard, the rising enrollments of children in private schools.

The focus on children and schools as sources of competitive advantage, represents the archetypical application of an instrumental outlook. Children are converted into tools which are to be machined in schools and polished at home. The notion that children are to be valued in and of themselves, and that they deserve an opportunity to creatively encounter the world and themselves through a stimulating and rich set of learning experiences, seems tragically to have fallen by the wayside in our society. Regaining this sense of wonderment about life, and allowing children to experience it, is the real reason why we need a reform of education.

Each of the transformations noted above, and others which can be listed, contribute to the modern malaise. But each paradoxically serves as a tonic to society. The separation of spheres of life has been a powerful engine for the release of creative energies, the achievement of excellence and the protection of rights. So too, the benefits of freedom cannot be won without a loosening of social bonds, including those within and between families. Being solely defined by one's family is problematic, for it can lead to a suffocation of one's identity as a person. Cultural diversity, and its press for recognition, provides a necessary challenge to a social order based upon the power and privilege of elites, however they are configured. Even an instrumental outlook has value, if it directs attention to the need to re-establish a common purpose as a way of effectively negotiating change.

The underlying roots of the modern problem lie in a situation in which an assertive self or group confronts an increasingly weakened cultural context. Many of the problems faced by families today — from spousal abuse to child neglect — are symptomatic of the relationship between individual assertiveness and a weakened cultural context. Women with children, who want the right to pursue a career, face a workplace designed on the premise that children are non-existent in the lives of employees. Childhood and family problems, moreover, have risen as the number of facilitating institutions has decreased. These facilitating institutions (extended families, caring neighbourhoods) have been replaced by commercial, curative, sometimes punitive, purely protective institutions — the juvenile justice system, child protection agencies, residential treatment centres. By their nature, such institutions come into play after a child's emotional or other problems have become severe. Persistence of this gap between assertiveness and a weakened cultural context not only does damage to the culture, but makes selfhood inevitably problematic.

The Modern Choice

The modern problem, as I have described it, generates the modern choice. That choice revolves around the individual and the social context in which he/she lives. For the better part of this century, the individual has been the focus of attention in our drive to modernize. To some extent, we have inadvertently extracted the individual from the context(s) of living, since the existing structures in those contexts were seen as barriers to rights and freedoms. It is not that individualism must be destroyed, but that a new relationship between the individual and the various communities of living must be forged. For the family, this leads to a new concept of rights — the right to be connected. It also redefines liberation, not as the act of breaking off from one another, but as a person's ability, whether child or adult, to live to the fullest potential because of the supportive strands that connect us.

The need to reconnect the person with the social contexts of life is no more evident than in the field of education and its relationship with the family. Education and formal schooling are integral aspects, indeed generators and products, of modernization. They tend to be conducted as separate spheres of activity, are highly individualistic in their ethos, instrumental in their purposes and unidimensional in their view of the learning potential of people. This model of education does not need to be reformed. It needs to be fundamentally transformed.

The transformation of education must begin with a reintegration of learning with society. To begin with, we must shift the focus of our attention from what learning can contribute to society to what society can contribute to learning. We must create a society of learning; one in which learning, fulfilment and becoming human are the primary goals and all institutions and processes are directed to this end. In this context, learning is not a segregated activity, conducted for certain hours in certain places. It is the core purpose of the society: its central and abiding project. The design of a society of learning rests upon principles which challenge a series of myths surrounding the separation of learning from social life. The estrangement of education from family is but one example of this split. The remainder of this chapter outlines four principles, which collectively call for the reintegration of learning with life contexts, and explores their implications for policies which can reconnect the family to education.

Learning in Multiple Contexts

Much of social science research seems to confirm the wisdom of everyday life. This wisdom, which Jerome Bruner has labelled "folk psychology," has persistently asserted that formal educational institutions provide only one context of and for learning and that judgements of competence in those settings are just that (Bruner, 1992). In Robert Sternberg's view, on the other hand, intelligence entails a kind of mental self-management — the mental management of one's life in a constructive, purposeful way (Sternberg, 1991). Three elements are central to this capacity for mental self-management: adapting to environments, selecting new environments and shaping environments.

Each environment demands a different set of adaptive strategies, and different people possess a differential ability to invent and exercise these strategies. Stephen Ceci and Jeffrey Liker, for example, studied handicappers in order to determine their success at the race track (Ceci & Liker, 1986:119-142). They found that most of these people were unremarkable in terms of formal IQ ratings. Yet, successful handicappers regularly used quite complex statistical models for predicting winners. Their ability to do this was unrelated to their IQ's. In this regard, it would be intriguing to compare the performance of young people in the complex skills of Nintendo with their school-based academic performance records.

The implication of Sternberg's view of intelligence is, again, a form of folk wisdom: there is no single set of behaviours or skills that are intelligent for everyone. Language learning is a case in point. Most children learn the elements of spoken, and in some cases written language, in the family (Donaldson, 1993:104-125). This is symbolic learning — one of the most complex and difficult of all tasks. It works in the family because the learning process is tied to authentic personal human experience — your own experience not someone else's. Schooling tends to do the opposite — to increasingly detach learning from authentic experience and narrow the range of contexts for that experience. The case of literacy is instructive. The most successful programmes in literacy training do not use professional teachers or schools. Programmes like those of Frontier College use friends, family members and volunteers in settings like the home, the street and work.

Research on what has come to be known as "everyday cognition" further highlights our narrow view of intellectual competence. Jean Lave, working with "just plain folks," describes how many people use mathematics and solve problems that they cannot solve in formal classroom settings (Lave, 1992). In one research study, Lave and her colleagues studied the mathematical thinking capability of a group of housewives in two settings: a formal classroom setting and a supermarket. What does a supermarket have to do with mathematics? The supermarket houses a range of products of different types, all of which have numbers (prices) and discounts (percentages) attached to them. The shopper, if he/she is "intelligent," calculates and compares these numbers and percentages in relation to their own budget or credit capability. The supermarket is a living mathematics lab.

Lave analyzed the mathematical knowledge needed in the supermarket and developed a formal test for these skills. The housewives took two tests: a classroom version and a live version. Performance in the live version, in the supermarket, far outstripped that of the classroom — even with formal instruction. In fact, housewives who were defined as "not knowing" a skill in the classroom actually practised it in the supermarket.

Contextual learning may be seen as new and different within the world of formal education, but it is descriptive of how most learning actually occurs in society. Consider the process of learning involved in the following sets of activities: a surgeon operating on a patient; an airforce pilot acquiring targets while flying an F-15 fighter jet; and a design team developing a new idea with aid of computer design tools. Several common patterns emerge from research analysis of learning in these settings.

The knowledge and skills in operation in these settings are not static and are not contained solely within the individual(s). Knowledge, in fact, is distributed throughout the environment – housed in computers, books, patient monitors, instruments and especially in other people. Pea has described this as "distributed intelligence" (Diggory, 1990:63). The heat monitors, airplane avionics and computer design programmes available to these real world problem-solvers all provide information, while continually signalling new problems and changing conditions. There is also teamwork involved, with people in different fields collaborating to define and solve problems. Each person's individual goals, values and beliefs, moreover, interact with these distributed sources of information, making each person's experience in the situation both similar and unique.

Compare these three learning contexts with what occurs in most classrooms. Learning in classrooms is competitive among individuals, the subject and nature of problems change on the hour in a predictable succession, and the major source of information is typically the teacher. This is not a context which transfers to many situations outside of the educational system, regardless of the level in the system.

Today there is criticism of education, at all levels, but much of this critique misses the point. Its focus is on content, what is learned, rather than on process, how it is learned. The central problem in formal education centres not so much on what is learned, although schools are remarkably timid in introducing students to alternate modes of knowing, but with the prevalent assumption that school settings are optimal contexts for learning (Gardner, 1992).

There is a test which needs to be applied to all levels of education, and that is authenticity: the degree to which the context of learning genuinely matches that which is to be learned in a way that it can be learned. To meet this test of authenticity, learning situations must exhibit some of the key attributes of real life problem solving: (1) ill-structured and complex goals; (2) an opportunity for the detection of relevant and irrelevant information; (3) active and generative engagement in finding, resolving, solving and dissolving problems; (4) an involvement of the learner's beliefs and values and; (5) an opportunity to engage in and be rewarded for collaborative interpersonal and problem-solving activities (Young, 1993:43-59).

The dimensions of the test of authenticity may seem familiar to you. If so, this is due to the fact that many emerge as attributes of familial learning. Familial environments, as we all know, tend to be messy and ill-structured, no matter how much we try to impose order. Values and beliefs are at the core of familial existence. Collaboration, which is constantly negotiated, is necessary in some form for familial survival. And problems are certainly actively created and acted upon.

Each setting in which we participate contains within it what James Wertsch calls a toolkit for learning; that is, the various mediational means through which we take action (Wertsch, 1991). These mediational means include technical tools (machines/artifacts), psychological tools (language, counting systems, signs, diagrams) and other people. As a result, each setting has its own learning code, its preferred way of structuring and making available its collage of learning tools and people available within it. Families house learning toolkits which are structured into learning codes. The kits and codes in various families vary. So too, schools house learning codes and toolkits. Although constant effort is expended in schools in the attempt to "standardize" these codes and kits, diversity within certain boundaries is also great.

When a child attends a school, two learning toolkits and codes confront one another. Typically, the learning code of the school and its associated toolkit gradually dominate and supplant that of the family in the school setting. The latent assumption in this process is that the learning code of the school is superior to that of the family and more relevant to the real world outside each of these institutions. As noted earlier, both of these assumptions are highly questionable and lead to a distorted conception of the capabilities and capacities of children as learners.

The educational system, rather than striving to find ways to incorporate families within its learning model, must explore ways in which it can mirror familial contexts of learning. Within the diversity of familial life, there is stored a tremendous source of untapped knowledge and skills about effective learning and an equally impressive body of educational expertise. The point is not to reverse the process and have the familial learning code triumph over that of the school, but to find vehicles through which both codes can co-exist, mutually expanding the learning potential of students. The dramatic rise in interest and involvement in home schooling, even though this is an ironic contradiction in terms, and the "success rates" of young people in these familial learning settings, is testimony to these principles. When parents say to teachers and others in formal education that "you really don't understand my child," they are right, and it is about time that we did.

From Passive to Active Learning

One of the most long-standing and cherished practices in all levels of education is the receptacle theory of learning. Put simply, the idea is that knowledge exists apart from the person and is transferred from one to another. Like a tea ceremony, one person pours and the others drink. Whether in a typical schoolroom, university lecture theatre, corporate training session or parliamentary hearing, the typical one-way process of receptacle learning is acted out. In this process, education is the conveyance of what experts already know to be true. It is not a process of inquiry, discovery or creation. The implicit assumption here is that one of education's key roles is to transmit society's culture from one generation to the next, not to critically examine it.

The receptacle model of education generates passive learning, a process which poses serious obstacles for human growth and development. Passive learning eliminates the opportunity for exploration, discovery and invention, with the result that students perceive learning as a thing not a process. Passive learning objectifies the educational process. People experience the world in two ways: as objects and as subjects. Passive learning, regardless of where it occurs, creates contexts in which students experience themselves as objects of the actions and plans of others. Constant passivity in learning robs the development of such "higher order" skills as creativity, problem-solving and initiative — the new skills of the new informational economy.

Cognitive change and development, contrary to the receptacle model of learning, are as much a social as an individual process. They occur in what Vygotsky termed the zone of the proximal development: the difference between the level of problem difficulty that a child could engage in independently and the level that could be accomplished with adult help (Vygotsky, 1978). More recently, Michael Cole and his associates have talked of a construction zone: an interactive system within which people work on a problem which at least one of them alone could not work on effectively (Newman, Griffin and Cole, 1992). Cognitive change takes place in this zone as a result of the interaction of the person, his/her capacities, and the people and cultural tools in the setting. The same learning task, as a result, will be approached differently by children in different settings, and no single setting is perfectly matched to learning any task. People construct knowledge together in various zones of proximal development. Learning is preeminently active, not passive. Moreover, there exists a broad range of construction zones for learning in our society and the family is one such setting.

Parents and other caregivers are teachers in the familial construction zone. They possess intuitive knowledge and skills related to the amount and type of help children need to learn particular things and the process involved in children being able to take over tasks on an independent basis. This poses a new opportunity for parenting education; not the education of parents by schools, but the education of schools by parents.

Contrary to the romantic rhetoric about the family, this setting can also contribute to passive or active learning, depending on its structure and the model of learning in use. Learning in families can be equally as passive as in formal educational institutions. In fact, familial conservatism in learning preference sometimes can act as a brake on the move toward active learning in schools. In other cases, rigid role and gender definitions within families, coloured by power relations, can generate extreme passivity in learning. Family choice in education, a popular notion in current reformist rhetoric, can be a problematic idea; that is, it can potentially act as a reinforcer of passivity. In other words, being born into a family is no guarantee of intellectual development or liberation. A transformation of schools and education without equal attention being paid to the developmental environment of families will lead only to false starts and social anxiety.

Thinking While Doing

We live in what can be described as a mind-centred and fragmented culture. Thinking takes precedence over doing and each is strangely seen as a separate process. Status differentials are built upon this dualism: mind work is valued higher than hand work; academic learning is preferred over vocational study; and athletes, although well paid at the professional level, are defined as intellectually inferior. Paradoxically, this very mind-centred culture has generated a new critique of education at all levels; that it is somehow divorced from practical reality and does not provide usable skills. If one designs an educational system around a disembodied mind and divorces that system from the realm of life experience, then is it any wonder what results are forthcoming (Varella and Thompson, 1993)?

We need to reexamine our culture and history to find contexts in which thinking and doing are integrated. Interestingly, history provides an enduring example of just such a context: apprenticeship. Apprenticeship has been the subject of renewed interest among learning theorists and researchers, since it provides a powerful way of organizing learning-in-context. The concept of cognitive apprenticeship is now being actively discussed and examined as a key to acquiring the higher order of thinking skills that are increasingly needed in a knowledge-based economy and society (Brown, Collins and Duguid, 1989:18; Rogoff, 1991). Apprenticeship provides a micro-world in which a person is immersed in learning and the application of learning to real problems and tasks. Apprenticeship provides for a renaissance, not merely a reform, of education.

In apprenticeship, learning centres on action rather than on mere discussion. It is concerned with ability to perform rather than merely the ability to talk about performing something. Apprenticeship is not separated from life, but is a way of life. In apprenticeship, work is the driving force and progressive mastery of tasks is not so much a step toward a distant symbolic or credential goal, as for immediate benefit. Apprenticeship entails a learning process in which the order of events and activities is derived from the organic structure of work and its real context. Apprentices typically work from the edges of a complex task toward its centre; rather than, as in school, from a linear model. Apprentices acquire skills in clusters and use chunks of knowledge. Apprenticeship is a community of learning practice, in which expertise is embedded not only in the master, but also in the tools and personal interactions in the environment. The process bears remarkable similarity to the way children learn, through play, in families.

Apprenticeship, however, has fallen into ill-repute over the years for two primary reasons. Firstly, it was associated with the historic exploitation of child labour. In the process of removing children from the exploitative practices of the workplace, however, we have unintentionally removed children from the experience of work itself and of the process of learning in a community of practice. The second reason for the disfavour shown to apprenticeship relates to its use, in formal training systems, as a vehicle for the education of trades and technical occupations. If one did not succeed in the mind-centred games of schooling, then apprenticeship was one's option. It is interesting to note, however, that many professions — presumably the highest order of mind-centred learning — continue to use apprenticeship as the final stage in induction, although the word apprenticeship is replaced by other terms. Lawyers and accountants enter "articling," doctors "intern," teachers and social workers engage in a practicum, and academics pursue post-doctorates.

The idea that a cognitive apprenticeship can serve as a new organizing principle for education is not a call to have the young participate in the world of work, whether paid or unpaid, or a demand for more career education. Rather, it is a metaphor for using responsibility and experience as vehicles for reintegrating thought and action in learning. The concept of cognitive apprenticeship transcends linear, sequential and lockstep models of learning, replacing those with an ecological framework. It highlights the messiness of the world and the various strategies people use to comprehend it. For this reason, the basic idea of a cognitive apprenticeship was not borne out of studies of schooling, but flows from a deeper appreciation of the role of learning in such settings as the workplace and family.

For years, researchers and others have attempted to design optimal learning experiences for children. The bulk of this research has focused upon two settings: the classroom and the research lab. Piaget, of course, is a noted exception; he studied children at home. Recent research by Michael Csikszentmihalyi and his colleagues is different; its focus has been on optimal learning in a range of contexts. Optimal learning blooms when a balance exists between abilities and responsibilities; when the skills one possesses are roughly commensurate with the challenges one faces; when one's talents are neither underused or overtaxed. It emerges in circumstances which are perceived as both problematic and soluble.

The Smart Environment

Reconnecting learners with the life contexts of learning, as a means of creating authentic and optimal learning experiences, is the single greatest challenge facing education and, in some ways, our entire society. For the better part of this century, however, we have focused our energies on capturing and storing knowledge within formal educational institutions and creating access channels to it. While this accumulation and access process was underway, new information technologies have been developing which are reversing this very process. Knowledge is increasingly dispersed and accessible in environments beyond formal educational institutions, as are the new tools to access it (Poser, 1990; Tapscott and Caston, 1993). The result is a growing gap between society's expectation of where one should learn and how it is now possible to learn. Learning is increasingly "out of control" and in this very phenomenon resides its greatest potential for social benefit.

Historically, human learning was limited to what could be accumulated in a single human brain in one lifetime. The invention of spoken and written language, then printing and electronic communications media, incrementally expanded the human ability to accumulate and share knowledge among people and across generations. These innovations, significant as they were, never expanded the storage of information outside the human brain. Today, technology is extending the learning process outside the human brain and into the environment (Perelman, 1993).

New technologies make possible transparent learning; that is, learning which is unbounded by time (when one learns), space (where one learns), mode (how one learns), pace (the rate at which one learns) and role (with whom one learns). An example of transparent learning is distance education, one of the most rapidly developing models of education in the world today. Distance learning systems reverse the historical flow in accessing education. Rather than having learners come to a central point to acquire knowledge and learn, distance learning systems take education to where people live, work or play (Morrison, 1992:19-56).

New computer and telecommunications technologies and the transparent learning models which they nurture are leading to a reinvention of the home and family as a context for learning and knowledge development. The home, in this regard, has the potential to emerge as an inquiry system orchestrating a multi-dimensional set of learning processes (Mitroff, 1993). Technology expands the communicational reach of the home almost on a global basis, in such a way that knowledge resident in other people and data bases can be accessed, interpreted, created and transmitted continuously. The home, often defined as a passive receptacle of social and technological change, is emerging as an active generator of change and a model of the future of learning.

The social implications of new information technologies becomes clear when one examines some of the central findings of a major study of computer competence conducted across the USA by the Educational Testing Service. Defining computer competence as one's ability to use a computer as a general purpose tool for the manipulation of information, communicating with other people and a medium for pursuing educational goals, the Educational Testing Service study reported the following conclusions: (1) Computer competence was directly related to having used a computer at school or in the home; (2) Most computer learning takes place outside of school, particularly in the home; (3) Males generally evidenced higher computer competence than females; (4) White students evidenced greater computer competence than black and Hispanic students; (5) Advantages in computer competence were greater for students whose parents were college graduates, who attend non-public schools and who are from high socio-economic groups.

As the Educational Testing Service study shows, access to a computer at home, one of the central tools of new information technology, exerts a powerful impact on computer competence. However, the Educational Testing Service study also portends the emergence of class, racial and ethnic gaps in access to information technology, which further highlights the central role of the family and home in crafting an information technology opportunity policy. Our society urgently needs to address access rights to new information technologies and the knowledge generating power they increasingly possess. The locus of these rights centres on both individuals and collectivities, particularly the home and families. Such a policy needs to guarantee, at a minimum, three access rights.

The first is an access right to knowledge tools; to the new informational hardware and software tools used in knowledge creation, transmission and analysis. Access to these new knowledge tools is the contemporary equivalent of guaranteeing access to books and literature, to reading and writing. Without such universal access, new information technologies inevitably become instruments for the generation and reproduction of inequality.

The second is access to knowledge pools. Increasingly knowledge is available in data bases of various kinds — pools of knowledge (de Sola Pool, 1992). These knowledge pools are being created with a speed and range that defies the imagination. They are highly dynamic, growing in depth and breadth and changing on a daily basis (Arnold and Mable Beckman Centre, 1993). Access to such knowledge pools is somewhat akin to providing access to libraries, and yet it must also encompass the right to participate in the actual creation as well as storage of knowledge. Restricting access to knowledge pools, a critical resource and basis of influence in the new economy, is from one perspective equivalent to the sanctioning of private armies. The difficult question is how to provide access without so controlling the knowledge generation process that creativity itself is destroyed.

A tentative answer to this dilemma rests in the third category of access rights — access to knowledge rules. Knowledge rules refer to creative thinking processes which convert inert information into meaningful knowledge. New information technologies, since they allow information to be represented in various ways — text, graphics, voice and images — dramatically expand the ways in which knowledge can be understood, created and transmitted. These new rules of knowledge call for inventive thinking and the capacity by learners to reflect on their thinking-in-progress. New educational technologies, for example, allow a student not only to create and solve problems, but to examine while they are problem solving how they approached the activity, how other students were simultaneously approaching it, and alternative ways it can be approached.

New technologies provide a potential link between schools as places of learning and a culture of personal responsibility. This sense of "doing something important," is visible in such projects as "Kidnet" (Papert, 1993:25). Developed in a collaboration between the National Geographic Society and Robert Tinker, Kidnet engages middle school students in the collection of data about acid rain. Individual schools send their data across electronic networks to a central computer where it is integrated and sent back to local sites, where it can be analyzed and discussed in the context of real and pressing global issues. The project suggests a vision of millions of children all over the world engaged in work that makes a real contribution to the study of a critical problem. Kidnet and other such projects represent the use of active learning by children, evaluating an idea by implementing it. Such a high involvement use of technology in education makes the student the subject rather than the object of the learning process.

A Learning-Focused Educational Policy

What can be done to facilitate a reconnection of learning to life? Of paramount importance is to shift the current focus of educational policy from inputs and outputs to process. Until the 1980s, the focal point of educational policy rested on such system inputs as the building and equipping of schools, teacher training, reducing staff-student ratios, and curriculum development and refinement. Expanding these inputs was seen to equate with growth in programme quality and student performance.

During the eighties, due more to international shifts in economic competitiveness and growth than well-researched educational studies, the public mood shifted. Now increasingly critical of schools, policymakers are seeking ways to remedy the presumed defects in institutional and student performance. Public policy in education has shifted from inputs to outputs of the system. Widespread performance testing of children and effectiveness ratings of schools has ensued, each being conducted within national and international comparison rankings. Performance-driven funding mechanisms have been introduced and curriculum is being redesigned to match various outcome measures. Test scores of students have marginally improved, but parallel to this has been a rise in non-academic problems in schools. Today, violence in schools is rising more rapidly than test scores.

There is a fundamental problem with a policy in education which focuses exclusively either on inputs or outputs. Neither provides any insight into why a particular effect occurs or offers a framework for an effective educational practice. The only possibility for long-term, comprehensible and sustained improvement in student and school performance is to re-focus educational policy on the learning process itself. Learning is the process which converts inputs, regardless of their quantity and scale, into performance, regardless of how that is measured. Learning is also the process which informs us about the nature of educational effectiveness and how to provide for and improve it.

It is ironic, indeed, that what is needed most at this time is a learning-focused educational policy. Such a policy is devoted to innovation in and strengthening of the learning process, using inputs as its resource base and outputs as an appropriate indicator of growth and development of students. Space does not permit an exhaustive outline of all the elements of a learning-focused educational policy. Based on the theme of this chapter, however, several critical elements of such a reformulated policy can be sketched.

The first element of a learning-focused educational policy is to recognize that the quality of human relationships matters every bit as much as individual ability and the level of available resources in generating effective learning. Effective learning hinges on the availability of three types of assets or capital. The first is physical capital embodied in buildings, dollars and technology. The second is human capital created by changes in individuals that result in new skills and capabilities allowing a person to act in new ways. Physical and human capital depend for their productive use, however, on social capital which inheres in the relationships among people.

Research is beginning to make clear that the social capital of the family plays a key role in the creation of human capital in the next generation (Coleman, 1988:95-120). Family background has long been associated with success or failure in school. The financial capital available to a family, typically defined as level of parental income, provides potentially for physical resources that can aid achievement: a fixed place in the home to study, materials and technology to aid learning and travel experience. Human capital, approximately measured by the level of education of the parents, provides the potential for a modelling environment which aids the motivation and learning of a child.

The social capital of a family is different from physical and human capital. It flows from the relations between parents and children. The social capital of the family is what gives the child access to the human capital of adults and this depends on the physical presence of adults in the family, the quality of attention given by adults to the child, and the degree of trustworthiness evident in parent-child relations. If the human capital possessed by parents is not complemented by social capital embodied in family relations, then it is irrelevant to the child's learning growth. Both the quality of family relationships and degree of parent-child interaction have been found to significantly affect school success, as well as dropout rates. To a degree, level of income and previous education, since they can set boundaries around family relationships, also affect the level of social capital in the family.

The level and quality of family relationships, in other words, matter very much in the learning success of the next generation. A learning-focused educational policy, therefore, must not be confused with a policy for schools, since it must be broader and strengthen the social capital of families. Such a learning-focused educational policy supports initiatives to reduce dramatically the income disparity among families through a guaranteed annual income, and the maintenance of key social programmes. Linked to financial bursary programmes, it is committed to a significant broadening of access opportunities to further education for adults. In addition, it encourages a redesign of work through such initiatives as parental leave, day care provision, flexible hours and working at home. In this era of performance indicators, a learning-focused educational policy calls for a new set of national accounts which charts our progress in building the social capital of this country.

The second element of a learning-focused educational policy is to supplement, if not replace, achievement testing with learning assessment. If a student scores on the 35th percentile on a standardized math test, what does this score tell about what the student knows and what he/she fails to understand? What does it tell about how to help the student? Why do some students with comparable abilities flourish and others wither academically? Answers to these questions require what cognitive scientists refer to as learning assessment: a portrait of developmental changes in a student's performance. Children and young people change dramatically and continuously as they mature. So too, their learning capacity is dynamic and changing. Achievement tests artificially freeze this dynamic process, producing results which are both static and misleading.

Learning assessment is ongoing and monitors performance in the larger environment in which it unfolds. The tasks used to assess what students know and can do are authentic. The evaluation framework: (1) reflects the tasks that students will encounter in the world outside of schools, not merely those limited to schools themselves; (2) reveals how students go about solving a problem, not only the solutions they formulate; (3) encompasses not only solo performances of children but also monitors this effectiveness in collaborative efforts; (4) permits students to select their preferred way of representing knowledge; and (5) relates to but is not bound by the curriculum as taught. Unlike achievement testing, learning assessment not only gives both students and teachers the tools for positive change, but also provides parents and others with a dynamic portrayal of the learning performance of students in this highly fluid period of their lives.

A third element in a learning-focused educational policy is to provide, within and through schools, for greater and richer opportunities for collaborative learning. Collaborative learning not only actively enhances learning but also reflects the reality of learning and work in the larger society. Collaborative learning need not be confined to students themselves, but can encompass activities which bring together people from different generations and walks of life. Families, in this regard, potentially provide natural settings for collaborative learning. Collaborative learning not only challenges our single-minded obsession with individual performance, but provides a route to the acquisition of a core skill requisite to effectiveness in our changing economy and society: learning with and through others.

A fourth aspect of a learning-focused public policy is to broaden substantially the contexts in which children learn. For years, schools have attempted to simulate the outside world for the young, with the result that success in learning has been defined as success at learning in school. This is a policy which, although not intentional, is prejudicial against those students who learn best in contexts other than school, and may also later in life work against those children who can only learn best in school.

To accomplish this broadening of the contexts of learning for the young, three changes are required, each of which seriously counters conventional thinking. The first is to reduce the number of instructional contact hours in schools and increase the amount and variety of out-of-school experience for children. The second is to remunerate teachers not exclusively on the basis of instructional time but on their overall capacity to design learning experiences for children. The third is to substantially increase the use of volunteers in schools who can function as community mentors of the young, introducing them to learning experiences outside of school.

A fifth prong in a learning-focused educational policy entails a system-wide and national strategic investment in networked learning. The potential of new information technologies, linked through electronic highways, to extend the communicational reach of individual schools and students and reduce existing inequities in access to knowledge and expertise, is immense. The national rail, highway and airline systems move people and goods across this country. They were and are central to the vitality of this nation's economy and identity. Both our economy and identity will require for their vitality, in the future, that we move information and knowledge to people in a way that develops our nation's capacity for continuous learning.

To have schools standing as isolated repositories of knowledge in a society in which information is exploding is not only to deny reality but to design redundancy into the education of the young. The centrepiece of a much needed telecommunications policy in this country must be the creation of an electronic learning highway accessible by any school, anytime, anywhere and funded as a core component of our national infrastructure.

The sixth component of a learning-focused educational policy is to provide a vehicle for families and schools to reconnect around the learning futures of the young. To date, many of the proposals in this area have called for empowering families through school choice or voucher schemes or urged the establishment of various parental advisory mechanisms for schools. These proposals tend to treat schools and families as separate if not adversarial entities. They have not explored the terrain of mutual and interdependent interest.

A modest proposal toward the fostering of mutual interest between families and schools would involve the creation, at each school, of a family learning account. The account, in the name of each child, would be funded to a given level and on an annual basis from a percentage of the provincial grants to school divisions. The sole purpose of the account and expenditures against it would be to enhance the learning potential of the child. Expenditures from the account could only be made on the basis of mutual agreement of parents (caregivers) and the individual teacher. Both parents and teachers, as well as the child, could bring forth proposals. Expenditures from the family learning account, moreover, would not be confined to activities within the school, but could encompass the family and other settings.

The establishment of a family learning account not only directs resources to the development of the learning potential of the child, but also requires for its use that parents and teachers discuss on an ongoing basis their mutual ideas about learning with reference to an individual child. It empowers the teacher, the parent and the child to make real decisions with real consequences. And it substantially enlarges the pool of ideas from which schools can draw in the education of students.

Conclusion

Today, there is constant talk of fiscal deficits and the need to balance our collective books. Unquestionably this is a problem which needs to be addressed. But fiscal balance, even if obtained, will not bring social balance. The reason is that there exist other deficits in our society which, if left unattended, bring with them even greater social upheaval. Large and growing opportunity deficits between the rich and poor are one example. Another, ironically, is the learning deficit in education: the growing gap between the potential of human learning and the capacity and willingness of formal education to learn about learning.

Learning in our society is outstripping the capacity of our educational systems to anticipate, respond and adapt. Lifelong learning, the new imperative of the modern age, demands a flexibility of mind, skill and spirit, and the ability to function in a multiplicity of contexts throughout the life cycle. Individuals of all ages are increasingly aware of these challenges. They are increasingly open to new ways of learning new things. Formal education, if it is to play a role in this emerging society of learning, must open itself to new ways of learning about learning. This challenge must be met, not by inviting society into the classroom, but by redefining society as the classroom.

CHAPTER FIVE

Families in Crisis

Brian Wharf

The problems of many families will not be solved by early intervention efforts but only by changes in the basic features of the infrastructure of our society. No amount of counselling, early childhood curricula or home visits will take the place of jobs that provide decent incomes, affordable housing, appropriate health care, optimal family configuration or integrated neighbourhoods where children encounter positive role models (Zigler, 1990:xiii).

The above quotation captures the essence of the argument advanced in this chapter: that the most significant crises which affect families arise from the absence of an adequate income and, as a consequence, having to live in substandard housing and in an unsafe neighbourhood. These crises are viewed here as public issues, whereas crises which are in large part untroubled by poverty and inadequate housing are viewed as personal troubles. The distinction between public issues and private troubles is pivotal for the case developed in the chapter.

The obvious point that all families experience crises through sickness, accidents and deaths is acknowledged at the outset. However, infrequent crises which are handled, albeit with difficulty at the time, are not the subject of this chapter. Rather the concern here is with severe crises which disrupt the lives of families on a continuing basis.

The chapter is organized in the following fashion. After a brief introduction, some theories and concepts are introduced which establish the overall direction and thrust of the chapter. The second section presents the views of a group of social and community workers in Victoria, British Columbia, about families in crisis. While a deeper appreciation of family crises would have been obtained by interviewing family members, these interviews would have been difficult to arrange. Reliance is then placed on professionals who work with families in crisis. The wisdom of these practitioners is confirmed by other pieces of evidence leading to the overall position of the chapter that current Canadian social policies do not recognize nor respond to the reality of family life in the 1990s.

Further, it is argued that the ruling arrangements* which prevail in Canada virtually guarantee that some Canadian families, and particularly those headed by women, will live in poverty and in a state of continuing crisis. The concluding section draws on the experience of practitioners and on the literature in outlining the case for policies and programs which would connect public issues and private troubles and thereby reduce crises for families.

---

* Ruling arrangements is a shorthand term used in this chapter to refer to those institutions, both public and private, which govern Canada's social, economic and tax policies. As will become apparent as the discussion unfolds, it is the author's view that the ruling arrangements are controlled by a relatively small group of men who occupy prominent positions and who share a distinctive perspective on how society should be governed and operate and how financial rewards should be distributed. In recent years this perspective or ideology has been known as neo-conservative and its most prominent public sector exponents have been Margaret Thatcher in Britain, Ronald Reagan in the United States and Brian Mulroney in Canada.

The Conceptual Base of the Chapter

Three interrelated concepts, which taken together go a long way to explaining the position taken in the chapter with respect to family crises, are presented below. The first outlines the distinction between public issues and private troubles, the second consists of information and evidence dealing with the issue of power in Canadian society, and the third concerns the relationships between the family and the state. These concepts combine to establish the central thesis of the chapter that public issues are a consequence of the ruling arrangements in Canadian society and that families in crises are the recipients of these arrangements. Hence they live in crises not of their own making.

The distinction between "the private troubles of milieu" and "the public issues of social structure" was developed by C. Wright Mills.

Troubles occur within the character of the individual and within the range of his immediate relations with others; they have to do with his self and those limited areas of social life of which he is directly and personally aware. Accordingly, the statement and the resolution of troubles properly lie within the individual as a biographical entity and within the scope of his immediate milieu – the social setting that is directly open to his personal experience and to some extent his wilful activity. A trouble is a private matter: values cherished by an individual are felt by him to be threatened.

Issues have to do with matters that transcend these local environments of the individual and the range of his life. They have to do with the organization of many such milieux into the institutions of an historical society as a whole, with the ways in which various milieux overlap and interpenetrate to form the larger structure of social and historical life. An issue is a public matter; some values cherished by publics are felt to be threatened (Mills, 1959:8).

While helpful, the distinction is incomplete. In the first place, Mills does not explicitly acknowledge the deep connections between public issues and private troubles. Feminist scholars have been instrumental in pointing out connections and the phrase "the personal is political" has now become part of everyday discourse. It is readily apparent that public issues such as poverty have an enormous impact on individuals and in turn public issues develop when private troubles are experienced by more than a few individuals.

A second weakness is that the distinction fails to appreciate the differential impact of public issues. The issues of race, class and gender divide members of society in very clear and inequitable ways. Thus women earn less than men and lone female parents are poorer than their male counterparts (Oderkirk and Lochhead, 1992). The differences in all social indicators are simply staggering when the lot of Canada's First Nations are compared to those of Anglo-Saxon descent.

A third weakness is that the framework is curiously untroubled by a discussion of power. It is a surprising omission because Mills is best known for his studies of power in the United States and his critiques of the power wielded by the military/industrial complex in that country. The framework tends to suggest that once "values cherished by publics are threatened", action to resolve these issues will occur in a relatively automatic fashion. This assumption fails to recognize that those in power will resist and effectively block actions which threaten their interests. In addition, public issues which affect other citizens will be reframed into private troubles!

Nevertheless, the distinction between public issues and private troubles is a useful one because it makes the crucial point that ruling arrangements are largely responsible for public issues and not the wilful activities of individuals. As will be apparent from the discussion which follows, the point is often obscured and sometimes deliberately.

The assertion that an elite group control the affairs of Canadian society is fundamental to the discussion in this chapter and while space limitations prohibit a full account, a skeletal body of evidence and references are noted below. The subject of power and its distribution in Canadian society has been studied in depth beginning with John Porter's pioneering research reported in *The Vertical Mosaic*, and continuing through the work of scholars such as Wallace Clement, Leo Panitch, David Ross, Bill Carroll and journalists like Peter Newman and Linda McQuaig. Perhaps the most readable accounts have been written by the latter who, in dealing with the relationship between taxes and wealth, provides detailed information on power and its distribution in Canada. McQuaig concludes that the most affluent one fifth of the population controls 68% of the nation's wealth whereas the bottom fifth has less than 1% (McQuaig, 1988).

One of the best examples of the power of the powerful comes from the combined efforts of the business community, neo-conservative governments and the media to lay the responsibility for the national debt on runaway spending on social programs. Thus a Financial Post editorial,(quoted in McQuaig, 1993:14) warned in ominous tones that:

The cause of most concern is Canada's welfare state. Two generations of Canadians have become spoiled because of the largesse of spendthrift politicians at all levels of government and with all parties. The chief economist of the Bank of Nova Scotia was more of an alarmist in his statement that "Canada's profligate social spending presents a tremendous moral hazard."

Despite the above claims, the studies of many scholars and reporters have shown that social program expenditures have not been responsible for the debt. Rather the principal reason has been the failure to collect revenue from individuals and corporations at the rate which was in effect in the 1960s. McQuaig argues persuasively that:

Government spending should not necessarily be seen as the villain of the deficit story. Equally responsible for our deficit plight is the reduction in tax revenues. Indeed if we had followed the example of Europe and maintained higher tax revenues, our deficit situation would be dramatically different. Neil Brooks notes that if Canada had simply maintained throughout the 70s the level of taxation that it had in 1974 our debt would have been roughly half of what it had become by the early 80s (McQuaig, 1993:150).

Edgar Epp's studies of taxation patterns reveal a similar conclusion.

It is startling to see how little income tax has been paid by Canadian corporations during the past fifteen years. A substantial portion of corporate profit used to be paid in tax. In 1946 corporations achieved profits of $1,721 million and paid $654 million in income tax. This was equivalent to 34.63% of profit....In 1986, however, corporations that could boast of $86,168 million in profit paid only $13,710 million in income tax – a measly 15.91% (Epp, 1989:9).

The above quotations represent only a fragment of the evidence that could be presented to establish the point that current tax policies favour the rich and powerful. It is also apparent that these and other economic policies which grant tax breaks to industry effectively set the overall framework for the collection and distribution of income in Canada. Given that these policies are controlled by those who have the most to lose by a radical redistribution of income, it is acknowledged that change is unlikely to occur in the near future. Nevertheless, the rather dim prospect of change should not allow us to blur the essential argument that public issues rather than personal troubles account for the most severe crises facing Canadian families.

The above discussion has outlined the societal context in which Canadian families live and has stressed the differences in power and wealth. It now remains to relate these contexts to the family. In doing so I rely on the work of Jane Ursel, who has traced the development of the relationships between social policies and the family. Ursel notes that:

while having babies and making love are intensely personal acts and decisions, the consequences of these acts have always been of great interest to governments in all societies....The exercise of our individual needs and preferences regarding family life is always directed and circumscribed by larger social circumstances: the state, its laws, policy and finances play a major role in determining these circumstances (Ursel, 1993:147).

The interest of governments in family life is, of course, brought about by that very basic of concerns – the need for societies to continue and to grow. But such a concern is too limited. It is suggested here that a higher order of concern for governments is to develop policies and create environments which will allow the caring, intellectual and artistic capacities of citizens to flourish. Thus a society characterized by arrangements which provide limited and unequal opportunities for citizens to achieve these capacities is a damaged society. The challenge is to bring the interests of families and individuals in line with the overall interests of society – a harmony rarely achieved in societies and particularly in those characterized by a disproportionate share of power and wealth.

Ursel argues further that while economic policies and arrangements have always been structurally separate from and unresponsive to the requirements of the family, social policies have attempted to "provide protection, support and regulation to the family as the reproductive unit" (Ursel, 1993:165). Protection is expressed in the form of legislation such as child labour and child welfare laws, support is provided through measures like the Child Benefits program, social assistance, Old Age Security and related transfer payments from government, and regulation refers to efforts to control behaviour in matters such as child maintenance. Ursel's overall view is that social policies have had a positive effect on Canadian families.

The most striking feature of the growth of the state's supportive function has been the growth of its generalized or universal commitment to the support of the Canadian population and its reproduction. This has the effect of broadening the scope and possibilities of individuals for exercising personal choice. For example, the existence of social support increases the likelihood of an elderly person being able to live independently, a wife being able to leave an abusive marriage and a child being provided with alternative care (Ursel, 1993:159).

A historical perspective supports Ursel's line of argument. However, the recent decisions to introduce a Goods and Services Tax, to reduce federal contributions to health, education and social welfare programs and to eliminate the Family Allowance program suggest that Canada's largely positive record in developing social policy supports for the family is coming to an end.

To conclude this section it is argued that the above concepts and explanations reinforce each other. Together they provide a convincing case that while the state must ensure that families have children, the current ruling arrangements also ensure an unequal distribution of income and opportunities. Some families enjoy a high income and standard of living and in so doing escape the ravages of public issues such as poverty.

The Views of Practitioners

As noted in the introduction, the writer assembled a group of practitioners to discuss the issue of families in crisis. The practitioners included two staff members of the Ministry of Social Services, the director of Transition House, the president of Capital Families, herself a retired social worker with many years of experience in the mental health field, a program supervisor of a multi-service centre, and three community development workers who have extensive and recent experience in working with client groups such as the homeless and youth on the street, and with a network of agencies serving families. In addition a separate meeting was held with the director of the Victoria branch of Parents in Crisis. The names and affiliations of the practitioners are listed at the end of the chapter.

The questions posed to the practitioners were:

1. Who are the families in crisis in Victoria? Do we have any information about them in terms of numbers, characteristics (income, race, residence, etc.,) and the kind of difficulties they experience?
2. How would you describe the network of services which provides assistance to families? Is it adequate, accessible and effective?
3. What might be done to prevent family crises? Are there any policies and programs which should be put into place?

The practitioners identified four characteristics of families in crisis: poverty and the related issue of the lack of affordable housing, parent/teen conflict, mental illness and First Nations ancestry.

Only the first two characteristics of families in crisis are dealt with for the following reasons. The condition of mental illness can be severe and disabling, but according to the practitioners affects only a relatively small number of individuals and families in the Greater Victoria area. It is acknowledged that had the discussion been dominated by mental health professionals, a greater sense of urgency and priority about mental illness would have emerged.

If the characteristic of mental illness affects only a relatively few families, the same cannot be said about First Nations families. The plight of these families is the consequence of generations of culturally inappropriate policies, and as the practitioners pointed out, the responsibility for developing new and appropriate responses is increasingly being assumed by First Nations people. The history of oppression of First Nations families is so extensive that it requires a more adequate discussion than can be provided within the space limitations of this chapter.

Before presenting the views of the practitioners, it should be noted that they were unable to answer the question about the numbers of families served by social and health agencies in Victoria. At the present time, no agency has been assigned or indeed sought the mandate of collecting information about families in crisis or seeking assistance. And the task would be formidable given the number of agencies in the Greater Victoria community. The list includes the statutory services of the Ministries of Social Services and Health; neighbourhood houses; a transition house; sexual counselling centres for children, women and men; the YM/YWCA; Salvation Army; and a large number of agencies and individuals providing a variety of counselling services.

Many of the latter agencies are of relatively recent origin and have come into being as a consequence of the philosophy of privatization. Given the need to compete for funds, the social service field in all provinces is dominated by competition rather than cooperation. It is not possible to gain an unduplicated count of the number of individuals and families being served by agencies in Victoria, and of course, not all of these clients could be described as experiencing a crisis. Further, the practitioners did not advocate establishing a central registry on the grounds that such a mechanism has the potential to invade the privacy of clients.

It should also be noted that the practitioners agreed that the present arrangement of services is not satisfactory. Services are not adequate, accessible nor arranged in a way that ensures continuity of service and accountability to clients. The practitioners' recommendations for change are woven into the discussion in the concluding section of the chapter.

Poverty as the Underlying Issue

The practitioners were unanimous in asserting that poverty dominates the lives of families in crisis. Virtually all of the families who come to the attention of the family and child welfare office of the Ministry of Social Services located in downtown Victoria are poor. While the correlation is not as high in other offices, Ministry staff reported that poverty is the single most significant factor in the child welfare and family support caseload of the Ministry. In addition, the largest group of families living in poverty are headed by women.

The practitioners identified the consequences of poverty in very precise terms. Being poor means that one has difficulty in finding and keeping suitable accommodation. Being poor means that one is forced to move frequently, and the reasons for moves vary from not being able to pay the rent on time due to unforeseen additional expenses, to the unsatisfactory nature of the current housing. Frequent moves result in the inability to establish roots in a neighbourhood, and in turn the consequence of frequent moves are feelings of being disconnected and isolated. Being poor means that one has insufficient income, time and energy to ensure that children are healthy, grow up in safe accommodation and neighbourhoods, receive a good education, and participate in athletic and cultural activities. Admittedly the views of a small number of practitioners in one city cannot be taken as a national portrait of families in crisis. But their opinions are supported by a report based on fifteen community consultations in Vancouver in 1992. The meetings sought to identify the needs of families and the similarity in views is striking, particularly with respect to the first two recommendations.

- Families need housing, jobs and adequate incomes. Without these necessities other family problems cannot be resolved.

- Services must be client-centred. The services must fit the client rather than making the client responsible for accommodating the needs of the service.

- Service integration is necessary to eliminate duplication of efforts and to ensure that money is used as effectively as possible.

- Prevention of family problems must be regarded as being at least as important as intervention.

- Services should be community-based and community-driven.

- The increasing multicultural diversity of Vancouver means that there are new priorities for services to families and children (Tracon Training Consultants, 1992:4).

In addition, the views of the practitioners are supported by a veritable volume of studies and projects reported in the social work literature. Perhaps the first and still the most common description is the "multi-problem family," a label applied by the numerous projects designed to serve these families in the 1950s and 1960s (see among other sources, Buell, et al., 1952; Schlesinger, 1963). Oscar Lewis referred to these families as lost in "a culture of poverty" (Lewis, 1966); Silverman called them "defeated" (Silverman, 1968) and in his study of the clients of multi-service centres, Perlman coined the adjective "buffeted" (Perlman, 1975). Perlman's colourful words portray the lives of families in crisis in a vivid fashion.

These are the people who seem to be caught in a windstorm in which everything is loose, flying about in an imminent threat to life itself. These are indeed the "buffeted" of our society, requiring help but fearful and suspicious. When troubles strike they have little leverage but react by using their smartness to try to manipulate the social institutions that seem to be manipulating them (Perlman, 1975:37).

In sum these families lack self-esteem, self-confidence and, above all, hope. Their children acquire these characteristics and thus perpetuate generations of buffeted families. While a variety of responses have been attempted to assist these families, they have fallen short of providing the most significant strategies – jobs, income and affordable housing. Indeed the unenviable task of providing help has fallen to child welfare agencies and I return to the notion of child welfare as "a poor family's social service" in a later section of the chapter (Meyer, 1985:101).

Parent/Teen Conflict

According to the Victoria practitioners, the second most significant characteristic of family crises is conflict between parents and adolescents, and this particular source of crisis is not confined by income. Parent/teen conflict can of course be exacerbated by the lack of an adequate income and housing, but is nevertheless prevalent in quite well-to-do neighbourhoods. Significantly, however, the conflict is not apparent in the most affluent areas, where residents avoid both public and voluntary social service agencies in favour of psychologists, psychiatrists and other counsellors in private practice, private schools, and other resources available only to the rich.

The practitioners described the parent/teen conflict as a smouldering issue which begins in the early years of childhood and explodes during adolescent years. The consequences of the breakdown of relationships between parents and children are often serious and long-term. They can result in children leaving home and school for a life on the street. Teenagers, mostly girls, who end up in prostitution as a way of surviving on the street face a dim and precarious future.

Explanations for parent/teen conflict vary and indeed no one explanation will adequately account for this complex matter. While it is often viewed as a personal trouble, the extent of the problem as identified by the practitioners argues that it merges into a public issue. Parent/teen conflict can be seen as the embodiment of a society/teen conflict whereby adolescents are exposed to a barrage of dismal information about wars on the international scene, intractable disputes on the national scene, violence on the local scene, and the destruction of the environment, to say nothing of their immediate future and the unlikely prospects of finding employment. Even college and university graduates face difficulties in locating work, and the price of housing in many communities renders their chances of home ownership very problematic.

Another factor contributing to family crises brought about by parent/teen conflict is the need for two incomes. If the combined income of both parents is sufficient only to take care of basic needs and not for day care, housecleaning, holidays and other supports, the two-income family can be isolated from neighbourhood and friends, and indeed from each other. Their life is dominated by work, frequently in low-paying and unsatisfactory jobs, leaving insufficient time and energy to fashion strong parent/child relationships. In no way is this discussion intended to blame parents, since the cost of raising a family often requires two wage earners. The point is that the need for two incomes can create undue stress in the lives of both parents and children.

According to the Victoria practitioners parent/teen conflicts are extraordinarily difficult to resolve. The seeds of the conflict were sown many years prior to the emergence of the problem, and relationships have deteriorated to such an extent that the traditional responses of mediation, family counselling and therapy usually prove to be ineffectual. More extreme responses like placement in a foster home are equally ineffective. The practitioners argued that priority should be given to prevention strategies and some suggestions are presented in the closing section of the chapter.

Social Policy and the Family

Having presented the views of some practitioners about families in crisis, I now turn to the larger social policy picture. The objective of this section of the chapter is to present information about the extent of poverty among Canadian families and to document the changing structure of families. From this base, I argue that a principal response of social policy has been to reframe the public issue of poverty into the private trouble of child neglect and abuse. The thesis is that a cultural lag exists between social policy and the realities facing Canadian families at the present time. The thesis is supported by a number of related pieces of evidence.

The first piece of evidence concerns the growing incidence of poverty in Canada. In 1980, 3,624,000 persons lived below the poverty line, resulting in a poverty rate of 15.3%. A decade later, in 1991, the poverty rate had increased to 16.0% with 4,227,000 persons in poverty. However, the most significant piece of data for this chapter is the fact that poverty among children grew at a more rapid rate. In 1980, the poverty rate for children under 18 was 14.9% and thus lower than the overall rate of 15.3%. By 1991 the poverty rate for children was 18.3% – an increase of 3.4% and again higher than the rate for all persons (National Council of Welfare, 1993).

The second source of support for the thesis is the lack of affordable housing, although it is difficult to obtain accurate estimates of the need for affordable housing on a national or provincial basis. Locally, the best data available allowed the Capital Region Housing Corporation to make a guesstimate that 20,000 to 30,000 households require subsidized housing in Victoria, British Columbia, but only 360 units were built in 1992 (BC Provincial Commission on Housing Options, 1992). Housing crises are most evident in urban areas and are brought about by a number of factors including increases in the price of land and the reluctance of federal and provincial governments to commit sufficient resources to social housing. The 1991/92 federal budget eliminated funding for the national cooperative housing program and reduced by half the funds for nonprofit housing despite the fact that an estimated 10,000 people are homeless in Canada (BC Provincial Commission on Housing Options, 1992).

The third piece of evidence concerns the changes which have occurred in the structure of families. "According to the 1991 Census there were almost one million lone-parent families with never married children of all ages representing 13% of all families, whereas in 1966, only 8% of all families were headed by a lone parent" (Oderkirk and Lochhead, 1992:16). The percentages and the changes are even more pronounced in B.C. where, in the space of a decade, the percentage of single parent families rose from 7% of all families in 1981 to 12% in 1991 (BC Ministry of Social Services, 1993:14).

Finally, the thesis is strengthened by pointing to the poverty of mother-led families. "During the late 1980s, 56% of lone mothers with children under age 18 and 20% of lone fathers with children under that age were living with incomes below the Statistics Canada Low Income Cut offs" (Oderkirk and Lochhead, 1992:18). By 1991 the situation facing single parent mothers had worsened. Sixty-five percent of children in mother-led families were living below the poverty line. The percentages varied only slightly between provinces, with Prince Edward Island having "only" 52.2%

below the poverty line and neighbouring Newfoundland having the highest percentage in the country with 74% (National Council of Welfare, 1993:20).

It is clear then that Canadian families are changing, and that a significant number are now led by single-parent women who cannot obtain sufficient income either from wages or from social assistance and other forms of transfer payments. A not infrequent consequence of lone parenthood coupled with poverty is the neglect of children. Although it is difficult to compile a comprehensive picture because provincial record-keeping systems differ, it is estimated that 66 – 75% of the children in care of child welfare agencies come from poor families...even though these families account for only about 20% of the population (Canadian Child Welfare Association et al., 1988). An even more startling but perhaps more accurate report comes from a study of the children in the care of a Children's Aid Society in Toronto. This study revealed that 83% of the families served lived in poverty and a further 11% were economically vulnerable (Novick and Volpe, 1989).

A recent research project on children in the care of the Ministry of Social Services in the province of British Columbia yields additional information about the relationship between women-led families and child neglect. The study found that half the children taken into care came from families led by women (Campbell, 1992). Commenting on this study and other trends in child welfare, Callahan observes:

> *The picture that emerges is striking. A major group of clients whose children are coming into care are very poor women on social assistance who are charged with neglecting their young children....The care of children also suffers, not just because their mothers have fewer economic resources but because mothers are less able to protect them from violence. There is ample evidence that violence against women and children is motivated by deeply held views of the inferiority of women and the rights of men to dominate them (Callahan, 1993:183).*

Indeed, while the child welfare system was developed with the intent of ensuring that children were not neglected, abused or abandoned, and as an instrument of social reform, some slippage in the reform agenda has occurred. One example of the early social reform efforts comes from the development of the Mother's Allowance program. Ursel claims that this income assistance program for mothers came into being "as a direct response to the reports of Children's Aid Societies in many provinces that many children who were taken into custody were apprehended primarily because of the poverty of their homes" (Ursel, 1993:156).

For many reasons, such reform efforts have been few and far between in recent years. In the first place, the time and energy of child welfare staff has been consumed in investigating complaints of neglect and abuse and the increase in these complaints has risen dramatically. From 1980 to 1990, complaints in the province of British Columbia rose from 3,500 to 32,000 (Ironmonger, 1993). Second, child welfare services are now provided by or financed by provincial governments which also have responsibility for income assistance, day care and housing programs. Hence, advocacy efforts by child welfare staff would involve criticism of their own employer. It is useful to point out that the most significant advocacy efforts have occurred in Ontario where child welfare services are provided by Children's Aid Societies. While these agencies receive almost all funding from the provincial government, their organizational structure ensures a degree of autonomy and separation from the government.

Third, the profession of social work, arguably the dominant profession in child welfare, has largely ignored the poverty-ridden lives of its clients in favour of a clinical approach to practice. Some evidence for this reframing of child welfare comes from a review of 84 articles in the volumes published 1990 – 1992 in *Child Welfare*. Despite its proclaimed intention of being a journal devoted to policy, practice and program, only two of the 84 articles dealt with the public issues of poverty, homelessness and unemployment. The majority of articles focused attention on developing and refining measures by which child welfare workers could detect symptoms of abuse and neglect. One prominent example will serve to illustrate this focus. In their article dealing with the application of a maternal characteristic scale to poor neglecting mothers and poor non-neglecting mothers, the authors report that the scale successfully distinguishes between the two groups on their ability to relate, their impulse control, their level of self-confidence and verbal facility (Polansky, Gaudin and Kilpatrick, 1992). Thus, the study can be seen as blaming the victims rather than inquiring into the impact of poverty and homelessness.

The above argument is supported by examining the contents of a recent Canadian book called *Child Maltreatment: Expanding our Concept of Helping* (Rothery and Cameron, 1992). The book consists of 17 chapters on various approaches to helping children and families, yet the public issues of employment, poverty and homelessness rate only a brief mention in one chapter!

It is difficult to escape the conclusion that rather than providing employment, income and adequate housing to poor families, they have been offered counselling, homemaker services and other forms of support. Should these fail, child welfare agencies apprehend their children. In effect, child welfare staff and academics have reframed the public issues facing their clients into private troubles and in so doing have served the dubious function of shielding public issues from the attention and responses they require. The matter receives further attention in the concluding section.

Tackling Public Issues

If, as argued in this chapter, poverty is the principal reason for family crises, what should and can be done? First, it must be acknowledged that a decidedly pessimistic tone shapes much of the following discussion. Based on his years of work at the National Council of Welfare, Ken Battle's most recent analysis of the changes in child benefits comes to the following gloomy conclusion:

> *This chapter has examined the complex series of changes by which the Mulroney government put in place a child benefit system that – while purporting to be fairer, simpler and more effective – in reality will become leaner and meaner with each passing year. Partial indexation – a veritable virus of social and tax policy – will remove in the order of $8 billion from the child benefits system on a cumulative basis between 1986 and 2000. All of the major objectives of the child benefit system – parental recognition, horizontal equity, anti-poverty – have been compromised. One of the defining philosophical premises of the Canadian welfare state – universality – was easily done away with not with a bang but a whimper. And social policy is firmly in the hands of the Department of Finance whose priority, not surprisingly, is cost cutting rather than social reform (Battle, 1993:51).*

As noted earlier, the social and economic policies of the recent federal government have been based on tackling the deficit without paying adequate attention to the income side of the budget. Thus, this government has reduced tax rates for wealthy individuals and corporations, has failed to close loopholes in the tax structure and has shrunk from the task of implementing new tax measures such as an inheritance tax. Two examples illustrate the priorities of this government. The first concerns the business entertainment deduction, which "allows business executives to deduct the cost of meals, drinks and sports tickets – even private boxes at the Sky Dome – at a cost to the federal treasury of more than $1 billion a year in lost revenue. That could pay for a lot of day care centres" (McQuaig, 1993:121). The second is illustrated by the cancellation of the universal family allowance program in January of 1993. It was left to critics to point out that while the government had defended the decision on the grounds that universal programs are too costly and inefficient, that changes to the RRSP deductions in 1988 which "provided most benefit to higher income Canadians

...resulted in total costs to federal and provincial treasuries of $4.5 billion annually" (Canadian Council on Social Development, 1992:12). In its brief to the House of Commons Legislative Committee studying child benefits the Canadian Council on Social Development asked:

> Critics of universal family allowance used to pose the following question: Why are Canadian taxpayers subsidizing bank presidents by providing them with a baby bonus they don't need? To be consistent these same critics should now ask the question: Why are Canadian taxpayers subsidizing the private pensions of those same bank presidents and many other upper income Canadians?

The combination of a neo-conservative national government, a business community with close connections to the government and a media largely controlled by business, united by a common interest in controlling inflation and reducing social benefits to the minimum, represents a powerful coalition dedicated to a residual approach to social policy. In its purest form, the residual or neo-conservative approach is based on a deeply held conviction that all citizens should be able to prosper on their own in a market-driven economic system and that to extend social benefits to anyone except the aged and disabled is to encourage dependency.

First we need an agenda for change and second a constituency. The agenda outlined here is based on McQuaig's comparison of social policies in North American and European countries. She concludes with the following recommendations:

1. Our social welfare system should be universal.
2. We should re-establish and strengthen our universal Family Allowance program.
3. There is also an urgent need to protect universality in health care and education.
4. We should establish universal day care.
5. We should make sex equality a top priority.
6. We should make fighting unemployment a top priority.
7. We should reform our social programs – not with the goal of cutting their costs – but with the goal of making them more effective and cost-efficient.
8. We should make our tax system fairer including an inheritance tax (McQuaig, 1993:21).

To this impressive and comprehensive set of reforms I would add that a reframing of work in Canadian society is in order. Among others, David Gil has argued for many years that:

> The way a society defines the concept "work" has important consequences for the circumstances of living of individuals. By excluding certain functions from the social and economic definition of work, persons assigned to those functions are deprived of economic rewards....Business executives who entertain prospective customers are "working" and so are professional ball players who throw balls, but volunteers who "entertain" patients in hospital or tutor slow-learning children in schools or women who clean their families' home, prepare meals and care for children are not "working" (Gil, 1990:103).

The particular reframing envisaged here is to define caring for children as work which deserves a wage. And while child care has traditionally been viewed as women's work for which pay has been unthinkable, some changes in attitudes can be discerned. Thus a Canadian organization, Wages for Housework, has been formed to push for wages for homemakers. "Ellen Woodsworth told a weekend conference on housework and family care that the $12 billion spent on Canada's defence budget would more than cover a wage for women working as home managers" (Times/Colonist, March 9, 1993:C2).

While some may dismiss this suggestion as impractical, particularly in view of the preoccupation with the deficit, the very existence of a deficit argues that we must rethink some basic and traditional assumptions. Why is it deemed appropriate to fund the defence budget from the public purse but not parental wages for child care? Why is it appropriate to support the Senate but not day care centres? Why is it deemed essential to spend $4.3 billion on military helicopters while at the same time eliminating $4.7 from federal contributions to post-secondary education (Andrews, 1992)?

Given this outline of a reform agenda to eliminate or reduce poverty and family crises, how might the agenda be implemented? I argue here that the changes are not likely to come from the national or even provincial levels of government but from social movements and from local institutions.

Connecting Public Issues and Personal Troubles

Despite awareness of the interconnectedness of public issues and private troubles through such theories as feminist, radical and ecological, social workers and other human service workers have found it extraordinarily difficult to implement their understandings in practice. The reasons are not difficult to identify and include policies which resolutely screen out connections between issues and troubles. For example, the assessment forms which child welfare workers in British Columbia are required to complete after investigating a report of alleged child abuse or neglect require information only about personal matters such as parent/child relationships and parenting skills. The assessment forms do not ask for information about income, housing and other socially relevant conditions. In addition, social workers experience working conditions characterized by heavy caseloads, crises and extensive reporting requirements, all of which make it difficult for them to give attention to the public issues side of their work.

Flowing from the above example, one strategy to connect public issues and private troubles is to require that human service agencies report on social conditions as part of their mandate. It would be relatively easy to change the reporting forms in child welfare agencies to include information on the socio-economic circumstances of their clients and to report this information on a regular basis. Indeed some agencies have extended this practice by establishing special projects to inquire into social and environmental conditions in the communities they serve. One example comes from a research study of the Public Health Department in Toronto, which examined the connections between socio-economic conditions and health. The report concluded that "we do not need more health care spending to create more health, we do not need more economic growth to create more health, but we do need more economic equity to create more health" (Toronto, City of, 1991:4).

A second strategy is to strengthen existing agencies and create additional ones which have as their raison d'être the connecting of issues and troubles. Some useful precedents come from feminist organizations like Transition Houses and Sexual Assault Centres which have combined services to women with public education and social reform. Other precedents with deep historical roots are settlement or neighbourhood houses. Indeed, the practitioners interviewed for this chapter argued that these agencies, providing as they do a range of programs, have the potential to overcome the deficiencies in the current arrangement of services.

Whether called neighbourhood houses, multi-service centres or family places, these agencies would provide family and individual counselling services nested within a range of self-help programs, day care, job readiness and employment training programs, and leisure time activities. Practitioners used adjectives like accessible, non-stigmatized, and comprehensive to describe the kind of agencies they had in mind. Further, these agencies would be organized on a neighbourhood basis, governed by boards of locally-elected citizens with representation from municipal and provincial governments. They would have the capacity to identify and respond to the needs of local residents and to advocate on their behalf. Such agencies might offer a range of preventive programs, including discussion groups for new parents and courses on child development and sexuality, and in so doing, encourage residents to deal with issues prior to the crisis stage.

An important dimension in this approach to human services is the need for close connections with and perhaps location in elementary schools. The rationale for connections is that schools provide the best universal auspices for services to children and families. Practitioners argued for reforms in school curricula to provide education for living, for schools to become centres of learning for adults as well as children, and for community governance of schools. They noted that transforming schools into community centres might alleviate some of the tensions which now characterize relationships between teachers and other human service workers. The tension frequently occurs when teachers, seeing only the plight of an individual child, push for child welfare workers to apprehend and the workers resist, knowing the ties which bind families and the often unsatisfactory nature of substitute care.

A third strategy is to develop new and innovative ways of providing service to these families. A joint project between the Ministry of Social Services and the School of Social Work at the University of Victoria is attempting the daunting task of changing child welfare practice from one characterized by investigation and casework with individual clients to a group and community work approach. In essence, the project requires that child welfare workers identify with the situation of their clients and work with them in obtaining the resources they require. The emerging evidence is that, while difficult to implement, the approach holds the promise of "protecting children by empowering women (Callahan, 1992)."

All of the above strategies have much in common with the mutual aid and social network approaches to working with families. These approaches are based on the assumption, noted in this chapter, that buffeted families live in isolation from family, friends and each other. Some carefully designed and evaluated projects have demonstrated that bringing isolated families together and assisting them to work together on issues of mutual importance can enhance self-confidence and reduce the incidence of child neglect and abuse. (See among others, Cochrane, 1988; Cameron, et al., 1992; Gaudin, et al., 1990/91; and Whittaker, 1986).

A fourth strategy of social learning can be implemented through neighbourhood houses and other agencies characterized by local governance. Here, I come to the closing argument of the chapter: that long-term change in societal priorities will come about only as ordinary citizens learn about the interrelatedness of public issues and private troubles. Such learning could include exposing poverty as a primary contributing factor to child neglect and thus advocate for increasing the finances available to poor families. It could also include striking neglect from child welfare legislation as a reason for apprehending children of poor families. Learning could include arguments for redefining work and providing a parental wage on the grounds that child care is work and work which should be valued by adequate recompense. It could include opportunities to learn about Canada's tax structure and the inequities which result from present arrangements. It could assist in the public education of citizens, and encourage citizens to become involved in social movements which push governments at all levels to bring about some fundamental changes in ruling arrangements. While no one would claim that the First Nations, women's and environmental movements have achieved all their goals, their gains have nevertheless been substantial.

The recommendations presented above are, to say the least, optimistic. It is apparent from the discussion that no single strategy will suffice to significantly alter the lives of buffeted families. The public issues of poverty and the lack of affordable housing can only be resolved by some fundamental changes in existing social policies and indeed in the ruling arrangements which govern social policy. However, one small step can be taken by establishing neighbourhood houses as the core component in the array of human services. Neighbourhood houses have the potential to provide effective responses to personal troubles and to ensure that public issues are not conveniently reframed as private troubles. By providing spaces for social learning, these and other locally-governed agencies can contribute to increased participation on the part of ordinary citizens and eventually, perhaps, to the reform of ruling arrangements.

PRACTITIONERS

Howie Anderson, District Supervisor, Ministry of Social Services, Province of British Columbia

Judy Burgess, Program Supervisor, James Bay Community Centre

David Letchford, Area Manager, Ministry of Social Services, Province of British Columbia

Dorothy Livingstone, President, Board of Directors, Capital Families Association

Barbara Loveday, Planning Associate, Community Social Planning Council

Linda Patterson, Planning Associate, Community Social Planning Council

Janet Rabinowitz, Social Planner, City of Victoria

Susan Robinson, Director, Transition House of Victoria

Sandra McConnell, Director, Parents in Crisis, Victoria

CHAPTER SIX

Crests and Crashes: The Changing Tides of Family Income Security

Sherri Torjman

INTRODUCTION

Describing family income security in Canada over the past few decades reads like a story of contradictions. On the one hand, average family income improved significantly in real terms. At the same time, many Canadian families suffered serious financial setbacks during the two recessions of the early 1980s and 1990s, which eroded long-term gains in average income and pushed up already-high rates of poverty. Moreover, Canadians face an uncertain future due to the fundamental restructuring of the economy and the growth of low-paid, casual employment. Changing family structures have also generated economic insecurity – especially for women and children.

Family income security has been buoyed to a certain extent by various government programs that supplement income and that provide a safeguard against absolute poverty. The security of families is also bolstered by a wide range of 'income in kind' delivered in the form of subsidies (e.g., rent supplementation, child care subsidies) and services (e.g., health services, licensed child care, counselling services, public housing). While this chapter focuses primarily upon income security programs, the contribution and support provided through subsidies and services must be recognized. Yet despite the help these programs provide, government cutbacks and 'reforms' to social programs over the past ten years in particular, have rattled family security and have exacted a high toll – especially upon low- and modest-income families (Battle and Torjman, 1993:1-7).

In short, the story of family income security is one of good news and bad news – of both crests and crashes.

The purpose of this chapter is to describe the major programs that supplement family income and that provide some protection in the event of unemployment, disability and retirement. It considers briefly the factors that influence income security and the role that governments have played in both supporting and shaking the family economic base. Finally, the chapter sets out policy options, including reference to international initiatives, that might be pursued to help stabilize and improve the income security of Canadian families.

Income Security

Canadian families rely primarily upon the labour market for their economic security. While the precise proportion varies from year to year, between 1982 and 1986 only about two percent of working-age adults belonged to families that had no income from paid employment for that five-year period (Economic Council of Canada, 1992:6).

But working in the labour force is no guarantee against poverty. One in five low-income families is headed by a man or woman who works full-time all year and another 34.3 percent are headed by someone working part-time (Statistics Canada, 1993:35, 176).[1] Many Canadians who work can find only low-wage jobs and part-time, casual or temporary employment. From 1982 through 1986, seven percent of families with income from work remained below the poverty line for the entire six-year period. The same percentage had work incomes that hovered just above the poverty line (Economic Council of Canada, 1992:5).

Clearly, employment earnings are not always sufficient or secure enough to protect against poverty. A wide range of social programs has been set up to supplement or replace work earnings. There are four categories into which income security programs fall: social insurances, universal programs, income-tested programs and needs-tested programs.

i. Social Insurances

Social insurances provide income protection by pooling contributions against designated risks such as unemployment, retirement and accidents on the job. Benefits are paid if contributors or eligible workers fall victim to the risk from which protection is ensured. Unemployment insurance, the Canada/Quebec Pension Plan and provincial workers' compensation plans – all employment-based programs – are the major social insurance programs in Canada.

ii. Universal Programs

Universal programs provide benefits to all households that meet certain criteria – such as old age or presence of children – regardless of their income. Benefits are not affected by the receipt of assistance from other income programs. Family allowances and the Old Age Security pension used to be delivered on a universal basis prior to the introduction of the "clawback" in 1989. These programs are discussed under Child Benefits and Retirement Benefits, respectively.

iii. Income-tested Programs

Income-tested programs deliver benefits to households that qualify on the basis of income. Households whose net incomes fall below a certain level called the 'threshold' receive the maximum benefit. Above the threshold, benefits decline relative to increases in net income. The 'reduction rate' is the amount by which benefits are reduced as income rises. Benefits end entirely when net incomes exceed a designated amount known as the 'cut-off point.'

Most income security programs in Canada are income-tested. The newly-introduced child tax benefit and the Guaranteed Income Supplement are examples of income-tested programs.

iv. Needs-tested Programs

Needs-tested programs take into account not only net income but also assets and extent of need. They are considered 'intrusive' because they require much more information than income-tested programs to determine eligibility. Social assistance – commonly referred to as 'welfare' – and the Quebec Parental Wage Assistance Program are needs-tested programs.

Income Security Programs

The programs described briefly below help offset the costs of raising children or provide a basic level of income in the event of unemployment, disability or retirement.

i. Child Benefits

a. Federal Child Tax Benefit

In 1992, the federal government announced the "Brighter Futures Initiative" which proposed a new child tax benefit that took effect January 1993.[2] The child tax benefit replaced the three major income programs for families with children: family allowances, the non-refundable child tax credit and the refundable child tax credit.[3]

The new child tax benefit is worth $1,233 for each child age 6 and under and $1,020 for each child age 7 to 17. Families with net incomes up to $25,921 in 1993 receive the maximum benefit. Both the benefits and threshold are partially indexed – by the amount of inflation less three percentage points. The third and each subsequent child receives an extra $75 a year.

Above the 'threshold', benefits are reduced by five percent for families with two or more children (five cents for every dollar above the income limit) and by 2.5 percent for families with only one child. The cut-off or disappearing point is $75,241 for a family with one or two children age 7 or under, $70,981 for a family with two children under and over age 7, and $66,721 for families with one or two children between the ages of 7 and 17. Families with employment earnings of $3,750 or more are eligible for an earned-income supplement worth a maximum $500 per family per year (Caledon Institute of Social Policy, 1992:7).[4]

b. Federal Tax Credits And Deductions

In addition to the child tax benefit, there are two other components to the child benefits system. The equivalent-to-married credit allows single parents to claim a non-refundable tax credit worth $915 in 1993 ($1,418 including average provincial income tax savings) in respect of the first child. The credit is equivalent to the amount permitted to married taxpayers whose spouses are not in the labour force.[5]

The child care expense deduction allows the lower-income spouse to deduct up to $5,000 per child age 6 and under and $3,000 per child age 7 to 17 in respect of receipted child care expenses. The maximum family limit of $8,000 for child care expenses was lifted in 1988. The value of the deduction increases with income.[6]

c. Provincial Benefits

Some provinces provide additional benefits to low-income families with children. Quebec grants an Allowance for Young Children as well as a birth allowance.[7] The province's Parental Wage Assistance Program or APPORT (Aide aux parents pour leurs revenus du travail) supplements the employment earnings of low-income families with children. The program provides an earnings supplement, a housing subsidy and an amount to offset child care costs. Assistance varies by family size, family type, income, child care costs, housing costs and other factors.[8]

Manitoba pays up to $30 a month per child under the Child-Related Income Support Program (CRISP). The maximum benefit goes to families with net incomes of $12,384 a year or less. The Family Income Plan (FIP) in Saskatchewan provides non-taxable cash assistance for eligible families with dependent children up to age 18. Up to $100 a month is paid for each of the first three children and $90 for each subsequent child. The maximum benefit goes to families with annual incomes below $8,700. Negotiations are underway between the federal and Saskatchewan governments to integrate the child tax benefit and FIP benefits into a single program.

In July 1993, Ontario announced its intention to dismantle its welfare system and to replace it by two new income programs: the Ontario Child Income Program and the Ontario Adult Benefit. While the "Turning Point" initiative provided no specific figures, it indicated that the new child benefit would be an income-tested program that would be delivered to all families (including welfare poor and working poor families) whose net incomes fall below designated levels. The benefit will vary not only by income but also by family size.

ii. Unemployment Benefits

Paid employment is the primary source of income for Canadian families. Unemployment insurance and welfare are the key programs that provide income support in the event of unemployment.

a. Unemployment Insurance

Unemployment insurance (UI) is a national program that provides income protection from temporary work absences arising from unemployment, illness, temporary disability, or birth or adoption of a child. The risk against which the insurance is afforded must be a temporary interruption; those unemployed over a prolonged period receive assistance under different programs – primarily welfare, described below.

In 1990, the federal government stopped contributing to the UI program, which is now funded entirely through employer and employee premiums. The qualifying period for benefits varies between 14 and 20 weeks, depending on the regional rate of unemployment. Eligible applicants receive 57 percent of their insurable earnings.[9] Eligible mothers may receive up to 15 weeks of UI maternity benefits worth 57 percent of insurable earnings. In addition, ten weeks of parental benefits are payable to the mother and/or father of a newborn or adopted child.[10]

b. Welfare

Welfare is the income program of last resort. It provides financial assistance to individuals and families whose resources are inadequate to meet their needs and who have exhausted other avenues of support.[11] While welfare generally is directed toward persons who are unemployed, it also can assist working households whose needs exceed their resources.

Each province and territory sets its own rules that govern eligibility for assistance, the amount of basic assistance, type and amount of special assistance, enforcement policies and provisions governing the appeal of decisions on individual cases. Despite the differences, all jurisdictions have several common features. Applicants must qualify according to provincial definitions and on the basis of a needs test, described earlier. Their liquid and fixed assets must not exceed designated levels. (As noted, Ontario announced in July 1993 its intention to dismantle the welfare system in that province and to replace it by two new income programs.)

Generally, provinces pay more generous benefits to single-parent mothers and to persons with disabilities than they do to employable households. Despite the higher levels of assistance for these recipients, welfare assistance falls well below the poverty line for all households in all parts of the country (National Council of Welfare, 1993:24-25).[12]

iii. Disability-Related Benefits

The disability income system is composed of a patchwork of programs. Eligibility is based on cause and severity of disability. Although the major disability-related income programs are identified here, there are several other important programs that provide income support including veterans' pensions, automobile accident insurance and private disability pension plans (Torjman, 1988).

a. Canada/Quebec Pension Plan Disability Benefits

The Canada/Quebec Pension Plan pays disability benefits to workers with severe and prolonged impairments who have made the required contributions. The disability benefit consists of two components: a flat-rate sum and an earnings-related portion worth a combined monthly maximum of $812.85 in 1993.

b. Workers' Compensation

Every province and territory has an employer-financed workers' compensation scheme to provide income in case of occupational injury, disability or disease. Employees receive compensation in the event of injury but abrogate their right to seek legal damages. Benefits are determined by the length and severity of the incapacity; lost earnings potential also may be taken into account. In addition to cash awards, workers' compensation plans include a variety of in-kind benefits, such as rehabilitation services.

c. Welfare

Persons with disabilities who have no other source of income or whose resources are insufficient to meet their needs may apply for welfare assistance, described earlier.

d. Tax Credits

There are two tax provisions that help offset disability-related costs: the disability credit and the medical expenses credit.[13] To qualify for the disability credit, claimants must be severely impaired in one or several of the major activities of everyday living.

Since 1990, the list of health-related items considered deductible under the medical expenses credit has expanded considerably (Torjman, 1993:56-59). Several provinces provide cash benefits or services for families caring at home for children with disabilities.[14]

iv. Retirement Benefits

Retirement benefits are provided through a three-tiered retirement income system (National Council of Welfare, 1989).

a. OAS/GIS/SPA

The first tier consists of the Old Age Security (OAS), Guaranteed Income Supplement (GIS) and Spouse's Allowance (SPA). The OAS pension is provided to all Canadians age 65 and over. While the OAS still is referred to as a 'universal' program, its universal foundation crumbled in 1989 when the federal government introduced a 'clawback' which requires upper-income pensioners to pay back all of their benefits.[15] In reality, Old Age Security is now an income-tested benefit. The income-tested Guaranteed Income Supplement helps lower-income elderly Canadians. The Spouse's Allowance is an income-tested benefit designed to help low-income Canadians ages 60 through 64 who are married to people 65 and older and who receive the Guaranteed Income Supplement.[16]

The second tier in the retirement income system is the Canada/Quebec Pension Plan (C/QPP). In contrast to the income-tested plans (OAS and GIS), the C/QPP is a social insurance program funded through employer and employee contributions. Benefits are paid to retired persons and to surviving spouses and children. Benefits vary according to the claimant's lifetime average earnings.[17]

Finally, there is a diverse range of employer-sponsored occupational pension plans that vary widely in terms of their benefits and features. While these private pensions are an important part of the retirement income system, they cover fewer than half of paid workers: most workers in the private sector, most women and most lower-paid employees work for employers that do not offer occupational pension plans.

Workers who do not belong to occupational pension plans (as well as those who do) may contribute to Registered Retirement Savings Plans. As with occupational pension plans, RRSPs are used largely by Canadians with above-average incomes.

Factors that Influence Income Security

i. Labour Market

The well-being of families is tied directly to the health of the economy (Baker, 1993:336-344). Since the mid-1960s, Canadian households have experienced both good times and hardship. Their incomes, and their well-being more generally, have risen and fallen in line with unemployment and interest rates.

Family income has increased substantially over the past 25 years. Figure 1 shows the steady rise in average family income from $33,000 in 1965 to $53,131 in 1991 (these figures are expressed in 1991 inflation-adjusted dollars). The only downturns reflect the two recessionary periods of the early 1980s and 1990s. The overall increase is due primarily to the dramatic rise in the labour force participation rate of women.[18] The presence of a second earner not only has bolstered family income but also has protected many families from impoverishment in the event that one earner falls unemployed.

Another important factor has contributed to the overall rise in incomes: the growth of average real (i.e., adjusted for inflation) wages. Between 1920 and 1970, in particular, there were substantial

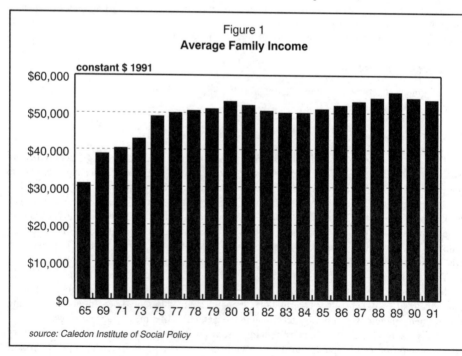

Figure 1
Average Family Income

source: Caledon Institute of Social Policy

increases in average real wages – from $6,773 in 1920 to $7,590 in 1930, $8,370 in 1940, $11,249 in 1950, $16,031 in 1960 and $21,928 in 1970 (Rashid, 1993:13). Overall, average wages in 1970 were 224 percent higher or more than triple what they were in 1920.

However, the steady and significant growth in real wages began to slow considerably after 1970, due primarily to rapidly-rising inflation. Between 1970 ($21,928) and 1980 ($23,791), the overall increase in average real wages was less than nine percent. The growth slowed even more dramatically between 1980 and 1990 – years marked by recession at both the beginning and close of the decade. Overall average real wages rose by only two percent during that period, from $23,791 in 1980 to $24,259 in 1990 (Rashid, 1993:13).

Moreover, for the first time, the average real wage of men fell slightly – from $29,871 in 1980 to $29,757 in 1990. Over the same period, by contrast, the average real wage of women grew substantially by 14 percent from $15,710 in 1980 to $17,933 in 1990, attributable partly to an increase in the proportion of women with higher levels of education and more work experience moving into better-paying jobs (Rashid, 1993:13). However, the wage gaps between the sexes remains wide; in 1990, women averaged only 60 percent of men's average wages (Rashid, 1993:19).

Despite the overall rise in average incomes, poverty remains high in Canada and has grown in response to the current recession. In 1991, 13.1 percent of all Canadian families were poor. Of these, 10.7 percent of two-parent families and 61.9 percent of single-parent families led by women were poor. See Figures 2 and 3. (Statistics Canada's low income cut-offs are used as the basis for poverty statistics.)

Moreover, Canadian families increasingly are insecure as a result of labour market changes. There is evidence of some polarization of the work force, with growth in both 'good' jobs and 'bad' jobs and a relative decline in middle-income employment (Economic Council of Canada, 1990). 'Good' jobs usually are associated with high salaries, a package of benefits and opportunities for

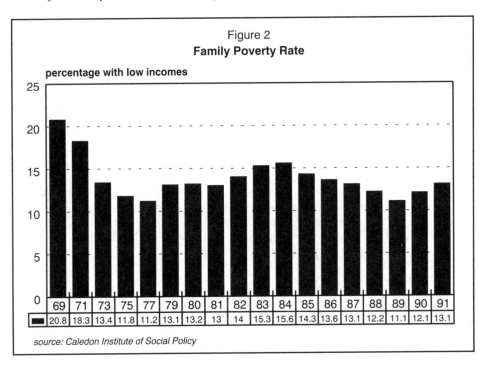

Figure 2
Family Poverty Rate

percentage with low incomes

69	71	73	75	77	79	80	81	82	83	84	85	86	87	88	89	90	91
20.8	18.3	13.4	11.8	11.2	13.1	13.2	13	14	15.3	15.6	14.3	13.6	13.1	12.2	11.1	12.1	13.1

source: Caledon Institute of Social Policy

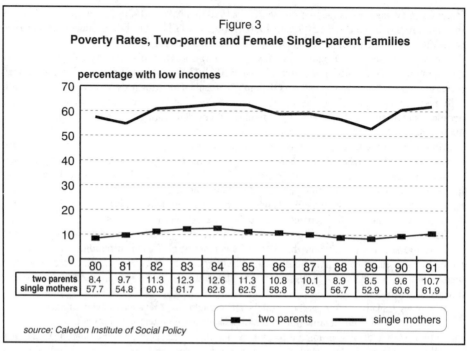

Figure 3
Poverty Rates, Two-parent and Female Single-parent Families

percentage with low incomes

	80	81	82	83	84	85	86	87	88	89	90	91
two parents	8.4	9.7	11.3	12.3	12.6	11.3	10.8	10.1	8.9	8.5	9.6	10.7
single mothers	57.7	54.8	60.9	61.7	62.8	62.5	58.8	59	56.7	52.9	60.6	61.9

━■━ two parents   ━━━ single mothers

source: Caledon Institute of Social Policy

training and promotion. 'Bad' jobs, by contrast, tend to have limited advancement and on-the-job training opportunities, are often unstable, demand little in the way of formal qualifications and rarely provide private pensions, union membership or job satisfaction, let alone security. Bad jobs not only generate insecurity but also give rise to uncertain, poverty-bound futures.

Finally, despite its positive economic impact, rising labour force participation by women also has created emotional stresses. Women remain primarily responsible for family-related matters, regardless of their employment status.[19]

One of the most serious stresses arises from the fact that Canada lacks an adequate system of high-quality, affordable child care. More than one-half of preschool-age children regularly need care while their parents work (Friendly, Rothman and Oloman, 1991). The demand for child care far outweighs the supply (Lero, Goelman, Pence, Brockman and Nuttall, 1992:14)

The federal government backed away from its promise to increase the availability of licensed child care spaces when it failed to pass the Child Care Act in 1988 and did not proceed with alternative legislation. Ottawa said it could not afford the additional funds for high-quality, licensed care; it did, however, raise the value of the child care expense deduction that favors high-income families. Poor and modest-income families that gain little or no benefit from the deduction must line up for scarce child care spaces and often must use unlicensed care of variable quality (Battle and Torjman, 1993:3).

ii. Family Structure

Labour market factors tell only part of the story. The high rate of poverty in Canada also reflects the dramatic rise in the number of single-parent families, due to the growth in separation and divorce rates and the small, but increasing, number of women raising their children without living with or marrying the father. In 1991, there were close to one million single-parent families in Canada, a 34 percent increase from 1981. The vast majority of lone parents in Canada are women; they represented 82 percent of all single parents in 1991 (Lindsay, 1992).

Single-parent families experience very high rates of poverty, regardless of the performance of the economy. In 1989, the 'best' year of the economic recovery from the 1981-82 recession, more than half (52.9 percent) of one-parent families led by women were poor. These families live far below the poverty line; in 1990, their incomes came to only 60.7 percent of Statistics Canada's low-income cut-offs (National Council of Welfare, 1991:42).

Single parents are more likely to be unemployed than two-parent families; in 1991, 16.8 percent of female and 15.7 percent of male lone parents were unemployed compared to 9.6 percent of women and 7.7 percent of men in two-parent families with children (Lindsay, 1992). The incomes of single parents also are lower than two-parent families. In 1991, the average income of female-led single-parent families was $22,186 or 38 percent of that ($59,014) of two-parent families with children (Statistics Canada, 1992a:27).

Single mothers who must rely on support payments are particularly insecure; child support default rates are as high as 80 percent in some provinces. Moreover, the average amount of these payments – $400 per month – is relatively small (Galarneau, 1993:9). As a result, many single parents must rely on welfare – a passport to poverty.

iii. Government Programs

Government programs in the form of both taxes and transfers (i.e., income security programs and tax credits) have a significant impact upon family income security. Figure 4 shows the 'wave-like pattern' of average family income between 1971 and 1991. The dotted line represents market income – i.e., income from employment, private pensions, interest and other private sources before

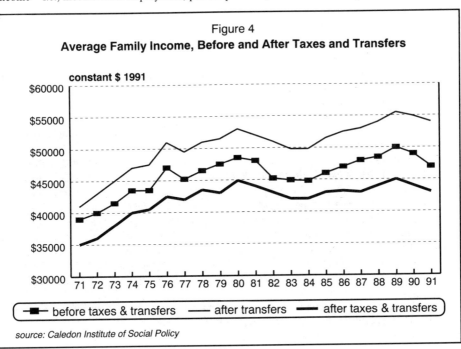

Figure 4
Average Family Income, Before and After Taxes and Transfers

constant $ 1991

legend: before taxes & transfers — after transfers — after taxes & transfers

source: Caledon Institute of Social Policy

income taxes and transfers such as child benefits, unemployment insurance and welfare. The long-term improvement is clear, as is the dampening effect of the two recessions that began and ended the 1980s. The impact of government programs described earlier is also readily apparent: they boost average family income, as depicted by the thin line. The thick line shows the combined effect of income taxes and transfers on average family income. The impact of income taxes is evident: they lower average income below the level of market income. However, their burden is offset partly by transfers.

Government taxes and transfers help lessen inequality. In 1991, families in the highest income quintile (those with incomes over $57,990) had 44.1 percent of all market income, while families in the bottom quintile (those with incomes below $23,132) got only 2.4 percent of market income. In other words, families in the highest income group had 18 times the share of market income of families in the lowest income group. However, once the redistributive effects of taxes and transfers are factored into the equation, the highest income families' share fell to 37.3 percent and the lowest income group's share rose to 7.7 percent. The gap between the top and bottom groups dropped to five times.

While transfers help raise family income and to some extent reduce income inequality, several factors have had the opposite effect. The federal government's changes to income taxes have increased substantially the tax burden and hit modest-income families and individuals particularly hard. The recent string of provincial budgets will weaken the moderating effect of government transfers as the taxperson dips further and further into the pockets of modest- and middle-income families. Many families would be destitute without transfer payments such as unemployment insurance and welfare. Yet these programs generally provide benefits that fall below poverty levels.

Moreover, cuts and amendments to major social programs have impeded seriously their ability to boost income – let alone make a dent in poverty. The poor were hurt by Ottawa's announcement, in 1990, of plans to limit federal transfers to Ontario, Alberta and British Columbia for cost-sharing welfare and social services under the Canada Assistance Plan (CAP) to an increase of five percent a year for 1990-91 and 1991-92. In 1991, this 'cap on CAP' was extended through 1994-95.

The elimination of family allowances and the non-refundable child tax credit through the introduction of the child tax benefit in 1993 destroyed the principle of horizontal equity – i.e., recognition of the fact that taxpayers who are parents have heavier financial responsibilities than taxpayers at the same income level who do not support children.

Moreover, the child tax benefit added only $500 a year to the former child benefit programs. Because the $500 is provided as an earned-income supplement for the working poor, families on unemployment insurance or welfare – the poorest of the poor – get no more child benefits than they did under the former programs. Only larger eligible families receive slightly higher benefits: an extra $75 for the third and each subsequent child. This will not help the vast majority of Canadian families that have only one or two children (Battle and Torjman, 1993:2). The new child tax benefit (like the programs it replaced) is not adequately protected against inflation, so that benefits will erode in future and fewer and fewer low-income families will be eligible for the maximum payment.

In short, the child tax benefit will have little impact on child poverty. In fact, its design allows families with two children under and over age 7 to continue to receive some benefits up to net incomes of $70,981. The problem is serious, given the rates of child poverty in Canada. In 1991, one in five children age 18 or under (1,210,000 children) was living in a poor family. The picture for children living in single-parent families was more bleak; in 1991, 66 percent of all children (496,000) raised by single mothers were poor.[20]

These figures represent a serious problem, given what we know about the impact of poverty upon children. There is evidence that children from poor families are twice as likely as children from non-poor families to suffer death in the first year, death from accidents, physical disabilities, grade failures, school dropout, and inadequate opportunities for recreation, skill and cultural development (Barnhorst and Johnson, 1991:100,105). The risks are especially high for Aboriginal children. Children from poor families experience a greater incidence of chronic health problems including bronchitis, asthma, digestive disorders, anemia, sight disorders, mental disorders, diabetes and heart disease. Low income all too often results in poor diets for pregnant women; inadequate nutrition, in turn, may result in low birth weight, which increases the risk for illness, poor development and infant death (Ryerse, 1990:21-25).

iv. Social Spending

Despite recent cuts and 'amendments' to social programs, overall social spending has continued to increase in real terms. The steady rise is due primarily to two factors.

The rapidly growing numbers of aged Canadians has driven up spending on elderly benefits. Figure 5 shows that the costs for the foundation of the pension system (OAS/GIS/SPA) rose from $14.9 billion in 1982 to $19.6 billion in 1993. Canada Pension Plan spending follows the same steady rise (Figure 6).

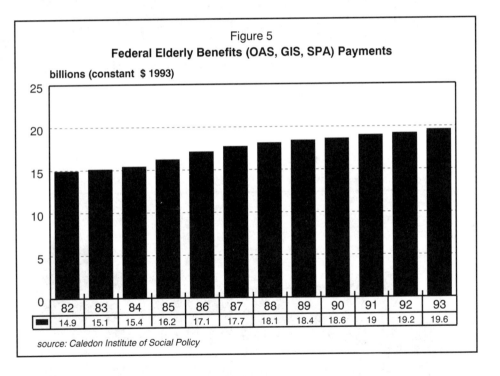

Figure 5
Federal Elderly Benefits (OAS, GIS, SPA) Payments

billions (constant $ 1993)

	82	83	84	85	86	87	88	89	90	91	92	93
■	14.9	15.1	15.4	16.2	17.1	17.7	18.1	18.4	18.6	19	19.2	19.6

source: Caledon Institute of Social Policy

The second major factor that accounts for the overall increase in social spending is the 'recessionary compensation' represented by the considerable growth in UI costs in the early 1990s (Figure 7) and in welfare spending through federal transfers under CAP (Figure 8). Welfare spending has gone up despite the 'cap on CAP', providing strong evidence of the cost pressures generated by rising caseloads (Figure 9).[21]

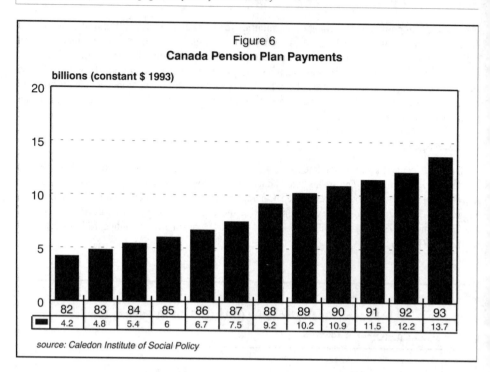

Figure 6
Canada Pension Plan Payments

billions (constant $ 1993)

	82	83	84	85	86	87	88	89	90	91	92	93
	4.2	4.8	5.4	6	6.7	7.5	9.2	10.2	10.9	11.5	12.2	13.7

source: Caledon Institute of Social Policy

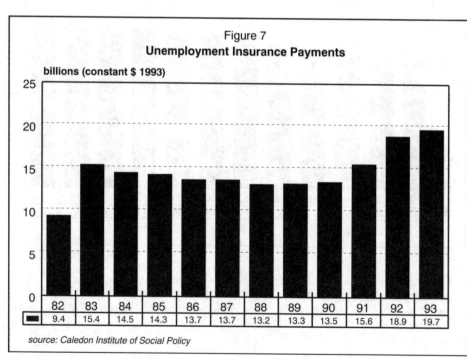

Figure 7
Unemployment Insurance Payments

billions (constant $ 1993)

	82	83	84	85	86	87	88	89	90	91	92	93
	9.4	15.4	14.5	14.3	13.7	13.7	13.2	13.3	13.5	15.6	18.9	19.7

source: Caledon Institute of Social Policy

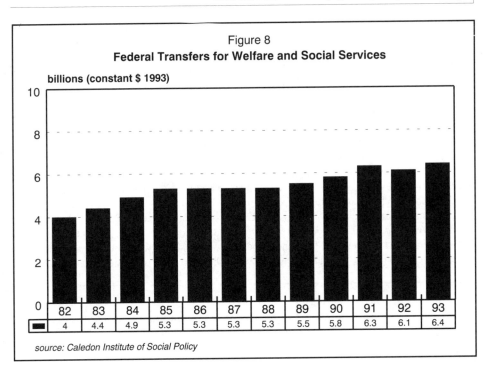

Figure 8
Federal Transfers for Welfare and Social Services

billions (constant $ 1993)

	82	83	84	85	86	87	88	89	90	91	92	93
	4	4.4	4.9	5.3	5.3	5.3	5.3	5.5	5.8	6.3	6.1	6.4

source: Caledon Institute of Social Policy

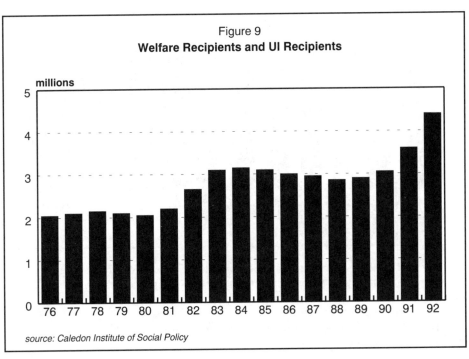

Figure 9
Welfare Recipients and UI Recipients

millions

source: Caledon Institute of Social Policy

The rise in federal payments to individuals does not represent a substantial increase in the adequacy of the program benefits these transfers represent. Nor is it due to any dramatic policy initiatives to provide greater assistance to Canadians. The rise in spending is a response to demographic and labour market factors that together exert substantial pressure on income security programs. In short, federal transfers to individuals have risen because there are more elderly and unemployed Canadians.

In contrast to the growth in spending for individuals, federal transfers to the provinces that help pay for health and post-secondary education have dropped considerably. In 1986, federal transfers under Established Programs Financing were partially indexed to the increase in GNP less two percentage points rather than the full change in GNP. In 1990, these payments were frozen at their 1989-90 level for two years. The freeze was subsequently extended until the end of 1994-95, after which the formula will be partially indexed to the increase in GNP less three percentage points.

This technical change to the funding arrangement will remove vast sums of federal money from these services – an estimated $98 billion on a cumulative basis between 1986 and 2000 (National Council of Welfare, 1991:18). Figure 10 shows the rapid and steady decline in federal transfers under EPF between 1984-85 and 1992-93. The withdrawal of transfers will impede Ottawa's ability to uphold the principles of accessible and comprehensive health care set out in the Canada Health Act.

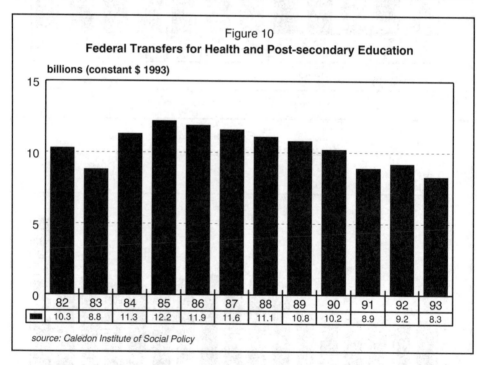

Figure 10
Federal Transfers for Health and Post-secondary Education

billions (constant $ 1993)

	82	83	84	85	86	87	88	89	90	91	92	93
▬	10.3	8.8	11.3	12.2	11.9	11.6	11.1	10.8	10.2	8.9	9.2	8.3

source: Caledon Institute of Social Policy

The impact of the cuts in transfers under EPF is profound. Provinces are being forced to cut back on health services, raise taxes or consider charging user fees to offset the shortfall. Cuts to post-secondary educational institutions may threaten future income security by hurting Canada's ability to compete in a fierce global economy.

The reduction in EPF transfers does not merely affect provincially-funded services. Its impact is more far-reaching in that it limits the amount of funds that provinces can transfer to municipalities for police and fire services, sewage treatment and water, and recreation as well as to school boards for education. In short, the infrastructure of many communities – in terms of both physical structure and public services – is being seriously eroded as a result of cuts in federal funding to the provinces.

The decline in public funds for human services creates pressures for the voluntary sector as well. At a time when the demand for these services is high and growing, voluntary organizations – such as family counselling agencies and food banks – are caught in a squeeze as funds for their support become increasingly scarce.

Policy Options

Income security has improved over the years for many Canadian families primarily because of the contribution to family incomes made by women and improvements in public pensions. Despite the rise in average family income, poverty in Canada remains high and the overall security of Canadian families has been shaken substantially by a radically different labour market and changing family structures. Recent changes in taxes and social programs have weakened federal support for families.

The most fundamental action that can be taken to reduce poverty and promote income security is to ensure that all families have access to the means to provide for their economic support. In short, the best form of income security is a good job. An economy which tolerates an unemployment rate of 11.5 percent translates into income insecurity for many Canadians.

Yet an adequate supply of jobs is only part of the answer. The income security system in Canada is based largely on social insurance programs which require labour force attachment. This means that jobs provide access not only to current income security but to future income security as well through retirement pensions. Many jobs coming on the market provide a wage but have no associated benefits – in particular, an occupational pension plan. Other labour market interventions – such as adequate and indexed minimum wages and human resource development in the form of apprenticeships, training and student employment - are key economic measures to help promote income security (Ross and Shillington, 1991).

Even when workers are 'fortunate' enough to be employed, they face a built-in 'wage bias.' Not surprisingly, young and inexperienced workers have lower earnings, on average, than older, more experienced workers. In 1991, males between the ages of 25 and 34, 35 and 44, and 45 and 54 earned an average $27,633, $37,417 and $39,728, respectively; women earned an average $19,138, $22,057 and $22,112 (Statistics Canada, 1993:43). The difficulty for families arises from the fact that the earnings of both men and women tend to be relatively low at a time when financial pressures – particularly in the form of child-rearing costs – are generally high. Young single-parent family heads face an especially onerous burden.

At the social policy level, the federal government should renew its commitment to high-quality, affordable child care by directing funds toward licensed child care rather than toward the child care expense deduction that provides the greatest benefit to higher-income families. Both public and private employers should recognize family needs through flexible work arrangements, leave for family responsibility and employer-supported child care subsidies or centres. Canada's maternity and parental leave provisions are less generous than most other industrialized nations (Townson, 1986).

The income security of one-earner families is equally important; the financial status, pension protection and child care needs of work-at-home mothers must be addressed. In an effort to measure the value of 'invisible' contributions – care of children and the elderly, housework and volunteer work – Statistics Canada plans to ask about unpaid work in the 1996 Census.

The Federal/Provincial/Territorial Family Law Committee should continue its efforts to reform the child support systems that govern child maintenance payments (Federal/Provincial/Territorial Law Committee, 1992). Child benefits and tax credits can be made more adequate and, at the very least, protected from erosion by restoring full indexation to the child benefits and personal income tax systems. Comprehensive income security reform might include a substantially higher, more-targeted child benefit; wage supplementation for families with children; or some form of guaranteed income that replaces several existing income security programs.

The federal government should stop removing funds from health care by restoring full indexation in transfers to the provinces. It should renew its commitment to social housing, recently shaken by a series of successive freezes and cuts.

Despite the need for substantial improvements, Canada does support a wider range of income security initiatives and social programs than many other countries of the world. Canada is well ahead of the U.S., for example, in the provision of universally accessible health care. The U.S. federal government, however, makes significant investments in Head Start and school lunch programs for poor children.

While the Canadian mix of cash transfers, tax deductions, parental leave provisions and services is similar to those of many European countries, there are some lessons to be learned from overseas initiatives (Dumon, 1992; Kamerman and Kahn, 1981). Several countries, notably France, Belgium and Sweden, explicitly recognize the collective responsibility for supporting working parents through a range of child care services, parental leave provisions and cash benefits.

Eleven of the 12 member states of the European Community have advance maintenance payment systems in which governments assume responsibility for collecting and distributing spousal and child support payments subsequent to separation or divorce. This represents a policy response to the high rates of default of these payments. Germany, for example, passed an Advance Payments Maintenance Act, effective January 1993, that raises the age of the child to whom maintenance payments are guaranteed from 6 to 12 years and the length of payment from three to a maximum six years.

In 1990, Spain introduced non-contributory pensions for retirement and permanent disability – a form of guaranteed income to fill in the gaps in the contributory insurances. France has brought in measures to 'economize' domestic forms of work through explicit recognition of 'family jobs.' Ireland's 'Plan for Social Housing' encourages low-income households to purchase houses through a co-ownership scheme with local authorities.

Unfortunately, substantial and substantive improvements to income programs, and to social programs more generally, are unlikely in these times of fiscal restraint. The problem is more serious than simply a lack of funds; the mindset of restraint also generates a poverty-of-ideas mentality that tends to stifle innovation.

Conclusion

The past 25 years have seen a steady real (after inflation) rise in average family incomes, declining only in the recessions of the early 1980s and 1990s. The rise is due primarily to the contributions to family incomes made by a second earner (i.e., wives); the growth in average real wages, by contrast, has slowed considerably since 1970. Moreover, the average wage of men fell slightly for the first time between 1980 and 1990. Despite the substantial rise in women's average real wages between 1980 and 1990, their average wages still are only 60 percent of men's average wages. In addition, the overall 'good news' of increasing average family incomes is tempered by the fact that poverty remains unacceptably high in Canada – especially for single-parent families – and has grown as a result of the current recession.

The primary source of economic security – the labour market – has become increasingly insecure as the globalization of production and trade force a restructuring of national economies. Meanwhile, another fundamental restructuring is under way: the profile of Canadian families has been substantially transformed in the areas of marriage and divorce, labour force participation and parenting.

To a certain extent, government programs have helped cushion the impact of this economic and social restructuring. Income security programs, in particular, supplement family income and provide protection in the event of job loss due to unemployment, disability or retirement. Yet the benefits they pay are often no higher than subsistence levels. In addition, family income security has been weakened by a series of changes to taxes and social programs that especially have hurt low- and modest-income families.

Canada will have to work hard to make good its signature on the UN Convention on the Rights of the Child that it ratified in 1991. Family income security should not read like a story of unpredictably rough tides. The federal government must take charge at the helm and chart a course through the current storm into calmer seas. It must pursue economic and social policies that actively promote, rather than shake, the foundations of family income security.

Endnotes

1. *Full-time work refers to 30 hours or more per week for 49 to 52 weeks. Part-time work refers to 29 hours a week or less for 49 to 52 weeks or less than 49 weeks.*

2. *As part of the "Brighter Futures Initiative" announced in 1992, the federal government established a Child Development Initiative Fund worth $500 million to promote the health and well-being of children at risk.*

3. *Family allowances had been delivered on a universal basis in that they provided a monthly benefit to all families with children, regardless of family income. In 1973, family allowances were made taxable; middle- and higher-income families were required to pay back part of the benefit. Nonetheless, the allowances were still universal in that all families with children continued to keep all or a substantial part of their benefits. In 1989, the universal foundation of family allowances crumbled when the federal government introduced the 'clawback', a tax measure which reduced benefits by 15 cents for every dollar of the higher-income parent's net income over $50,000. The clawback was phased in by one third over three years so that affected families paid back only one third in 1989; by 1991, the clawback was fully in place.*

4. *As with the former family allowances, Quebec varies the rate of the child tax benefit – worth $72.41 per month for the first child, $83.33 for the second child and $138.08 for the third and each additional child in 1993. These benefits are increased by $8.58 per month for each child age 12 and over. Quebec also provides its own family allowances worth $10.91, $14.54, $18.18 and $21.78 a month in 1993 for the first, second, third and each subsequent child, respectively.*

5. *Non-refundable tax credits act to reduce federal and provincial tax payable. Refundable credits, by contrast, reduce federal tax payable and provide a cash benefit for low- and modest-income families.*

6. *A $5,000 deduction, for example, is worth $1,318 in federal and average provincial income tax savings for a claimant earning $35,000, $2,015 for a taxfiler earning $50,000 and $2,248 for a parent earning $75,000.*

7. *The Allowance for Young Children is worth $9.77 a month in 1993 for the first child age 6 and under, $19.53 for the second such child and $48.83 for each additional child. The Quebec birth allowance is worth $500, $1,000 and $8,000 for the birth or adoption of the first, second and third child, respectively.*

8. *In 1993, the maximum annual assistance for single-parent families with one child is $3,030 as an earnings supplement, $1,675 for partial reimbursement of child care, $1,080 as a special housing allowance – for a total annual maximum of $5,785. Two-parent families with two children may receive up to $7,085 a year: $4,330 as an earnings supplement, $1,675 in respect of child care and $1,080 as a housing allowance. In general, the earned-income component of the benefit supplements earnings by 33 percent up to designated thresholds. Beyond these levels, the supplement is reduced by 42 percent. The base benefit for child care is calculated by taking 67 percent of child care costs; the benefit is reduced by 25 percent of the lesser of child care costs or the amount by which total income exceeds the designated threshold for that family.*

9. *Effective April 4, 1993, UI benefits were reduced from 60 to 57 percent of average weekly insurable earnings. UI benefits were denied to employees who quit their jobs without 'just cause.' In 1992, the maximum weekly benefit was $426; the average weekly benefit was $261.09.*

10. *Parental benefits may be extended to 15 weeks where the child is six months or older upon arrival at the claimant's home and suffers from a physical, emotional or psychological condition.*

11. *Although welfare often is referred to as though it were one single program, there are 12 welfare programs in Canada – one in every province and territory. In fact, there are actually hundreds of welfare programs because these are administered by municipalities in the two-tier provinces of Nova Scotia, Ontario and Manitoba. 'Two-tier' refers to the fact that the provincial government provides benefits to recipients considered to be unemployable over prolonged periods of time and municipal governments provide assistance to persons considered to be temporarily unemployed. In July 1993, Ontario announced its intention to dismantle its welfare system and replace it by two new income programs.*

12. *In 1992, welfare benefits for single parents with one child, for example, ranged from a low of 55 percent of the poverty line in New Brunswick (annual welfare income of $9,956) to a 'high' of 80 percent in Ontario (welfare income of $16,517). Welfare incomes for a couple with two children ranged from $11,932 (45 percent of the poverty line) in New Brunswick to $21,977 (73 percent of the poverty line) in Ontario.*

13. *The disability credit is worth an estimated $720 in 1993 ($1,116 when federal and average provincial income tax savings are taken into account). The medical expenses credit permits the deduction of up to 17 percent of allowable health-related costs (e.g., attendant care) in excess of three percent of net income.*

14. *Families in Newfoundland may be eligible for a special allowance of up to $424 per month. Prince Edward Island grants financial support on a sliding scale. The In-Home Support Program in Nova Scotia provides financial support and other services to help families with children with severe disabilities. Up to $300 a month may be granted to help cover costs such as medications, equipment and services. In-home training helps parents with children's spe-*

cial needs. In Quebec, parents receive assistance to care for their children with severe disabilities under the program "Soutien aux familles des personnes ayant une déficience physique ou présentant une déficience intellectuelle". Quebec also grants a non-taxable allowance worth $119.22 a month as of January 1993 for families with children who are severely disabled. Ontario families may qualify for a Handicapped Children's Benefit of between $25 and $375 a month to help offset disability-related costs. The Children's Special Services program in Manitoba makes available respite, child development services, transportation in rural areas, supplies and equipment for families whose children have complex, lifelong needs. Under the Handicapped Children's Services Program in Alberta, families may receive counselling related to the child's disability, assistance for medically-prescribed diets, prescription drugs, dental and orthodontic services if required as a result of the disability, day care fees for extraordinary disability-related costs, rehabilitation services and non-education fees such as registration for community programs. The benefits under the At Home Program in B.C. include Pharmacare and medical services, premium coverage, health care supplies, medical transportation and ambulance costs, optical equipment, prosthetics and orthotics, and respite.

15. The old age pension is reduced by 15 cents for every dollar of the senior's net individual income between $50,000 and $76,333, above which the full pension must be repaid. Because the clawback is partially indexed, it will catch more pensioners every year as it drops in value relative to inflation.

16. From October to December 1993, the Old Age Security pension was worth $384.66 a month; the benefit is indexed quarterly. The Guaranteed Income supplement for a single person was $457.13 between October and December 1993. The Spouse's Allowance was worth $682.42 a month from October to December 1993 and $753.38 for a married recipient.

17. In 1993, the maximum C/QPP retirement benefit was $667.36 a month.

18. Over the past two decades, women ages 15 and over accounted for 72 percent of the rise in employment between 1975 and 1991. During this period, the total number of working women increased 65 percent from 3.4 million to 5.6 million. The proportion of married women with children, in particular, has risen dramatically. In 1991, 63 percent of mothers with children under 16 were employed – up from 50 percent in 1981.

19. A recent national study (reported in "Canadian Social Trends", Spring 1993, Catalogue 11-008E, p. 6) found that women are more than twice as likely as men to be absent from work because of personal or family responsibilities. During an average week in 1991, 3 percent of employed women versus 1.2 percent of employed men lost some time from work for these reasons. While employers are increasingly aware of the need for family-responsive policies, only a small percentage have actually introduced policies and programs that help employees balance their work and family responsibilities.

20. Figures provided by Ken Battle, President of the Caledon Institute of Social Policy.

21. While this includes the transfers for both welfare and social services, the greatest proportion of CAP spending goes toward the payment of welfare.

CHAPTER SEVEN

Families, Health and Health Care

Jane Fulton

Acknowledgement

   The author wishes to acknowledge the contribution of Dr. R.W. Sutherland in the sourcing of information for this chapter.

INTRODUCTION

The decisions made by governing bodies affect our safety, our opportunities, and our social and economic institutions, all of which affect our health. These decisions are the product of the talent and values of decision-makers as well as the pressures acting upon them. The actions taken to improve health have changed over time. The first big advances in health status were due to socioeconomic and public health measures which included improvements in housing and water supply, the preservation of food, the pasteurization of milk, sewage control, garbage disposal, and control of communicable disease. These were followed by an acceleration of scientific and technological progress, by the prevention and cure of infectious diseases and by a greater understanding of mental health problems and endemic chronic diseases. Associated with the onslaught of chronic diseases was the need for new treatment and prevention strategies but especially for new attitudes toward the relative importance of state of mind as distinct from state of body. A third phase of health protection is related to the burgeoning volume of social and environmental pathology. We are still adapting to these and are not, as yet, skilful at dealing with them or at recognizing how and why they develop.

Good health is difficult to maintain in individuals who must act and live in communities shaped by forces beyond their control. Yet the total health of Canadians is influenced heavily by those factors that strengthen and promote such things as mental health, security, nondestructive lifestyles, safer workplaces and a healthier environment. In any discussion of health in Canada, we should remember that increasing our material standard of living may not increase our level of health proportionately. At the moment, we measure national success in terms of gross national product (GNP) or balance of payments; we should also be developing measures of quality of life, including group tolerance, capacity for compassion and willingness to share.

The major determinants of health are today, as always, outside of the purview and mandate of the health care system. They include the level of employment, the quality of interpersonal interaction, the quality of our social and physical environments, and the safety of our workplaces. At this time, we often ignore major threats to health while lavishly supporting selected health services whose impact on health is much smaller than we might believe.

Defining Health

Protection and improvement of the health of Canadians are the most basic objectives of Canadian public policy and health services. Health will be considered to be, first of all, a reasonably optimistic and contented state of mind. This definition is preferred because state of mind is usually the major determinant of quality of life, and an acceptable quality of life is what makes life worth living. The greatest threats to the health of Canadians are therefore not necessarily those things which end our lives or interfere with our physical perfection, but those things which ruin the quality of life. To concentrate on preserving life can be discouraging because in the end, everyone must die; concentrating on preserving quality of life is, however, apt to be rewarding because quality can almost always be improved. None of this is meant to suggest that the preservation of life and of physical health is not important. Obviously, poor physical health can seriously damage the quality of life.

If the protection and improvement of state of mind, or quality of life, are the primary objectives of health services, then these services will be delivered with enthusiasm and purpose even if a life is near its end, although the nature of the services may change. Because quality of life is subjective, health workers cannot protect or improve it until they know what is important to each patient. Services can then be offered in ways that are compatible with, and in support of, the priorities of the patient and his or her family.

Recently the World Health Organization, European Region, has defined health as a resource for everyday living, and as the extent to which an individual or group is able to realize aspirations and satisfy needs while also changing with, or coping with, the environment. Others have defined health as physical and mental well-being; as freedom from disease, pain, or defect; and as normal physical and mental functioning. In contrast to this broad definition, health care professionals tend to think of health as the absence of physical abnormalities.

Mental health and emotional health can be used synonymously but there is also, at times, a degree of difference. Mental health carries a more psychiatric connotation. Mental ill health, therefore, tends to be associated with institutional care and inability to function in society. Emotional ill health, on the other hand, may be seen as the depression or anxiety or panic that happens to "normal" people. Emotional disorders are predominantly a reaction to some situation, like bereavement, unemployment, failure, loss of independence, lack of socialization, or continuing insecurity.

Social health is a collective term applying to populations rather than individuals. Social pathology exists when too many members of a population experience undesirable states or characteristics, such as fear or anxiety. Social health, as well as individual health, is threatened by such things as unemployment, war or the threat of war, starvation, or natural disaster.

Not only do we have trouble with the word "health," but the definitions of "disease" and "illness" are also unclear. Because health services have been created to respond to ill health or injury, our network of services will change as our concept of ill health changes.

There is no clear distinction between health and ill health, normal and abnormal, the point where no external support or care is needed and the point where it is justified. What is called disease or illness obviously changes with the perceptions of the victims, caregivers, observers or policymakers involved. There can be disagreement as to whether or not disease or sickness exists. Disease is often described as the biomedically demonstrable condition, whereas illness is considered to be what the patient experiences.

Measures of Healthiness

Mortality data are still often used as measures of the healthiness of a population. Mortality data tell us about what appears to have caused us to die but they do not tell us much about how healthy we are. About 200,000 Canadians die annually: of these about one half die from diseases of the circulatory system. Within this category the biggest killer is coronary artery disease. Another 20-25 percent of deaths are caused by cancer (Sutherland and Fulton, 1992).

A different picture emerges if one counts the extent to which different hazards shorten life as well as end it. This approach gives added emphasis to deaths that are premature. A death at age 45 represents about 30 years of life lost, whereas a death at age 70 represents a loss of only 5-6 years from average life expectancy. Using this approach of "potential years of life lost," the big two (circulatory disease and cancer) are joined and sometimes surpassed by the effects of injuries. Accidents and suicide are the big killers of children and young adults (Statistics Canada, 1992).

The five greatest contributors to loss of potential years of life of males are coronary heart disease, car accidents, suicide, lung cancer and perinatal mortality. This is the order of importance of these causes of premature deaths in most parts of Canada, although in the Yukon and the Northwest Territories suicide is first. This information is critical when considering how to improve the health of Canadians and how to avoid premature deaths. The first four of the five conditions respond better to prevention than treatment and the fifth is partially the result of avoidable factors. The picture for females is essentially the same with the exception that breast cancer is usually in the top five (Greenwald, 1992; Statistics Canada, 1992).

Physical fitness and those programs to promote it will, for many people, reduce morbidity and mortality. For other persons, morbidity and mortality will be increased, but the net effect of physical activity is very positive. It seems likely that most persons who participate regularly in recreational physical fitness activities find them enjoyable and emotionally rewarding as well as physically useful. It is quite possible that fitness activities are more important as sources of improved quality of life than of lengthened life.

The relationship between income and health is a direct one. People who live in impoverished families tend to have higher rates of morbidity and mortality at all ages (National Council of Welfare, Autumn 1990: 6). Low incomes make it difficult for families to eat nutritious meals, to protect their children from crime and accidents, to take well-needed holidays, to pay for prescriptions and nutritional supplements, and to afford safe and comfortable accommodation. Living on inadequate incomes over time affects people's feelings of optimism and efficacy. For Canadians who are not employed, public policy determines their level of income through pensions, welfare payments, unemployment insurance and workers' compensation. Yet neither levels of social assistance nor minimum wages in most provinces have kept up with rising living costs (National Council of Welfare, 1992).

Canada's Health Care System

The current philosophical underpinnings of Canada's health services are, to a large extent, a product of former decades. Canada has, in theory, opted for: (a) egalitarian rather than elitist or market-based access to health care; (b) the right of every individual to approve or reject recommended care, to approve or reject a healthy/unhealthy lifestyle, or to accept or reject almost any form of risk; (c) greater societal response to physical ill-health or injury than to mental or psychosocial difficulty; (d) protection of children against public or individual decisions which are not in their best interests; and (e) collective priorities and practices determined increasingly through public policy rather than by providers.

There is uncertainty regarding the extent to which access to services should relate to potential for benefit, although to date the decision has usually been to provide unlimited service if such is prescribed by a physician. Patients have the freedom to choose a physician, access to any number of physicians, and physicians have the freedom to reject any patient except in selected situations. It is current practice to give much greater weight to the needs of people who are already receiving services than to those who are waiting in line. The rationing of health care is regularly mentioned, and usually condemned, although the practice is with us and always has been.

The overall goal of a civilized society should be the highest possible health status within the means of both present and future populations. This global goal does not imply that the highest quality or maximum consumable amount of health care or health protection will be available routinely to everyone or anyone. It does not mean that the life of everyone will be the longest it could possibly be or that every hazard will be eliminated.

Legislation for Funding Health Services

The Hospital Insurance and Diagnostic Services Act of 1957 and the *Medical Care Act* of 1966 are still understood as the vehicles through which universal health insurance (Medicare) was brought to Canada. They are perhaps our most famous pieces of health legislation, but they are now largely historical documents. The funding arrangements in the two famous statutes were replaced in 1977 by the *Federal Provincial Fiscal Arrangements and Established Programs Financing Act* (EPF), and by the *Canada Health Act* of 1984. These two acts spell out the terms and conditions required for the provinces to receive federal financial assistance since 1977 and 1984 respectively.

Under EPF unconditional transfers from the federal government to the provinces were sharply increased. Actually, transfer payments under EPF are not entirely unconditional, because five principles must be met in order to receive federal funding: provincial health insurance programs under Medicare must be universal, accessible, portable, comprehensive and publicly administered. Nevertheless, the degree of federal control certainly decreased in 1977. EPF terminated federal responsibility for a fixed portion of provincial expenditures for selected health services, and for practical purposes eliminated federal control over provincial medicare and hospitals. EPF also reduced federal financial risk. As compensation, the provinces were given a per capita block grant, per capita payments tied to the gross national product, additional income tax points, and full flexibility to financially support various health services to whatever extent they wished.

From 1977 to 1984, predictable sums were transferred from the federal government to the provincial treasuries, with the provincial governments being, for practical purposes, able to spend these monies in any way they wished. The amounts transferred continued to rise, but not as rapidly as they would have risen if the 1977 costsharing arrangement were still in place.

Bill C-69 *The Federal Restraint Law*, passed in 1991, has created a relative reduction of federal contributions to the total cost of education and health, as costs have risen. For example, federal transfers to Ontario for post-secondary education and health care have fallen from 52 percent of the total cost in 1979-80 to 31 percent in 1991-92. In dollar terms, Ontario has lost $12.3 billion in expected revenue (Ontario Provincial Budget Estimates, 1992).

In addition to the legislation regarding the funding of health services and establishing the delivery of health services as provincial jurisdiction, there are various statutes and treaties which establish federal responsibility for health care to the First Nations and Inuit. There is disagreement, however, about the range of responsibility and who is entitled to care. Yet, a relatively unchallenged relationship, based on a combination of contract, precedent, legal decision and acceptance of obligation, exists between the native peoples and the federal government. This relationship includes an obligation for health and other social services, although the federal government continues to seek devices through which native peoples can, at least for the purposes of health care, be seen as provincial residents. Provinces have varied in their willingness to accept natives as regular beneficiaries under provincial medical and hospital insurance, but in most provinces this administrative absorption has occurred.

In Quebec, the organization of health and social services is significantly different from the rest of Canada. In 1972, *Bill 65* reorganized and regionalized health and social services, establishing a province-wide network of regional councils. The Quebec system is a network of facilities and programs, each with a specific population for which they are responsible and to which they are somewhat accountable. Each institution has a responsibility to offer a defined range of services to its specified population. The boundaries do not restrict client access to other physicians and hospitals, but they do give the institutions an obligation to be available to the population in their area.

Sources of Health Funding

Health care costs are met from five sources, with the importance of the sources varying by province. The contributions are 27 to 36 percent from the federal government, 38 to 50 percent from the provinces, 0 to 5 percent from local government, 0.4 to 1.3 percent from Workers Compensation Boards, and about 25 percent from private sources. Alberta, British Columbia, Ontario and the Yukon have required residents to pay health insurance premiums, but only the former two have retained them.

After the introduction of universal hospital insurance, municipalities felt they were permanently relieved of responsibility for hospital capital and operating costs. However, in response to pressure from hospitals, which are faced with rising costs and shrinking government funding, some municipalities are once again contributing to hospital costs. This trend is likely to continue, although the residential property tax is fully needed for other expenditures that are also important to health, including recreation, urban planning, police and fire protection, sewage, water and garbage services, daycare and low-income housing.

In Canada, there is ongoing discussion of whether further expenditures on institutions and physicians is a reasonable way for society to spend its health dollars. The basic conclusion is that to improve or maintain health status, we should direct money to activities and workers other than hospitals and doctors. If the costs of hospitals and physicians are controlled, however, there will be continuing complaints about longer hospital waiting lists and the absence of the latest technology. There is increasing evidence that Canada should accept these problems because expenditures in other areas will produce greater improvements in the health status of Canadians, and will bring more social return per dollar spent than hospital or physician expenditures. Some argue that these two sources of traditional health care are already overfunded rather than underfunded in comparison to community and home care services and health prevention (Roos and Roos, 1990).

Health Expenditures

Although health services are not the largest component of social spending in Canada, they represent about one third of total provincial government budgets. Three quarters of health expenditures are for institutional and physician services. In 1992, Ontario spent $17 billion on publicly financed health care for about eight million residents. These costs are not typical of other parts of the world, as Canada has the most costly publicly funded system of the industrialized countries in Table 7.1, which compares per capita spending.

Despite the increase in the percentage of GNP devoted to health care in both Canada and the U.S., shown in Table 7.2, the pressure for additional funds for health services continues to increase. The critics of universal programs no longer complain about the threat of uncontrollable costs; they speak of underfunding. User fees are being vigorously proposed and hospital fundraising campaigns have once again become common.

Provincial Health Insurance Programs

According to the Canadian Constitution, each province is responsible for the delivery of health services, including priority-setting, policy selection, planning, financing, regulating, administration,

Table 7.1

Per Capita Health Expenditures,
Life Expectancy and Infant Mortality, 1987

COUNTRY	PER CAPITA	LIFE EXPECTANCY	INFANT MORTALITY PER 1000 LIVE BIRTHS
United States	$2,051	75.0	10.1
Canada	$1,483	76.8	7.3
Sweden	$1,233	77.2	6.1
France	$1,105	77.1	7.8
Germany	$1,093	75.9	7.5
Netherlands	$1,041	77.1	6.8
Japan	$ 915	78.9	5.0
United Kingdom	$ 758	75.4	9.0

Source: 1987/88 O.E.C.D. and World Health Organization data.
Note: All in U.S. dollars.

Table 7.2

Health Expenditures as Percentages of Gross National Product,
Canada and the United States, 1960-1990

Year	Canada	U.S.A.
1960	5.5	5.3
1965	6.0	5.9
1970	7.1	7.3
1975	7.3	8.3
1980	7.5	9.2
1985	8.7	10.5
1986	9.1	10.7
1987	9.0	10.9
1988	8.9	11.2
1989	9.0	11.6
1990	9.5	12.2

Source: Health and Welfare Canada, National Health Expenditures in Canada 1960 - 1992; Policy, Planning and Information Branch, Ottawa: March 1992.

resource allocation, evaluation, standard-setting and delivery of any type of health service. These services include physician services, dental services, ambulances, hospitals, and public health. To varying degrees, the provinces have chosen, by act or omission, to delegate certain managerial and delivery functions to quasi-governmental, voluntary, professional or commercial entities, but all provincial governments are directly active in most major aspects of health care.

As part of Medicare, the provinces operate their health insurance programs. Public insurance always covers hospital services and physician services because this was a condition of federal financing. Public insurance may also cover drugs, ambulance services, long-term care, dental services, prosthetics, glasses, home care, optometry, and chiropractics.

All provinces take a direct interest in the standards and costs of health care, with hospitals, physicians' services, public health, home care, long-term care institutions and ambulances being most routinely under scrutiny and control. Control of drugs, dental services and the supply of health personnel receive varying attention. Provincial governments tend to require standardized reporting with respect to selected aspects of institutional or other operations and care delivery.

Health insurance operates within the same principles as any other insurance: it is a means whereby people replace unpredictable major expense by predictable regular expense. A beneficiary facing a risk makes regular payments to an insurer, who agrees to meet the unpredictable costs if they materialize. Public health insurance differs somewhat from private insurance in that it is usually compulsory and the beneficiary may make all the payments through the tax system. When health care costs are paid out of general revenues, the payments made by each person vary with their level of taxation rather than their level of risk.

Public insurance systems have major advantages for most taxpayers and families. Public administration costs are low compared to those of private and competing insurance companies. Multiple carriers, on the other hand, are inefficient and bring no benefit to users. Governments have excellent data which increase their ability to identify unreasonable billing patterns and, as the only major funding agency, are in a better position to regulate payments and patterns of practice by using negotiation as well as statutory powers. Because the insurance programs have public service as their motive, low-income families need not worry about losing coverage if costs are too high; their insurance will not be cancelled. It is unlikely that major expenses will fall to the user, as is common with the exclusions, deductions and indemnity payments in profit-based plans.

Charges to the System

Despite the fact that Canada is presently in the midst of a recession, physicians are billing more in some provinces. For example, the 1990-91 Alberta annual report shows that doctors' services rose 8 percent ($60 million) to a record $836 million, while the population increased less than 2 percent. Alberta has 560 patients per doctor and data show that a 15 percent increase in utilization occurred in 1991 (Alberta Health Annual Report, 1991).

The number of admissions to hospitals per 1000 population is falling steadily. The number of days of acute hospital care per 1000 population is also declining, but the amount of the decrease is not easily identified because of the mixing of acute and long-term days of care; many hospitals provide both types. The number of hospital admissions per 1000 involving surgical procedures and treatments is rising despite a reduction in the availability of surgical beds. Shortened lengths of stay for inpatient surgery have more than made up for the reduced bed supply. In addition to the increase in hospital surgery, there has also been a steady increase in the number of surgical procedures performed as day surgery, outpatient surgery and office surgery (Evans and Stoddart, 1990).

Utilization of long-term care institutions is increasing steadily per 1000 population in Canada, but there is not much recent change in utilization if expressed as use per 1000 population over 65. In some locales, such as Ottawa-Carleton, there has been a decrease in the percentage of those over 65 who are in institutions. Home support services such as palliative care, friendly visiting and Victorian Order of Nurses (VON) have grown rapidly from their formal beginnings in the 1950s and before. Emergency visits and the use of ambulances continue to grow.

Constraint

Controlling the cost of health care is part of the distributive justice practised in Canada. It is the limiting of the resource consumption by health care so that social spending for other valued goods and services can occur. The capping of budgets, which is the most common regulatory tool for the control of expenditures (a global budget is one form of 'cap'), is quick and easy. Capping ends open-ended expense. It was, and is, a rational policy choice if health care professionals will routinely make good spending choices and when it is believed that professionals know which choices are best. Programs which are not capped are a threat to cost control, including, for example, private laboratories, drug insurance programs and fee-for-service practitioners.

There are two ways to improve spending:

1. lower production costs (i.e. be more efficient; produce the same service but at less cost per unit of service);
2. buy only those products (services) which bring significant benefits per dollar spent.

The desirable combination is to buy only the most beneficial services at the lowest possible cost per unit. The administrators and evaluators of health care have for several decades been concentrating on lower unit costs. This can occur through a change of location, a change of process, the elimination of some elements within the unit cost, the use of less expensive personnel, and the use of lower-cost generic drugs. Use of outpatient surgery to replace inpatient surgery, and the centralization of services such as obstetrics or pediatrics to achieve economies of scale, are examples of lowering cost through a change of location. Shortening the length of hospital stay or the reduction of unnecessary laboratory tests are examples of elimination of items which formerly added to the total unit cost. Group purchasing is a new way to perform the same tasks, as in the lowering of energy costs.

Many information systems have been developed to allow better measurement of cost and better comparison of costs. Provinces routinely compare the cost of various elements of care in one hospital with the cost of the same service elsewhere. The same attention and energy, however, has not been applied to reforming the services that are delivered. Evidence of inappropriate health care has been accumulating for some time, but efforts to reduce it have been made mostly in teaching hospitals and include limited access to certain drugs and services, routine review of selected services, and a requirement to justify some forms of care.

Utilization of Health Care Services

Age and Gender

The use of health care services varies by age and gender. Babies, the elderly and females during their reproductive years are heavy users of health services. Before age 5, males use more health services than females. From 5 to 14 years and after age 45, males and females consume relatively equal amounts of care per capita whether measured in number of services or cost in dollars. In most provinces, 80 to 85 percent of the population see a physician at least once a year. For optometrists and chiropractors, the figures are 10 to 20 percent and 5 to 15 percent respectively.

The utilization of health care is affected by many social and demographic characteristics, including low birthrates, the increasing number of one-person households, the rising percentage of one-parent families, the urbanization of the population, the rise of females to 45% of the labour force and the increasing percentages of children living in households below the poverty line. These changes demand policy response from government departments not usually affiliated with the health care system. Yet, healthy public policy in education, nutrition and labour become as crucial as policy in health departments.

Societal aging brings new demands for social support and health services, primarily for those over age 75. Canada will face its most serious challenge in responding to the health care needs of its seniors population in the years when the first of the baby boomers reach age 75, at about the year 2025. The pressures will fall by the year 2045 when the percentage of elderly is likely to decrease to about 20% of the population. There is little reason to panic about these new requirements, however; about 19% of the Swedish people are now over age 65 and the country is handling the demands comfortably. In Victoria, British Columbia, 14% of the population is 65 or over, and seniors comprise about 25% of the population of some small Canadian villages and towns (Fulton, 1993).

Despite the likelihood that the "crisis" of aging is being overstated, aging does bring new demands. The percentage of seniors with significant disabilities increases from 20% in the age group 65 to 74 to 49% in the age group 85 and older (Statistics Canada, 1992). Persons aged 65 to 84 use hospitals about three times as much as persons 25 to 64, whereas persons 85 and over use hospitals five times as much (Mustard and Frank, 1991).

It may no longer be reasonable to consider age 65 to be of any medical significance: health care demands change very little in the first ten years after age 65. Sweden in 1992 raised its retirement age to 66, partially a recognition of the capacity of individuals at that age, but also a money-saving measure. Canada may also raise the age at which persons will be classified as `old' and at which they qualify for a variety of special programs. Yet, at the same time, we need to rethink the wisdom of placing so many of our health care services into acute care rather than chronic care services.

Reproductive Health

Although midwives and home births formed an important part of our Canadian past, physicians and hospitals have dominated the culture of reproductive health for nearly a century. Over the past few decades, advocates for reform have pressed for greater consumer choice in childbirth location and professionals, arguing that midwife-assisted births tend to be less costly, less interventionist and more satisfying to women and couples experiencing low-risk births (Baker, 1990). In addition, the presence of fathers during the birthing has been successfully encouraged by reformers, and is now a common practice in Canadian hospital births.

In 1993, midwifery is beginning to receive official recognition in some provinces, although these services have been excluded from Medicare and must therefore be paid by the family. Reproductive services provided by physicians or birth control clinics have also been covered by Medicare in most provinces. Well-baby care and childbirth training are most commonly delivered under the jurisdiction of health departments.

New reproductive technologies have been the subject of a controversial Royal Commission, and provinces are now questioning the major financial investments in programs with controversial success rates. Most provinces require some user co-payment for services such as in vitro fertilization, which is a barrier to access for some consumers. In addition, the possible long-term negative outcomes of the process on the health of women have not yet been fully explored.

Health Status of Children and Adolescents

The concerns of individuals are a part of their health status, and these concerns vary greatly between age groups. In 1984-85, the Canada Health Attitudes and Behaviours Survey of over

30,000 children nine, twelve, and fifteen years old reported lifestyles and feelings that are considered to indicate a less than optimal health status. Twenty to thirty percent of the children reported difficulty sleeping because of worrying, and among 15-year-olds, 30 percent used alcohol at least twice a month, 25 percent were smokers and 20 percent reported use of cannabis. Sugar- and fat-dominated diets were common and activity levels were often very low; television was more popular than exercise. Children with higher activity levels reported less depression, a happier home life, and a more optimistic attitude towards life.

The Report on the Health of Canada's Children, which was released in 1989 by the Canadian Institute on Child Health, supports greater emphasis on prevention. The report states that 6% of babies born had a low birth weight. This risk factor is associated with increased mortality and disability. Low weight is often preventable through reductions in smoking and alcohol consumption and by improved prenatal care. Children born to teenagers or to mothers living in poverty are more likely than others to have low birth weight. About 20% of premature low birth weight babies have long term disabilities which result in personal, family, social and economic costs (Werner and Smith, 1992). Statistics are even more unfavourable for native children.

Of children who die in motor vehicle accidents, one third were pedestrians, one third were passengers and 20% were cyclists. A one-year study in Washington State found that 40% of child deaths from motor vehicle accidents were caused by parents backing up over their child, usually in the driveway. Death of children on farms is most likely to occur when they are run over by a tractor. Premature mortality among children tends to be related to low family income.

A number of diseases of childhood have largely disappeared; these include rheumatic fever, pernicious anaemia, rubella, measles, mumps and polio. However, a major new disease, AIDS, has appeared, although it is not yet prevalent in children.

In North America, one fifth of children live in poverty, and poverty is the most common predictor of poor health. Countries such as Sweden have implemented programs to eliminate poverty with resulting improvements in health status. Countries such as Japan, where the gap has been narrowed between the rich and the poor, have improved infant mortality, which is one measure of population health. Table 7.3 shows how infant mortality rates have declined in selected industrialized countries throughout the 1980s.

Table 7.3
Infant Mortality Rates Among Selected Nations
Per 1000 Live Births

	1980-82	1983-85	1986-87
Canada	9.8	8.3	7.6
United States	12.2	10.9	10.1
Japan	7.2	6.0	5.3
Germany	9.8	8.8	8.2
U.K.	11.5	10.1	9.4

Source: WHO Geneva 1991

Mental Health Services

The environments of our homes, workplaces, communities, recreation sites, and institutions are important in the preservation of reasonable mental health, as are the actions of individuals. Preventative programs that assist children and adults in tolerating differences of others, and modifying their own performances so that they are more easily tolerated by others, are likely to produce better mental health.

Caregivers, regardless of the nature of their services, can both promote and damage the mental health of their clients. The way the medical news is delivered, the degree of respect shown for the client's opinions, the tolerance with which client fear or anger are handled, the extent of the family's involvement, the patience with which instructions are explained all affect the self-image and the level of stress of the client and his or her family.

Community-based mental health services provide a broad range of advocacy, education, advice, protection, and therapy. The networks tend to be dominated by nonprofit, low-budget sources of care. Children's mental health services and facilities consist largely of quite expensive and usually residential treatment units associated with psychiatric hospitals, children's hospitals, or child protection agencies such as the Children's Aid Societies.

Child psychiatry is a rapidly growing specialty as is psychogeriatrics. Major problems in children include hyperactivity, eating disorders, adolescent depression, suicide and sexual abuse.

Long-Term Care (LTC)

Much of the evolution of LTC merely reflects the larger events in society. Three phases have occurred in this evolution. The first phase was characterized by social disinterest. Families cared for their frail and disabled members as well as they could. The objectives of government, to the extent that it was involved through funding or by means of legislation, were to keep costs down and keep disabled persons and indigent elderly out of sight. Institutionalized persons were treated as inmates and frequently referred to as such.

The second phase was firmly in place by the 1960s. It brought benevolent paternalism characterized by family, professional and societal protection and dominance of the less fortunate. Patronizing institutions and professionals using the medical model became surrogate parents, regardless of the mental competence of the dependent persons. The concept of second childhood became enshrined in our processes of assessment, placement and care of frail elderly people. Professionals evaluated the patient, decided the appropriate location for care, and then planned its delivery; the role of the user and the family in decision making was minimal.

In the early stages of this period of benevolent paternalism, the LTC institutions copied the hospital model through the use of regular schedules, professional control, uniformed staff, prohibition of alcohol and limited visitation. As phase two has matured, serious efforts have been made to make institutions more stimulating, flexible, personal and pleasant, that is, more homelike, and to recognize client individuality. Many institutional professionals and administrators and many families, however, still believe that some institutionalized adults, regardless of their mental competence, need someone to make sure they do not do anything foolish.

Paternalistic phase two is steadily and peacefully merging into phase three. In the third phase of LTC evolution, the dependent adult is treated as an adult rather than a child. This phase is guided by the idea that adult status is not compromised by physical dependency. The extent to which this latest phase has arrived, how its full arrival can be hastened, and the implications of its arrival are all questions now open for discussion. Home care is also an emerging formal component of both acute and long-term care services. Both short-term and continuous support are available in many communities where early hospital discharge and delayed institutionalization of elderly or disabled persons are goals. Home care services are growing in both type and quantity as restructuring and reallocation occur of their health funding. Effective home care services can become a valuable support for families, if the traditional caregiver is part of the labour force or is frail or elderly herself.

Communities and Consumers

Consumers increasingly believe the health services network exists to work for them, and the services have been obliged to be more responsive, less paternalistic, and more sensitive to individual needs. Changes have occurred in patients' rights statements and legislation, in obtaining access to records, and in the composition and roles of boards of trustees. Through influence on public policy, consumers could, if they chose, limit resource availability and utilization, control professional supply and function, determine rates of pay and directly influence a broad range of professional decisions.

Consumers have always been able to complain to caregivers, institutions, the police, the media or anyone else about the quality or availability of health care. Historically, however, they seldom complained, and were seldom listened to if they did. Complaints now are not only more apt to receive attention, but they are being delivered in more ways. Patient satisfaction surveys and questionnaires are routine, and institutional ombudspersons are increasingly available to help identify patient problems or abuse, and to implement acceptable response. Self-help or advocacy groups are now prevalent; legislation and court decisions have spelled out the rights of patients to information and choice, and professional complaints committees and higher appeal mechanisms have public members. The existence of these devices encourages institutions and individual caregivers to be aware of the wishes, preferences, and values of patients and their families. Boards, discipline committees, payment agencies and courts now routinely decide whether professional or institutional service and conduct is adequate or merits discipline.

The rise in public participation and influence can be endorsed as a means of strengthening democracy through the production of a more informed and less cynical population. It also can counterbalance the power of professionals and bureaucrats and more decisively insert the priorities of users and payers into the decision-making process.

Services Which Preserve Families and Households

When a family requires levels or types of care that cannot be delivered through existing programs or by other family members, the person in need will either not get the care or will lose the pleasure of staying with friends and/or family. In speaking of the preservation of families and households, one must remember that the dependent person is only one of the individuals to be considered. Other family members also face financial, career, and personal challenges. The long-term care network must consciously identify and work to meet these challenges if the household is to be preserved and the quality of life of all members protected. Additional stress may be placed on women, as traditional caregivers, as more also work outside the home.

Stress to the family caregiver(s) arises from the dependent person's wandering, aggression and incontinence, from the additional expense, from the destruction of quality of life of the caregiver, from the inability to obtain short-term relief, and from fear of injury or illness. Supporting family caregivers would seem to be logical both to reduce these stresses and in the interest of cost control through continued involvement of unpaid family caregivers. Unfortunately the system has, in the past, often failed to welcome or support family caregivers.

Fifteen years ago in many Canadian provinces, a family with a developmentally handicapped or autistic child either provided care without support from the health care system or admitted the child to an institution. The caregivers were isolated and exploited. In recent years, several devices have been used to support household caregivers:

1) Financial aid.
   a) In B.C., funds are provided by government to families who care for their severely retarded children at home. The amount to be paid is determined by a voluntary agency (The Living Society) acting as an assessor, counsellor, and quality control vehicle within Ministry guidelines.

   b) A number of states in the U.S. provide tax incentives. At best these are not very effective, and are of no value to individuals or families who pay no tax.

   c) When the dependent person is mentally competent, money can be given to him/her to purchase required services. This practice is followed in some European countries.

2) Legislated or voluntary sabbaticals from work without penalty and with job protection to enable people to care for family members.

3) Training and education regarding caregiving skills, understanding the situation and coping with stress.

4) Respite care programs which provide family caregivers with relief for a few hours, days or weeks; the respite care may be scheduled in advance to allow vacations, or available without prior scheduling if the caregiver becomes ill.

Respite care arrangements in most provinces are currently inadequate, as one bed is typically set aside in a home for the aged or a nursing home. It may not always be available, and it usually is poorly publicized. Too often there are rules that limit access to not less than one week or not more than two to four weeks a year, and there is minimal availability of regular weekend relief.

Administrators tend not to welcome personalized arrangements. Just as there is little effort to help institutionalized persons to regularly spend time with family, there is not much imagination applied to the question of how to help dependent persons stay at home for 30 to 50 weeks a year, or for 4 to 6 days a week. The family is routinely expected to adapt to bureaucratic rigidities instead of the system adapting to family problems and constraints. The same attitudes are seen in day care programs that serve a major relief function but are useful only to those caregivers who can adapt to 9:30 to 5:30 service. For selected persons, in particular those who are confused or acutely distressed by new caregivers and surroundings, consideration should be given to respite care in which the alternate caregivers are persons who are known and will provide care in familiar surroundings.

Any service which allows anyone to be independent in any respect obviously increases that individual's opportunities for control. Examples of such services might be a seeing-eye dog, a ramp, a telephone adaptation for the hearing impaired, an electric wheelchair, or additional disposable income. Conversely, things that reduce the individual's opportunity for control or prevent him or her from exercising independence include: institutional regulations regarding pets, plants, visitors, outside visiting, or how one may spend available wealth.

Families have an important role to play in the management and provision of health services in the future. With fewer dollars and fewer services to go around, the family is emerging as a key player in promoting health and in managing illness and disease.

Our expectations of continued levels of traditional hospital-based services may need to adapt to the new fiscal reality. At the same time, health reform at the provincial and regional level should aim to reduce barriers to appropriate health care and reallocate resources to community-based services. This change offers the potential to improve the health of Canadian families by increasing prevention and health promotion activities.

Improving the health of families also requires emphasis on individual well-being in all aspects of life. Since health care is only one contributor to health, energy will be well spent on many other social policies and programs including antipoverty programs, antismoking programs and child care, which also impact on people's health.

CHAPTER EIGHT

Quebec's Pro-Active Approach to Family Policy: "Thinking and Acting Family"

Céline Le Bourdais
Nicole Marcil-Gratton
with the collaboration of Danièle Bélanger

One might wonder why, in a book on Canadian family policy, it was thought advisable to devote an entire chapter to the approach taken by Quebec. In other words, what factors distinguish the Quebec family policy from that of other provinces, both with regard to the type of government intervention and the objectives of their policies?

First, Quebec is without doubt the only Canadian province in which family policy is governed by a complete set of coherent measures aimed specifically at the well-being of families. To achieve its goal, Quebec has set in place an administrative structure and mechanisms that call upon the services of numerous participants in a myriad of governmental sectors of activity, all with one goal: improving the well-being of the family.

Second, at the root of Quebec government intervention in family policy was a sudden and intense change in a variety of socio-demographic indicators of family life: a drop in the birthrate, a decline of legal marriage, an increase in marital instability and a dramatic rise in the number of working mothers. All these were factors which have brought radical change to the structure of today's families, and although they are not exclusive to Quebec, the rate of change in the province makes it stand out within Canada and even internationally.

Finally, the family policies developed in Quebec have the additional special feature of being aimed both at correcting demographic trends deemed negative for the future of its population and its place within the Canadian confederation, and at helping families attain social equity. This dual perspective is clearly apparent in the series of measures adopted, some obviously in response to the objective of increasing the birthrate, others being targeted more at supporting families in their varied functions. In this article we shall try to shed some light on this dual perspective, by examining the recent history of family policy in Quebec.

1. The Socio-demographic Context: Questioning the "Traditional" Family

In order to better understand the factors that have contributed to the recognition of the family as a sphere of government intervention, as well as the sometimes controversial but always strong measures taken to assist the family, we must examine the Quebec situation in the context of the socio-demographic changes that have occurred over the past 30 years.

Quebec has experienced a severe drop in its fertility, indeed among the most rapid in all of Canada or the rest of the Western world. The total fertility rate, which measures the average number of children that a woman would have in her lifetime if current trends were maintained, fell from 4.0 children per woman in 1959 to 2.1 children in 1970 (Duchesne, 1992; Dumas, 1990). Since then the rate has remained below the population replacement threshold, continuing to fall throughout the eighties to reach a low of 1.34 children[1] in 1987. This rate is among the lowest observed in the world today, putting Quebec on a par with Italy (1.27 in 1990) and Portugal (1.43 in 1990) (Monnier and de Guibert-Lantoine, 1991). There is therefore quite a gap in fertility rates between Quebec and the rest of Canada, which had a rate of 1.7 children per woman throughout the eighties; even in 1990, the Quebec average of 1.6 children per woman was below the Canadian average of 1.8 children (Dumas with Lavoie, 1992).

Taken in conjunction with a positive but still weak net migration rate since 1985 (Duchesne, 1992), the drop in the birthrate appeared to be the cause of a series of negative impacts on the demographic future of Quebec (Baker, 1993). A more rapidly aging population, and above all the setbacks for the French language and the demographic weight of Quebec within Canada, which fell from 28% in 1971 to 25% in 1991 (Duchesne, 1992), have become a matter of growing concern. This concern has been heightened by the fact that at the very same time the behaviour of couples was changing, causing an upheaval in the structure of family life and consequently in the conditions in which reproduction is organised (Le Bourdais, 1989).

As Baker has said in Chapter 1, the divorce rate shot up in Canada after the Canadian Parliament passed the Divorce Act in 1968. In Quebec, the current divorce rate rose from less than 100 divorces per 1000 marriages in 1969 to almost 500 per 1000 in 1990 (Duchesne, 1992), and is now very close to that observed elsewhere in Canada and among our American neighbours. This astonishing increase is the result of the easing of criteria for access to divorce, but also reflects the fact that fewer and fewer couples choose to confirm their commitment with a legal marriage.

In Quebec, the decline in the marriage rate has been especially severe: none of the countries for which we have marriage statistics have indices lower than Quebec's (Duchesne 1992; Monnier and de Guibert-Lantoine, 1991). The marriage rate, which indicates the proportion of singles who would marry for the first time before the age of 50 if present trends continue, was 920 marriages per 1000 single men in Quebec in 1970, and 878 per 1000 single women. In 1987, at its low point, the rate had fallen to 413 and 449 marriages respectively (Duchesne, 1992). One can hardly speak of a subsequent recovery, since in 1990 the indices were 421 per 1000 for men and 467 for women. The rest of Canada has also experienced a drop in the marriage rate, but less pronounced than in Quebec, and since 1988 the Canadian rate has climbed slightly to 685 marriages per 1000 single men and 735 for single women (Dumas, 1990).

The drop in the marriage rate does not necessarily mean that people no longer form couples. In Quebec especially, the drop in legal marriages has been accompanied by a sharp rise in common-law marriages, which have now become the choice of the majority of young couples. Approximately 50% of Quebec women aged 20-24 and 30-34, and almost 70% of 25-29 year-olds questioned in the General Social Survey in 1990, stated that they had lived in common-law relationships. The percentages are markedly lower for the rest of Canada, where 42% of female respondents aged 25-29 reported that they had lived in common-law relationships (calculations by the authors).

Quite apart from the fact of couples living together, the common-law marriage seems to have become the preference for a growing number of new families, as is shown by the growing proportion of out-of-wedlock births in Canada, which increased from about 5% in the mid-sixties to 10% in the early seventies and doubled again, reaching 22% in 1988. Indeed, children born out of wedlock are not always born outside of families – far from it. The percentage of births attributable to mothers without spouses has in fact hardly varied over time, and in Quebec, as in the rest of Canada, remains at about 5% (Duchesne, 1992; Marcil-Gratton, 1993). The rise in the number of children

---

[1] Figure supplied by the Bureau de la statistique du Québec (Quebec Bureau of Statistics) (Duchesne, 1992); for the same year Statistics Canada gives the total fertility rate as 1.4 children per woman (Dumas, 1990).

born outside of marriage in the whole of Canada is largely attributable to the increase in the number of births in common-law marriages, particularly in Quebec. If 38% of all children born and 48% of first-born children in Quebec in 1990 are classified as "out-of-wedlock", it is estimated that 90% of them are born to common-law couples; this was true of only 5% of children born 15 years earlier (Duchesne, 1992; Marcil-Gratton, 1993).

These changes in married life lead not only to a greater diversity in the types of families into which children are born, but also to a profound shift in the direction that families will take over the course of their lives. As Baker points out in the first chapter of this volume, the face of the family has greatly changed. A not inconsiderable proportion of parents and children will experience life in a one-parent family, for an indeterminate duration and number of periods (Desrosiers, Le Bourdais and Péron, 1993; Marcil-Gratton, 1993); a growing number of them will at some point belong to a blended family, that is, a family having at least one stepparent (Desrosiers and Le Bourdais, 1992; Marcil-Gratton, 1993).

Among the other factors which have contributed to the change in the ways in which families and family responsibilities are organised, the rapidly increasing labour force participation of mothers of young children has played a significant role. In Quebec the rate of working mothers with at least one child under three years at home rose from 28% in 1976 to 60% in 1990 (Duchesne, 1992); in the last census, almost two out of three mothers of preschool children were in the labour force in Quebec and Canada (Statistics Canada, 1993). Finally, it is important to stress that the economic recessions of 1982 and 1992 have impoverished families and individuals, especially the young, and have brought on a new financial crisis for the government. These difficult economic times appear to have convinced many young people to delay having a family or even perhaps to abandon the idea altogether; they have also been at the root of the government's gradual withdrawal from a number of sectors of activity that directly or indirectly affect the family (see chapters three and six of this book).

2. The State Awakens: The Pro-family Approach at the Beginning of the Eighties

In response to the fears caused by the changes in socio-demographic indicators, the Quebec government announced in the early eighties that it wished to adopt a family policy for the province. Some time later an interministerial committee on the family was created and a Green Paper was tabled in 1984 by Camille Laurin, then minister of Social Affairs (Dandurand, 1987). In this document, the Quebec government position was characterised by its neutral approach to individual choices, reflecting a growing diversity and a distancing from the "traditional" view of the family. A broader definition of family was proposed, and it was stressed that the government should not take the place of the family. A number of observers were to note that "the document contained few firm proposals and many generous ideas" (Dandurand and Kempeneers, 1990: 88).

The Green Paper was followed in 1985 by a major round of consultations, leading to the publication of a two-volume report; the first, entitled *"Le soutien collectif réclamé pour les familles québécoises"* ("The Collective Support Demanded for Quebec Families"), summarized the consultations, and the second, *"Le soutien collectif recommandé pour les parents québécois"* ("The Collective Support Recommended for Quebec Parents"), contained the committee's recommendations (Comité de consultation sur la politique familiale (Consultation Committee on Family Policy), 1985; 1986) . In responding to the Green Paper, this report stressed that "though the government should not take the place of parents, it should make serious efforts to assist them" (Dandurand and Kempeneers, 1990: 88). The report recognizes that raising children is not just a private and individual matter, but is also a societal responsibility, and that the government therefore "has a duty to support Quebec families" (Comité de consultation sur la politique familiale, 1986: 40). It was recommended that support be provided to parents rather than to families: the report thus gives preference to a policy targeted at parents and their dependent children, rather than to a broad social policy aimed at the extended family, and whose purpose would be to mitigate the government's lack of programs for the elderly and the sick. Finally, the consultation committee concludes that there is no "crisis of the family," but rather a "crisis in the collective and individual relationships between men and women" (Comité de consultation sur la politique familiale, 1986: 31). Following this diagnosis, it was proposed that family policy pursue the goals of solidarity and equity between men and women (Dandurand, 1987).

The report contains a number of concrete recommendations: a single, universal transfer of all allowances and tax exemptions for children, adapted to the age of the child and its position in the family; the creation of a maternity leave fund; and the improvement of maternity and parental leave. It was also recommended that the government show its commitment to families by naming a ministre d'État à la politique familiale (Minister of State for Family Policy), which would be responsible to a Secrétariat à la famille (Family Secretariat), directly attached to the ministère du Conseil exécutif (Ministry of the Executive Council), and also by creating a Conseil national de la politique familiale (National Family Policy Council), distinct from the existing Conseil des affaires sociales et de la famille (Social Affairs and Family Council), which still had responsibility for the family.

Until that time, concerns with the low birthrate were noticeably absent from the proposed objectives, and feminist groups as well as family agencies expressed their satisfaction with the proposals, reassuring as they were in light of concerns expressed in 1982 by the President of the Conseil du statut de la femme (Advisory Council on the Status of Women), Claire Bonenfant, who feared a return to a pronatalist policy that would drive women back to "kitchen and cradle" (Dandurand and Kempeneers, 1990: 87).

3. The 1987 Policy Statement: A Family Policy in Line With Original Principles

In December 1987, the Quebec Cabinet adopted an "Énoncé sur l'orientation et la dynamique administrative de la politique familiale" ("Statement on the Approach and the Administrative Process for Family Policy"). This statement was the first step in the government's plan to support family life, and the basic principles of the policy did not seem to be dictated by a wish to increase the birthrate, any more than in the report on the 1985 consultations. It stated that "family policy has its own goals and (that) *whether or not there is a problem of a falling birth rate[2]*, we must adopt this policy" (Quebec, 1987: 7). The emphasis on the birthrate would only become clear in the selection of the measures that would be given priority when implementing the policy.

The basic principles of the Statement flow from those of previous reports. They call for:
- recognition of the family as a fundamental value;
- willingness to help make the family more stable and cohesive;
- willingness to support parents, the primary caretakers of children, while protecting the interests of the child (Quebec, 1987: 8).

The general approach following from these principles stipulates that the government must provide support to parents by encouraging harmonious relationships between family members: liberty, equality and family solidarity would therefore be the underpinnings of the new policy. Moreover, the Policy Statement proposed as principal functional objectives both the coordination between government agencies and the involvement of families in order to formulate a policy whose general

---

[2] Our emphasis

objective would be to "recognize the importance of the family as an institution and as a living environment... in particular, to support the parent-child relationship, which is the nucleus common to all forms of families" (Quebec, 1987: 9-10). Family diversity is therefore recognized, and it is the function of parenting that must receive governmental support.

The policy was to be applied in thirteen sectors, justifying the description of the family policy as "multisectorial." These sectors (see Table 1) cover the expected areas of child-care services, justice and family law, and labour insofar as it concerns balancing the roles of working parents, but it also covers more remote sectors such as immigration, housing and "cultural agents, particularly the media and advertising" (Quebec, 1987: 11).

Table 1
Quebec family policy: Sectors for intervention

1987 STATEMENT	1989-1991 ACTION PLAN	
Sectors	Sectors	No. of measures
1. Economic support for parents	1. Economic support for families	4
2. Work: ways to balance the roles of parents and workers	2. Parental responsibilities and the labour market	8
3. Family housing	7. Family housing and habitat	6
4. The family and the educational system	5. Families and school	7
	6. Families and higher education	**
5. Immigration, the cultural communities and the family	10. Families in the cultural communities	3
6. Social and health services for the family	4. Families and health, social and community services	14
7. Native family services		
8. Child care services	3. Families and child care services	*
9. Family and leisure	8. Family leisure and cultural activities	4
10 Justice and family law	11. Family law	6
11. Family safety (family violence and youth problems)		
12. Research and cooperation on family development and family policy	12. Family research and experimentation	2
13. The family and cultural agents, especially the media and publicity	9. Families and the media	3
	13. Recognition of large families	1

* This sector contains no measures but repeats 12 commitments in l'Énoncé de politique sur les services de garde (Policy Statement on Child Care Services) adopted in 1988.

** No new measure proposed; repeat of earlier measures to improve the student financial aid plan and encourage access to post-secondary education.

On the administrative side, the statement also created the structures first proposed in the 1985 consultation report, enabling the government to "think and act family" (Quebec, 1987: 13). A Minister responsible for the family was appointed, with a mandate to develop Quebec family policy and act as spokesperson on the family for the government. A Secrétariat à la famille was established to provide the Minister with the services required to implement the multisectorial family policy within the government; among its roles were the analysis of the socioeconomic development of families and their needs and the study of the impact of government actions on the family. Finally, the Quebec government amended the act governing le Conseil des affaires sociales et de la famille, so as to create an agency with the sole mandate of studying family matters. The members of the Conseil de la famille (Advisory Council on the Family), appointed by the government after consultation with family associations, were given a dual mandate to receive and to transmit to the government requests and suggestions submitted to them, and to issue public statements on matters relating to family policy. The Conseil de la famille therefore acts as a "watchdog" over family policy, its mission being to formulate constructive criticism of measures proposed by the government. Finally, a network of respondents, not in the original Policy Statement, was set up in 1989; this appeared necessary after the First Action Plan was adopted that year, so as to create a liaison between the Secrétariat à la famille and all ministries; the network would make it possible to identify actions affecting families that are taken by the various ministries, to ensure the implementation of the Action Plan, and to develop future Plans. This network provides the intra-governmental coordination recommended in the 1987 Statement.

From the outset, Quebec has created the structures needed to make support of family life a major priority. Political implementation, however, and measures adopted since this crucial phase, have revealed that the response to the basic principles could take on quite a different and more pronatalist tone, in other words that the pro-family approach could give way to more "populationist" objectives. Nonetheless, the structures that have been created make it possible to make any necessary corrections: Quebec's brief experience with family policy has shown that, to a certain extent, the system is working.

4. The 1988 Budget and the First Action Plan (1989-1991): Applications With a Pronatalist Flavour

The 1988 budget

The 1988 Budget was the first in a series of steps actually taken by the Quebec government, showing its willingness to act on family policy and to put its ideas into action. The steps taken in this first budget were to be followed a year later by the publication by the Secrétariat à la famille of its first action plan entitled "Familles en tête" ("Families First").

Essentially, the 1988 budget stressed economic support for families. Among the measures announced were the abolition of the recovery of Quebec family allowances through income taxes, the change of "availability" allowances into allowances for young children, an increase in child-care tax deductions, and a program to help families with two or more children to buy a home. The highlight of the budget was undoubtedly the introduction of a system of non-refundable birth allowances ("baby bonuses" as they would be called), calculated according to the child's order in the family. An amount of $500 is granted at the birth of each of the first two children; starting with the third child, assistance increases to $3000, paid in quarterly instalments over the two years following the child's birth (Dandurand et al., 1989).

In spite of the large number of measures proposed, the budget was roundly criticised. First, the proposed measures did not seem as generous as was claimed: in several sectors (family allowances, for example) the budget aimed mainly at catching up on ground lost over the previous years; in other areas such as housing, the proposed program was in fact less generous than earlier existing programs (Dandurand and Kempeneers, 1990; Dandurand et al., 1989). Second, the birth allowance was diametrically opposed to the proposals of the Comité de consultation and the Conseil du statut de la femme (1990) and from the outset provoked criticism by numerous women's groups who saw it as a measure aimed at increasing the birthrate and as an incentive to procreate, rather than a way to support individuals who become parents (Dandurand et al., 1989; Le Bourdais, 1989). The nature of this birth allowance was condemned, as it supports parents for only two years after the child is born. And finally, the premises of such a policy were challenged, as it takes for granted that the first and second children would come automatically in any case; demographic indicators show a relative decline of first and second births, and so from a strictly demographic viewpoint, they would also deserve additional support (Rochon, 1992).

The 1989-1991 Action Plan

The "Familles en tête" Action Plan published by the Secrétariat à la famille at the end of 1989, was the real kick-off to the Quebec family policy. The plan contained the pro-family perspective which from the outset motivated the various government initiatives; to that was added the pronatalist approach of the 1988 budget.

The Action Plan was striking in its breadth. It presented no fewer than 58 measures, contained in 13 "chapters" for action (See Table 1), responsibility for which was conferred on various government ministries and agencies. The plan was also surprising in the diversity of the measures that it proposed (awareness, prevention, policy, financial contributions, support for research, etc.) and the diversity of family functions on which it focused.

From the start in 1990, the Conseil de la famille presented an in-depth response to this first plan, not hesitating to support or criticise the measures proposed. In general, the Council considered the plan to be "an excellent starting point." It pointed out that "Familles en tête" flowed from the general objectives laid down in the Family Policy Statement. In addition it noted and approved of the Quebec government's willingness to implement a multisectorial family policy structure, with real involvement and coordination of some twenty ministries and agencies. On the other hand it identified "a lack of coordination in the Action Plan" and noted that no timetable had been set and no evaluation system developed. It further noted a gap between the scope of the changes hoped for and the measures proposed. As was observed: "the good intentions often run up against limited measures or research" (Conseil de la famille, 1990: 8).

In view of the specific measures contained in the Plan, the Conseil de la famille reacted positively to the variable birth allowances structure, but warned against the pronatalist perception of the measure which the public seemed to have, even though the Council did not itself take that view. To counterbalance the pronatalist view, it encouraged the government to give greater importance to the birth of the first and the second child and above all, to continue the financial assistance for the third or subsequent child until age six. The Council also stressed that the measures aimed at balancing parental and work responsibilities are more likely to change people's attitudes and to support parents, and deplored the fact that these were not more generous. It pointed out the serious need for child care and regretted the absence of a policy "which considers all the needs of parents and children" (Conseil de la famille, 1990: 10). Finally, it pointed out that some actors, especially in the health and social service sectors, were developing a strategy that is more individual- than family-oriented, and expressed astonishment that the question of the collection of support payments had not been tackled.

Several aspects of the implementation phase of the First Action Plan are noteworthy, in particular the economic support measures and the birth allowances: for the third or subsequent child, the allowance rose sharply from $3,000 in the 1988 budget to $7,500 in 1991 (and to $8,000 in 1992) but remained at $500 for the first child and increased to $1,000 for the second child. It should be noted here that the child's rank in the family is calculated on the basis of the number of dependent minor children in the home where the birth occurs, and is not based on the fertility of the mother. This is an innovative approach, in that it recognized the reality of "new families" and supported dependent children, whatever the type of family. The spectacular nature of the birth allowance brought it much publicity and made it the trade mark of the Quebec family policy, overshadowing many other aims and achievements of the Plan.

The Plan did not just remain a matter of good intentions, however; action was taken in several strategic areas. A number of measures aimed at adapting minimum labour standards to the parental responsibilities of working parents were adopted in the framework of la Loi sur les normes du travail de 1990 (Labour Standards Act): introduction of 34 weeks of unpaid parental leave, added to the existing 18 week maternity leave; lengthening of paternity (or adoption) leave from two to five days, with the first two days now being paid; creation of a five-day unpaid parental leave for activities related to child care, health and education. These measures may still seem inadequate, but they do have the merit of having been implemented, sometimes in addition to the federal system, in a context of economic crisis which left the Quebec government little latitude. Some features such as leave for parental obligations, applicable to either parent, met the criterion of equality and family solidarity put forward in the 1987 Statement.

A series of preventive measures dealing with prenatal care, teenage pregnancy, violence in the family, adoption and new reproductive technologies were put in place. One also notes the concern with adapting family policy to the new types of families being formed; an interministerial task force will thus examine the consistency of various programmes and laws as they affect common law couples.

In short, no one has ever denied the "pronatalist" aim of the Quebec family policy. Implicit in the 1987 Statement, in which family policy is seen as the "catalyst in a population policy," it became explicit in the 1988 budget and was affirmed by the first action plan. This approach to family policy is similar to that developed in France and pursued since the end of the Second World War; it is proof of the demographic concerns of both peoples.

5. The Second Action Plan (1992-1994): Readjusting the Family Focus

Before launching its second action plan, the Secrétariat à la famille (1992a) took stock of the objectives of the first plan, and as the results proved positive, decided to include in the second plan most of the few measures that had not been implemented between 1989 and 1991.

In the light of numerous criticisms about the pronatalist approaches in the 1989-1991 plan, the second plan was more careful in tone, and attributed to the Quebec family policy the mission of providing parents with better opportunities to "realize their desire to have children." In this same spirit, the thirteenth feature of the first plan, aimed more specifically at support for large families, was abandoned (Secrétariat à la famille, 1992b).

The 1992-1994 Action Plan was somewhat different from its predecessor: 88 measures were grouped under five headings: prevention, reconciling family and work, economic support for the family, improving the family living environment, and pursuing the family focus. There is no doubt that the desire to see the whole of society become family-oriented is connected to the emphasis put on measures to promote the idea and to inform families and government, municipal and community actors (see graph No. 1). On the other hand, the plan is disappointing because it contains very few legislative or financial measures likely to bring real change in the situation of families. A comparative study of the proposals in the two plans reveals a great increase in information and promotion activities and administrative studies, and a net decrease in legislation, regulation and funding for families (see graph No. 1).

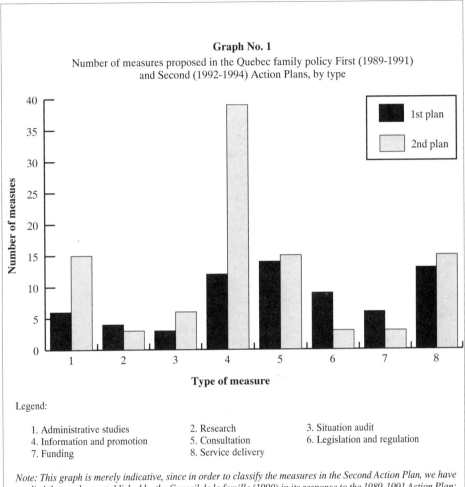

Graph No. 1

Number of measures proposed in the Quebec family policy First (1989-1991) and Second (1992-1994) Action Plans, by type

Legend:

1. Administrative studies   2. Research   3. Situation audit
4. Information and promotion 5. Consultation   6. Legislation and regulation
7. Funding   8. Service delivery

Note: This graph is merely indicative, since in order to classify the measures in the Second Action Plan, we have applied the typology established by the Conseil de la famille (1990) in its response to the 1989-1991 Action Plan; there may therefore be differences of interpretation between the two classifications.

The birth allowance (baby bonus), which is very high from the third child on, remained in place, and as we saw was even increased to $8,000 in 1992. It is then spread over a five-year period following the birth of the child, thus responding to the wishes of the Conseil de la famille; the latter remains in favour of the provision, which it sees to some extent as compensating for the income lost when a third child is born and one parent quits work or child-care expenses increase. The Conseil du statut de la femme, however, continues to oppose this approach, seeking instead to rechannel these resources into better-paid parental leave.

In the new plan, as in the first, reconciling family and employment responsibilities remains an important objective. Whereas the first plan concluded by stating that "the most significant measures in the 1989-1991 period are without doubt those aimed at the labour market" (Secrétariat à la famille, 1989:57), the second major focus of the new plan, after prevention and before financial support for families, is how to reconcile family and work. However, an examination of the proposals shows that the first plan took more vigorous action in this area. We must not forget that publication of the 1989-1991 plan coincided with the passage of the new Loi sur les normes du travail en 1990, which, as we have seen, proposed several changes, especially to parental leave. In the new plan, the chapter on balancing work and family contains only two specific objectives and nine measures, four of which are aimed at consultation, information and prevention. The only two direct support measures for parents deal with creating new day-care places and services; as we shall see later, the announced commitments were only partially achieved.

In general, one notes a willingness in the Second Action Plan to decentralise initiatives to a more local level. The Secrétariat à la famille and the Conseil de la famille maintain their role of animation, consultation and coordination, but there is also a desire to increase awareness among family agencies, municipalities and other social actors and to have them more involved in responding to the needs of families with dependent children. For example, the second plan "seeks to increase commitment to families by municipalities" (Secrétariat à la famille, 1992b:39) and to encourage increased collaboration between municipalities and family organizations. These objectives are all in line with the text of the agreement signed in 1988 by the leaders of two Quebec municipal unions (l'Union des municipalités et l'Union des municipalités régionales de comté) (the Union of Municipalities and the Union of Regional County Municipalities) and the Minister Responsible for the Family, continuing the initiatives undertaken by the government in the framework of the First Action Plan. In this context we might point out a successful experiment: the Carrefour "Action municipales et familles" (Crossroads "Municipal Action and Families") undertaken by the Fédération des Unions de famille (Federation of Family Unions), which, in conjunction with the municipalities, organizes an annual conference on this theme and awards a prize to recognize the small and large municipalities that make positive impacts on family life.

As the end of 1993 approaches, the emphasis placed on animation and consultation is once again present in the document preliminary to the Third Action Plan, entitled "Canevas de réflexion sur les familles. Situations, acquis, défis" ("Reflections on Families: Conditions, Characteristics, Challenges") (Secrétariat à la famille, 1993c). This document will be the object of a first round of consultations with family and community organizations; this initial step will be followed by a forum bringing together actors from the private, community and government sectors.

6. Discussion: The Merits of a Policy Which Outweigh its Demerits

In taking stock of Quebec family policy since the 1987 Statement, it would be unfair to give it a negative rating without recognising its merits, or to point out only positive features without mentioning its shortcomings. Points of view will of course vary, depending on one's sensibilities, but the overall picture clearly seems positive, even if we must point out some limitations.

Several groups or organizations, of which the Conseil du statut de la femme is the most visible and the most credible, continue to criticise the Quebec family policy on the grounds that it is more concerned with increasing the birthrate than with families. In the government's defense, one can certainly point out the troublesome nature of Quebec's demographic trends over the past thirty years.

Hence, some authors have argued that the future of Quebec is tied to the growth of its population, and that this future cannot be assured without the participation of the individuals and families which make up that society. (see Commission parlementaire sur la culture (Parliamentary Commission on Culture), 1985; Mathews, 1987).

To the extent that the types of support provided for families met the real needs and aspirations of today's parents, there would be no need to worry about the emphasis put on the birth of a third child; the response to demographic-type concerns would simply be complementary to the expectations of families with dependent children. However, studies that have attempted to estimate the costs associated with the birth of children show that this is not the case – far from it. No one would dare claim that the financial assistance provided to parents can cover the full costs incurred for dependent children (Gauthier, 1989; Fortin, 1989). Yet, what is most galling is that the assistance given does not necessarily go where it is expected; for example the assistance for a third child is much higher than for the first two, although studies have shown that the costs for later children decrease (Gauthier, 1989); similarly, governmental assistance is stronger in the first five years after the child is born, whereas maintenance costs for children do not necessarily decrease with age (Dandurand et al., 1989). The major approach taken by the Quebec family policy thus seems to favour an increase in the birthrate, as "its aims are more numerical than qualitative"; in other words it tries to "encourage women (and couples) to bring more children into the world, without necessarily being concerned about how to support them once they are born" (Dandurand and Kempeneers, 1990:87).

In the opinion of the Secrétariat à la famille and the Conseil de la famille, the cornerstone of the family policy should consist of a broad reform of the labour sector. The Loi sur les normes du travail de 1990, which instituted or improved various forms of parental leave and which attempted to strengthen job guarantees for women returning to work after maternity leave are without doubt an important step forward in recognising parental responsibilities, but it is still only the first step. As soon as the First Action Plan appeared, the Conseil du statut de la femme (1990:5) noted that women who stop "work to have a child receive less favourable treatment than that accorded under Quebec social insurance plans to people on workers' compensation, who suffer from work-related illnesses, or who are victims of criminal acts or highway accidents." For its part, the Conseil de la famille (1990:10) concluded that "these minimum standards should be much more generous and provide more adequate compensation for income replacement," since in order to "have the right to take leave without risk of being penalised, one must be in a position to do so."

Indeed one of the main shortcomings of the Quebec family policy is that it does not tackle the problem of income replacement for working men and women on parental or maternity leave, although that is a major factor in reconciling work and family. Apart from the compensation paid to working women to cover the waiting period for maternity benefits administered under the federal Unemployment Insurance Plan, the Quebec government pays no compensation for wages lost due to having to care for dependent children. Such losses can be serious, since a high proportion of working women (self-employed and part-time workers) are not eligible for unemployment insurance, and maternity leave benefits are only 57% of the gross weekly insurable income. In order to make up for these losses, the Conseil du statut de la femme recommended to the Quebec government in 1990 that it adopt a policy of universal and adequately remunerated parental leave. The total absence from the Second Action Plan of measures to compensate parents for absences from the job market is extremely disappointing, in a context where two incomes have become a necessity for most families.

Balancing employment and family responsibilities is also facilitated by easy access to high quality child-care services; yet according to the Conseil de la famille (1993: 57), the Quebec government "is far behind in respecting all the commitments it made in its child-care policy" adopted in 1988. The goal of achieving a better balance between the needs of parents and the supply of services that might satisfy them does not appear to have been reached. The Council therefore put forward nineteen recommendations on improving accessibility to day-care services, and their quality and funding. In particular it pleads with the government to "speed up the creation of new places, in order to meet the accumulated backlog and to make it possible to reach the goal set in its child-care services policy by the target date" (Conseil de la famille, 1993: 45). The Council also encourages government to give real financial help to families by revamping the tax system.

In view of the deficiencies in government action, the objective of promoting equality and solidarity among family members, especially men and women, seems to have been the major element forgotten by the Quebec family policy. Although one aim of the second plan is to "identify and promote initiatives that would encourage greater sharing of family responsibilities between men and women" (Secrétariat à la famille, 1992b: 47), this effort seems negligible when we consider what a serious problem this is in our society. When the time comes to leave work to take care of the children, it is still usually the women who have to do it. That is hardly surprising, when we realise that women tend to occupy the most precarious, part-time, badly-paid jobs; in view of the low coverage rate of parental leave, it does indeed appear "more rational for a couple to prefer to keep the man working, since he earns more and his career prospects are brighter" (Le Bourdais, 1989:94). The effect is to reinforce the differences between men and women when it comes to caring for the children, and to force women back into the senseless quandary of having to choose between wanting to have a child or to work.

In spite of these limitations, a number of positive features in the Quebec family policy should be emphasized. Joint government action, undertaken through the network of respondents in the various ministries, encourages the adoption and development of coherent policies and programs for supporting parents. The will to decentralise and to bring government closer to local organizations and communities is also positive, since it can result in concrete solutions better suited to the real needs of families in their own environments; however, this requires that financial compensation accompany the delegation of responsibilities. Faced with ever-shrinking resources, the government also seems to want to expand its role as animator for the private sector employers, encouraging them to better organize the services most likely to help their employees reconcile work and family life; business productivity and profitability and the quality of family life could only benefit from it. Moreover, the recent publication by the Secrétariat à la famille (1993a), the *Guide québécois de la famille* (Quebec Family Guide), is a powerful and very useful tool for disseminating a great deal of information relevant to contemporary families, as it deals with themes as varied as child care, the death of a family member, security, education and leisure.

The willingness of the Quebec government to act on family policy, in conjunction with a solid administrative structure linking the entire governmental apparatus, allows for true efficiency and the ability to react rapidly when intervention is necessary, something unequalled in the rest of Canada. The organization of the *1994 International Year of the Family* is a striking example. When in the summer of 1993 the Canadian government undertook actions to oversee Canada's participation in the event, Quebec had already created an independent agency, the *Bureau québécois de l'année internationale de la famille* (Quebec Bureau for the International Year of the Family), seconded six staff members to the Bureau, given it a budget of $1.35 million, defined its mandate and appointed a board of directors from various sectors of society. An action program had also been drawn up and the activities for 1994 were already being planned, at the local as well as the provincial level, thanks to the regional coordination committees involving not only government agencies but also employer and union organizations, as well as various para-public organizations.

Finally, the approach put forward by Quebec places the province at the forefront of family policy in Canada. In Quebec, as we have seen, support for families is the subject of a truly integrated approach which takes into consideration the whole of family life. The government can of course be criticised for not investing sufficient new money to adequately respond to the real needs of families, but we must also recognize that given that the current fiscal situation is not very encouraging, Quebec has clearly shown that it is willing to take firm and coordinated action.

In the rest of Canada one cannot find the same type of family policy, since support for families is still delivered though sectoral welfare measures aimed at responding to the problems of families in difficulty. The development of government initiatives observed over the past fifteen years not only confirms, but strengthens this approach taken by the federal government. Since the mid-seventies, in fact, the financial contribution of the Canadian government to compensation for dependent children has steadily declined, while that of the Quebec government has risen. Moreover, the federal government has reduced the universality of several of its family support programs, limiting them entirely to low- or mid-income families (Secrétariat à la famille, 1993b). In 1974, for example, it made family allowances taxable, and in 1989 began to recover allowances above a pre-determined income threshold. In 1979 it dropped the allowances to their 1974 level, and counterbalanced this with a refundable child tax credit, accessible to low-income families. In 1993 it replaced family allowances and both tax credits for dependent children with an integrated and non-taxable allowance for low- or middle-income families.

With regard to reconciling family and work, the federal government contribution lies mainly in administering the maternity benefits instituted in 1971 in the framework of the unemployment insurance program. In 1987 it announced its intention to draw up a national child-care strategy, but the very next year withdrew the proposal. The maternity benefits program has been progressively widened; since 1984, for instance, adoption leave has been covered, and since 1990, a ten-week maximum parental leave. Over the years the total assistance paid by the Canadian government for maternity and parental leave benefits has risen, but only because the number of recipients has increased, the result of a greater participation of women in the labour force. The real assistance given to women workers on maternity leave has actually decreased with the successive amendments made to the rates for unemployment insurance benefits (Secrétariat à la famille, 1993b).

On the whole, Quebec family policy is growing ever more distinct from the approach taken by the Canadian government. From a financial viewpoint, the Quebec government has increased its support to families over the past few years, while the federal government has reduced its financial assistance. In the administrative sector, the Quebec government has set up the necessary structure to implement a multisectorial family policy, while the federal government continues to intervene on a piecemeal basis. These varying approaches reveal diametrically opposed concepts of the family, which are subsequently reflected in the general orientation taken by those policies. Thus in Quebec families are something to be valued and given collective support because of their fundamental contribution to the continuation of society; conversely, the federal government sees the family as belonging essentially to the domain of the individual's private life. Consequently, its initiatives are limited almost exclusively to "looking after" families in difficulty. This approach, while we might describe as "reactive," is in contrast with the "proactive" role which Quebec has sought to play by seeking to achieve better prevention through support to the family.

This article has been written in the context of a research program on the study of family transformations. This program is supported by the following funding agencies: Fonds pour le développement académique du réseau (FODAR) de l'Université du Québec; Fonds pour la formation de chercheurs et l'aide à la recherche (FCAR) - Équipes; Social Sciences and Humanities Research Council of Canada (SSHRCC); the Donner Canadian Foundation.

Note: Quotations contained in this chapter are translated from the original French language.

CHAPTER NINE

Family Policy: International Comparisons

Frédéric Lesemann
Roger Nicol

Over the past half-century, most industrialised countries have developed more or less explicit family policies, or at least the rudiments of such policies. Far from considering the family as a purely private sphere, the welfare states, depending on their particular characteristics and national differences, have each in their own way recognized that the family is a basic and essential structure in society. It is mainly in and through the family that social norms are produced and transmitted, and that mechanisms are established to integrate individuals into the group and to protect them against the risks and hazards of life in society.

More than ever before, today's industrialized societies are confronted with the problem of preserving social links and group solidarity, which are constantly threatened with fragmentation and disintegration. In fighting against the inequalities that threaten social cohesion, the welfare state is inevitably forced to deal with family structure, which it sometimes attempts to promote as an ally in its support functions, and at other times to control, either symbolically or directly, when it does not fulfil its role of social integration and regulation, or when it plays that role badly.

In this chapter, we aim to provide a general outline and propose an interpretation of the various trends in family policy in a number of countries usually said to represent differing concepts of the relationships between family and state. We shall identify the historical and ideological origins of these concepts and end by presenting the main issues revealed through a comparative analysis. This will enable us to better identify and put in perspective the main features of the debate on this topic, now under way in Canada. In conclusion, we shall discuss the seemingly growing trend, in all countries today, towards policies that are focused much more on children than on families, and not just on children, but especially those who are "at risk," whether economic, physical or emotional. We hypothesize that this development is not exclusive to the realm of family policy, but indeed reflects a profound change in the way in which the welfare state intervenes in our societies, or if one prefers, a sign of the emergence of new forms of social regulation that are replacing the outmoded forms of public intervention we have known for the past fifty years.

1. A Major Divergence: Family-oriented[1] or Privacy-oriented[2] Concepts of Social Policy

Comparative studies all agree on two major historical models of state intervention in the family: the French model and the English model, the latter being associated here with the American model.

The first comes out of a centralist, unifying and interventionist tradition, in which the state intervenes not only in the family, but in society as a whole. This republican tradition is based on the con-

---

[1] Family-oriented: any programme aimed at providing comfort to the family as such, bearing in mind its role and its functions in the personal development of individuals and of society (Ribes, 1991: 84).

[2] Privacy-oriented: the principle of respect for the privacy of the individual and of non-interference by the state in the private lives of individuals.

cept of public authority which has no qualms about establishing private family programs for objectives such as increasing the national birthrate for demographic purposes. If we recall the major postwar reforms to social security, we see that a considerable range of measures were developed to assist and protect the family: generous family allowances, use of a family income-family size ratio to calculate income tax, housing allowances, creation of day care centres, kindergartens, support for secondary and higher education, multiple reductions for large families using public services, consideration of the numbers and ages of children when calculating the tax rate or granting various child-care allowances, including childbirth allowances (Belgium, Portugal, Luxembourg), maternity benefits, home child-care allowances, educational scholarships: these all reflect the idea that "to raise a child is to discharge an obligation; it is to make a financial sacrifice for the benefit of the nation as a whole" (Messu, 1991: 279). The family and the nation were thus closely intertwined, at least at the end of the 1940s and in the early 1950s.

The social dynamic was to undergo dramatic developments from the end of the 1960s, moving towards more selective support for the most disadvantaged families, and towards measures to combat social inequalities. But the debate remained very much alive in France until the 1980s, led by family associations (which are naturally in favour of a vigourous family policy), and focused on the opposition between a vertical redistribution concept much favoured by social programs and a horizontal concept aimed at providing support to families, whatever their socioeconomic status, and for the sole reason that the family looks after the children and thus contributes to the future of the nation. The socialist government of the 1980s reinvigorated the debate by attempting, in the name of "national solidarity," to reconcile the demographic objectives of support for large families and the goals of social justice by vertical redistribution to the less advantaged. So it created the "API" or single-parent allowance, granted to single mothers, the amount being at about the level of the minimum wage. Such a measure was in the tradition of French family policy of increasing the birthrate, and tended to compete with income from labour force activity, while of course being aimed at mothers whose income depends exclusively on this allowance, which makes it a form of social assistance (Messu, 1991: 285-6).

Even though family policies have today become essentially selective, they nonetheless remain part of an overall approach whose goal is to defend and support the institution of the family itself. This approach is also found in Belgium and Luxembourg, and to a lesser extent in Portugal.

The second model fits into the grand philosophical tradition of liberalism which tends to consider state intervention as a potential threat to the freedom of the individual. It is mainly in Great Britain, and to an even greater extent in the United States, that this so-called "privacy-oriented" model is found. Common law favours the respect of privacy, hence in Great Britain the well-being of the individual is assured, without explicit reference to the family (Ribes, 1991: 83): the presence of children in a household is not considered when determining the tax rate, nor is there any tax relief for dependent children, any recognition of rights associated with being a parent, or any specific allowances, except to the most disadvantaged parents, and then only in the form of welfare and not as a recognition of families with dependent children. As Barbier (1991: 78) points out, the absence of family policies and related allowances in Great Britain explains why, for example, three quarters of one-parent families collect welfare and the "one-parent benefit,"[3] while in France less than a third of single-parent families have to depend on such last-resort programs (Barbier, 1990: 351).

In the United States, neither maternity benefits, parental leave or family allowances are provided: the sole support given to families is social assistance (the AFDC), which is given only to single-parent families in amounts that vary considerably from State to State, and is often less than the min-

---

[3] Or that in the United States the vast majority of recipients in the "Aid to Families with Dependent Children" (AFDC) program, which is the main social assistance program, are single mothers with dependent children.

imum required by most families (Kamerman and Kahn, 1981: 66). Only those poor families which are recognized as such by means tests receive assistance (income-tested benefits), and in some cases, limited financial support to enable mothers to obtain day care services. They are also entitled to food stamps. On the other hand, the United States does grant tax exemptions and a tax credit to low-income parents. In addition, working parents can deduct a part of their child-care expenses from their taxes. As in Great Britain, there is no day care policy at the federal or state level. When day care services exist locally, they are provided by community groups (local councils, churches, charities), which in some cases benefit from federal subsidies granted in the framework of anti-poverty policies. They are not usually aimed at responding to the needs of working parents (Kamerman and Kahn, 1981: 106), but rather at preventing the worsening of the living and learning conditions of children endangered by the poverty of their surroundings. One example of this policy is the "Head Start" programs for pre-schoolers.

As for the development of child-care services, that is largely left up to the private sector (Lesemann, 1988: 157). Some employers, especially large corporations in Great Britain and the United States, do offer on-the-job day care facilities, as well as maternity leave and parental leave as fringe benefits to employees. This practice is, however, restricted to a limited number of privileged wage earners, and occurs in countries which have no legislation on maternity leave, far less on paid maternity leave (Kamerman, Kahn and Kingston, 1983: 137).

The entire question of the relationships between public and family policies is basically reduced to that of the relationships between social assistance policies and poor families, the main concern in the United States being to determine to what extent transfer policies (especially the AFDC program) help keep the families concerned mired in poverty and in economic dependence on public assistance (Cherlin, 1988). Thus the main debate on family policy now under way in the United States is centred on the 1988 Act sponsored by Senator Daniel Moynihan, the Family Support Act, which is aimed entirely at measures to reduce welfare-dependency, especially for children in poverty whose fathers fail to meet their financial and moral obligations. The law authorizes the deduction at source of a portion of the father's salary, having in many cases first obliged him to recognize paternity. The law also promotes basic training for parents in order to help them find and keep a job. In such a case, the Act obliges states to guarantee access to day care services for children whose parents are in training and are rejoining the labour force (Focus, 1988-89: 15-19). Furthermore, it compels states to adopt a Child Support Assurance program by 1994, based on the affirmation that it is parents and not the government who are responsible for their children. This legislation would provide assistance to children who suffer a lack of income due to the absence of a parent, not as a result of death, but because of divorce, separation or non-marriage (Garfinkel, McLanaham and Robins, 1992), once all efforts have been made to find the legitimate father and make him pay up.

Even if we agree that the first two social policy models show us the major approaches to the family taken in public policy, it is still relevant to mention a third, which we might describe as "statist" or state-based, whose very existence adds further complexity to the debate on the relationships between state and family. This is the Swedish model, whose main characteristic has to do not with a choice between whether to deal first with the family or with the individual, but with the fact that it refers to employment and access to employment as the basis of all social policy in the country, including family policy. Its principle is that every individual is entitled to a job and consequently to be remunerated on the basis of wage parity, which requires that the same wage be paid for jobs requiring similar skills and effort, independent of productivity or the market position of the business (Groulx, 1990: 17). Based on this employment principle, the programs and services which ensure employment are established in opposition to the principle of financial assistance, over which they always take priority. This political philosophy established in the early 1950s directly governs relationships between the state and the family (Kamerman and Kahn, 1981: 46). Indeed the principle of access to jobs for women, on an equal footing with men, encourages a very high rate of female participation in the labour force.

Consequently, working mothers in Sweden can take advantage of day care services provided by the government, and which are widespread and greatly used. These services are provided not only for children but for elderly dependents, and are highly developed in Sweden, to the detriment of direct day care allowances, a phenomenon which is explained partly by the job creation opportunities provided by a services policy.

In addition to broad access to day care services, families also benefit from a whole range of family allowances: parental allowances, support for one-parent families, very extensive and generous parental leave, schooling and housing allowances, whose basic philosophy is first of all to compensate for potential income lost because of the need to care for children (Groulx, 1990: 80), rather than to support the family as an institution. Above all, the aim is to allow parents to balance employment and family life (Kamerman and Kahn, 1981: 223), since in Sweden the government is in no way concerned with the regularity of the marital situation (common-law relationships are frequent and most children are born "out of wedlock") but rather with the emotional and educational quality of the family environment provided for the child (Trost, 1989: 94).

The Swedish model has been much criticised since the early 1980s, mainly in connection to the crisis in salaried work, but also because of the runaway costs of the service systems. There has therefore been a steady reduction of services, a relative increase in cash allowances and an increase in social assistance benefits, to the detriment of wage incomes, particularly in one-parent families, which run counter to the very principle of keeping welfare payments to the minimum and allowing every adult to obtain their income from employment. The result is a growing use of forms of family day care or direct compensation for child-care expenses, rather than further development of public day care services.

This third, state based model, in which the government guarantees the right of everyone to have paid employment, thus giving the individual dignity, is found not only in other nordic countries such as Norway, but was in part the basis for many of the social measures in the former east-bloc countries. The former German Democratic Republic (DDR), for example, passed a law in 1949, stating that "the equality of women and mothers in the labour force should be achieved through public institutions" (Schultheis, 1991: 106), and established, especially from the early 1970s on, a heavily used network of child-care services, parental leave and high family allowances (Kamerman and Kahn, 1981: 61), in short, a whole range of supports for working parents. A number of surveys done before the reunification of the German Democratic Republic and the Federal Republic of Germany, showed that the vast majority of East German women were very attached to these services (Kamerman and Kahn, 1981: 84). Of course that model was eliminated in the collapse of the communist states, but it is also experiencing the difficulties we have mentioned in the nordic countries, because the crumbling opportunities for guaranteed full employment and hence the right to waged work leave behind a certain disenchantment with this form of intervention by the welfare state.

2. The Rise of the Privacy-oriented Model; From Family Policy to Social Policy; From Family Policy to Child Policy

Quite apart from these concepts which differ so widely, both in their historical and ideological roots and in the resultant practices, and which have prevailed for several decades, there is today a noticeable weakening of the family-oriented model in favour of more selective, targeted measures, at least as far as transfer policies are concerned. This is partly due to a political preoccupation with the increased efficiency of social policy measures in a context of scarce resources, but also because of an ideological retreat from governmental claims to regulate certain aspects of civil society.

Among the factors which contribute to this displacement and the reformulating of public family policy, we might mention the following:

- Universal changes in the industrialized societies, relating to demography and familial behaviour: a sharp drop in the birthrate and the total fertility rate; an increase in the number of family lifestyles; new communal living practices; higher divorce rates; marital instability; common-law relationships; blended families; an increase in the number of children born out-of-wedlock. These societal phenomena make it useless to try to give a single definition of "the" family.
- Governments are more inclined to take note of the diverse range of family lifestyles that now co-exist. This phenomenon of familial pluralism makes it more and more difficult to devise any family policy statement, and tends to encourage an approach more focused on the individual as a unit for administrative management or taxation.[4] Rather than promoting one or more models of the family, governments are tending to play a much more modest role of assisting the most vulnerable, in this case mostly one-parent families. One therefore finds a strong correlation between some types of family (especially lone-parent families) and precarious living conditions.
- The increased participation by women in the work force, with the special feature that they occupy mainly precarious and poorly paid jobs. This participation reveals a profound transformation in the roles of men and women vis-à-vis the family, and the relative disappearance of the single-provider model. But it also bears testimony to the deteriorating living conditions of families which, over the past ten years, have depended more and more on two incomes to maintain their standard of living. This immediately raises the question of child care and the compatibility between parental and employment responsibilities.
- An indirect but very real and growing demand for autonomy among individuals in their choice of behaviour, lifestyles, organization of their behaviour as consumers and as participants in society; this all helps to limit and discredit the outdated government approaches to familial behaviour, as concerns the birthrate or the planning of child-care services, since, for example, families expect to be able to choose the kind of child care they want for their children.
- The need to control public expenditures on social protection functions, and to reassess the relevance of various programs (health, unemployment, old age, training and social assistance), as they affect family policies. In this reassessment, however, family policies seem to be less and less of a priority; in these times of economic crisis and demographic change, social programs seem to be oriented mainly towards the "risks" of unemployment, poverty and old age.

All these changes in society largely determine the current reorientation of family policies that is taking place world wide.

It is noticeable that when it comes to granting financial benefits and services to families or individuals, social policies dealing with the family have grown more selective, both in those countries with family-oriented traditions, as well as in those with privacy-oriented traditions. The development during the 1960s and 1970s (and in some cases even earlier) of universal benefit systems aimed at all households, has gradually if not suddenly, in some countries, been reduced or halted over the past decade, and the emphasis placed on specific beneficiaries: one-parent or large families, the elderly or the most disadvantaged. The aim of transfer payments today must be to redistribute scarce resources, concentrating on the poorest groups, applying resource criteria, and very often assessing need, which

---

[4] Which does not prevent governments faced with fiscal crises from considering a "familial" unit in their taxation practices when that might be to their advantage.

may depend on the number of children and their position in the family. From this viewpoint, family policies everywhere are tending to become social policies in the fight against inequality.

Another noticeable worldwide phenomenon is the switch from a family policy approach, be it explicit or implicit, to a more child-centred approach (Dumon, 1992). In order to escape from the deadlock that inevitably occurs when a normative definition of the family is applied to specific administrative forms of assistance (since such a definition is quite simply impossible to adhere to or to apply in view of the vast numbers of different types of families), those countries with a family-oriented tradition have tended throughout the 1980s to focus their assistance on the child, and have defined policies based on standards for the well-being and security of children. In countries with a privacy-oriented tradition, where assistance is granted as a last resort, especially to one-parent families, who make up the bulk of welfare recipients, it is more and more in the name of children's well-being and of preventing further deterioration in their material and emotional conditions that assistance is provided. Invoking the child's well-being lends greater legitimacy to the policy than the concept of meeting the needs of welfare mothers, who are always suspected of being responsible for their own problems by a population of taxpayers exasperated at having to maintain marginalized social groups in deeply dualized societies. Thus for a wide variety of political and economic reasons, and depending on the specifics of the country in question, childhood becomes the point where old family policies now being revamped all converge. "The notion of the child's interest represents a powerful theoretical abstraction and an ambiguous concept which easily lends itself to becoming a legal and political open sesame" (Schultheis, 1991: 178). In that sense, family policy is tending to become child policy.

These two major transformations of family policy are implemented in various but coherent ways, depending on the dominant tradition of the country in question. Greater selectivity has led in Great Britain and the United States to a willingness to target those groups and individuals on social assistance who deserve the support of the state, and to track down missing fathers and make them fulfil their obligations. In France, Belgium and Portugal, the decision has been made to be more selective by concentrating assistance on the third child in the family. This has been based on the idea of the threshold effect (Ribes, 1991: 87; Lattès, 1991: 323) which seems to be created by the birth of a third child: after her third child the mother will often decide to quit work temporarily or permanently; the house becomes too small; or if the country is concerned about increasing the birthrate, there will be attempts to counter the feared threshold effect that could dissuade parents from having a third child, by providing them with ad hoc financial support. In Great Britain, of course, such policies are seen as an undue attempt to influence private behaviour, and even as an attempt to reduce the woman to the sole function of mother, thus limiting her freedom of choice to be a mother or to have a career. But that measure is also an expression of a growing awareness that poverty is often linked to the special status of some families (such as lone-parent families) or to those with more dependents than they can afford, because of the deteriorating wage conditions for many such women.

As for the focus on the child's interests, this is expressed in France and in countries with comparable traditions, as well as in "statist" countries such as Sweden, through policies which consider the fact that a majority of mothers also work. In such countries child-care policies are highly developed. Of course, in countries such as France, the practice of placing children in day-nurseries and kindergartens has been well-established since the immediate postwar era, and the vast majority of parents make use of these facilities, whatever their social status. Ninety percent of children over three attend day-nursery or kindergarten fulltime, these being public institutions that are free, or to which parents make only minimum payments. Such measures are found in countries where a high proportion of women are in the labour force (85% in Denmark and Sweden, 72% in France) and child-care services attempt to meet the needs of children and of working parents. In principle, they allow women to choose between working in or outside the home. Other policy initiatives are also related to the care of young children, from parental leave to guarantees of flexibility for wage earners, and measures to regulate and protect work in the home, all aimed at ensuring that working parents can be available to their children.

The United Kingdom and the United States, however, are notable exceptions to this trend towards support for child care, and as we have seen, on the rare occasions in those countries where child-care facilities are found, they are generally linked to the "welfare" concept, and are reserved for disadvantaged children, who make up a population potentially "at risk." Indeed, in 1990, Mrs. Thatcher warned of the danger for Great Britain of "a generation of day-nursery children" (quoted by Barbier, 1990: 352). Even though the employment rate for women in those two countries is also very high, their governments stubbornly refuse to become involved in creating day care facilities, placing the responsibility squarely on the private sector. The practice of some employers of providing day care for their employees as a fringe benefit is the exact opposite of the French and Swedish models, which require employers to contribute to a fund used to develop local services (Moss, 1991: 103), and therefore require the state to mediate between the interests of private groups and those of the community. It is conservative governments which for ideological reasons have consistently opposed any involvement by the public sector in this field, opening wide the gates of entrepreneurship to the private sector and sending women back home. The governments which criticised the pro-natalist policy of some countries, deeming it conservative for women, are in turn criticised by the latter as conservative when they refuse to organise large-scale child care services, thus forcing women to stay home to look after their own children.

3. "Privacy-oriented" and "Family-oriented" Approaches to Family Policy in Canada and Quebec

In Canada, the privacy-oriented tradition, deeply rooted in the early years of the century, delayed until the mid-forties the introduction of family allowances, which already existed in over 35 countries before 1944. The French tradition served as an important benchmark for several Canadian social groups demanding such a system (Vaillancourt, 1988: 106, 361). Even though family allowances might seem to fit into a family-oriented perspective, they were above all a means of stabilizing the economy and reducing the social tensions brought about by the end of the war (Jean, 1988: 51-62). In addition, even though the program implemented had a strong impact on large families, it was far from providing them with the minimum of well-being that the politicians had promised. The latter feared that family allowances would make people lazy and cause a drop in productivity. The allowances were tacked on to a form of non-refundable child tax credit, which was changed at the end of the forties into a tax exemption for dependent children. By the early 1960s, family allowances already had little more than symbolic value in the support they provided families to help them maintain their children. Gradually, with changing family lifestyles as well as the development of social services, the way in which the welfare state intervened also changed, moving instead towards strategies to fight poverty, with priority being given to supporting poor families. It is true that family allowances underwent a major reform in 1974: the amount was almost tripled and then indexed to the cost of living. This reform must undoubtedly be seen in the light of the political tensions between the federal and provincial governments of the day, but above all it made family allowances part of a strategy for redistributing wealth between the provinces and for implementing a minimum income policy.

In Quebec, it was in the 1960s that the provincial government first showed a willingness to play a central role in correcting economic inequalities and to affirm its jurisdiction over social affairs. It established universal schooling allowances, the loans and scholarships plan and its own family allowances program, aimed at greater vertical equity of incomes and at correcting the impact of dependent children on the family. That was also one of the aims of the 1969 Social Assistance Act, which included implicit family policy measures, since it paid special attention to family composition. Its harmonization with the 1974 family allowances reform and the minimum wage laid the groundwork for a minimum income formula for families. Over the years, however, the central aspect of the obligation to work was to take precedence over the social and family aspects of the policy. Assistance was to remain exceptional and conditional.

Family allowances are viewed in Quebec as a tool for horizontal redistribution, because of the universal nature of the benefits, and as a vertical measure, at the point where benefits become taxable. Moreover, to the extent that they are adjusted according to the numbers and positions of the children, they help support an increase in the birthrate, either by recognizing the contribution parents make to the future of the nation or through incentives for people to have more children, tendencies that can be explained by Quebec's preoccupation with maintaining its demographic weight within the Canadian confederation. Maternity benefits for working women, to compensate for the two-week waiting period for federal benefits; unemployment insurance; universal Availability Allowances for parents of children under six; child care allowances; training tax credits for mothers: these are all measures aimed at improving family living conditions, and all the result of pressure from family groups, as well as from women's groups, who see the financial allowances in particular not just as material compensation but as the beginnings of a family salary.

It is paradoxical that the family seems simultaneously to be recognized and supported by the government, especially in its reproductive aspects (birth allowances, increased deductions for child care) and abandoned by it, that is designated to take over from the government some of the responsibilities it is abandoning in the areas of family poverty and youth unemployment (restrictions to the social assistance program, increased responsibility of families for unemployed youth, increases in school fees, restrictions on educational loans and grants). What is more, categories of families which do benefit from government transfer payments are only penalized if they share their homes with others or if they obtain marginal incomes.

At the federal level during the 1980s, family policy has been much clearer. Obviously inspired by neo-conservative philosophy, which is concerned mainly with deficit reduction, with harmonizing social programs with those of their free-trade partners, and with wanting to control and reduce social assistance spending, the policies, or rather the measures aimed at families, have become explicitly selective and targeted, visibly weakening the few family-oriented symbols which had survived till then. Even more, the social solidarity that had existed between society and family was destroyed by the establishment of two categories of family, through the use of a standard based on family income. Just having dependent children is no longer sufficient qualification; family income must now be below a certain threshold. With the formal disappearance of family allowances in 1992 and the establishment of the child tax credit and exemption, Canada has finally turned its back on any family policy, and now considers only the problem of reducing poverty and providing last resort measures aimed mainly at children living in low-income households. The total disengagement by the federal state, under the aegis of the Conservative government, from a national child-care program, despite its earlier promises and very elaborate plans, has confirmed its complete and utter abandonment of any federal involvement with Canadian families, unless they are in extreme poverty.

Conclusion

The trend now so clearly seen in all industrialized countries, and quite explicitly in Canada, to opt for very selective principles and to target "at risk" categories, has had as its consequence a severe reduction in, if not the total disappearance of, family policy measures aimed at recognizing the contribution that families make to society by raising children. This political choice, which does of course reflect an increased demand for autonomy from individuals, as regards their lifestyles and consumer habits, as well as a symbolic and financial bankruptcy of welfare state policies and programs, is paradoxically occurring at the very time when societies are more than ever seeking new ways to achieve social cohesion. Subjected to the logic of "the market," to the breakdown of traditional values, to the increasing disappearance of employment as a factor in social integration, societies urgently need to find new means of achieving solidarity. Moreover, in the ageing industrialized societies world wide, interest in support for families, so as to ensure a certain demographic age balance, should more than ever be on the political agenda. The stakes are not only financial, but social and ethical: who is going to take care of ageing family members? Cohesion in a society is not simply achieved by "verticality" or by managing inequalities in incomes, but also through "horizontality," through recognising the family's contribution to the future of the society, through balanced and dynamic relationships between age groups and generations. That is the price of quality of life in a society.

CHAPTER TEN

The Effectiveness of Family and Social Policies

Maureen Baker

INTRODUCTION

Although some provinces, most notably Quebec, have developed more explicit family policies than others, Canada, as a nation, does not have an explicit or consistent set of family policies. Instead, values and ideals about family life are implicit in family law, the income tax system, income security programs, Medicare, educational systems, and family benefits. Within these laws, programs and benefits, the assumptions sometimes differ about what constitutes a family and what role the state should play in family life. Inconsistency in family policies can be traced to the fact that the legislation governing these policies and programs was introduced in different historical eras and jurisdictions, by political parties with different ideologies, to resolve a variety of situations considered to be social problems at that time.

In comparison with European countries, Canada is not very generous to parents rearing children. Compared to the United States, however, Canada looks somewhat more generous. The types of social and family policies which a nation generates depend on many variables, including economic, political, demographic, legal and social factors. The next section will include an examination of some of the factors influencing and constraining policymakers when they attempt to create or reform social policies relating to families and children.

Constraints Influencing Policy Making

Why have some jurisdictions introduced social programs that are very supportive to families, despite their cost, while others have expected family members to assist one another with minimal government support? This is not an easy question to answer but one which social scientists have debated for many years. Explanations for the welfare state's uneven development in different parts of the world have focused on political pressures placed on governments to resolve problems created by industrialization, the state of their economies, constraints on national governments from economic globalization, the structures of political decision making, the importance of political ideology, and public perceptions about social policy needs. Each of these arguments will be discussed separately.

The first explanation, which is essentially an economic one, relates to the development of social security programs. Proponents argue that rapid social change resulting from urbanization and industrialization led to political pressure on governments to resolve new social problems, such as displacement of older workers, work-related injuries and "latch-key" children. However, political pressure was not enough to encourage the development of new social programs. The economic prosperity of both governments and citizens, resulting from industrialization and wage labour, allowed for the expansion of the public sector. Although social problems might be evident and political pressure is strong to resolve those problems, only in times of economic prosperity and expansion can nations afford to develop major social security programs (Cameron, 1978).

Since the mid-1970s, when the world economy took a downturn, most industrialized countries have not expanded their social programs but rather cut back or at best maintained them (Mishra, 1990). Now that many governments such as Canada are concerned about deficit reduction and spending cuts, expansion of social programs is considered by many to be economically impossible. For example, those who argue for a national child care program in Canada are usually presented with this rationale by politicians, that the country cannot afford it at this time.

While economic prosperity may be necessary for the expansion of social programs, it is clearly not a sufficient reason. For example, economic prosperity did not translate into more generous social programs in all countries during the 1960s and early 1970s. The prime example is the United States, which despite prosperity failed to develop social insurance programs such as unemployment insurance and maternity benefits, a public health care system, or a universal family allowance. This is in contrast to most European countries, Australia and Canada. Instead, the United States government invested in defence, space exploration, freeways, expansion of the public service, and other projects unrelated to social welfare.

Another prevalent economic argument is that federal government policies in nations such as Canada increasingly are constrained by economic globalization or the expansion of world markets, as well as the plans and preoccupations of multinational corporations and foreign investors. Most Canadian political parties now share the concern about the size of the deficit and growing national debt because interest rates are swallowing up an increasing amount of money which governments collect in taxes and require in order to provide services. If interest rates rise for governments who need to borrow, because bond-rating organizations lose confidence in that government's ability to reduce the deficit, the problem worsens (Courchene, 1987; Gray, 1990). Yet there are varying ideas about what has caused the debt to rise, whether the deficit should be reduced through spending cutbacks or reforms to the tax system, and how best to establish priorities in government spending (Ternowetsky, 1987).

Expanding this economic argument to add issues relating to the structure of decision making, some social scientists have suggested that political ideology has become less important than it used to be in influencing government decisions. As mentioned above, there are economic constraints on decision makers, such as a "globalized economy" dependent on foreign control and markets. In addition, parties need to win elections and if certain ideologies are not popular, parties must modify their policies to accommodate the ideas of their electorate, in order to stay in power. Furthermore, as the size and complexity of government increases, changes are more difficult to make. Established political structures such as federalism also make reform time-consuming and cumbersome. And entrenched social and economic programs make it difficult for political parties to change policy or even maintain different ideological positions. These economic and political constraints have led some to argue that ideology is less important than concrete economic reality and entrenched structures in deciding policy. For this reason, the argument has been called "the decline of ideology" thesis (Banting, 1987; Smardon, 1991).

In opposition to this theory, others would argue that political ideology, both from the platforms of prevailing political parties and from mass support, remains a decisive factor in explaining the development or maintenance of social programs (Castles, 1978). Over the years, political parties were developed precisely because different philosophical assumptions exist about: 1) the role of government in personal life, 2) how best to keep a nation and its citizens prosperous, and 3) whether and how wealth should be redistributed from the rich to the poor, or from those without children to families caring for dependent children. Traditionally, various political parties have supported different kinds of policies. Some parties have placed more emphasis on social policy than economic policy; some have provided more generous benefits to families with children while others have been more supportive to individuals regardless of their family status.

Recently, there has been ideological convergence among Canadian political parties on certain economic and labour issues. This convergence may represent some acceptance of the economic and political constraints on policy, and may to some extent mirror changes in popular attitudes. For example, provincial New Democratic Parties have become more concerned with issues such as reducing the deficit, down-sizing government and reducing labour costs. Traditionally these concerns have been associated with Conservative Party ideology. Yet, this apparent convergence has not necessarily translated into explicit changes in family policy but has reduced family incomes for many people.

Aside from the ideology of political parties, how a country is governed and which groups influence policy making also affect the introduction of social programs. Sweden has been successful since the 1930s in developing social insurance programs, a guaranteed minimum income and full employment policies because it has a strong central government, a relatively homogeneous population, an alliance between the labour movement and the Social Democratic Party, and established procedures that guide negotiations among employers, government and employees (referred to as corporatism) (Traves, 1991; Smardon, 1991).

In Canada, the federal system and division of powers between federal and provincial governments have served as barriers to the development of several social programs (Banting, 1987). The introduction of Unemployment Insurance, for example, required an amendment to the Constitution in the 1940s because initiating such a program was outside federal jurisdiction. In addition, the population of Canada is very heterogeneous, with strong regional concerns. Cultural and language differences, as well as regional inequalities, are accompanied by different ideas about which social programs are needed and how existing programs should be implemented. In addition, some advocacy groups are more effective than others in making their concerns heard. Also, there is no strong, visible and continuing alliance between labour unions and any political party which has ever held power in Ottawa. As well, there is no formal procedure, except consultations in Parliamentary Committees, for governments to negotiate with advocacy groups or employer/employee representatives, and no legal obligation for the government to consider the wishes of advocacy groups in new legislation.

The difficulty of creating a stronger family policy in Canada can be illustrated by the attempt to change the funding formula for child care. In 1988, the federal government proposed that child-care funding be removed from the federal/provincial cost-sharing agreement called the Canada Assistance Plan, through which the federal government matches provincial spending (with no spending ceiling). The plan was to establish a new funding arrangement under the Canada Child Care Act, in which more child-care costs were to be shared but only up to a spending ceiling for each province. One problem with this proposal was that child care falls under provincial jurisdiction. The federal government therefore required the support of ten provinces and two territories in order to change the legislation, especially if they wanted to pursue some national objectives with the new program. Because child-care services have developed unevenly and some provinces have been spending more money than others, a few provincial governments would have gained more money under the new plan while the more prosperous provinces would probably have lost if the new funding formula had become law. The federal government consulted with various advocacy and cultural groups, including unions, child care advocacy groups, feminist groups, "pro-family" groups, religious groups and First Nations People and all groups suggested amendments. Although none of these obstacles were necessarily insurmountable, considerable political will was required to overcome them. Apparently, the political will was lacking to resolve the issues, as an election was called before the legislation passed and it was not reintroduced in the next Parliament.

Another category of explanations about the development of social or family policy relates to mass support. People's ideas about the need for policy reform are influenced by changing social and economic circumstances. When people see that government programs are no longer protecting themselves, their family members or their friends, they are more likely to press for policy reform (Wilensky, 1975). There are several changes in Canadian society which have altered people's family and economic circumstances and motivated reform movements.

The Emergence of Family Policy Debate in Canada

One of the most important social changes influencing family policy is the entrance of mothers into the paid labour force. The impetus for this is related to the erosion in the value of the family wage, the expansion of the service sector of the labour force, the development of part-time work, widespread use of birth control, higher educational levels for women and the impact of feminist ideologies. As Duxbury and Higgins argue in Chapter Three, the increase in the numbers of working women and parents has created the need for a variety of new employment-related programs. These include:

- leave for employees with family responsibilities (including maternity/parental leave and benefits),
- public child care services, and
- equal pay for work of equal value.

In addition, as Julien Payne notes in Chapter Two, changes resulting from the increase in two-income families and rising divorce rates have also led to the need for reform in family law, including:

- divorce law,
- laws relating to child custody,
- the division of matrimonial property,
- laws relating to child support and spousal support,
- better enforcement mechanisms for child support.

Other demographic and social changes including declining birth rates, population aging and rising rates of cohabitation have required amendments to family law and policy or the creation of new programs.

The second societal change motivating policy reform is the relatively high rate of immigration, which has made Canadian society more heterogeneous in terms of culture, race and religion. Cultural diversity has encouraged new ideas about what a family is, about the role of government in family life, and about what kinds of social programs are necessary and desirable. At the same time, governments are becoming more concerned that the interests of new Canadians be represented in policy decisions. Yet, as more people from different cultural backgrounds become involved in social policy debates, gaining consensus becomes more complex because both new social issues and new standards of behaviour are introduced.

While some cultural groups in Canada have remained relatively uninvolved politically, other groups have pressed for policy alternatives. Variation in the interests of advocacy groups makes any one point of view less powerful in influencing government, especially when there are few formal structures for the public to express their views. Furthermore, controversy among advocacy groups can lead to a situation in which the government is allowed to pursue its own agenda with minimal consultation, because of the sheer complexity of consultation, negotiation and final agreement.

All these factors together have influenced the development of social programs in industrialized countries. As we previously mentioned, a prevalent explanation of why France and Sweden developed a family policy with more generous benefits than Canada at an earlier time relates to a combination of demographic trends, political ideologies and the structure of government. As birth rates declined and life expectancy increased in France and Sweden, especially after the Second World War, population aging led people in these countries to worry about whether the future of social insurance programs could be assured if the percentage of the working-age population was shrinking. Concern about declining fertility led to the implementation of pronatalist policies in France, and policies to more effectively combine work and family appeared in Sweden from the 1930s to the 1950s. Later, in the 1960s and 1970s, these programs were expanded and improved.

The differences between Canada and Sweden can be largely explained by the fact that, in Sweden, the population has always been more homogeneous, women entered the labour force in larger numbers in earlier decades, and rates of divorce, unmarried parenthood and one-parent families have been higher for a longer period of time. All these trends reinforced the demand for policy changes. In addition, the political alliance between labour unions and the Social Democratic Party, and the formal role of unions, employers and government in policy formation led to more effective work and family policies, initiated at an earlier date.

There are several factors which could encourage greater support for policies to enhance family life in Canada. First, the population is aging and there is concern about financing future social programs. This could lead to greater social support for childbearing and childrearing, as higher birth rates would delay population aging. Second, the typical family now has two incomes. This suggests that more people will need policies and supports to resolve their own work/family conflicts and therefore mass support for such policies will grow. Third, international comparisons have indicated that child poverty rates in Canada are much higher than in most industrialized countries, except the United States. Publicizing this fact could encourage the Canadian government to improve Canada's record with new programs designed to reduce child poverty.

On the other hand, there are factors which may impede the development of family policies in Canada. A globalized economy could lead to greater similarity between U.S. and Canadian social programs. Although this convergence may not be apparent in all areas of social policy, it is already visible in family benefits with the recent abolition of the universal family allowance and the new reliance on tax benefits (Banting, 1993). In addition, the problem of gaining consensus for national programs in a federalist state remains as long as the provinces have jurisdiction over social assistance, child care, child welfare, education, and the provision of health services. This will make the creation of new national programs, such as child care, very challenging. Increasingly, linguistic and cultural heterogeneity and regional inequality make consensus on any issue complicated. Finally, it is becoming more difficult to design a policy that treats all family structures equally, given the variety in present lifestyles, the social acknowledgement of difference, and the growing legitimacy of varying family forms.

Family Policy Options

From an analysis of Canadian and international policies, there are clearly some effective ways for governments to invest in the full development of children, to keep families out of poverty, and generally to enhance family life. An examination of the variety of policy options used by Canada and other countries to support families and children shows that several conclusions can be reached.

First, some jurisdictions have been more successful in gaining widespread support for the idea that bearing children and caring for dependent children and adults make an important contribution to society. In many cases, public acceptance of this idea has grown with declining fertility and an aging population, leading to concern about the future of social programs or population/cultural decline. In other jurisdictions, the idea of redistributing the cost of childraising has been strengthened by concluding that the consequences of child poverty, lack of day care services, and work/family conflicts are more costly than the solution. As Duxbury and Higgins suggest in Chapter Three, when employers realize that employees with child-care problems have higher absenteeism rates and lower productivity, they may become more supportive of workplace child-care services and other family support programs. Similarly, when governments realize that dealing with children's behavioural, health and educational problems arising from child poverty are complicated and expensive to resolve, they may reconsider the cost of expanding child benefits and public day care, and reforming child welfare services.

Those jurisdictions which see raising children and caring for dependent adults as important societal contributions are more likely to have created and maintained universal programs, rather than targeting benefits to particular categories of children or families. Countries using universal programs clearly have been more effective than those using targeted programs in keeping families with dependent children above the poverty line (Smeeding, Rein and Rein, 1988; Baker, Hunsley and Michetti, 1993). Social insurance programs require contributions from all employees and employers, and this enables larger sums of money to be accrued and more generous benefits to be provided than through programs based on general taxation. France, for example, funds its child allowance through a social insurance program which has been in place since 1932 (Ray, 1990). As Lesemann notes in Chapter Nine, the French model of family policy is based on the assumption that childrearing costs should be shared by all French residents.

Most social insurance programs, however, were not designed for natural events such as childbearing and infant care. With the exception of retirement pensions (such as the Canada Pension Plan), most social insurance programs were developed to cover employees in the event of unfortunate and unforseen circumstances such as lay-offs, job-related accidents or illness. Consequently, using social insurance to cover events which occur in the lives of most adults, such as childbirth and parenting, raises considerably the cost of these programs.

Some social insurance programs cover only those in full-time continuing positions in the labour force while those in more temporary employment positions fall through the cracks. In many countries, such as Canada, Australia, Britain and Germany, those who are self-employed or maintain only a casual attachment to the labour force are not eligible for maternity or parental benefits. Not all pregnant women in Canada are eligible for maximum maternity benefits, either because they are not working full-time, haven't worked for an employer for long enough, or have worked too few hours per week to qualify.

Governments need to view children as a future resource who must be supported now, regardless of their parents' incomes, in order to prevent future problems. Governments presently provide financial assistance to the arts, sports, self-employed people, and those who invest in Registered Retirement Savings Plans, regardless of the income of the users or investors. Under these circumstances the argument that support for all children is unaffordable and too expensive would seem to be inconsistent. Governments need to acknowledge that prevention may actually save money in the future.

Family policies could become more generous and enhancing if Canadian governments and the public accepted the idea that assisting all families to raise children and helping all children to develop fully is not only collectively advantageous but is also a public responsibility. Unfortunately, the prevailing attitude that it is parents who are solely responsible for their children may only change if birth rates remain well below replacement levels and public concern about the aging population increases.

Another conclusion is that family policies need to be reinforced by employment policies. Providing a child tax benefit is helpful to middle- and lower-income parents, but as Wharf argues in Chapter Five and Torjman in Chapter Six, having a full-time job which pays above the minimum wage will have a greater impact on keeping families out of poverty. Encouraging parents into the labour force, however, can only be effective if other supports are also in place. These include:

- a public child-care system which offers affordable care for extended hours;
- enforceable legislation to require employers to base wages on comparable worth rather than gender, marital status or family status;
- minimum wages which are above the poverty line;
- job training for real jobs, and job creation programs; and
- a guaranteed minimum income for those who cannot find work or are unable to work.

As Lesemann indicates in Chapter Nine, countries such as Sweden have been very successful in keeping families with children out of poverty because they have promoted a policy of full employment, focused on employment equity, and provided subsidized child care services for working parents.

Another change that is needed is to make income tax regulations more consistent with family benefits, but not necessarily deliver these benefits through the income tax system. Canada has shifted the delivery of more social benefits to the income tax system in order to promote efficiency and save resources. As Sherri Torjman notes in Chapter Six, the federal government now delivers all federal family benefits through the income tax system and targets most to middle and lower income families.

There are advantages and disadvantages of delivering family benefits through the income tax system. Among the advantages, benefits can be efficiently calculated along with income tax returns, and can be targeted to those families who need them most. With tax credits, there is higher take-up rate than for benefits requiring application. Furthermore, benefit levels can be altered easily as changes do not require a debate in Parliament.

This lack of public scrutiny, however, could be considered problematic as it is less democratic. In addition, taxation officials become more involved in social policy without sufficient background and knowledge in social policy or family trends. With an education in economics or accounting, taxation officials are probably less likely than those working in departments of social services or health and welfare to value universal programs or to argue that children should receive a minimum level of support regardless of their parents' income. Similarly, taxation officials would probably be unwilling to increase benefit levels beyond a basic level.

Countries which deliver family benefits through the income tax system, as Canada does, tend to provide a lower level of benefits than those who rely on universal family allowances delivered monthly or bimonthly (Baker, Hunsley and Michetti, 1993). If family benefits are delivered as tax deductions, or as child-care expenses deductions, they tend to be more advantageous to those with higher incomes and higher marginal tax rates. If they are delivered as non-refundable tax credits they do not benefit those whose incomes are too low to pay tax.

Canada also needs policies which respect the variation in family structure, the differences in cultural backgrounds, and the sometimes opposing needs of individual family members. Not all families are the same, and not all members have identical interests. This has led some researchers and writers, such as Brian Wharf in Chapter Five, to argue for a variety of community-based services rather than more centralized child welfare services, and for services delivered under different auspices rather than only by governments. On the other hand, this variety of services could lead to a complicated system with many opportunities for inequality among different groups. It could also be more expensive to operate and monitor than unified government services.

Although many politicians have pronounced that children are the nation's future resource, it has not always followed that policies have reflected this attitude. A comparison between federal money spent directly on children and money spent on elderly people indicates that children are obviously not taxpayers or voters! Although Canada has established public health care and education systems, there has not been a willingness to finance publicly the care of preschool children or afterschool care. Neither has there been a willingness to provide income security for all children.

Canada created a universal pension (recently "clawed back" from those with higher incomes) plus a guaranteed supplement for low-income seniors, but now provides a benefit only for children living in middle- and lower-income families. It has been assumed that families will pay the cost of child care themselves, although the government also provides tax concessions for working parents if they produce official receipts. In failing to provide child care, mothers are expected to forfeit employment opportunities and income in order to care for their children at home. Although non-parents are required to pay school taxes or non-drivers to pay for road maintenance, all citizens are not required to share the cost of child care or child support.

The high cost of parenting needs to be reconsidered in Canada's social policies. Parents are asking for a viable choice of whether to care for their own children at home or enter the labour force. At the present time, some mothers are being forced into the labour force for economic reasons, without adequate social supports, without equal opportunity to earn a living, and at a time of high unemployment. Consequently, high percentages of single parents are living on low incomes or welfare, and high percentages of working parents are experiencing serious conflict over child-care issues.

Does Canada Need More Explicit Family Policies?

Although there have been major changes in Canadian social programs over the past twenty years, families with dependent children (especially one-parent families) have not been the major beneficiaries. With the introduction of the new federal Child Tax Benefit, the government has chosen to target income security benefits only to middle- and lower-income families. This implies a retreat from the view that government has a role to play in supporting childrearing, and a reaffirmation of the ideology that governments should only intervene when family members cannot look after themselves.

Few researchers and policy experts would suggest that the growing problem of work/family conflicts and the continuing poverty of children and their parents can be resolved easily through modifications to child benefits. Instead, it has been suggested in this book that these problems require a more comprehensive overview of all policies and programs in order to consider their impact on the family unit and on individual family members. In addition, family programs, tax policies and employment strategies need to be internally consistent and consistent with each other in their goals and outcomes. Some of the problems of inconsistency relate to the fact that certain programs are federal while others are provincial. Others are perpetuated because of lack of consensus even within the same level of government. However, consistency among policies is an important goal.

Numerous studies have indicated that poverty is related to unemployment and low-paying jobs. More specifically, it is related to declining minimum wages, the loss of full-time permanent jobs to part-time and temporary positions, childrearing responsibilities and lack of child support, shortage of public child care services, and inequities in the labour force such as job segregation and lower pay for female workers (National Council of Welfare, 1990).

Throughout this volume, there has emerged some consensus among the various authors that new policies are needed to assist parents to care for their dependents while earning a living. In fact, there is a need to reconsider the implications which all social policies and programs have for family and personal life.

In revising social policies to make them more supportive of family life, it is important to:

1. Attempt to reduce the adversarial nature of separation and divorce procedures, perhaps by supporting more non-legal mediation;
2. Reduce judicial discretion in cases of spousal and child support after divorce by preparing and enforcing the use of more explicit guidelines for judges;
3. Develop government-initiated enforcement procedures for court-ordered child support pay-

ments after divorce;

4. Provide affordable child care services which are culturally sensitive, available for extended hours, and operate within the residential neighbourhood or at or near the workplace. This could be financed through tax incentives to employers to create child care, through the creation of a contributory social insurance program, or by merging the day care and education systems.

5. Remove some of the conflicts between work and family responsibilities by legislating (at both federal and provincial levels) adequate leave provisions for family illness and other family responsibilities. This could include statutory days off for sickness in the family and raising the wage replacement levels for maternity and parental benefits in Canada to make them comparable to those of European countries.

6. Make learning and education more relevant to real life to encourage children to stay in school, and incorporate more skills training into educational programs.

7. Develop a child welfare system which recognizes the role of poverty and unemployment in influencing childrearing practises and family interaction, and tries to deal with the causes of poverty rather than its symptoms.

8. Try to diminish the income gap between men and women (and for visible minorities, native persons and persons with disabilities) through proactive legislation not based on complaints. By this we mean legislation which requires employers to practise employment equity, with regular monitoring and enforcement procedures built into the system, rather than enforcement initiated only by employee complaints.

9. Ensure that provincial minimum wages and social assistance rates keep pace with the rising cost of living.

10. Equalize and prorate the wages and benefits associated with full-time and part-time work.

11. Fully index child benefits to the rising cost of living and consider the possibility of raising the level of these benefits to make them more comparable to European nations.

12. Examine more closely the relationship between poverty and ill health, focusing more on healthy environments and child development, and viewing the quality of family and personal life as an important factor in health promotion.

13. Consider remunerating the important but unpaid work of childrearing and caring for adults with disabilities.

If these policies were introduced and enforced, fewer families would be living in poverty and more people with caregiving responsibilities would be able to combine work and family life. Lone parenting would not disadvantage children as much as it now does.

These policy changes require the reallocation of government spending, which undoubtedly will generate controversy and debate in these times of fiscal restraint. Yet even if governments do not take the initiative to reform social programs and family policies, eventually they will be forced to change by the sheer number of families experiencing difficulty, by declining birth rates, and by the increasing demands of family members and the groups which advocate on their behalf.

As noted throughout this book, some countries and some jurisdictions within Canada have already made the first steps to create a more conducive environment for childrearing and family life. Hopefully this book will provide some inspiration and concrete suggestions to motivate others to reconsider their policies for families and children.

BIBLIOGRAPHY

Adams, O., and Nagnur, D. (1990). "Marrying and Divorcing: A Status Report for Canada." In C. McKie and K. Thompson (eds.) *Canadian Social Trends.* Toronto: Thompson Educational Press: 142-145.

Alberta Government (1991). *Alberta Health Annual Report.* Edmonton: Queen's Printer.

Aldous, J. (1990). "Specification and Speculation Concerning the Politics of Workplace Family Policies." *Journal of Family Issues* 11: 355-367.

Andrews, A. (1992). "Letter to the Editor." Ottawa: *The Ottawa Citizen.* (23 July).

Arnold and Mable Beckman Centre of the National Academics of Sciences and Engineering (1993). *Technology, Scholarship and The Humanities: The Implications of Electronic Information.*

Baines, C., Evans, P., and Neysmith, S. (eds.) (1991). *Women's Caring. Feminist Perspectives on Social Welfare.* Toronto: McClelland and Stewart.

Baker, M. (1990). "A New Status for Midwifery: Women and Public Policy." *Canadian Review of Social Policy* 26: 1-10.

Baker, M. (ed.) (1990a). *Families: Changing Trends in Canada* (2nd edition). Toronto: McGraw-Hill Ryerson.

Baker, M. (1990b). "The Perpetuation of Misleading Family Models in Social Policy: Implications for Women." *Canadian Review of Social Work* 7 (2) Summer.

Baker, M. (1993). *Families in Canadian Society.* (2nd edition) Toronto: McGraw-Hill Ryerson.

Baker, M. (1993b). "Family and Population Policy in Quebec : Implications for Women." *Canadian Journal of Women and the Law* 6 (2).

Baker, M., Hunsley, T., and Michetti, A. (1993). "The Use of the Income Tax System to Deliver and Target Family Benefits: A Cross-National Comparison." Presented at the 6th Biennial Conference on Social Welfare Policy. St. John's, Newfoundland: (June 29).

Banting, K. (1987). *The Welfare State and Canadian Federalism.* Montreal and Kingston: McGill-Queen's University Press.

Banting, K. (1993). "Globalization, The Labour Market and Social Welfare Spending." Address to plenary session of 6th Biennial Social Welfare Policy Conference. St. John's, Newfoundland: (June 29).

Barbier, J. C. (1990). «Comment comparer les politiques familiales en Europe.» *Revue internationale de sécurité sociale* 13/90: 342-357.

Barbier, J. C. (1991). «Politiques familiales ou politiques sociales.» *Informations sociales* 15-17: 72-80.

Barnhorst, R., and Johnson, L.C. (eds.). (1991). *The State of the Child in Ontario*. Toronto: Oxford University Press.

Battle, K. (1993). "The Politics of Stealth: Child Benefits Under the Tories." In S. Phillips (ed.), *How Ottawa Spends*. Ottawa: Carleton University Press.

Battle, K., and Torjman, S. (1993). *Federal Social Programs: Setting the Record Straight*. Ottawa: Caledon Institute of Social Policy.

BC Ministry of Social Services (1993). *Bulletin*. Victoria, British Columbia.

BC Provincial Commission on Housing Options (1992). *New Directions in Affordability*. Vancouver: City Space Consulting Ltd.

Beaujot, R. (1990). "The Family and Demographic Change in Canada: Economic and Cultural Interpretations and Solutions." *Journal of Comparative Family Studies* XXI (1) (Spring): 25-38.

Berger, P., and Berger, B. (1983). *The War Over The Family*. New York: Doubleday.

BNA (1988). *Employers and Elder-Care: A New Benefit Coming of Age*. Washington, D.C.: The Bureau of National Affairs.

BNA (1989). *The 101 Key Statistics on Work and Family for the 1990s*. Washington, D.C.: The Bureau of National Affairs.

Brown, J. S., Collins, A., and Duguid, P. (1989). "Situated Cognition and The Culture of Learning." *Educational Researcher* 18 (1).

Bruner, J. (1992). *Acts of Meaning*. Cambridge: Harvard University Press.

Buell, B., and Associates (1952). *Community Planning for Human Services*. New York: Columbia University Press.

Burch, T. K., and Madan, A. (1986). *Union Formation and Dissolution: Results from the 1984 Family History Survey* (Catalogue 99-963). Ottawa: Statistics Canada.

Burke, M., Crompton, S., Jones, A., and Nesser, K. (1991). "Caring For Children." *Canadian Social Trends* (Autumn): 12-15.

Caledon Institute of Social Policy (1992). *Child Benefit Primer: A Response to the Government Proposal*. Ottawa.

Callahan, M. (1992). *Protecting Children by Empowering Women*. A research submission to the Ministry of Social Services. Province of British Columbia.

Callahan, M. (1993). "Feminist Approaches in Child Welfare." In B. Wharf (ed.), *Rethinking Child Welfare in Canada*. Toronto: McClelland and Stewart.

Cameron, G., Hayward K., and Mamatis D. (1992). *Mutual Aid and Child Welfare: The Parent Mutual Aid Organizations in Child Welfare Demonstration Project*. Waterloo, Ontario: Centre For Social Welfare Studies, Faculty of Social Work, Wilfred Laurier University.

Cameron, D. R. (1978). "The Expansion of the Public Policy." *The American Political Science Review* 72: 1243-1261.

Campbell, J. (1992). *An Analysis of Variables in Child Protection, Apprehensions and Judicial Dispositions in British Columbia Child Welfare Practice*. Vancouver, BC: M.S.W. Thesis, School of Social Work, University of British Columbia.

Canada, Department of Justice (1990). *Evaluation of the Divorce Act*; Phase II: Monitoring and Evaluation (May). Ottawa.

Canada, Department of Justice and Status of Women Canada (1992). *An Economic Model to Assist in the Determination of Spousal Support*. (prepared by Richard Kerr). Ottawa.

Canadian Child Welfare Association et al. (1988). *A Choice of Futures: Canada's Commitment to its Children*. Ottawa.

Canadian Council on Social Development (1992). *Presentation to the House of Commons Legislative Committee on Bill C-80*. Ottawa.

Canadian Mental Health Association (1984). *Work and Well-being: The Changing Realities of Employment*. Toronto: The Canadian Mental Health Association.

Canadian Research Institute for Law and the Family. (1989) *How Much and Why? Economic Implications of Marriage Breakdown: Spousal and Child Support*. Pask, E.D., and McCall, M.L. (eds.).

Castles, F. G. (1978). *The Social Democratic Image of Society*. London: Routledge and Kegan Paul.

Ceci, S., and Liker, J. (1986). "Academic and Non Academic Intelligence." In R. Sternberg and R. K. Wagner (eds.), *Practical Intelligence*. New York: Cambridge University Press.

Cherlin, A. J. (1988). *The Changing American Family and Public Policy*. Washington, D.C.: The Urban Institute Press.

Cleveland, H. (1993). *The Birth Of A New World*. San Francisco: Jossey Bass.

Cochrane, M. (1988). "Between Cause and Effect: The Ecology of Program Impacts." In A. Pence (ed.), *Ecological Research with Children and Families*. New York: Teachers College Press.

Coleman, J. S. (1988). "Social Capital In The Creation Of Human Capital." *American Journal of Sociology* 94: 95-120.

Comité de consultation sur la politique familiale (1985). *Le soutien collectif réclamé pour les familles québécoises. Rapport de la consultation sur la politique familiale* (Tome I). Québec : Gouvernement du Québec.

Comité de consultation sur la politique familiale (1986). *Le soutien collectif recommandé pour les parents québécois. Rapport de la consultation sur la politique familiale* (Tome II). Québec : Gouvernement du Québec.

Commission parlementaire sur la culture (1985). *Étude de l'impact culturel, social et économique des tendances démographiques actuelles sur l'avenir du Québec comme société distincte* (rapport French). Québec : Gouvernement du Québec.

Conseil de la famille (1990). *Réaction au Plan d'action gouvernemental en matière de politique familiale 1989-1991 «Familles en tête.»* Québec : Gouvernement du Québec.

Conseil de la famille (1993). *Les services de garde au Québec : un équilibre précaire.* Québec : Gouvernement du Québec.

Conseil du statut de la femme (1990). *Pour une politique québécoise de congés parentaux. Avis du Conseil du statut de la femme.* Québec : Gouvernement du Québec.

Courchene, T. J. (1987). *Social Policy in the 1990s: Agenda for Reform.* Toronto: Prentice-Hall.

Dandurand, R. (1987). «Une politique familiale : enjeux et débats.» *Recherches sociographiques XXVIII* (2-3): 349-369.

Dandurand, R., et M. Kempeneers. (1990). «Femmes et politiques familiales entre l'ambivalence et l'implication.» *Santé mentale au Québec* XV (1): 85-99.

Dandurand, R., Kempeneers, M., et Le Bourdais, C. (1989). «Quel soutien pour les familles?» *Options politiques* 10 (2): 26-29.

de Sola Pool, I. (1992). *Technologies Without Boundaries.* Cambridge: Harvard University Press.

DeSousa, D. (1991). *Illiberal Education.* New York: Free Press.

Desrosiers, H., et Le Bourdais, C. (1992). «Les familles composées au féminin : évolution, ampleur, caractéristiques.» Dans G. Pronovost (éd.), *Comprendre la famille. Actes du premier symposium québécois de recherche sur la famille.* Québec: Presses de l'Université du Québec: 71-95.

Desrosiers, H., Le Bourdais, C., et Péron, Y. (1993). «La dynamique de la monoparentalité féminine au Canada.» *Revue européenne de démographie* 9: 197-224.

Diggory, S. F. (1990). *Schooling.* Cambridge: Harvard University Press.

Donaldson, M. (1993). *Human Minds.* New York: Penguin.

Drakich, J. (1988). "In Whose Best Interest? The Politics of Joint Custody." In B. Fox (ed.), *Family Bonds and Gender Divisions*. Toronto: Canadian Scholars' Press: 477-496.

Duchesne, L. (1992). *La situation démographique au Québec. Édition 1991-1992*. Québec: Bureau de la statistique du Québec.

Dumas, J. (1990). *Rapport de l'évolution de la population du Canada 1990* (No 91-209 au catalogue). Ottawa: Statistique Canada.

Dumas, J., avec Lavoie, Y. (1992). *Rapport de l'évolution de la population du Canada 1992* (No 91-209 au catalogue). Ottawa: Statistique Canada.

Dumas, J., with Lavoie, Y. (1992). *Report on the Demographic Situation in Canada 1992*. For Statistics Canada (Catalogue 91-209). Ottawa: Ministry of Industry, Science and Technology.

Dumon, W. (1992). *Les politiques familiales des États membres de la communauté européenne en 1991*. Leuven: Observatoire européen des politiques familiales, Katholieke Universiteit Leuven.

Dumon, W. (ed.) (1992). *National Family Policies in EC-Countries in 1991*. European Observatory of National Family Policies. Brussels: Commission of the European Communities, 1 and 2.

Duxbury, L., Higgins, C., and Lee, C. (1992). *Balancing Work and Family: A Study of the Canadian Public Sector*. Ottawa: The Department of Health and Welfare Canada (NHRDP).

Duxbury, L., Higgins, C., Lee, C., and Mills, S. (1992). "Balancing Work and Family: An Examination of Organizational and Individual Outcomes." *Optimum* 23: 46-59.

Dworkin, R. (1993). *Life's Dominion*. New York: Knopf.

Economic Council of Canada (1990). *Good Jobs/Bad Jobs*. Ottawa: Supply and Services Canada.

Economic Council of Canada (1992). *The New Face of Poverty: Income Security Needs of Canadian Families. A Summary*. Ottawa.

Edmonds, Cote-O'Hara, and MacKenzie. (1990). *Beneath the Veneer*. Ottawa: Supply and Services Canada.

Eichler, M. (1988). *Families in Canada Today* (2nd edition). Toronto: Gage (1st edition, 1983).

Epp, E. (1989). "Thinking the Unthinkable: The Fair Tax of Corporations." *Canadian Review of Social Policy*: 24.

Evans, R. G., and Stoddart, G. L. (1990). *Producing Health, Consuming Health Care*. Toronto: Canadian Institute for Advanced Research, Population Health Working Paper #6.

Federal/Provincial/Territorial Family Law Committee (1992). *The Financial Implications of Child Support Guidelines*. Research Report.

Fernandez, J. (1986). *Child-Care and Corporate Productivity: Resolving Family/Work Conflicts.* Lexington: Lexington Books.

Focus (1988-89). "The Family Support Act of 1988." Madison: Institute for Research on Poverty, University of Wisconsin 11 (4) (Winter): 1519.

Fortin, P. (1989). «Les allocations pour enfants et la politique des naissances au Québec : principes directeurs et proposition concrète de réforme.» Dans *Dénatalité : des solutions : Colloque international sur les politiques familiales.* Québec: Publications, du Québec: 161-180.

Friedman, D. (1987). "Work Versus Family: War of the Worlds." *Personnel Administrator*: 36-38.

Friedman, L. (1990). *The Republic of Choice.* Cambridge: Harvard University Press.

Friendly, M., Rothman, L., and Oloman, M. (1991). *Child Care for Canadian Children and Families: A Discussion Paper.* Ottawa: Canada's Children: The Priority for the 90s.

Fukuyama, F. (1992). *The End of History.* New York: Oxford.

Fulton, J. (1993). *Canada's Health Care System: Bordering on the Possible.* Washington, D.C.: Faulkner and Gray.

Gaffield, C. (1990). "The Social and Economic Origins of Contemporary Families." In M. Baker (ed.), *Families: Changing Trends in Canada* (2nd edition). Toronto: McGraw-Hill Ryerson: 23-40.

Galarneau, D. (1992). "Alimony and Child Support." *Perspectives on Labour and Income* 4 (2) (Summer): 8-21.

Galarneau, D. (1993). "Alimony and Child Support." *Canadian Social Trends.* Ottawa: Statistics Canada (Spring): 9.

Galinsky, E. (1989). *Business Competitive Policies and Family Life: The Promise and Potential Pitfalls of Emerging Trends.* New York: Families and Work Institute.

Galinsky, E., and Stein, P. (1990). "The Impact of Human Resource Policies on Employees: Balancing Work and Family Life." *Journal of Family Issues* 11: 368-383.

Galinsky, E., Friedman, D., and Hernandez, C. (1991). *The Corporate Reference Guide to Work Family Programs.* New York: Families and Work Institute.

Gardner, H. (1992). *The Mis Education of the Mind.* New York: Basic Books.

Garfinkel, I., McLanaham, S., and Robins, P. H. (1992). *World Support Assurance Design, Issues, Expected Impacts and Political Barriers.* Washington, D.C.: The Urban Institute Press.

Gaudin, J. M. Jr, et al. (1990/91). "Remedying Child Neglect: Effectiveness of Social Network Interventions." *The Journal of Applied Social Sciences* 15 (1).

Gauthier, A. H. (1989). «Des enfants, mais à quel prix?» (Une estimation du coût des enfants). Dans *Dénatalité : des solutions, Colloque international sur les politiques familiales*. Québec: Publications, du Québec: 123-135.

Gauthier, P. (1991). "Canada's Seniors." *Canadian Social Trends* 22 (Autumn): 16-20.

Gil, D. (1990). *Unravelling Social Policy*. Revised Fourth Edition. Rochester.

Government of Canada (1992). *Inventing Our Future : An Action Plan For Canada's Prosperity*. Ottawa.

Graff, G. (1993). *Culture Wars*. New York: Basic Books.

Gray, G. (1990). "Social Policy By Stealth." *Policy Options*. (March): 17-29.

Greenhaus, J., and Beutell, N. (1985). "Sources of Conflict Between Work and Family Roles." *Academy of Management Review* 10: 76-88.

Greenwald, H. P. (1992). *Who Survives Cancer?* Berkeley: University of California Press.

Groulx, L. H. (1990). *Où va le modèle suédois?* Montréal: Presses de l'Université de Montréal.

Gupta, N., and Jenkins, D. (1985). "Stress, Stressors, Strains, And Strategies." In T. A. Beehr and R. S. Bhagat (eds.), *Human Stress and Cognition in Organizations*. New York: John Wiley and Sons: 141-176.

Health and Welfare Canada (1991). *Status of Day Care in Canada in 1990*. Ottawa: Supply and Services Canada.

Higgins, C., Duxbury, L., and Lee, C. (1993). *Balancing Work and Family: A Study of the Canadian Private Sector*. London: National Centre for Research, Management and Development, University of Western Ontario.

Hobson, B. (1990). "No exit, No voice: Women's Economic Dependency and the Welfare State." *Acta Sociologica* 33: 235-250.

Hughes, D., and Galinsky, E. (1988). "Balancing Work and Family Lives: Research and Corporate Applications." In A. Gottfried and A. Gottfried (eds.), *Maternal Employment and Children's Development*. New York: Plenum Press: 233-268.

Ironmonger, W. (1993). *Personal Communication*.

Jean, D. (1988). *Familles québécoises et politiques sociales touchant les enfants, de 1940-1960*. Thèse Ph. D. Université de Montréal.

Kamerman, S. B., and Kahn, A. J. (1981). *Child Care, Family Benefits and Working Parents, A Study in Comparative Policy*. New York: Columbia University Press.

Kamerman, S. B., Kahn, A. J., and Kingston, P. (1983). *Maternity Policy and Working Women.* New York: Columbia University Press.

Kanter, R. (1977). *Work and family in the United States: Critical Review and Agenda for Research and Policy.* New York: Sage Publications.

Kingston, P. (1990). "Illusions and Ignorance About the Family Responsive Workplace." *Journal of Family Issues* 11: 438-454.

Lattès, G. (1991). «Le coût de l'enfant.» Dans F. de Singly (éd.) *La famille, l'état des savoirs.* Paris: La Découverte: 320326.

Lave, J. (1992). *Cognition In Practice.* New York: Cambridge University.

Le Bourdais, C. (1989). «Politique familiale ou politique nataliste : un enjeu de taille pour les femmes.» *Revue canadienne de santé mentale communautaire* 8 (2): 83-102.

Le Bourdais, C., Hamel, P.J. et Bernard, P. (1987). "Le travail et l'ouvrage. Charge et partage des tâches domestiques chez les couples québecois", *Sociologie et Sociétés* XIX (1) avril: 37-55.

Lee, M. D., and Kanungo, R. (1984). "Work and Personal-life Coordination in a Changing Society." In M. D. Lee and R. N. Kanungo (eds.), *Management of Work and Personal Life: Problems and Opportunities.* New York: Praeger: 1-9.

Lee, C., Duxbury, L., Higgins, C., and Mills, S. (1992). "Strategies Used by Employed Parents to Balance the Demands of Work and Family." *Optimum* 23: 60-69.

Lero, D., Goelman, H., Pence, A., Brockman, L., and Nuttall, S. (1992). *Canadian National Child-Care Study: Parental Work Patterns and Child-Care Needs.* Ottawa: Health and Welfare Canada.

Lesemann, F. (1988). *La politique sociale américaine.* Paris: Syros and Montréal: St. Martin.

Lewis, O. (1966). "The Culture of Poverty." *Scientific American* (October).

Lindsay, C. (1992). *Lone-Parent Families in Canada* (Catalogue 89-522E). Ottawa: Ministry of Industry, Science & Technology.

Louv, R. (1991). *Childhood's Future.* Boston: Houghton, Mifflin.

MacBride-King, J., and Paris, H. (1989). "Balancing Work and Family Responsibilities." *Canadian Business Review* (Autumn): 17-21.

Marcil-Gratton, N. (1989). *Transition* 19 (September): 4-7.

Marcil-Gratton, N. (1993). "Growing Up with a Single Parent, a Transitional Experience?" Some Demographic Measurements. In J. Hudson and B. Galaway (eds.), *Single Parent Families. Perspectives on Research and Policy.* Toronto: Thompson Educational Publishing: 74-90.

Marshall, K. (1990). "Household Chores." *Canadian Social Trends* 16 Spring: 18-19.

Mathews, G. (1987). «Le choc démographique : *pas seulement une affaire de famille.*» *Revue internationale d'action communautaire* 18/58: 9-16.

Mattis, M. (1990). "New Forms of Flexible Work Arrangements for Managers and Professionals: Myths and Realities." *Human Resource Planning* 13: 133-145.

McQuaig, L. (1988). *Behind Closed Doors*. Toronto: Penguin Books.

McQuaig, L. (1993). *The Wealthy Banker's Wife*. Toronto: Penguin Books.

Messu, M. (1991). «Les politiques familiales.» In F. de Singly (ed.), *La famille, l'état des savoirs*. Paris: La Découverte: 278287.

Meyer, C. (1985). "The Institutional Context of Child Welfare." In J. Laird and A. Hartman (eds.), *A Handbook of Child Welfare: Content Knowledge and Practice*. New York: The Free Press.

Millar, W. (1991). "Divorce, Canada and the Provinces 1989." *Health Reports* 3 (2) (June): 83-86.

Mills, C. W. (1959). *The Sociological Imagination*. New York: Oxford University Press.

Mishra, R. (1990). *The Welfare State in Capitalist Society. Policies of Retrenchment and Maintenance in Europe, North America and Australia*. Toronto: University of Toronto Press.

Mitroff, I. (1993). *Breaking The Boundaries Of Traditional Business Thinking*. New York: Oxford.

Monnier, A., et De Guibert-Lantoine, C. (1991). «La conjoncture démographique : l'Europe et les pays développés d'outre-mer.» *Population*, 46 (4): 941-964.

Morgan, R. (1984). *Disabling America: The Rights Industry In Our Time*. New York: Basic Books.

Morrison, T. R. (1992). "Learning, Change and Synergism." In Suk-Chang (ed.), *The Role Of Open Universities In Promoting Education For All*. Korean Open University Press.

Moss, P. (1991). «Les modes de garde de l'enfant.» *Informations sociales* 1617: 98103.

Moynihan, D. P. (1993). *Pandemonium*. New York: Oxford University Press.

Mustard, F. J., and Frank, J. (1991). *The Determinants of Health*. Toronto: Canadian Institute for Advanced Research, Paper #5.

National Council of Jewish Women (1988). *Accommodating Pregnancy in the Workplace*. New York: NCJW Centre for the Child Report.

National Council of Welfare (1989). *A Pension Primer*. Ottawa: Supply and Services Canada.

National Council of Welfare (1990). *Health, Health Care and Medicare*. Ottawa: Supply and Services Canada (Autumn).

National Council of Welfare (1990). *Women and Poverty Revisited*. Ottawa: Supply and Services Canada (Summer).

National Council of Welfare (1991). *Poverty Profile 1980-1990*. Ottawa: Supply and Services Canada.

National Council of Welfare (1992). *Welfare Incomes 1991*. Ottawa.

National Council of Welfare (1993). *Poverty Profile: Update for 1991*. Ottawa: Supply and Services Canada.

National Council of Welfare (1993). *Welfare Incomes 1992*. Ottawa: Supply and Services Canada.

Newman, D., Griffin, R., and Cole, M. (1992). *The Construction Zone: Working For Cognitive Change In School*. New York: Cambridge University Press.

Novick, M., and Volpe, R. (1989). *Perspectives on Social Practice*. Toronto: Laidlaw Foundation.

Oderkirk, J., and Lochhead, C. (1992). "Lone Parenthood: Gender Differences." Ottawa: *Canadian Social Trends* 27 (Winter): 16-19.

Ontario Government (1992). *Ontario Provincial Budget Estimates*. Toronto: Queen's Printer.

Ontario Women's Directorate (1991). *Work and Family Fact Sheet*. Toronto.

Papert, S. (1993). *The Children's Machine*. New York: Basic Books.

Perelman, L. T. (1993). *School's Out: Hyperlearning, The New Technology And The End Of Education*. New York: Morrow.

Perlman, R. (1975). *Consumers and Social Services*. New York: Wiley and Sons.

Piotrkowski, C. S., Rapoport, R. N., and Rapoport, R. (1987). "Families and Work." In M. Sussman and S. Steinmetz (eds.), *Handbook of Marriage and the Family*. New York: Plenum Press: 251-283.

Pleck, J. (1985). *Working Wives/Working Husbands*. Beverly Hills, CA: Sage Publications.

Polansky, N., Gaudin J., and Kilpatrick, A. (1992). "The Maternal Characteristics Scale: A Cross Validation." *Child Welfare* LXXI (3).

Porter, J. (1965). *The Vertical Mosaic*. Toronto: University of Toronto Press.

Poser, M. (1990). *The Mode Of Information*. Chicago: University of Chicago.

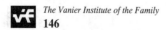

Québec (1987). *La politique familiale. Énoncé des orientations et de la dynamique administrative.* Québec: Gouvernement du Québec.

Ram, B. (1990). *New Trends in the Family. Demographic Facts and Figures.* Prepared for Statistics Canada (Catalogue 91-535E). Ottawa: Supply and Services Canada (March).

Rashid, A. (1993). "Seven Decades of Wage Changes." *Perspectives on Labour and Income* (Catalogue 75-001E). Ottawa: Statistics Canada (Summer): 9-21.

Ray, J. (1990). "Lone Mothers, Social Assistance and Work Incentives: The Evidence in France." In *Lone-Parent Families. The Economic Challenge.* Paris: OECD.

Reich, R. (1991). *The Work of Nations.* New York: Norton.

Ribes, B. (1991). «Les politiques familiales.» *Informations sociales* 1617: 8190.

Rochon, M. (1992). «Évolution récente de la fécondité selon le rang de naissance au Québec, en Ontario et en France.» Dans *Démographie et différences*, Actes du Colloque international de l'Association internationale des démographes de langue française. Paris: Presses universitaires de France: 85-93.

Rogers, F., and Rogers, C. (1989). "Business and the Facts of Family Life." *Harvard Business Review*: 121-129.

Rogoff, B. (1991). *Apprenticeship In Thinking.* New York: Cambridge.

Roos, N. P., and Roos, L. L. (1990). *Limiting Medicine.* Toronto: Canadian Institute for Advanced Research, Paper #17B.

Ross, D., and Shillington, R. (1991). Child Poverty and Poor Educational Attainment: The Economic Costs and Implications for Society." In *Children in Poverty: Toward a Better Future.* Standing Senate Committee on Social Affairs, Science and Technology. Ottawa: Supply and Services Canada: 51-85.

Rothery, M., and Cameron, G. (1990). *Child Maltreatment: Expanding our Concepts of Helping.* Hillsdale: Lawrence Erlbaum Associates.

Ryerse, C. (1990). *Thursday's Child: Child Poverty in Canada. A Review of the Effects of Poverty on Children.* Ottawa: National Youth in Care Network.

Schlesinger, B. (1963). *The Multi Problem Family: A Review and Annotated Bibliography.* Toronto: University of Toronto Press.

Schultheis, F. (1991). «Dans l'Allemagne réunifiée.» *Informations sociales* 1617: 104111.

Schwartz, F. (1991). *Breaking With Tradition, Women and Work and The New Facts of Life.* New York: Warner Books.

Secrétariat à la famille (1989). *Familles en tête. Plan d'action en matière de politique familiale 1989-1991.* Québec: Gouvernement du Québec.

Secrétariat à la famille (1992a). *Bilan du Premier plan d'action en matière de politique familiale «Familles en Tête.»* Québec: Gouvernement du Québec.

Secrétariat à la famille (1992b). *Familles en tête. 2ᵉ plan d'action en matière de politique familiale 1992-1994.* Québec: Gouvernement du Québec.

Secrétariat à la famille (1993a). *Guide québécois de la famille.* Gaëtan Morin éditeur. Boucherville.

Secrétariat à la famille (1993b). *Interventions des gouvernements fédéral et québécois en matière de soutien aux familles pour la présence d'enfants.* Document non publié. Québec: Gouvernement du Québec.

Secrétariat à la famille (1993c). *Canevas de réflexion sur les familles. Situations, acquis, défis.* Québec: Gouvernment du Québec.

Selznick, P. (1993). *The Moral Commonwealth.* Berkeley: University of California Press.

Silverman, P. R. (1968). *The Client Who Drops Out: A Study of Spoiled Relationships.* Unpublished doctoral dissertation. Waltham, Mass.: The Florence Heller Graduate School for Advanced Studies in Social Welfare, Brandeis University.

Smardon, B. (1991). "The Federal Welfare State and the Politics of Retrenchment in Canada." *Journal of Canadian Studies* 26 (2) (Summer).

Smeeding, T. M., Rein, B. B., and Rein, M. (1988). "Patterns of Income and Poverty: The Economic Status of Children and the Elderly in Eight Countries." In J. L. Palmer, T. Smeeding and B. B. Torrey (eds.), *The Vulnerable.* Washington D.C.: The Urban Institute.

Statistics Canada (1992). *Labour Force Annual Averages, 1991.* (Catalogue 71-220). Ottawa: Ministry of Industry, Science and Technology (February).

Statistics Canada (1992). *Causes of Death.* Ottawa: Department of Industry, Science and Technology.

Statistics Canada (1992). *Low Income Persons.* Ottawa: Supply and Services Canada (January).

Statistics Canada (1992a). *Income Distributions by Size in Canada,* 1991 (Catalogue 13-207). Ottawa: Supply and Services Canada.

Statistics Canada (1993). *Earnings of Men and Women 1991* (Catalogue 13-217). Ottawa: Supply and Services Canada.

Statistics Canada (1993a). *The Daily* (March 2).

Statistics Canada (1993b). *The Daily* (April 13).

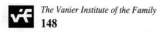

Statistique Canada (1993). *Activité des femmes selon la présence d'enfants, Recensement de 1991* (No 93-325 au catalogue). Ottawa: Statistique Canada.

Sternberg, R. (1991). *The Triarchic Mind.* New York: Viking.

Stout, C. (1991). "Common-Law: A Growing Alternative." *Canadian Social Trends* 23 (Winter): 18-20.

Sutherland, R., and Fulton, M. J. (1992). *Health Care in Canada: A Description and Analysis of Canada's Health Services.* Ottawa: The Health Group.

Tapscott, D., and Caston, A. (1993). *Paradigm Shift.* New York: McGraw-Hill.

Taylor, C. (1989). *The Ethics of Authenticity.* Cambridge: Harvard University Press.

Ternowetsky, G. W. (1987). "Controlling the Deficit and a Private Sector Led Recovery." In J. Ismael (ed.), *The Canadian Welfare State: Evolution and Transition.* Edmonton: The University of Alberta Press: 372-389.

Thurow, L. (1992). *Head To Head.* New York: Free Press.

Times-Colonist (1993). *Homemakers Push for Pay.* Victoria. (9 March).

Torjman, S. (1988). *Income Insecurity: The Disability Income System in Canada.* North York: The Roeher Institute.

Torjman, S. (1993). *Nothing Personal: The Need for Personal Supports in Canada.* North York: The Roeher Institute.

Toronto, City of. (1991). *Health Inequalities in the City of Toronto.* Toronto: Department of Public Health, Community Health Information Section.

Townson, M. (1986). *Paid Parental Leave Policies: An International Comparison with Options for Canada.* Ottawa: Status of Women Canada, Task Force on Child Care.

Tracon Training Consultants Corp. (1992). *What do Families Need? Report on Consumer and Stakeholder Consultation Meetings Held in the City of Vancouver.* Vancouver.

Traves, T. (1991). "The Canadian Insurance State: A Comparative Note on Olsson's 'Planning in the Swedish Welfare State'." *Studies in Political Economy* 34 (Spring).

Trost, J. (1989). «Les conséquences politiques de l'évolution de la famille, l'exemple suédois.» Dans *Actes du colloque Familles d'Europe sans frontières.* Paris: (Décembre): 7380.

Ursel, J. (1992). *Private Lives, Public Policy. 100 Years of State Intervention in the Family.* Toronto: Women's Press.

Ursel, J. (1993). "Family and Social Policy." In G.N. Ramu (ed.), *Marriage and Family*. Scarborough: Prentice-Hall.

Vaillancourt, Y. (1988). *L'évolution des politiques sociales au Québec, 1940-1960*. Montréal: Presses de l'Université de Montréal.

Vanier Institute of the Family (1992a). *Canadian Families in Transition: The Implications and Challenges of Change*. Ottawa.

Vanier Institute of the Family (1992b). *Transition* (September).

Vanier Institute of the Family (1992c). *Transition* (March).

Varella, F., and Thompson, E. (1993). *The Disembodied Mind*. Cambridge: MIT Press.

Voydanoff, P. (1987). *Work and Family Life*. Newbury Park, CA: Sage Publications.

Vygotsky, L. S. (1978). *Mind In Society*. Cambridge: Harvard University Press.

Weitzman, L. J. (1985). *The Divorce Revolution: The Unexpected Social and Economic Consequences for Women and Children in America*. New York: Free Press.

Werner E. E., and Smith, R. (1992). *Against the Odds, High Risk Children from Birth to Adulthood, Part 1*. Ithaca: Cornell University Press.

Wertsch, J. (1991). *Voices Of The Mind*. Cambridge: Harvard University Press.

Whittaker, J. (1986). "Formal and informal helping in child welfare services: Implications for management and practice." *Child Welfare* 65 (1).

Wilensky, H. (1975). *The Welfare State and Equality*. Berkeley: University of California.

Wirth, A. (1993). *Education And Work For The Year 2000*. San Francisco: Jossey Bass.

Wolfe, A. (1993). *The Human Difference*. Berkeley: University of California Press.

Young, M. (1993). "Instructional Design For Situated Learning." In *Educational Technology Research And Development* 41: 43-59.

Zigler, E. (1990). "Foreword." In S.J. Meisel and J.P. Shenkoff (eds.), Handbook of Early Childhood Intervention. New York: Cambridge University Press.

Zimmerman, S. L. (1992). Family Policies and Family Well-Being. The role of Political Culture. Newbury Park, California: Sage Publications.